June 25–26, 2012
Copenhagen, Denmark

I0060957

Association for Computing Machinery

Advancing Computing as a Science & Profession

EICS '12

Proceedings of the 2012 ACM SIGCHI Symposium on

Engineering Interactive Computing Systems

Sponsored by:
ACM SIGCHI

Supported by:
IFIP & IT University of Copenhagen

Association for Computing Machinery

Advancing Computing as a Science & Profession

The Association for Computing Machinery
2 Penn Plaza, Suite 701
New York, New York 10121-0701

Notice to Past Authors of ACM-Published Articles
ACM intends to create a complete electronic archive of all articles and/or other material previously published by ACM. If you have written a work that has been previously published by ACM in any journal or conference proceedings prior to 1978, or any SIG Newsletter at any time, and you do NOT want this work to appear in the ACM Digital Library, please inform permissions@acm.org, stating the title of the work, the author(s), and where and when published.

ISBN: 978-1-4503-1168-7 (Digital)

ISBN: 978-1-4503-1878-5 (Print)

Additional copies may be ordered prepaid from:

ACM Order Department
PO Box 30777
New York, NY 10087-0777, USA

Phone: 1-800-342-6626 (USA and Canada)
+1-212-626-0500 (Global)
Fax: +1-212-944-1318
E-mail: acmhelp@acm.org
Hours of Operation: 8:30 am – 4:30 pm ET

Printed in the USA

Foreword

It is our great pleasure to welcome you to the 4th ACM SIGCHI Symposium on Engineering Interactive Computing Systems – EICS'12 held in Copenhagen (25–28 June 2012). EICS is an international conference devoted to all aspects of engineering usable and effective interactive computing systems. Topics of interest include multi-device interactive systems, new and emerging modalities (e.g., gesture), entertaining applications (e.g., mobile and ubiquitous games), safety critical systems (e.g. medical devices), and design and development methods (e.g., extreme programming).

EICS focuses on tools, techniques and methods for designing and developing interactive systems. The conference brings together people who study or practice the engineering of interactive systems, drawing from Human-Computer Interaction (HCI), Software Engineering, Requirements Engineering, Computer-Supported Cooperative Work (CSCW), Ubiquitous & Pervasive Systems, Game Development, and Cognitive Engineering communities. The conference is the legatee of a number of conferences and workshops series: EHCI (Engineering Human Computer Interaction), DSV-IS (International Workshop on the Design, Specification and Verification of Interactive Systems), CADUI (International Conference on Computer-Aided Design of User Interfaces) and TAMODIA (International Workshop on Task Models and Diagrams).

Since its beginning EICS has witnessed a growing number of submissions. This year the program contains 21 full papers carefully chosen from a total of 95 submissions (22% acceptance rate). There are also 12 late breaking papers (five of which presented as posters) as well as a number of doctoral reports, workshop reports, tutorial abstracts and demonstration descriptions. The published material originates from 15 countries, including New Zealand, North and South America, and Europe. In addition, keynote addresses will be offered by Robert Jacob (Tufts University, USA) and Jakob Bardram (IT University of Copenhagen, Denmark).

We believe that for this fourth EICS edition we obtained an exciting and interactive program, which stimulates fruitful discussion in the relevant research fields. Topics range from model-based approaches to the design, analysis and generation of user interfaces, to toolkits supporting their development. A diversity of interaction styles and application areas is covered including multimodal, multidevice or multi-touch interfaces, ubiquitous computing, and health.

We hope that you will find this year program interesting and thought provoking. The symposium aims to provide you with a valuable opportunity to share ideas with other researchers and practitioners from institutions around the world. We also wish the best to the next edition, EICS 2013 to be held in London, UK, in June 2013.

Many people have contributed to EICS 2012 with their hard work and we would like to thank them all, from the different chairs to the Program Committee and the many external reviewers listed in the proceedings. Lastly, we would like to especially thank our sponsors, ACM SIGCHI and IFIP WG 2.7/13.4, for their continued support and endorsement of EICS symposiums.

José C. Campos   **Philippe Palanque**   **Michael Harrison**
Simone D. J. Barbosa   **Rick Kazman**   **Steve Reeves**
EICS'12 General Co-chairs   *Long papers Co-chairs*   *Late Breaking Results Co-chairs*

Table of Contents

Session 5: Formal Methods

Session 6: WWW & Visualization

Session 7: Models

Session 8: Task Models

Session 9: Engineering 2

Session 10: Health

Demonstrations

Poster Session

Doctoral Consortium

Tutorial

Workshop

EICS 2012 Symposium Organization

General Chairs: Simone D. J. Barbosa *(PUC Rio de Janeiro, Brazil)*
José Creissac Campos *(University of Minho, Portugal)*

Long Papers Chairs: Rick Kazman *(Carnegie Mellon University and University of Hawai'i, USA)*
Philippe Palanque *(University of Toulouse 3, France)*

Late Breaking Results Chairs: Michael Harrison *(Newcastle University, UK)*
Steve Reeves *(University of Waikato, New Zealand)*

Demonstrations Chairs: Lutz W. H. Krauß *(Porsche, Germany)*
Gerrit Meixner *(DFKI, Germany)*

Doctoral Consortium Chairs: Alan Dix *(Lancaster University, UK)*
Laurence Nigay *(University of Grenoble, France)*

Workshops Chairs: Panos Markopoulos *(TU/e, The Netherlands)*
Kevin Schneider *(University of Saskatchewan, Canada)*

Tutorials Chairs: Anke Dittmar *(University of Rostok, Germany)*
Gavin Doherty *(Trinity College Dublin, Ireland)*

Local Organization Chairs: Jakob Bardram *(ITU, Denmark)*
Morten Borup Harning *(Dialogical, Denmark)*

Publicity Chair: Greg Phillips *(Royal Military College of Canada, Canada)*

Registration Chair: José Luís Silva *(University of Minho, Portugal)*

Steering Committee Chair: Nick Graham *(Queen's University, Canada)*

Steering Committee: Simone D. J. Barbosa *(PUC Rio de Janeiro, Brazil)*
Gaëlle Calvary *(University of Grenoble, France)*
José Creissac Campos *(University of Minho, Portugal)*
Prasun Dewan *(University of North Carolina Chapel Hill, USA)*
Gavin Doherty *(Trinity College Dublin, Ireland)*
Peter Forbrig *(University of Rostock, Germany)*
Morten Borup Harning *(Dialogical, Denmark)*
Kris Luyten *(Hasselt University, Belgium)*
Philippe Palanque *(University of Toulouse 3, France)*
Fabio Paternò *(CNR-ISTI, Italy)*
Jean Vanderdonckt *(Université Catholique de Louvain, Belgium)*

Additional reviewers (continued):

Andrew Morrison
Wolfgang Müller
Miguel Nacenta
David Navarre
Michael Nebeling
Patrick Oladimeji
Stefan Oppl
Oscar Pastor
Heiko Paulheim
Andriy Pavlovych
Simon Perrault
Emmanuel Pietriga
Andreas Pleuss
Benjamin Poppinga
Costin Pribeanu
Angel Puerta
Muhammad Musaddique Ali Rafique
Roberto Ranon
Alberto Raposo
Janet C. Read
Madhu Reddy
Luis Roalter
Mario Romero
Rimvydas Ruksenas
Alan Said
Daisuke Sakamoto
Vagner Santana
Stefan Sauer
Johannes Schöning
Daniel Schreiber
Marc Seissler

Marcos Serrano
Orit Shaer
N. Sadat Shami
Dvijesh Shastri
José Luís Silva
Daniel Sinnig
Sandra Smith
Jean-Sébastien Sottet
Lucio Davide Spano
David Stotts
Chiew Seng Sean Tan
Franck Tarpin-Bernard
Keng Soon Teh
Mathura Thapliyal
Eliane Tozman
Hallvard Trætteberg
Daniela Trevisan
Philippe Truillet
Ullmer, Brygg
Jan Van den Bergh
Peter Van Roy
Davy Vanacken
Radu-Daniel Vatavu
Jo Vermeulen
Markel Vigo
Chris Vincent
Dong-Bach Vo
Chui Yin Wong
Min Wu
Chuang-wen You
Rui Zhang

EICS 2012 Sponsor & Supporters

Sponsor:  SIGCHI

Supporters: 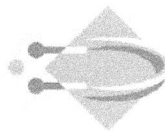 ifip wg 2.7/13.4 on user interface engineering

IT University of Copenhagen

Keynote Talk

Engineering Next Generation Interfaces — Past and Future

Robert J.K. Jacob

Department of Computer Science

Tufts University

Medford, MA 02155 USA

jacob@cs.tufts.edu

Abstract

Tools, abstractions, models, and specification techniques for engineering new generations of interactive systems have tended to follow the development of such systems by about half a generation. In each case, hackers first start experimenting with new types of systems. Then the model developers and tool builders enter as requirements and paradigms solidify. And ultimately the tools and abstractions become so widely accepted and commonplace that they are no longer an open research area. This has happened with conventional graphical user interfaces, and it continues through new generations of interaction styles. It poses a continuing challenge to our community to focus ahead on the tools and techniques needed for each new emerging future interaction style.

I will discuss research projects on specifying previous and current genres of "next generation" user interfaces and how each has been matched to its target domain and has followed this pattern. I will also describe a new genre of adaptive, lightweight brain-computer interfaces as an example of the kinds of next generation interfaces that I see emerging. I offer it as a challenge to our community -- to think about tools and techniques for engineering a new generation of interfaces of this sort.

Categories & Subject Descriptors: H.1.2 [Models and Principles]: User/Machine Systems - Human Factors - UIMS

Author Keywords: Next-generation; interaction styles; virtual reality; ubiquitous computing; tangible interfaces; multimodal; context-aware; post-WIMP interfaces; reality-based interaction; user interface software; UIMS; UIDL.

Bio

Robert Jacob is a Professor of Computer Science at Tufts University, where his research interests are new interaction modes and techniques and user interface software; his current work focuses on adaptive brain-computer interfaces. He was also a visiting professor at the Universite Paris-Sud and at the MIT Media Laboratory. Before coming to Tufts, he was in the Human-Computer Interaction Lab at the Naval Research Laboratory. He received his Ph.D. from Johns Hopkins University, and he is a member of the editorial board of Human-Computer Interaction and the ACM Transactions on Computer-Human Interaction. He was Papers Co-Chair of the CHI 2001 and CADUI 2004 conferences, Co-Chair of UIST 2007 and TEI 2010, and Vice-President of ACM SIGCHI. He was elected to the ACM CHI Academy in 2007, an honorary group of the principal leaders of the field of HCI, whose efforts have shaped the discipline and industry, and have led research and innovation in human-computer interaction.

Keynote Talk

Distributed Interaction

Jakob E. Bardram

IT University of Copenhagen
Rued Langgaards Vej 7, DK-2300 Copenhagen, Denmark
bardram@itu.dk

Abstract

The personal computer as used by most people still – to a large degree – follows an interaction and technological design dating back to Allan Kay's Dynabook and the Xerox Star. This implies that interaction is confined to a single device with a single keyboard/mouse/display hardware configuration sitting on a desk, and personal rather than collaborative work is in focus.

The challenges of "moving the computer beyond the desktop" are being addressed within different research fields. For example, Ubiquitous Computing (Ubicomp) investigates how computing can be embedded in everyday life; Computer Supported Cooperative Work (CSCW) researches collaborative interaction; and many researchers in the CHI and EICS community explores basic infrastructure and technologies for handling multiple devices and displays in e.g. smart room setups.

In this talk, I will present our approach to these challenges. Specifically, I will introduce the term of "distributed interaction," which is a research agenda focusing on researching theory, conceptual frameworks, interaction design, user interfaces, and infrastructure that allow interaction with computers to be distributed along three dimension:

1. Devices – computers should not be viewed as single devices but as (inter)networked devices. Hence, interaction is not confined to one device, but should encompass multiple devices.

2. Space – computers are distributed in space and time, and are not confined to one setting. This includes mobility, but more importantly that devices are to be found in all sorts of odd settings where they need to adapt to, and collaborate with, their surroundings, including other devices, people, interaction devices, etc.

3. People – computers are to a large degree the primary way of collaboration in distributed organizations. Hence, a lot has changed since the personal computer was designed for small office collaboration and there is a need for incorporating support for global interaction as a fundamental mechanism in the computing platforms.

I will present our current approach for supporting distributed interaction called "activity-based computing" (ABC). Based on a strong theoretical foothold in Activity Theory, ABC provides a conceptual framework, interaction design, user interface, and a distributed programming and runtime infrastructure for distributed interaction. I will present ABC and show how it has been applied in building support for clinical work in hospitals and for smart space technology.

Categories & Subject Descriptors: H.5.2 [Information Interfaces and Presentation]: User Interfaces—Theory and methods; H.5.3 [Information Interfaces and Presentation]: Group and Organization Interfaces— Theory and methods.

Author Keywords: Distributed Interaction, Ubiquitous Computing, Global Interaction, Smart Spaces.

Bio

Jakob E. Bardram [www.itu.dk/~bardram/] is a professor at the IT University of Copenhagen (ITU) and runs the Pervasive Interaction Technology (PIT) Laboratory [pit.itu.dk]. Prior to this position, he was an associate professor at the Computer Science Department, University of Aarhus and the co-founder and first manager of the Danish Centre for Pervasive Healthcare. His research interests are Pervasive/Ubiquitous Computer Systems, Object Oriented Software Architecture, Computer Supported Cooperative Work (CSCW); and Human-Computer Interaction (HCI). The main application areas of this research are healthcare, biology, and global collaboration.

In the summer of 2006 he co-founded the company Cetrea A/S, which specialize in the development of pervasive computing technology for hospitals. He also helped found CLC Bio A/S, which develops bioinformatics software. Dr. Bardram has previously held positions as project manager and IT architect at IBM, and he has been an industrial research fellow at CSC, where he worked with software architectures for cooperative systems in hospitals.

Dr. Bardram received his PhD in computer science in 1998 from the University of Aarhus, Denmark. Since returning to academia in 2001, he has been involved in several R&D Projects with industry. He has co-edited a book on Pervasive Healthcare and has co-edited a special issue of Pervasive Healthcare in the IEEE Transactions on Information Technology in Biomedicine. Dr. Bardram is a senior member of the Association for Computing Machinery (ACM) and member of the Institute of Electrical and Electronics Engineers (IEEE). He was the conference co-chair and organizer of the ACM UBICOMP 2010 conference in Copenhagen and was the Papers and Notes co-chair for the ACM CSCW 2011 conference. He has served on numerous program and organizing committees for both ACM and IEEE conferences.

Increasing Kinect Application Development Productivity by an Enhanced Hardware Abstraction

Bernardo Reis, João Marcelo Teixeira, Felipe Breyer, Luis Arthur Vasconcelos,
Aline Cavalcanti, André Ferreira, Judith Kelner
Virtual Reality and Multimedia Research Group – Computer Science Center
Federal University of Pernambuco, Recife – Pernambuco – Brazil
{bfrs, jmxnt, fbb, lalv, asc3, amf2, jk}@cin.ufpe.br

ABSTRACT

Designing and implementing the interaction behavior for body tracking capable systems requires complex modeling of actions and extensive calibration. Being the most recent and successful device for robust interactive body tracking, Microsoft's Kinect has enabled natural interaction by the use of consumer hardware, providing detailed and powerful information to designers and developers, but little tooling. To fulfill this lack of adequate tools for helping developers in the prototyping and implementation of such interfaces, we present Kina, a toolkit that makes the development not fully conditional to the existence of a sensor. By providing playback capabilities together with an online movement database, it reduces the physical effort found while performing testing activities.

Author Keywords

Application testing; development methodology; interaction database.

ACM Classification Keywords

D.2.5 Software Engineering: Testing and Debugging - Testing tools

INTRODUCTION

Microsoft's Kinect sensor was originally developed as an accessory for the Xbox 360 videogame console that would allow interaction without touching a game controller, through natural postures and gestures [9]. Soon enough the scientific community realized that it could be applied to a wide range of applications, from robot navigation support [1] to high quality dense 3D reconstruction [10].

To test such applications is often a hard and time consuming activity because it is difficult to redo tests using the same reference input, and furthermore it requires considerable physical effort from the users to perform movements and body gestures.

Some issues are particularly interesting in the field of developing Kinect-based applications:

- Equipment restriction - the development phase demands a Kinect sensor to be available all the time. For example, a development team consisting of 4 users should have 4 different sensors in order to make possible different and independent tests at the same time;

- Physical effort during tests - testing applications requires at least one user to be placed on the view area of the sensor and to perform some specific movements. To repeat the same tests means that the user must perform the same physical actions over and over, which can cause physical weariness resulting from exertion;

- Some body gestures require specific knowledge - while developing health support applications, for example, such as functional exercises or physiotherapy evaluations, the support of a specialist is needed in order to verify whether the movement being used as input is correct. Therefore, the figure of a specialist is required during most of development and testing phases.

Some work has been done concerning the first issue, but only few are applied specifically to the Kinect device itself. One way of sharing the same device for more than just one user is to adopt the concept of virtual USB ports [3]. This way, the device is connected to a single PC and its information is passed over the network to any of the connected users. Unfortunately, it does not solve the problem of simultaneous accesses, since only one access is permitted at a time. In [14], the authors propose an open source tool for distributing data from Kinect over the web. By using their solution it is possible to share and access the data independently, which solves the first issue. However, scalability and data transmission still are bottlenecks, as they limit the number of simultaneous users that can access the device.

The second and third issues, regarding physical effort and specialized information, respectively, could be solved by recording user input and then reproducing the data that was captured. This way, during the development test phase, a single user input would be necessary for each different movement. The Fakenect library [2] is an existing solution that captures the dump of the Kinect sensor and later reproduces the information to the application (more details about this library will be given in the next sections). One problem regarding to this solution is that data capture happens apart from the application being developed, which means that the input generation must be performed previously, without any feedback from the application. This way, it is difficult to generate the input that is exactly as required by the application.

In order to make the development of Kinect applications more accessible and help to improve the test experiments regarding them, this paper proposes Kina, a toolkit that (1) reduces the physical effort found while testing applications by recording user actions directly from the sensor and (2) softens the requirement of having a device available during the entire development phase, because the real-time Kinect data can be replaced by the previously recorded one.

In summary, the main contributions of this paper are:

- a toolkit for improving the test development productivity of Kinect applications by simplifying the testing phase, and

- a database of movements captured using the Kinect sensor, which can benefit developers by freeing them of having a sensor physically installed on the development PC.

DEVELOPMENT TOOLS AND SDKS

Being released as only an accessory for the Xbox 360 console, Kinect was not expected to be used for such a variety of purposes. The first effort in the direction of using depth data from Kinect was made by the open-source community, which hacked the communication protocol between device and Xbox 360. They were able to capture and correctly identify the information travelling through the channel, and then produce a driver that would allow reading the color camera images and depth data. Along with the driver, libraries for body tracking have been developed. Nowadays, there are three major SDKs available for Kinect-based application development: the open-source OpenKinect + libfreenect [11], derived from the aforementioned driver; the also open-source OpenNI + SensorKinect [12], based on PrimeSense's (the original Kinect manufacturer) code; and the proprietary Microsoft Kinect for Windows SDK [8].

These SDKs have the same intent, which is to provide means for using the Kinect device on a PC platform. However, they differ from top to bottom. In order to clearly expose the differences among them, we have compiled Table 1.

Table 1. Differences between available Kinect SDKs.

	Kinect for Windows SDK	OpenNI + SensorKinect	Libfreenect
Skeleton tracking	✓	✓	✗
Audio capture	✓	✗	✗
Elevation motor access	✓	✗	✓
Multiple sensors	✓	✓	✗
Other sensors	✗	✓	✗
Infrared image access	✗	✓	✓
Color and depth registration	✓	✓	✗
Rec/Play from HDD	✗	✓	✓
Supported OSes	Windows	Windows, Mac, Linux	Windows, Mac, Linux

Although the output provided by the sensor is the same for every SDK, each one has a different subset of features that are made available for the developer. Microsoft's is the only one capable of accessing the full 1024x768 px color image resolution, while others can only access up to 800x600 px images. The libfreenect is the only one that does not provide body tracking, while only OpenNI cannot access the audio stream. Microsoft's only runs on Windows, while the others can also be used on most major Linux distributions and OSX.

A very useful feature of libfreenect is a side project, known as Fakenect, which provides the capability of recording color, depth, and accelerometer streams from the sensor and using them later as input for the library. It enables the experimentation of Kinect without actually having one attached to the computer, and furthermore, it is possible to test an application that has been developed without the need to stand up in front of the device, which can be physically exhausting. Another good Fakenect feature is the ability to provide a way to specify input behaviors on a body tracking system, allowing the programmer to perform simple tests without a designer or a specialist close by.

Fakenect replicates libfreenect library signatures, so that the decision to use either one can be done at run time, and not during the programming stage. Instead of dynamically linking to libfreenect, the developer links to the Fakenect library, which loads data from a dump file. The application code remains the same to access both of them. The dump is actually a package with header file information enumerating the available data by their file name, describing its type and timestamp. Each data frame is stored in a different file grouped together in the same folder. A color frame is stored in Portable PixMap format (PPM) and a depth frame in Portable GrayMap format (PGM), both of them without any sort of compression. This lack of compression results in large amounts of data even for a few seconds of recording. It grows as big as 30MB/s for 640x480 px color image resolution and 320x240 px depth data resolution.

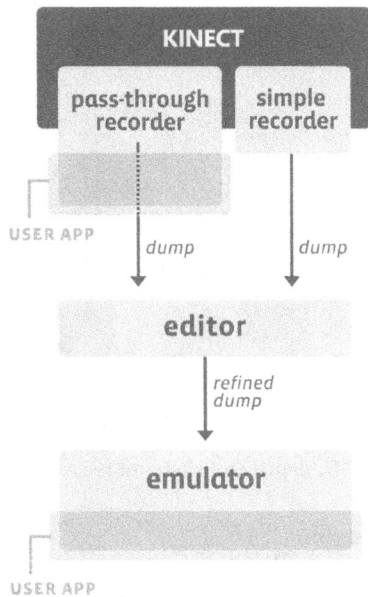

Figure 1. Kina Toolkit architecture.

A tool such as Fakenect provides interesting improvements to the development of interactive body tracking applications, being one of the most evident the fact that the developer no longer needs to stand up and perform the desired movement repetitively during the tests phase. However, it lacks some characteristics that should aggregate much more to Kinect-based development, such as a dump editing tool, skeletal recognition support and pass-through recording.

In spite of Fakenect, libfreenect is a very low level library for Kinect-based applications, which lacks some important features, for example, skeletal recognition and color/depth mapping. This way, the development of an interactive application with such poor support is time-consuming and complex.

OpenNI also features record and playback capabilities, for purposes quite similar to those of Fakenect. They are already included in the core of the framework, but it requires some code modifications for recording or using playback in the session. By virtue of a complex, but well-structured architecture of the framework, it is possible to record data while using it in the user application. The data is saved in an uncompressed .oni file, capable of storing any data streamed by OpenNI, including raw infrared information.

THE KINA TOOLKIT

The Kina Toolkit is a group of tools that enhance the development process of applications that use the Microsoft Kinect SDK. The Microsoft SDK was chosen because it possesses a simple and clean API, has an easy installation procedure and performs skeletal recognition, a feature that was considered crucial for body gestures based applications.

The current version of Kina is compatible to version 1.0 Beta 2 of Kinect for Windows SDK, which only executes on Windows, therefore so does Kina. The SDK is available only on C++ and C#, thus the toolkit was implemented on C++. Any application that makes use of Kinect for Windows SDK should be compatible to Kina, given the current restrictions of our toolkit.

Some project goals defined in the beginning of the Kina project have guided its implementation. One of them was to reduce the effort of the programmer in every possible way. In this direction, it had to be easily interchangeable with the SDK. In order to achieve that, our solution was to create a library that replicates the Kinect for Windows API, just as Fakenect did with libfreenect, and dynamically links to it instead of to the SDK libraries. It was also expected to have a temporal behavior similar to Microsoft library, so a major effort was done to adjust the response times and to synchronize the various data streams. This library is called Kina Emulator, a key part of the proposed toolkit.

The playing mechanism must be supplied with visual information, so a data recorder was also implemented. Actually, two recorders were made, as different situations require different solutions. The recorded information should also be adaptable, thus Kina Editor was created. These tools compose the Kina Toolkit and they interact as illustrated in Figure 1. Detailed information describing how each tool works is provided in the following subsections.

Kina Toolkit is available for download at http://www.gprt.ufpe.br/grvm/kina, along with a step-by-step tutorial explaining how to use it.

Kinect Data Recording

When using the Kinect sensor, it is possible to access three distinct types of data: visual (from color and depth images), audio (from the microphone array), and motor angle. Visual data comprehends all information that comes from both color and infrared sensors. This includes color image, depth image, and detected skeleton information. There is other visual information, such as the image that comes directly from the infrared sensor, instead of the calculated depth. Currently it is not possible to access such information using Microsoft Kinect SDK. Audio information comprises the audio stream from the 4 microphones located on Kinect and also an approximate direction of the beam that generated the current sound. At last, the motor information gives the angle that maps to the current inclination of Kinect tilt motor. Since the focus of Kina is on visual information, only this type of data is recorded. In case the user tries to access non-visual, the return is null.

The recording of the information can happen in two different ways. The conventional one, as occurs with Fakenect, is to use a specific application to simply record the wanted data. Kina offers a recording application capable of capturing and visualizing sensor data at the same time, as shown in Figure 2.

7

Figure 2. Kina Recorder capturing data from Kinect (left) and its corresponding RGB, depth and skeleton representations (right).

This approach frees developers of having to code an application for performing the recording, just by choosing the desired type of data and resolution. This type of recording is useful for establishing an initial data input stream for applications that are in an early stage of development. The disadvantage of this approach is that, while it presents visual feedback of what it is capturing, it doesn't have any relation to the user application whatsoever. So, in order to record a dump that fits the application, the user must be aware of all interactions expected and perform the movements simulating the interactions.

The second way of capturing data from Kinect is through the pass-through recording capability of the toolkit. Differently from the previous approach, this one enables developers to first work on a subset of their application and only then record the user movements, this time while running the application. This means that the application receives data that comes from the sensor and this same data is being stored on file, for further use. The synchronization between user input and application feedback is significantly easier to perform in this way, because the user receives the feedback as the user performs the body gestures/movements. When using the pass-through recording mode, it is not necessary to initialize the recording with specific parameters as done in the conventional recording. The toolkit simply stores every information accessed by the application, using the configuration passed as parameter on its initialization. As happens with the conventional recording, the result is the same: a file containing the dump information. There is no distinction between files generated by the two capture modes. Both can serve as input to any application using the toolkit in "play" mode.

Figure 3 illustrates the layout in the dump file for storing a 640x480 px color image and a 320x240 px depth image, together with the corresponding skeleton information.

Data Compression
In order to decrease the amount of memory needed to store the information captured, a compression scheme had to be adopted. Instead of using a video compression algorithm, we decided to use single image compression for both color image and depth information. This is due to the fact that two video streams, one for color and other for depth information, would generate more overhead to the application that uses the toolkit while accessing the recorded dumps in real time. By compressing frame by frame independently does not take into consideration the temporal relationship between frames for compression, but there are gains on performance.

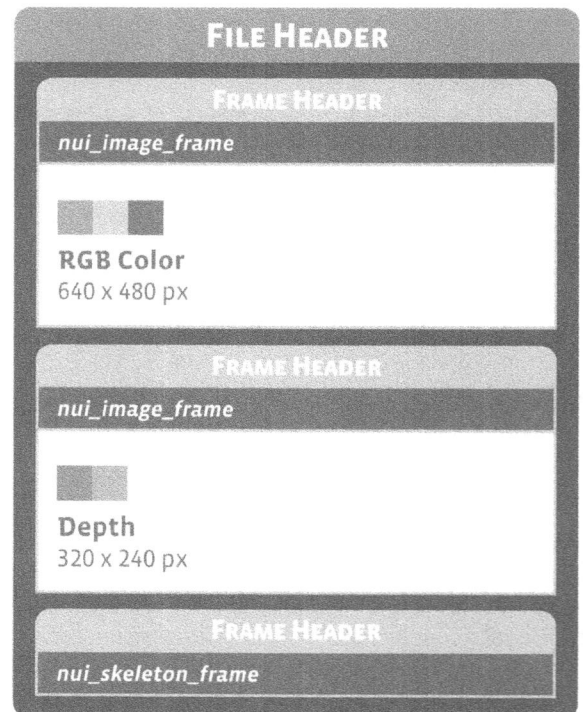

Figure 3. Space required by the dump file to store uncompressed (left) and compressed (right) data.

It is important for the toolkit that it should be as light as possible in a way that it does not interfere significantly on the application performance, so that it could be executed almost as if it was accessing the data directly from the Kinect device.

Since the depth data must be as accurate as possible, it is advisable to use a lossless compression scheme while processing this type of data; therefore, PNG compression is used for depth data. Differently, artifacts in the color image result in less damage to the data, when using it for visualization purposes, as the human vision cannot perceive some small variations in brightness frequency. This way, the color data is compressed with JPEG, a lossy algorithm, saving a considerable amount of memory space. The chosen parameters allowed a compression of about 93% without damaging visualization quality.

The data compression, in order to not compromise the Kinect data capture, is only performed when the application is finalized. This way, the data captured is stored in its original format (raw) on memory. At the end, a process iterates over all data and performs the compression using the specific algorithm for every frame found (JPEG for color and PNG for depth image). After compression, the resulting data is stored in the dump file. It was not necessary to compress the skeleton information, since it represents a small percentage of the entire frame size when compared to both color and depth images. Using 90% of JPEG quality, it was possible to maintain an almost non-perceivable visual difference between original and compressed images with a satisfactory amount of data compression. A single block of data containing compressed 640x480 px color image, 320x240 px depth image, together with the skeleton information, occupies an average of 92KB.

Kinect Data Playing

A dump file can have up to three types of information: color image, depth information, and skeleton data. According to how the data was captured, some information may not be present. A configuration file named "kina.ini", located at the same folder as the application executable, contains information about which dump file should be opened and two extra parameters detailing how it should be read. One of the additional parameters indicates whether the content in the dump file should be read repeatedly or just once. The other parameter provides the toolkit with the size of the read buffer to be used (how many frames should be read from file before asked by the application).

The Kina Emulator possesses a thread that runs in background and is responsible for allocating, reading and decompressing the data stored in the dump file. Once initialized, it performs the following task sequence:

- if read buffer is not full, read frame from dump file;
- decompress information based on its type (JPEG or PNG);
- store information in the read buffer.

If the read loop is not activated in the configuration file, once it reaches the end of the dump file, it stops feeding the read buffer. After that, the application should receive an error indication every time it asks for a new frame.

The Kina Emulator thread starts working as soon as the application calls the initialization function of the SDK. Because of the fact that different frames can have different sizes due to the compression scheme adopted, the thread starts by reading the entire dump file and saves the initial address of each frame. This information will be used later for fast indexing of the stored data. The emulator can return an error signal as result every time one of these situations happens:

- the dump file is not found during initialization;
- the SDK is initialized requesting data that is not present in the current dump file (for instance, data with different resolutions);
- a specific data cannot be found inside the dump file (for example, the application asks the toolkit for skeleton data, but the file only contains color image and depth information);
- the application tries to read a frame from the toolkit but there are no more frames available (the option that enables the continuous read from the dump file is disabled).

The timestamp of each data provided by the SDK is essential in order to maintain the temporal coherence between sensor and emulator. Based on the timestamps, it is possible to simulate the waiting time between two consecutive frame reads. For example, in order to access two sequential frames, one must wait until the difference between timestamps is equal or higher than the current time. Only then the information is made available to the application. This mechanism is used in order to guarantee the capture frame rate of Kinect data. By using this, it is possible to read a certain amount of frames almost at the same time, independently if they are read from SDK or Kina Emulator. Microsoft Kinect SDK provides two different ways of reading data from the sensor: polling- and event-based. Currently, only the first one is available on Kina Emulator. Event-based reading is a work in progress and should be available soon. Despite that, the current state of the toolkit allows the creation of fully functional Kinect-based programs, such as games and data visualization applications (more detail will be given about these applications on the remaining sections).

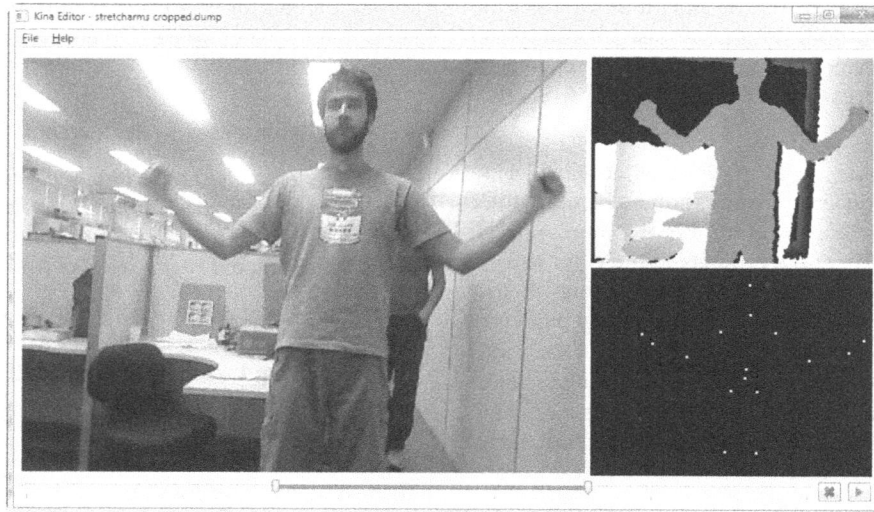

Figure 4. Kina Editor interface.

Dump Editor

Another important component of the Kina Toolkit is the Kina Editor. It was created in order to help editing a dump that was previously captured using the Kina Recorder tool or the pass-through mode. One of the tool features is the possibility of removing undesirable frames from the dump file, in order to make it smaller and more succinct. This procedure occurs by selecting a range of frames using the graphical interface of the application and then removing the undesired group of frames from the entire sequence. There is no limitation regarding the number of times this operation can be done. Another feature is that it also enables users to combine two or more dump files by joining together their data. Using only these two operations, "removal" and "join", it reduces even more the work during the test phase, since it is possible to record a single sequence of all user movements and later divide the captured data into relevant segments. Based on the Kina Editor, an online movement database was created in order to help developers construct their own applications without the need of having a real Kinect device available.

The Kina Editor supports every data format (color image, depth and skeleton, using any resolution) that can be stored in a dump file. In other words, it supports all formats available on Microsoft Kinect SDK. The tool was implemented using the Qt library [13] for the graphical interface and specifically the libqxt [7] component for the slider, and libjpeg [5] and libpng [6] for decompressing the compacted data. There is a fixed space on screen for each one of the three data types available. The color image is shown on the left, occupying most of the screen space, while depth and skeleton information are shown on the right side of the screen. Apart from the resolution being used, the content is adjusted to fit the screen accordingly. Kina Editor interface is illustrated in Figure 4.

When a dump file is opened by Kina Editor, all frames are decompressed and stored into memory. Therefore, it demands a high amount of memory available in order to allow the selection and navigation through different frames in a smooth way. After the frames are edited, either removed or added to the main sequence, the remaining frames are not re-compressed. What happens is a direct copy of the original frames that still are at the new sequence. This prevents the loss of image quality by compressing over and over again the same frame with JPEG while saves processing time. If necessary, the timestamps are adjusted in order to maintain the temporal coherence between frames.

Seamless Integration

When designing Kina Toolkit, one of the main concerns was that it should be easy to use and require the minimum knowledge as possible from the developer. Assuming that the developer is familiar with Microsoft Kinect SDK, the Kina Toolkit requires no additional knowledge to be used. This was possible by a direct mapping between Microsoft Kinect SDK and the toolkit functions. This way, it is possible to use the toolkit as if the developer was using the SDK itself. The expected result of the functions is the same, and all functions regarding visual data are fully functional. This is a notorious advantage of the Kina toolkit, because it is possible to switch between it and Microsoft Kinect SDK by simply changing the header file being included on code. Consequently, the remaining application code does not need to be altered. Once the application has the expected behavior during tests using the Kina toolkit, the developer can switch again to Microsoft's header file, in order to perform the final tests using the Kinect device itself.

In addition to the easiness of use, the toolkit also offers very low overhead to the application when executing on "play mode", reading data from the dump file. This happens because an internal thread is responsible for reading the dump data, instead of intensively processing the depth data looking for skeleton matches, as performed by the SDK. The toolkit is available as a dynamic library, containing a respective DLL (Dynamic Link Library) and header file. When in pass-through recording mode, the toolkit itself accesses the Microsoft Kinect SDK in order to capture data from the sensor. Only in this case the SDK is required to be installed at the system as well.

DEVELOPMENT MODEL

The development model of applications for Kinect is not different from any other application development model. Regardless of which one is used and the size of the project, it almost invariably requires design, implementation, and evaluation steps. However, when applied to Kinect development, it becomes unsuitable, especially for developers.

The first issue is right at the beginning of a project, as it is not simple for designers and specialists to specify input behaviors that the applications should answer to when dealing with gestures and body movements. The most common solutions, textual and pictorial specifications, are not enough to inform the programmer how the movement should be executed. Movies are a better solution, but they lack depth information and cannot be used as input for Kinect. All of those fail to be used on the definition of an input reference.

A second issue arises at the testing phase, when it is necessary to have a Kinect device available and attached to the development machine. In order to test a feature, it is required to stand up in front of the Kinect and perform the desired movement. This can become physically exhausting after several repetitions.

Those issues degrade the process of development in a remarkable way, and therefore we propose the use of Kina Toolkit to help solving all of the issues presented previously. Being able to record the desired movement and use it as a specification component is a great advancement in the design and prototyping of body tracking interaction systems, as it is useful for designers and programmers. Designers may use it as a definitive reference of their input modeling, this way avoiding the need to be present in some evaluations. Programmers take advantage by using it as the input of their programs, avoiding the need to place him/herself within sight of the sensor during tests, thus softening the physical effort required. Additionally, with Kina it is possible to perform tests even without a Kinect.

These adjustments can be summarized in a revised development model as illustrated in Figure 5. After finishing the concept of the application, the designers specify the input behaviors by using Kina Recorder to create dumps and Kina Editor to precisely select what is desired (step 1). This procedure requires the use of Kinect, but if it is not available at the moment, the online

Movement Database may also be used. Dumps are used by the programmer during the development and testing of the feature set, being loaded using Kina Emulator (steps 2 and 4), without any need for Kinect. Eventually it may be required to perform more captures (step 3). When a feature is implemented, it is then taken to be tested (step 4). If the result is not yet satisfactory, it goes back to development (step 5); otherwise, it is marked as completed (step 6). When a set of features is completed, it shall be taken to be tested with Kinect (step 7) for a real-world testing scenario. If it fails, it goes back to development (step 8); otherwise, it can be pushed to release (step 9).

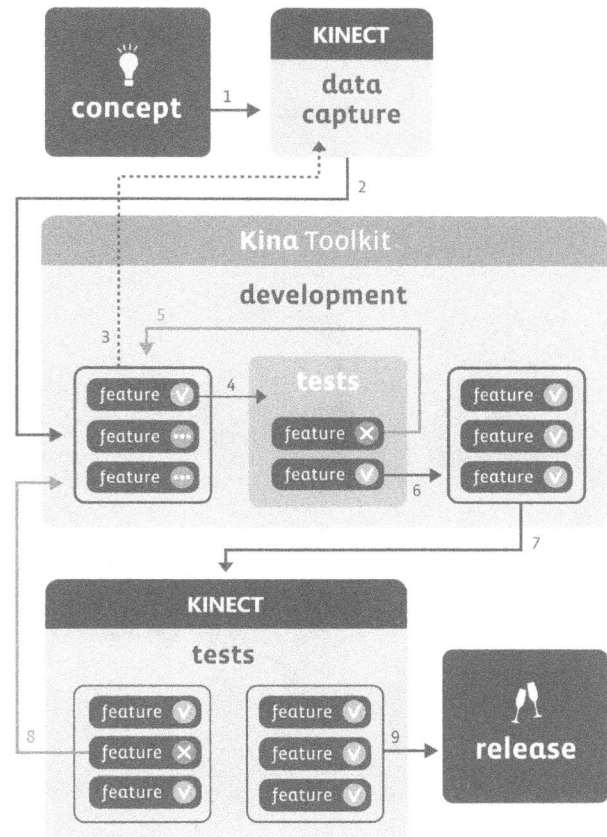

Figure 5. The revised development model for Kinect-based applications using the Kina Toolkit.

MOVEMENT DATABASE

It is already known the possibility of using Kinect sensor dumps with Kina Toolkit, which relieves the developer from having a Kinect on the majority of the development phase. However, dump files are created by using the sensor itself and capturing its data, therefore it must be utilized at least once on the beginning of the project. In order to abstract the need of a Kinect sensor during the development phase, a movement database was created. It is composed by a collection of different dump files, each one representing a single body gesture/movement. A consequence of having generic dump files that represent common movements is the possibility of using them as reference for different tests and projects. This way, it would be possible to evaluate the applications using some metric that considers the exact same input for different scenarios.

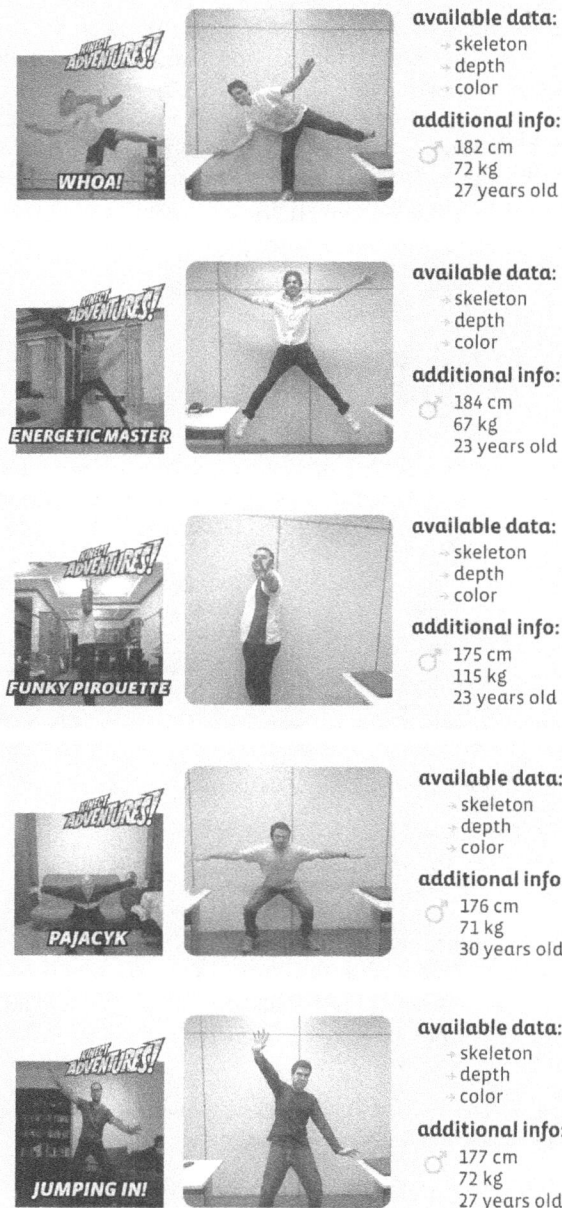

Figure 6. Samples found on Kina Movement Database. On the left, images of users playing Kinect Adventures that were used as inspiration for populating the database. On the right, the corresponding movements captured in a controlled environment.

The movement database is formed by a set of simple movements, which can be combined using Kina Editor in order to generate complex sequences of movements. The initial set of movements to be part of the database was defined by analyzing the most common body gestures/movements performed by Kinect-based game players, specifically when using the Kinect Adventures game [4]. Based on user screenshots, it was possible to replicate the most common movements and add a dump containing each one of them to the database. Figure 6 illustrates some dump samples that were placed on the database based on their similarity to common movements of users when playing Kinect Adventures.

Besides the dump files, the database also takes into consideration the specificity of some applications (for example, related to health or sports) and provides some textual attributes that help classifying and searching for a specific dump file. This is achieved by a tag-based system for identifying the nature of the behavior on the dump file, and some attributes of the person performing the movement, such as: number of people performing the movement, gender, height, weight, age, etc. There was no exhaustive study as for how to classify the movements, but great effort was done to provide sufficient information. Examples of tags are: "circular left hand", "raising arms", "jumping".

The Kina Movement Database is currently online and was made to be collaborative, which means that other researchers can produce and send their own movements captured using the toolkit, in order to make the database even more complete. It can be accessed on the address mentioned in the Kina Toolkit section.

RESULTS
Kina was designed to help in the development of Kinect-based applications, with emphasis in those that make use of body-tracking interaction. In order to fulfill its goals, it addresses a series of issues in this development process that is believed to be flawed or that could be enhanced. Some of the improvements are already covered by tools for other SDKs, such as the possibility to develop without an attached Kinect, the comfort of remaining seated while testing or the indispensable deterministic testing procedure. Others, such as the ability to edit large sequences of data, the movement database and the revised development model are contributions of this work that are unique, until now, to Microsoft SDK.

One of the main concerns when implementing Kina Emulator was that it had to provide a temporal response similar to the one of the SDK. The most compute intensive operations performed by the toolkit are the compressing and decompressing tasks. The libjpg and libpng compression libraries take in average 14.73 ms and 1.45 ms to decompress a 640x480 px color image and a 320x240 px one, respectively. That is short enough to supply a real time data stream. This way, the approach chosen was to execute the decompression of a buffered frame in a background thread while the user manipulates previous data. By doing so, the initialization time of the toolkit is short and the temporal response throughout the execution is kept equivalent to the SDK.

Another concern was the memory overhead of the emulator, as it is desired to be minimal. If the whole dump was decompressed and kept in memory, it would have a very fast response, but would demand hundreds of MBs. The current design, by keeping only two buffered frames of each type of image, requires only 11 MB of RAM, while the SDK itself makes use of 158 MB. It is not clear why the SDK consumes so much memory, but it is probably due to the skeleton recognition phase, where it tries to match a segmented part of the depth image with a database of body positions [15].

The simple recorder has milder memory requirement, since it is supposed to be used by itself (separate from the user application). The pass-through mode is more complex as it has to share memory with the user application. The current solution keeps all the frames in memory and hence needs a better memory management.

Kina Toolkit was tested and experimented in a computer course, namely Advanced Topics in Media and Interaction, where the students had to develop a body tracking interaction project based on Kinect. The purpose of the course was to introduce nonconventional interaction systems and techniques, and to provide means for the students to develop their own applications in this regard.

In the experiment, there were 12 computer science students, from 20 to 27 years old, of which only one was a woman. None of them reported previous knowledge of natural interaction development, but they were familiar to general purpose programming. They were divided in 3 diverse groups, based on acquaintance to each other. The experiment with the toolkit lasted for 2 months, but previously the students had other 2 months of classes about interaction.

As most of the students did not own a Kinect device, the toolkit happened to become extremely useful for a proper unravel of the projects. Unfortunately, it was not possible to compare the development of application with and without Kina, since the quality of the resultant application influenced the student's grades, and it could create an unfair situation. The outcome of the course were several interesting projects shown in Figure 7, including: a bug-smashing casual game, in which the player gains power-ups if he/she kills the right sequence of insects; a functional training program, that instructs the user to execute functional training positions, indicating how well positioned he/she is; and an art experiment, where the user paints in a virtual canvas using his/her own body as a brush.

Figure 7. Example applications developed using Kina Toolkit: (1) a game in which the player must use his/her hands to kill insects; (2) an application for conditioning the user to perform functional exercises; (3) an art experiment of painting using body parts.

In the end of the course, the students were asked to provide a feedback about their experience with the Kina Toolkit. In summary, they reported that the toolkit was indispensable during the test phase, where they used it to properly calibrate the response of the program. They were pleased by the fact that they could easily develop and test even without the Kinect and that it notably relieved the fatigue of testing. They also suggested that in the emulator it should be possible to dynamically change its input dump and that the recorder should provide a GUI for setting its parameters.

CONCLUSION

According to the feedback given by developers, the Kina Toolkit was able to successfully achieve its goals. The experience of using the developed tools as support for a course inside the university was fundamental in order to validate its adoption by a variety of users, from less experienced to advanced ones. The proposed development model was shown to be well suited for Kinect applications while effectively enhancing developers' productivity.

An ongoing work focuses on the implementation of event-based capture, so that it will be possible for the application to use Kina and be notified every time information is available.

As future work, we intend to perform more tests involving different resolutions to guarantee that there is no combination between color and depth information that fails when stored and played by the toolkit. We also intend to implement some features suggested from developers, such as the ability of changing the input dump file in real time. The amount of different movements available on the online Movement Database should be incremented. At last, event-based capturing should be implemented, broadening the compatibility of the toolkit.

In order to combine short movement sequences in a smoother way, to have as result complex movement sequences, different interpolation techniques will be researched and implemented so that the transition between distinct dump information be the least perceptible possible.

ACKNOWLEDGMENTS

The authors would like to thank CAPES, FINEP and CENPES Petrobras for financially supporting this research (TechPetro process 3662/2006).

REFERENCES

1. Bouffard, P., and Tomlin, C. Quadrotor Autonomous Flight and Obstacle Avoidance with Kinect Sensor, http://hybrid.eecs.berkeley.edu/starmac, 2011.

2. Fakenect. http://openkinect.org/wiki/Fakenect.

3. Hirofuchi, T. USB/IP PROJECT. http://usbip.sourceforge.net/

4. Kinect Adventures! http://www.xbox.com/kinectadventures.

5. Libjpeg. http://libjpeg.sourceforge.net.

6. Libpng. http://libpng.org.

7. LibQxt. http://libqxt.org.

8. Microsoft Kinect for Windows SDK beta 2. http://research.microsoft.com/kinectsdk.

9. Microsoft Kinect for Xbox 360, http://www.xbox.com/kinect, 2012.

10. Newcombe, R. A., Molyneaux, D., Kim, D., Davison, A. J., Shotton, J., Hodges, S., and Fitzgibbon, A. KinectFusion : Real-Time Dense Surface Mapping and Tracking, in Proceedings of ISMAR 2011, ACM Press, 127-136.

11. OpenKinet project. http://openkinect.org.

12. OpenNI Framework. http://www.openni.org.

13. Qt Framework. http://qt.nokia.com/products.

14. Reis, B., Teixeira, J. M., and Kelner, J. An open-source tool for distributed viewing of kinect data on the web, in Proceedings of WRVA 2011.

15. Shotton, J., Fitzgibbon, A., Cook, M., Sharp, T., Finocchio, M., Moore, R., Kipman, A., and Andrew Blake. Real-Time human pose recognition in parts from single depth images, in Proceedings of CVPR 2011.

Fusion in Multimodal Interactive Systems: An HMM-Based Algorithm for User-Induced Adaptation

Bruno Dumas
WISE Lab
Vrije Universiteit Brussel
Pleinlaan 2
1050 Brussels, Belgium
bdumas@vub.ac.be

Beat Signer
WISE Lab
Vrije Universiteit Brussel
Pleinlaan 2
1050 Brussels, Belgium
bsigner@vub.ac.be

Denis Lalanne
DIVA Group
Université de Fribourg
Boulevard de Pérolles 90
1700 Fribourg, Switzerland
denis.lalanne@unifr.ch

ABSTRACT

Multimodal interfaces have shown to be ideal candidates for interactive systems that adapt to a user either automatically or based on user-defined rules. However, user-based adaptation demands for the corresponding advanced software architectures and algorithms. We present a novel multimodal fusion algorithm for the development of adaptive interactive systems which is based on hidden Markov models (HMM). In order to select relevant modalities at the semantic level, the algorithm is linked to temporal relationship properties. The presented algorithm has been evaluated in three use cases from which we were able to identify the main challenges involved in developing adaptive multimodal interfaces.

Author Keywords

Multimodal interaction, multimodal fusion, HMM-based fusion, user interface adaptation

ACM Classification Keywords

H.5.2 Information Interfaces and Presentation: User Interfaces—*Graphical user interfaces, Prototyping, Theory and methods*

General Terms

Algorithms; Human Factors.

INTRODUCTION

Multimodal interaction has been shown to enhance human-computer interaction by providing users with an interaction model that is closer to human-human interaction than standard interaction via mouse or keyboard. By providing users with a number of different modalities and by offering them the possibility to use these modalities either in a complementary or in a redundant manner, multimodal interfaces take advantage of the parallel processing capabilities of the human brain [25]. Furthermore, due to the different ways on how modalities can be combined, multimodal interfaces have the potential to adapt to a user, by offering them one or multiple preferred schemes of interactions. However, research on the combination or fusion of different modalities has progressed slower than the appearance of new modalities. In particular, fusion-related topics such as the dynamic adaptation of fusion engines, for example with help of machine learning techniques, still need to be addressed in more detail by the scientific community [21].

In this article, we present a novel algorithm for the fusion of input modalities in multimodal interfaces. In the past few years, we focussed on studying different aspects of multimodal input fusion. To this end, a framework for the prototyping of multimodal interfaces, called HephaisTK, has been developed. HephaisTK allows developers to focus on the creation of their multimodal applications, without having to worry about the integration of input libraries, input data normalisation, concurrency management or the implementation of fusion algorithms. The HephaisTK framework comes along with a number of fusion algorithms for managing input data. Among the different algorithms, a symbolic-statistical fusion algorithm based on hidden Markov models (HMMs), which offers the possibility to take a user's feedback into account, has been developed. While this novel multimodal fusion algorithm represents a first major contribution of our paper, a second contribution is the identification of a number of challenges to be overcome for the introduction of user-induced automatic multimodal interface adaptation based on some of our initial explorations.

We start by presenting related work on prototyping tools and multimodal fusion algorithms with respect to the adaptation to the user and context. The following section introduces the HephaisTK framework and its architecture, as well as the SMUIML language, on which the presented algorithm has been built. The HMM-based fusion algorithm that we used for the user adaptation is then presented and we describe how to integrate such an algorithm in a typical multimodal system. This is followed by an evaluation of our HMM-based algorithm. Finally, we provide some conclusions and outline possible future work.

RELATED WORK

Research on fusion algorithms and prototyping tools for multimodal interactive systems has been an active field during the last two decades. In this section, we are going to introduce the state of the art on fusion algorithms for multimodal interactive systems, provide a summary of notable results on prototyping tools and give an overview on adaptation to user and context.

Fusion of Multimodal Input Data

On a conceptual level, Sharma et al. [29] consider the data, feature and decision levels for the fusion of incoming data. Each fusion scheme can operate at a different level of analysis of the same modality channel. *Data-level fusion* considers data from a modality channel in its rawest form, where fusion is generally used on different channels of the same modality, in order to enhance or extract new results. Adaptation of data-level fusion typically focusses on taking into account contextual information to improve results. *Feature-level fusion* is used on tightly coupled, synchronised modalities, such as speech and lip movement. Low-level features extracted from raw data are usually processed with machine-learning algorithms. Adaptation on the feature level can be used when multiple data sources provide data for the same modality. *Decision-level fusion* is the most common type of fusion in interactive multimodal applications, because of its ability to extract meaning from loosely coupled modalities. Complex forms of adaptation can be applied on the decision-level, including the adaptation to the number of users, user profiles or device. On an algorithmic level, typical decision-level fusion algorithms are frame-based fusion, unification-based fusion and hybrid symbolic-statistical fusion.

- *Frame-based fusion* [18] uses data structures called frames or features for the meaning representation of data coming from various sources or modalities.

- *Unification-based fusion* [30] is based on the recursive merging of attribute/value structures to obtain a logical meaning representation. However, both frame-based as well as unification-based fusion rely on a predefined and non-evolutive behaviour.

- *Symbolic-statistical fusion* [6, 31] is an evolution of standard symbolic unification-based approaches, which adds statistical processing techniques to the fusion techniques described above. These hybrid fusion techniques have been demonstrated to achieve robust and reliable results. A classical example of a symbolic-statistical hybrid fusion technique is the Member-Team-Committee architecture used in Quickset [9]. However, these techniques need training data specific to the targeted application.

On a modelling level, the CARE properties as defined by Coutaz and Nigay [10] show how modalities can be composed. Note that CARE stands for *complementarity, assignment, redundancy* and *equivalence*. Complementary modalities will need all modalities for the meaning to be extracted, assigned modalities allocate one and only one modality to each meaning, redundant modalities state that all modalities can lead to the same meaning and equivalent modalities assert that any modality can lead to the same meaning. The difference between redundancy and equivalence is the way in which cases with multiple modalities occurring at the same time are dealt with.

Multimodal Authoring Frameworks

Quickset by Cohen et al. [9] is a speech/pen multimodal interface based on the Open Agent Architecture[1], which served as a test bed for unification-based and hybrid fusion methods. The integration of multimodal input fusion with the modelling of multimodal human-machine dialogues was introduced by IMBuilder and MEngine [4], which both make use of finite state machines. In their multimodal system, Flippo et al. [14] use a parallel application-independent fusion technique, based on a software agent architecture. In their system, fusion has been realised by using frames. After these original explorations, the last few years have seen the appearance of a number of fully integrated tools for the creation of multimodal interfaces. Among these tools are comprehensive open source frameworks such as OpenInterface [28] and Squidy [20]. These frameworks share a similar conceptual architecture with different goals. While OpenInterface targets pure or combined modalities, Squidy was created as a particularly effective tool for streams composed of low level data. Finally, in contrast to the linear, stream-based architecture adopted by most other solutions, the Mudra [16] framework adopts a service-based architecture. However, few of these tools provided services to test, use and compare multiple fusion algorithms.

Adaptation to User and Context

When considering user adaptation, different ways of adapting the user interface can be considered. On the one hand, the user interface can be created in such a way that it will adapt automatically and without any user intervention. The adaptation can thus be performed automatically to the context of use or to the user. On the other hand, users can be given the possibility to modify the user interface in a proactive way. More formally, Malinowski et al. [23] proposed a complete taxonomy for user interface adaptation. Their taxonomy is based on four different stages of adaptation in a given interface, namely *initiative, proposal, decision* and *execution*. Each of these adaptations at the four different stages can be performed by the user, the machine or both. López-Jaquero et al. proposed the ISATINE framework [22]. This framework introduces seven stages of adaptation including the goals, the initiative, the specification, the application, the transition, the interpretation as well as the evaluation of adaptation. Interestingly, while adaptation has been investigated for traditional WIMP interfaces [5] or context-aware mobile interfaces [1], less work has been devoted to user-induced adaptation in the context of multimodal interfaces. Octavia et al. [24] explored adaptation in virtual environments, especially on how to build the user model.

The HephaisTK framework that we are going to present in the next section and in particular a novel adaptive multimodal fusion algorithm, contribute to this currently not much explored research on user-induced adaptive multimodal interfaces.

HEPHAISTK FRAMEWORK

Before we present our new solution for user-induced adaptation in multimodal interaction, we introduce the framework in

---

[1]http://www.openagent.com

which the new algorithm has been integrated, since its architecture, modules and scripting language influenced the choice we made in terms of our user adaptation solution.

HephaisTK is a framework that has been built to help developers in creating multimodal interfaces via a range of tools [12]. The HephaisTK framework shown in Figure 1 offers engineers a framework which manages, stores and presents data coming from a number of input recognisers in an uniform way, with the possibility to query past input events. Second, the tool provides different multimodal input data fusion algorithms, including a classical implementation of frame-based fusion as well as our novel algorithm presented in the next section. Third, multimodal human-machine dialogue is described by means of a high level modelling language, called SMUIML, which is linked to the CARE properties [10]. Compared to the tools in the related work section, HephaisTK focusses on the study of fusion algorithms, as well as on the high level modelling of multimodal human-machine interaction through the SMUIML language.

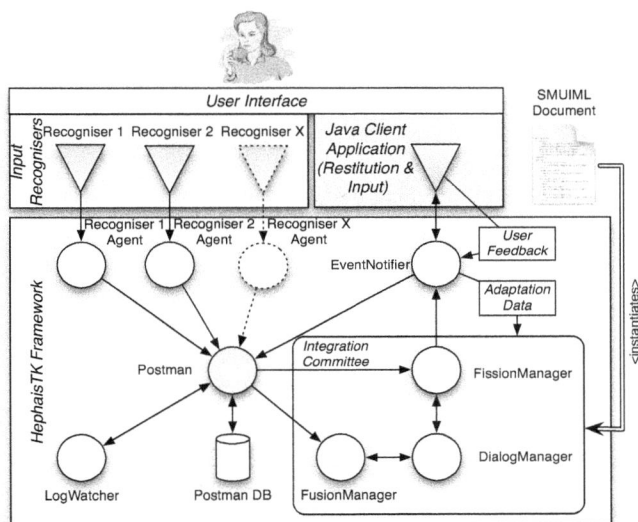

Figure 1. HephaisTK architecture

Developers of multimodal interfaces define the behaviour of their multimodal interface in a configuration file loaded by HephaisTK. This configuration file defines which recognisers to use (*input/output level*), how an event is triggered and how it is linked to the human-machine dialogue (*event level*), and the various states of the dialogue and the transitions between these states are specified (*dialogue level*). The *adaptation level* links the dialogue with contextual and user information. To model this human-machine dialogue for a specific client application, the SMUIML language has been developed [13].

The SMUIML language is divided in three different layers dealing with different levels of abstraction as shown in Figure 2. The lowest level specifies the different modalities which will be used in the context of an application, as well as the particular recognisers to be used to access the different modalities. The middle level addresses input and output events. Input events are called *triggers* whereas output

events are called *actions*. Triggers are defined per modality and therefore not directly tied to specific recognisers. They can express different ways to trigger a particular event. For example, a speech trigger can be defined in such a way that "clear", "erase" and "delete" will all lead to the same event. Actions are the messages that the framework will send to the client application. The highest level of abstraction in Figure 2 describes the actual human-machine dialogue by means of defining the contexts of use and interweaving the different input events and output messages between those different contexts, as well as link to adaptation-related information. The resulting description takes the form of a state machine, in a similar way as Bourguet's IMBuilder [4]. The combination of modalities is defined based on the CARE properties as well as the (non-)sequentiality of input triggers.

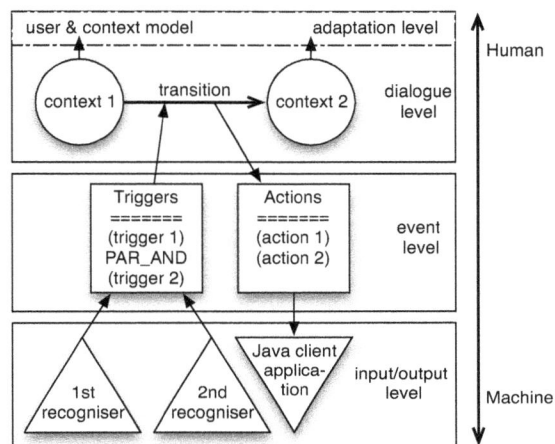

Figure 2. SMUIML and its three levels of abstraction

To come back to the overall HephaisTK architecture, an integration committee is in charge of interpreting the multimodal input data in order to create a suitable answer for the user. The different components of the integration committee are shown in Figure 1. The `FusionManager` and `FissionManager` are linked to the `DialogManager` which informs them about the current state of the interaction and what they can expect as input information. The `DialogManager` relies on the interpretation of the application-specific SMUIML script for managing the interaction. The `FusionManager` focusses on the interpretation of incoming input data based on information provided by the `DialogManager`. It also encapsulates the different available fusion algorithms. In addition to a classic frame-based multimodal fusion algorithm, we have developed an HMM-based multimodal fusion algorithm which is described in the next section.

HMM-BASED MULTIMODAL FUSION ALGORITHM
As presented in the previous section, the HephaisTK framework has been designed to serve as a test platform for multimodal input data fusion algorithms. Based on HephaisTK, different algorithms including our new machine learning-based fusion algorithm have been implemented and tested.

The idea of mixing the adaptiveness of machine learning-based recognition algorithms with the expressive power of higher level rules is getting more attention recently, with examples demonstrating the overall effectiveness in recognition rates and expressiveness of such hybrid approaches [7]. However, symbolic-statistical approaches, such as the ones mentioned in the related work section, tend to not take into account temporal relationships between modalities, which we believe is a necessary feature of fusion algorithms for multimodal interactive systems. Furthermore, the adaptation to user behaviour has only been sparsely studied. We also have to stress that machine learning algorithms have mainly been used for multimodal input fusion at the feature level to typically improve the recognition results of a specific modality or in offline analysis systems such as biometrics or meeting browsers. However, at the decision level, purely rule-based approaches such as frame-based or unification-based fusion have been the norm so far.

Goals of the Algorithm

When considering which type of machine learning should be used, hidden Markov models have been prioritised because of their easy adaptation to time-related processes. Hidden Markov models have historically been used in temporal pattern recognition tasks, such as speech [19, 26], handwriting or gesture recognition. Since the fusion of input data also focusses on time-dependant patterns, HMMs have been seen as one of the obvious choices when considering the different alternatives among statistical models. Due to the fact that SMUIML models the human-machine interaction via states, the transition from the dialogue model to a Markov process is relatively straightforward. Hidden Markov models have already been used for tasks such as video segmentation [17] or biometric person recognition [8] using multimodal input data at the data or feature level. However, to the best of our knowledge, HMMs have not yet been applied for the fusion of multimodal input events at the decision level in the context of real-time multimodal human-machine interfaces.

Our goals when designing the new multimodal fusion algorithm were threefold:

1. Consider a class of machine learning algorithm which has shown its efficiency at modelling the flow of time events and thus is ideally suited for the modelling of multimodal human-computer interaction.

2. In the fusion recognition process take into account a set of the most likely results from probability-based modality recognisers, such as speech or gesture recognisers.

3. Be able to adapt and correct results from the fusion algorithm on-the-fly based on user feedback.

Hidden Markov Models

As presented by Rabiner [26], hidden Markov models are based on discrete Markov processes, in particular discrete time-varying random phenomenons for which the Markov property holds. In place of directly observing the states of the discrete Markov process, a hidden Markov model observes the (hidden) states through a set of stochastic processes that produce the sequence of observations. The most likely sequence of states, given a set of observations, is extracted by the Viterbi algorithm [15]. Finally, the training of hidden Markov models is achieved with help of the Baum-Welch algorithm [2], a particular case of a generalised expectation-maximisation algorithm.

Algorithm in Action

The first challenge when integrating HMMs as fusion algorithms for multimodal interaction is to map the features and states to the actual human-machine interaction model. In our case, data fed to the HMM will be semantic-level information, such as a speech utterance or the high-level description of a gesture such as "flick left". For our implementation of the algorithm, the Java Jahmm HMM library[2] was used. Scripts written in the SMUIML modelling language [13] serve as high-level descriptions of the HMMs topology. A second challenge was to minimise the need for training the algorithm before being able to actually use the system. As we explain later, a pre-training of our system is achieved through the simulation of expected inputs described in SMUIML.

As an example to explain how the algorithm works, let us consider the *"put that there"* example by Bolt [3]. In this example, a user is seated in front of a wall on which different shapes are displayed. To move a shape from one place to the other, the user points to the shape and utters *"put that there"* while pointing to another place on the wall. Five different input events are expected, including three speech related triggers (*"put"*, *"that"* and *"there"*) and two gesture related triggers (i.e. pointing events). Note that in our example, the two pointing events will be considered as events of the same type.

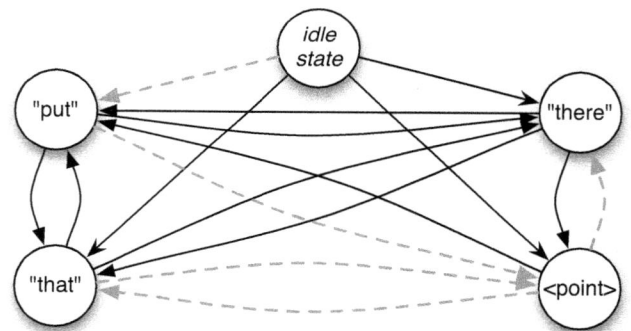

Figure 3. A sequence of states for a *"put that there"* multimodal event

The step from the high-level human-machine interaction description to the actual implementation of the HMM-based fusion algorithm is achieved as described in the following. In SMUIML, the `<context>` element is used to describe different application states. For example, in a drawing application, free line drawing and shape editing could be modelled as different states of the application. Different application states in SMUIML are modelled with help of one HMM for each state. This implies that changing states in an application created with HephaisTK, corresponds to changing from one

---

[2]http://code.google.com/p/jahmm/

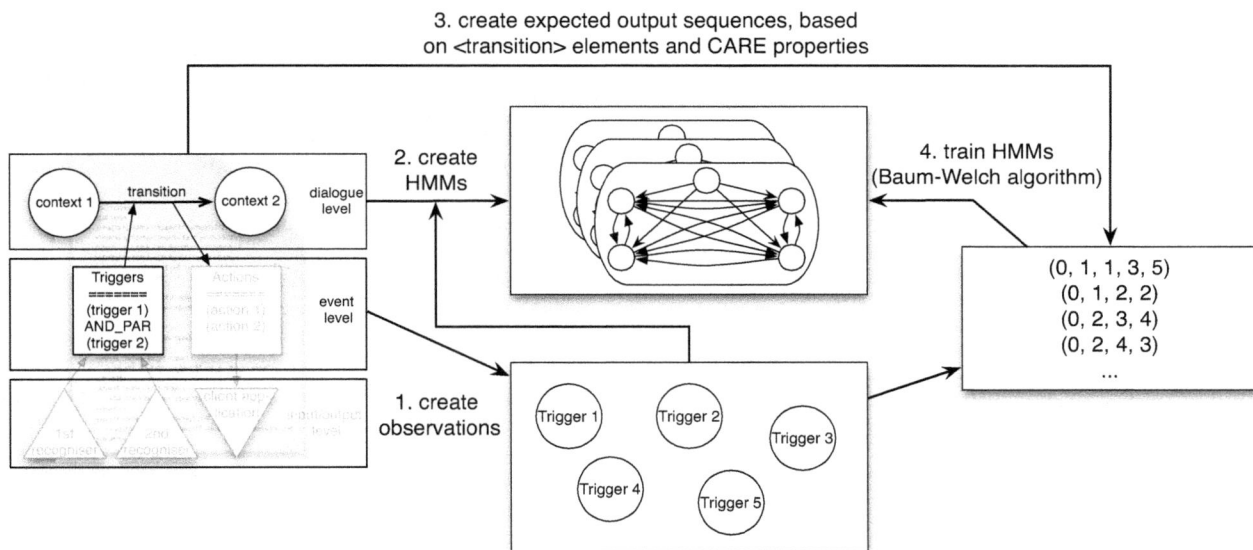

Figure 4. Instantiation of the HMM-based fusion algorithm with observations and HMMs created and trained based on a SMUIML script

<context> element to another in SMUIML. This in turn is equivalent to switching from one HMM to another HMM. The *"put that there"* example consists of a single interaction with only one context and thus a single HMM. In the current implementation of the algorithm, any adapted training done after the initialisation phase will not transfer directly during context switching.

At runtime, input events such as a speech utterance or a gesture are modelled as individual observations. Basically, one input event described in the SMUIML script corresponds to one observation of the HMM. Every time an input event is processed by the HephaisTK framework, it is sent to the FusionManager. For the list of all input events happening in a specified time window, the FusionManager considers potential combinations. Those combinations are then injected into the HMM. The Viterbi algorithm is subsequently used on the HMM to extract the most probable state sequences. These state sequences are compared to a set of expected observation sequences which are defined by the <transition> elements of the current <context> in the SMUIML script. For example, the following succession of input events: *"put"* *point* *"that"* *point* *"there"* would generate a state sequence as illustrated by the red dashed arrows in Figure 3. If a match is found, the information that a sequence of events corresponding to the SMUIML script description has been found is passed to the client application.

Instantiation of the HMM-Based Fusion Algorithm

The instantiation of HMM-based fusion in HephaisTK is performed based on a given SMUIML script as highlighted in Figure 4. First, all triggers defined in the script are parsed and states are created based on this list of triggers (step 1). Basically, one state corresponds to one trigger definition, with the addition of an idle state which serves as a starting state. Then, for each defined <context> element, one HMM is instantiated with the number of states correspond-

ing to $T + 1$; T being the number of triggers declared for the current <context> (step 2). All states are initially interconnected, except the idle one. A discrete output observation distribution is used to connect the hidden layer with the observations. All <transition> elements declared in the SMUIML script are then parsed and, based on the synchronicity rules, a set of all expected output sequences is generated for each context (step 3).

The input events processed by HephaisTK all come from users interacting with a multimodal interface, for example by means of speech, gestures or gaze. Therefore, correlated input events generally happen within relatively small time windows of less than 10 seconds. Synchronicity and time ordering of modalities is modelled via the CARE property-based <par_or>, <par_and>, <seq_or> and <seq_and> elements in SMUIML. These elements are in turn used to create the list of expected output sequences for all HMMs. For example, a <transition> declared as equivalent means that any of the modalities in the transition will lead to the same next <context>.

Finally, each HMM undergoes a pre-training stage, with automatically created sequences of observations injected into their applicable HMM. The Baum-Welch algorithm is used to find the unknown parameters of the HMM, hence allowing the fusion algorithm to be directly used (step 4). Basically, the internal structure of an HMM trained this way corresponds to the weighted state machine representation of the human-machine dialogue defined in the SMUIML script. The HMM can then stay this way, as a "luxury" weighted state machine, or be refined with real training data or user feedback at runtime. The HMM can also be trained at instantiation time with real training data, if it is available.

The particular strength of HMMs for the implementation of this human-machine dialogue in comparison to ad-hoc methods lies in the possibility to adapt the HMM behaviour at runtime. As pointed out in the introduction of this subsection, the main goal when creating an HMM-based fusion algorithm was to lay the foundations in HephaisTK for adding the ability to adapt to context and user feedback. HephaisTK was therefore modified to support a simple *"I am not ok with that result"* feedback from the user. If no particular result is specified, HephaisTK assumes that the last result has to be corrected. The HMM is then re-trained in order to give less weight to the erroneous result. An illustration of this feedback process is provided in the next section.

Our description of the HMM-based fusion algorithm integration is based on the SMUIML modelling language. However, the presented algorithm could be integrated into any multimodal system considering input events as normalised information atoms at the semantic level. A full modelling of the entire human-machine dialogue is not mandatory, but helps to map the interaction flow to Markov models and improves results. Also, without such a model, the training of the algorithm with help of recorded sequences would be required.

EVALUATION

The evaluation of our new multimodal fusion algorithm has been conducted in three steps. First, a qualitative evaluation using existing multimodal applications that were created based on HephaisTK has been performed. Then a more formal evaluation using the framework's integrated benchmarking tool [11] was carried out. These two tests were designed to assess the accuracy and performance of our HMM-based fusion algorithm. Third, the adaptation to user input was also tested. In addition to these three evaluations, explorations of user-induced adaptation in the context of a particular application are presented. Initial conclusions based on the results of these explorations are then discussed.

Qualitative Test Using Real-World Applications

The first task was to check whether the HMM-based algorithm aligned itself correctly with the expected results for applications that had already been developed with the HephaisTK framework based on a classic frame-based fusion algorithm. Those applications did not take into account user adaptation but were good illustrations of use cases considering the CARE-based combination of modalities. Among the tested applications, a multimodal music player application was chosen to illustrate redundancy versus equivalence cases. Another application, a tool for document management in smart meeting rooms called Docobro [12], was used for the cases of sequential and non-sequential complementarity between modalities.

Both of these two applications were migrated to the HMM-based fusion algorithm. Only a single line in the HephaisTK XML configuration file, specifying the fusion algorithm to be used, had to be changed. No other code in the SMUIML modelling script or the client Java application had to be modified. More importantly, since the SMUIML modelling script which defines the human-machine dialogues is used as preliminary training for the HMM-based fusion algorithm, no explicit training is required before the applications can be used. In fact, applications can even hot swap fusion algorithms while

they are running, since context switching information is propagated in real-time to every fusion algorithm. While this was only a qualitative evaluation, the goal was to check whether the overall behaviour of the HMM-based fusion algorithm would at least be comparable to the frame-based one. Three expert users were presented with the two applications, first running with the frame-based fusion algorithm, then with the HMM-based fusion algorithm. Users were given five minutes with each of the condition to work with the application. Then an interview was conducted with them after each condition. During these interviews, users reported a coherent behaviour between both algorithms, with less false positives in the case of the HMM-based algorithm. Overall, sequenced and unsequenced complementarity, redundancy as well as equivalence cases were managed in a similar way by both algorithms. Regarding the responsiveness of the HMM-based fusion algorithm, users did not report a noticeable difference between both algorithms.

Quantitative Assessment Through an EMMA Benchmark

HephaisTK's integrated benchmarking tool [11] has been used to validate our initial observations. The benchmarking tool simulates various recognisers for a number of modalities and feeds this input data into the framework at predefined times, which have been previously recorded from a user session. The benchmarking tool then collects the fusion results in place of the client application. In the test setting shown in Figure 5, the HephaisTK framework works as if real modalities and a real client application were used.

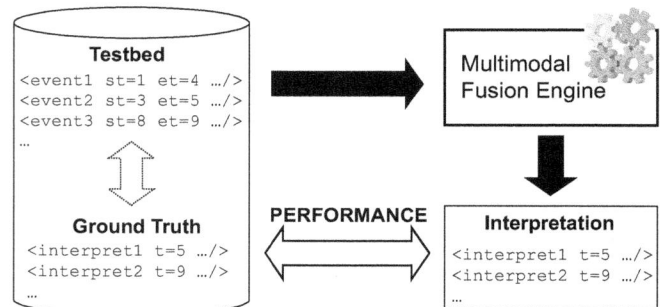

Figure 5. Benchmark test setting

The HephaisTK benchmarking tool allows for reproducible testing of the overall behaviour of the framework and of its performance and enables a comparison of different multimodal fusion algorithms. The benchmarks themselves are described via the XML EMMA language[3] which has been defined by the W3C Multimodal Interaction Working Group. Benchmarking tests were preferred over live user testing in order to compare the performance of two fusion algorithms working under the same conditions in a framework.

The results of our tests are illustrated in Figure 6 and Figure 7. Note that the screenshots of the benchmarking tool were slightly altered by adding horizontal black lines to differentiate the steps of each test. Each line corresponds to a

---

[3]http://www.w3.org/TR/emma/

single input sent to the HephaisTK framework. Details are, from left to right: the time in milliseconds when the data was sent with 0 being the start of the test, the used modality, the content of the data and the expected answer from the fusion engine. In green or red is the answer which was effectively sent (or not) by the framework, whether this was the correct answer and finally how much time (in milliseconds) elapsed between sending the piece of data and receiving the result.

Start time	Modality	Content	Awaited Answer	Actual Answer	Correct?	Delay
0	gesture	hello_wave	hello_message	hello_message	yes	227
2000	speech	hello	hello_message	hello_message	yes	21
4000	gesture	hello_wave	hello_message	hello_message	yes	10
4200	speech	hello	hello_message	hello_message	yes	17
6000	speech	to_par_or	to_par_or	to_par_or	yes	6
8000	gesture	hello_wave	hello_message	hello_message	yes	5
10000	speech	hello	hello_message	hello_message	yes	19
12000	gesture	hello_wave	hello_message	hello_message	yes	227
12200	speech	hello	hello_message	hello_message	yes	26
13000	speech	to_seq_or	to_seq_or	to_seq_or	yes	4
14000	speech	whatever			yes	0
14100	gesture	hello_wave	hello_message	hello_message	yes	16
16000	gesture	begging_gesture			yes	0
16100	speech	please			yes	0
18000	speech	to_par_or	to_par_or	to_par_or	yes	9
20000	speech	hello	hello_message	hello_message	yes	19
20100	gesture	thumbs_up			yes	0
22000	gesture	begging_gesture			yes	0
22100	speech	please			yes	0

Figure 6. Equivalence and redundancy tests

Note that some delays are well above 100 ms. These delays represent in fact the delay between the time when the first single modality data of a complex command was fed into the framework and the time when the final multimodal command was fused. For example, the *"put"* command on the first line of Figure 7 was sent to the framework 318 ms before the complete *"put that there"* command was fused.

Start time	Modality	Content	Awaited Answer	Actual Answer	Correct?	Delay
0	speech	put	put_that_there		yes	318
100	gesture	object_pointed	put_that_there		yes	216
150	speech	that	put_that_there		yes	165
200	gesture	object_pointed	put_that_there		yes	115
300	speech	there	put_that_there	put_that_there	yes	14
2000	speech	put	put_that_there		yes	307
2100	speech	that	put_that_there		yes	206
2150	gesture	object_pointed	put_that_there		yes	155
2200	gesture	object_pointed	put_that_there		yes	105
2300	speech	there	put_that_there	put_that_there	yes	4
4000	speech	put			yes	0
4100	speech	that			yes	0
4200	gesture	object_pointed			yes	0
4300	speech	there			yes	0
6000	gesture	object_pointed			yes	0
6100	speech	there			yes	0
6200	speech	that			yes	0
6300	speech	put			yes	0
6500	gesture	object_pointed			yes	0

Figure 7. Sequential and non-sequential complementarity tests

The CARE properties were used as a basis to test the accuracy of the HMM-based fusion algorithm. Each CARE property was first modelled with a correct case and then with some noise introduced. Finally, erroneous commands were fed into the system to check its resistance against false positives. Figure 6 shows the results for the equivalence and redundancy cases. *"Hello"* messages were input in different modalities, first sequentially and then at the same time. The test was executed in four sequences with an increasing number of noise along the legitimate data. As shown in Figure 6, the HMM algorithm managed to pass all tests with or without added noise. The second part of this series of tests was to check

whether sequential and non-sequential complementarity fusion was correctly managed by the fusion algorithm. The results are shown in Figure 7. The well-known *"put that there"* case was used to model these tests. Listing 1 shows the modelling of the command in SMUIML with parallel and sequential temporal constraints used. Four variants of the command were used: two legit variants, then an incomplete command and finally a garbled command. As outlined in Figure 7, the two correct commands were successfully fused while the incomplete and garbled commands were both rejected by the algorithm.

Listing 1. *"Put that there"* expressed in SMUIML.

```
<transition leadtime="1500">
    <seq_and>
        <trigger name="put_trigger" />
        <par_and>
            <trigger name="that_trigger" />
            <trigger name="object_pointed_event" />
        </par_and>
        <par_and>
            <trigger name="there_trigger" />
            <trigger name="object_pointed_event" />
        </par_and>
    </seq_and>
    <result action="put_that_there_action" />
</transition>
```

Finally, a challenging multimodal fusion task was tested in the form of the *"play next track"* example discussed in [11]. This task involves the differentiation between three different nuances of meaning, only based on the order of the input events. In [11], the frame-based fusion algorithm was used and could not correctly differentiate the various cases, because frames cannot easily represent this level of temporal nuances. There was a slightly better behaviour when sequential constraints were taken into account.

Start time	Modality	Content	Awaited Answer	Actual Answer	Correct?	Delay
0	gesture	track_pointed	play_next_of_pointe...		no	406
300	speech	play	play_next_of_pointe...	play_pointed_track	no	104
400	speech	next track	play_next_of_pointe...	next	no	4
3000	speech	play	play_pointed_track		yes	255
3250	gesture	track_pointed	play_pointed_track	play_pointed_track	yes	5
3500	speech	next track	next	next	yes	65
6000	speech	play	next		yes	436
6100	speech	next track	next		yes	335
6400	gesture	track_pointed	next	next	yes	35
Start time	Modality	Content	Awaited Answer	Actual Answer	Correct?	Delay
0	gesture	track_pointed	play_next_of_pointe...		yes	413
300	speech	play	play_next_of_pointe...		yes	112
400	speech	next track	play_next_of_pointe...	play_next_of_pointe...	yes	11
3000	speech	play	play_pointed_track		yes	258
3250	gesture	track_pointed	play_pointed_track	play_pointed_track	yes	8
3500	speech	next track	next	next	yes	12
6000	speech	play	next		yes	419
6100	speech	next track	next		yes	319
6400	gesture	track_pointed	next	next	yes	19

Figure 8. *"Play next track"* example without sequential constraints in the upper part and with sequential constraints in the lower part

Figure 8 shows the same tests but this time with the new HMM-based fusion algorithm. The first case without sequential constraints is still not completely solved but at least provides a consistent answer compared to most results returned by frames. The two other cases are correctly fused. As for the test run with sequential constraints, the HMM-based algorithm scores perfectly. We think that these challenging cases of ambiguous input sequences emphasise the advantage HMMs have over other classes of fusion algorithms, due to their ability to model time-related processes. However, we think that a full user evaluation would be needed in order to further assess the effects on usability of the different algorithms since our evaluation primarily focussed on the accuracy of recognition.

Performance

Multimodal interfaces should be responsive and therefore the fusion algorithms have to demonstrate reasonable performance. A full test run using the same list of commands as the tests of Figure 6 and Figure 7 was used. In total, the test run fed 40 different pieces of information into the system and expected 20 different fusion results. The full test was run 5 times with each algorithm and the delays between the input of data and the retrieval of the corresponding results were measured. 100 different measures were thus taken for each algorithm. The average computation time over these 100 measures for the frame-based fusion algorithm was 18.2 ms, with a standard deviation of 12.7 ms. On the other hand, the average computation time for HMM-based fusion algorithm was 16.6 ms, with a standard deviation of 11.6 ms, which is not significant. Further examination showed that the actual computation time of the fusion algorithms is much lower than these average values and a significant amount of the time is used by other HephaisTK computations. In fact, it appeared that most of HephaisTK's computation time is devoted to information storage and retrieval in the internal database as well as the information passing between the different software agents. In the future, we therefore intend to also test the algorithms with more complex situations and events.

User-Induced Adaptation

As presented in the related work section, adaptation can take a multitude of shapes. We are particularly interested in what is called user-induced automatic adaptation in Malinowski et al.'s framework [23]: Initiative from the user and Proposal-Decision-Execution from the machine. In this form of adaptation, the user signals to the machine that a given output was not what they expected and implicitly asks the machine to accordingly revise its judgement. The identification of the "wrong" result, the decision about a correction as well as the execution of the necessary changes are left to the machine and only the error detection part depends on the user as shown in Figure 9. The user is also not explicitly asked to select which result they would have preferred which guarantees minimal intrusion. Of course such a semi-automatic adaptation introduces some challenges for the machine processing.

In HephaisTK, the definition of the human-machine dialogue through SMUIML and the HMM-based fusion algorithm allows to explore user-induced automatic adaptation. User feedback was experimentally tested in the following way: vibration sensors were attached to the computer screen of a machine running the HephaisTK framework. When the computer screen is gently slapped, the vibration sensors are activated and provide input to the framework. Those vibration sensors events are tagged in the dialogue manager as user feedback expressing dissatisfaction from the user. The correction is sent to the HephaisTK `FusionManager` which adapts the behaviour of the HMM-based fusion algorithm accordingly. The erroneous result was in our test case simply

considered to be the last output produced by the fusion algorithm. The HMM for the current context is trained to give less weight to the particular transition which triggered this erroneous result.

We have conducted some tests of this setting with help of the benchmarking tool, in order to verify the correct behaviour of the algorithm. The same tests as explained above were used, but in the case of a wrongly recognised result, simulated user feedback was injected into HephaisTK. Three different cases were tested and in all three cases the algorithm adapted successfully its behaviour. The same setting was then used "live" with the Docobro document browser and the multimodal music player.

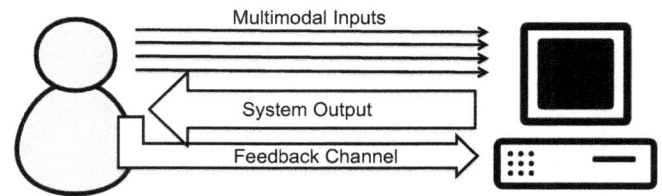

Figure 9. User-based error detection and feedback

Based on our tests, we can draw the conclusion that the integration of user-induced automatic adaptation in multimodal interfaces raises the following challenges: the identification of the problematic fusion result, the identification of the source of the error and the creation of a meaningful correction as well as the possibility for undo operations.

When the user indicates the wish for a fusion result to be corrected, other fusion results might already have been processed before the user's feedback reaches the fusion engine. In the presented test environment, the erroneous fusion result was always considered to be the last one. Evidently, this strategy proved soon to be error prone. Since the HMM-based fusion algorithm provides a probability for the correct recognition with each fusion result, this probability score was used to try to give less weight to the least probable fusion result among the most recent ones. This strategy was not satisfactory either and the identification of the erroneous fusion behaviour among the latest results without further input from the user is still an open issue.

The identification of the source of error is also an open issue. Indeed, the fusion algorithm works with interpretations coming from different recognisers. If the erroneous fusion behaviour originates from a recognition mistake of a particular modality (e.g. speech recogniser), downgrading a fusion result at the fusion algorithm level could worsen the fusion results rather than improving them. On the other hand, if the source of the error is correctly identified, the individual modality recognisers have the possibility to make use of a user's feedback to correct their results. We assume that extensive testing could help to identify thresholds at which "bad" results should be delegated either to the fusion algorithm or to individual recognisers, or be simply ignored if no source could be assigned.

The meaningful correction was satisfactory throughout the tests achieved with the previously described setting. When incorrect results originating from the latest fusion result were produced by the HMM-based fusion algorithm, a retraining of the current context's HMM lead to a reduction of false positives. However, if the error did not originate from the latest fusion algorithm result, the lack of some "undo" functionality showed to be problematic. Keeping two copies of each HMM and having one version trained one step later than the other should help to introduce this "undo" mechanism at the technical level.

CONCLUSION

We presented our work on a novel algorithm for decision-level fusion of input data in the context of multimodal interactive systems. Our algorithm is based on hidden Markov models and has been implemented and tested in the HephaisTK framework. A qualitative as well as quantitative assessment of the algorithm has been conducted with HephaisTK's integrated benchmarking tool. We conducted repeated tests of two multimodal fusion algorithms by feeding them with multimodal inputs organised in a series of examples. These examples represented different cases of unambiguous and ambiguous time-synchronised multimodal input. With similar processing time, our new HMM-based fusion algorithm demonstrated similar or better accuracy than a classic frame-based fusion algorithm. This improvement in accuracy, coupled with the capability of our new HMM-based algorithm to take temporal combinations of modalities into account, makes it a promising solution for decision-level fusion engines of interactive multimodal systems. Furthermore, the algorithm demonstrated its strength in adapting fusion results based on user and context information. Our initial explorations on automatic user-induced adaptation in multimodal interfaces revealed three main challenges to be overcome before the presented type of adaptivity can be fully employed in multimodal interfaces: 1) the identification of the problematic fusion result, 2) the identification of the source of error and 3) error correction and learning.

In the future, we plan to explore automatic user-induced adaptation, based on the challenges identified in this paper. We will do further evaluations through tests on specific tasks and hypotheses, as well as a user study with more users. We further plan to focus on making full use of probability scores provided by individual modality recognisers and go beyond the simple integration in HMMs. The robust handling of inputs with uncertainty needs to be tackled not only on the algorithm level but also on the dialogue level. To this end, we plan to integrate a variant of the framework proposed by Schwarz et al. [27] into HephaisTK, which should complement the management of the probability scores at the algorithm level.

ACKNOWLEDGMENTS

The work on HephaisTK and SMUIML has been funded by the Hasler Foundation in the context of the MeModules project and by the Swiss National Center of Competence in Research on Interactive Multimodal Information Management via the NCCR IM2 project. Bruno Dumas is supported by MobiCraNT, a project forming part of the Strategic Platforms programme by the Brussels Institute for Research and Innovation (Innoviris).

REFERENCES

1. Arhippainen, L., Rantakokko, T., and Tähti, M. Navigation with an Adaptive Mobile Map-Application: User Experiences of Gesture- and Context-Sensitiveness. In *Proceedings of the 2nd International Conference on Ubiquitous Computing Systems (UCS 2004)* (Tokyo, Japan, November 2005), 62–73.

2. Baum, L., Petrie, T., Soules, G., and Weiss, N. A Maximization Technique Occurring in the Statistical Analysis of Probabilistic Functions of Markov Chains. *The Annals of Mathematical Statistics 41*, 1 (1970), 164–171.

3. Bolt, R. A. "Put-that-there": Voice and Gesture at the Graphics Interface. In *Proceedings of the 7th Annual Conference on Computer Graphics and Interactive Techniques (SIGGRAPH 1980)* (Seattle, USA, July 1980), 262–270.

4. Bourguet, M.-L. A Toolkit for Creating and Testing Multimodal Interface Designs. In *Companion of the 15th Annual Symposium on User Interface Software and Technology (UIST 2002)* (Paris, France, October 2002), 29–30.

5. Cesar, P., Vaishnavi, I., Kernchen, R., Meissner, S., Hesselman, C., Boussard, M., Spedalieri, A., Bulterman, D. C., and Gao, B. Multimedia Adaptation in Ubiquitous Environments: Benefits of Structured Multimedia Documents. In *Proceedings of the 8th ACM Symposium on Document Engineering (DocEng 2008)* (São Paulo, Brazil, September 2008), 275–284.

6. Chai, J., Hong, P., and Zhou, M. A Probabilistic Approach to Reference Resolution in Multimodal User Interfaces. In *Proceedings of the 9th International Conference on Intelligent User Interfaces (IUI 2004)* (Funchal, Madeira, Portugal, January 2004), 70–77.

7. Chen, Q., Georganas, N. D., and Petriu, E. M. Hand Gesture Recognition Using Haar-Like Features and a Stochastic Context-Free Grammar. *IEEE Transactions on Instrumentation and Measurement 57*, 8 (August 2008), 1562–1571.

8. Choudhury, T., Clarkson, B., Jebara, T., and Pentland, A. Multimodal Person Recognition using Unconstrained Audio and Video. In *Proceedings of the International Conference on Audio- and Video-Based Person Authentication (AVBPA 1999)* (Washington DC, USA, 1999), 176–181.

9. Cohen, P. R., Johnston, M., McGee, D., Oviatt, S., Pittman, J., Smith, I., Chen, L., and Clow, J. QuickSet: Multimodal Interaction for Simulation Set-Up and Control. In *Proceedings of the 5th Conference on Applied Natural Language Processing (ANLC 1997)* (Washington DC, USA, April 1997), 20–24.

10. Coutaz, J., Nigay, L., Salber, D., Blandford, A., May, J., and Young, R. M. Four Easy Pieces for Assessing the Usability of Multimodal Interaction: The CARE Properties. In *Proceedings of the 5th International Conference on Human-Computer Interaction (Interact 1995)* (Lillehammer, Norway, June 1995), 115–120.

11. Dumas, B., Ingold, R., and Lalanne, D. Benchmarking Fusion Engines of Multimodal Interactive Systems. In *Proceedings of the 11th International Conference on Multimodal Interfaces (ICMI-MLMI 2009)* (Cambridge, USA, November 2009), 169–176.

12. Dumas, B., Lalanne, D., and Ingold, R. HephaisTK: A Toolkit for Rapid Prototyping of Multimodal Interfaces. In *Proceedings of the 11th International Conference on Multimodal Interfaces (ICMI-MLMI 2009)* (Cambridge, USA, November 2009), 231–232.

13. Dumas, B., Lalanne, D., and Ingold, R. Description Languages for Multimodal Interaction: A Set of Guidelines and its Illustration with SMUIML. *Journal on Multimodal User Interfaces: "Special Issue on The Challenges of Engineering Multimodal Interaction" 3*, 3 (February 2010), 237–247.

14. Flippo, F., Krebs, A., and Marsic, I. A Framework for Rapid Development of Multimodal Interfaces. In *Proceedings of the 5th International Conference on Multimodal Interfaces (ICMI 2003)* (Vancouver, Canada, November 2003), 109–116.

15. Forney Jr, G. The Viterbi Algorithm. *Proceedings of the IEEE 61*, 3 (1973), 268–278.

16. Hoste, L., Dumas, B., and Signer, B. Mudra: A Unified Multimodal Interaction Framework. In *Proceedings of the 13th International Conference on Multimodal Interfaces (ICMI 2011)* (Alicante, Spain, November 2011), 97–104.

17. Huang, J., Liu, Z., Wang, Y., Chen, Y., and Wong, E. Integration of Multimodal Features for Video Scene Classification Based on HMM. In *Proceedings of the 3rd IEEE Workshop on Multimedia Signal Processing (MMSP 1999)* (Copenhagen, Denmark, September 1999), 53–58.

18. Johnston, M., Cohen, P., McGee, D., Oviatt, S., Pittman, J., and Smith, I. Unification-Based Multimodal Integration. In *Proceedings of the 35th Annual Meeting of the Association for Computational Linguistics (ACL 1997)* (Madrid, Spain, July 1997), 281–288.

19. Juang, B., and Rabiner, L. Hidden Markov Models for Speech Recognition. *Technometrics 33* (1991), 251–272.

20. König, W. A., Rädle, R., and Reiterer, H. Squidy: A Zoomable Design Environment for Natural User Interfaces. In *Proceedings of the 27th International Conference on Human Factors in Computing Systems (CHI 2009)* (Boston, USA, April 2009), 4561–4566.

21. Lalanne, D., Nigay, L., Palanque, P., Robinson, P., Vanderdonckt, J., and Ladry, J. Fusion Engines for Multimodal Input: A Survey. In *Proceedings of the 11th International Conference on Multimodal Interfaces (ICMI-MLMI 2009)* (Cambridge, USA, September 2009), 153–160.

22. López-Jaquero, V., Vanderdonckt, J., Montero, F., and González, P. Towards an Extended Model of User Interface Adaptation: The Isatine Framework. In *Engineering Interactive Systems*, J. Gulliksen, M. B. Harning, P. Palanque, G. C. Veer, and J. Wesson, Eds., vol. 4940 of *LNCS*. Springer Verlag, 2008, 374–392.

23. Malinowski, U., Thomas, K., Dieterich, H., and Schneider-Hufschmidt, M. A Taxonomy of Adaptive User Interfaces. In *Proceedings of the Conference on People and Computers VII (HCI 1992)* (York, United Kingdom, September 1992), 391–414.

24. Octavia, J., Raymaekers, C., and Coninx, K. Adaptation in Virtual Environments: Conceptual Framework and User Models. *Multimedia Tools and Applications 54* (2011), 121–142.

25. Oviatt, S. Human-Centered Design Meets Cognitive Load Theory: Designing Interfaces That Help People Think. In *Proceedings of the 14th ACM International Conference on Multimedia (ACM MM 2006)* (Santa Barbara, USA, October 2006), 871–880.

26. Rabiner, L. A Tutorial on Hidden Markov Models and Selected Applications in Speech Recognition. *Proceedings of the IEEE 77*, 2 (1989), 257–286.

27. Schwarz, J., Hudson, S., Mankoff, J., and Wilson, A. D. A Framework for Robust and Flexible Handling of Inputs with Uncertainty. In *Proceedings of the 23nd Symposium on User Interface Software and Technology (UIST 2010)* (New York, USA, October 2010), 47–56.

28. Serrano, M., Nigay, L., Lawson, J., Ramsay, A., Murray-Smith, R., and Denef, S. The OpenInterface Framework: A Tool for Multimodal Interaction. In *Proceedings of the 26th International Conference on Human Factors in Computing Systems (CHI 2008)* (Florence, Italy, April 2008), 3501–3506.

29. Sharma, R., Pavlovic, V., and Huang, T. Toward Multimodal Human-Computer Interface. *Proceedings of the IEEE 86*, 5 (1998), 853–869.

30. Vo, M., and Wood, C. Building an Application Framework for Speech and Pen Input Integration in Multimodal Learning Interfaces. In *Proceedings of the IEEE International Conference on Acoustics, Speech, and Signal Processing (ICASSP 1996)* (Atlanta, USA, May 1996), 3545–3548.

31. Wu, L., Oviatt, S., and Cohen, P. From Members to Teams to Committee – A Robust Approach to Gestural and Multimodal Recognition. *IEEE Transactions on Neural Networks 13*, 4 (2002), 972–982.

User Interface Engineering for Software Product Lines – The Dilemma between Automation and Usability

Andreas Pleuss
Lero
University of Limerick, Ireland
andreas.pleuss@lero.ie

Benedikt Hauptmann
Technische Universität
München, Germany
benedikt.hauptmann@in.tum.de

Deepak Dhungana
Siemens AG Austria
Corporate Technology
deepak.dhungana@siemens.com

Goetz Botterweck
Lero
University of Limerick, Ireland
goetz.botterweck@lero.ie

ABSTRACT

Software Product Lines (SPL) are systematic approach to develop families of similar software products by explicating their commonalities and variability, e.g., in a feature model. Using techniques from model-driven development, it is then possible to automatically derive a concrete product from a given configuration (i.e., selection of features). However, this is problematic for interactive applications with complex user interfaces (UIs) as automatically derived UIs often provide limited usability. Thus, in practice, the UI is mostly created manually for each product, which results in major drawbacks concerning efficiency and maintenance, e.g., when applying changes that affect the whole product family. This paper investigates these problems based on real-world examples and analyses the development of product families from a UI perspective. To address the underlying challenges, we propose the use of abstract UI models, as used in HCI, to bridge the gap between automated, traceable product derivation and customized, high quality user interfaces. We demonstrate the feasibility of the approach by a concrete example implementation for the suggested model-driven development process.

Author Keywords

User Interface Engineering; Model-driven development; Software Product Lines; Usability Engineering

ACM Classification Keywords

D.2.2 Software Engineering: Design Tools and Techniques—*User interfaces*; D.2.9 Software Engineering: Management—*Software configuration management*; H.5.2 Information Interfaces and Presentation: User Interfaces—*Theory and methods*

INTRODUCTION

A *Software Product Line* (*SPL*) aims for the development of a family of similar software products from a common set of

shared assets by making use of the commonalities among them [6, 16]. By applying SPL practices, organizations are able to achieve significant improvement in time-to-market, engineering and maintenance costs, portfolio size, and quality [6]. SPLs have been commercially applied in many industry domains [20] including highly interactive applications like e-commerce software [2] or mobile games [1].

The fundamental premise of an SPL is that the initial investment in a family of products pays off later by allowing systematic, efficient derivation of products. This can be achieved by using techniques from model-driven engineering [21, 23] like automated model transformations to derive the final product from a given product configuration. While this works well for deriving most parts of the product implementation [8, 24, 25], it has limitations for the product's user interface (UI) part: A high quality UI must not only adhere to certain functionality defined by a product configuration (e.g., the presence or absence of UI elements) but also meet usability requirements like adequate layout, composition into screens, and choice of UI element types. This requires to customize the UI beyond purely automated derivation [15, 4]. A simple solution is to design the UI manually for each product [2]. However, as practice shows, this can result in serious drawbacks regarding error rate and maintenance [4].

This paper investigates these problems based on real-world examples and analyses the development of product families from a UI perspective. The paper is structured as follows: We first show the basic SPL concepts followed by their application to UIs. Then we discuss solution alternatives and their benefits and drawbacks. As it turns out, there is a dilemma between support for systematic, automated SPL concepts and usability of the resulting UIs. As we show, this challenge can be addressed by a model-driven SPL process with specific support for UI customization. In the remainder of the paper, we first analyze the different aspects of a UI to be customized and then describe a resulting model-driven SPL process for interactive applications.

GENERAL SPL CONCEPTS

A SPL is used for the efficient development of a family of related products from a shared set of software assets. A common example is online shop software: As different online

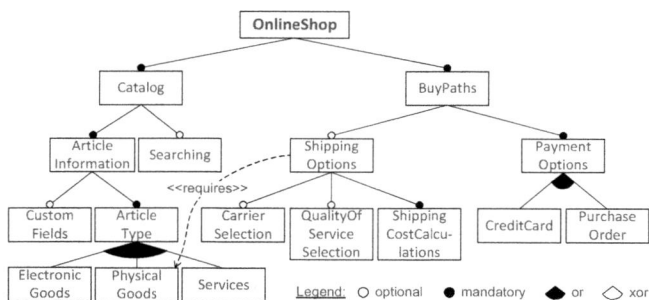

Figure 1. Example feature model for online shops.

shops (as commonly found in the web) have large commonalities in their functionality they can all be built from a common set of software assets. However, there are also variations between them, like the supported payment methods or the way the articles sold in the shop are organized. The core idea of SPL is to systematically manage this variability so that (ideally) a concrete product can be derived by just selecting its desired options.

The commonalities and variability in a SPL are usually specified in terms of a variability model. In this paper we use *feature models* [18] as a very common variability modeling concept but there are several other approaches, e.g., decision models [17] or OVM [16], which are used analogously.

A feature model specifies all features supported by the SPL and the dependencies between them. Figure 1 shows a small example feature model for online shop software[1]. Each node represents a feature that can be supported by the software, like a Catalog, Searching or different ArticleTypes[2]. The relationships between parent features and child features are constrained as *mandatory* (the child feature is always required), *optional* (the child feature is optional), *or-group* (at least one of the child features must be selected), or an *xor-group* (exactly one of the child features must be selected).

For instance, in Figure 1 each online shop must support a Catalog (mandatory feature) which includes ArticleInformation and optionally Searching. ArticleInformation includes the ArticleType from which at least one child has to be selected (or-group). By definition, selecting a child feature requires its parent to be selected as well. In addition, cross-tree constraints can be defined, such as *requires* and *excludes*. For instance, in Figure 1 ShippingOptions requires PhysicalGoods as otherwise there is no need to support shipping.

A feature model allows specifying a concrete product by configuring the product, i.e., selecting and deselecting features according to the constraints in the feature model. Each feature is mapped to SPL assets (the implementation of a feature; depending on the target platform) so that a given feature configuration (ideally) allows direct derivation of the corresponding implementation. For instance, there might be a software

component Shipping which implements the different shipping options and is only included into the implementation if the feature Shipping was selected.

Figure 2a shows the basic (model-driven) SPL process (Figures b) and c) shown in comparison will explained later). The upper part shows the *domain engineering* which refers to creation of the whole SPL based on domain knowledge and market analysis. This includes defining the feature model, the SPL assets, and a mapping between them (called *feature mapping*). The lower part shows the *application engineering* which refers to derivation of concrete products based on the SPL. A product is developed by defining a *feature configuration*, i.e., selection of features. From this, the product implementation is derived based on the feature mappings.

The product derivation can be automated using model transformations. Usually, the transformation is performed on the model level, i.e., the implementation is represented by a model ("code model") which can read and write the actual code, to reduce the complexity of the transformation and to ensure traceability of code changes [8, 2]. The derivation itself is performed either by composing the selected SPL assets ("positive variability") or by starting with an implementation of the whole SPL and selectively deleting deselected SPL assets ("negative variability"). Whether an SPL asset is selected or deselected is defined by the feature mapping. However, usually the mapping is not a 1:1 mapping between features and SPL assets but more complex and is specified, e.g., by constraints. We will show a concrete example applied to UIs in the next section.

APPLICATION OF SPL CONCEPTS TO THE UI

The initially most natural way to realize a SPL for interactive applications is a straightforward application of SPL concepts to all its parts, including the UI. This means that the application's UI is just considered as an SPL asset like any other application part. This section shows how this can be realized.

In the following we illustrate how to specify a mapping between UI elements and features which enables product derivation. To this end, we use the approach described in [7]. It uses the principle of "negative variability" [25] which means that product derivation starts from a superimposed model (created manually) which contains the implementation for all features in the whole SPL. The model elements are annotated with *presence conditions* over features. During (automated) product derivation, all model elements are removed whose presence condition is false based on the current feature configuration. Presence conditions can be specified as boolean constraints over features and more complex constraints can be specified using arbitrary XPath[3] expressions. The default present condition is "true", i.e., model elements without an explicit presence condition always remain present in a product.

Figure 3 shows an extract of a potential (manually designed) UI for the example online shop SPL annotated with presence

---

[1]See, e.g., [12] for a more realistic example with 225 features.
[2]Please note that to avoid misunderstanding we use the term "product" to refer to products developed with a SPL while we use "article" to refers to the items sold in an online shop.

[3]http://www.w3.org/TR/xpath/

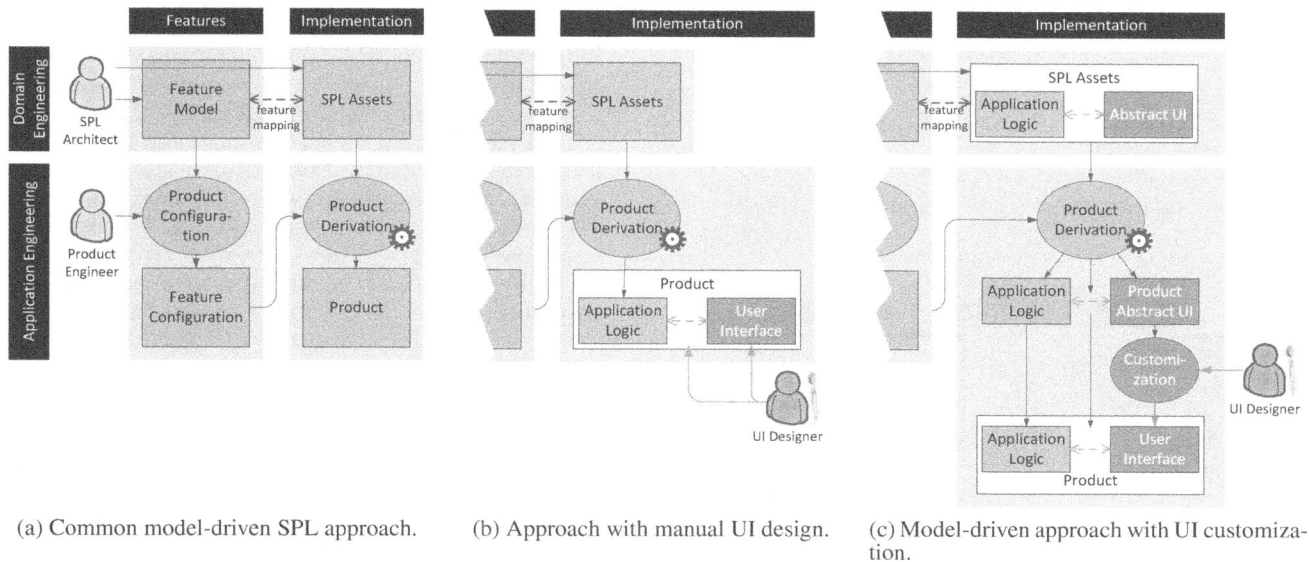

(a) Common model-driven SPL approach.   (b) Approach with manual UI design.   (c) Model-driven approach with UI customization.

Figure 2. Model-driven product derivation in SPLs.

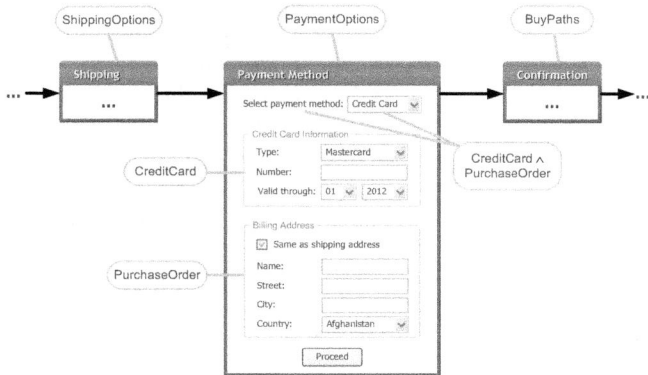

Figure 3. Example for a feature mapping for a UI.

conditions over the features from Figure 1[4]. It shows three screens Shipping, Payment Options, and Confirmation, the basic navigation between them (represented by arrows), and the associated presence conditions. For instance, the screen Shipping is removed from a product (together with all its content) if the feature ShippingOptions is deselected in the feature configuration. A slightly more complex constraint is specified for the the combo box Select payment method: it remains only present in a product if the features CreditCard and PurchaseOrder are both selected as otherwise there is nothing to select for the user.

In this approach, presence conditions are evaluated according to the containment hierarchy, i.e., if a container is removed (e.g., a screen or a grouping) all contained elements are removed as well. For instance, if the feature PaymentOptions is

---

[4]For the product derivation, the information in the figure needs to be specified as a model using an appropriate modeling language but this is not important at this stage. We will discuss appropriate modeling approaches later in this paper.

deselected the screen Payment Method is removed with all its contents.

In addition, [7] allows specifying rules for post-processing steps. An example is the navigation (represented by arrows in Figure 3): if a screen is removed, incoming and outgoing arrows are merged to close the navigation flow. Of course, this can be customized by attaching presence constraints to navigation flows.

In this way, the whole UI for a product can be derived from a feature configuration including its behavior specification. For instance, [7] shows derivation of Activity Diagrams, which might be used to specify the behavior of a UI. Figure 4 illustrates an example. The upper part in Figure 4a shows a feature configuration based on the feature model from Figure 1 (only those parts of the feature model relevant for the example). In this example, ShippingOptions are deselected and CreditCard is the only payment option. The lower part in Figure 4b shows the resulting UI, which was derived based on the feature mapping (from Figure 3) and the derivation rules explained above.

THE DILEMMA BETWEEN AUTOMATION AND USABILITY – SOLUTION ALTERNATIVES

In the preceding sections we introduced the general concepts of SPLs and their potential applications to the UI. While SPL concepts work very well in practice (see, e.g., [20]), the specific challenges of the UI in SPLs for interactive applications have mostly been neglected in software engineering community. In fact, the UI aspect differs from other SPL assets insofar as a high quality UI must not only provide a certain functionality but also must provide high usability which is much more difficult to satisfy with automated techniques.

In this section, we discuss the challenges when applying SPL concepts to the UI. There are two experience reports from in-

(a) Feature configuration.

(b) Resulting UI.

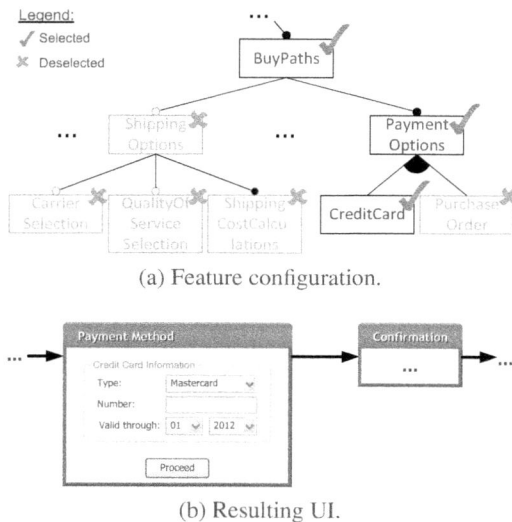

Figure 4. Example product for the online shop SPL.

dustry that mention the UI aspect and which we hence use for our discussion: [2] presents the experience from a company called *SystemForge* with their model-driven SPL for online shops for small and medium businesses. In [4], the company *HIS* reports on challenges arising with their product *HISinOne*, a web-based university management software supporting, e.g., management of students, human resources, and financial accounting. HISinOne is not a SPL in the strict sense (i.e., there is no SPL approach fully applied) but is still a highly variable ecosystem providing different customized products for their customers.

In the remainder of this section, we will first discuss the benefits and problems of existing solution alternatives and then we present a third solution alternatives to address the identified problems.

On the Need for UI Customization

The approach described in the previous section (Figure 3) directly applies the common SPL concepts (as shown in Figure 2a) to the application's UI part. This means that the UI is considered like any other software artifact as part of the SPL assets in Figure 2a. The main advantage is that in this way all existing strengths of SPLs – like efficiency, reuse, and a high degree of automation – apply to the UI part as well. Moreover, existing further SPL concepts can be applied, like concepts for SPL validation or maintenance.

However, this approach has limitations. The quality of a UI is not only determined by functional requirements (i.e., presence or absence of UI elements and behavior) but also by its usability which is influenced by many other factors like the decomposition into screens, the layout, and the detailed visual appearance [19]. All such UI properties must hence be customized to the specific needs and requirements of a specific product.

In context of a SPL, two levels of UI customization can be distinguished, which we discuss in the following.

Customization according to general usability requirements: In real SPLs, feature models become usually large and complex and consist of many hundreds or even thousands of features. Hence, it is often impossible to foresee the consequences of all different combinations of feature configurations in advance. For the UI this can mean that usability issues arise after automated product derivation. For instance, removing elements from a screen (as in negative variability) can lead to screens which are almost empty and are no longer useful as screens of their own [4]. To some extent this might be addressed by additional rules or heuristics during the product derivation, e.g., that a screen with very few content is merged with other screens. In practice, it depends on the complexity of the UI and the desired degree of usability whether such heuristics are sufficient enough.

Customization according to product-specific UI requirements: The most obvious part of an UI which often needs to be customized is its visual appearance. For instance, in case of an online shop, each shop's visual appearance should reflect the shop owner's corporate identity. Customizing the visual appearance is often unproblematic as this can be achieved without changing the derived UI implementation, e.g., by using stylesheets and dynamic loading of custom text and graphics. However, other UI properties like its general structure (e.g., decomposition into screens and screen layout) cannot be customized in this way. For instance, HIS reports that universities want to have input fields in the same order as they appear on their paper forms to increase the input speed [4].

To some extent, such product-specific customization might be captured by extending the feature model with UI specific options, e.g., to provide several standard layouts to choose between [2]. However, as pointed out by [2], this alone is not sufficient as all their customers want more control over their UI. Similarly, [4] clearly states that, according to their experience, the complexity of UI customizations and their interdependencies cannot be captured in a feature model.

Summary: In summary, customization needs of the UI within a SPL can be addressed to some extent by applying heuristics or capturing UI-specific options in the feature model. However, for interactive applications where the UI is important and highly variable, this is often not sufficient in practice.

On the Need for Automation

The preceding section has shown that interactive applications often need individual UI customization. On the other hand, the application logic of, e.g., online shops is well understood and can be derived very efficiently using model-driven SPL techniques. One way to solve this conflict is a two-fold development approach: The application logic is generated using a SPL while the corresponding UI is developed manually. Figure 2b illustrates this alternative in comparison to the basic SPL approach in Figure 2a. For instance, this solution is applied by SystemForge [2] by generating only UI templates (providing variables to access the application logic) while the UI is developed manually by the customer herself on that base. Similarly, HIS allows the customers unrestricted manual modifications of the UI code [4].

However, this solution results in new problems. While the manual design allows unrestricted customization according to the product-specific usability needs, it does no longer comply to the overall model-driven SPL approach. This means that systematic SPL concepts can no longer be applied to the application's UI part. For instance, the feature configuration still contains lots of information which is relevant for the UI, but this information is no longer used in a purely manual UI design approach. Moreover, the UI's compliance to the feature model as well as the correct linkage between UI and application logic now has to be ensured manually which can be tedious and error-prone.

The most important drawback is in evolution and maintenance. Concepts from model-driven SPL, like traceability, can no longer be applied to a manually designed UI. Updates on the software which require changes on the UI can no longer be automatically applied. For instance, HIS reports on these difficulties when, e.g., adding new input fields to the UI of the whole SPL, e.g., due to new laws for Universities [4]. In a manually designed UI, each change has to be integrated manually to each single product which is error-prone and lacks of efficiency.

In addition, other benefits of model-driven SPLs, like support for multiple target platforms, can no longer be applied to the UI. For instance, an online shop might be provided in several versions for the desktop and for different mobile devices. In a model-driven SPL, all these versions can be derived consistently from a given feature configuration. Having purely manual UI design, each version must be created and maintained separately and consistency between them must be ensured manually.

In summary, there is a dilemma between usability and automation. It is desired to have an approach which provides full support for UI customization but still integrates with the systematic model-driven SPL concepts. We propose such an approach in the next section.

A Model-driven Approach Supporting UI Customization

We propose to use abstract UI models which allow all required manual customization on the model level and fully integrate into a model-driven SPL approach. For this, we make use of the existing concepts defined in the research area of *model-based user interface development* (*MBUID*) [22, 5, 10]. These approaches provide models on different abstraction levels to specify the UIs and to support multi-platform development. They do not address SPLs but we can reuse their basic concepts of abstract UI modeling for our purpose.

The types of models typically used in MBUID are Task Model, Domain Model, Abstract UI Model, and Concrete UI Model (see, e.g., [5]). We briefly introduce them in the following[5].

The most abstract models are the *Task Model* and the *Domain Model*. The *Domain Model* is a conventional model to describe domain concepts and the corresponding application structure, e.g., in terms of a UML class diagram. A *Task Model* describes the user tasks to be supported by the application (like "Choose Articles" in an online shop application) and the temporal relationships between them. A concrete approach for task models is, e.g., CTT [14].

An *Abstract UI Model* describes the UI in terms of abstract UI elements, which are platform-independent abstractions of UI widgets, like *input* element, *output* element, *selection* element, or *action* element (abstraction of a button). Each abstract UI element realizes tasks from the *Task Model* and is associated with properties or operations from the Domain Model. Abstract UI Elements are contained in *Presentation Units*, which are top-level containers like Windows/Frames, and other *UI containers* (abstractions of, e.g., panels). The *Abstract UI Model* also describes the navigation between the *Presentation Units* and an (abstract) layout.

A *Concrete User Interface Model* refines the *Abstract UI Model* by specifying concrete UI elements, i.e., concrete UI widgets, and their layout. It can still abstract from a specific GUI API (e.g., providing a generalized "List Box" widget).

The final implementation, sometimes represented as a model as well, is referred to as the *Final UI Model*.

To solve the dilemma described in the previous sections, we propose to perform product derivation for UIs on an appropriate level of abstraction (i.e., derivation of more abstract UI models instead of a final UI) which allows to specify all required UI customizations using the models. From these abstract UI models it is then possible to move down to the final implementation using a model-driven process. The approach is shown in Figure 2c.

In this way, it is possible to overcome all drawbacks described in the previous sections: On the one hand, there is now support for full UI customization provided, on the other hand all advantages of a model-driven approach still apply like efficiency, consistency, traceability, support for maintenance, and even support for multiple target platforms. Due to the automated derivation of the (abstract) UI, also the consistency with the feature configuration and the correct linkage of the UI with the application logic is automatically ensured.

In the next section, we analyze which is the right abstraction level, which UI elements need to be potentially customized and which can always be derived. Afterwards, we present on that base the details of the proposed approach.

ANALYSIS OF UI CUSTOMIZATION NEEDS

In this section we discuss the different aspects which make up a UI and analyze them regarding their potential need for customization within an SPL. This is necessary for our approach to identify the right abstraction level for the UI models to be used and, in particular, which aspects of a UI can be directly derived from a feature configuration and for which aspects we need to support customization.

---

[5]Please note that advanced properties of UIs, like context-sensitive behavior or multimodality, as discussed in [5], are beyond the scope of this paper and not further considered.

Development UI Aspect	Customization	Customization Specification
Tasks and Temporal Operators	No	-
Abstract UI (AUI) Elements	No	-
Relationships to Domain Model	No	-
Presentation Units	Yes	AUI Model
Navigation	No	-
Concrete UI (CUI) Elements	Yes	AUI to CUI Transformation
Layout	Yes	AUI Model or AUI to CUI Transformation
Visual Appearance & Adornments	Yes	Stylesheets
Other CUI properties	Yes	AUI to CUI Transformation

Table 1. UI aspects and their need for customization.

Table 1 lists the different aspects of UIs as they typically appear in MBUID models. *Other CUI properties* refers to element-specific properties of concrete UI elements like if a text field provides word-wrapping or a if list box allows multi-selections. The second column of Table 1 specifies whether there is a need for product-specific customization in a SPL (in contrast to purely automated derivation from a feature configuration). The third column specifies on which level of abstraction the customization should be supported within a model-driven process. In the following, we discuss each row in detail.

Tasks and temporal operators: The tasks are directly related to the functionality of an application. Customizing the tasks within a SPL would contradict the SPL approach where the functionality of a product is specified by a feature configuration. Hence, there is no need for customization. (Of course, it is possible that a product of a SPL is extended with new custom functionality but this means to change the application logic and goes beyond the scope of UI customization.) The temporal operators between tasks are directly associated with them and there is no need to customize them as long as the tasks do not change.

Abstract UI elements: The abstract UI elements are still on a very generic level (such as input, output, selection, action) and, hence, determined by the tasks. For instance, a task "select payment method" will always be realized by a selection element while "input credit card number" will be realized by an input element. Thus, as there is no need for customizing the tasks, the abstract UI elements do not need to be customized.

Relationships to the domain model: Abstract UI elements are associated with properties or operations from the domain model to specify the information which they represent or the operation they trigger. Therefore, these mappings to the domain model are directly related to the corresponding tasks and do not require customization.

Presentation Units: The decomposition of the UI into Presentation Units (i.e., top-level UI containers that cluster other UI elements into logical groups) needs to consider product-specific constraints. As described above, product derivation can lead to almost empty (or overfull) presentation units due to removal (or addition) of UI elements. Moreover, product-specific layout and space constraints can require customiza-

tion of presentation units as well. For instance, in some online shops the description of articles might require extra space or a specific layout which influences the distribution of UI elements to the presentation units. Related to that, there might be product-specific requirements on which presentation unit a specific information should be presented. An example is the decision, which information about the articles to show on an "Article Details" page only, which information in the "List of Articles", and which in the "Shopping Cart". For instance, in an online shop selling business software, the number of licenses to buy and the resulting prices can be very important. In contrast, in a shop selling computer games, most customers will buy only a single license, so that the input field to set the number of licenses might be displayed on a less prominent place (e.g., in the "Shopping Cart" only but not in the "List of Articles").

The product-specific customization of Presentation Units should be supported early on abstract level (i.e., abstract UI model) as many further development steps, like navigation and layout specification, rely on the definition of the Presentation Units.

Navigation: Once the Presentation Units are defined, the navigation between them can be derived based on the temporal operators from the task model. Thus, in most cases the navigation does not need to be customized itself.

Concrete UI elements: The choice of concrete UI elements implementing the abstract UI requires customizations as well. On the one hand the choice of concrete UI elements is often considered by the user as part of the visual design and thus subject to customer requirements, e.g., when using tabbed menus instead of classical menu bars. On the other hand, the choice of a concrete UI element depends on the actual content (e.g., the articles in an online shop). For instance, for a small number of choices, radio buttons might be desired while a large number of choices might be represented by a list or by even more sophisticated custom widgets, as used in Rich Internet Applications.

The choice of concrete UI elements can be customized efficiently by adapting the model transformation which defines the mappings from abstract UI Elements to concrete UI Elements. In SPL context, this transformation is defined once for the SPL and provides the default mapping. There are several ways to adapt a model transformation, either just by extension, or by using an additional "mapping model" to define custom mappings, or by other mechanisms provided by current model transformation languages (like ATL[6] or ETL[7]) like parameterization or rule inheritance.

Layout: As the Presentation Units and the concrete UI elements can require customizations, the layout need to be customized as well. This can either be performed in the abstract UI model to specify general layout rules on abstract UI level or in the model transformation from abstract UI model to concrete UI model (using the same techniques like for the con-

---

[6] http://www.eclipse.org/atl/
[7] http://www.eclipse.org/gmt/epsilon/doc/etl/

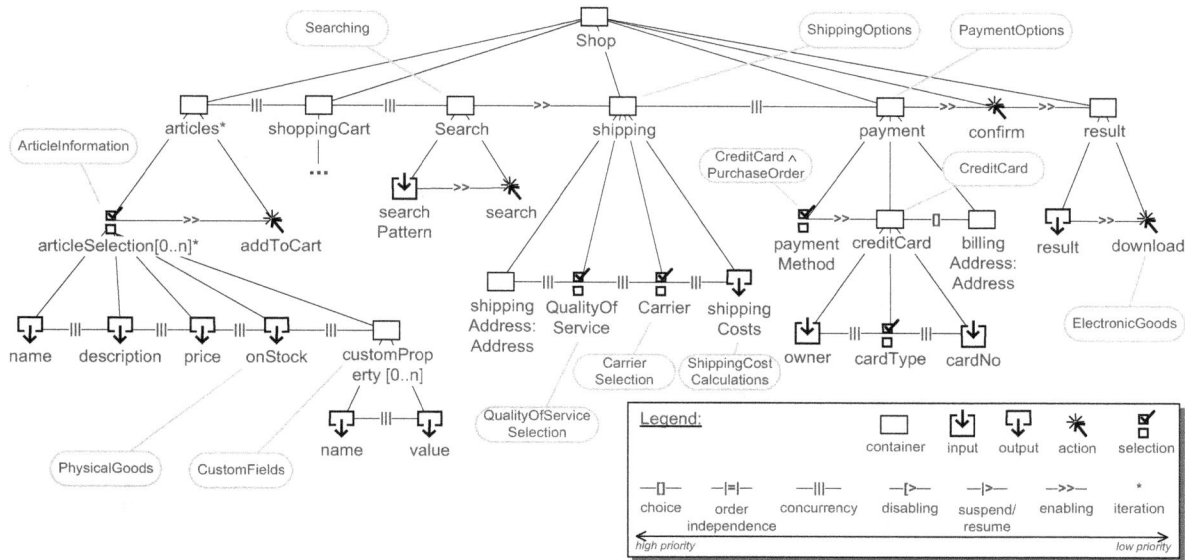

Figure 5. Abstract UI model for a online shop product line including presence conditions.

crete UI elements). Fine-tuning of single layouts can be specified in the concrete UI model.

Visual appearance: The visual appearance has often to be customized, e.g., to make different applications look less uniform or according to concrete customer requirements like the corporate identity. Customizing the visual appearance can be performed without changing the UI itself using, e.g., stylesheets and dynamic loading of text and images at runtime.

Other CUI properties: Properties of UI elements which are directly related to functionality, e.g., whether a list allows multiple selections, should be derived automatically during product derivation. Other properties are set during the transformation from abstract to concrete UI and can be customized there in the same way as described for the concrete UI elements.

PROPOSED DOMAIN ENGINEERING CONCEPTS

In the remainder of the paper we show how the proposed process from Figure 2c can be realized in detail based on the analysis results in the previous section. We have implemented the complete proposed approach to ensure the feasibility of the concepts proposed. Due to space limits we will focus in this paper on the most important concepts only. Interested readers can find all implementation details in [9].

In this section we explain the domain engineering (see Figure 2c), i.e. definition of an appropriate abstract UI model and a feature mapping. Thereby, according to our approach, we need to distinguish between the application logic and the (abstract) UI.

Abstract User Interface Modeling: According to the analysis in the previous section, tasks, temporal operators, abstract UI elements, and their relationships to the domain model do not require customization. Hence, they need to be specified just once and can afterwards automatically be derived using

the common SPL product derivation concepts. Moreover, as in MBUID the abstract UI elements are a more concrete representation of tasks, the tasks can be omitted here as they contain no extra information. This means that for the product derivation we need a model which contains the abstract UI elements, their relationships to the domain model, and the temporal operators. In the following, we introduce such a model.

Figure 5 shows our abstract UI model for the online shop example SPL. It is annotated with exemplary presence conditions analogous to Figure 3. The nodes in this model are the abstract UI elements. They are structured using the concepts from CTT task models [14], i.e., in a tree hierarchy and with temporal operators between them. The abstract UI elements supported are the same like in common model-based UI development approaches, like *input*, *output*, *selection*, and *action*, which must be leaves in the tree. All non-leaf nodes are UI containers. An exception is the selection element which can be either used as simple abstract UI element or as special container. In the former case, it is used for a simple value selection, in the latter case it is used to select from a list of objects represented by its children. For instance in Figure 5, the selection element articleSelection allows to select from a list of articles, which are represented by multiple children.

The abstract UI model also supports specification of multiplicities for elements whose number is not specified yet as it is either product-specific or calculated at runtime (like the number of articles in the articleSelection). It is also possible to reuse a container multiple times by defining multiple copies. For instance, shippingAddress and billingAddress are both copies of the container Address (defined elsewhere) which is denoted by a colon after the container name followed by the name of the copied container.

The semantics of the temporal operators refers to the task associated with the abstract UI Element, i.e., input of data for input elements, output of data for output elements, etc. The available operators are the same like in CTT [14] (see legend in Figure 5)[8]. Abstract UI elements required for the navigation (like a "Submit" button in a web application) are not specified in the abstract UI model here as those have to be generated based on the navigation which is specified later.

Each leaf is associated with a property or operation from the application logic (not visualized in the figure). This can also be non-persistent helper classes used only for return values or for database queries, etc. We briefly introduce a model for the application logic in the next section.

Application Logic: The models and model transformation used to specify and generate the application logic in a SPL are often specific to the domain and the target platforms. For instance, a SPL for web applications uses a different approach than a SPL for infotainment systems in a car.

We use here an existing model-driven approach for web applications as example, called *UWE (UML-based Web Engineering)* [11]. UWE supports, in conjunction with its extension UWE4JSF[9], model-driven development of Rich Internet Applications based on *Java Server Faces (JSF)*.

UWE provides five kinds of platform-independent models, three of which can be considered as application logic in terms of Figure 2c: The UWE *Content Model* and the UWE *User Model* describe the application structure in terms of extended UML class diagrams, whereas the UWE *Process Model* specifies the application logic in terms of extended UML activity diagrams.

As UWE supports generation of complete web applications, it comes also with its own models to describe the application's UI. These are the UWE *Navigation Model* (describes the navigation structure between web pages) and the UWE *Presentation Model* (specifies the UI of pages). This means that our model-driven process for the UI has to end up with these two models (instead of generating a UI implementation directly) to be able to leverage the UWE approach.

Feature Mapping and Derivation Rules: For the feature mapping and the resulting derivation, we use the "negative variability" approach based on [7] as previously explained by Figure 3. Each abstract UI element can be mapped to a feature. If containers are removed their content is removed as well.

For the temporal operators we use the following derivation rule: If a deleted abstract UI Element has two neighbor siblings (in the tree structure) then the temporal relationship with the *higher* priority (see legend in Figure 5) is deleted and the remaining one is used to connect the two siblings. If a deleted abstract UI element has only one neighbor sibling (i.e., it is a leftmost or rightmost sibling in the abstract UI tree), then its temporal relationship to its neighbor is deleted as well.

---

[8]In CTT, additional operators allow to specify whether information is passed between two tasks. We do not need this distinction here, as information passing is managed by the application logic anyway.
[9]http://uwe.pst.ifi.lmu.de/toolUWE4JSF.html

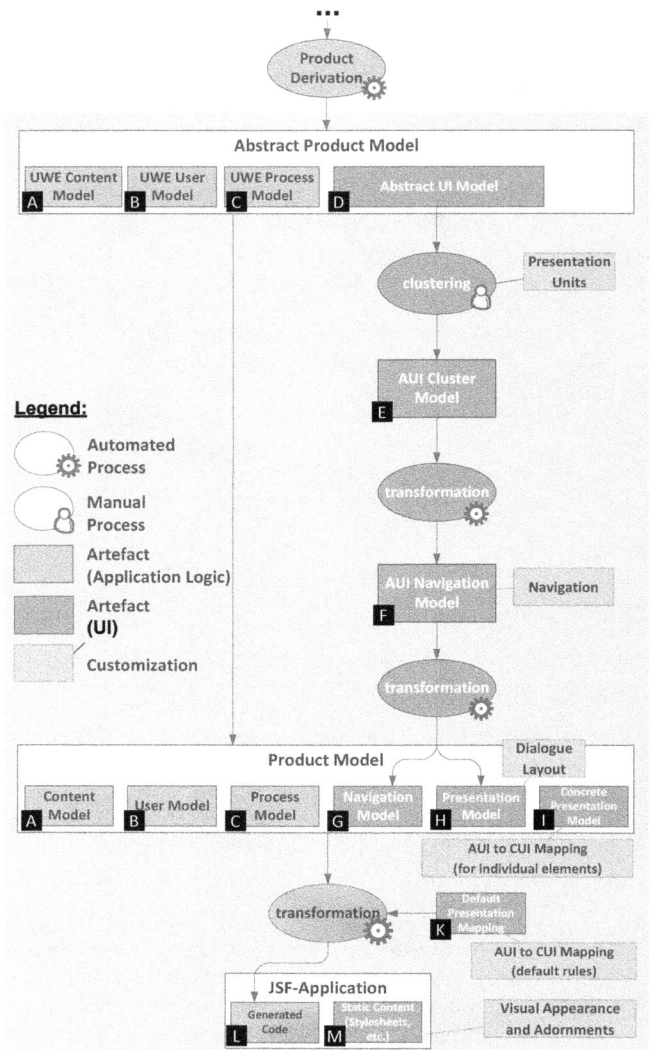

Figure 6. UI Model transformation process.

For the application logic, the negative variability approach is applied as well (derivation of UML class and UML activity diagrams in case of UWE) but this is not further discussed here.

PROPOSED APPLICATION ENGINEERING CONCEPTS

This section shows the application engineering within our model-driven process (see Figure 2c), i.e. the derivation of concrete products with support for UI customization on model level. This process is shown in more detail in Figure 6. It starts with the derivation of the product-specific abstract model UI model based on the feature mapping and the derivation rules described in the previous section. The product derivation performed so far resulted in an abstract, product-specific UI model (**D** in Figure 6) and an incomplete UWE model containing only the application logic **A B C** for the configured application. The result of the process should be the complete UWE model including the UI specification, i.e., UWE navigation **G** and UWE presentation model **H I**.

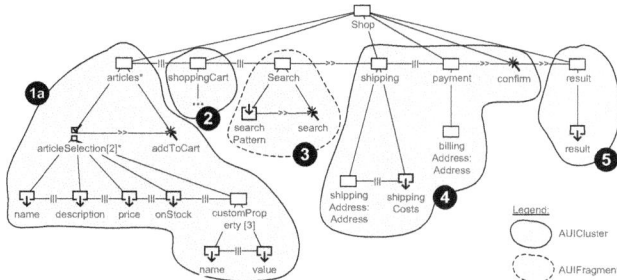

(a) Single cluster for article list and article details   (b) Article details in a separate cluster.

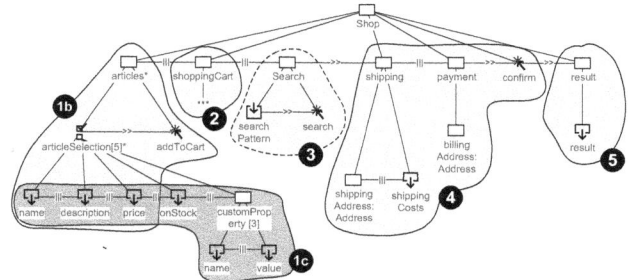

Figure 7. Two alternative clusterings for a product-specific UI.

The steps in between should support customization of the UI for all aspects identified in Table 1. We describe them in the following.

Presentation Units and Navigation: As discussed before, the decomposition of the UI into Presentation Units (i.e, the single windows or web pages) often needs to customized due to spatial and other product-specific constraints. We support this on the level of the abstract UI model by specifying clusters which results in a so-called *Abstract UI Cluster Models* **E** (inspired by [3]) shown in Figure 7. Abstract UI Cluster Models support two cluster types: *AUI-Clusters* are the basic cluster type to group several abstract UI elements. They will become a single Presentation Unit later on. *AUI-Fragments* are also used to group various abstract UI elements but will not become independent Presentation Units in the later UI. Instead, they will become reusable components that can be embedded into AUI-Clusters, to realize (sub-)views which are available within multiple other views, like a "search bar" available on multiple web pages.

Figure 7 gives an example for two alternative clusterings of a product-specific abstract UI. For instance, the UI containers shoppingCart **2** and result **5** (and their children) are clustered into AUI-Clusters of their own. The UI containers shipping and payment (and their children) are clustered together with the action element confirm into a single AUI-Cluster **4**. The container Search and its children are clustered as an AUI-Fragment **3** which means that it will be embedded into other clusters. The two alternatives (Figure a) and b)) differ in the clusters used to present the products in the shop (UI container products and its children): In Figure 7a there is a single cluster **1a** to display the list of products, including product details. The multiplicity of productSelection is set to "2" which means that two products are displayed at once. Figure 7b shows an alternative decision where the product list is more condensed (showing only the product's name, description, price) so that five products are displayed on a single view **1b**. Instead, an additional view (dark colored cluster **1c** in Figure 7b) is used to show the product details.

Based on the clustering and the temporal operators, the Presentation Units and the navigation between them are calculated in a model transformation. The result is stored as an *Abstract UI Navigation Model* **F** which specifies the navigation between Presentation Units as a simple kind of state diagram

and allows the developers to perform manual refinements, if desired. The calculation extends the algorithms used in [14, 13] to calculate Presentation Units based on the temporal operators. For instance, if multiple clusters are defined as concurrent (e.g., because they are connected by a concurrency operator) they must be accessible at the same time. Therefore, the UI must allow the user to switch between the resulting Presentation Units for example by providing links for navigating between them. AUI-Fragments are a special case in this calculation: An AUI-Fragment will never become an independent Presentation Unit, instead it is included into all concurrent AUI-Clusters. The details of the transformation are described in [9].

Concrete UI Elements: While the basic UWE models are platform-independent, UWE provides transformations to different target platforms like JSF. The concrete UI elements are hence generated by this transformation. Therefore, UWE defines a *Default Presentation Mapping* **K** which maps UWE UI elements to JSF elements. In addition, UWE provides a so called *Concrete Presentation Model* **I** containing mappings for individual UI elements. Both mappings can be adapted to customize either the default mapping or the mapping for individual UI elements.

Layout: The layout of presentation units is specified in the UWE Presentation Model **H** by assigning *UWE presentation groups*. By hierarchical nesting, it is possible to equip several web pages at once with an equal layout or to define templates for the general site layout.

Visual Appearance and Adornments: The generated JSF application **L** has to be extended with static, not generated artifacts like images, stylesheets and property files **M** which allow to easily customize the final visual appearance and adornments.

CONCLUSIONS AND OUTLOOK
Model-driven SPLs are highly efficient and have strong industrial relevance when developing a family of products. However, although SPL concepts have been applied to various types of interactive applications, like online shops, the specific challenges caused by the UI have been neglected so far. In this paper we provide the following contributions:

1. We demonstrate how SPL concepts can be applied to the UI (p.2/3).

2. We expose (and classify) general practical problems of applying SPL concepts to UIs (p.4). This analysis is based on reports from industry like [4].

3. We point out the problems of purely manual UI design within an SPL (p.4/5) based on reports from industry.

4. We develop a general model-driven SPL approach for UIs which overcomes the problems identified in 2) and 3) (p.5–9).

We demonstrate the feasibility of the approach by an example implementation based on UWE which is described in more detail in [9].

To our knowledge, UI development within SPLs has not been addressed by existing work so far (except our first work in [15]). In turn, a SPL approach differs from existing generative approaches for UIs (like MBUID) as the initial UI (for the whole SPL) is designed manually which prospectively results in higher quality UIs than purely generated UIs.

A more detailed evaluation – like empirical studies on the impact of the process proposed – is planned for future projects. For this, future work includes the development of more advanced tool support to create and manage the models and, ideally, to provide early visual feedback on the resulting UIs. In addition, SPLs in practice will use their own modeling languages instead of UWE as used in our implementation so the overall process has to be adapted accordingly. This requires mainly to adapt the final transformations from the AUI Navigation model to the final UI specification.

Acknowledgments

This work was supported, in part, by Science Foundation Ireland grant 03/CE2/I303_1 to Lero, http://www.lero.ie/ and by Siemens Corporate Technology CT T CEE.

REFERENCES

1. V. Alves, P. M. Jr., L. Cole, P. Borba, and G. Ramalho. Extracting and evolving mobile games product lines. In *SPLC'05*, 2005.

2. P. Bell. A practical high volume software product line. In *OOPSLA'07*, 2007.

3. G. Botterweck. A model-driven approach to the engineering of multiple user interfaces. In *MoDELS Workshops*. 2006.

4. H. Brummermann, M. Keunecke, and K. Schmid. Variability issues in the evolution of information system ecosystems. In *VaMoS'11*, 2011.

5. G. Calvary, J. Coutaz, D. Thevenin, Q. Limbourg, N. Souchon, L. Bouillon, M. Florins, and J. Vanderdonckt. Plasticity of user interfaces: A revised reference framework. In *TAMODIA'02*, 2002.

6. P. Clements and L. M. Northrop. *Software Product Lines: Practices and Patterns*. Addison-Wesley, 2002.

7. K. Czarnecki and M. Antkiewicz. Mapping features to models: A template approach based on superimposed variants. In *GPCE'05*, 2005.

8. J. Greenfield, K. Short, S. Cook, and S. Kent. *Software factories: assembling applications with patterns, models, frameworks and tools*. Wiley, 2004.

9. B. Hauptmann. Supporting derivation and customization of user interfaces in software product lines using the example of web applications. Master's thesis, Technische Universität München, October 2010. http://www4.in.tum.de/~hauptmab/pub/Hauptmann2010.pdf.

10. H. Hussmann, G. Meixner, and D. Zuehlke, editors. *Model-Driven Development of Advanced User Interfaces*. Springer, 2011.

11. N. Koch, A. Knapp, G. Zhang, and H. Baumeister. Uml-based web engineering: An approach based on standards. In *Web Engineering: Modelling and Implementing Web Applications*. Springer, 2007.

12. S. Q. Lau. Domain analysis of e-commerce systems using feature-based model templates. Master's thesis, University of Waterloo, 2006 2006.

13. K. Luyten. *Dynamic User Interface Generation for Mobile and Embedded Systems with Model-Based User Interface Development*. Phd, Transnationale Universiteit Limburg, Belgium, 2004.

14. F. Paternò. *Model-Based Design and Evaluation of Interactive Applications*. Springer, London, UK, 2000.

15. A. Pleuss, G. Botterweck, and D. Dhungana. Integrating automated product derivation and individual user interface design. In *VAMOS'10*, 2010.

16. K. Pohl, G. Boeckle, and F. van der Linden. *Software Product Line Engineering*. Springer, 2005.

17. K. Schmid, R. Rabiser, and P. Grünbacher. A comparison of decision modeling approaches in product lines. In *VaMoS'11*. ACM, 2011.

18. P.-Y. Schobbens, P. Heymans, and J.-C. Trigaux. Feature diagrams: A survey and a formal semantics. In *RE'06*, pages 136–145, 2006.

19. B. Shneiderman and C. Plaisant. *Designing the User Interface*. Addison Wesley, 4th edition, 2004.

20. Software Engineering Institute. SPL Hall of Fame. Web site, 2008. http://splc.net/fame.html.

21. T. Stahl and M. Voelter. *Model-driven software development : technology, engineering, management*. John Wiley, 2006.

22. P. A. Szekely. Retrospective and challenges for model-based interface development. In *DSV-IS*, 1996.

23. J.-P. Tolvanen and S. Kelly. Defining domain-specific modeling languages to automate product derivation: Collected experiences. In *SPLC'05*, 2005.

24. M. Voelter and I. Groher. Product line implementation using aspect-oriented and model-driven software development. In *SPLC'07*, 2007.

25. M. Voelter and E. Visser. Product line engineering using domain-specific languages. In *SPLC'11*, 2011.

Autonomic Management of Multimodal Interaction: DynaMo in action

Pierre-Alain Avouac, Philippe Lalanda and Laurence Nigay
Université Joseph Fourier Grenoble 1
Laboratoire d'Informatique de Grenoble LIG UMR 5217, Grenoble, F-38041, France
{Pierre-Alain.Avouac, Philippe.Lalanda, Laurence.Nigay}@imag.fr

ABSTRACT

Multimodal interaction can play a dual key role in pervasive environments because it provides naturalness for interacting with distributed, dynamic and heterogeneous digitally controlled equipment and flexibility for letting the users select the interaction modalities depending on the context. The DynaMo (Dynamic multiModality) framework is dedicated to the development and the runtime management of multimodal interaction in pervasive environments. This paper focuses on the autonomic approach of DynaMo whose originality is based on partial interaction models. The autonomic manager combines and completes partial available models at runtime in order to build multimodal interaction adapted to the current execution conditions and in conformance with the predicted models. We illustrate the autonomic solution by considering several running examples and different partial interaction models.

Author Keywords

Multimodal interaction; Autonomic computing; Model-based engineering; Service-oriented components.

ACM Classification Keywords

D.2.2 Software Engineering: Design Tools and Techniques – User interfaces.

General Terms

Algorithms; Human Factors.

INTRODUCTION

Pervasive environments lead people to reconsider the way they interact with digitally controlled equipment. Indeed, facing the proliferation of communicating devices in the environments, the users will express their needs or desires with any available interaction modalities, expecting the environment and its equipment to react accordingly [26]. As motivated in [2], multimodal interaction fits very well in pervasive environments because multimodality offers (i) a natural way to interact with equipment including gesture, speech and direct manipulation [6] (ii) flexibility in letting

the users select the modalities according to different contexts (tasks to be performed, interaction devices availability, social context, etc.).

In order to develop and autonomically manage multimodal interaction in service-based pervasive settings, we designed and developed the DynaMo framework. Autonomic in the context of DynaMo means that management decisions are taken and realized by the framework itself. The overall architecture of the underlying platform of DynaMo is described in [2] and a simple scenario illustrating the appearance of an interaction device and therefore a new interaction modality is presented in [3]. After a declarative description of the underlying platform and its software layers in [2], this paper focuses on the management of multimodal interaction by the autonomic manager (i.e., the platform in action). We describe a complete example highlighting the dynamic aspect of multimodal interaction

Based on the dynamic capabilities of the underlying platform, the DynaMo autonomic manager creates and modifies the multimodal processes at runtime. A multimodal process for input multimodality defines the interpretation function and is made of a sequence of input transformations: Information acquired by input digital channels (physical interaction devices) is transformed and abstracted to obtain a meaningful application task through multiple process activities characterized with four intertwined ingredients: level of abstraction, context, fusion/fission, and parallelism [21]. In order to create and update these multimodal processing chains, the autonomic manager contains domain-specific knowledge. The originality of our approach relies on the definition of partial interaction models in order to specify the autonomic manager knowledge and constraints. The interaction models are characterized as partial with respect to the complete multimodal transformation chain which ranges from raw data captured by devices to elementary tasks. A partial interaction model will thus define a sub-part of this transformation chain. In this paper we present these partial interaction models organized according to the ARCH software architectural model [1] and illustrate how they are used by the autonomic manager.

The structure of the paper is as follows: first, we motivate the adopted approach for designing DynaMo at the intersection of two domains, multimodal engineering and pervasive computing. We then recall the overall architecture of DynaMo fully specified in [2] before describing and illustrating the autonomic manager and the manipulated partial interaction models.

DYNAMO: PERVASIVE COMPUTING FOR MULTIMODAL ENGINEERING

On the one hand, several frameworks have been defined for developing multimodal interaction including ICON [11], ICARE [5], OpenInterface [24], Squidy [18] and MUDRA [16]. Such frameworks are mainly based on a component-based approach, which allows the easy and rapid development of multimodal interfaces. Indeed the designer specifies multimodal interaction dedicated to a given task of the interactive system under development by assembling components, the corresponding code being automatically generated. Such frameworks predominantly take on a data-flow approach that has been shown to be adapted for specifying multimodal interaction: indeed the assembling of components defines the data-flow from interaction devices to application tasks. Figure 1 presents an example of a data-flow as an assembly of generic and tailored software components from the OpenInterface framework [23].

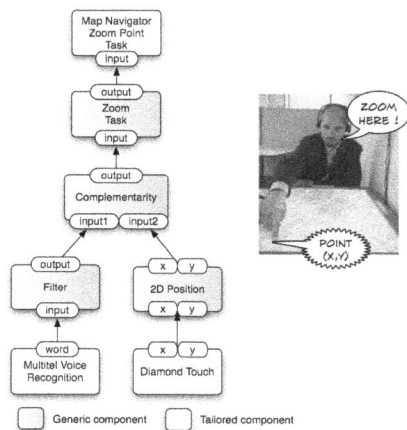

Figure 1: Multimodal processing as an assembly of components describing the data-flow from devices to tasks. (from [23]).

Some existing frameworks include a graphical editor that allows direct manipulation and assembling of components in order to specify multimodal interaction. Figure 2 presents a screenshot of the Squidy graphical editor [18].

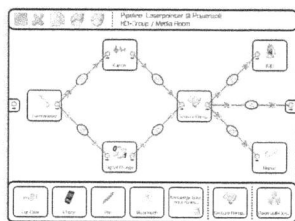

Figure 2: Screenshot of the graphical editor of Squidy (from [18]).

To fully understand the scope of these frameworks we show in Figure 3 where the corresponding code is located within the complete code of the interactive multimodal system structured along the ARCH software architectural model [1].

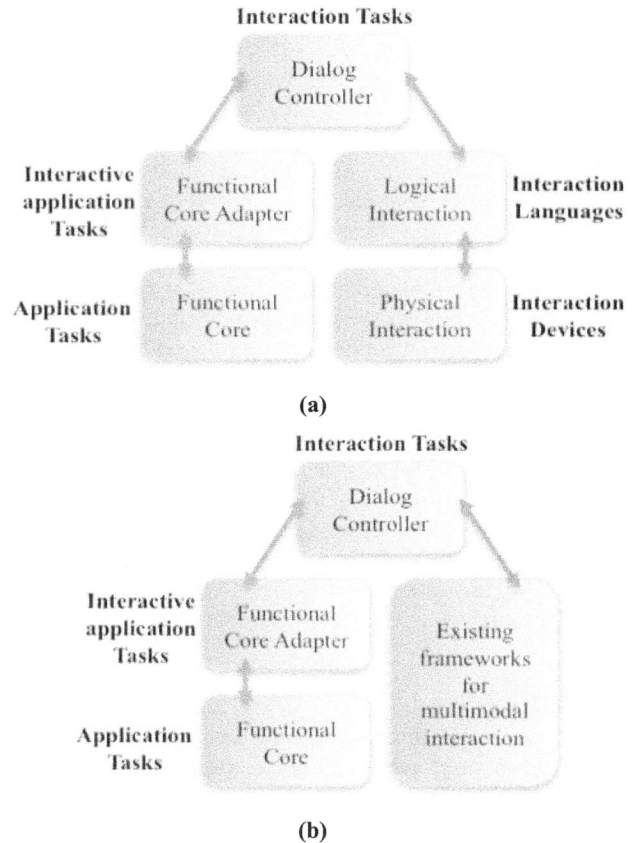

(a)

(b)

Figure 3: (a) Multimodality and the ARCH software architectural model: An interaction modality is defined by the couple: (device, language). The Physical Interaction component is device dependent and the Logical Interaction component is device independent but language dependent. (b) Existing frameworks for multimodal interaction within an ARCH software architecture.

Finally some frameworks support the dynamic discovery of input devices. Such frameworks therefore provide some flexibility by defining adaptable multimodal interaction. Such adaptation is made possible by defining at design time equivalence modalities for a given task. Equivalence of modalities for a given task is defined in [21] as one of the CARE properties. But multimodal adaptable interaction is completely defined at design time. One example is the COMET interactors [10]. COMET interactors are dedicated to plastic user interfaces. In particular for input multimodality, a COMET interactor includes a facet called *physical model* that describes input and output. For input, several equivalent devices can be defined at design time. At runtime the user can then switch between modalities.

Such approaches, however, are made for well-delimited environments where application tasks to be controlled and interaction devices to be used are known in advance. The existing frameworks cannot handle highly dynamic environments where devices, applications, and the way multimodal interactions unfold, are rapidly evolving. For multimodal interaction not fully defined at design time, more dynamic features are needed both at the design language level and the runtime execution framework level. Figure 4 schematizes the highly dynamic context that we addressed with DynaMo according to the ARCH software architectural model.

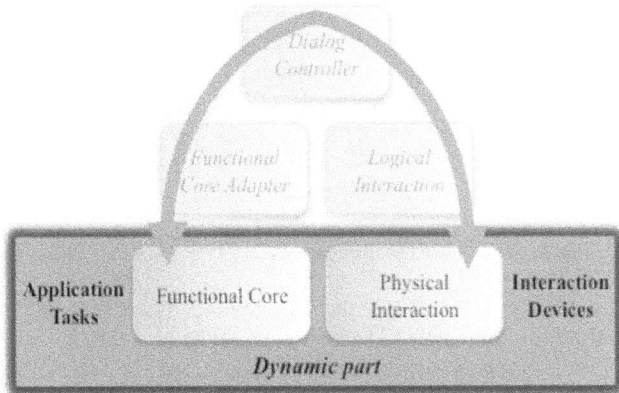

Figure 4: Dynamic context addressed by the DynaMo framework.

On the other hand, pervasive computing is influenced by advances in service-oriented computing [22] whose purpose is to build systems through the late composition of independent software elements called services. Service-oriented computing allows us to manage highly dynamic pervasive environments. Our approach then considers service-based applications (Functional Core of ARCH in Figure 4) and service-based interaction devices (Physical Interaction of ARCH in Figure 4). Multimodal interaction with pervasive applications is then a truly illuminating case. It requires us to dynamically bind service-based interaction devices like mobile phones, TV remote controls and wiimotes and service-based applications like media players and games. Composition is context aware in the sense that it relies on the available interaction devices and on the currently running applications. The situation can change at anytime. It is not possible to anticipate all the eventualities in a design time composition, even through abstraction. Multimodal interactions between service-based devices and applications require the integration of heterogeneous information sources in a timely fashion implying a number of operations, including communication, synchronization, fusion, syntactic and semantic alignments as defined in the previous section (i.e., the interpretation function [21]). In the pervasive computing field, these operations are called mediation operations [27], and demand some middleware support to be correctly developed, executed, and maintained. Enterprise Service Buses (ESBs) have been developed in order to allow richer and better controlled interactions between clients and servers. An ESB appears as a communication bus providing a unique interface to service providers and consumers. It can host mediation operations organized as processing chains transporting requests from consumers to providers and back. Mediation chains are generally decomposed into specific components that implement mediation operations. A number of products have been recently developed, including open source versions such as Apache ServiceMix or Codehaus Mule for instance. Many existing solutions are built on dynamic platforms like OSGi, which allows for runtime adaptation.

Current ESBs are not adapted to the management of multimodal interfaces. There are at least two reasons for that. First, current solutions are big in size. They target Information Systems, not pervasive infrastructures. Also, current solutions are still very technical and technology-driven. The development, deployment and management of mediation chains generally require highly skilled people. Last, but not least, current solutions are not autonomic. Adaptations cannot be decided and performed by ESBs themselves. Towards this goal of flexibility to be managed by autonomic managers, we have designed and developed a service mediation framework for dynamic applications called Cilia [14]. We added mechanisms in order to build adaptable mediation solutions (i.e. adaptable multimodal interpretation processes) based on structural and behavioral reflection [13] that can be used by external managers in charge of performing adaptations at runtime. Cilia is the mediation framework of DynaMo and is built on top of a service integration platform called iPOJO [12].

The design and development of the DynaMo framework is therefore based on results from both multimodal engineering and pervasive computing. DynaMo combines recent advances in component-based multimodal engineering, service-oriented component engineering as well as adaptable service mediation mechanisms. In the following sections, we recall the overall architecture of DynaMo before describing the model-based autonomic manager and its models.

DYNAMO: OVERALL ARCHITECTURE

As shown in Figure 5, DynaMo is made of three main parts.

First DynaMo relies on a service integration platform (based on OSGi and IPOJO [12]) that monitors the environment in order to trace any computing evolution. In particular the ROSE module [4] captures services (i.e., interaction devices or applications) in the computing environment and reifies them as iPOJO components in an advanced service registry. Various protocols are supported including Web services, Zigbeee, Bluetooth, UPnP and DPWS.

Second DynaMo includes a lightweight component-based mediation framework called Cilia as introduced above. Cilia allows the execution of adaptable multimodal processes. An assembly of Cilia mediators also called Cilia mediation chain corresponds to the data-flow from interaction devices to application tasks as specified at design time with the existing multimodal frameworks (Figures 1 and 2).

The third constituent of DynaMo is a model-based autonomic manager that creates and adapts the multimodal interaction using the dynamic capabilities of the underlying Cilia component model.

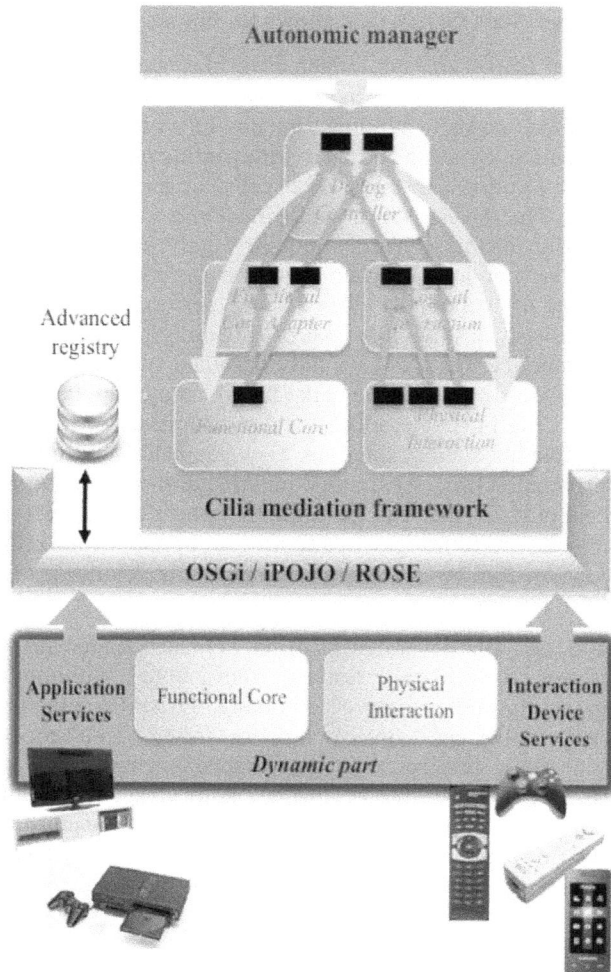

Figure 5: DynaMo overall archiecture.

As a conclusion, the DynaMo framework is built on top of readily available and proven software elements, which is required in order to attain the expected level of quality. OSGi is an industrial framework providing flexibility and service orientation on top of Java. We are using Felix, the reference open source implementation hosted by Apache. IPOJO is a service-oriented component model facilitating the development of OSGi-based applications. It is also available on Apache and is widely used today. CILIA leverages OSGi and iPOJO to provide a dynamic Enterprise Service Bus and, more generally a solution for data

mediation. Cilia is also available in open source and is successfully used in collaborative projects (including industrial projects with France Telecom and Schneider Electric). Finally, ROSE is an iPOJO-based framework conceived to handle distribution in dynamic and heterogeneous environments. ROSE is made available on the OW2 forge and used in industrial settings (to provide eBooks for instance). All these software elements have been designed by the same team in the last decade and are carefully integrated.

While the two first constituents of DynaMo, the service integration platform and the mediation framework are fully described in [2], the following section focuses on the autonomic manager and its models. We articulate the presentation of the autonomic management of interaction by adopting an original point of view based on the levels of abstraction of the Arch model: Arch provides us with a structured way (i) to explain the different cases for the autonomic manager and (ii) to present a complete example.

AUTONOMIC MANAGER AND ITS MANIPULATED MODELS

Autonomic systems are made of managed artifacts and an autonomic manager. Managed artifacts are the software entities that are automatically administered by the system. Here the managed artifacts are clearly the mediation chains implementing multimodal processes. The autonomic manager is the module in charge of the runtime administration of the managed artifacts. The purpose of the DynaMo autonomic manage is to build and maintain multimodal interactions at runtime. To make its decisions, the manager uses semantics-related knowledge defined by interaction experts and contextual information provided by the execution machine. It builds multimodal interaction through the composition of predefined components conforming to the component model of Cilia presented in [2]. When a modification occurs in the environment (e.g., a new device or a new application) the manager is reactive and computes a new mediation chain or adapts the current one. Based on the dynamic capabilities of the Cilia mediation framework, the autonomic manager can manage a mediation chain at a very fine grain (i.e. the component level): when a component is replaced, the new component receives the state of the replaced one.

The manager is first driven in its decisions by high-level goals, namely policies, that can be set by the user. Moreover the user can modify the policy at runtime. Two policies are currently defined: <simple> and <bind-all>. With the <simple> policy, the goal of the manager is to bind each task of the current active application with available devices. With the <bind-all> policy, the manager starts from the devices and its goal is to bind all the devices to the tasks. This <bind-all> policy likely implies that multiple equivalent modalities (Equivalence of the CARE properties [21]) are defined for a given task.

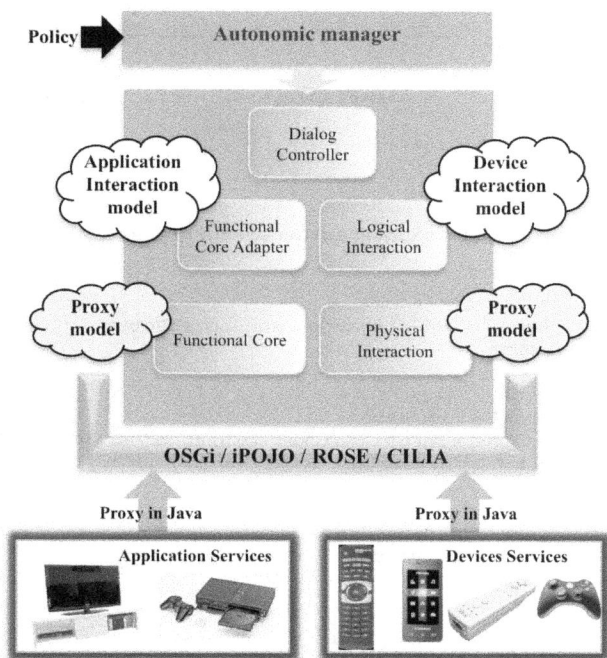

Figure 6: Models used by the autonomic manager within an ARCH software architecture.

The developers first create proxies in Java (Figure 7) and proxy models expressed in a xml language (Figure 8). The proxy meta-model is described in [2].

```
// Called by iPOJO when the instance becomes valid
private void start() {

  conn = DBusConnection.getConnection
  (DBusConnection.SESSION);

  remoteVlc=conn.getRemoteObject("org.mpris.vlc",
   "/Player",MediaPlayer.class);
}

// Called by iPOJO when the instance becomes
invalid
private void stop() {
  conn.disconnect();
}

public void playPause() {
  remoteVlc.Pause();
}

public void volume(int vol) {
  remoteVlc.VolumeSet(vol);
}
```

Figure 7: Java proxy of VLC media player (downloadable at www.videolan.org/vlc) that includes the life-cycle related code that handles the connection with VLC, and the two entry points "playPause" and "volume".

A proxy model contains information used by ROSE to track the services (devices or applications) and to start the corresponding proxies. A proxy model also contains information about the protocol (e.g., inter-process communication system D-Bus in Figure 8) as well as the ports and their types (e.g., port `playPause` and type `event` in Figure 8). Based on the proxy models, the autonomic manager is able to bind the proxies to the endpoints (i.e., an application or an interaction device) of the mediation chain. Figure 9 graphically presents the proxy models of the application VLC and the device Wiimote as endpoints of the mediation chain.

```
<name>vlc</name>

<discovery>
  <discriminator>org.mpris.vlc</discriminator>
  <factory>VLC</factory>
  <location>vlc-0.1.jar</location>
  <protocol>dbus</protocol>
</discovery>

<port>
  <codereference>playPause</codereference>
  <datatype>event</datatype>
  <direction>in</direction>
  <name>playPause</name>
</port>
...
</dynamo>
```

Figure 8: Excerpt of the xml proxy model of VLC: description of the communication protocol and the port playPause. VLC being an existing application, the xml proxy model describes the ports and types defined in VLC.

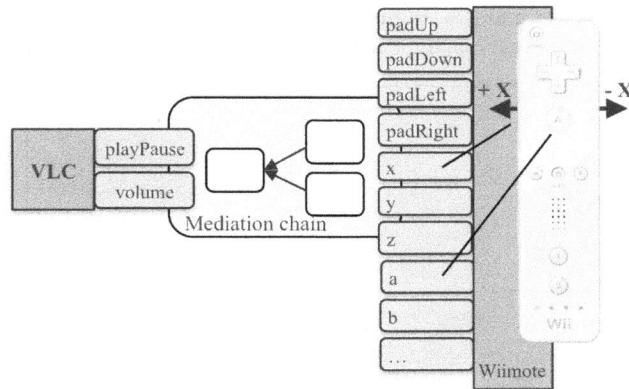

Figure 9: Excerpt of VLC and Wiimote proxy models represented as endpoints in the mediation chain.

Based on only the proxy models, the autonomic manager will generate a mediation chain from information about data type. Based on the ARCH model, this corresponds to the case where the manager directly links the Physical Interaction component to the Functional Core component as depicted in Figure 10-a. For example, the autonomic manager will bind the port x of the wiimote to the port `volume` of VLC, and the port a of the wiimote, to the port `playPause` of VLC. By moving the Wiimote horizontally, the volume will be increased or decreased, and the user must select the button "a" of the wiimote to stop the movie. In this case, the autonomic manager only performs syntactic alignments to generate this mediation chain. For instance, when dealing with interaction devices providing numbers, adaptors are often necessary to align the provided values and the ones expected by the applications. In the example, the Wiimote x port provides values in [-180, +180] and the VLC volume port needs values in [0, +100], so an adaptor is introduced to perform linear transformation.

Finally in order to go beyond syntactic alignment, the manager relies on semantics-related knowledge called interaction models. An interaction model contains information about data processing, data path and data semantics. They describe the way an application and a device can be used from an interaction point of view. As opposed to proxy models, no programming skill is required for defining interaction models in a xml language. A graphical editor of interaction models is provided. An interaction model describes a partial interaction that has to be completed by the autonomic manager. An interaction model is partial because it describes only a sub-part of the transformation chain which ranges from raw data captured by devices to elementary tasks. In structuring this transformation chain along the levels of abstraction of ARCH, we defined two partial interaction models. Indeed Application interaction models and Device interaction models respectively correspond to the Functional Core Adapter component and the Logical Interaction component of ARCH (Figure 6). According to the availability of the interaction models, Figure 10-(b,c,d) depicts three cases for the autonomic manager when building a mediation chain.

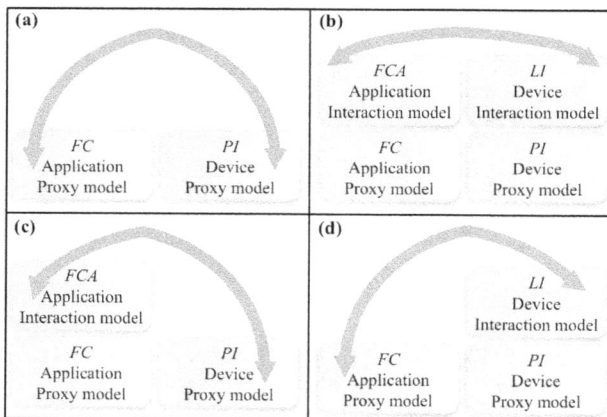

Figure 10: Four cases for the autonomic manager according to the availability of interaction models.

For applications, the interaction model plays the role of the ARCH Functional Core Adapter as described in [7]. For instance semantic reparation can be performed by adding a new application task. By considering the VLC example, the application interaction model can add a new task to mute the volume of VLC. Figure 11 presents an excerpt of the VLC interaction model. It includes a constant generator that generates the value 0 sent to the port volume of VLC. Constant generator is one example of a generic

function that can be used by the designer, for defining interaction models.

```
<dynamo>
  <interactionClass>mediaplayer</interactionClass>
  <proxy>vlc</proxy>
  <component>
    <baseComponent>constantGenerator</baseComponent>
      <port>
        <name>in</name>
        <connectedPort>mute</connectedPort>
      </port>

      <port>
        <name>out</name>
        <connectedPort>volume</connectedPort>
      </port>

      <property>
        <key>constant</key>
        <value>0</value>
      </property>
  </component>
  ...
</dynamo>
```

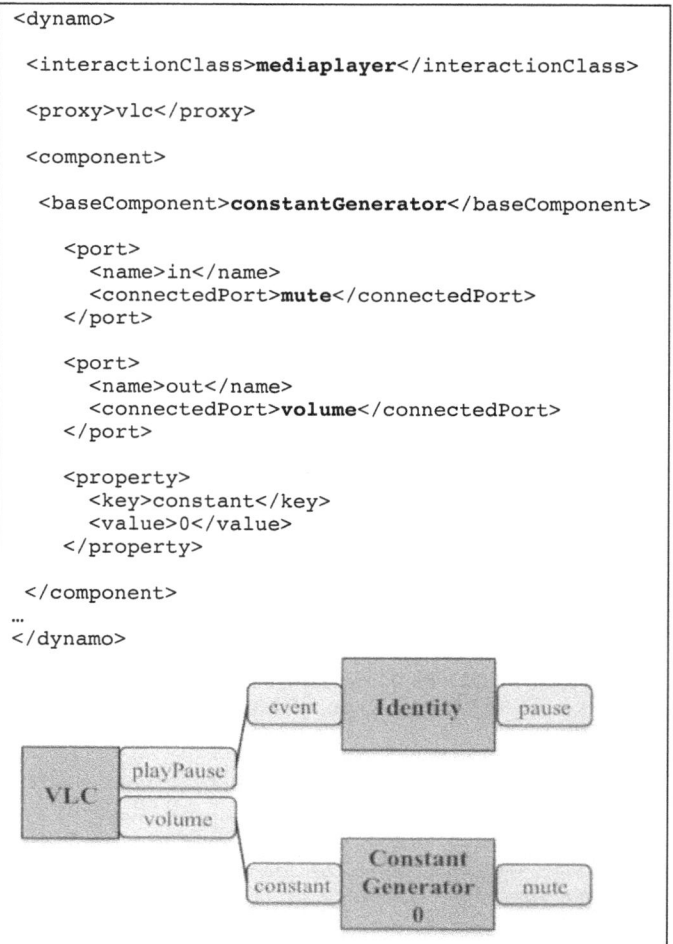

Figure 11: Excerpt of the interaction model of VLC.

For devices, the interaction model plays the role of the ARCH Logical Interaction component. It describes how to abstract events from devices. It is the right place to abstract or standardize different types of events from devices (identifier and/or parameters of a command). It depends on the syntax of the interaction language. It does not, however, depend on the semantic level of the application. As for application interaction models, the designer can use predefined processing functions within a device interaction model. For example, a triggering function sends an event as soon as it receives a value greater than a specified value. In addition generic fusion functions are provided based on the CARE properties (Redundancy and Complementarity). These generic functions are implemented by mediators developed with reuse concerns in mind and are similar to the generic components manipulated in the OpenInterface framework [23] (e.g., the Filter and Complementary generic components of Figure 1). Moreover more complex components can be used including gesture or speech recognition. The designer declares which components are to be used and bind their ports within the graphical editor. At this stage of the specification, data types can generally be ignored because the autonomic manager will be able at runtime to infer each port data type. Such inference leads to the completion of component configuration, and adds a data type converting component if necessary. For example, we have developed the multimodal map navigator as described in [23] (Figure 1) using a generic speech recognizer and a complementarity component, two mediators specific to multimodal processing. These components can be directly inserted in the interaction models, with a given configuration.

Application and device interaction models not only contain information about data processing (mediator class) and data path (bindings) but also data semantics. Indeed the autonomic manager needs to match meanings defined in the different interaction models. The current state of DynaMo supports simple semantics matching by defining interaction classes. An interaction class defines several meanings that make sense together. For example in Figure 11 and 12-a, we use the interaction class MediaPlayer that defines the two meanings *pause* and *mute*. Another interaction class is called GamePad and defines the meanings: *up*, *down*, *left* and *right*. Only one interaction class is referenced by an interaction model. The interaction designer can nevertheless define several interaction models based on different interaction classes for a given device for example, as shown in Figure 12 for the TV remote control.

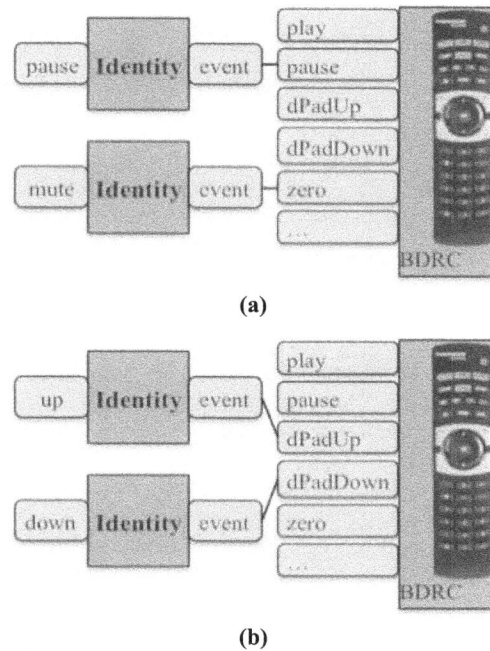

(a)

(b)

Figure 12: Excerpt of two interaction models of the BDRC TV remote control: (a) MediaPlayer interaction class (b) GamePad interaction class.

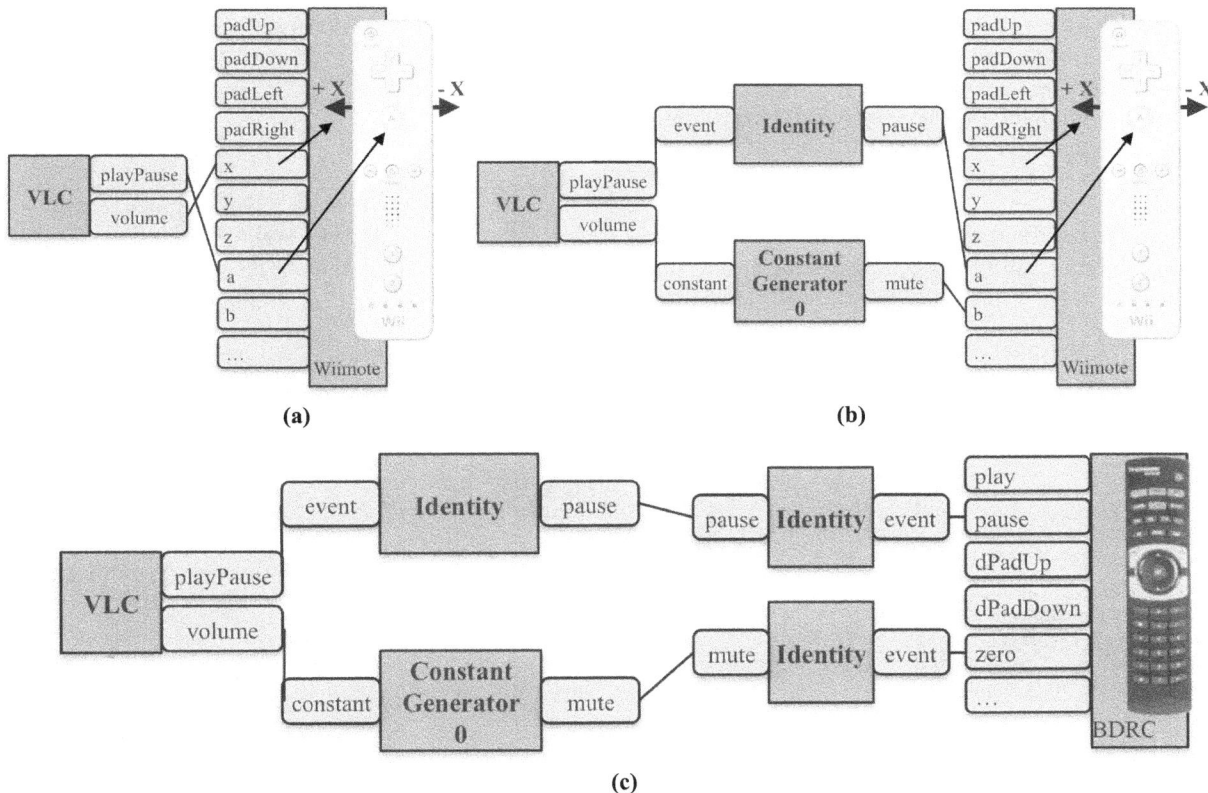

(a)

(b)

(c)

Figure 13: VLC - Generated mediation chains (a) without interaction model (b) with an application interaction model (c) with application and device interaction models.

41

Figure 13 illustrates how the interaction models guide the autonomic manager by considering the VLC example. Figure 13-a shows the case of Figure 10-a without interaction models. The autonomic manager only performed syntactic alignments to generate this mediation chain that links the wiimote to control VLC. Figure 13-b shows the case of Figure 10-c, with a VLC interaction model only. Since no interaction model is defined for the wiimote, the autonomic manager links port b of the wiimote to the new port mute of VLC that extends the tasks that can be performed with VLC. Finally Figure 13-c considers the case of Figure 10-b with application and device interaction models. We consider that the BDRC TV remote control has been activated. The autonomic manager receives a discovery notification about BDRC, hence it downloads the BDRC binary proxy from the repository and starts it. Amongst the interaction models of BDRC, it selects the one that uses the MediaPlayer interaction class (Figure 12-a) since VLC also has a MediaPlayer interaction model. Simple semantics matching is then performed by the autonomic manager in order to define the complete mediation chain, since the application and the device interaction models belong to the same class, namely MediaPlayer. If the interaction policy is set to <bind-all>, the wiimote will still be connected to VLC and the user can select one of the two equivalent modalities for specifying VLC tasks.

To conclude on the autonomic manager, we focus on the complementarity of modalities that imply fusion mechanisms. In DynaMo complementary modalities can be defined by using a fusion component. The complementarity generic mediator combines events close in time based on a temporal window that is a configuration parameter of the component. On the one hand, such a component can be declared within an interaction model as explained above for the example of the multimodal map navigator that combines speech with pointing gestures. On the other hand, the complementary component can be automatically added to the mediation chain by the manager.

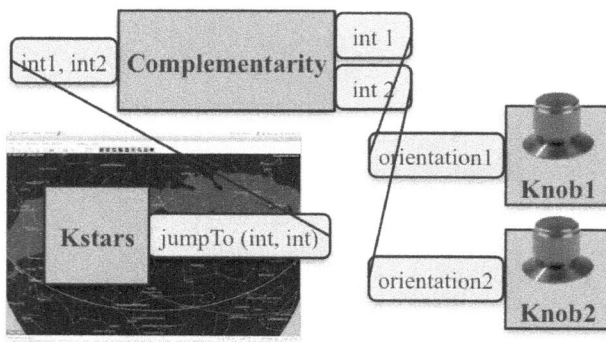

Figure 14: KStars application (downloadable at http://edu.kde.org/kstars/): Automatically generated combined usage of two knobs for selecting a point on the night sky map.

Figure 14 illustrates this case: We consider another application, KStars, that is a downloadable application that simulates the night sky, including stars and planets. The proxy of this service includes a port jumpTo with two integers as parameters. We consider that we have two control knobs as interaction devices for interacting with KStars. The two control knobs provide an orientation as output (the two ports orientation1 and orientation2). Without interaction models, the autonomic manager will define a multimodal interaction corresponding to the combined usage of the two knobs for manipulating the night sky map. The corresponding generated mediation chain includes a complementarity component.

CONCLUSION AND RESEARCH AGENDA

The autonomic DynaMo framework is dedicated to the development and the runtime management of pervasive multimodal interaction. In pervasive environments with highly dynamic and heterogeneous applications and interaction devices, DynaMo is able to analyze and understand multiple communication means and reconfigure itself in real-time. To do so the autonomic manager uses Proxy models and Interaction models to generate and maintain a mediation chain that defines multimodal interaction techniques. The underlying execution machine then concretely realizes the mediation chain.

The clear distinction between the management of the dynamic computing infrastructure and that of multimodal interaction enables us to identify two distinct roles:

- that of the developers that define proxies so that applications and devices can be managed by DynaMo, and,

- that of the interaction designers that define interaction models at a high level of abstraction without knowing the implementation of the applications and device drivers.

Proxy models as well as interaction models guide the autonomic manager in order to define the mediation chain corresponding to the multimodal interaction processes. On the one hand, the autonomic manager has all the information to build a mediation chain: the interaction models are then complete and defined at design time. DynaMo then corresponds to the existing multimodal frameworks for which multimodal interaction is defined at design time. On the other hand, the autonomic manager is also able to build a mediation chain with incomplete interaction models. This is the case of multimodal interaction not fully defined at design time: for example a device not initially planned to be used to control a particular application is now linked to a task of this application.

DynaMo is fully operational and stable. In particular the execution machine is robust and used by our industrial partners (Schneider Electric and France Telecom especially). Its robustness and its clear distinction of concerns within its architecture enable us to build a research agenda on pervasive multimodal environments that we organize along three main axes.

Populate the DynaMo framework for experimental evaluation: We plan to add new devices and new applications to DynaMo by defining new proxies. The goal is to be able to perform experimental evaluation. DynaMo is currently studied within the Medical project (medical.imag.fr). Medical is a project that focuses on smart homes for the elderly. Its overall purpose is to provide a middleware, based on iPOJO and Cilia, allowing the development of pervasive applications. Applications are hosted by so-called "Internet boxes" and can be extended to the cloud. Interaction needs are immense in such contexts. In current settings, we are using remote control, speech commands, mouse and tactile tablets as input modalities. For instance one primary need is the configuration of applications on a tablet. While several equivalent modalities are defined at design time for configuring the applications on the tablet, it also possible to interact with applications on the tablet from far away, by using the remote control. Such interaction was not fully defined at design time. Moreover for Health applications for which values of physiological parameters must be regularly captured, multiple modalities based on different sensors (passive or active modalities) are defined. The autonomic manager may make this multimodal process of capturing values of physiological parameters more efficient, robust and safe.

Enrich the autonomic manager: We identify several research avenues to better guide the autonomic manager in its decisions. First further contextual information [8] can be used by the autonomic manager. For instance the autonomic manager could learn from the users' interaction (inputs): her/his preferences in terms of devices and/or coupling of devices with applications. This learning approach can be directly implemented in DynaMo since our architecture supports the sensing and actuating at a fine grain. Moreover situational contextual information including spatial relationships as in proxemic interactions [15] could guide the manager, for instance in selecting the devices closer to the user. A more general approach to enrich the autonomic manager and its knowledge is also to define ontologies instead of interaction classes, which correspond to very simple light-weight ontologies. As explained in [25], several ontologies for pervasive environments have been proposed. For example the European project SOFIA (Smart Objects For Intelligent Applications) explored ontology-based mechanisms for pervasive environments [19]: In this context, the Semantic Media Ontology [20] is closely related to the interaction class Media Player used in DynaMo. By using ontologies, in DynaMo, correspondences between application and device ontology entities will then be based on ontology matching mechanisms (equivalence or subsumption relations between ontology entitites).

Make the decisions observable and controllable by the user: The autonomic solution of DynaMo is appealing since autonomic adaptation does not require the user to explicitly manage her/his pervasive environment and could ideally only focus on her/his intention. Nevertheless as stated in [9], the user needs at least to understand the state of its environment and furthermore control or tune the decisions made by the autonomic manager (i.e. mixed initiative approach [17]). For these purposes a meta-UI as described in [9] must then be defined. The current meta-UI of DynaMo is basic and requires further studies: appearance and disappearance of a service (i.e., an application or a device) are notified to the user by a pop-up window and we provide partial observability of the available modalities by graphically displaying which sensors of the devices are connected to the tasks of the current active application. The ReWiRe framework [25] adopts a more advanced mixed initiative approach by displaying a "pervasive menu" that allows the users to observe and modify the current state of the pervasive environment. In DynaMo, the meta-UI to be designed must (1) make observable the current application tasks and the corresponding available modalities as well as show how to perform actions with the modalities (e.g., the symbolic 3D gestures that can be perfomed) (2) let the users modify the decisions made by the autonomic manager that could in turn learn from these modifications. It is a vast research agenda that we can explore with the current implemented architecture of DynaMo.

REFERENCES

1. A metamodel for the runtime architecture of an interactive system: the UIMS tool developers workshop. *ACM SIGCHI Bulletin, 24, 1* (1992), 32-37.

2. Avouac, P-A., Lalanda, P., Nigay, L. Service-Oriented Autonomic Multimodal Interaction in a Pervasive Environment. In *Proc. ICMI 2011*, ACM Press (2011), 369-376.

3. Avouac, P-A., Lalanda, P., Nigay, L. Adaptable multimodal interfaces in pervasive environments. In *Proc. CCNC 2012*, IEEE Consumer Communications and Networking Conference, IEEE (2012).

4. Bardin, J., Lalanda, P., Escoffier, C. Towards an Automatic Integration of Heterogeneous Services and Devices. In *Proc. APSCC 2010*, IEEE Asia-Pacific Services Computing Conference, IEEE (2010), 171-178.

5. Bouchet, J., Nigay, L., Ganille, T. ICARE software components for rapidly developing multimodal interfaces. In *Proc. ICMI 2004*, ACM Press (2004), 252-258.

6. Carrino, S., Péclat, A., Mugellini, E., Omar Abou Khaled, O-A, Ingold, R. Humans and Smart Environments: A Novel Multimodal Interaction Approach. In *Proc. ICMI 2011*, ACM Press (2011), 105-112.

7. Coutaz, J., Balbo, S.Applications: a dimension space for User Interface Management Systems. In *Proc CHI 1991*, ACM Press (1991), 27-32.

8. Coutaz, J., Crowley, J., Dobson, S., Garlan, D. Context is Key. *Communications of the ACM 48, 3* (2005), 49-53.

9. Coutaz, J. Meta-User Interfaces for Ambient Spaces. In *Proc. TAMODIA 2006*, Springer (2006),1-15.

10. Demeure, A, Calvary, G., Coninx, K. CO-MET(s), A Software Architecture Style and an Interactors Toolkit for Plastic User Interfaces. *In Proc. DSVIS 2008*, LNCS 5136, Springer (2008), 225-237.

11. Dragicevic, P., and Fekete, J. D. ICON: Input Device Selection and Interaction Configuration. *Companion Proc. UIST 2002*, ACM Press (2002), 47-48.

12. Escoffier, C., Hall, R. S., Lalanda, P. iPOJO: an Extensible Service-Oriented Component Framework. In *Proc. SCC 2007*, IEEE Conference on Services Computing, IEEE (2007), 474-481.

13. Garcia, I., Morand, D., Debbabi, B., Lalanda, P., Bourret, P. A reflective framework for mediation applications. In *Proc. ARM 2011*, 10th Middleware Workshop on Adaptive and Reflective Middleware, ACM Press (2011), 22-28.

14. Garcia, I., Pedraza, G., Debbabi, B., Lalanda, P., Hamon, C. Towards a service mediation framework for dynamic applications. In *Proc. APSCC 2010*, IEEE Asia-Pacific Services Computing Conference, IEEE (2010), 3-10.

15. Greenberg, S., Marquardt, N., Ballendat, T., Diaz-Marino, R., Wang, M. Proxemic interactions: the new ubicomp? *ACM Interactions, 18, 1* (2011), 42-50.

16. Hoste, L., Dumas, B., Signer B. Mudra: a unified multimodal interaction framework. In *Proc. ICMI 2011*, ACM Press (2011), 97-104.

17. Horvitz, E. Principles of Mixed-Initiative User Interfaces. In *Proc CHI 1999*, ACM Press (1999), 159-166.

18. König, W. A., Rädle, R., Reiterer, H. Interactive Design of Multimodal User Interfaces - Reducing technical and visual complexity. *Springer Journal on Multimodal Interfaces, 3,3* (2010), 197-213.

19. Niezen, G., van der vlist, B., Hu, J., Feijs, L. From Events to Goals: Supporting Semantic Interaction in Smart Environments. In *Proc. ISCC 2010*, IEEE Symposium on Computers and Communications IEEE (2010), 1029-1034.

20. Niezen, G., van der vlist, B., Hu, J., Feijs, L. Using semantic transformers to enable interoperability between media devices in a ubiquitous computing environment. In *Proc. of S3E 2011*, International Workshop on Self-managing Solutions for Smart Environments at the 6th International Conference on Grid and Pervasive Computing (GPC 2011).

21. Nigay, L., Coutaz, J. Multifeature systems: the CARE properties and their impact on software design. *Multimedia Interfaces: Research and Applications, chapter 9*, AAAI Press (1997).

22. Papazoglou, M. P., Georgakopoulos, D. Service-Oriented Computing: Introduction. *Communications of the ACM 46, 10* (2003), 24-28.

23. Serrano, M., Nigay, L. A Three-dimensional Characterization Space of Software Components for Rapidly Developing Multimodal Interfaces. In *Proc. ICMI 2008*, ACM Press (2008), 149-156.

24. Serrano, M., Nigay, L., Lawson, J-Y., Ramsay, A., Murray-Smith, R., Denef, S. The openinterface framework: a tool for multimodal interaction. *Ext. Abstracts CHI 2008*, ACM Press (2008), 3501-3506. www.oi-project.org.

25. Vanderhulst, G., Luyten, K., Coninx, K. ReWiRe: Creating Interactive Pervasive Systems that cope with Changing Environments by Rewiring. In *Proc. of IE 2008*, the 4th International Conference on Intelligent Environments, IEEE (2008), 1-8.

26. Weiser, M. The computer for the 21st century. *Scientific American, 265, 3* (1991), 66-75.

27. Wiederhold, G., Genesereth, M. 1997. The Conceptual Basis for Mediation Services. *IEEE Expert: Intelligent Systems and Their Applications 12, 5* (1997), 38-47.

A Logical Framework for Multi-Device User Interfaces

Fabio Paternò, Carmen Santoro
CNR-ISTI, HIIS Laboratory
Via G. Moruzzi 1, 56124 Pisa
Italy
{fabio.paterno, carmen.santoro}@isti.cnr.it

ABSTRACT

In this paper, we present a framework for describing various design dimensions that can help in better understanding the features provided by tools and applications for multi-device environments. We indicate the possible options for each dimension, and also discuss how various research proposals in the area are located in our framework. The final discussion also points out important areas for future research.

Keywords: Multi-device User Interfaces; Logical Framework; Distributed and Migratory User Interfaces.

ACM Classification Keywords
H.5 Information Interfaces and Presentation;
H.5.2 User Interfaces

General Terms: Design, Human Factors.

INTRODUCTION

Nowadays, it is extremely common to see users performing their tasks using various devices ranging from the traditional stationary desktop platform to mobile devices with various multimodal interaction resources. However, by now, users' expectations have not yet been adequately fulfilled. Often all this technological offering is not exploited as it could be, and when users perform cross-device service access they encounter various usability issues: poor adaptation to the context of use, lack of coordination among tasks performed through different devices, inadequate support for seamless cross-device task performance. For example, one potential source of frustration for users is the inability to continue to perform their tasks when they have to move about and change the interaction device. In such cases, users either have to manually perform some activity in the first device in order to save the up-to-date interaction state and then reconstruct it afterwards on the new device, or, in the worst case, they have to start their activities over again from scratch when moving to the second device. A study reported in [4] aimed to achieve a better understanding of why and how people use multiple devices in their everyday life. The authors

found out that users already employ a variety of techniques for accessing and managing information across devices. However, there is still room for improvements, especially from the user experience viewpoint: participants in the study reported that managing information across devices is the most challenging aspect of using multiple devices. To this end, various approaches are possible. In distributed User Interfaces (UIs) we have solutions that allow users to exploit user interfaces distributed across multiple devices at a given time to access their applications. In migratory UIs users can change device and still access the application with some level of continuity, which means that at least some parts of the original user interface preserve their state after changing device. More generally, it is important to reach a better understanding of how we can design tools and applications exploiting multi-device UIs, which is the main goal of the framework that we propose.

In this paper, after discussing some relevant work in the area, we first suggest a logical framework in order to describe the range of possibilities that multi-device UIs offer, by identifying ten dimensions that have been judged relevant for such systems based on our analysis of the state of art and experience in designing multi-device environments. Then, we summarise the main points of the framework by also providing a table supporting an analysis of some proposals in this field. Finally, we conclude with some summary remarks and indications for areas that are currently underexplored and need more research work.

STATE OF THE ART

The *recombinant computing* approach [7] has been proposed and investigated to facilitate users in exploiting multiple technologies in a composite manner (rather than in isolation). On the one hand, the approach does not require the involved components to have mutual awareness, but on the other hand the components have to specify how they exchange information (thus, they need to have a recombinant implementation). A recent study [17] aimed to investigate the key elements that characterise the User eXperience (UX) when users exploit Web-based applications through different computing platforms (mainly desktop and mobile devices). This study also identified an initial framework for cross-platform service UX, in which the central elements include i)fit for cross-contextual activities (the structure of the application across different devices matches the user's activity, leading to an effective fit for tasks in different contexts), ii)flow of interactions and content (the transitions across the devices are experienced as fluid and connected), and iii)perceived service coherence (the application and its components are perceived as consistent and coherent, as part of the same service). In our paper we aim to provide a more structured framework, which is also able to highlight the main technical issues in multi-device User Interfaces (UIs).

Demeure et al. [5] have investigated distributed user interfaces (DUIs). The introduced reference framework defines four possible dimensions for the distribution: what is distributed, who is distributing it, when, from/to where. According to the authors, the framework does not consider the collaboration among users since this dimension is assumed to be "a natural extension" of DUI when several users are involved in the distribution. Some analogies can be found between that framework [5] and ours: the computation dimension, which introduces the notion of splittability, defines which parts of the interface can be distributed and is similar to our "granularity"; coordination is related to the "trigger activation type"; communication corresponds to "UI generation phase". However, the main difference with our proposal is that our framework addresses multi-device UIs in more general terms (including also e.g. as resulting from migration) and is not limited to DUIs.

A problem space for UI plasticity is proposed in [3]. The problem space is defined by a few dimensions and an interactive system is modelled as a graph of models that can be dynamically manipulated by, and/or encapsulated as services. Their approach to this problem is to bring together MDE (Model Driven Engineering) and SOA (Service Oriented Approach). In our case, we provide a more detailed set of dimensions in which the tool support for multi-device environments can also be analysed, and we do not limit our analysis to model-based approaches.

Myngle [15] is a support that facilitates device change (e.g. desktop to mobile) in Web navigation. It provides an easy way to revisit content previously accessed, by providing a unified web history from multiple personal devices, and allowing users to filter their history based on high-level categories. Since it is proposed as a browser extension (Firefox, Chrome) and as a native application for a few mobile platforms, thus it lacks portability. Also, it cannot support access to resources (e.g. session cookies, JavaScript variables, …) that are not usually mapped in the URL.

Multi-device applications are important in many domains. In [9] the authors investigated how to improve learnability in ubiquitous systems (e.g. multi-device museum guides). Authors claim that one design principle to promote the learnability of such systems is to improve their UI consistency. They identified three types of consistency, in order to better address the issues of multi-device, multi-user contexts: i)*within-device consistency*, which occurs when the UI design is consistent with the design of previous applications developed for a specific mobile device; ii)*across-device consistency*: it occurs when the UI design is consistent with the design developed on other mobile devices; iii)*within-context consistency*: when consistency is applied to the context, including aspects that are not strictly connected with the devices. For instance, a museum is a social, informal context in which interactive learning is supported: therefore, the user interface should reflect these characteristics to some extent. To this goal, the authors have compared three different interaction styles (gamepad controller emulation, mobile multi-touch, and Wii-based emulation) and they concluded that the within-device consistency generally gives better results for museum applications (these results can be also generalised to other similar ubiquitous contexts).

Previous work by the research community has coped with multi-device access to applications. Olsen et al. [13] studied techniques to combine multiple clients working on the same task, and have introduced the concepts of "Join" and "Capture". *Join* refers to collaborations with other users, whose clients can subscribe to data associated to a particular task; clients are promptly notified whenever data change. *Capture* consists of assembly of interactive resources to address specific problems, for instance by exploiting different modalities, with the aim to improve interaction. The authors claim that their integrated approach of multi-client interaction and multi-user collaboration is able to provide synchronization among tasks. This aspect is related in some way to the migration dimension of our framework. However, the paper does not consider a scenario where multiple users, independently from their physical position, share application interfaces. The authors also state that, although the multiple devices involved share the same network and are integrated in the same task, they are not aware of each other.

In general, we found a variety of research contributions in the area of multi-device user interfaces, and we cannot mention all of them. However, despite the increasing interest on this topic, when designers and developers want to support users in accessing applications (or parts of them) through various devices, they have often difficulties in identifying the possibilities and aspects that should be considered. The main goal of our framework is to provide a set of dimensions that allow users, designers, and developers to analyse the possibilities of tools and applications accessed in multi-device environments. This is useful both in the design of new multi-device environments and in the evaluation of existing ones.

A LOGICAL FRAMEWORK FOR MULTI-DEVICE UIs
A number of factors enable the analysis, design and comparison of multi-device user interfaces. Such factors have been identified by analysing related work in the area, emerging applications, and carrying out research in tools for supporting multi-device environments.

There are many ways to support multi-device applications. They range from accessing them through different devices at different times (one device at each time), to situations in which users access multiple devices at the same time through a UI that dynamically changes its distribution across them. Other cases could occur when the user changes the interaction device and the user interface supports (or not) the possibility to preserve the interaction state. Thus, with this framework we want to systematically analyse the various possible situations in which cross-platform access can be performed. These dimensions are described in the following subsections in which we consider various types of multi-device UIs. A solution can assume just one value in each dimension (when applicable). We have not identified particular dependencies between dimensions and the range of the possible values is specified for each framework dimension.

UI Distribution

This aspect analyses whether the solution considered is able to support the distribution of the user interface elements across various devices at a given time. We have distributed UIs when the UI elements of a given application are distributed across more than one device. In such distribution some elements can be even duplicated. Therefore, since at each time there are (at least) two devices involved in the rendering of the UI, UI distribution implies the existence of some coordination across the involved interactive devices supporting the access to the application logic by exploiting input/output from/to the various devices involved in the distribution. An example is when people access large screens to see large amount of information and use a mobile device to enter some queries. As for the range of values, the distribution can be *dynamic* (when the user interface elements can vary their allocation to the devices during a user session) or *static* (when the distribution configuration cannot change during a session).

An approach for *dynamic* distribution of UIs at run-time is discussed in [1], where the authors highlight the availability of diverse devices that characterise smart networked environments. Among the potentialities of distributed user interfaces in such contexts, there is the possibility for the user to enhance the interaction, for instance by increasing the communication bandwidth.

Although not mentioned explicitly as distribution, an early example of interface splitting among several devices was also tackled in [12]: Pebbles SlideShow Commander allowed users to control a PowerPoint presentation running on a laptop through a handheld with wireless connection. Multibrowsing [10] is an example of dynamic UI distribution, as it enables users to move existing pages among multiple displays.

UI Migration

This dimension analyses whether there is some continuity when users change device and still access the same application. Users should be enabled to change the current device in use (the source device) and then have available the application on a different device (the target device) while the system automatically preserves the interaction state reached with the first device and offers an adapted UI

on the new device. It is worth pointing out that distributed UIs and migratory UIs are two independent concepts: there may exist distributed UIs which are also able to migrate, but we can also have only distributed user interfaces (which do not migrate at all), or migratory UIs that are not distributed across multiple devices. In addition, multi-device UIs are different from distributed UIs: the latter is just an example, a particular case of the former. The range of values for this dimension is represented by the elements whose state can be preserved and transferred from one device to another: UI elements, functions, history, bookmarks, etc. However, it is worth noting that the state of the interactive application that can be captured/preserved depends on the implementation environment considered. For example, in Web applications it can include the state of forms, JavaScript variables, cookies, sessions, history, bookmarks, etc. An example of this is [8], which supports state persistence of web application in terms of state of HTML forms, session cookies, and JavaScript variables. Other types of applications (e.g. those supported by cloud computing) are able to preserve the state of only server-side information, others do not provide any support at all to UI continuity.

According to [17] continuity is considered to depend on how well the system supports cross-platform transitions, task migration and synchronization. An automatic solution for migrating UIs and preserving their state has recently been presented [2]. This approach, called Deep Shot, allows the migration of a user interface (or parts of it) by simply "shooting" it with a mobile phone camera. The authors claim that Deep Shot is compatible even with applications that are not Web-based. One limitation of this tool is that extra work is needed by developers to enable deep shooting/posting within an existing application.

UI Granularity

In this case we consider the granularity of the user interface that is manipulated (through e.g. distribution or migration) across various devices. As for the range of values we have:

- *entire UI*: the UI is seen as a single monolithic item, which can be e.g. moved/copied between devices;

- *groups of UI elements*: in this case we consider the possibility of e.g. distributing structured parts of user interfaces (e.g. navigation bars, articulated content areas with text and images, …) across various devices;

- *single UI elements*: in this case, single UI elements are distributed across devices;

- *components of UI elements*: interactive elements, which are usually characterised by *prompt*, *input*, and *feedback* are distributed across devices. For example, the user enters an input through a mobile device and the resulting feedback is shown on a large screen.

Some levels of granularity were addressed in [8], where a platform for totally/partially migrating Web pages across devices is described. Various levels of granularity were also addressed in [11] to support UI distribution.

Trigger Activation Type

This dimension analyses how the request for a change in the cross-device user interface is triggered. This change could then activate e.g. a migration or a (re-)distribution of the UI. The simplest case is user-initiated: the user actively selects when, to which device and what should be changed. With automatic trigger the system autonomously activates the change when it recognises the verification of suitable contextual conditions (e.g. in case of a high battery consumption level and a simultaneous user's proximity to another device). Therefore, the system might decide that a device change is appropriate and then select the new device to be used. This type of automatic trigger can be related to the work on implicit human-computer interaction driven by the context discussed in [14], in which the system acts proactively on the basis of context information. Another option is a mixed type of trigger activation (partially suggested automatically and partially determined by the user): the system first automatically suggests a change to the user who is still able to modify some parameters in the request. In the case of the user-generated trigger we further distinguish between *push* and *pull* modalities depending on whether the triggered migration is from the local device to a remote one or vice versa. Therefore, the range of values is: *user* (which can be further decomposed into *push/pull* modality), *system*, and *mixed*.

In [8] both user (push and pull) and automatic migration triggering are available.

Device Sharing between Multiple Users

Multi-user interaction raises a wide variety of issues and possible solutions. Our framework is focused on support for multi-device environments. Thus, here we want to consider only the cases in which there are various devices and some of them can be shared by multiple users. This can happen either because the same device is targeted by the user interfaces of their applications (an example could be when two users use the same large display as a target for a migration from their mobile devices) or different users access the same interface on the same device (e.g. when two or more users exploit the same wall-sized interactive screen by using their own devices).

The multi-user/device framework discussed in [6] and the related scenarios explicitly consider the situation of several users concurrently accessing the same UI on a public display. Sharing implies that the supporting environment is able to indicate what the shareable devices are, whether there is any conflict in their use, and provide some information regarding their state. Thus, the possible levels of sharing considered are: multiple users can move information on that device (*sharing by moving*), or can even interact with that device (*sharing by interacting*).

Timing

Here the aspect considered is the time when a device change should occur in a multi-device configuration. An example typical case is a migration that has to be carried out as soon as the migration trigger is sent from the source device (*immediate* effect) in order to achieve seamless continuity. Another case covers the possibility for the user to specify the time when to defer the change in the multi-device configuration (*deferred* effect). This could be useful when the target device is temporarily unavailable to the user, hence the effect will be delayed until a more appropriate time. In this case the support should enable users to specify the device to be used as target, even if it could be temporarily unavailable in the current environment. The deferring time is implicitly managed in Deep Shot [2], which allows launching on a different device an application with a previously captured work whenever the user needs it. Myngle [15] could also be seen as an example of system that handles this possibility, since it lets the user choose when to restore the previous state of a Web application on a different device. Thus, the range of values for this dimension includes: *immediate*, *deferred, and mixed* (when both the previous ones are possible).

Interaction Modalities Involved

This dimension analyses the modalities involved in the multi-device UI. There are three possible values. *Mono-modality* means that the devices involved in the cross-device access support the same, (single), interaction modality. *Trans-modality* means that different devices can support different modalities, but any device supports only one modality at a given time. *Multi-modality* occurs when the multi-device interface simultaneously supports two or more interaction modalities in one (at least) of the devices involved. Various modalities have been considered in the dynamic interactors distribution proposed in [1], where the authors assume that each device category available in a smart environment has specific interaction resources (IRs). The approach is based on distribution of UI interactors among available IRs (devices). Distribution is performed automatically according to context information and developer/user settings. In their work, the authors refer to multi-modality as the combined use of multiple modalities within a (distributed) UI. However, they do not report on supporting more than one modality within the same device.

UI Generation Phase

This dimension specifies the phase when the user interface is obtained so as to be rendered on the target device(s). On the one hand, in the *design-time* case the UI is built in advance for each type of device, and then at run-time only the state has to be updated, in case of migration. On the other hand, the *run-time* case covers the situation where a run-time engine dynamically generates the user interface, according to the features of the target device. Also an intermediate approach (*mixed* case) is still possible where the supporting engine dynamically generates the user interfaces for the different devices by exploiting some logical descriptions which have been created at design time. Therefore, we have three possible values.

The aspects related to the design time are discussed in [16], which presents Dygimes, a testbed for model-based UI development. Networked cooperating devices potentially offer a set of interaction resources to the mobile user. The authors distinguish between static and dynamic approaches for UI distribution, i.e. for distributing interaction resources (IRs) among UI components. The static approach would require knowing at development time the runtime context peculiarities, which is rather difficult since it implies to know which IRs are available in the environment and to which IR every part of a UI will be distributed. The dynamic approach allocates at runtime UI components to IRs, either automatically by the system or manually upon user request. The authors propose a possible solution describing the UI using a model-based approach. Different models are used to create descriptions at development time, while the actual UIs are generated at runtime starting from the models.

UI Adaptation Aspects

When changing the device(s) currently used, user interface adaptation is usually required. The adaptation process can have an impact at various granularity levels: either the entire application is changed depending on the new context, or just some logical UI parts (presentation, navigation, content) or even single UI components are adapted. There is also the case that no adaptation is provided, often generating low usability results.

By adaptation at the presentation level we mean, for example, the possibility to change the presentation layout. There are various ways to adapt the presentation ranging from simple scaling to applying information visualization techniques (e.g. semantic zooming, fisheye, …). Navigation refers to the connections among the different presentations: for example, when the number of presentations increases or decreases then the connections between them will be adapted accordingly. Content adaptation refers to when some information is removed, added, or modified (e.g. summarised) in order to produce a more usable UI depending on the resources of the device. One proposal [8] concerns a platform for partial migration of Web UIs with adaptation capabilities particularly useful when Web pages are migrated towards small devices: pictures are scaled, content can be split into several presentations, interaction components can be replaced by more suitable ones.

We identify three main approaches to adaptation: *Scaling*, in which the user interface is just linearly scaled according to the interaction resources of the available device, as it happens with Safari on IPhone; *Transducing*, an approach preserving the initial structure while translating the elements into other formats, and compressing/converting images to match device characteristics; *Transforming* goes further to modify both contents and structures originally designed for desktop systems to make them suitable to display on small screens. The multi-user/device framework previously cited [6] also tackles UI adaptation: transformation modules convert information into different representations (e.g. visual to audio) according to user's preferences. Transformations rely on previously defined annotations specifying how to convert resources at runtime.

Architecture

Two different strategies can be considered with regard to the architecture of a possible platform supporting a multi-device environment: *client/server*, in which there is an intelligent unit managing all requests and sending all data to target devices, thus controlling the user interface allocated across various devices; *peer-to-peer*, where the devices directly communicate and negotiate the distribution parameters. Within this type of coarse-grained distinction, it is still possible to identify more refined approaches for managing some phases, one of this being the interaction state preservation (when supported). For example, with a client-side approach we have some (client-side) mechanisms such as plug-ins or scripts that gather the interaction state data on the client and then send the collected data to the migration engine for further processing. With a server-side approach there is a server which is able to gather requests from the client side and consequently stores the relevant information. However, the choice between client/server and peer-to-peer may be driven by other aspects of the platform. For instance, if UI adaptation features are included in the platform, then the server support is highly desirable, since the computational effort needed to transform/generate the target interface might be too huge for a mobile device.

The migration platform described in [8] is based on a server which creates logical description of the source UI, adapts it to the target device capabilities and generates on-the-fly a specific implementation. The cross-device infrastructure of DeepShot [2] also relies on an instant messaging protocol which is server-based, even the devices involved in migration are usually co-located. On the contrary, a peer-to-peer strategy could offer more flexibility. For example, a set of devices equipped with peer-to-peer clients in the same network that do not rely on an external Web server could exchange information locally. This simplified architecture also leads to lower communication latencies between devices. An example of peer-to-peer implementation for distributed user interfaces is in [11], which requires the use of a specific development toolkit in order to benefit from this feature.

DISCUSSION and CONCLUSIONS

Table 1 provides a concrete example of how our logical framework can be used to analyse various proposals. For sake of brevity and lack of space we only consider a small set of tools.

The table shows that there are various points in the framework that are partially covered by most proposals and can be the topic for new research work. For example, there is a lack of solutions able to exploit peer-to-peer communication among sets of devices that are opportunistically accessed. Another part that has received limited attention, also for its complexity, is the ability to preserve the state of UI functionalities in migration.

Aspect\Tool	Web Migration [8]	DeepShot [2]	Myngle [15]	Peer-to-peer DUIS [11]	Dygimes [16]	Multimodal distribution [1]
Distribution	Not Supported	Not Supported	Not Applicable	Dynamic	Dynamic	Dynamic
Migration	UI elements / functions	UI elements	Web history	UI elements	Not Applicable	UI elements
Granularity	Entire UI / Groups	Entire UI / Groups	Entire UI	Entire UI / Groups /	Entire UI / Groups /	Entire UI Groups /
Trigger	User / Automatic	User	Automatic	User	Automatic	Automatic
Sharing	Move informat.	Not supported	Not supported	Move informat.	Not applicable	Not applicable
Timing	Immediate	Mixed	Mixed	Immediate	Immediate	Immediate
Modalities	Transmod.	Monomod.	Monomod.	Monomod.	Monomod.	Multimodal
Generation	Run-time	Mixed	Runtime	Runtime	Mixed	Mixed
Adaptation	Transduc./ Transf.	Scaling	Scaling	Transduc.	Transduc./ Transf.	Transducing/ Transfor.
Architecture	Client/Serv	Client/Serv	Client/Serv	Peer-peer	Client/Serv	Client/Serv.

Table 1: Example Application of the Logical Framework

Another topic that deserves further study regards users' attitudes towards multi-device UIs when the context is shared with other users, and while performing tasks with privacy concerns. This is a research direction that we also plan to further investigate in the future. In addition, the support of richer set of interaction modalities and their various combinations seem an area that needs to be better explored also considering the recent technological improvements for modalities such as voice and gesture.

To conclude, we can say that despite the increasing number of research proposals in the area of multi-device UIs, there is still need for further solutions able to address the parts of the logical space proposed that are still underexplored, such as the support for multimodal distributed user interfaces or peer-to-peer architectures for migration of Web applications.

ACKNOWLEDGMENTS

This work has been partly supported by the SMARCOS Project, http://www.smarcos-project.eu/

REFERENCES

1. Blumendorf, M., Roscher, D., and Albayrak, S. Dynamic User Interface Distribution for Flexible Multimodal Interaction, in *Proceedings of ICMI-MLMI'10*, Acm New York, 2010.

2. Chang, T.H., and Li, Y. Deep Shot: A Framework for Migrating Tasks Across Devices Using Mobile Phone Cameras, in *Proceedings of CHI 2011*, ACM Press, 2011, 2163-2172.

3. Coutaz J., Balme L., Alvaro, X., Calvary, G., Demeure, A., Sottet, J.: An MDE-SOA Approach to Support Plastic User Interfaces in Ambient Spaces. HCI (6) 2007: 63-72.

4. Dearman, D., and Pierce, J. It's on my other Computer!: Computing with Multiple Devices, in *Proceedings of CHI '08*, ACM Press, 2008, 767-776.

5. Demeure, A., Sottet, J.-S., Calvary, G., Coutaz, J., Ganneau, V., and Vanderdonckt, J. The 4C Reference Model for Distributed User Interfaces, in *Proceedings of ICAS '08*, IEEE, 2008, 61-69.

6. Ding, Y., and Huber, J. Designing multi-user multi-device systems: an architecture for multi-browsing applications, in *Proceedings of MUM '08*, ACM Press, 2008, 8-14.

7. Edwards W. K., Newman M. W., Sedivy J. Z., Smith T. F. Experiences with recombinant computing: Exploring ad hoc interoperability in evolving digital networks. ACM Trans. Comput.-Hum. Interact. 16(1): (2009)

8. Ghiani, G., Paternò, F., and Santoro, C. Push and Pull of Web User Interfaces in Multi-Device Environments, to appear in *Proceedings AVI 2012*, Capri, 2012, ACM.

9. Jimenez Pazmino, P., and Lyons, L. An exploratory study of input modalities for mobile devices used with museum exhibits, in *Proceedings of CHI 2011*, ACM Press, 2011, 895-904.

10. Johanson, B., Ponnekanti, S., Sengupta, C. and Fox, A. Multibrowsing: Moving Web Content across Multiple Displays, in *Proceedings of Ubicomp 2001*, Springer-Verlag, 2001, LNCS 2201, 346-353.

11. Melchior, J., Grolaux, D., Vanderdonckt, J., and Van Roy, P. A toolkit for peer-to-peer distributed user interfaces: concepts, implementation, and applications, in *Proceedings of EICS 2009*, ACM, 2009, 69-78.

12. Myers, B.A. Using handhelds and PCs together, *Communications of the ACM*, 44 (11), 2001, 34-41.

13. Olsen, D.R., Nielsen, S.T., and Parslow, D. Join and Capture: a Model for Nomadic Interaction, in Proceedings of UIST '01, ACM, 2001, 131-140.

14. Schmidt, A. Implicit Human Computer Interaction Through Context. *Personal and Ubiquitous Computing* 4(2/3), 2000, 191-199.

15. Sohn, T., Li, F.C.Y., Battestini, A., Setlur, V., Mori, K., and Horii, H. Myngle: unifying and filtering web content for unplanned access between multiple personal devices, *Proceedings UbiComp* 2011, ACM, 257-266.

16. Vandervelpen, C., and Conix, K. Towards Model-Based Design Support for Distributed User Interfaces, in *Proceedings of NordiCHI 2004*, ACM, 2004, 61-70.

17. Wäljas, M., Segerståhl, K., Väänänen-Vainio-Mattila, K., and Oinas-Kukkonen, H. Cross-Platform Service User Experience: A Field Study and an Initial Framework, *Proceedings of MobileHCI 2010* (Lisboa, Portugal, September 2010), ACM Press 219-228.

PuReWidgets: A Programming Toolkit for Interactive Public Display Applications

Jorge C. S. Cardoso

CITAR – Portuguese Catholic University,
Rua Diogo Botelho 1327, Porto, Portugal
jorgecardoso@ieee.org

Rui José

Algoritmi – University of Minho,
Campus de Azurém, Guimarães, Portugal
rui@dsi.uminho.pt

ABSTRACT

Interaction is repeatedly pointed out as a key enabling element towards more engaging and valuable public displays. Still, most digital public displays today do not support any interactive features. We argue that this is mainly due to the lack of efficient and clear abstractions that developers can use to incorporate interactivity into their applications. As a consequence, interaction represents a major overhead for developers, and users are faced with inconsistent interaction models across different displays. This paper describes the results of a study on interaction widgets for generalized interaction with public displays. We present PuReWidgets, a toolkit that supports multiple interaction mechanisms, automatically generated graphical interfaces, asynchronous events and concurrent interaction. This is an early effort towards the creation of a programming toolkit that developers can incorporate into their public display applications to support the interaction process across multiple display systems without considering the specifics of what interaction modality will be used on each particular display.

Author Keywords

Human-Computer interfaces; User Interface Design; Programming toolkits; Public displays

ACM Classification Keywords

D.2.2 [Software Engineering]: Design Tools and Techniques – Software libraries, Modules and interfaces;

INTRODUCTION

Public digital displays have become increasingly ubiquitous artefacts in public and semi-public spaces. Most of them, however, do not support any interactive features, even though interaction is clearly recognised as a key element in making them more engaging and valuable. A key reason behind this apparent paradox is the lack of efficient and clear abstractions for incorporating interactivity into public display applications. While interaction can be achieved for a specific display system with a particular interaction modality, the lack of proper interaction abstractions means that there is too much specific work that needs to be done outside the core

application functionality to support even basic forms of interaction. This is an effort that must be replicated by each developer, representing a wasted effort. This also leads to inconsistent interaction models across different displays and, as a result, people are not able to develop, based on previous experiences, any expectations and practices regarding their interaction with public displays.

It seems reasonable to make an analogy between this situation and the time when desktop computer programmers had to make a similar effort to support their interaction with users. This was quickly recognised as a problem and addressed with the emergence of reusable high-level interaction abstractions, such as the WIMP model and its associated controls, that provided consistent interaction experiences to users and shielded application developers from low-level interaction details [12]. Nowadays, with the wide availability of interaction widgets, developers can benefit from ready-to-use interaction elements that deal with input, encapsulating behaviour and visual appearance, and users have learned to interpret their affordances in a way that enables them more easily to tackle new interfaces and programs by building on their previous experience.

In this work, we studied new interaction abstractions for the development of interactive applications for public displays. Our early results are instantiated in a programming toolkit that developers can incorporate into their public display applications. The main contributions of this work are the elicitation of the requirements for public display interaction abstractions and an architecture and software library system for application developers that provides high-level abstraction that can be incorporated into interactive public display applications.

This paper is organized as follows. We first characterize the interaction environment of public display applications; then we describe the main steps that we took while developing this work; we present work related to our own; then we define the requirements that an interaction abstraction should meet; we present the design of PuReWidgets; we provide an initial evaluation of the toolkit; and, finally, we conclude.

Interactive Public Display Applications

Applications for interactive displays are still an emerging topic with a lack of widely accepted and well-defined concepts. In this section we characterise our assumptions regarding the properties of the ecosystem of interactive public display applications.

Display ecosystem

Using the concept of "ecosystem of displays" introduced by Terrenghi et al. [22], we could generally describe the public display environment as perch/chain[1] sized ecosystems for many-many interaction: and environment composed of displays of various sizes (from handheld devices, to medium/large wall mounted displays), and where "many people can interact with the same public screens simultaneously". The different sized displays afford different types of interaction but they can function in an integrated way in this ecosystem. The bigger displays (perch/yard sized) can function as the main information outlets of a place, providing a shared information and interaction point for the whole place – they are public, visible to everybody at all times (usually located in high-visibility locations), and can function as the reference display in a place. Normally, these displays are not meant to be appropriated by single users; they should be perceived as always available to everybody [9]. Medium-size displays (yard/foot sized) can also be present and dedicated to particular uses such as for allowing users to interact with the information on the main display, or for presenting some particular kind of information. These smaller public displays can be used, for example, to provide an interaction point (e.g., using touch interaction) that shows some of the most important interactive features that are locally available. The person that is responsible by the place – to whom we will refer to as the place owner – typically owns both large and medium displays. Small displays (foot/inch sized) are typically the personal mobile devices such as smart-phones, tablets, or laptop computers. Users that own these kinds of devices will want to take advantage of them to interact with their environment, including the available public display applications. The small personal devices will most likely be used as input devices to the public display application, allowing users to interact in a more opportunistic way by sending an SMS message to the application, using Bluetooth naming, or even a custom mobile application to interact. Personal tablets and laptops will most likely be used for more lengthy interactions allowing users to interact with an application via a place web page or directly through the application's web page, perhaps for configuring a user profile, or for upload or downloading large content files.

Applications

We want this display environment to be open to place owners, to application providers (or more generally, content providers), and to users. We have targeted our toolkit at web-based public display applications that can be hosted on third-party servers to serve content to many displays, but take advantage of the locally available interaction resources. Software developers will create these applications and will want to be able to distribute them globally. Place owners will be able to browse, select, and configure the applications they want to display in a given location. An application selected

for a place will be sometimes visible on a public display. We assume that each display will show content from multiple applications and will iterate through those applications based on some pre-defined scheduling criteria. Even though an application may not be continually visible on the public display, it will be accessible via many other displays and interaction mechanisms. Once selected for a place, the public display application will be able to receive and process interaction events and produce place specific content that can be accessed in different ways (on a public display, through a web page, through a custom mobile application, etc.).

RELATED WORK

Interactive public displays are not new, and there are many systems that explore different interaction mechanisms that can be used by applications for public displays. For example, Rohs [4] has implemented a set of widgets for visual marker-based interaction that allows users to activate actions or select options encoded in a visual marker and send it via SMS (using a custom mobile application). The visual marker encodes the type (menu, radio or check button list, sliders, etc.) and layout (vertical or horizontal menu, number of options, etc.) of the widget, so that the mobile phone application can immediately superimpose graphical information about the currently selected item or value. Dearman & Truong [4] developed Bluetone: a widget that is activated through dual tone multi-frequency (DTMF) over Bluetooth. Users interact with an application by changing the Bluetooth name of their device to a system command, wait for the display to pair with the user's phone as an audio gateway, and then pressing the keys on the keypad of their phone. Bluetone supports several users, being limited only by the Bluetooth protocol. This widget is limited to the DTMF interaction mechanism, and has been developed for an environment where a single application executes at a time; graphically, it consists of a single widget that encapsulates all the interactive features of the application. SMS interaction has also been used frequently with public display applications. Jumbli [11], for example, is a word puzzle game that allows users to form words with the letters presented on the public display and send those words, via an SMS message with the word sent to a pre-defined number. Bluetooth (BT) naming is another approach for providing interactivity to public displays. Lancaster University's e-Campus display system [21], for example, explored Bluetooth naming as an explicit input mechanism. BT scanners on each display continually discover devices in the vicinity and send these sightings information to a content scheduler. To interact, users need only to change the BT name of their personal mobile device using a pre-defined command structure and wait for the BT scanner in the place to pick up the change.

All these are good examples of how to provide users with specific interaction channels to public displays. However they do not address the question of providing useful interaction abstractions to applications so, they don't help the application developer who wishes to deploy a public display application without worrying about the specificities of the

---

[1] 1 chain ≈ 20 meters; 1 perch ≈ 5 meters; 1 yard ≈ .9 meters; 1 foot ≈ .30 meters; 1 inch ≈ 0.025 meters (or ≈ 2.5 cm)

available interaction mechanisms of the various places where his application may run. In all the previous examples, the assumption was that a specific mechanism would be available.

There has also been much work on input middleware for ubiquitous systems. Magic Broker [7], for example, is an event-based input infrastructure that allows applications to subscribe to input from different sources such as SMS, Voice (using Voice XML), and web interactions. However, it provides a lower level of abstraction than the one we wish to achieve. For example, it does not define how users can address individual applications or interactive features, or how the web interface would be generated. Other input middleware such as ICON [6], allow the dynamic mapping of input devices to applications. However, these mappings are created for individual applications, and they work for local input devices. Also, it does not defined high-level controls suitable for public display applications.

Various interaction abstraction models have been used for different purposes and computing platforms. In the WIMP widget based interaction abstraction for GUI, widgets provide a high-level interface to the application in the form of widget events, triggered by user actions, which invoke callback functions in the application. The application does not know the specific action that was used to trigger the event; it has only access to the high-level data exposed by that specific widget. In the dynamic user interface generation, more appropriate for smart environments, programmers describe the application/service interface using an abstract language, which is then used to generate various interfaces for different devices (e.g. widgets for graphical devices; speech interfaces; etc.). Communication between the device and application is usually accomplished via some form of remote method invocation. The abstract language usually allows developers to specify which functions and parameters are associated with a particular interactive feature. There is also the data-driven interaction approach, usually used in cases where we want a single application to be able to receive input from various, different, "dumb" input devices. This approach is usually implemented using a tuple space data structure where input devices and application programmers define their own tuples and a mapping software component maps tuples from input devices to tuples for applications. Thus, programmers are free to define whatever tuples they need and applications simply react to the data-type (and parameters) of the incoming tuples.

SCENARIOS
To provide a better image of the type of interaction we envision of public display applications, we describe next some usage scenarios.

John is a software developer in charge of creating an interactive public display application that will integrate with an existing social news platform developed by the same company. The existing platform allows an institution to post news items on a web page and allows users to "like" and

discuss on those individual items. There are already two clients that want to use this new public display application: a university's communication department and a local coffee shop. John has already developed much of the logic for the application and is now on the process of adding the "like" feature. He fires up his favourite IDE – Eclipse, and opens up the application project. In the project settings he configures the application to use an interaction library for public displays. The application creates and displays a list of text items and for each item John needs to associate a "like" action by instantiating an action widget which, when activated, will contact the server to update news platform with the indication that a user liked the news item. He does not need to worry about the specific input mechanisms that will be used to "press" the action button; the interaction library handles all that...

Sophia is waiting for her friends at the university's main hall. Looking at the large display across the hall, one of the entries of the school-related news catches her eye - it's about Adam, a friend on the robotics class, which has won the national robot-dancing contest. There is a button next to the news entry's header that Sophia recognizes: is a ``like'' button with three letters underneath. The instructions on the top of the display tell her how to interact so she fetches her mobile phone and sends a text message to the number on the instructions. A few seconds later, a popup near the button appears with a phone number. Some digits do not show, but she recognizes it as her own. She knows her ``like'' will increase the news visibility on the school's website and on the display. Adam deserves it!

Sarah and George took a break from work to grab a snack at the coffe shop across the street. They sit down and order an entry from the menu that is on their table – the latte+muffin menu. While they're eating and talking, Sarah notices a familiar symbol next to each entry in the menu: a QR code. The description says that they can post a comment. George is not sure how that works, but he pulls his smartphone, launches the default app for visual codes, and scans the code. A webpage opens with a textbox. He enters: "Best blueberry muffin, ever!" and presses Send. A confirmation message pops up thanking and telling him that he can check the result of his interaction in a nearby display. A few moments later they notice that the display in the coffee shop is showing photos of the various menu entries and comments from customers: George's comment appears next to the latte+muffin entry!

RESEARCH METHODOLOGY
This work proceeded in three phases. In the first phase, we elicited the main requirements for interaction abstractions for public displays. For this, we collected academic publications about interactive public display systems by searching online databases (such as ACM, IEEE, Google Scholar) and filtering publications by keywords such as "public display", "interactive display", from the last 20 years. In our analysis dataset, we also included references from these publications to other public display systems (in total, we analyzed about

50 different display systems). We focused on the descriptions of the requirements, functionalities, and properties of the described display systems to extract relevant common features and synthesize them in a set of high-level requirements (cf. Requirements for Public Display Interaction section).

In a second phase, we investigated existing ways of providing interaction abstractions to application programmers, taking note of their main properties and paying particular attention to how they could support our requirements. We analyzed specifically the widget abstraction model, the dynamic interface generation model and the data-driven interaction model (cf. Related Work section). This phase resulted in a set of design guidelines that incorporated features from the various existing interaction abstractions to form a new interaction abstraction for interactive public displays.

In a third phase, we re-analyzed the interactive public display systems of phase 1, but this time focusing on analyzing the types of high-level data generated by different types of interactions with public displays [2], and then examining various interactive features proposed in different display system to extract the fundamental properties of those features. This resulted in a set of control types that serve as the basis for the various controls in our toolkit (cf. PuReWidgets System section). While designing the toolkit we made a decision to support control types that would not impose a direct manipulation interaction style.

REQUIREMENTS FOR PUBLIC DISPLAY INTERACTION

The main objective of an interaction abstraction is to facilitate the programmer's task of developing an interactive public display application by abstracting away the details of the multiple interaction mechanisms that may exist in a place, and which may vary across places. At the same time, the abstraction should allow developers to specify what kind of high-level interaction data their applications need. Achieving this objective for public display applications entails addressing several requirements. Some of these requirements are common to other interactive systems, but others are very specific to public displays.

Multiple interaction mechanisms

Unlike desktop systems, which usually rely on a very small set of input devices – most often just a keyboard and mouse – public display interaction can take advantage of several, very different input mechanisms. Many public displays have been developed that use very different input mechanisms, such as SMS [24], email and instant messaging [16], Bluetooth naming [10], Twitter [11], RFID [13], body movement [18], gestures [23], face detection [8], custom mobile applications [19], etc. These different input mechanisms have different costs and requirements and a single place cannot be expected to provide all of them nor can we expect to encounter the same set of input mechanisms in all places. Additionally, not all input mechanisms have the same data capabilities so they may not all be capable of providing the same high-level input

controls. Application programmers, however, should be able to specify their interaction necessities in a way that is independent from the specific interactive modalities or input mechanism that will be available at each specific place. A good interaction abstraction should be applicable, in a consistent way, to multiple input mechanisms.

Concurrent interaction

Given the many-many nature of the social interaction with public displays, public displays must explicitly support multiple, concurrently interacting users, possibly using different input mechanisms. Many applications will, at least, require information about the input events that allows them to differentiate users. An interaction abstraction for public displays should give support for concurrent input by multiple users, possibly using different input mechanisms. This is in sharp contrast to desktop systems were the assumption is that, generally, a single user is interacting – in control of the keyboard and the mouse – and applications are indifferent to which user is interacting. This has implications in the public display system support for the interaction because it means that there is a need to differentiate input events for different users.

Shared interaction

Shared interaction works on two levels: the first means that users are aware of each others interactions and, so, may decide to adapt their own behaviour in light of what others are doing; the second means that the display system is able, not only to accept concurrent interaction, but also to conciliate those interactions in its response. In a many-many interaction setting, being aware of each others actions is fundamental to the success of the interaction because it can act on two important aspects of public display interaction: attention and motivation [14]. The first barrier to interaction with a public display is understanding that it is interactive – moving from an unwitting bystander to a witting bystander (as defined by Dix and Sas [5]). If the display system provides some kind of public awareness regarding interactions, it can help attracting users' attention and making users aware that the display is interactive. It can also add to the collaboration motivation factor for interacting with public display, because "collaboration is especially motivating if individual behaviour is recognized by others" [14].

Asynchronous interaction

Our assumptions regarding the life cycle of a public display application are very different from traditional desktop applications. The life-cycle of a desktop application is completely controlled by the desktop user, which decides when the application should run, when it should be in the foreground receiving input, and when it should be terminated. In a public display ecosystem, users may not, in general, control applications. Once an application is associated with a particular place, it should be available for interaction at all times, or at least have that possibility. Also, a public display application should generally be available for users independently of whether there any public display currently showing any of its content. Contrary to desktop applications, the display is not the only interaction point with a public display application. A good interaction abstraction for public displays must support this kind of asynchronous interaction environment and allow interaction to happen at any time. This kind of interaction can help mitigate the "conflict of pace" mentioned by Dix and Sas [5], which happens because users are not in full control of the public display. An asynchronous interaction environment guarantees that, at least, the display's scheduling does not impose the pace for the interaction with an application.

Clear and decoupled affordances

The interaction abstraction should convey clear affordances in a way that people may easily learn to recognize, enabling potential users to become aware of the existence of the interactive features and their properties. Even when facing a display or an application for the first time, the interaction alternatives should always be clear, even if the semantics of the operation for an unknown application are not. This is a generic interaction guideline and a key function of an interaction abstraction, common to other interactive systems. It responds to the basic interface design principle of visibility, which helps bridging the gulf of evaluation of a system [15]. It is especially important for public displays because, unlike what happens with desktop computers where people are aware of the computer, when facing a public display, users may not even realize it is interactive. The interaction abstraction can partly address these issues and help users move from unwitting bystanders to participants, by providing identifiable graphical representations for widgets on the public display. However, given the environment in which public display applications will operate, we can't expect applications to be continuously shown on a public display nor to have the ideal screen space available to display an application's content. This requires that the affordances for the interactive features be decoupled from the public display screen, because it may not always be possible or desirable to show the graphical representations for the interactive features on the public display. The interaction abstraction should be flexible enough to allow the interactive features of applications to be rendered in other platforms such as web pages, or mobile devices. Ideally, this should be done with minimal or no extra effort needed from the application developer.

Multiple, public display specific, interactive features

A good interaction abstraction for public display must allow applications to have many different and individually addressable interactive features, just like standard desktop applications. Desktop applications typically need several interactive features of different types of controls. A single desktop form screen, for example, may require several text boxes, list boxes, radio buttons, and action buttons. The different types of controls allow programmers to choose the ones that best fit the application's data needs. There are many different controls for desktop applications such as data entry, selection, imperative, and display controls [3], and each type may have several variations that provide applications with different high-level data and give users

different affordances. Public display applications also need a set of controls for developers to choose from, but these controls must be appropriate for public display interaction. An interaction abstraction should provide a set of useful control types that allow a wide range of meaningful interactions. Programmers should be able to specify any number of interactive features that the application needs, and users should be allowed to address those features individually.

PUREWIDGETS SYSTEM

The PuReWidgets system is composed of a widget library and web service that handles interaction events. A widget is an interaction abstraction that: provides developers with high-level interaction data, hides the specific details of the underlying input mechanism; and can have different graphical representations in different platforms. The development process of a public display application that uses PuReWidgets is similar to the development of a regular web application. The developer includes an external code library in his project and uses the available functions of the library to code the application, instantiating widgets and registering interaction event callback functions. The developer then deploys the set of HTML, CSS, and Javascript files on a web server. The life cycle of a public display application (start, stop, and reacting to input events), however, is very different from the life cycle of a traditional application: the application is instantiated and terminated by a scheduler software that drives all the content of the public display, and interaction events can be generated via multiple local or remote sensors. When a widget is instantiated by an application, some metadata about the widget are sent to the PuReWidgets service. A remote I/O infrastructure is responsible for accepting raw input events from users. This I/O infrastructure can serve multiple displays, or even places, and its function is mainly to provide an initial abstraction over several sensor data such as SMS, Bluetooth naming, OBEX, etc. These input events are then used by the PuReWidgets service, which routes them to the application/widget that was addressed by the user. This service acts as an input event queue, storing the widget input until the application is ready to receive them, allowing applications to receive widget events even if they were generated when the application was not executing at the public display. When the PuReWidgets library asks for input, the service replies with the stored input. The library (running within the application) then forwards the input to the correct widget instance so that it can trigger the high-level application event. This requires a distributed architecture in which some widget information is kept by remote services, effectively decoupling widgets from applications. PuReWidgets provides two application models depicted in Figure 1, and described next.

PuReWidgets Library

The library provides high-level interaction abstractions to applications (widgets), and it is actually composed of two separate libraries: one for server-side code, and one for client-side code. This allows programmers to develop

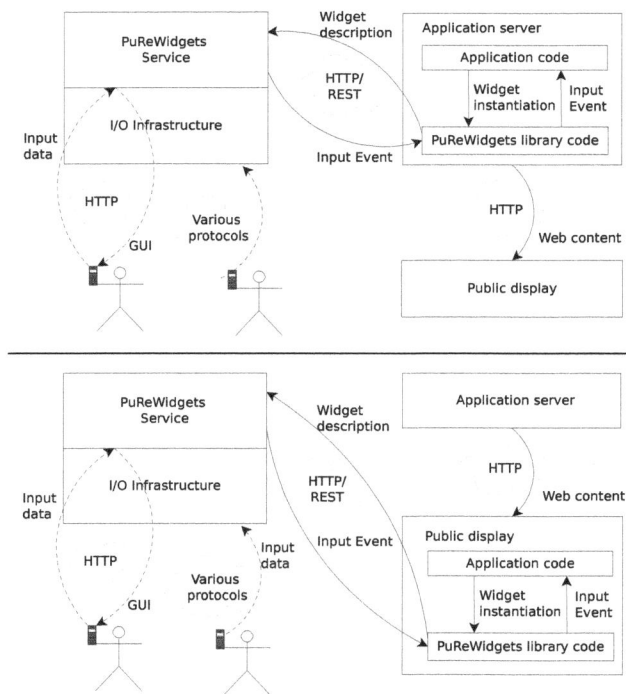

Figure 1: Application models for the PuReWidgets toolkit.

different types of applications, depending on the particular needs. The server-side library (Figure 1, top) allows developers to create applications than run mainly on the web server (i.e., their main logic resides on the server). These applications can run independently of the public display scheduling, e.g., they react immediately to user input, updating their internal state or calling external services, that may affect the content that it will display next, even if the application is not currently showing content on the display. The client-side library (Figure 1, bottom) allows developers to create applications that are more tightly coupled with the public display in the sense that their main, or even only, content output is on the display itself. These applications may not need to react immediately to interactions if they are not currently showing content on the public display so the widget life cycle, in this case, is coupled to the scheduling of the application in the public display. For these cases, it makes more sense for the main application logic to reside in the client code that is transferred to the public display so that it can create and control the necessary widgets. The PuReWidgets toolkit support this development mode by providing a client-side library (even though the code is still transferred from the application server in the form of Javascript, HTML, and CSS).

Control types

Widgets are provided in the form of an object-oriented library in which each widget has a type that defines the type of high-level data that it exposes to the application. Programmers can choose which widgets to use, according to the application's data needs (in some case there may be alternative widgets for the same data need), by instantiating

the respective widget class and registering a callback to receive the high-level events generated by the widget instance. The toolkit also allows programmers to extend the existing widgets and provide new ones, more suited to some specific interactive features needed by a particular application. We have based our toolkit's controls on the analysis of different types of high-level information generated by interaction with public displays [2], and categorized them in five categories: imperative/selection, entry, download, upload, and check-in controls.

Imperative/Selection controls

Imperative/selection controls allow users to trigger actions or select options in the public display application. From the abstraction point of view, an imperative control can be viewed as a selection control with just one option. The high-level event generated by these controls just needs to identify the option that the user selected. Many concrete widgets such as different types of buttons, list boxes, and check boxes, are of this type. Currently, PuReWidgets provides a button and a listbox widget.

Entry controls

Entry controls allow users to input simple data such as free text or bounded values. These controls generate high-level events that contain the input data. In this category we can include widgets such as textboxes, but also bounded data widgets such as number boxes. We have currently implemented a textbox widget that accepts unbounded text.

Upload controls

An upload control allows users to submit media files to the public display application. The high-level event generated by these controls includes an URL to the uploaded file so that the application can then process it. Concrete widgets can be specialized in particular media types, providing high-level events only is the media type of the uploaded file matches the required one.

Download controls

Download controls allow the application to provide files that users can download to their personal devices, or forward to their email, etc. This type of control generates a high-level event that simply signals that a user wants to download the item. The process of actually sending the file to the user is handled transparently by the toolkit. When instantiating the widget, applications are required to specify the location (an URL) of the associated media file.

Check-in controls

Check-in controls allow users to signal the application that they are present. In this case, the high-level event is just the identification of the user that has just checked-in.

Decoupled widgets

Decoupled widgets are widgets that do not depend on the application that created it for graphical representation or interaction. A decoupled widget allows the public display system to provide alternative graphical representations and interaction points to a widget created by an application. PuReWidgets provides automatic generation of desktop, mobile, and QR code interfaces for all widgets. The desktop and mobile interfaces are web-based and provide a rich graphical interface to an application's widgets (the interfaces are kept in synchronization with the widgets created by the application). The QR code generation can be used by place-owners who wish to draw attention to specific interactive features by printing the codes and distributing them locally. The codes can also be explicitly used by applications that wish to provide an alternative QR code based graphical interface on the public display itself.

This decoupling is accomplished by using a PuReWidgets service that stores metadata and input information about the instantiated widgets and exposes this information to system applications. All this is done transparently to the application and to the application developer. Whenever a widget is instantiated or updated by an application, the PuReWidgets toolkit sends the widget description data to the PuReWidgets service. The data that is sent to the server includes the widget unique id within the application, the type of control (imperative, entry, upload, download, check-in), a short and long textual description of the widget (used to give contextual information to the user), and a list of possible widget options (for widgets with several options). A widget option is composed of an option id, and short and long descriptions.

Public display applications are still responsible for creating and destroying widgets, during the course of their lifetime, allowing applications to behave much like desktop applications, which are responsible for graphically laying out their widgets and rendering them on the display, but it also allows the display infrastructure to keep track of the widgets that each application is using and providing alternative interaction points. It should be noted, however, that this does not preclude application developers from creating a custom web or mobile interface to their applications. Both can even be integrated in the display system, which can provide users with the custom application web or mobile interface, but fall back to the dynamically generated one if the former does not exist.

Addressing an input routing

PuReWidgets takes advantage of an I/O infrastructure that provides input data acquisition and basic level parsing to third-party components. This infrastructure manages a variety of sensors and input mechanisms and pre-processes the data input coming from these sensors. The I/O infrastructure works on two levels. On the lower level, the infrastructure is able to parse the raw input data and structure it into abstract "commands", using a pre-defined command syntax. As an example, the SMS, email or even Bluetooth

modules can be used to send keywords to a public display, which the I/O structures into a "keyword" command, with a parameter consisting of the actual keywords. A client of the I/O service is able to request a list of "keyword" commands issued and respective parameters (along with other metadata, such as timestamp, input mechanism id, etc.). The I/O infrastructure is also able to extract and store media files received via OBEX or through other mechanisms, and provide them on request to clients. On a higher level, the I/O infrastructure is able to associate individual input data with user identities. This optional service allows users to register and associate several personal input mechanisms (phone number, Bluetooth MAC address, etc.), which the infrastructure uses to identify which user is interacting. Depending on the available level, the PuReWidgets service is able to get a user id and associated nickname, or at least an input mechanism id (such as an anonymised phone number or Bluetooth MAC address) that allows it to differentiate among users.

PuReWidgets relies on this I/O service to support several low-level input mechanisms such as SMS, Bluetooth naming, etc. We use an I/O service developed for another project [10], but other I/O middleware such as the one by Paek et al. [16] could have been used. For these interactions, our approach to addressing is based on a simple referencing scheme that relies on unique textual reference codes that are generated for each widget instance and that become the address of the widget. These reference codes are small (3 or 4 alphanumeric characters), and are generated automatically by the PuReWidgets service. Widgets can have several distinct reference codes to allow addressing options within a single widget. These reference codes can be used explicitly by users on an SMS, Bluetooth naming, email, and other text-based mechanisms.

In some cases, routing behaves a little differently. For example, the check-in widget is naturally global to the place: users check-in to a place, not a specific application. In these cases, routing must also be global in the sense that all widgets of that particular type, regardless of in what application they were instantiated, will receive the input. This kind of routing is applied on an input mechanism basis or using place generated reference codes. For example, all input from a magnetic card reader may be interpreted as global data that should be sent to all check-in widgets. In these cases, routing the input data is a matter of associating the input with all applications that are currently using these types of controls.

When using the rich graphical interfaces or the QR codes for interactions, routing is more simple: the generated interfaces use the widget id and communicate directly with the PuReWidgets service to create input events directly associated with a widget instance from a particular application.

The input sequence from the time the user issues the input to the instant the application receives the input event is illustrated in Figure 2.

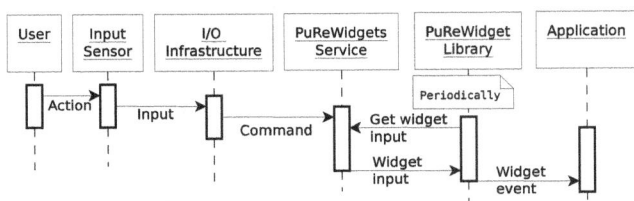

Figure 2: Sequence diagram of user sending input.

Graphical input feedback to users' actions

An important aspect of desktop widgets is the system-level feedback they provide and that helps users understand the response of the system, independently of how the application will react.

For public displays, feedback can also be used as a way to convey a sense of awareness about other users' actions. Displaying input feedback on the public display effectively helps creating a shared interaction environment independent of the application itself. This is an important aspect for creating more engaging public displays [1]. However, public display interaction also imposes practical considerations that may require other solutions for input feedback. In some cases, providing feedback through the main display itself may not be the best solution, in part because the available screen real-estate may dictate other priorities, but also because there are other feedback channels that can be more efficient considering the multi-user and multi-modality nature of the interaction.

Our approach is to provide a base mechanism for presenting feedback on the public display: the graphical representation of a widget includes the associated graphical input feedback. This is similar to what happens for the desktop, with the difference that, given the multi-user scenario, feedback information must be much more explicit for public displays, providing an indication of which user is responsible for the input. The feedback mechanism ensures that in a shared interaction environment, users are able to identify the feedback to their own input. Also, feedback can be decoupled from the graphical representation of the widget: programmers can choose to display feedback for a particular widget, even if the widget itself is not displayed on the public display.

Implementation

PuReWidgets was implemented using Google's App Engine platform (http://code.google.com/appengine) and Google's Web Toolkit (http://code.google.com/webtoolkit). The library is provided as a GWT module that developers can include in their GWT projects and the service is implemented as an App Engine application that exposes a REST API to the library. The graphical components of the widgets take advantage of the standard GWT widgets.

Current set of interaction mechanisms

PuReWidgets is designed in a way that allows the user of multiple interaction mechanisms. Currently, PuReWidgets supports the following interaction mechanisms: SMS, email, Bluetooth naming, Bluetooth OBEX, QR codes, mobile application, and desktop web application.

Using the toolkit

To show how PuReWidgets can be used to create a display application, we now describe a simple Hello World public display application. Using Google's GWT platform and PuReWidgets, the main application class would simply be the one in Listing 1. The code is very similar to what we would need if we were developing a desktop application.

```
1  public class HelloWorld implements EntryPoint {
2      @Override
3      public void onModuleLoad() {
4          PublicDisplayApplication.load(this, "HelloWorld", true);
5          GuiButton guiButton = new GuiButton("helloButton",
6                                              "Hello World");
7          guiButton.setShortDescription("Say hello!");
8          guiButton.setLongDescription("Say hello to be greeted
9                                        by the HelloWorld application");
10         guiButton.addActionListener(new ActionListener() {
11             @Override
12             public void onAction(ActionEvent<?> e) {
13                 PopupPanel popup = new PopupPanel();
14                 popup.add( new Label("Hello " +
15                                      e.getPersona() + "!") );
16                 popup.show();
17             }
18         });
19         RootPanel.get("main").add(guiButton);
20     }
21 }
```

Listing 1: Hello World application main class.

The main differences are in line 4, which initializes some background data structures and processes to communicate with the PuReWidgets service. Line 5, which creates a button with an application defined-named 'helloButton'. This name is needed so that the PuReWidgets service is able to distinguish widgets and to make sure that, if a widget was already created, it is not recreated. Lines 7 and 8 are needed to provide some application-specific context information in case the widgets are used in other platforms (see Figure 3-c for the mobile interface). Figure 3 shows the output of the Hello World application: a) the regular output; b) the reaction to a user input from the mobile interface; and c) the automatically generated interface for a mobile device. The popup on top of the button is the input feedback provided by PuReWidgets (which can be disabled by applications).

EVALUATION

Evaluating a programming toolkit like PuReWidgets is challenging, mainly because interactive public display applications are a new thing, and there are no programming communities for this platform. Given the current state of this field, our best approach to begin evaluating the toolkit was to develop some applications that could be deployed as real public display applications, and try to assess, through hands-on experience, whether the main requirements are met. We have implemented two interactive public display applications: a public video player, and voting application.

Public video player application

The public video player is an application that searches for, and plays youtube videos. Search is based on tags taken from a tag cloud that is built using tags defined by the place owner, suggested by users, and extracted from videos that users liked. The application is composed of three screens (Figure 4) which iterate over time: (left) a screen for playing the current video in full screen, (center) a screen that shows the recent activity (played videos, liked videos, and

a) Application output   b) Reacting to input   c) Mobile interface

Figure 3: Hello World application.

Figure 4: Public video player and voting applications.

suggested tags), and (right) a screen which shows alternative videos to play next along with a video play queue; the last two screens also display the current tag cloud. The application's interactive features are: 1) allow users to suggest tags. This was implemented using a custom tag cloud widget that incorporates a textbox widget. The tag cloud widget accepts keywords and automatically creates a tag visualisation. 2) Allow users to "like" videos. This feature was implemented with an action button that is displayed on the activity screen and allows users to "like" a specific video. 3) Allow users to download a reference to a recently played video. This feature was implemented with a download widget by providing a link to the corresponding youtube page. 4) Allow users to select a video to play from the list of search results. Action buttons are displayed to allow this. Selected videos are put in a play queue.

Voting application

The voting application is composed of two screens, depicted in Figure 5: (left) an open polls screen which iterates through the open polls, showing their description and options, and (right) a closed polls screen which iterates through the closed polls and shows their voting results. Polls are created by the place owner in a backoffice interface. The application offers the following interactive features to users: 1) Vote on a specific poll. The options of a poll are presented using a poll widget, which was built on top of a listbox widget but additionally shows a graphical representation of the votes when someone interacts. 2) Suggest a poll. A textbox widget is displayed briefly after someone interacts and on the closed polls screen, to signal that users can also suggest questions for polls.

Analysis

Developing these two applications enabled us to observe some important properties of PuReWidgets. The transparent support for multiple mechanisms, for example, enabled the place owner to create QR codes for some of the long running polls and to place them in wall posters or flyers drawing

more attention to those polls. This was done transparently to the application; while developing it we paid no specific attention to this possible use.

The identification of users/interaction mechanisms was also an important aspect of the interaction abstraction. Without it the poll application would not be possible. In this application, we used this identification to determine if a user had already voted on a specific poll, thus allowing a more correct voting count (there is still the problem of a single user voting using different input mechanisms, in which case multiple votes will be counted). This feature was also used in the youtube application, allowing us to create a play queue when multiple users selected a video to play next.

Support for asynchronous interaction was also an important feature, specifically for the voting application. This application is only shown on the display for a brief period at a time, but because the toolkit supports asynchronous interaction, users can still be aware of this application through the printed QR codes, for example, and vote on the existing polls.

While developing the youtube application we also demonstrated the flexibility of the widget classes, namely the possibility of creating new widgets by composing existing ones. We composed the tag cloud widget by incorporating the existing textbox widget into a new widget that automatically keeps a list of tags and tag frequencies and displays a tag cloud visualisation. From the point of view of the application, this is a widget just like any other.

CONCLUSION

We have created a toolkit for developing interactive public display applications, which handles much of the work a developer would have to deal with to develop even the simplest interactive public display application. PuReWidgets provides high-level interaction abstractions that suit the kind of interaction one normally does with public display applications and transparently supports various interaction mechanisms. The toolkit provides a widget addressing and an input routing mechanism, supports concurrent, asynchronous interaction and provides decoupled graphical affordances that can be used directly on the public display, or on alternative platforms. This toolkit fills a clear gap in the area of interactive public displays. Having a foundational tool like PuReWidgets allows designers and programmers to focus on the real creative work of designing interesting applications and user experiences.

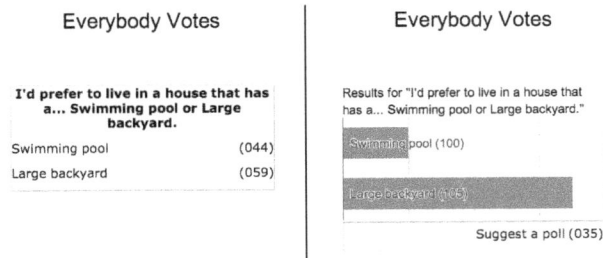

Figure 5: Voting application.

ACKNOWLEDGMENTS

Jorge Cardoso has been supported by "Fundação para a Ciência e Tecnologia" (FCT) and "Programa Operacional Ciência e Inovação 2010" co-funded by the Portuguese Government and European Union by FEDER Program and by FCT training grant SFRH/BD/47354/2008. This research has also received funding from the European Union Seventh Framework Programme (FP7/2007-2013) under grant agreement no. 244011 (PD-Net).

REFERENCES

1. Brignull, H., & Rogers, Y. (2003). Enticing People to Interact with Large Public Displays in Public Spaces. In M. Rauterberg, M. Menozzi, & J. Wesson (Eds.), *INTERACT'03* (pp. 17-24). IOS Press.

2. Cardoso, J. C. S., & Jose, R. (2009). A Framework for Context-Aware Adaptation in Public Displays. In R. Meersman, P. Herrero, & T. Dillon (Eds.), On the Move to Meaningful Internet Systems: OTM 2009 Workshops (Vol. 5872/2009, pp. 118-127). Vilamoura, Portugal: Springer Berlin / Heidelberg. doi:10.1007/978-3-642-05290-3_21

3. Cooper, A., Reimann, R., & Cronin, D. (2007). About face 3: the essentials of interaction design. New York, NY, USA: John Wiley & Sons, Inc.

4. Dearman, D., & Truong, K. N. (2009). BlueTone. Proceedings of the 11th international conference on Ubiquitous computing - Ubicomp '09 (p. 97). New York, NY, USA: ACM Press.

5. Dix, A., & Sas, C. (2008). Public displays and private devices: A design space analysis. Workshop on Designing and evaluating mobile phone-based interaction with public displays. CHI2008. Florence.

6. Dragicevic, P., & Fekete, J.-D. (2001). Input Device Selection and Interaction Configuration with ICON. In P. G. A. Blanford, J. Vanderdonkt (Ed.), People and Computers XV Interaction without Frontiers: Joint proceedings of IHM 2001 and HCI 2001 (IHM-HCI '01) (pp. 543-558). Springer Verlag.

7. Erbad, A., Blackstock, M., Friday, A., Lea, R., & Al-Muhtadi, J. (2008). MAGIC Broker: A Middleware Toolkit for Interactive Public Displays. 2008 Sixth Annual IEEE International Conference on Pervasive Computing and Communications (PerCom) (pp. 509-514). IEEE.

8. Grasso, A., Muehlenbrock, M., Roulland, F., & Snowdon, D. (2003). Supporting communities of practice with large screen displays. In K. O'Hara, E. Perry, E. Churchill, & D. M. Russel (Eds.), Public and Situated Displays - Social and Interactional Aspects of Shared Display Technologies (pp. 261-282). Kluwer.

9. Huang, E.M., Mynatt, E.D., and Trimble, J.P. When design just isn't enough: the unanticipated challenges of the real world for large collaborative displays. Personal Ubiquitous Comput. 11, 7 (2007), 537-547.

10. José, R., Otero, N., Izadi, S., & Harper, R. (2008). Instant Places: Using Bluetooth for Situated Interaction in Public Displays. IEEE Pervasive Computing, 7(4), 52-57.

11. LocaModa. (2010). LocaModa App Store. Retrieved March 2011, from http://locamoda.com/apps/

12. McCormack, J., & Asente, P. (1988). An overview of the X toolkit. Proceedings of the 1st annual ACM SIGGRAPH symposium on User Interface Software - UIST '88 (pp. 46-55). NY, NY, USA: ACM Press.

13. McDonald, D. W., McCarthy, J. F., Soroczak, S., Nguyen, D. H., & Rashid, A. M. (2008). Proactive displays. ACM Transactions on Computer-Human Interaction, 14(4), 1-31. New York, NY, USA: ACM.

14. Müller, J., Alt, F., Michelis, D., & Schmidt, A. (2010). Requirements and design space for interactive public displays. Proceedings of the international conference on Multimedia – MM'10 (pp. 1285-1294). New York, NY, USA: ACM Press.

15. Norman, D. A. (2002). The Design of Everyday Things. Basic Books.

16. Paek, T., Agrawala, M., Basu, S., Drucker, S., Kristjansson, T., Logan, R., Toyama, K., et al. (2004). Toward universal mobile interaction for shared displays. Proceedings of the 2004 ACM conference on Computer supported cooperative work (pp. 266-269). New York, NY, USA: ACM.

17. Rohs, M. (2005). Visual Code Widgets for Marker-Based Interaction. 25th IEEE International Conference on Distributed Computing Systems Workshops (pp. 506-513). Washington, DC, USA: IEEE.

18. Sawhney, N., Wheeler, S., & Schmandt, C. (2001). Aware Community Portals: Shared Information Appliances for Transitional Spaces. Personal and Ubiquitous Computing, 5(1), 66-70. London, UK: Springer-Verlag.

19. Scheible, J., & Ojala, T. (2005). MobiLenin combining a multi-track music video, personal mobile phones and a public display into multi-user interactive entertainment. Proceedings of the 13th annual ACM international conference on Multimedia (p. 199). New York, NY, USA: ACM Press.

20. Shneiderman, B., & Plaisant, C. (2005). Designing the User Interface: Strategies for Effective Human-Computer Interaction (4th ed.). Addison Wesley.

21. Storz, O., Friday, A., & Davies, N. (2006). Supporting content scheduling on situated public displays. Computers & Graphics, 30(5), 681-691.

22. Terrenghi, L., Quigley, A., & Dix, A. (2009). A taxonomy for and analysis of multi-person-display ecosystems. Personal and Ubiquitous Computing, 13(8), 583-598.

23. Vogel, D., & Balakrishnan, R. (2004). Interactive public ambient displays. Proceedings of the 17th annual ACM symposium on User interface software and technology - UIST '04 (p. 137). New York, NY, USA: ACM Press.

24. Vogl, S. (2002). Coordination of Users and Services via Wall Interfaces. (PhD Thesis). University of Linz, Linz, Austria.

jQMultiTouch: Lightweight Toolkit and Development Framework for Multi-touch/Multi-device Web Interfaces

Michael Nebeling and Moira C. Norrie
Institute of Information Systems, ETH Zurich
CH-8092 Zurich, Switzerland
{nebeling,norrie}@inf.ethz.ch

ABSTRACT

Application developers currently have to deal with the increased proliferation of new touch devices and the diversity in terms of both the native platform support for common gesture-based interactions and touch input sensing and processing techniques, in particular, for custom multi-touch behaviours. This paper presents *jQMultiTouch*—a lightweight web toolkit and development framework for multi-touch interfaces that can run on many different devices and platforms. jQMulti-Touch is inspired from the popular jQuery toolkit for implementing interfaces in a device-independent way based on client-side web technologies. Similar to jQuery, the framework resolves cross-browser compatibility issues and implementation differences between device platforms by providing a uniform method for the specification of multi-touch interface elements and associated behaviours that seamlessly translate to browser-specific code. At the core of jQMulti-Touch is a novel input stream query language for filtering and processing touch event data based on an extensible set of *match predicates* and *aggregate functions*. We demonstrate design simplicity for developers along several example applications and discuss performance, scalability and portability of the framework.

Author Keywords

Multi-device interface toolkit; multi-touch framework

ACM Classification Keywords

H.5.2 Information Interfaces and Presentation: User Interfaces—*Input devices and strategies, Interaction styles*

General Terms

Design, Human Factors

INTRODUCTION

Application developers face the increased proliferation of new touch devices, nowadays ranging from smartphones, tablet PCs and touch notebooks to all-in-one touchscreen solutions,

tabletop systems and interactive walls. Unless an application is to be designed for a specific device only, it is becoming increasingly difficult for developers to create interfaces that cater for the wide range of possible settings. In particular, there are three major technical and design challenges for current multi-touch frameworks: **1) Many technological differences between touch devices**: Multi-touch devices vary in terms of the amount of touch points they can track simultaneously as well as the tracking speed and the support for other advanced sensing techniques based on accelerometers or tilt sensors. Some devices such as the Microsoft Surface[1] tabletop system provide additional tracking support for tangible objects in the form of physical tokens, while others are limited to finger tracking. Available frameworks are therefore often designed for a specific technological setup, e.g. DiamondSpin [21] or DTFlash [7] for the DiamondTouch system [5], and tend to focus their support on either finger or tangible object tracking [13]; **2) Different software architectures and implementation methods**: Developers require a wide range of skill sets and experience with different programming languages and software development kits (iPhone, Android, etc.) in order to build applications for the latest generation of smartphones and tablet computers [3]. Some frameworks such as PyMT [9] and MT4j [16] therefore instead build on cross-platform programming languages such as Python or Java and protocols such as TUIO [12] to achieve a higher degree of interoperability between different platforms and devices, but this comes at the cost of additional abstraction layers and requires device-specific drivers that implement the protocols [6]; **3) Limited support for extensibility**: Existing frameworks are often designed for a single class of applications only. For example, most of the aforementioned frameworks are specifically designed for either mobile platforms or tabletop systems and are therefore not easily extended towards other settings. In addition, the implementations typically provide a fixed set of basic gestures and are generally difficult to extend with support for custom and application-specific multi-touch behaviours. Recent solutions such as Midas [20] or Proton [14] introduce domain-specific languages with the aim of supporting developers in the design and implementation of new gestures, but do not share our specific goal of supporting multi-touch interface development for many different devices.

We propose *jQMultiTouch*—a lightweight web toolkit for creating multi-touch interfaces that can run on multiple devices.

---

[1]http://www.surface.com

Our framework directly builds on top of modern browser engines, such as WebKit[2] or Mozilla's Gecko[3], and therefore carries the potential of providing a lightweight solution for multi-touch application development based on established and widespread web technologies. jQMultiTouch is similar in implementation to two recently developed web frameworks, jQTouch[4] and Sencha Touch[5], but more general in terms of the concepts and features it supports since both these frameworks are primarily designed for mobile application development. More importantly, they suffer from rather limited support for multi-touch in that interactions can involve only one screen object at a time. While this may be sufficient on small-screen devices usually operated by a single user, the potential benefits of larger interactive surfaces, where multi-finger, multi-hand or even multi-user input can play an important role [11, 24], are not leveraged. jQMultiTouch therefore aims to be a more general framework that addresses the core requirements of multi-touch and gesture-based interactions within interfaces, but at the same time, does not limit itself to a specific platform or type of device.

jQMultiTouch is inspired from jQuery[6], one of the most popular web toolkits that has arguably changed the way developers nowadays implement web interfaces. jQuery is designed to simplify web scripting tasks such as the selection and manipulation of DOM elements and handling of events through the help of callbacks, as well as creating advanced interfaces and interactions with animations and visual effects that typically involve sliding and fading of web page elements. jQuery provides powerful abstractions from low-level implementation details and resolves cross-browser compatibility issues, which contributes to the ease of use and design simplicity for developers. jQMultiTouch is not only similar to jQuery in terms of the idea of providing a lightweight and general framework, but also because of the fact that we have adopted ideas from jQuery and applied them to some of the core concepts. The main technical contributions of our work include (1) a device-independent method for the processing and handling of multi-touch events within web interfaces, (2) a novel concept of a touch history that functions as the central source for event handling which is particularly useful given the more complex event flows with multi-touch and gesture-based interactions, as well as (3) a toolkit and multi-touch framework based on only native web technologies that do not require external browser plug-ins.

Applications based on our framework have been successfully deployed on many new touch devices, including Apple's iPhone and iPad or other Android-based smartphones and tablets, the TouchSmart[7] all-in-one PC and tabletop systems such as Microsoft's Surface, without the need for switching between special software development kits. Our decision to build on web technologies also has other advantages. In particular, active support for touch input or gesture-based modality *within* web interfaces is still in its infancy in that multi-touch interaction in a web context is generally limited to gestures for scrolling and zooming of content as interpreted by web browsers. The fact that most modern browsers have recently started to integrate support for processing touch input is promising as it means that multi-touch support will no longer be limited to specific browsers or require additional plug-ins such as Flash or Silverlight. However, the problem remains that native browser support still varies considerably in terms of touch event models and default browser behaviour due to the lack of standards. For example, Firefox 4 introduced custom `MozTouchDown`, `MozTouchMove` and `MozTouchUp` events[8] with minimal information in terms of touch coordinates relative to the viewport of the browser and a unique identifier to track continuous touches of the same input source. On the other hand, WebKit-based browsers, such as Apple's Safari which is used on the iPhone and iPad, only trigger handlers associated with `touchstart`, `touchmove` and `touchend` which provide additional information that is absent in Firefox, such as scale factors and degree of rotation if the commonly associated gestures are currently being performed on the target element. Moreover, the event callback mechanism differs considerably and touch event data is separated into all active touches on the screen, touches only related to the current target element and changed touches since the last time an event was handled. Again, in Firefox this important information is missing. For developers, this means that applications are presented with different input data depending on the browser and therefore considerable effort is required to eliminate cross-browser compatibility issues. We argue that solving these problems can enable a new generation of web interfaces that will start to include carefully designed multi-touch features and therefore bring real benefits to users when working with applications on a touch device.

We begin by presenting the concepts of jQMultiTouch and its main features as well as the implementation. This is followed by an evaluation of the framework in two parts. First, we present two applications that we developed based on jQMultiTouch and discuss them in more detail. We then sketch the range of possible applications and the framework support for rapid prototyping by showing more examples created by students as part of an assignment. We close with a discussion of the performance and extensibility of our framework.

JQMULTITOUCH

In the spirit of jQuery, jQMultiTouch provides abstractions from low-level multi-touch event handling details as well as cross-browser support for custom and default gesture-based interactions with interface elements. Figure 1 shows the four-layered architecture for applications based on our framework as well as the main components responsible for multi-touch support. The framework builds on basic browser support for multi-touch events available in modern browsers and extends it with customisable event handlers and attachable behaviours.

---

[2]http://www.webkit.org

[3]http://developer.mozilla.org/en/Gecko

[4]http://www.jqtouch.com

[5]http://www.sencha.com/touch

[6]http://jquery.com

[7]http://www.hp.com/touchsmart

[8]Note that, since Firefox 6, the touch event API has aligned with the W3C proposal. However, W3C's Touch Events specification is under active development and browser support not always consistent.

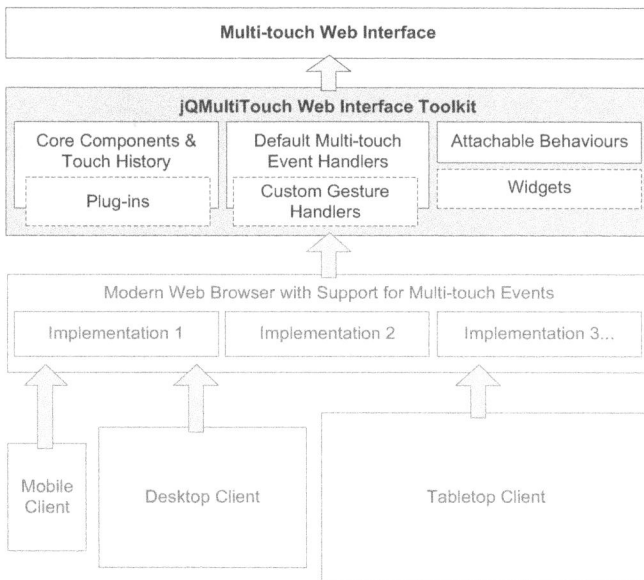

Figure 1: Four-layered architecture for multi-touch web applications based on our framework with support for different mobile, desktop and tabletop platforms as well as customisable multi-touch event handlers and attachable behaviours.

Applications developed with our framework can run on a number of different mobile, desktop and tabletop platforms. jQMultiTouch therefore functions as both a run-time environment and an extensible platform for developers to meet application-specific requirements.

To illustrate how jQMultiTouch can be used for multi-touch interface development, we refer to the simple picture viewing application shown in Figure 2. The code uses a simple jQuery statement `$('img')` to select all images loaded into the web interface and attaches the `touchable` behaviour provided by jQMultiTouch (Figure 3). Doing this first of all transforms all images into touch areas and then associates corresponding handlers by setting options for the default behaviour. In the example, we allow users to tap and hold images in order to perform unconstrained drag-n-drop operations by setting `draggable` to `true`. This means that pictures can be moved around by translating their x and y coordinates relative to the viewport. We further enable scaling using pinch/spread gestures so that users can enlarge or shrink the pictures within a certain range for the scale factor. This is achieved by setting the `scalable` option accordingly. Finally, we set the `rotatable` option to allow rotation of images by steps of 15 degrees. All features are enabled based on the attachable `touchable` behaviour provided by jQMultiTouch.

Core Features

Our framework consists of four components for touch event handling, touch event tracking and coordination, touch event capture and delegation and touch device detection (Figure 3). The core features of jQMultiTouch are built around a unified method for touch event handling independent of the specific platform and browser used to execute the interface. For this, we introduce browser-neutral `touchDown`, `touchMove` and

```
$('img').touchable({
    draggable: true, scalable: { min: 0.4,
    max: 2.0 }, rotatable: { step: '15deg' } });
```

Figure 2: Simple picture viewing web application supporting multi-touch based on our framework, enabling controlled drag-n-drop, scale and rotate actions for images by assigning the new `touchable` behaviour.

`touchUp` events that are then mapped to the specific events used in browsers. Moreover, the touch data associated with touch events is normalised so that rotation and scale properties are provided independent of native browser support. This is achieved with the help of additional methods for measuring the angle and distance between touch points in order to determine the scale factor and degree of rotation. The event callback handlers provided by jQMultiTouch will be fed with separate information about all active touches and only target-related ones. This data can then be used to determine whether users interact with other components and to define interactions between them. In addition to the standard callback mechanism that may require to create and pass on custom data between touch events, e.g. for data initialisation at `touchDown`, manipulation during `touchMove` and clean-up after `touchUp` events, our framework also provides a separate gesture callback handler. This handler can then be used to manage custom data in a central place. Also, methods are provided to control default browser behaviours and prevent conflicting actions, e.g. for scaling only specific content, such as images in the previous example, rather than the entire page. Finally, the framework defines a method for detecting if the particular device in use supports touch input. If it does, this will then trigger attached behaviours for touch elements. Also included is a method for determining the orientation of the device and a callback mechanism for handling changes.

Touch History Concept

One of the core concepts of the framework addresses the need for touch event tracking and coordination which is required in the case of multiple consecutive or simultaneous touches on one or more interface elements, e.g. for dragging several images at the same time similar to the previous example. To track the position of active touches and the order in which these have appeared and changed over time, jQMultiTouch introduces the concept of a central touch event history (Figure 5). While most existing frameworks internally also work

Component	Features
Touch event handling	Unified touch event listeners that work across different browser implementations
	Common touch event properties and multi-leveled information about active touches
	Configurable default handlers for common dragging, scaling and rotation operations
Touch event tracking and coordination	Touch history for keeping track of touch events and changes in touch data
	Separate gesture callback handler
	Mechanisms to control default browser behaviour and prevent conflicting actions
Touch event capture and delegation	Event capture for simultaneous touches on one or more target elements
	Event delegation to transfer capture to other elements
	Automatic capture release after timeout if no new touch data available for an active touch
Touch device detection	Method to detect whether device is touch-enabled
	Method to determine orientation of device as well as callback handler for changes

(a) Feature Overview

Feature	Examples	Description
$.fn.touchable	$(element).touchable({ draggable: true, scalable: true, rotatable: true });	Marks the element as touchable and registers default dragging, scaling and rotation behaviours
$.fn.touches	if ($(element).touches().length > 1) { … }	Returns true if more than one touch was registered on the DOM element
$.touchHistory	$.touchHistory.each(function() { … })	Keeps a record of the entire touch history and can be used for global analysis
$.touchPrevent Default	$.touchPreventDefault = false;	Enables default browser behaviour (default is to prevent default behaviour)
$.touchEnabled	if ($.touchEnabled()) { … }	Checks whether touch input is available on the device
$.touchReady	$.touchReady = function() { … }	Registers a callback to be executed on startup if device supports touch
$.orientation Changed	$.orientationChanged = function(orientation) { … }	Registers a callback to handle changes of the device's orientation

(b) Features

Figure 3: jQMultiTouch consists of four different components for touch input processing on touch devices. These components are implemented as a set of jQuery extensions specifically for multi-touch interface development.

Predicate	Examples	Description
type	history.filter({ type: 'touchMove' })	Constrains history to a single type or set of down/move/up events
	history. filter({ type: ['touchDown', 'touchUp'] })	
target	history.filter({ target: element })	Constrains history to one or several DOM elements
	history.filter({ target: [element1, element2] })	
touch	history.filter({ touch: $.touches[0] })	Filters history by the first touch only
finger	history.filter({ finger: '0..2' })	Filters history by the first three fingers
time	history.filter({ time: '1..100' })	Constrains history to a 100ms time window
	history.filter({ time: '<100' })	

(a) Filter predicates

Predicate	Examples	Description
clientX/ clientY	history.match({ clientX: '>550' })	Returns true if every touch in the history is within the position constraints
	history.match({ clientX: '500..550' })	
deltaX/ deltaY	history.match({ deltaX: '>100' })	Returns true if the difference between the positions of the first and last touch event in the history is within constraints
	history.match({ deltaX: '>100', deltaY: '+-10' })	
netX/ netY	history.match({ netX: '>100' })	Returns true if the finger has moved at least 100 pixels to the right over the series of touch events in the history
All filter predicates	history.filter({ finger: 0, time: '1..100' }).match({ deltaX: '<-100' })	Supports also filter predicates as a shorthand to first constrain and then match the history
	history.match({ finger: 0, deltaX: '<-100', time: '1..100' })	

(b) Match predicates

Figure 4: One of the core components is jQMultiTouch's touch history. The touch query language provides an extensible set of filter and match predicates as well as aggregate functions for online gesture recognition based on the history of touch events.

with some kind of touch event buffer, we formalise the concept and provide several new ways of making use of it for uniform touch event handling across different devices.

History Keeping

Figure 5a shows an example of a touch history for the start of a simple swipe-left gesture. For every new source indicated by a different touch id, a separate stream will be created in the history and updated with consecutive touchDown, touchMove and touchUp events. Each of the entries in the history stores touch data such as the position together with the target touch area and the time when the touch occurred. The target is by default locked in consecutive events which enables a simple form of multi-capture for all active touches.

History Evaluation

To make working with the touch history easier for developers, jQMultiTouch provides methods for querying and filtering the entries according to a combination of criteria. Figure 4 shows several example queries. In particular, the framework

provides an extensible set of *match predicates* (e.g. type, target, touch, finger, time, clientX/Y) and *aggregate functions* (e.g. deltaX/Y, netX/Y, angle, area) for evaluating the current touch history. With the help of these, the history can be filtered by touch id, input source and target elements as well as limited to only return touch data of previous events within a certain window of time. For example, it is possible to compute the delta for a series of touch points and from that to see how each touch has changed within a given time frame. Figure 5b shows how the touch query mechanisms can be used to detect simple swipe left/ right gestures. The code implements an example gesture callback handler that is provided with the current touch event e that triggered the handler and a touch history related to the target element that binds it. The basic mechanism, in the example used to process the history and look for swipe left/right gestures, is inspired by the way jQuery allows developers to

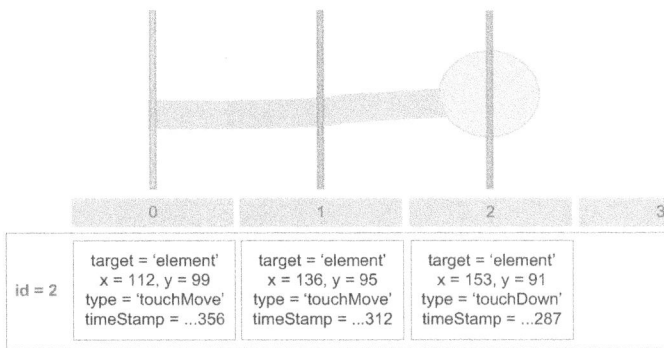

(a) Excerpt of touch history

```
function gestureHandler(e, history) {
  if (history.match({ finger: 0, deltaX: '<
    -100', time: '1..100' })) {
    // TODO swipe left handler
  } else if (history.match({ finger: 0,
    deltaX: '> 100', time: '1..100' })) {
    // TODO swipe right handler
  }
}
```

(b) Simple gesture handler

Figure 5: Illustration of touch history for a swipe left gesture on element and a possible gesture handler.

script animations.[9] In jQMultiTouch, we apply this concept to define simple gesture templates programmatically using relative values for variables to be tracked and compared. The match method of the touch history therefore takes a gesture template as an argument and returns true if it matches against the touch history. In the example, we define two simple templates that look for touch changes of the horizontal position. The evaluation then first computes the delta between the first and the last touchMove events within the last 100 milliseconds (indicated by the 1..100 range expression). This delta is then compared to the provided value, i.e. swipe left is then recognised if the x position in the touch data has decreased by at least 100 pixels, and swipe right if the delta for x is greater than 100.

Note that the gesture callback handler can be used for registering additional gestures, potentially giving priorities to certain gestures as well as resolving conflicts between them, and to execute corresponding actions. For more complex gestures, the match method of the touch history can also take an array of gesture templates and will then return true only if they all match the given criteria. Distinct or partly overlapping periods defined for the time variable in templates can then be used to define composed or sequential gestures and to increase sensitivity of gesture recognition. In addition, the templates used for gestures can also be shared between different callback handlers by using global variables instead. Rather than relying on comprehensive gesture recognition frameworks, such as iGesture [22] or the 1$ gesture recogniser [23] for more complex stroke-based gestures, this provides a simple way of detecting basic online gestures as they are executed on one or multiple touch elements, such as pinch-to-zoom, panning and tilting which are typical for multi-touch interaction [11, 24].

History Manipulation
Finally, the touch history provides several methods for manipulating the touch history. For example, overriding the target of a touch event provides a basic mechanism for delegating touch events so that the capture can be transferred to elements other than the original target. This can, for instance,

be useful to support dragging of a dynamically created intermediate representation of the dragged element rather than the original target on which the touchDown event occurred. The same mechanism can also be used for controlling multi-capture and automatically releasing event capture after a certain timeout, i.e. if no further updates on touch data have been received. This is necessary for cases where an active touch leaves the browser window and hence does not fire the expected touchUp event.

Attachable Behaviours
As mentioned earlier, our framework provides default implementations for basic interactions with touch-enabled web interface elements, such as drag-n-drop, zoom and rotate actions. The underlying gestures, i.e. moving two fingers apart/ toward each other for enlarging/shrinking elements, and using one finger to pivot around another or moving two fingers in opposing directions for rotation, are thereby detected and interpreted either based on native support, as in the case of Safari, or using features of the touch history component to compare the distance and angle between consecutive touch events, e.g. in Firefox. The default handlers provided by jQMultiTouch therefore enable the basic set of interactions supported in many multi-touch applications [14, 20]. However, to provide developers with a richer set of features, their behaviour is also customisable through a number of parameters as illustrated in Figure 2. For example, it is possible to limit the scope for drag-n-drop operations to only certain areas or special components of the web interface, as well as the scale factors for zoomable elements and the degrees and steps by which elements can be rotated. Finally, jQMultiTouch also allows for intercepting the chain of events through various before/during/after callback handlers, or even completely replacing the default behaviour with custom implementations.

One of the advantages of having attachable behaviours similar to jQuery is that they can be associated with any interface component. This allows developers to reuse custom behaviours, bundle them with new, maybe application-specific components and share them between different applications.

Legacy Support and Extension Mechanisms
Touch input shares some commonalities with mouse input since both trigger a series of down/move/up events with point

---
[9]http://api.jquery.com/animate

coordinates of where the input occurred. In all modern web browsers, single touch input is per default mapped to mouse events with the benefit that traditional implementations remain operational also on touch devices. On the other hand, simultaneous touches are usually not translated to mouse events and can therefore not be processed by traditional event handlers. This raises two major problems for application developers. First, the fact that single touches also fire mouse events is not always convenient, especially when mouse input should be treated differently from touch. Second, even the most advanced implementations for interacting with web interface elements offered by the jQuery UI framework[10] will not work properly with multiple objects at the same time even if the respective event handling methods are linked to touch events. The reason for this is that current implementations typically rely on the fact that there is normally only one variable to track for the mouse, i.e. the position of the mouse cursor. Hence, often a single global variable is used to store the current position, which would then be overridden with every other touch event being processed. To prevent such conflicts, it is important that touch-related data is cleanly associated with the target it concerns, but this requires fundamental changes in the code of most existing solutions.

jQMultiTouch essentially provides two solutions to this problem. First, the attachable behaviour mechanism can be used to override existing implementations. For example, jQMultiTouch's `draggable` and `scalable` behaviours could be used to override similar `draggable` and `resizable` behaviours of the standard jQuery UI framework. This provides a simple way of automatically extending existing applications with support for multi-touch and could also provide the basis for turning single-user web interfaces into multi-user applications. Second, building on jQMultiTouch's `touchDown`, `touchMove` and `touchUp` events in addition to traditional mouse handlers provides a way of supporting advanced multi-touch features as well as maintaining legacy support. jQMultiTouch's ability to control default browser behaviour can then be used to disable default browser behaviour so that touch events will not automatically fire mouse events.

Finally, the basic support for gesture recognition based on the touch history could be easily extended by registering new match predicates and aggregate functions. It is also possible to combine jQMultiTouch with existing gesture recognition libraries. To this end, jQMultiTouch provides a method for converting the data stored in the touch history to a format supported by the recogniser and vice-versa. We have used this technique to integrate jQMultiTouch with the lightweight JavaScript implementation of the popular 1\$ unistroke recogniser [23][11].

IMPLEMENTATION

jQMultiTouch is implemented as an extension of jQuery. The implementation consists of three main components: a class `touchHistory` for history keeping, evaluation and manipulation, the `touchable` behaviour for elements to be associated with basic multi-touch interactions, as well as a default

---

[10]http://www.jqueryui.com
[11]http://dev.globis.ethz.ch/jqmultitouch/dollar.html

gesture callback handler. jQMultiTouch has been tested and is compatible with WebKit-based browsers such as Safari on iPhone/iPad, the Android browser and Firefox on Windows 7 touch PCs.

The touch history relies on basic JavaScript array operations for maintaining a history of events. The touch history prototype class provides two methods, `start` and `stop`, for segmenting the touch history using match predicates. Each segment can then be further constrained and evaluated using the `filter` and `match` methods shown in Figure 4. Because each of these functions returns a new touch history object similar to the way it is done in jQuery, it is possible to specify multiple different processing steps in sequence.

As already mentioned, elements marked as `touchable` can be configured with a number of options for touch event handling, such as custom callback handlers as well as default dragging, scaling and rotation behaviours. Each element will be associated with a CSS marker class `ui-state-touchable`, which can also be used for formatting and styling, and bind to the default gesture event handler with cross-browser compatible implementations of the standard behaviours.

The default gesture handler processes a browser-specific touch event e and tries to map the type of the event to the uniform touch events `touchDown`, `touchMove` and `touchUp`, or exits if the event cannot be matched by our implementation. For every changed touch, it updates the data or creates a new touch object in the case of a `touchDown` event. In the next step, the touch event will be cached and associated with a `timeStamp`. The uniform `touchEvent` object created in this way will then be passed on to associated touch event handlers of the target elements together with a history of the active touch. The handler also triggers an event for custom gestures, which is instead given a touch history related to the current target rather than only the touch that triggered the event. This excerpt of the history can therefore be used to recognise gesture-based interactions that involved multiple active touches. Each new touch event is appended to the touch history, the size of which is constrained by a configurable maximum size. The touch will remain active until a `touchUp` event is received.

APPLICATIONS

We have used jQMultiTouch for the development of a number of applications as part of our research as well as in teaching and student projects. In this section, we present selected applications based on our framework. The first is FBTouch, an extension of the Facebook picture tagging interface with adaptations for touch and multi-touch. The second is TFlickr, an adaptation of Flickr's picture editing application with more advanced multi-touch handlers compared to FBTouch. The first application was created by the first author and lead developer of the framework to evaluate the feature support, while the second was created in a two-months internship project of a Bachelor student to test the ease-of-use for new developers. Our preliminary evaluation therefore aims to demonstrate the flexibility and potential of the framework as well as providing first insights concerning usability.

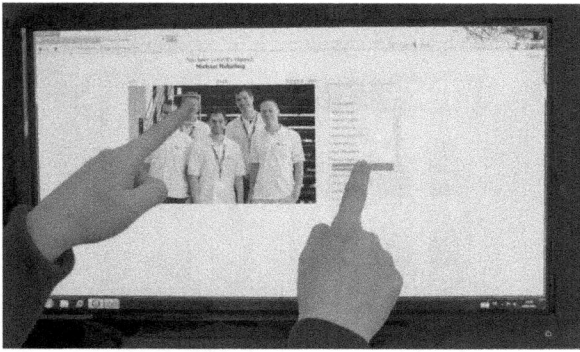

Figure 6: One of the multi-touch versions we have designed and evaluated for a simple picture tagging application similar to Facebook, here using a two-point tagging interaction.

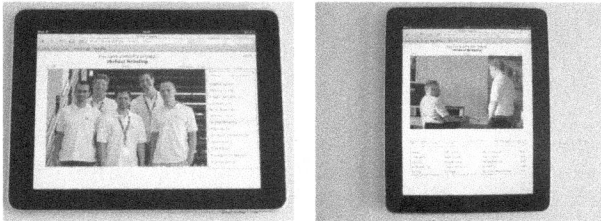

(a) Landscape mode using the two-point tagging interaction

(b) Portrait mode using drag-n-drop interactions instead

Figure 7: Another FBTouch prototype for the iPad using different multi-touch interfaces according to device orientation.

FBTouch

As shown in Figure 6, FBTouch provides a multi-touch web interface for tagging people in pictures. The two main components of the FBTouch application are the picture viewing control and the list of selectable tags. The design is based on the picture tagging application known from Facebook, but has been extended to experiment with two new multi-touch interfaces. Both interfaces enable multi-touch gestures not available in the original Facebook interface, i.e. swipe right or left to navigate to the previous or next picture, spread to overlay a larger version of the picture and pinch to hide the overlay again. The first interface shown in Figure 6 uses a two-point tagging interaction that requires two hands with one finger touching the picture and the other a name in the list. The second version of the interface uses a drag-n-drop interaction that requires dragging a name from the list and dropping it on a person shown in the picture.

Interestingly, Windows 7 on the TouchSmart with which the interfaces were developed and tested, did not allow for simultaneously touching the picture and interacting with Windows standard controls such as the list control used for the name tags. We therefore enhanced the scrolling mechanism in the list of names to support scrolling when users touch the picture at the same time and to prevent accidental tagging/untagging when scrolling occurred prior to the interaction. Not to remove names from the list via drag-n-drop in the second interface, we built on the touch delegation features of jQMulti-Touch to drag a thumbnail of the person's photo as an inter-

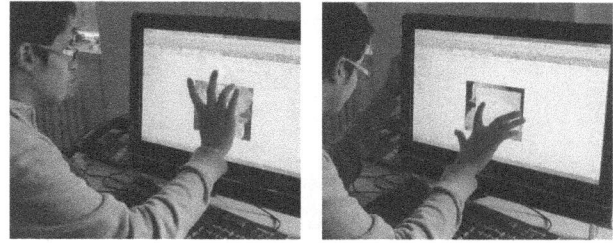

(a) Rotate interaction

(b) Crop interaction

Figure 8: The Flickr interface recreated using features of jQ-MultiTouch for common picture editing tasks such as rotate and crop using multi-touch interactions.

mediate representation of the original touch target. We also exploited multiple touch event captures so that simultaneous dragging of two or more photo tags is generally possible using multi-finger/multi-hand interaction. To support this, we switched to a horizontal layout to instead place the list below the picture. Also here the default scrolling mechanism was adapted for horizontal scrolling not to interfere with active dragging operations. In another version we developed for the iPad, we make use of both layouts as we switch between the interfaces when the device is rotated (Figure 7).

TFlickr

Like FBTouch for Facebook, TFlickr is a multi-touch version of Flickr's interface for common picture editing tasks. As mentioned before, the project was carried out in an internship which consisted of three parts. First, the student was asked to explore various adaptations and new multi-touch interactions as possible extensions of the original application. Second, since this project built on an earlier version of jQ-MultiTouch, the task was to overcome current limitations by making small adjustments to the implementation in order to meet the requirements of the new application. Third, the implementation of several of the new prototype interfaces was simplified by building on the advanced framework support. The final TFlickr application was then composed of the most promising prototypes.

In the first phase, the student created multiple versions of the interface, e.g. for rotate and crop picture editing tasks as shown in Figure 8. The framework support was already considered fairly comprehensive at this stage. However, the project still identified the need for more callbacks, e.g. to provide entry and exit points for extending the rotate function with step-wise behaviour and allowing for more precise selection of the crop area. In addition, a mechanism for temporarily overriding default behaviours and to disable/enable them as required was considered necessary as well as additional parameters for configuring the new features and required thresholds. These requirements led to the latest version of jQMultiTouch reported in this paper with the support for customisable default behaviours mentioned earlier.

RAPID PROTOTYPING WITH JQMULTITOUCH

To further evaluate the framework and its support for multiple different devices, we created an assignment as part of an HCI class designed for Bachelor computer science students.

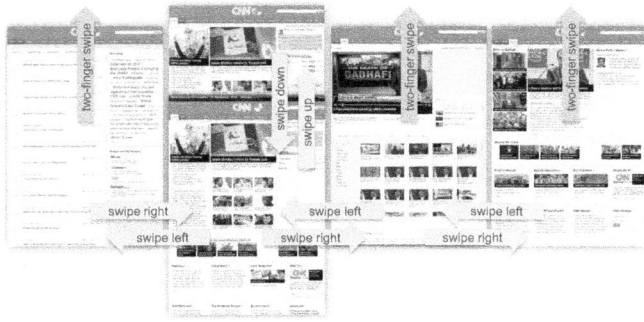

Figure 9: CNN example application implementing several gestures for navigating between screens.

The assignment was divided into two parts and ran over three weeks. First, students were asked to think of an application that could potentially benefit from multi-touch interaction and to first create story boards and paper prototypes before starting with the implementation. In the second part, students were given an introduction to jQMultiTouch and its main features using code examples and were shown how they could use their own devices for development. Since we wanted to minimise the coding effort and given that not all students had a lot of experience with jQuery, they were encouraged to build on the following simple example application as a starting point for their own solutions.

The CNN application shown in Figure 9 consists of a set of five screens with simple gesture-based interactions for navigating between screens (using swipe left/right), setting the news site edition (swipe down on the homescreen) and going to the front page from all other screens (via two-finger swipe). To demonstrate some of the other features of jQMultiTouch, the application automatically adapts to landscape mode when the device is rotated and adjusts the content to fit different screen dimensions and resolutions. Most importantly, the implementation is based on a very lightweight skeleton that makes heavy use of images rather than complex HTML and CSS. We found that this would require less programming skill and, while still using many features of jQMultiTouch, would focus the students' attention on the rapid prototyping of interactions and multi-touch behaviours rather than other implementation details.

Finally, to further guide the design process, we encourage students to use the following method which we found useful for creating the FBTouch and TFlickr prototypes.

1. Basic touch enhancements

2. Extension of interaction model towards multi-touch

3. Alternative designs to meet user preferences and skills

4. Optional adaptations to meet special device characteristics

While the assignment was not mandatory and required to complete the course, it still attracted the interest of 8 groups with a total of 24 of around 50 students registered in the course. The most popular devices included the iPhone and Android-based phones HTC Desire, Sony XPERIA and Samsung Galaxy SII.

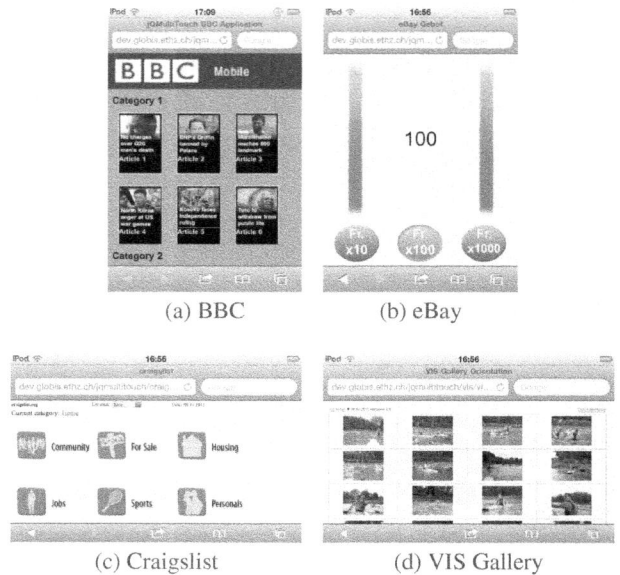

(a) BBC

(b) eBay

(c) Craigslist

(d) VIS Gallery

Figure 10: Student solutions based on the CNN application that range from simple modifications for the BBC web site, over experimental interfaces for eBay to more complex adaptations of existing web sites for multi-touch.

Students reported no major issues and most were able to test and build their solutions using their own touch devices. We show a selection of the submitted assignments in Figure 10. The first shown in Figure 10a is a variant of the example application which was extended for the BBC web site using simple gestures for flipping through different articles and browsing categories within the same screen rather than navigating between different pages. The second application shown in Figure 10b was created from scratch and not based on the example code we provided. It is not a complete implementation of the anticipated interface, but the general idea was to provide a multi-touch interface for bidding on auction platforms such as eBay by using multiple fingers to select and sliders to adjust the price in steps of 10, 100 or 1000 Francs. The third application is a more complete adaptation of the Craigslist web site for mobile touch devices (Figure 10c). Users are provided with a number of gestures to ease navigation between different categories and narrowing down the search results. The last application is in implementation more similar to the example we provided, but creates a whole new experience when translating the concepts to a photo gallery with multi-touch support as an adaptation of an existing student union web site (Figure 10d). In addition to flick left/right gestures for browsing through the pictures, users can also swipe down on a picture to download it to their device. The application also makes use of the layout orientation features provided by jQMultiTouch as the photo gallery shows more or less pictures in horizontal direction according to device orientation.

In general, the assignment was well received by students and led to a number of simple, yet interesting, solutions. The informal feedback concerning jQMultiTouch was positive and gives reason to believe that the framework is both of practical and research value. One student explained: "I found the framework fairly easy to work with, but our group did not apply it in very much depth. Conceptually though, I found the framework easy to understand, and it seems capable of supporting projects of all different complexities."

DISCUSSION AND RELATED WORK

We have demonstrated that jQMultiTouch can cater for a wide range of applications and enable the rapid prototyping of multi-device/multi-touch interfaces. We have promoted a web-based approach to designing multi-touch applications that can run on different types of devices. Many of our examples, however, relate to mobile application development and therefore add to the ongoing debate on web *vs.* native implementations [3]. Proponents of the first argue for reduced implementation and maintenance cost, while advocates of the latter see benefits in terms of performance and interface design. One of the main benefits of jQMultiTouch is that developers can build on the web programming stack that they may already be familiar with and therefore only have to learn one method of specifying multi-touch and gesture-based interactions that is compatible with many different devices. While our specific focus with jQMultiTouch leaves out the widget support for emulating the look-and-feel of native mobile applications, it could still provide a complete development environment when integrated with other existing jQuery-based frameworks such as jQTouch. Moreover, while several works have contributed the design of a general multi-touch architecture, e.g. [6, 13], our solution seems more lightweight and direct since we leverage native browser support as much as possible. The current lack of support for tangible widgets in our framework could be mitigated by other techniques similar to CapWidgets [15].

From a more general perspective and given the examples in the paper, jQMultiTouch also provides new ways of adapting existing interfaces for touch and multi-touch. The adaptation of web sites to different devices is a popular topic in web engineering, but research has often aimed at fully automatic methods, e.g. for retargeting existing web interfaces to mobile phones [4, 10]. Other research has mainly looked at different models of user interface abstraction, e.g. CAMELEON [1], and model-driven approaches for generating interfaces adapted to different user, platform and environment contexts [2, 8, 18]. In particular, the authoring of adaptive and multi-modal user interfaces has been the subject of extensive research. However, the focus has tended to be on logical descriptions of user interfaces and the design of domain-specific languages rather than leveraging existing solutions [17]. Of the various existing approaches only MARIA [19] has included support for the new generation of touch devices, but this is limited to a mapping of concepts at the concrete user interface level. A critical goal of our work has therefore been to find more lightweight solutions that, in particular, build on only native web technologies, i.e. HTML, CSS and JavaScript, and integrate well with existing web scripting toolkits such as jQuery.

Our discussion addresses three remaining important topics with respect to the proposed framework: development effort, performance of applications and extension mechanisms.

Design Simplicity

It is difficult to carry out direct comparisons between implementations based on jQMultiTouch and other existing multi-touch frameworks due to fundamental differences. However, especially when compared to browser-specific code, the abstractions provided by jQMultiTouch lead to cleaner implementations and therefore add to the design simplicity for developers. In particular, the history concept with its query and evaluation mechanisms as well as the lookup table for active touches require less helper variables in event handlers because custom state can be attached to the touches or the history object and therefore be tracked more easily between callbacks. While this may not be so obvious from the simple code examples given in the paper, this has been recognised as a major issue [14] and can become particularly complex in larger applications.

Execution Performance

As already mentioned, jQMultiTouch has been used on many different mobile devices including iPhone 3G/4G, iPod 1G/2G, iPad 1G/2G, EeePad transformer tablet/notebook, as well as the TouchSmart all-in-one desktop computer. While it is difficult to cross-test all possible configurations and provide reliable data due to considerable differences between many of these devices and available browser implementations, we did not see major performance issues in terms of the multi-touch interaction on any of the devices. The simple picture viewing application from the first example executed on a modern smartphone performs almost as well as on the full-blown desktop PC showing very high refresh rates, but starts to drop in frequency the larger the images are scaled. However, this is a limitation of current browser support for CSS3 2D Transforms and not an issue related to our framework.

Scalability and Portability

While we can therefore argue that the current implementation of jQMultiTouch has the potential to scale across many different devices ranging from mobile phones to large interactive surfaces, we have to critically note that this may change if more browser vendors start to build on proprietary methods for touch event handling rather than aiming at standards. We therefore welcome recent efforts to create a W3C recommendation for common touch event models[12]. In the meantime, however, jQMultiTouch can provide a viable alternative and allow developers to build applications for a range of devices, as well as contributing an advanced framework for handling touch and other input data in a consistent way.

jQMultiTouch is available for download from the project web site[13]. We hope this encourages interested developers to experiment with existing framework support in their own applications and contribute refinements or new extensions building on the different mechanisms we have built into the framework for exactly this purpose.

CONCLUSION

In this paper, we presented jQMultiTouch, a lightweight framework for the rapid prototyping and development of multi-touch web interfaces that can run on many different devices.

---

[12] http://www.w3.org/TR/touch-events
[13] http://dev.globis.ethz.ch/jqmultitouch

We have shown how this framework was used to improve the interaction of existing applications on touch devices as well as for providing application-specific support for gesture-based modalities and multi-touch interaction techniques that go beyond basic zooming and panning actions.

In our ongoing research, we are building on the multi-touch framework in several projects to develop new methods for web interface adaptation as well as exploring novel touch and gesture-based interaction techniques especially useful in a web context. In addition, we believe that the extensible query-based input processing techniques presented in this paper can cater for other kinds of continuous input data, e.g. for handling 3D skeletal tracking data of Microsoft Kinect.

ACKNOWLEDGMENTS

We would like to thank Sai Swaminathan and Max Speicher for their help with the implementation of jQMultiTouch and some of the example applications. Special thanks go to the HCI class 2011 at ETH Zurich who also contributed several example applications. This work was supported by the SNF under research grant 200021_121847.

REFERENCES

1. Calvary, G., Coutaz, J., Thevenin, D., Limbourg, Q., Bouillon, L., and Vanderdonckt, J. A Unifying Reference Framework for Multi- Target User Interfaces. *IWC 15* (2003).

2. Ceri, S., Daniel, F., Matera, M., and Facca, F. M. Model-driven Development of Context-Aware Web Applications. *TOIT 7*, 1 (2007).

3. Charland, A., and LeRoux, B. Mobile Application Development: Web vs. Native. *CACM 54*, 5 (2011).

4. Chen, Y., Ma, W., and Zhang, H. Detecting Web Page Structure for Adaptive Viewing on Small Form Factor Devices. In *Proc. WWW* (2003).

5. Dietz, P. H., and Leigh, D. DiamondTouch: A Multi-User Touch Technology. In *Proc. UIST* (2001).

6. Echtler, F., and Klinker, G. A Multitouch Software Architecture. In *Proc. NordiCHI* (2008).

7. Esenther, A., and Wittenburg, K. Multi-User Multi-Touch Games on DiamondTouch with the DTFlash Toolkit. In *Proc. INTETAIN* (2005).

8. Frăsincar, F., Houben, G.-J., and Barna, P. Hypermedia presentation generation in Hera. *IS 35*, 1 (2010).

9. Hansen, T. E., Hourcade, J. P., Virbel, M., Patali, S., and Serra, T. PyMT: A Post-WIMP Multi-Touch User Interface Toolkit. In *Proc. ITS* (2009).

10. Hattori, G., Hoashi, K., Matsumoto, K., and Sugaya, F. Robust Web Page Segmentation for Mobile Terminal Using Content-Distances and Page Layout Information. In *Proc. WWW* (2007).

11. Hinrichs, U., and Carpendale, S. Gestures in the Wild: Studying Multi-Touch Gesture Sequences on Interactive Tabletop Exhibits. In *Proc. CHI* (2011).

12. Kaltenbrunner, M., Bovermann, T., Bencina, R., and Costanza, E. TUIO: A Protocol for Table-Top Tangible User Interfaces. In *Proc. GW* (2005).

13. Kammer, D., Keck, M., Freitag, G., and Wacker, M. Taxonomy and Overview of Multi-touch Frameworks: Architecture, Scope and Features. In *Proc. EICS, Workshop on Engineering Patterns for Multi-Touch Interfaces* (2010).

14. Kin, K., Hartmann, B., DeRose, T., and Agrawala, M. Proton: Multitouch Gestures as Regular Expressions. In *Proc. CHI* (to appear).

15. Kratz, S. G., Westermann, T., Rohs, M., and Essl, G. CapWidgets: Tangible Widgets versus Multi-Touch Controls on Mobile Devices. In *Proc. CHI Extended Abstracts* (2011).

16. Laufs, U., Ruff, C., and Zibuschka, J. MT4j - A Cross-platform Multi-touch Development Framework. In *Proc. EICS, Workshop on Engineering Patterns for Multi-Touch Interfaces* (2010).

17. Nebeling, M., Grossniklaus, M., Leone, S., and Norrie, M. C. XCML: Providing Context-Aware Language Extensions for the Specification of Multi-Channel Web Applications. *WWW 15*, 4 (2012).

18. Niederhausen, M., van der Sluijs, K., Hidders, J., Leonardi, E., Houben, G.-J., and Meißner, K. Harnessing the Power of Semantics-Based, Aspect-Oriented Adaptation for AMACONT. In *Proc. ICWE* (2009).

19. Paternò, F., Santoro, C., and Spano, L. MARIA: A Universal, Declarative, Multiple Abstraction-Level Language for Service-Oriented Applications in Ubiquitous Environments. *TOCHI 16*, 4 (2009).

20. Scholliers, C., Hoste, L., Signer, B., and Meuter, W. D. Midas: A Declarative Multi-Touch Interaction Framework. In *Proc. TEI* (2011).

21. Shen, C., Vernier, F., Forlines, C., and Ringel, M. DiamondSpin: an extensible toolkit for around-the-table interaction. In *Proc. CHI* (2004).

22. Signer, B., Kurmann, U., and Norrie, M. C. iGesture: A General Gesture Recognition Framework. In *Proc. ICDAR* (2007).

23. Wobbrock, J. O., Wilson, A. D., and Li, Y. Gestures without Libraries, Toolkits or Training: A $1 Recognizer for User Interface Prototypes. In *Proc. UIST* (2007).

24. Wu, M., and Balakrishnan, R. Multi-Finger and Whole Hand Gestural Interaction Techniques for Multi-User Tabletop Displays. In *Proc. UIST* (2003).

ToyVision: A Toolkit for Prototyping Tabletop Tangible Games

Javier Marco
Madeira-ITI
University of Madeira, Portugal
javier.marco@m-iti.org

Eva Cerezo, Sandra Baldassarri
Advanced Computer Graphics Group (GIGA)
Computer Science Department,
Engineering Research Institute of Aragon (I3A)
University of Zaragoza, Spain
{ecerezo, sandra}@unizar.es

ABSTRACT

This paper presents "ToyVision", a software toolkit aimed to make easy the prototyping of tangible games in visual based tabletop devices. Compared to other software toolkits which offer very limited and tag-centered tangible possibilities, ToyVision provides designers and developers with intuitive tools for modeling innovative tangible controls and with higher level user's manipulations data. ToyVision is based on Reactivision open-source toolkit, which has been extended with new functionalities in its Hardware layer. The main design decision taken has been to split the Widget Layer from the lower abstraction layers. This new abstraction layer (the Widget layer) is the distinguishing feature of ToyVision and provides the developer with access to a set of encapsulated classes that give the status of any playing piece handled in the tabletop while the game is running. The toolkit has been complemented with a Graphic Assistant that gathers from the designer all the information needed by the toolkit to model all the tangible playing pieces. As a practical example, the process of prototyping a tangible game is described.

Author Keywords

Tabletop; toolkit; tangible; games; playing pieces; widget; architecture

ACM Classification Keywords

H5.2. [Input devices and strategies]: User Interfaces

General Terms

Design.

INTRODUCTION

Horizontal computer-augmented surfaces (tabletops) enable simultaneous and co-located access to digital content to multiple users around the table. Until recently, the use of

these devices were restricted only to research environments [29] [31] [9], but now private companies are offering tabletop solutions [26], and also there is a growing community of hobbyist designers of tabletops [27] thanks to new affordable hardware techniques [34]. Games and entertainment emerge as very promising applications for these devices, since tables are popular spaces for social games due to their physical affordances that engage face to face interaction between players [32].

Recent expansion of tabletop devices gives rise to a new generation of physical and social videogames which mix traditional board games with the new possibilities of digitally augmenting the area of interaction with computer image and audio. Most of the tabletop games are based on multitouch interaction [6] [2] in which playing pieces are virtually projected on the surface and players manipulate them dragging their fingers on the table.

Several tabletop devices are not only capable of detecting user fingers and hands, but also of supporting the identification and tracking of conventional objects placed on the active surface. Thanks to this functionality, physical tabletop games based on tangible interaction are also feasible [11] [20]. By keeping playing pieces in the player's physical environment, emotional impact of videogame is reinforced [16] [14] and digital technology becomes accessible to other user profiles such as very young children [24], users with disabilities [21] and the seniors [1].

On the other side, the creation of a tabletop game usually implies to "hardcode" complex algorithms to process raw data from tabletop in order to detect and track each playing piece manipulated on the active surface. This situation brings a breach between tangible interaction design and the corresponding implementation tasks, i.e., between designers and developers. To tackle the problem, several software toolkits are emerging with the aim of isolating developers from tabletop hardware, so that they can implement their application in a higher abstraction level. These toolkits offer the developer processed data of users' interactions on the table, both tactile and through objects, but unfortunately, for the moment, in a very basic form: tangible interaction is described though simple events (object placed, moved or removed). This simplistic approach is constraining the designer to use playing pieces that can be just moved on the table, and therefore, this situation limits the exploration of more rich tangible interaction possibilities.

This paper proposes ToyVision, a toolkit for the rapid prototyping of tangible tabletop games. ToyVision can be seen as an expansion to already existing and in development "simplistic" toolkits based on TUIO [16] (such as reacTIVision [30] or CCV [5]), created to facilitate designers and developers the implementation tasks. This is done by supplying them with high processed data centered in the function that every playing piece plays in the game. ToyVision proposal is based on Reactivision open-source toolkit [18], which has been extended with new functionalities which are oriented to the rapid prototyping of tabletop games in Action Script 3 (AS3) development environments (Adobe Flash, Air and Flex). Nevertheless, the approach exposed in this paper can be easily translated to other tabletop toolkits and other development environments different from Reactivision and AS3.

The paper first goes through the current state of tabletop toolkits, and then proposes a classification of the different playing pieces to be used in board games. Next, ToyVision toolkit is presented, followed by a comparison of the design of a tangible game with and without the use of ToyVision. Finally, conclusions and future work are outlined.

RELATED WORK

Due to the recent success of multitouch devices, several toolkits have emerged aimed to implement applications in the most popular development environments with independence of the hardware. While earlier multitouch toolkits merely informed developers about raw-tactile events (finger added, moved, left from the table) [36] [3] [22] [35] [23], recent toolkits isolate finger gesture recognition from developers, by sending high abstraction events (zoom, rotation, delete…) [13] [12] [28].

The addition of tangible interaction functionalities to tabletop surfaces requires identifying and tracking conventional objects placed on the interactive surface area. In visual based multitouch surfaces [34] this can be achieved by attaching a printed visual tag (fiducial) [7]. Fiducial recognition is based on a simple principle: a fiducial is composed of infrared light (IR) reflective and non-reflective areas, and the visual software detects the reflective areas as white blobs. Each fiducial has a unique distribution of blobs, so it is possible to distinguish different fiducials, and also to track their position and orientation on the tabletop surface. Using this technique, several multitouch tabletop toolkits are also supporting interaction with tagged objects [4] [30] [5] [37].

Software architecture of tabletop toolkits has been described by Echtler and Klinker [10] using four layers, from lowest to highest abstraction:

- *Hardware*
- *Calibration*
- *Event Interpretation*
- *Widget*

A toolkit that follows a layered architecture (see fig. 1) offers, at least, the Hardware layer in order to hide the visual hardware and blob recognition algorithms. Optionally, the toolkit can add the Calibration layer to correct the position coordinates of each detected blob due to camera optics aberrations. With the Event Interpretation layer, the toolkit keeps track of blob events (added, moved or removed from the tabletop surface). Finally, by adding the Widget layer, the toolkit may associate sequences of events in tabletop regions with predefined actions in the tabletop application.

As toolkits include more abstraction layers, developers receive higher abstraction processed data from user interactions. By separating the toolkit from the developing environment, tabletop applications can be translated to other devices based on different hardware and even different toolkit. This is provided by the use of standard communication protocols between the toolkit and the development environment. In this context, the TUIO protocol [16] has become very popular and has been adopted by most tabletop toolkits [30] [5] [38] [36] [22]. However, TUIO protocol is designed to transmit processed data from the Event Interpretation Layer (EIL): the toolkit sends, embedded in TUIO packets, multitouch and tangible events to the tabletop application (see fig. 1). TUIO support of tagged objects are limited to three simple events (add, remove and move/rotate tagged objects) (see fig.1 left). Although the soon expected launch of the TUIO 2.0 specification is announcing a better support for tangible tabletop applications, this will actually consist in the support of untagged objects [18], keeping toolkits that will support TUIO 2.0 in the same EIL architecture.

There are also some toolkits specific for Tangible User Interfaces which isolate developers from the intrinsic complexity of managing several kinds of sensors hidden in objects. Most of these toolkits use an EIL approach [19], but also there are some interesting proposals of tangible toolkits with a Widget Layer architecture [8]. The work here presented contributes to the state of the art of tabletop toolkits with the addition of a Widget layer in a toolkit based on an EIL architecture in order to support advanced tangible interaction with playing pieces in tabletop games with a high abstraction development approach.

The challenge of designing a toolkit which includes a Widget abstraction layer relies in the huge collection of different existing objects that can be placed on a table. Nevertheless, this work focuses in board games and, therefore, the range of playing pieces should be approachable, as it will be detailed in next section.

CLASSIFYING PLAYING PIECES IN BOARD GAMES

Holmquist et al. [15], pioneers on modeling the relationship between physical objects and an ubiquitous computer system, proposed the term Tokens to describe any object used to represent some stored digital information. Later, Ullmer and Ishii [39] refined the Token definition for Tangible User Interfaces (TUI), and additionally proposed a new kind of object, a constraint; both were defined and related as following:

- Token: any piece that can be placed, moved and removed to interact with the application.

- Constraint: any physical area in which tokens are restricted in translation or rotation.

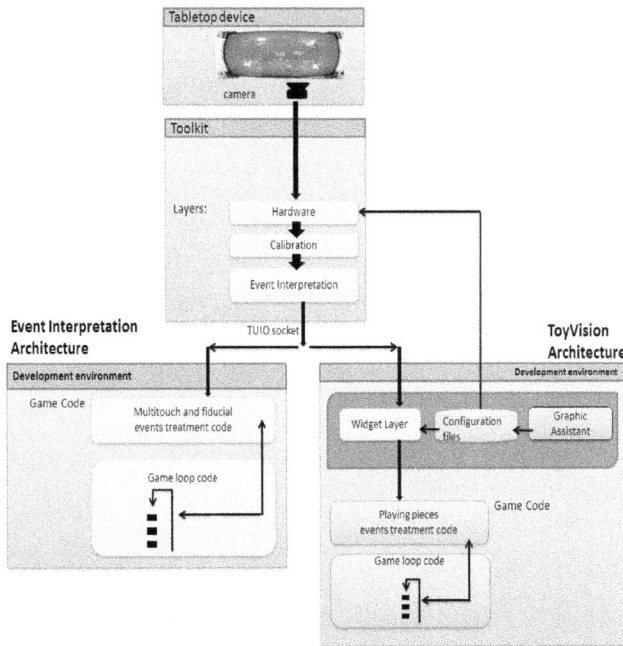

Figure 1. Tabletop toolkits architecture. Left: Current toolkits's architecture characterized by only three layers of abstraction. Right: ToyVision toolkit architecture.

Two kinds of relationships can emerge between Tokens and Constraints to define the kind of interaction that the user is able to carry out with the tokens in the limits of the constraint:

- Associative: The user is limited to place and remove the tokens inside the constraint area.

- Manipulative: the user is able to manipulate (move and rotate) the tokens inside a limited area of the constraint.

Later on, Shaer and Jacob [33] expanded this work, by proposing a Tangible User Interface Description Language (TUIDL) also based on tokens and constraints, so that any kind of object involved in a TUI could be modeled in UML, and translated into a XML specification. Our proposed Widget layer can be seen as a practical implementation of a TUIDL for tangible tabletops in which every playing piece

is automatically modeled in an XML specification, as it is explained in next section.

Starting from precedent classifications and trying to adapt them to the tabletop tangible context, we propose four categories of playing pieces: Simple Tokens, Named Tokens, Constraint Tokens and Deformable Tokens. These categories try to cover the wider spectrum of possible playing pieces that may be used in tangible board games (in a very broad sense, considering any ludic activity that could be played on a table such as painting or clay modeling), but should be seen as a starting point to future innovative game designs.

Simple Tokens

Simple Tokens are the most common playing pieces in board games: checkers, marbles, chips… Players arrange a limited amount of playing pieces on the board according to game rules (e.g. Checkers, Ludo, Stairs and Ladders, Roulette…) In general, Simple Tokens can be physically described as small flat cylindrical pieces, all identical with the exception of the colour used to distinguish the piece of each player, or to give different values (money, points…). Usually, most board games need a lot of Simple Tokens to be played, but grouped in few categories (Checkers only uses black and white pieces, Ludo uses four colors…).

Named Tokens

Other kind of playing pieces get from game rules a very specific role and unique name, which are perceived by the player through their physical appearance. A classic example is the Chess game: the Tower piece has a different appearance and rules than the Pawn. It is possible to have more than one instance of a kind of Named Token in a game (Chess has four Towers and sixteen Pawns), or to have unique instances of each playing piece (in card games, each card is unique in the game, and has a unique *name* such as Ace of Diamond, Three of Spade …). A Named Token physically identifies the player it belongs to (usually by colour) and the role it has in the game.

Constraint Tokens

A Constraint Token can be described as a playing piece that acts as a physical constraint of a set of smaller Simple Tokens. The bigger piece can be moved in the game board as any other playing piece, but with the manipulation of the Simple Tokens associated with it, the Constraint Token gets new meanings. For example, the playing piece of the Trivial Pursuit game is composed of six triangular small pieces (Simple Tokens) which can be placed inside a bigger circular piece (Constraint Token) (see fig. 4) which represents the progress of each player during the game. In this particular case, handling of the playing piece is based on *associating* (placing/removing) Simple Tokens inside a Constraint Token. Other playing pieces require more complex manipulations, for example, in the Roulette game, players spin a little marble (Simple Token) inside a circular plate (Constraint Token); in this case the playing piece is based on *manipulating* (moving/rotating) a Simple Token inside the Constraint Token.

Deformable Tokens
Finally, there are other playing pieces which do not have a constant shape, as they change with the manipulations of the player, as they are made of malleable materials, such us clay, cardboard, cloth… In a table, children use these materials in crafts.

Our proposal related to use Deformable Tokens in a game is that they cannot be identified, but characterized by their size, shape…

Next section details ToyVision's distinguishing features and how the four categories of tokens previously presented are related to the toolkit.

TOYVISION TOOLKIT
ToyVision is a toolkit aimed to prototype tangible games in vision based tabletop devices. The architecture proposed is shown in figure 1 right. The Hardware, Calibration and Event Interpretation layers are based on the open-source Reactivision toolkit. However, new functionalities have been added in the Hardware layer in order to support the identification of the four categories of playing objects presented in the previous section. Besides, a Graphic Assistant tool has been developed in order to allow the designer to easily model each tangible control involved in the tabletop game. This Graphic Assistant outputs the configuration files needed by toolkit to identify and model all the playing pieces. The other distinguishing feature of ToyVision toolkit is the Widget layer, created to support high abstraction coding of games in AS3 development environment.

Following, the new functionalities of the Hardware layer, the Graphic Assistant tool, and the new Widget layer are explained in detail.

Hardware Layer
Original Reactivision's Hardware layer identifies fingers and a collection of fiducials placed on the tabletop surface. These functionalities have been adapted and upgraded in order to accomplish some new requirements raised from the proposed classification of playing pieces (see previous section).

Simple Tokens
Simple Tokens can be visually tracked in the toolkit Hardware layer using the shape and size of the blob generated by its base when placed on the table surface. In order to identify each Simple Token with its player, a fiducial is needed to be attached to their base. Original Reactivision's collection of fiducials can support a large amount of different objects (up to 180), but fiducial designs are too complex to be reliably tracked when printed at sizes

smaller than 4 cm diameter when using a normal 640x480 px. resolution camera. For that reason, Reactivision's fiducial tracking algorithms have been expanded to track a new collection of Simple Token's fiducials, with a design adequate to be used in small playing pieces (see fig. 2).

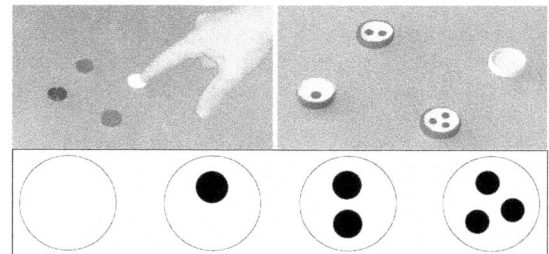

Figure 2. Different Simple Tokens (up-left); with Simple Token's fiducials attached (up-right); detail of the Simple Token's fiducial design (down).

In should be pointed that that fiducials shown in Fig. 2 could be recognized in Reactivision just by extending the mapping tree file but this would led to confusions between two and three topological levels fiducials. The implementation of specific tracking algorithms enables Reactivision to reliably recognize original fiducials together with the extended ones.

Named Tokens
In order to develop tabletop games that use Named Tokens, each playing piece needs a fiducial attached to the base of the object. That way, toolkit's Hardware layer can identify each fiducial by its unique arrange of blobs. ToyVision uses original Reactivision's fiducial collection to identify Named Tokens (see fig. 3).

Figure 3. Animal toys used as Named Tokens (left). Reactivision fiducials used to identify them (right).

Constraint Tokens
ToyVision Hardware layer can identify Constraint Tokens by combining the Simple Token and Named Token identification features previously described. In this case, the Constraint Token has a unique Reactivision fiducial attached to its base, and each Simple token is identified with a Simple Token's fiducial (see fig. 4).

Deformable Tokens
As these playing pieces do not have constant shape or size, it is not possible to attach a fiducial to their base. The original Reactivision's Hardware layer tracks these playing pieces as unidentified white blobs. New functionalities have

been implemented in the Hardware layer in order to extract their geometrical attributes: area, perimeter, inertial angles, and contour segmentation (see fig. 5).

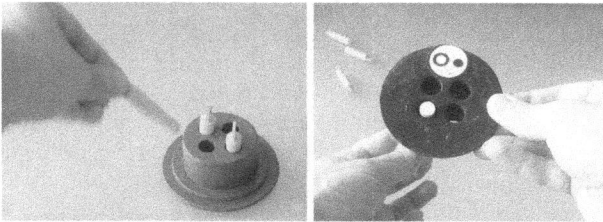

Figure 4. Example of Constraint Token: a "Trivial Pursuit" playing piece (left). Piece's base with the fiducial and a Simple Token placed inside the constraint (right).

Figure 5. Hardware layer identification of Deformable Tokens. Clay models placed on the tabletop surface (a). White blobs detected by the toolkit Hardware layer (b). Contour segmentation of each blob (c).

Graphic Assistant and XML specification

ToyVision's Graphic Assistant has been designed following a similar approach to that of existing graphic tools included in most popular development environments oriented to code WIMP based applications. These tools enable developers to graphically arrange controls on an application frame and to define attributes for each control. After that process, developers can access to the instantiated classes belonging to each control in the application code. Our Graphic Assistant allows the designer to model, in an easy way, all the data needed by the toolkit (in particular by the Hardware and Widget layers) to detect and track all the different playing pieces involved in the game. The procedure is as follows:

First, the new tangible control must be added to the game by choosing the category it belongs to: Simple Token, Named Token, Constraint Token or Deformable Token (see fig. 6).

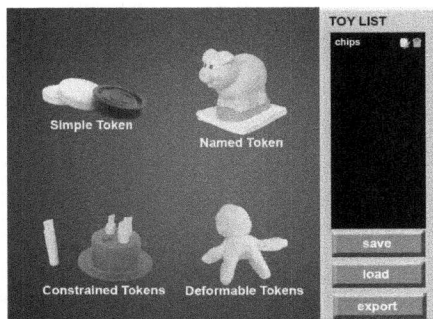

Figure 6. Graphic Assistant: Main menu.

Once the category is chosen, the assistant requires the name of the new tangible control, in order to be identified in the Widget layer.

Next, the assistant enables the designer to graphically model the tangible control. To do that, the designer places the playing piece on the tabletop surface, and an image of the base of the object is captured by the tabletop camera and displayed in the assistant. Then, the assistant asks the designer to graphically introduce all the data needed to model that playing piece. These data are automatically translated into an XML specification. This process varies depending on each token category:

- **Simple Tokens** (see fig. 7): From the image of the base of the pieces, the designer defines the size of the token and a tolerance. This way, any object with a size within the range of tolerance, will be identified as this particular tangible control. Also, the designer sets the number of different kinds of Simple Tokens that will be used in the game and the total number of pieces of each kind.

  These data are automatically translated into XML format to be kept in the configuration files using the following specification:

  ```
  < SimpleTokens name="text" size="number"
  tolerance="number" players="number"\>
  ```

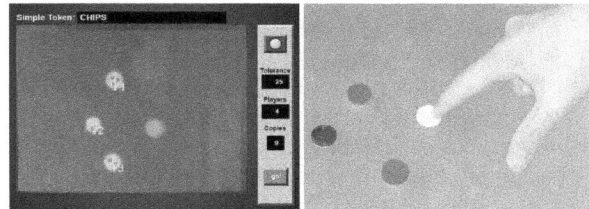

Figure 7. Graphic Assistant: Defining the size (left) of Simple Tokens (right).

- **Named Tokens** (see fig. 8): On the image of the object's base captured by the camera, the designer graphically draws the available area to place a fiducial. The designer also sets the number of copies of that object to be used in the game. These data are translated into XML in the following format:

  ```
  <NamedTokens name="text"
  fidID="number_of_fiducial_asigned"\>
  ```

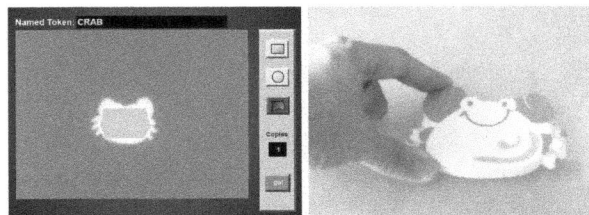

Figure 8. Graphic Assistant: Defining the fiducial area (left) of a Named Token (right).

- **Constraint Tokens**: In this case the first step is similar to the Named Token case; the designer draws the available area for placing a fiducial on the object's base. Then, the designer draws the constrained areas, choosing from two different options: associative or manipulative areas.

  o Associative areas (see fig. 9): The designer draws the areas in which one or more Simple Tokens can be placed or removed.

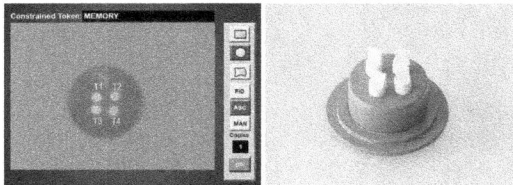

Figure 9. Graphic Assistant: Defining the Associative Constraint areas (left) of a Constraint Token composed of four Simple Tokens in four Associative areas (right).

  o Manipulative areas (see fig. 10): The designer draws the areas in which one or more Simple Tokens can be moved or rotated.

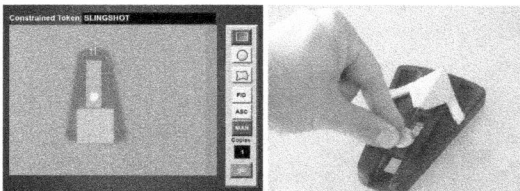

Figure 10. Graphic Assistant: Defining the fiducial area (red square) and the Manipulative Constraint area (yellow rectangle) (left) of a Constraint Token composed of a Simple Token that can be moved along an axis (right).

The position of the constrained areas are converted to polar coordinates relatives to the center and the orientation of the fiducial. Finally, all these data are translated into XML format using the following specification:

```
<ConstraintToken name="text" fidID="num">
    <AssociativeArea name="text" size="num"
    distance="num" angle="num"\>

    <ManipulativeArea name="text"
    areaType="rect" distance="num" angle="num"
    width="num" height="num"\>

    <ManipulativeArea name="text"
    areaType="circ" distance="num" angle="num"
    radio="num"\>
    ...
</ConstraintToken>
```

- **Deformable Tokens**: In this category, the assistant only asks for an interval of minimum and maximum size of blobs belonging to deformable objects to be tracked, and these data are translated into XML:

```
<DeformableToken minSize="number"
maxSize="number"\>
```

After the designer has created all tangible controls involved in the game, the Graphic Assistant exports the XML specification into configuration files. These files, needed by the Hardware and Widget layer, are loaded by the toolkit at launch. The assistant also creates an Adobe PDF document with all the fiducials required to be attached to each playing piece. This PDF is ready to be printed, and each fiducial can be cut and glued on the base of its respective playing piece (see fig. 11), so that it is ready to be used in the tabletop game.

Figure 11. Adapting a playing piece to be used in a tabletop game: Cutting the printed fiducial (a), gluing it (b), attaching the fiducial to the base of the toy (c).

Widget Layer

The new Widget abstraction layer offers all the programing tools needed by the developers to access the status of all the playing pieces placed on the tabletop surface at any moment of the game. ToyVision Widget layer has been integrated in the development environment, Action Script 3 (AS3) in our case. This decision allows the use of the Widget layer with other tabletop toolkits, as far as they use the same communication protocol, TUIO, as the Widget layer receives the raw-events from lower abstraction layers through a TUIO socket.

The developed Widget layer consists of a package of AS3 classes for the Adobe development environments (Flash, Air, Flex). The main class of this package is "ToyList". When this class is instantiated at the beginning of the game code it loads the XML configuration files exported by the graphic assistant (see figure 12). With the data recovered from the XML files, each AS3 class relative to each modeled tangible control is automatically instantiated. While the game is running, the "TabletopEvent" function is automatically triggered each time a tangible control changes its status (placed, moved or removed). In the particular case of Constraint Tokens, an event is also triggered each time any of its associated constraint areas changes. By using the name given in the graphic assistant tool, the developer identifies the tangible control which triggered the event, and writes the code necessary to take appropriated actions in the game.

```
public function Game() {
  //instantiate List of Toys
  gameToys= new ToyList('path to
                 configuration XML file');
  While (true) {//game loop}
}
public function TabletopEvent(toy, eventType)
{
  switch (toy.name) {
    case 'name1':
      if (eventType="add") {//toy placed}
```

```
        if (eventType="removed")
                          {//toy removed}
        if (eventType="updated")
                          {//toy moved/rotated}
        If (eventType="constraint")
           {//toy.updatedConstraint
           // is the area that triggered
           //the toy.constraintEvent
           Switch (toy.updatedConstraint) {
             Case 't1':
               if toy.constraintEvent="add"
                   {//a simple token has been
                    //added into this area
                   }
               if toy.constraintEvent="removed"
                   {//a simple token has been
                    //removed from this area
                   }
               if toy.constraintEvent="updated"
                   {//a simple token has been
                    //moved in this area
                   }
               Break;
               Case 't2';
               …
           break;
        case 'name2':...
        ...    } }}
```

Figure 12: Widget layer: Sketched AS3 code for a ToyVision tabletop game.

DEVELOPING A TANGIBLE TABLETOP GAME

In order to show ToyVision usefulness and its advantages in terms of simplicity and versatility, the process of prototyping a tangible tabletop game is outlined in this section. The AS3 code needed when using a conventional Event Interpretation Layer (EIL) toolkit, and when using ToyVision Widget Layer will also be compared.

The game chosen to show this process is a "Pirates" game which has been developed for the NIKVision tabletop [25]. "Pirates" is a cooperative game in which players have to work together to sail a pirate ship and to sink other enemy ships. These actions are carried out by manipulating a set of toys that take advantage of the tangible interaction possibilities of computer augmented tabletops:

- A fan toy is used to control the speed and direction of the ship by spinning the blades of a small fan toy (see fig. 13A), simulating that the toy is virtually blowing the ship's sails.

- A compass toy is used to point in what direction the player ship should sail to find a ship that can be attacked. The toy is a small cylindrical hash of optic fibers which transmits the image projected from the base of the toy to the top face of the cylinder. A projected needle points to the nearest enemy ship (see fig. 13B).

- A set of black and white chips are used to aim the cannons (see fig. 13C). When a chip is placed on the tabletop surface, ship's cannons fire a burst of cannonballs to the chip direction. Black chips fire

cannonball bursts that spread covering a wide area but travel short distances, and white chips fire precise long distance cannon balls.

These playing pieces belong to different token categories due to their different game functionalities. Next, the way these functionalities are implemented in the game is detailed.

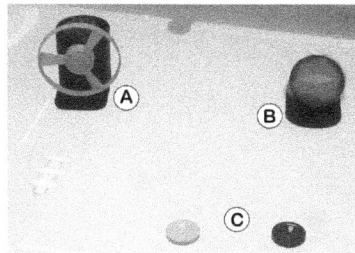

Figure 13. NIKVision Pirates game and playing pieces: A. fan toy, B. compass toy, C. chips

Chips and compass (Simple and Named Tokens)
The first thing to do with these tokens is to attach a printed fiducial on each toy's base, so that they can be tracked by the toolkit's Hardware layer.

In an EIL toolkit, the ID associated with the fiducial will be the only way for the developer to handle the corresponding object in the development environment. The TUIO protocol will send an event each time the Hardware layer detects that a fiducial has been placed, moved or removed from the table. The developer has to handle these three types of events and the fiducial IDs to implement the adequate game actions (see fig. 14).

```
Public function AddTuioObject(tuioObject) {
  //triggered when any fiducial is placed
  Switch (tuioObject.ID) {
    Case 0: //fiducial of white chip
      fireLong(tuioObject.x, tuioObject.y);
    case 1: //fiducial of black chip
      fireShort(tuioObject.x, tuioObject.y);
    case 2: //fiducial of compass toy
      drawNeedle(tuioObject.x, tuioObject.x,
        tuioObject.angle, calcNeedleAngle());
  }}
Public function UpdateTuioObject(tuioObject) {
    //Triggered when fiducial is moved/rotated
    If tuioObject.ID==2
      drawNeedle(tuioObject.x, tuioObject.x,
        tuioObject.angle, calcNeedleAngle());
}
Public function RemoveTuioObject(tuioObject){
    //Triggered when fiducial is removed
    If tuioObject.ID==2 eraseNeedle();}
```

Figure 14. Pirates game: schematic AS3 game code for compass toy and chips in EIL toolkits.

In ToyVision, the developer first uses the Graphic Assistant to give a name to each toy and to model it depending on its category. With these data, the Assistant automatically generates a PDF with the fiducials ready to print, cut and glued on the playing pieces' base. In the ToyVision Widget layer, a single tabletop event is sent with all the information needed by the developer (name of the toy involved and kind of event) to implement the adequate game actions (see fig. 15).

```
public function TabletopEvent(toy, event) {
   //toy has changed its status
   switch (toy.name) {
    case 'COMPASS':
      if (event=="add" or event=="update")
        drawNeedle(toy.x, toy.y, toy.angle,
          calcNeedleAngle());
    }
      if (event="remove") eraseNeedle();
    case 'CANNON':
      if (event=="add") {
        if (toy.fiducial==0) //white chip
       fireLong(toy.x, toy.y);
      if (toy.fiducial==1) //black chip
        fireShort(toy.x, toy.y);
    }}
```

Figure 15. Pirates game: schematic AS3 game code for compass toy and chips in ToyVision.

Fan toy (Constraint Token)

The action of spinning the blades is detected by the Hardware layer thanks to a half black-white dented wheel in the base of the toy that spins, which is tracked as a white blob appearing and disappearing at the speed the blades are spinning (see fig. 16). In consequence, toolkit's Hardware layer detects two different blobs related to the fan toy: one, the attached fiducial, and the other, the white blob that appears and disappears when the blades spin.

Figure 16. Pirates' Fan toy modeled as Constraint Token (left) with a fiducial and an associative area in its base (right).

In an EIL toolkit, the TUIO protocol sends toy's movement and blades' spin events independently: events related to fiducials are sent as tuioObject events while events related to white circular blobs (blades's spin) are sent as tuioCursor events (see fig. 17). In consequence, when coding the fan toy behavior using the data sent by the EIL, the developer has to implement robust code to find if a tuioCursor event is related to user's manipulations of the fan toy to handle it properly.

On the other hand, using ToyVision, the developer first models the fan toy in the Graphic Assistant as a Constraint Token tangible control. In the AS3 environment, a TabletopEvent is triggered each time the status of the toy changes, either because it has been placed, moved, or removed, or because its constraint areas have changed due to Simple Token manipulations. All the information about the event is available to the developer: name of the toy, type of event, ID of the constraint area that has changed, and the Simple Token status change that may have caused the modification of the constraint area (see fig. 18).

```
Public function AddTuioObject(tuioObject) {…}
Public function UpdateTuioObject(tuioObject) {
     //Triggered when fiducial move or rotate
     If tuioObject.ID==fan_fiducial {
       //update position of fan toy
       fan.x=tuiObject.x; fan.y=tuioObject.y;
       fan.angle=tuioObject.angle;
     }
}
Public function RemoveTuioObject(tuioObject){…}
public function addTuioCursor(tuioCursor) {
   //new circular white blob appeared
   //lots of trigonometric calculations to
   //determine if tuioCursor.y and tuioCursor.y
   //is in the right position and orientation
   //in relation with fan.x, fan.y, fan.angle
   //if true then impulse fan
}
public function UpdateTuioCursor(tuioCursor){}
public function removeTuioCursor(tuioCursor) {
   //circular white blob disappeared
   //lots of trigonometric calculations to
   //determine if tuioCursor.y and tuioCursor.y
   //is in the right position and orientation
   //in relation with fan.x, fan.y, fan.angle
   //if true then impulse fan
}
```

Figure 17. Pirates game: schematic AS3 game code for treating raw tangible TUIO events in an Event Interpretation based toolkit.

```
public function TabletopEvent(toy, event) {
   //toy has changed its status
   switch (toy.name) {
     case 'FAN':
      if (event=="constraint")
        and (toy.updatedConstraint=="t1")
          and (toy.constraintEvent=="add")
        {impulseShip(toy.x, toy.y, toy.angle);}
      If (event=="update")
        {fan.x=toy.x; fan.y=toy.y;
         fan.angle=toy.angle;
      break; }
}
```

Figure 18. Pirates game: schematic ToyVision AS3 game code for the fan toy.

In contrast to other toolkits, ToyVision is also capable of handle tabletop events from un-tagged and deformable objects. To develop a game that uses this kind of materials in ToyVision, developer first uses the Graphic Assistant to create a new playing piece of the Deformable Token kind, giving a name to it. In the AS3 environment, the developer can extract the geometrical data (e.g. a list of segments that compound the perimeter) of any untagged objects manipulated on the tabletop surface (see fig 19).

```
public function TabletopEvent(toy, event) {
  //toy has changed its status
  switch (toy.name) {
   case 'deformable':
    if event=="add" or event=="update" {
      for each (segment in toy.perimeter) {
      //create virtual representation of
      // the un-tagged object}
  }}
```

Figure 19. Schematic ToyVision AS3 game code to treat Deformable Tokens.

The consideration of this kind of playing pieces opens innovative opportunities for tabletop games for using materials and toys in which attaching a fiducial is not suitable. In particular, we have used this new kind of tokens in two simple games developed with ToyVision:

- The Paint game uses conventional brushes to paint on the table (see fig. 20 left). The brush is modeled as a Deformable Token: the width of the stroke will depend on the pressure applied with the brush.

- In the Bugaboo game the players use any kind of deformable material (clay, cardboard…) to build a path so that a virtual flea can jump and climb to reach the fruits (see fig. 20 right).

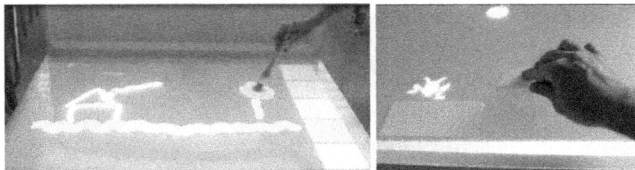

Figure 20. The Paint game (left) and the Bugaboo game (right).

CONCLUSIONS

ToyVision toolkit provides developers and designers of tabletop games with a tool that allows the easy prototyping of games using a great variety of playing pieces, opening new possibilities for tangible interaction in tabletop devices. This has been achieved by adding new functionalities to the Reactivision Toolkit (in the Hardware layer), developing a Graphic Assistant to model each playing piece that automatically generates its XML specification, and adding a new abstraction layer (the Widget layer) that enables designers to face in a high abstraction level the development of a new tangible tabletop game. ToyVision's Widget layer provides access to a set of AS3 classes that give the status of any playing piece handled in the tabletop while the game is running.

Compared to other software toolkits which offer very limited and tag-centered tangible possibilities, ToyVision offers developers with intuitive tools for modeling tangible controls with richer tangible interaction and user manipulations data of higher level.

A beta version of the ToyVision toolkit can be downloaded from http://webdiis.unizar.es/~jmarco/?page_id=297 and can be used and modified under open-source license. The

modifications added to the Hardware layer of Reactivision can be easily replicated in other tabletop toolkits based in the TUIO protocol. Likewise, the Widget layer implemented in AS3 may be implemented in other developing environments, and thus, may broaden the number of designers and developers that could take benefit of these new tools. In the near future, ToyVision will be expanded to other environments and to other kind of tangible tabletop games and applications.

ACKNOWLEDGMENTS

This work has been partly financed by the Spanish Government through the DGICYT contract TIN2011-24660.

REFERENCES

1. Al Mahmud, A., Mubin, O., Shahid, S. and Martens, J.B. 2008. Designing and evaluating the tabletop game experience for senior citizens. 5th Nordic conference on Human-computer interaction(NordiCHI '08) pp403-406.

2. Antle, A.N., Bevans, A., Tanenbaum, J., Seaborn, K., and Wang, S. 2010. Futura: design for collaborative learning and game play on a multi-touch digital tabletop. Fifth international conference on Tangible, embedded, and embodied interaction (TEI '11). Pp. 93-100.

3. Bespoke: http://www.bespokesoftware.org/multi-touch

4. Bollhoefer, K. W., Meyer, K., and Witzsche, R.. Microsoft surface und das Natural User Interface (NUI). Technical report, Pixelpark, Feb. 2009.

5. CCV: Community Core Vision Web: http://nuicode.com/

6. Cooper, N., Keatley, A., Dahlquist, M., Mann, S., Slay, H., Zucco, J., Smith, R., and Thomas, B. H. 2004. Augmented Reality Chinese Checkers. Proc. of the 2004 ACM SIGCHI international Conference on Advances in Computer Entertainment Technology (2005). ACE '04, vol. 74. 117-126.

7. Costanza, E., Shelley, S. B., Robinson, J. Introducing audio d-touch: A tangible User Interface for Music Composition and Performance. DAFx '03 Conference.

8. Dey, A.K., Abowd, G.D., Salber, D. 2001. A conceptual framework and a toolkit for supporting the rapid prototyping of context-aware applications, Human-Computer Interaction, v.16 n.2, p.97-166, December 2001

9. Dietz, P. and Leigh, D. DiamondTouch: a multi-user touch technology. In UIST '01: Proc. of the 14th annual ACM symposium on User interface software and technology, pages 219–226. ACM, 2001.

10. Echtler, F., Klinker G. A multitouch software architecture. In Proc of NordiCHI '08. 2008. pp. 463-466.

11. Heijboer M, and van den Hoven, E. 2008. Keeping up appearances: interpretation of tangible artifact design. Proc. of the 5th Nordic conference on Human-computer interaction: building bridges (NordiCHI '08) pp162-171.

12. Hansen, T.E., Hourcade, J.P., Virbel, M., Patali, S. and Serra, T. 2009. PyMT: a post-WIMP multi-touch user interface toolkit. Proc. of the ACM International Conference on Interactive Tabletops and Surfaces (ITS '09). Pp. 17-24.

13. Heng, X., Lao, S., Lee, H., and Smeaton, A. A touch interaction model for tabletops and PDAs. Proc. PPD '08, 2008.

14. Hinske, S. and Langheinrich, M. 2009. W41K: digitally augmenting traditional game environments. Proc. of the 3rd international Conference on Tangible and Embedded interaction (2009). TEI '09, 99- 106.

15. Holmquist L.E., Redström, J., Ljungstrand, P. 1999 Token-Based Access to Digital Information, Proc. of the 1st international symposium on Handheld and Ubiquitous Computing (1999), p.234-245

16. Iwata, T., Yamabe, T., Poloj, M., and Nakajima, T. 2010. Traditional games meet ICT: a case study on go game augmentation. Proc. of the fourth international conference on Tangible, embedded, and embodied interaction (TEI '10). Pp. 237-240.

17. Kaltenbrunner, M., Bovermann, T., Bencina, R., and Costanza, E. TUIO: A protocol for table-top tangible user interfaces. In 6th Int'l Gesture Workshop, 2005.

18. Kaltenbrunner, M. 2009. reacTIVision and TUIO: a tangible tabletop toolkit. Proc. of the ACM International Conference on Interactive Tabletops and Surfaces (ITS '09). Pp. 9-16.

19. Klemmer, S.R., Li, J., Lin, J., Landay, J.A. 2004. Papier-Mache: toolkit support for tangible input. Proc. of the SIGCHI conference on Human factors in computing systems (CHI '04). Pp. 399-406.

20. Leitner, J., Haller, M., Yun, K., Woo, W., Sugimoto, M., Inami, M., Cheok, A. D., and Been-Lirn, H. D. 2010. Physical interfaces for tabletop games. Comput. Entertain. 7, 4, Article 61 (January 2010), 21 pages.

21. Li, Y., Fontijn, W., and Markopoulos, P. 2008. A Tangible Tabletop Game Supporting Therapy of Children with Cerebral Palsy. 2nd International Conference on Fun and Games, Springer-Verlag, pp. 182-193.

22. Libavg web http://www.libavg.de/

23. Lin H.-H., and Chang, T.-W. A camera-based multi-touch interface builder for designers. In Human-Computer Interaction. HCI Applications and Services, 2007.

24. Marco, J, Cerezo, E., Baldassarri, S., Mazzone, E., Read, J. Bringing Tabletop Technologies to Kindergarten Children. 23rd BCS Conference on Human computer Interaction (2009). British Computer Society, Swinton, UK, UK, ISBN:978-1-60558-395-2. pp.103-111.

25. Marco, J., Cerezo, E., Baldassarri, S. Tangible Interaction and Tabletops: New Horizons for Children's Games International Journal of Arts and Technology (IJART). Vol. 5, Nos. 2/3/4. 2012. pp.151-176 ISSN: 1754-8853. Ed. Inderscience.

26. Microsoft surface: http://www.microsoft.com/surface/en/us/default.aspx

27. NUI Group web: http://nuigroup.com

28. Openexhibits web: http://openexhibits.org/

29. Patten, J., Ishii, H., Hines, J.,and Pangaro, G. 2001. Sensetable: a wireless object tracking platform for tangible user interfaces. Proc. of the SIGCHI conference on Human factors in computing systems (CHI '01). Pp. 253-260.

30. Reactivision: http://reactivision.sourceforge.net/

31. Rekimoto, J. and Saito. M. Augmented Surfaces: a spatially continuous work space for hybrid computing environments. Proc. of the ACM Conference on Human Factors in Computing System (CHI'99), pp. 378–385.

32. Rogers, Y. and Rodden, T. 2004. Configuring spaces and surfaces to support collaborative interactions. In O'Hara, K., Perry, M., Churchill, E. and Russell, D. (eds.) Public and Situated Displays. Kluwer Publishers. pp. 45-79.

33. Shaer, O. and Jacob, R.J.K. 2009. A specification paradigm for the design and implementation of tangible user interfaces. ACM Trans. Comput.-Hum. Interact. 16, 4, Article 20 (November 2009), 39 pages.

34. Schöning, J., Hook, J., Motamedi, N., Olivier, P., Echtler, F., Brandl, P., Muller, L., Daiber, F., Hilliges, O., Löchtefeld, M., Roth, T., Schmidt, D. and von Zadow, U. 2009. Building Interactive Multi-touch Surfaces. JGT: Journal of Graphics Tools. Springer.

35. Shen, C., Vernier, F., Forlines, C., and Ringel, M. DiamondSpin: an extensible toolkit for around-the-table interaction. In Proc. CHI '04, pages 167–174, 2004.

36. TouchLib: http://nuigroup.com/touchlib/

37. Trackmate: http://trackmate.sourceforge.net/

38. Touché: http://gkaindl.com/software/touche

39. Ullmer, B., Ishii, H., and Jacob, R. J. 2005. Token+constraint systems for tangible interaction with digital information. ACM Trans. Comput.-Hum. Interact. 12, 1 (Mar. 2005), 81-118.

MyUI: Generating Accessible User Interfaces from Multimodal Design Patterns

Matthias Peissner, Dagmar Häbe, Doris Janssen, and Thomas Sellner
Fraunhofer Institute for Industrial Engineering IAO
Nobelstr. 12, 70569 Stuttgart, Germany
{matthias.peissner, dagmar.haebe, doris.janssen, thomas.sellner}@iao.fraunhofer.de

ABSTRACT

Adaptive user interfaces can make technology more accessible. Quite a number of conceptual and technical approaches have been proposed for adaptations to diverse user needs, multiple devices or multiple environments. Little work, however, has been directed at integrating all the essential aspects of adaptive user interfaces for accessibility in one system. In this paper, we present our generic MyUI infrastructure for increased accessibility through automatically generated adaptive user interfaces. The multimodal design patterns repository serves as the basis for a modular approach to individualized user interfaces. This open and extensible pattern repository makes the adaptation rules transparent for designers and developers who can contribute to the repository by sharing their knowledge about accessible design. The adaptation architecture and procedures enable user interface generation and dynamic adaptations during run-time. For the specification of an abstract user interface model, a novel statecharts-based notation has been developed. A development tool supports the interactive creation of the graphical user interface model.

Author Keywords

Adaptive user interfaces; design patterns; accessibility

ACM Classification Keywords

D.2.11 [Software Engineering]: Software Architectures – Patterns; H.5.2 [Information Interfaces and Presentation]: User Interfaces – User-centered design.

General Terms

Design; Human Factors.

INTRODUCTION

Adaptive user interfaces have been widely recognized as a promising means towards accessible technology (e.g. [11] [29] [30] [35]). Identifying individual and situational user needs and providing dynamically personalized user interfaces can overcome significant barriers of use. Despite

the big potentials and the long research tradition of adaptive user interfaces, current approaches are still far from being adopted in the market. We argue that effective approaches to adaptive user interfaces for increased accessibility must satisfy a couple of requirements to gain significant attention beyond the scientific community:

They will require a conceptual and technical framework which allows for *extensive adaptations* to cover diverse user capabilities and needs, devices and contexts of use. Approaches that address only certain types of adaptations or disabilities and approaches for cross-platform interfaces may have their justification for other specific purposes or only parts of the problem. But they will not overcome the challenge of providing universal access for the widest range of users, devices and contexts of use.

Adaptations to such an extent require a huge knowledge base or extremely complex adaptation algorithms. It will hardly be possible to provide this in a monolithic system. *Modularity* will be needed to manage the complexity. For practical reasons, an *extensible* approach is regarded important to support starting with a manageable subset of design solutions and successive extensions.

Many users have problems with customization dialogues [15]. For users with disabilities and lower levels of ICT literacy the need for customization will be a significant barrier. Therefore, personalization which aims at increasing accessibility must include system-initiated adaptations and self-learning mechanisms to identify individual needs. *Adaptations during use* [6] can support an immediate adaptation to newly available knowledge about the user and the environment and can overcome problems of use directly when they occur. This will also help to cover altering capabilities in the course of aging and rehabilitation.

System-initiated adaptations during use can produce problems for the users. Confusing inconsistencies and the feeling of losing control can lead to bad usability and low acceptance [34]. Therefore, mechanisms to assure *transparency and controllability* of automatic interface adaptations are essential for the success of adaptive systems.

On the other hand, also developers and designers have reservations against generated and adaptive user interfaces. Main drawbacks include the relatively demanding work with abstract user interface specifications and the loss of control over the appearance of the generated user interface [15]. Hence, the popularity of adaptive systems in industrial software development will depend on *intuitive and efficient* approaches for the creation, *comprehensible* generation and adaptation mechanisms, and opportunities for *customizing* and modifying the resulting interfaces.

- Our MyUI system supports the further development and mainstreaming of accessible and adaptive user interfaces by addressing these above mentioned requirements. This paper makes the following contributions:

- We describe the MyUI framework and infrastructure to generate individualized user interfaces and perform adaptations to diverse user needs, devices and environmental conditions during run time. This approach relies on an extensible design patterns repository which includes adaptation rules and modular building blocks for user interface generation.

- We present mechanisms to increase the transparency and user control of system-initiated adaptations during use.

- We present MyUI development tools and a graphical user interface specification format for the efficient creation of adaptive applications.

- We evaluate our approach in preliminary studies from three perspectives: (1) effectiveness of the technical infrastructure, (2) usability and acceptability from an end user's point of view, and (3) initial feedback from developers.

RELATED WORK

Adaptation frameworks for accessibility
There have been a number of systems for generating and adapting user interfaces. Most of them concentrate on one specific purpose of adaptation: individual user needs and disabilities [5] [31], multiple devices and modalities, e.g. [26] [21] [2] or context conditions [12] [13]. SUPPLE automatically generates interfaces adapted to a person's device, preferences and physical abilities [11]. Adaptations in the SUPPLE system rely on optimizing a cost-function which includes all aspects to be considered for personalization. This cost function might provide opportunities for extensions to cover also perceptual and cognitive capabilities and environmental factors. However, already the generating of interfaces which reflect individual motor capabilities exceeds acceptable performance times for run time adaptations. Some frameworks have been proposed for extensive adaptations [8] [17]. But none of them has proven their practical feasibility in a complete implementation.

Motti [17] has recognized the importance of extensibility for generic adaptation frameworks. However, only little attention has been targeted towards open frameworks which explicitly aim at engaging other external experts to collaborate in the refinement and extension of the used adaptation mechanisms and rules.

Run-time adaptations and usability
Only few systems provide automatic run-time generation and adaptation (cf. [11] [23]). Nevertheless, a lot has been written about the potential problems of self-adaptive user interfaces, particularly the lack of transparency and the lack of controllability. However, mechanisms to overcome these shortcomings have received relatively little attention in the literature. In a recent paper, Dessart et al. describe a first attempt to improve the transparency of run-time adaptations by animated transitions. They propose a taxonomy of adaptation categories and suitable transitions [7]. For the problem of controllability, not much specific guidance is available. Findlater and McGrenere provide an overview of some empirical studies which compare adaptable and adaptive user interfaces. On the basis of their own study on personalized menus they conclude that a mixed-initiative design which combines adaptable and adaptive mechanisms in one system will be the best to satisfy diverse users [10]. MICA is a good example for a modern mixed-initiative system which recommends customizations but leaves the decision to the user [4]. However, adaptive user interfaces that aim at accessibility improvements might need approaches where the system takes a more proactive role.

Developing adaptive user interfaces
The growing need for user interfaces that run on multiple devices has motivated a lot work in the field of interface generation and abstract user interface descriptions. The most prominent approaches include MARIA [27] and the earlier TERESA [26] with ConcurTaskTrees [25], the Personal Universal Controller (PUC) [21] as used in Huddle [23] and Uniform [22], UIML [1] and canonical abstract prototypes (CAP) with recent modifications in CAP3 [33]. Trewin et al. present requirements for abstract languages to support accessibility. They examine four languages and conclude that extensions will be needed to meet the specific requirements of universal usability [32].

For the case of PUC, Nichols et al. have shown that user interface generation can increase the usability of interfaces for multiple devices [20]. However, support for branding and customization of generated user interfaces is a weak spot in PUC – and most other systems. In many systems for user interface generation, not only controlling the final appearance of the user interface is difficult but also understanding the connection between the specification and the final result [18]. Another frequently mentioned problem is the high threshold of learning a new language [18] – even if for many approaches a graphical editor is available to support the creation of an abstract user interface model. Finally, model-based tools require design activities at an unusually high level of abstraction. Gummy [16] and Damask [14] are notable attempts to better align model-based user interface development with current design practice. Both tools allow developers working on a concrete design for one device as a starting point for later abstractions. Gummy builds a corresponding UIML description from the concrete design. Damask uses higher-level design patterns selected by the designer to generate designs for other devices which can then be modified if desired. Both tools are not ready to be used for the specification of accessible and adaptive interfaces. They are restricted to cross-device design. The pattern approach in Damask might allow for extensions. However, as the used patterns work on a very specific level it would be very difficult to extend the approach to accessibility in general. Moreover, Damask generates designs, not complete interfaces. User interface adaptations are not addressed.

OVERVIEW OF THE MYUI SYSTEM

MyUI provides individualized user interfaces which are accessible to a broad range of users. The conceptual framework of MyUI contributes to the further development in the field of adaptive user interfaces by focusing on the following aspects (cf. [28]):

- *Generic framework for manifold adaptations:* The MyUI technical framework allows for adaptations to diverse user needs, different devices[1] and changing context conditions. Therefore, MyUI user interfaces adapt their presentation formats and modalities, the interaction mechanisms and the navigation paths.

- *Modular, extensible and open:* A modular approach is taken to manage the huge amount of possible user interface solutions. For practical reasons, extensibility is important to support a quick start with a manageable subset of design solutions and later extensions. Modularity and extensibility are achieved by a design patterns approach to adaptive user interfaces. The MyUI design patterns repository is publically available [19]. Thus, the underlying adaptation rules can be reviewed, refined and extended by other experts in the field.

- *Self-learning and adapting during use:* The model for MyUI user interface adaptations is the gradual adaptation between two human communication partners. In the beginning, both show quite careful and neutral behaviors. Over time, they learn to know each other better and better. A mutual understanding is established and improved by perceiving the partner's feedback to one's own communication acts, e.g. explicit remarks, emotional facial expressions, etc. Without an explicit interview to capture personal preferences and attitudes, human communicators adapt to each other in a quick, natural and smooth way during the interaction. MyUI strives to imitate such a smooth and natural adaptation process in

---

[1] The current MyUI application prototypes run on a web-based iTV platform and iPhone. The MyUI technical framework, however, is generic and not restricted to iTV.

accessible and highly individualized user interfaces. For this purpose, the MyUI system is collecting information about the user during the interaction and updates the user profile accordingly. In order to cover dynamic user profile changes, the MyUI framework supports run-time rendering and run-time adaptations of the user interface.

- *Transparent and controllable:* To assure high levels of usability and user acceptance, MyUI provides mechanisms to help the users to recognize and understand user interface adaptations.

- *Development infrastructure:* The mainstreaming of accessible and adaptive user interfaces is supported by a set of tools to facilitate easy and efficient design and development processes.

GENERATING AND ADAPTING USER INTERFACES

MyUI adaptive user interfaces are generated and adapted in a three-stage process (see figure 1).

User Interface Parameterization

User interface parameterization is the first step in the MyUI user interface generation and adaptation process. The result (output) of this first step is the *MyUI User Interface Profile* which defines general characteristics of the user interface. Examples for variables include bodyTextFontSize, displayMode (with values from "text only" over "mainly text" etc. to "graphics only") and voiceInput (on/off). The settings of the user interface profile are valid throughout the entire user interface and in all interaction situations of an application. During user interface parameterization information from three different input sources is processed:

- Information about the currently available and used I/O devices from the *Device Profile.*

- Information about the user and the current environment from the *User Profile.*

- Customization settings as defined by the developer of a MyUI application in the *Customization Profile.*

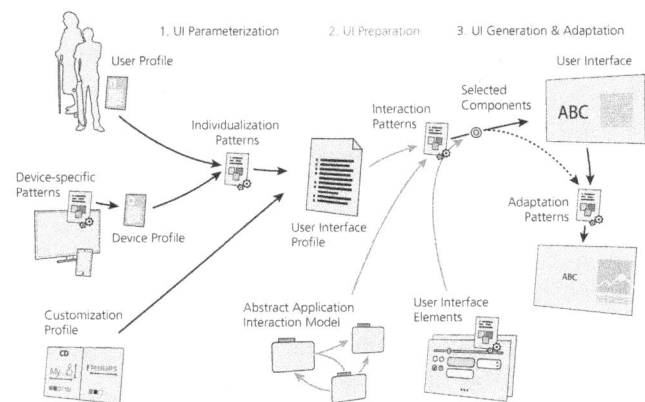

Figure 1 MyUI user interface generation and adaptation

User interface parameterization can be regarded as a transformation of these profiles into the User Interface Profile. A *MyUI User Interface Profile* is initiated at the beginning of a new interaction session with a MyUI application. A repeated user interface parameterization (i.e. user interface profile update) is triggered when the available information about the user, the environment or the available devices changes significantly.

User Interface Preparation

User interface preparation denotes the process of selecting the most suitable user interface components and elements for the current situation. The major input of this process step includes

- the *Abstract Application Interaction Model* (AAIM) which defines active interaction situations for each state of the application and

- the *User Interface Profile* which reflects the specific requirements related to the current user, environment and device setup (see above).

User interface preparation is triggered every time when a new state in the AAIM is entered or when changes have occurred to the user interface profile. The AAIM is described in later sections of this paper.

User Interface Generation and Adaptation

The selected user interface components are rendered to an individual user interface. The major input to this step is the set of selected user interface components as a result of the user interface preparation. The output is a complete user interface which is consistent with the currently available knowledge about individual user needs and context requirements at any time during the interaction.

Dynamic and system-initiated user interface adaptations during run time are a main feature of the MyUI system. Run-time adaptations can be considered as a repeated user interface generation with mechanisms to switch from one instance of a user interface to another instance. In summary, the last step in the MyUI user interface generation and adaptation process includes the following three activities which all take place during run-time:

- *User interface generation*: At the beginning of a new interaction session, a complete user interface is created and rendered on the basis of the selected components (result of user interface preparation).

- *Profile updates:* In a permanent process during an interaction session, relevant events from the interaction are fed back to the Context Manager to update the user profile and device profile. Profile updates trigger the entire three-stage adaptation process again.

- *User interface adaptations during use:* When new user interface components and elements have been selected in a repeated user interface preparation process, user interface adaptations are triggered and executed.

MYUI DESIGN PATTERNS

Design patterns as modular building blocks

To cover the great heterogeneity of users, environments and devices, MyUI follows a modular approach to user interface development which relies on multimodal user interface design patterns. The MyUI design patterns contain the knowledge needed to perform the described three-stage process of user interface generation and adaptation. Individual accessibility is achieved by composing design patterns which provide proven solutions for specific interaction situations and characteristics of the user, environment and device. Adapting the user interface means switching from one design pattern of a bundle (e.g. all patterns for single selection from a list of options) to another pattern of the same bundle which is hypothesized to be the most appropriate for the current context.

MyUI Design Patterns Repository

The MyUI patterns repository includes the design patterns in a human-readable description format. The repository is maintained as a publicly available media wiki (see figure 2) [19]. Hence, the entire body of knowledge and rules engaged in the MyUI user interface generation and adaptation is easily accessible and transparent to everyone. Each pattern is described in a defined structure as proposed by Borchers [3] and related to other patterns of different types and levels of abstraction. Each pattern is linked to a reusable software component and associated with a source code representation of the described solution to put the recommended guideline into action in the MyUI adaptive user interface.

Extensibility is an important aspect of the design patterns repository. The current body of design patterns reflects the interaction requirements of initial MyUI demo applications, i.e. email service and instant messaging. For future applications, additional patterns will be needed. These can be simply added to the pattern repository without requiring a new version of a monolithic patterns document. Also new knowledge about the current patterns can lead to modifications and refinements. The human-readable and

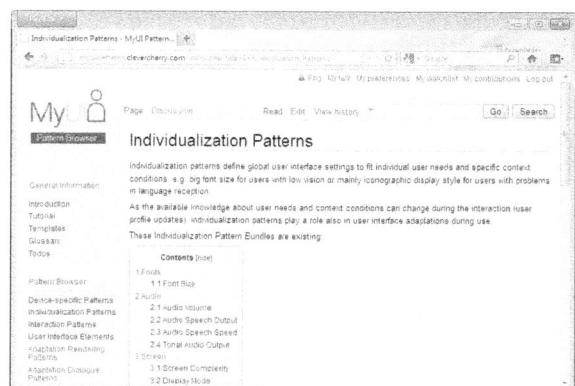

Figure 2 The MyUI Pattern Browser is the developer's access to the MyUI Pattern Repository

easy format, the well-known wiki platform and the little effort for changes lead to a low barrier for the community to use, discuss and improve the design patterns. With both, a machine-readable and a human-readable part, the MyUI design patterns repository bridges the gap between guidelines for accessible design and generative user interfaces.

Types of design patterns

The MyUI design patterns repository includes different categories of patterns. Each pattern type fulfills distinct functions in the MyUI adaptation framework (see figure 1):

Device-specific patterns create the device profile on the basis of primitive device features as provided by the used I/O devices. The device profile variables prepare the step of user interface parameterization by providing device-specific ranges of user interface settings from which individualization patterns select the most suitable (e.g. potential font sizes). Changes in the device setup will lead immediately to updating the device profile.

Individualization patterns define global user interface settings to fit individual user needs and environmental conditions, e.g. big font size for users with low vision or iconographic presentation for users with problems in language reception. As the available knowledge about the user and environment can change during the interaction, individualization patterns play an important role for user interface adaptations during use.

These first two pattern types work on a general level of the user interface. Together, they are responsible for setting and adjusting global variables in the user interface profile. An additional input to the user interface profile comes from the customization profile which allows for corporate-, project- or brand-specific customizations, e.g. colors or font styles. The customization settings are used in the user interface profile in a 1:1-manner without transformations. Therefore, no specific patterns are needed for customization.

Interaction patterns provide suitable user interface components for a current interaction situation as specified in the AAIM, e.g. a list element for an interaction situation in which a user can select from a set of options. For each interaction situation, a bundle of different interaction design patterns exists. They differ in appearance or interaction modality to support different user needs and context conditions. The selection of the best suitable interaction pattern from a current bundle is done on the basis of specific variables of the user interface profile.

User interface elements are the building blocks for the interaction patterns. While interaction patterns can be regarded as components to support a given interaction situation, the user interface elements provide generic primitives required to compose the interaction patterns.

Adaptation patterns cover the dynamics of the adaptation processes. They define the mechanisms of switching from one instance of a user interface to another. Adaptation patterns are described in more detail in a later section.

MyUI Design Patterns Language

According to Borchers' understanding, patterns are not isolated but refer to other patterns. In a hierarchical pattern language, larger patterns refer to smaller-scale patterns for the solution they describe. And smaller-scale patterns can only be used in a certain type of context which is the result of applying larger-scale patterns [3]. In the MyUI design pattern language, references between patterns play an important role. For a systematic use of references a classification of relations between patterns has been defined. Table 1 provides an overview of the relations used in the MyUI pattern language.

Table 1 Relations between MyUI design patterns

Relation	Description
A substitutes B	Both patterns A and B serve the same purpose in the MyUI framework and both patterns can never be active at the same time.
	This relation is used to create bundles of related patterns which support different user needs or context conditions.
A requires B	Pattern B describes parts of the higher-level solution addressed by pattern A.
	This relation is used to structure the design patterns repository in a vertical way. It links higher-level patterns to lower-level patterns for a detailed description of the solution.
A is required by B	This is the inverse relation of requires.
A sets <variables> as required by B	Patterns of bundle A set one or more global MyUI variables which specify (parts of) the solutions as provided by the patterns of bundle B.
A requires <variables> as set by B	This is the inverse relation of sets <variables> as required by.
A sets <variables> as used by B	Patterns of A set one or more global MyUI variables which are used to select the most suitable pattern from bundle B.
A uses <variables> as set by B	This is the inverse relation of sets <variables> as used by.

ADAPTATION PATTERNS FOR TRANSPARENCY AND CONTROLLABILITY

User interface adaptations are executed by the MyUI adaptation engine. The adaptation engine recognizes mismatches of the user interface components currently displayed and the components currently selected by the user interface preparation process. A mismatch triggers a runtime adaptation. Adaptations are performed by two types of MyUI adaptation patterns:

- *Adaptation rendering patterns* specify the graphical rendering process to smoothly but obviously switch from one user interface instance to another, e.g. animated transitions to grow small fonts to bigger fonts.

- *Adaptation dialogue patterns* specify the interaction dialogue which takes place around the actual adaptation to make sure that the user is aware of the adaptation and can control the system's adaptation behavior.

Adaptation rendering patterns

MyUI adaptation rendering patterns make extensive use of animations. They support orientation by creating continuity between the user interface before and after the adaptation. Animated transitions shall draw the end user's attention to the screen areas where adaptations occur and shall help them to understand that and how the new user interface is a modification of the former user interface. When, for example, an increased font size results in hiding menu options which were directly available before the adaptation, an animation can communicate to the user that the hidden options are now available via the »more« button.

Adaptation dialogue patterns

Adaptation dialogue patterns specify the dialogue between the user interface and the MyUI user in the course of an adaptation. This dialogue typically includes a notification and interaction options for the user to influence the system's adaptation behavior. In MyUI, two types of adaptation dialogue patterns are distinguished:

- *System-initiated adaptation dialogue patterns* are triggered by the system.

- *User-initiated adaptation dialogue patterns* describe customization dialogues in which the user modifies the user profile or the user interface profile.

The latter make MyUI a mixed-initiative system with adaptive and adaptable components. More interesting, however, are system-initiated adaptation dialogue patterns. They aim at increasing the usability and acceptability by making system-initiated adaptations more transparent and controllable. The MyUI patterns repository includes the following system-initiated adaptation dialogue patterns.´

Explicit Confirmation before Adaptation

Before performing the adaptation the system requests the user to accept or reject the adaptation. The user's decision is supported by a preview of the adaptation effect (figure 3). If the user rejects the adaptation, the dialogue box is closed and the user interface is not changed. If the user accepts the adaptation or if the system receives no user input (time-out), the dialogue box is closed and the adaptation is carried out. The MyUI context management infrastructure is informed about the user's decision to refine the user profile.

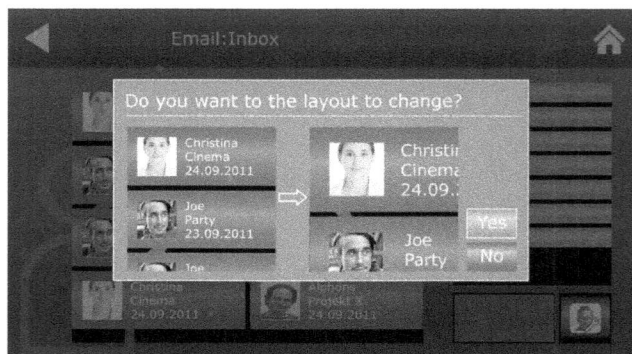

Figure 3 Explicit Confirmation before Adaptation: Dialogue box with preview (UI concept sketch)

Explicit Confirmation after Adaptation

The adaptation is triggered and performed automatically. After the adaptation a dialogue box asks the user if the changes shall be kept or undone. If the user rejects, the adaptation is undone. If the user accepts or a time-out event is recognized, the adaptation is kept. The user's decision is fed back to the context management infrastructure.

Automatic Adaptation with Implicit Confirmation

The adaptation is triggered and performed automatically. While rendering the adaptation, the system provides an icon-based notification in a dedicated adaptation area. Moreover, the adaptation area offers buttons to undo the adaptation and to access to the user interface profile and the user profile. Figure 4 shows a sequence of three screens before, during and after an automatic adaptation with implicit confirmation.

(1) Before adaptation
Permanent access to user profile and user interface profile via adaptation area (bottom right)

(2) During adaptation
Pulsing icon (here chameleon) indicates on-going adaptation.

(3) After adaptation
The user can undo the adaptation via button with curved backwards arrow.

Figure 4 Automatic adaptation with implicit confirmation

DEVELOPING AN ADAPTIVE APPLICATION WITH MYUI

MyUI provides a development toolkit which supports developers in the creation of adaptive applications. It is implemented as a plugin for the well-established Eclipse platform to facilitate the later integration into industrial settings. It supports creating, customizing, previewing and simulating adaptive applications. In addition, it provides access to tutorials, design patterns and information about the pattern-based adaptation process.

Automatically generating user interfaces changes the application developers' role significantly. Their impact on the specific user interface appearance is minimized in favor of an automated and rule-based user interface generation process which includes the provision of different user interfaces for users with different needs. The developers' main responsibility in MyUI is defining the functionality and application logic in an AAIM.

Abstract Application Interaction Model (AAIM)

The AAIM describes the interaction between the user and the application in a way which is independent of a specific appearance and concrete interaction mechanisms. It serves as a basis for the generated and adapted user interfaces by defining the common ground of all possible user interfaces. The MyUI AAIM extends the UML 2 State Machine Diagram [24]. Statecharts allow modeling the interaction without going into details about the presentation modalities or used control elements. These aspects are subject to adaptations in MyUI and therefore not part of the AAIM specifications. Figure 5 presents a part of the AAIM for the MyUI email application.

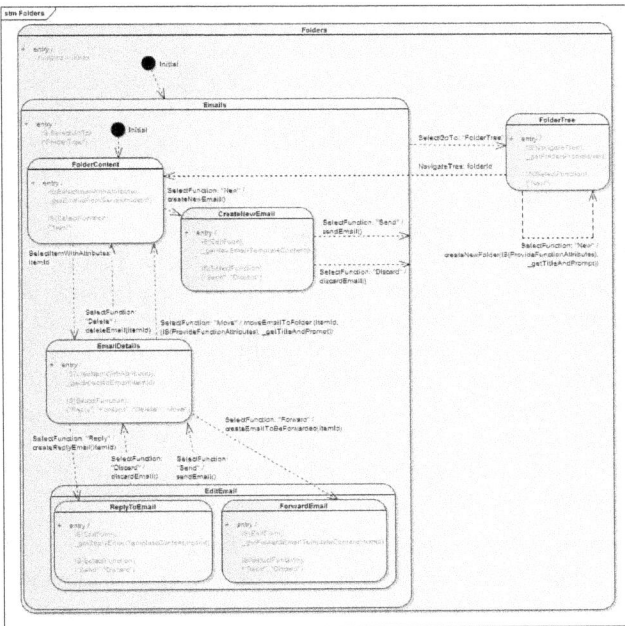

Figure 5 AAIM of the MyUI email application (excerpt)

Interaction situations as basis for adapting the user interface

The concept of interaction situations is essential for the MyUI adaptation framework. An interaction situation is an abstract super-set of user interface components and controls which serve the same interaction purpose. Interaction situations represent the interaction options a user has at a certain point in the application. Interaction options include all activities a user can perform in the application, e.g. perceiving information, providing specific input, selecting options, etc. Typically, more than one user interface component or element can be used in one certain interaction situation, e.g. selecting a single item from a set of items can be supported by a selection list, a drop-down list or even an audio menu. This flexibility is an essential basis for user interface adaptations in MyUI. Depending on individual user needs, the most suitable interaction pattern can be selected for a given interaction situation. The different variants of user interface components for a common purpose are referred to as bundles of interaction patterns.

Interaction situations in states and transitions

Every state includes one or more interaction situations. Interaction situations apply to the state in which they appear. Interaction situations in a composite state refer to all sub-states of the composite state and persist as long as one of the sub-states is active. This can be used also for the definition of generic navigation options which are available throughout an entire application or even across different applications, e.g. home navigation and back navigation.

An interaction situation of a state can be associated with respective transitions from the state to other states. An interaction situation, for example, which provides a set of functions from which the user can select in the current state, is always associated with a set of transitions from the state to other states in which the triggered functions are executed.

Interaction situations can appear in states and as arguments of transitions between states of the AAIM. Interaction situations at transitions are needed to retrieve confirmation or additional information from the user needed to perform the transition and to enter the next state. As an example, some interaction situations SelectFunction require arguments for executing the selected function, e.g. the destination folder of the "move to folder" function or an explicit user confirmation before the execution of an irreversible action. These arguments are then collected by a separate interaction situation, e.g. a dialogue box which requests the needed information from the user.

Development Toolkit

The main view of the MyUI Development Toolkit (see figure 6) in Eclipse includes the MyUI Editor (right side), a project explorer and a list of available interaction situations (upper and lower left side).

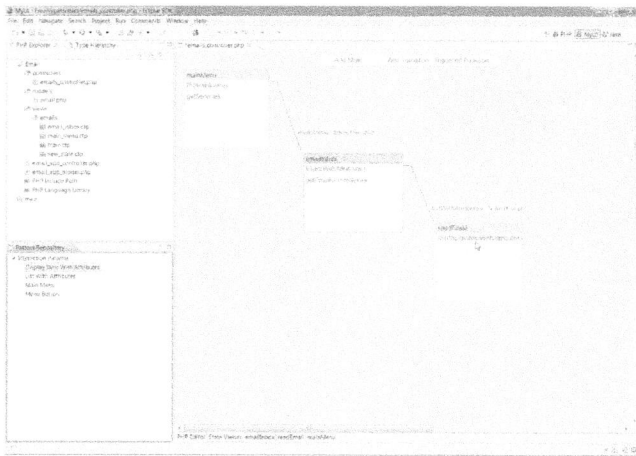

Figure 6 MyUI Development Toolkit

The MyUI Editor supports the easy creation of an AAIM by providing a graphical model view. A wizard helps to build the application skeleton by specifying general application properties. As a result, the generated file and folder structure of the application appears in the project explorer. The developer can then create new states in the model editor and add interaction situations by drag-and-drop from the list view in the lower left area. Thereby, specific parameters such as references to data sources can be entered. The related bundle of interaction patterns appears in the state. Associated transitions are automatically generated and can be connected to other existing states. In this way, the entire adaptive application can be successfully modeled. The MyUI Editor also allows switching between the model view and the source code view. The designer can chose to create and refine the model in any of both views which are kept consistent.

Another component of the development toolkit is the MyUI pattern browser. Integrated into the Eclipse-based development toolkit, the pattern browser provides direct access to the MyUI pattern repository with detailed information about the design patterns and their roles within the generation and adaptation process. Thus, the developer can easily explore the available patterns and identify the needed interaction situations.

In order to support a deep understanding of the relationships between the abstract model and the resulting interfaces for different users and contexts, the development toolkit has integrated preview functionality. The developer can select and load user profiles and see how the generated user interfaces would look for these specific users.

Finally, the development toolkit offers some opportunities for customizing the generated user interface. Simulation facilities make it possible to validate the feasibility of customized font styles, color schemes, etc. for disabled users by providing a what-you-see-is-what-others-get view on the customized user interface.

EVALUATION

Framework validation

The practical feasibility of the technical framework has been evaluated in the development of a first adaptive iTV-based web application. This demonstrator includes a main menu for service selection and an email service.

The developed prototype covers extensive adaptations to individual perceptual, physical and cognitive capabilities and environmental conditions such as ambient noise and ambient light. Device-specific adaptations were not tested in this first cycle. The adaptation to individual user needs was tested by the use of two different personas with different levels of perceptual, physical and cognitive impairments. The functional tests yielded satisfying results. At any time, the MyUI system generated a meaningful and consistent user interface. Relevant updates in the user and context profile during the interaction always resulted in the expected run-time adaptations. The recorded system performance for user interface generation and adaptations during run-time was excellent. The time needed to generate a new instance of the user interface was equal to the (very short) time for loading a new page of the web application without adaptations.

User Studies

A couple of preliminary informal user studies were carried out to evaluate specific user interface solutions for users with certain limitations as documented in the MyUI design patterns. Especially, patterns which could not be substantiated by the literature were tested with older adults.

In an early paper prototype study with four participants (three female, one male, aged 70-89) we wanted to explore the ways in which older people respond to the concept of adaptive interfaces. The participants were presented a series of pages which set out representations of interfaces based on an interactive TV screen. The interface depicted was chosen mainly for its ability to demonstrate various forms of adaptation rather than as a representation of a proposed device. Simple tasks were assigned and according to selections made, the 'screen' layout changed. Participants were asked for their opinions on the changing layouts, and for any suggestions they wished to make. A main result of this study was that it was very hard to get feedback on the specific concept of adaptation. Older persons with low ICT literacy seem to have difficulties in understanding and recognizing system-initiated adaptations at all [9]. This finding challenges the overall concept of adaptive and accessible interfaces for a major target user group of MyUI.

Currently, we are preparing a user study to evaluate the proposed adaptation dialogue patterns. We assume that their effectiveness and acceptability depend on the subjective cost-benefit of the adaptation. Predominant costs might be associated with a higher wish for user control and therefore, a preference for explicit confirmations. But in situations where the benefits outweigh the costs, users might prefer automatic adaptations because of their higher comfort of use. In our case, adaptations can cause further costs, e.g., when the adapted user interface requires additional interaction steps, e.g. increasing the font size requires extra scrolling. Benefits occur when an adaptation can increase the accessibility by eliminating a barrier of use. Besides these situational factors, also personal traits might influence the subjective cost-benefit ratio and the preference of one of the adaptation patterns. Users with lower ICT literacy or a higher need for security might tend to over-estimate the costs and therefore prefer explicit confirmations.

The current study will address the following questions:

- Which adaptation dialogue patterns are most effective in terms of transparency, controllability and acceptance?

- Which pattern is preferred by the users?

- Do these measures differ in different cost-benefit conditions and for different users?

The results will help us to design the mechanism for selecting the most appropriate adaptation pattern for different situations and user profiles.

Developers' feedback

Eight software developers participated in a preliminary study to collect feedback from the developers' perspective in a focus group setting. The participants were presented basic concepts of the MyUI project, a video which explains the work with the development toolkit and the AAIM of the email application. After a discussion and a round of questions and answers, the participants completed a questionnaire to evaluate the MyUI system on a number of Likert-scales. Figure 7 summarizes the results. Besides the relatively good overall assessment, a major finding was that some of the developers had severe problems in estimating the usefulness of the MyUI system. Due to the early stage in the development process the participants could not try a functional system but had to rely on the presented material. Therefore, it is not clear if these problems are due to the

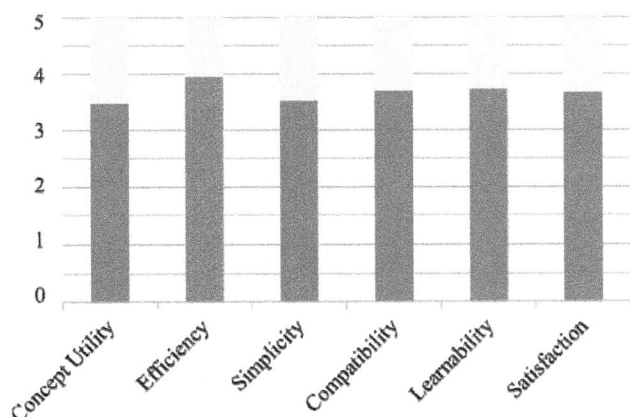

Figure 7 Initial developer feedback (mean ratings, n=8)

framework itself or to the presented material. Nevertheless, they pointed us to the importance of easy-to-understand instruction material to support an easy start with MyUI.

CONCLUSION

We have presented an overview of MyUI, a novel system which generates adaptive user interfaces to support the mainstreaming of accessibility. MyUI focuses on major requirements of adaptive interfaces for accessibility which have been neglected by previous systems in the field. MyUI provides a framework for extensive run-time adaptations to user characteristics, environmental conditions and used devices. Modularity and extensibility are achieved by a design patterns approach to adaptive user interfaces. Increasing the usability and acceptance of automatic run-time adaptations is a major topic in MyUI. Current user studies will help us to design transparent and controllable mechanisms. Finally, a statecharts-based approach to graphical user interface modeling with a dedicated toolbox aims at tackling current acceptance problems in the industrial software development.

ACKNOWLEDGMENTS

The research leading to these results has received funding from the European Union's Seventh Framework Program under grant FP7-ICT-248606. The authors acknowledge the help of other partners in the MyUI consortium in this work.

REFERENCES

1. Abrams, M., Phanouriou, C., Batongbacal, A.L., Williams, S. & Shuster, J. (1999), UIML: An Appliance-Independent XML User Interface Language. In Proc. WWW'8, Amsterdam: Elsevier, 1695-1708

2. Ali, M.F., Pérez-Quiñones, M.A., Abrams, M., & Shell, E. (2002). Building Multi-Platform User Interfaces with UIML. In Proceedings CADUI 2002, 255-266.

3. Borchers, J. O. (2001). A pattern approach to interactive design. Chichester, UK: John Wiley & Sons Ltd.

4. Bunt, A., Conati, C., & McGrenere, J. (2009). A Mixed-Initiative Approach to Interface Personalization. AI Magazine 30(4).

5. Coelho, J., Duarte, C., Biswas, P., & Langdon, P. (2011). Developing accessible TV applications. In Proceedings ASSETS '11. New York: ACM, 131-138.

6. Dieterich, H., Malinowski, U., Kühme, T. & Schneider-Hufschmidt, M. (1993). State of the Art in Adaptive User Interfaces. In: M. Schneider-Hufschmidt, T. Kühme & U. Malinowski (Eds.): Adaptive User Interfaces: Principles and practice. Amsterdam: North-Holland, 13–48.

7. Dessart, C.-E., Motti, V. G. & Vanderdonckt, J. (2011). Showing user interface adaptivity by animated transitions. In Proc. EICS '11. New York: ACM, 95-104.

8. Duarte, C. & Carriço, L (2006). A conceptual framework for developing adaptive multimodal

applications. In Proc. IUI '06. New York: ACM, 132-139.

9. Edlin-White, R., Cobb, S., Floyde, A., Lewthwaite, S., Wang, J. & Riedel, J. (2012). From guinea pigs to design partners - involving older people in technology design. In: P. Langdon, J. Clarkson, P. Robinson, J. Lazar & A. Heylighen (Eds.): Designing Inclusive Systems. London: Springer-Verlag, 155-164.

10. Findlater, L. & McGrenere, J. (2004) A comparison of static, adaptive, and adaptable menus. In Proceedings CHI'04, New York: ACM, 89-96.

11. Gajos, K. Z., Weld, D. S., & Wobbrock, J. O. (2010). Automatically generating personalized user interfaces with Supple. Artificial Intelligence 174, 12-13. 910-950.

12. Kane, S. K., Wobbrock, J. O. & Smith, I. E. (2008). Getting off the treadmill: evaluating walking user interfaces for mobile devices in public spaces. In Proceedings MobileHCI '08. New York: ACM, 109-118.

13. Lehmann, G., Blumendorf, M. & Albayrak, S. (2010). Development of context-adaptive applications on the basis of runtime user interface models. In Proceedings EICS '10. New York: ACM, 309-314.

14. Lin, J. & Landay, J. A. (2008). Employing patterns and layers for early-stage design and prototyping of cross-device user interfaces. In Proceedings CHI '08. New York: ACM, 1313-1322.

15. Mackay, W. E. (1991). Triggers and barriers to customizing software. In Proceedings CHI '91, New York: ACM, 153–160.

16. Meskens, J., Vermeulen, J., Luyten, K. & Coninx, K. (2008). Gummy for multi-platform user interface designs: shape me, multiply me, fix me, use me. In Proceedings AVI '08. New York: ACM, 233-240.

17. Motti, V. G. (2011). A computational framework for multi-dimensional context-aware adaptation. In Proceedings EICS '11. New York: ACM, 315-318.

18. Myers, B., Hudson, S. E. & Pausch, R. (2000). Past, present, and future of user interface software tools. ACM Trans. Comp.-Hum. Interact. 7, 1, 3-28.

19. MyUI Design Patterns Repository. Available at http://myuipatterns.clevercherry.com

20. Nichols, J., Chau, D. H., & Myers, B. A. (2007). Demonstrating the viability of automatically generated user interfaces. In Proceedings CHI '07. New York: ACM, 1283-1292.

21. Nichols, J & Myers, B. A. (2009). Creating a lightweight user interface description language: An overview and analysis of the personal universal controller project. ACM Trans. Comp.-Hum. Interact. 16, 4, 37 pages.

22. Nichols, J., Myers, B. A. & Rothrock, B. (2006). UNIFORM: automatically generating consistent remote control user interfaces. In Proceedings CHI '06. New York: ACM, 611-620.

23. Nichols, J., Rothrock, B., Chau, D. H. & Myers, B. A. (2006). Huddle: automatically generating interfaces for systems of multiple connected appliances. In Proceedings UIST '06. New York: ACM, 279-288.

24. Object Management Group (2011). Unified Modeling Language Superstructure, V 2.4.1, available at http://www.omg.org/spec/UML/2.4.1/Superstructure

25. Paterno, F. (1999). Model-Based Design and Evaluation of Interactive Applications. London: Springer-Verlag.

26. Paterno, F., Santoro, C., Mantyjarvi, J., Mori, G. & Sansone, S. (2008). Authoring pervasive multimodal user interfaces. Int. J. Web Eng. Technol. 4, 2, 235-261.

27. Paterno, F., Santoro, C. & Spano, L. D. (2009). MARIA: A universal, declarative, multiple abstraction-level language for service-oriented applications in ubiquitous environments. ACM Trans. Comp.-Hum. Interact. 16, 4, 30 pages.

28. Peissner, M., Schuller, A. & Spath, D. (2011). A design patterns approach to adaptive user interfaces for users with special needs. In Proceedings HCII'11, Berlin: Springer-Verlag, 268-277.

29. Ringbauer, B., Peissner, M., & Gemou, M. (2007). From "design for all" towards "design for one"– A modular user interface approach. In: C. Stephanidis (Ed.): Universal Access in HCI, Part I, HCII 2007, LNCS 4554, Berlin: Springer-Verlag, 517–526.

30. Savidis, A. & Stephanidis, C. (2004). Unified user interface design: Designing universally accessible interactions. Int. J. Interacting w. Comp. 16, 2, 243–270.

31. Stephanidis, C., Paramythis, A., Sfyrakis, M., Stergiou, A., Maou, N., Leventis, A., Paparoulis, G. & Karagiannidis, C. (1998). Adaptable and adaptive user interfaces for disabled users in the AVANTI project, in: IS&N 98 Proceedings, Springer-Verlag, 153-166.

32. Trewin, S., Zimmermann, G. & Vanderheiden, G. (2002). Abstract user interface representations: how well do they support universal access? SIGCAPH Comput. Phys. Handicap. 73-74 (June 2002), 77-84.

33. Van den Bergh, J., Luyten, K. & Coninx, K. (2011). CAP3: context-sensitive abstract user interface specification. In Proceedings EICS '11. New York: ACM, 31-40.

34. Weld, D., Anderson, C., Domingos, P., Etzioni, O., Lau, T., Gajos, K. & Wolfman, S. (2003). Automatically personalizing user interfaces. In Proceedings IJCAI'03. San Francisco: Morgan Kaufmann, 1613-1619.

35. Wobbrock, J. O., Kane, S. K., Gajos, K. Z., Harada, S., & Froehlich, J. (2011). Ability-based design: Concept, principles and examples. ACM Transactions on Accessible Computing, Vol. 3, No. 3, Article 9.

An Automated Layout Approach for Model-Driven WIMP-UI Generation

David Raneburger, Roman Popp
Institute of Computer Technology
Vienna University of Technology
Gusshausstrasse 27-29
A-1040 Vienna, Austria
{raneburger, popp}@ict.tuwien.ac.at

Jean Vanderdonckt
Université catholique de Louvain
Louvain School of Management
Place des Doyens 1
B-1348 Louvain-la-Neuve, Belgium
jean.vanderdonckt@uclouvain.be

ABSTRACT

Automated Window / Icon / Menu / Pointing Device User Interface (WIMP-UI) generation has been considered a promising technology for at least two decades. One of the major reasons why it has not become mainstream so far is that the usability of automatically generated UIs is rather low. This is mainly because non-functional requirements like layout or style issues are not considered adequately during the generation process. This paper proposes an automated layout approach that supports the explicit specification of layout parameters in device-independent and thus reusable transformation rules. Missing layout parameters are completed automatically, based on 'Layout Hints' under the consideration of scrolling preferences. We are aware that human intervention in the context of UI development will always be required to create high-quality UIs. Therefore, we aim to improve the generated UI by considering hints and applying heuristics, rather than solving a problem for which we believe that there is no generic solution.

Author Keywords

Automated Layout; WIMP-UI Generation; Model-driven

ACM Classification Keywords

D.2.2 Design Tool and Techniques: User Interfaces

INTRODUCTION

Millions of people world wide use Window / Icon / Menu / Pointing Device User Interfaces (WIMP-UIs) to interact with all different kinds of devices (e.g., smartphones, tablets, ticket vending machines, etc.) on a daily basis. Model-driven UI generation offers the methodology to generate UIs for multiple devices from one high-level model, and thus reduce the development effort in comparison to traditional methods. Such high-level models are ideally device and platform independent and therefore, on a higher level of abstraction than UI models. Hence, they do not provide the means to specify details concerning the layout or style of a specific widget.

These details can only be considered during the transformations, in particular when the high-level model is transformed into a concrete UI model. The additional specification of rendering details based on a device independent model is not a very illustrative task and in most cases not even possible, because such details are device specific. Additionally, their specification requires extra effort and they are frequently only supported to a limited extent by the transformation frameworks. Full automation, in particular inferring such details through heuristics, makes the outcome of most approaches "unpredictable" for designers. This inhibits the designer from achieving the exact look that she desires. Myers et al. state that automated UI generation usually implies that the designer compromises usability - the most determining factor of a UI - for the sake of automatic generation [24]. This is still true for current approaches and results in a low usability of automatically generated UIs [21].

Layout is one of the crucial parts for good UI usability, as the following statement from the Microsoft User Experience Guidelines underlines: "Layout is the sizing, spacing, and placement of content within a window or page. Effective layout is crucial in helping users find what they are looking for quickly, as well as making the appearance visually appealing. Effective layout can make the difference between designs that users immediately understand and those that leave users feeling puzzled and overwhelmed" [23]. Similar UI guidelines are provided by major software companies/platforms (e.g., Apple [1], Eclipse[1], KDE[2], etc.), to ensure a certain level of usability for their applications and consistency between them.

The research community took up the challenge to automate layout creation in the course of model-driven WIMP-UI generation about two decades ago. For example, scientist investigated layout techniques [32] and definded metrics for layout appropriateness [31]. However, the interest in the research community seemed to cease about one decade ago. Today most model driven UI generation approaches use manually created presentation or layout models. Automatisms are only applied to a very limited extend. Why? The key problems seem to be to select the right one out of a multitude of options and the direct impact of the layout on the usability of the

---

[1] http://wiki.eclipse.org/User_Interface_Guidelines
[2] http://techbase.kde.org/Development/Guidelines

generated UI. Kennard and Leany even suggest that the layout of a widget on the screen is perhaps the most intractable issue in UI generation, because layout "exposes a myriad of small details around UI appearance, navigation, menu placement and so on. The problem is so difficult, in fact we believe it insoluble" [13]. They argue that a non optimal layout that comprises the final product in usability or even only aesthetics, comprises automated generation in general. We also think that the problem of automated layout creation is too complex to be solved in a generic way. It is impossible to generate a specific UI without specifying the details.

Our approach aims to specify as much layout information as possible upfront, before the transformation, in a reusable way. The designer provides all layout information on concrete UI level of the Cameleon Reference Framework [4], which we consider the most appropriate level to specify layout information. To make these specifications reusable, they are part of the right hand side (RHS) of transformation rules. These RHSs are the UI model parts that the transformation rules create. Usually one screen of the UI is composed of the UI model parts of several transformation rules. These UI model parts are composed according to the structure of the high-level model. Such high-level models do not contain any layout specifications, thus its hierarchical structure is the only characteristic that is available for consideration for layouting. The rule that creates the container for the children does not consider their number, otherwise it would already be dependent on a certain high-level model. What we propose is to add hints for each child container that specify where it shall be placed in its parent container and to complete the layout data automatically, based on these hints. Thus, we support a seamless transition from fully automated to semi-automatic UI generation with human involvement. Our mixed-initiative approach will most probably not enable the designer to generate the UI she desires fully automatically in the first run. However, as we also think that iterative design is a crucial component of achieving high-quality user interfaces [25] and aim to reduce the number of iterations that a designer needs to develop the UI she desires in the long run. So the focus of this paper is on what makes automated UI generation an appropriate context for mixed-initiative layout.

The remainder of this paper starts with a short overview of layout mechanisms in state of the art UI generation approaches. We explain our automated layout approach in detail before we illustrate its integration in a UI generation framework. We will present the experiences gained through the implementation of our approach and discuss several issues that we consider worth for further investigation, before we draw the conclusions from our work.

STATE OF THE ART
The Layout of a UI can be created at design or at runtime. Compared to each other, design time approaches better support human intervention and run time approaches require less effort. This section contrasts design and runtime approaches that paved the way for our own work.

Lok and Feiner present a survey of automated layout techniques for information presentation in [18]. They state that

"A presentation's layout can have a significant impact on how well it communicates information to and obtains information from those who interact with it." Furthermore, they underline the necessity to consider high-level relationships and spatial constraints, and to provide a grammar based language to specify them. The authors admit that however powerful and expressive grammars may be, they may be difficult to use.

Vanderdonckt and Gillo summarize techniques from the area of visual design, to make them exploitable for UI design [32]. Their work gives a good overview of the multitude of options and provides layout guidelines to cope with the corresponding complexity. Further suggestions for a dynamic strategy for computer-aided visual design are provided in [3]. This work compares different placement strategies and concludes that in any case, generation may be considered as a fair starting point for manual refinement.

Designer intervention is supported by DON: the user interface presentation design assistant [16]. This approach applies design rules to generate menu and dialog box presentations, which can be customized by the designer to influence widget positioning.

Most model-driven UI development approach or frameworks that operate at design time use manually created layout or presentation models [27, 29]. Noteworthy in this context is SketchiXML [5] that provides an approach to transform hand drawn UI sketches, also known as wireframes or mock-ups, in UI specifications based on UsiXML[3]. This approach does not work on the UI layout, but enables designer to express such a layout without much effort.

A model-based approach for layout generation at runtime is introduced by Feuerstack et al. [10]. Their layout model consists of a list of ordered statements which is interpreted at runtime. A layout model generator with a graphical editor is provided to facilitate the layout model creation for the designer. The runtime interpretation of the layout model makes their approach adaptable to new contexts of use, but it also makes the resulting UI less predictable for the designer. The same goes for the approach of Keränen and Plomp [14]. They adapt existing layouts to devices with a smaller screen size through splitting.

The Automated Interface Layout (AIL) [20] approach creates the layout of digital library query results for a given screen size. This approach works at runtime and assigns vertical space to each query result, before creating its horizontal layout. AIL automatically scrolls vertically if insufficient screen real estate is available. SUPPLE, by Gajos et al. [11], is another runtime UI generation approach that automatically generates the UI layout based on a hierarchical model of widgets, having weights for selection and placement. Gajos et al. suggest that users may be willing to sacrifice predictability if the alternative has a large-enough improvement in adaptation accuracy.

Kennard and Leaney [13] define five key characteristics that any UI generation technique would need before it should

---

[3] http://usixml.org

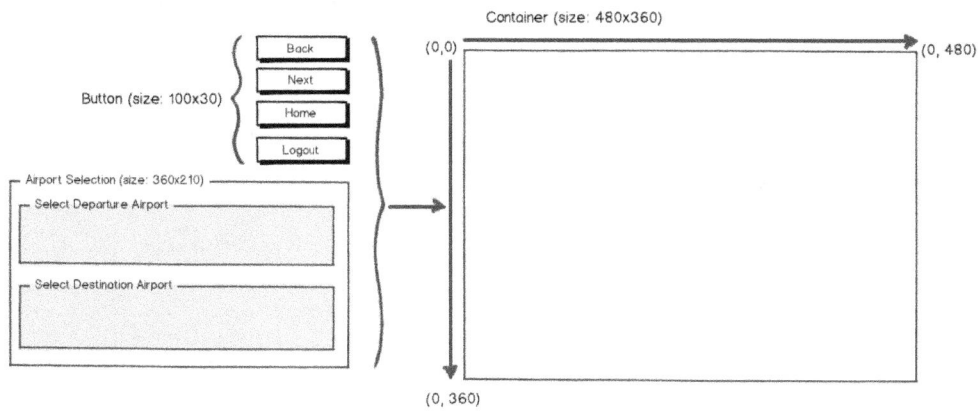

Figure 1. Flight Selection UI Widgets

expect wide adoption and built their Metawidget approach upon them. Of particular interest in the context of layout is their fifth principle: applying multiple, and mixtures of layout. They explicitly negate the use of heuristics, as heuristics would decrease the usability of the resulting UI. Furthermore, heuristics would make the approach more unpredictable for the designer, which is especially problematic if you try to replace manually created UIs with identical, but generated ones (i.e., retrofitting). For these reasons, they exclude automated layout generation from their focus and consciously limit their approach to deriving only layout facts that are constrained by the back-end architecture. This is possible, as their Metawidget approach operates at runtime.

Runtime approaches in general have the advantage that more information is available (e.g., number of list entries). Rendering and layout decisions can be based on this knowledge. The drawback is that the outcome is less predictable for the designer. Moreover, layout creation at runtime may lead to a performance degradation. Our approach is applied at design time, to give the designer control over the *look & feel* of the resulting UI, without having to create an application specific layout model.

OUR AUTOMATED LAYOUT APPROACH

This section presents our automated layout approach. We will introduce a small running example of a flight selection UI to illustrate the problem and our solution. In particular, we will use this example to describe our approach and the effects of different configuration criteria and our "Layout Hints".

Basic Layout Criteria

WIMP-UIs use containers to group widgets and are therefore structured in form of a tree. The root node of such a UI tree must be a container (e.g., a frame) and the leaf nodes are the concrete interaction widgets (e.g., buttons, labels, etc.). The intermediate levels are populated by containers that group widgets, which can again be containers or concrete interaction widgets. Each of these containers specifies the layout for its direct children. Hence, the overall screen or frame layout is composed of the layout of all its sub containers.

Our automated layout approach exploits the hierarchical UI structure and creates the overall screen layout bottom-up, in

steps for each level. By creating the overall layout step wise, we can reduce the complexity of the problem to placing a container's direct children. Creating more complex UIs is a matter of applying our technique with a larger number of steps, because more complex UIs have a deeper hierarchical structure. This is adequate for supporting scalability.

Let us illustrate the problem of placing a container's direct children with a simple flight selection UI. The left side of Figure 1 depicts the widgets that are on the same structural level of this UI. In particular, they are the direct children of the container depicted at the right side of the figure. The selected level contains four buttons (*Back*, *Next*, *Home* and *Logout*) and one container (*Airport Selection*). This container contains the two containers Select Departure Airport and Select Destination Airport, which contain the concrete interaction widgets (e.g., drop-down lists) to select the departure and the destination airport. These widgets are not depicted and the containers are grayed out, because they are on lower levels in the UI hierarchy.

Our layout approach is built on the assumption that the size of each widget that shall be laid out is available. We will show how we satisfy this requirement in the next section. For now, the challenge is to fit the widgets displayed on the left side of Figure 1 into their container. So, how to start? We implemented our approach analogously to the real world problem of how to fit your stuff in your suitcase. Most probably you will start with the big things first, because you can fit in the smaller ones later more easily. So what does big in our context mean? We opted for three different criteria: widget *area*, *width* and *height*. The widgets can now be ordered according to one of these criteria and placed in their container. Overall we try to avoid scrolling. Therefore, we start placing the widgets on the upper left corner. In case that the widgets don't fit in the container we try to rather exceed the container height than the container width, because UI guidelines [23] and other state of the art approaches [14, 20] suggest that users prefer vertical over horizontal scrolling.

After the insertion of each widget, we use a right-bottom strategy [3] to get the next placement options. Figure 2 illustrates this strategy with our running example. The Airport Selection container in Figure 1 is the widget with both,

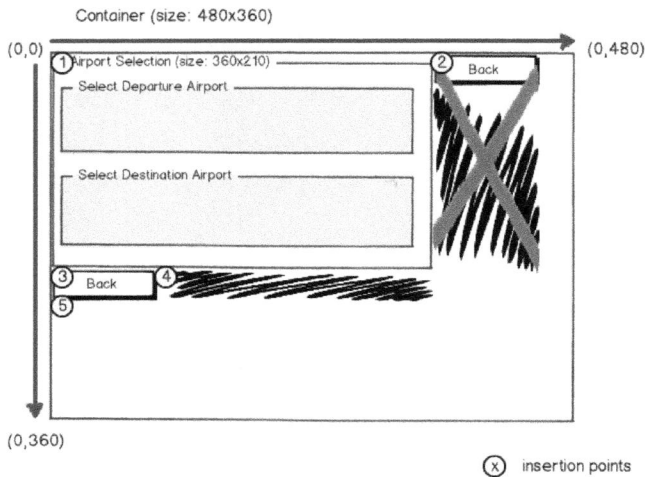

Figure 2. Placement Options and Evaluation

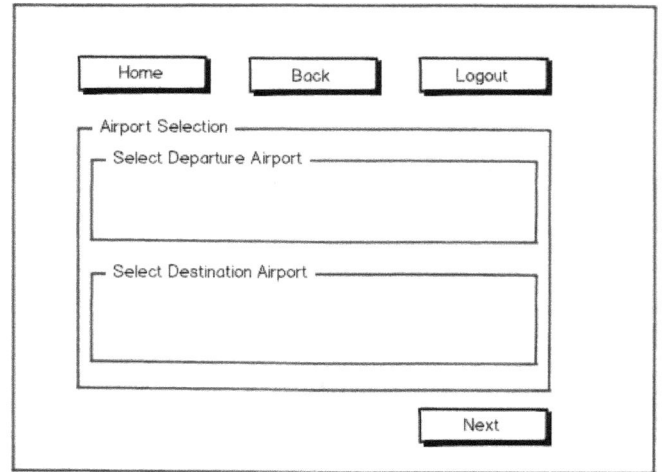

Figure 3. Flight Selection UI with Layout

the largest width and height, and thus also the largest area. Therefore, we have to insert this widget first at insertion point 1 (i.e., position (0,0)), independently of sorting criteria. The new placement options for the next widgets according to the right-bottom strategy are insertion point 2 (position (361,0)) and insertion point 3 (position (0,211)). Insertion point 1 is already occupied and therefore removed. The next widget according to our criteria is one of the buttons. Our approach offers the designer to choose between the criteria *smallest waste space* and *best ratio*, to influence the selection of the insertion point. To find the best option, we insert the new widget at each point and subsequently cut the container at the right most and the lowest widget edge. Next, we evaluate each insertion point according to the selected criteria. *Smallest waste space* means that we compare the space that is left empty in the cut containers (see the scratched out areas in Figure 2). *Best ratio* means that we compare the width/height ratio of the cut containers with a given value.

We used the least waste space criteria to insert the back button at insertion point 3 in Figure 2 (the second best option is crossed out). After inserting each widget, we update the available insertion points. This means that the right - insertion point 4 (position (101,211)) - and the bottom point - insertion point 5 (position (0,241)) - are added after the insertion of the back button. The now occupied point (insertion point 3) is not available anymore and therefore removed. Our approach repeats these steps for each widget. In case of the running example, we are able to fit all widgets in the container. The resulting UI will nevertheless not satisfy the user, because all buttons will be placed beneath the Airport Selection container and the next button will not be in the lower right part, where users might most probably expect it.

Figure 3 shows what we consider an adequate layout for our running example. Unfortunately, simply reversing the widget ordering criteria from biggest to smallest first will not lead to this UI either for two reasons. First, our criteria cannot distinguish the buttons. This makes their sequence arbitrary and most probably not the desired one. Second, the next but-

ton will be placed above the Airport Selection container instead of below. We think that figuring out the right sequence of interaction objects without the consideration of their functionality is not possible. So far, we use the ordering of the corresponding high-level model elements that they represent as a heuristic. According to our experience, this does still not lead to the right order in most cases. One reason might be that the order of elements does not matter for temporal operators that model concurrency in high-level models (e.g., the CTT [28] concurrency operator, or the Joint in discourse-based Communication Models [7]). The position of a widget on the screen however, is closely related to its functionality. To the best of our knowledge, there is no standard to specify a widget's behavior. To solve the problem of where to place a child widget, we introduced 'Layout Hints'.

Layout Hints

Our Layout Hints can be used to assign any UI widget to a certain region in its parent container. They support the divide and conquer principle, which means that they split a container in different regions and distribute the widgets to them. Our reasoning is that if you have less widgets to place, you have less options. This increases the chance to create the desired option, or at least an option that is as close to the desired one as without splitting.

The left side of Figure 4 shows that we distinguish three different sections - TOP, MIDDLE, BOTTOM. Each of these section is divided in three regions - LEFT, CENTER, RIGHT. Thus, we can distinguish nine different regions in total. Our Layout Hints introduce the vertical alignment options *top* and *bottom* and the horizontal alignment options *left* and *right* to identify each of these nine regions. Figure 4 depicts how these options need to be combined to target a certain region. The NO_ALIGNMENT region contains all widgets without Layout Hints. Our Layout Hints also support the specification of an integer as *z-index*. The z-index is used to refine the widget order of widgets within the same region. A widget with a higher z-index gets placed first. Layout Hints can be assigned to widgets either by the designer, when creating

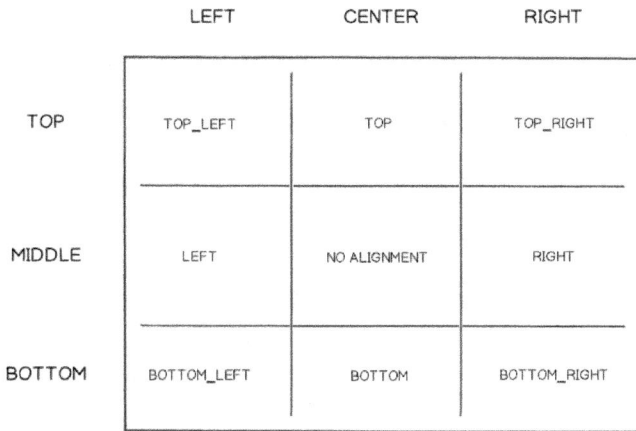

Figure 4. Container Division

a transformation rule, or by the framework, when it creates new widgets during the transformation process (e.g., buttons for navigation in case that containers are split). Our layout module evaluates these Layout Hints and places each widget in the specified region of its container.

The regions of a container are rarely equally populated. A common scenario is a crowded NO_ALIGMNENT region and empty LEFT or RIGHT regions. This means that the width and height of each region have to be adapted for each container. Our approach uses two steps to perform this adaption. First, we split the container's height between *top*, *middle* and *bottom* section. The width of each section is equal to the container's width. In the second step, we split each section's width between their *left*, *no_alignment* and *right* region. We use the minimum area required by each region (i.e., the sum of all its child widget areas) for this calculation. We then use our automated layout approach to place the widgets in each region. After each region, we refine the width calculation for the subsequent region(s). After we finish one section, we refine the height calculation for the subsequent section(s). This way we create the layout for each container stepwise, through layouting each of its regions.

Table 1 shows which Layout Hints would create the layout of our "ideal" flight selection UI in Figure 3. The table shows that each region contains only one widget, which makes the problem trivial and leads to the desired layout for sure. Alternatively, the designer could use the Layout Hint alignment-y top for the home, back and logout button and ensure the correct sequence through different z-index values.

Widget	Layout Hint
Home Button	alignment-y: top
	alignment-x: left
Back Button	alignment-y: top
Logout Button	alignment-y: top
	alignment-x: right
Next Button	alignment-y: bottom
	alignment-x: right

Table 1. Layout Hints for Flight Selection UI

Our example illustrates that our Layout Hints enable the designer to capture non-functional requirements concerning the layout that cannot be captured in high-level models. Layout Hints only demand less effort, in comparison to a manually created layout model, if they are reusable. We therefore support their incorporation in the RHS of transformation rules. Advantages of Layout Hints with regard to the state-of-the-art are the following:

- Layout Hints are attached to the child element of a container, thus requiring no further specification in the container.

- This simply requires copy and paste of a transformation rule and the adjustment of the Layout Hint, in comparison to creating a specific layout, specified in a transformation rule, for each container.

- Layout Hints express layout specifications at the same level of abstraction than constraint-based approaches, but with less effort because of their propagation.

- Layout Hints are incremental. As opposed to algorithms and constraint-based approaches, it is not necessary to process the whole algorithm or set of constraints to be satisfied in order to obtain a layout.

- First tests suggest that our approach requires less effort than fully manual development, especially if more than one UI is developed for the same application.

The integration of our layout approach into a model-driven WIMP-UI generation framework is presented in the next section.

INTEGRATION IN A WIMP-UI GENERATION FRAMEWORK

We incorporated our layout approach in the *Unified Communication Platform*[4] *User Interface generation framework (UCP:UI)* [8]. This UI generation framework uses its own EMF[5]-based rule language to transform discourse-based Communication Models [7] into Structural UI models. We integrated our new approach in this framework in two steps. First, we extended the rule language to incorporate our Layout Hints. Second, we extended the framework's layout module [17]. In particular, we refined its widget size calculation and adapted it to incorporate our Layout Hints.

Widget Size Calculation

We use a depth first algorithm to traverse the UI structure and create the layout bottom up. This means that only the size for non-container widgets has to be provided, as they are the leaf nodes of the UI tree. The size of containers is calculated after their layout has been created.

The most direct way to specify width and height of a widget is to set the corresponding attributes of the widget in the transformation rule. Additionally, we support the specification of width and size in Cascading Style Sheets (CSS). This allows style specifications via id, class and element. However, designers rarely use these option, because most transformation

---

[4]http://ucp.ict.tuwien.ac.at

[5]http://www.eclipse.org/modeling/emf/

95

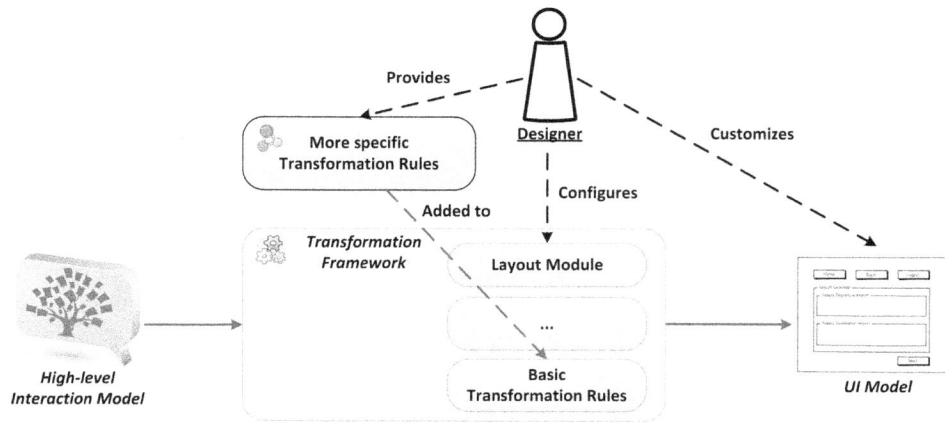

Figure 5. Integration of our Approach in UCP:UI

rules transform content that is only known at the time when they are applied and not at the time when they are designed. This means that a size specification at rule design time is not possible. To add flexibility in this regard, we introduced support for only width or height specifications. We then calculate the missing value automatically during the transformation process. This calculation is either based on static text, or default character numbers for widgets that handle text. Static text can be specified in the transformation rule, or is completed at the time of transformation. Default character numbers can be specified at the corresponding attributes in the domain model elements.

Width and height for a container are calculated after it has been laid out. List widgets are special containers in this regard. Their size, except for drop down lists, is determined by how many of their entries shall be visible. Our approach creates the layout for one entry and calculates the list's size, using default values for the number of visible entries. The layout module also uses default values for each widget type's size and width, in case that no other specification is available. All default values are defined in a configuration file, which can be adapted by the designer according to her needs.

Layout in UCP:UI

The integration of our layout approach in UCP:UI is illustrated in Figure 5. The layout module is part of the transformation framework, among other modules, and provides the implementation of the above presented concepts. The designer configures the layout module according to her needs.

Table 2 summarizes the configuration options for the designer. The *scrolling* options do not contain the value *none*. The reason is that this would lead to containers that have no valid layout, in case that the widgets cannot be fit in the given size. The available scrolling options guarantee that our approach is able to create a layout for any container. The *widget ordering* options influence the sequence in which widgets are inserted in their container. The designer can use the z-index in our Layout Hints to directly influence this widget order. Generic ordering options are hard to find, because the placement of widgets is highly dependent on their functionality

and therefore application specific. The *insertion strategy* options are evaluated to sort potential insertion points for a widget. Which insertion points are available is influenced by the scrolling option. Finally, the designer can adapt the *default widget property* values for width and height of each widget type.

Property	Options
scrolling	both, horizontal, vertical
widget ordering	biggest/smallest first according to width, height, area
insertion strategy	smallest waste space, best ratio
default widget properties	width, height

Table 2. Layout Module Configuration

Model driven UI generation approaches usually consider device constraints, like screen size or widget toolkit, during the rendering process. This means that information like the size of the root container (i.e., frame or screen) is usually available, while the size of its sub containers is typically unknown. Designers rarely use the option to explicitly specify the size for a sub container at design time, because the exact number or type of its child widgets depends on the structure of the high-level model and is thus not available at rule design time. Our Layout Hints resolve this problem, because they are attached to the child element instead of the container. However, an exact size calculation of a container is impossible without a valid layout. So, we need the exact size of each container to calculate its layout and we need the layout to calculate its exact size. This is the good old chicken or the egg causality dilemma. We solved this problem by using the *best ratio* option in case that no size is available for a container. We obtain the size of the root container from a target device specification and calculate the size for each region based on the minimum area of the direct children. The minimum area for a container is simply the sum of all its child areas and can always be calculated, as the size of the leaf nodes is always available.

Figure 5 shows that UCP:UI provides a set of basic transformation rules. These rules are independent of a certain Communication Model and guarantee that every correctly specified Communication Model can be transformed into a UI Model. The independence of a certain Communication Model is provided through a two step transformation process [12] and supports the reuse of the transformation rules. UIs that are generated with the basic rule set are fully functional and allow early testing of the application logic, but they hardly ever satisfy the user. Figure 5 shows that the designer can additionally provide more specific transformation rules. These transformation rules are added to the existing rules and usually render application domain specific concepts in the desired way. If the designer used mockups or wireframes during an initial design phase she can include the layout specifications in the UI model part (RHS) of a specific transformation rule. Direct layout specifications can be defined only within one UI model part of a transformation rule. This means that direct specification is not possible in case that one transformation rule creates the container, and other transformation rules create the UI model parts that populate it. Our Layout Hints can be used in this situation, to roughly specify the placement for a child in its container.

Let us illustrate the implications of the two-step transformation process and the effect of our Layout Hints with our running example. Figure 6 shows a transformation rule that transforms a *ClosedQuestion-Answer Adjacency Pair*. The upper part of the figure shows the Communication Model pattern that this rule matches (i.e., the rule's left hand side(LHS)). The root of the LHS is the Discourse element, which contains an Adjacency Pair with an opening Communicative Act of the type *ClosedQuestion* and the corresponding *Answer* as closing Communicative Act. The content of the Closed Question is specified as `many EObject`. This discourse pattern models the interaction, where the system provides a list of objects and the user selects one. Our running example uses this construct to model the airport selection. The objects are Airport concepts with the two String attributes *name* and *code*.

The UI model part that is created by this transformation rule (i.e., its RHS) is depicted in the lower part of Figure 6. The root container of this rule is the `ClosedQuestion-Answer` panel. The attached Layout Hint assigns this panel to the top region of its parent container. Its direct children are the `Heading` label, the `ClosedQuestion` foldout list and the `Send Answer` button. A fold out list is a container, which in case of our transformation rule contains an abstract `Output Placeholder`. All Placeholders are substituted through concrete widgets during the second step of the transformation process [12]. Placeholders are quite useful, because they support the specification of generic transformation rules, independently of domain elements. On the other hand, they make the direct layout specification within one UI model part of a transformation rule tricky, because it can be replaced by more than one widget.

Figure 6 shows that the layout has been specified explicitly for each widget in the rule's UI model part. All containers use a `Grid Layout` and their direct children have the corresponding `Grid Layout Data` attached. Each placeholder

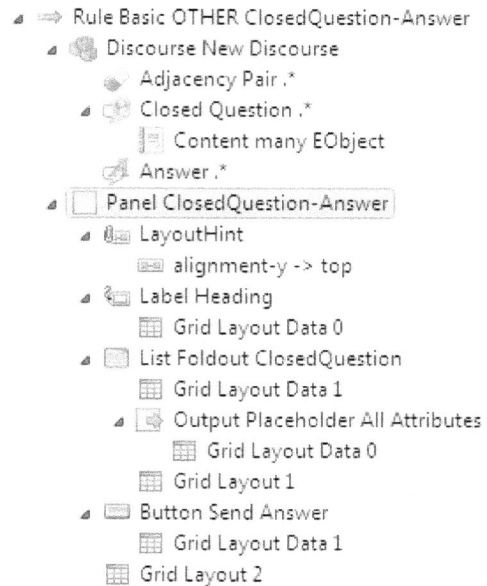

Figure 6. Transformation Rule

specifies an OCL statement that is evaluated on the domain model object that is transformed by the transformation rule, during the second transformation step. This step creates concrete interaction widgets according to the result of the OCL statement. For example, the OCL statement *"eAllAttributes"* leads to the creation of one widget for each attribute of the domain model object that is transformed. In case of our running example a label for the (Airport) *name* and one for the (Airport) *code* is created. At rule design time, however, layout data can only be specified for the placeholder widget. In case that a placeholder is replaced by more than one widget, the layout needs to be completed and adapted after the second transformation step.

In UCP:UI the transformation is completed before the resulting UI is passed on to the layout module. It is not possible for the layout module to distinguish between widgets that have been created in the first and the second step. This means that partial layout is difficult to achieve without adding extra information during the transformation. We opted for the solution to adjust the layout data directly after each second transformation step. To achieve this, we added the possibility to specify a *replacement direction* (either *vertical* or *horizontal*) for each placeholder widget. After the second step has been completed, we add layout data to the widgets created by this step and adjust the layout data for all widgets that need to be moved due to the new ones. We additionally added the possibility for the designer to explicitly specify whether a container shall be laid out or not after the transformation process has been completed. This ensures that the manually specified layout in the transformation rule is preserved. Furthermore we gain performance, as our approach can easily recognize whether a layout shall be created or if the size of the container can be calculated directly.

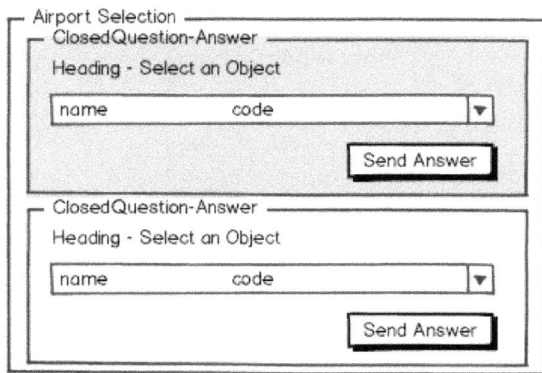

Figure 7. Transformation Result

The gray part of Figure 7 shows the resulting UI after the application of our transformation rule. Our Grid Layout Data offers similar characteristics as Java Swings's GridLayoutData. This means that alignment and fill options can be defined in addition to the positioning (i.e., row, column, rowspan, colspan). The drop down list shows that the Output Placeholder was substituted by two labels, and that the layout was adjusted horizontally (as defined by the corresponding attribute of the Output Placeholder).

If we apply the same rule again, to transform another Adjacency Pair that models the ClosedQuestion for the Destination Airport, we would create the lower part of Figure 7. The repeated application of the same transformation rule assigns the destination airport selection again to the top region of the container. If the designer wanted to explicitly assign it to the bottom, she would have to copy the rule and adjust the Layout Hints of the container. Another problem where our Layout Hints are quite useful, are the two Send Answer buttons. Here, the user would most probably expect one button to send both answers (i.e., selected airports) at the same time. Our framework combines these buttons based on the dynamic model of the UI [30]. In effect, it creates a new button that sends all answers. This button is added to the original buttons' closest common parent for which a layout is created. Our Layout Hints provide the possibility to assign this button to the bottom right region, which is presumably the area where a user would expect a button to submit her data or to proceed to the next screen.

Figure 3 shows the concrete UI for our running example. This UI results from applying the transformation rule in Figure 6 twice, combining the *Send Answer* buttons in Figure 7 to a *Next* button and using the Layout Hints of Table 1 in the transformation rules that create the *Back*, *Home* and *Logout* buttons. The Layout Hint for the *Next* button is automatically attached by the framework when it combines the *Send Answer* buttons.

Our running example illustrates that the initial layout is brought to UI models in UCP:UI in three steps. First, layout data can be defined manually in the UI model part of each transformation rule. Second, the layout data is completed and adjusted by the transformation framework after the comple-

tion of each second transformation step. Third, missing layout data is calculated and added by our layout module. Figure 5 shows that the designer can finally perform additional layout modifications on the UI model. This is important, as we do not think that a specific layout can be generated fully automatically and we therefore want to provide a good entry point to compensate still existing shortcomings.

DISCUSSION & OUTLOOK

This section discusses issues that we consider worth improving and underlines decisions that we took during the development of our approach. We also highlight challenges that we see for future development and give a short outlook on our next steps.

Regarding our automated layout approach, we think that the widget ordering strategies should be extended. The challenge here is to relate the ordering to the function of each widget. One possible solution is to provide further hints or annotations (e.g., "Ordering Hints") in the high-level model. What troubles us is that this information belongs to another level of abstraction. As a justification for this idea we can report on our experience with interaction designers in previous projects. Most of them used mock-ups that they refined iteratively in various analysis and design phases. Mock-ups can be easily created and provide the possibility to get early feedback from end users. They can then be adapted without much effort in each iteration. Additionally, they provide the advantage to capture non-functional (e.g., style or layout) requirements and explore different options. High-level task or interaction models provide the means to capture the sequence and content of the interaction, but there is already more information available if these models are created based on mock ups. The layout information for example could be encoded in such "Ordering Hints" that are attached to the corresponding high-level model elements.

Another idea in this context is to weaken the impact of the ordering strategy. This could be achieved through a second iteration that automatically evaluates and improves the outcome of the first layout cycle. Further iterations and different evaluation criteria [3] and techniques [19] would even add more flexibility. Many evaluation approaches [26, 9] however, need to be applied at runtime, as they are based on log data which is not available at design time. Additionally, they focus more on the interaction technique than on the layout. The most important problem with automated evaluation for us is that the feedback depends on the evaluation technique and criteria [3]. Therefore, a powerful approach has to provide different placement strategies and a variety of evaluation options. It will probably take some time for the designer to figure out the right criteria and technique. In the worst case this will take even longer than the manual customizations would have taken (assuming that the result is equal in the end). We think that the probability to create a desired layout through a generic strategy is rather low. Therefore, we rather pursue the aim to automate as much as *reasonable* [6], and give the designer the possibility to provide layout hints or to override the automatically calculated values and to specify layout data on an appropriate level of abstraction manually.

Human intervention requires adequate support. We claim that manipulating layout data in our graphical tree editor is more illustrative than specifying grammar based layout constraints, but we agree that a graphical "*what you see is what you get*" editor, probably similar to the Gummy [22] UI builder, would bring a considerable improvement. Such an editor should support the creation of transformation rules and the manual adaptations of the resulting UI model through direct manipulation of layout and style data. Another important feature would be easy support for rule duplication. This allows the designer to copy a transformation rule from the basic rule set and adapt or refine it according to her needs (e.g., the same rule with different Layout Hints).

We see one of the biggest chances for improvement in automatically ensuring a basic amount of layout consistency between screens. We plan to exploit traces between widgets and high-level model elements to achieve this. Screen consistency will make manual customizations more complicated, because all other screens need to be checked for consistency in case of modification. We plan to take up this challenge based on the work of Egyed et al. [6] after we have provided adequate support for manual customizations. Adequate design support and automation will also be crucial to handle large scale UIs with many screens.

Internationalization is another point worth investigating. Flippable UIs have been introduce by Khaddam et al. [15] to adjust the layout to different ethnic backgrounds. We see here an additional challenge in different space requirements by the widgets due to different text lengths, which we will take up first.

We think that iterative design together with human intervention is required in any case for achieving high-quality UIs in a long term perspective. This is especially true for UIs that are large in terms of screen estate (i.e., screen size and resolution), because aesthetic issues are impossible to automate. Therefore, we plan to put our effort in providing adequate support for the designer in our next step. We plan to support direct layout manipulation together with adding/removing widgets through the implementation of the dynamic UI space management approach by Bell and Feiner [2]. Subsequently, we will refine our configuration properties based on the feedback that we gain through the application of our approach and include support for automated change propagation. The overall challenge related to human intervention will be to find the right balance between automation and manual changes with adequate guidance.

CONCLUSION

The layout of a UI is a crucial component for good usability. Fully automatic layout creation is possible. The downside is that such UIs will hardly ever be satisfying for the end user. The problem is that it is hard, if not impossible, to generate a specific UI based on heuristics. Specifying details however, is a cumbersome and labour-intensive task. Our approach uses heuristics that can be selected by the designer through configuration. Moreover, we provide the option to specify additional information in the form of Layout Hints. Layout Hints are part of a transformation rule's UI model part. This means

that they are reusable through reapplication of the transformation rule. The UI model part of such a transformation rule is on concrete UI level, which we consider the most appropriate one for layout specifications. The integration of our approach in UCP:UI proved the feasibility of our concepts and showed that it is sensible to accomplish the layout stepwise. Our approach can be used to efficiently create UIs for rapid prototyping and initial user evaluation. It is independent of a specific high-level model and can thus be incorporated in any model driven UI generation framework using transformation rules.

REFERENCES

1. Apple Inc. *Apple Human Interface Guidelines - User Experience*, May 2011.

2. B. A. Bell and S. K. Feiner. Dynamic space management for user interfaces. In *Proceedings of the 13th annual ACM symposium on User interface software and technology*, UIST '00, pages 239–248, New York, NY, USA, 2000. ACM.

3. F. Bodart, A.-M. Hennebert, J.-M. Leheureux, and J. Vanderdonckt. Towards a dynamic strategy for computer-aided visual placement. In *Proceedings of the workshop on Advanced visual interfaces*, AVI '94, pages 78–87, New York, NY, USA, 1994. ACM.

4. G. Calvary, J. Coutaz, D. Thevenin, Q. Limbourg, L. Bouillon, and J. Vanderdonckt. A unifying reference framework for multi-target user interfaces. *Interacting with Computers*, 15(3):289 – 308, 2003. Computer-Aided Design of User Interface.

5. A. Coyette, S. Faulkner, M. Kolp, Q. Limbourg, and J. Vanderdonckt. Sketchixml: towards a multi-agent design tool for sketching user interfaces based on usixml. In *Proceedings of the 3rd annual conference on Task models and diagrams*, TAMODIA '04, pages 75–82, New York, NY, USA, 2004. ACM.

6. A. Egyed, A. Demuth, A. Ghabi, R. Lopez-Herrejon, P. Mäder, A. Nöhrer, and A. Reder. Fine-tuning model transformation: change propagation in context of consistency, completeness, and human guidance. In *Proceedings of the 4th international conference on Theory and practice of model transformations*, ICMT'11, pages 1–14, Berlin, Heidelberg, 2011. Springer-Verlag.

7. J. Falb, H. Kaindl, H. Horacek, C. Bogdan, R. Popp, and E. Arnautovic. A discourse model for interaction design based on theories of human communication. In *Extended Abstracts on Human Factors in Computing Systems (CHI '06)*, pages 754–759. ACM Press: New York, NY, 2006.

8. J. Falb, S. Kavaldjian, R. Popp, D. Raneburger, E. Arnautovic, and H. Kaindl. Fully automatic user interface generation from discourse models. In *Proceedings of the 13th International Conference on Intelligent User Interfaces (IUI '09)*, pages 475–476. ACM Press: New York, NY, 2009.

9. S. Feuerstack, M. Blumendorf, M. Kern, M. Kruppa, M. Quade, M. Runge, and S. Albayrak. Automated usability evaluation during model-based interactive system development. In *Proceedings of the 2nd Conference on Human-Centered Software Engineering and 7th International Workshop on Task Models and Diagrams*, HCSE-TAMODIA '08, pages 134–141, Berlin, Heidelberg, 2008. Springer-Verlag.

10. S. Feuerstack, M. Blumendorf, V. Schwartze, and S. Albayrak. Model-based layout generation. In *Proceedings of the working conference on Advanced visual interfaces*, AVI '08, pages 217–224, New York, NY, USA, 2008. ACM.

11. K. Z. Gajos, D. S. Weld, and J. O. Wobbrock. Decision-theoretic user interface generation. In *Proceedings of the Twenty-Third AAAI Conference on Artificial Intelligence*, 2008.

12. S. Kavaldjian, J. Falb, and H. Kaindl. Generating content presentation according to purpose. In *Proceedings of the 2009 IEEE International Conference on Systems, Man and Cybernetics (SMC2009)*, San Antonio, TX, USA, Oct. 2009.

13. R. Kennard and J. Leaney. Towards a general purpose architecture for UI generation. *Journal of Systems and Software*, 83(10):1896–1906, October 2010.

14. H. Keränen and J. Plomp. Adaptive runtime layout of hierarchical ui components. In *Proceedings of the second Nordic conference on Human-computer interaction*, NordiCHI '02, pages 251–254, New York, NY, USA, 2002. ACM.

15. I. Khaddam and J. Vanderdonckt. Flippable user interfaces for internationalization. In *Proceedings of the 3rd ACM SIGCHI symposium on Engineering interactive computing systems*, EICS '11, pages 223–228, New York, NY, USA, 2011. ACM.

16. W. C. Kim and J. D. Foley. Don: user interface presentation design assistant. In *Proceedings of the 3rd annual ACM SIGGRAPH symposium on User interface software and technology*, UIST '90, pages 10–20, New York, NY, USA, 1990. ACM.

17. M. Leitner. Space-saving placement using a structural user interface model. Master's thesis, Vienna University of Technology (TU-Wien), Faculty of Electrical Engineering and Information Technology, Institute of Computer Technology, E384, 2010.

18. S. Lok and S. Feiner. A survey of automated layout techniques for information presentations, 2001.

19. S. Lok, S. Feiner, and G. Ngai. Evaluation of visual balance for automated layout. In *Proceedings of the 9th international conference on intelligent user interfaces*, IUI '04, pages 101–108, New York, NY, USA, 2004. ACM.

20. S. Lok and S. K. Feiner. The AIL automated interface layout system. In *Proceedings of the 7th international conference on Intelligent user interfaces*, IUI '02, pages 202–203, New York, NY, USA, 2002. ACM.

21. G. Meixner, F. Paternò, and J. Vanderdonckt. Past, present, and future of model-based user interface development. *i-com*, 10(3):2–10, November 2011.

22. J. Meskens, J. Vermeulen, K. Luyten, and K. Coninx. Gummy for multi-platform user interface designs: shape me, multiply me, fix me, use me. In *Proceedings of the working conference on Advanced visual interfaces*, AVI '08, pages 233–240, New York, NY, USA, 2008. ACM.

23. Microsoft Corporation. *User Experience and Interaction Guidelines for Windows 7 and Windows Vista*, Sept. 2010.

24. B. Myers, S. E. Hudson, and R. Pausch. Past, present, and future of user interface software tools. *ACM Trans. Comput.-Hum. Interact.*, 7:3–28, March 2000.

25. J. Nielsen. *Usability Engineering*. Morgan Kaufmann Publishers Inc., San Francisco, CA, USA, 1993.

26. P. Palanque, E. Barboni, C. Martinie, D. Navarre, and M. Winckler. A model-based approach for supporting engineering usability evaluation of interaction techniques. In *Proceedings of the 3rd ACM SIGCHI symposium on Engineering interactive computing systems*, EICS '11, pages 21–30, New York, NY, USA, 2011. ACM.

27. O. Pastor, S. España, J. I. Panach, and N. Aquino. Model-driven development. *Informatik Spektrum*, 31(5):394–407, 2008.

28. F. Paternò, C. Mancini, and S. Meniconi. ConcurTaskTrees: A diagrammatic notation for specifying task models. In *Proceedings of the IFIP TC13 Sixth International Conference on Human-Computer Interaction*, pages 362–369, 1997.

29. F. Paternò, C. Santoro, and L. D. Spano. Maria: A universal, declarative, multiple abstraction-level language for service-oriented applications in ubiquitous environments. *ACM Trans. Comput.-Hum. Interact.*, 16:19:1–19:30, November 2009.

30. D. Raneburger, R. Popp, H. Kaindl, J. Falb, and D. Ertl. Automated Generation of Device-Specific WIMP UIs: Weaving of Structural and Behavioral Models. In *Proceedings of the 3rd ACM SIGCHI Symposium on Engineering Interactive Computing Systems*, EICS '11, pages 41–46, New York, NY, USA, 2011. ACM.

31. A. Sears. Layout appropriateness: A metric for evaluating user interface widget layout. *IEEE Transactions on Software Engineering*, 19:707–719, 1993.

32. J. Vanderdonckt and X. Gillo. Visual techniques for traditional and multimedia layouts. In *Proceedings of the workshop on Advanced visual interfaces*, AVI '94, pages 95–104, New York, NY, USA, 1994. ACM.

Systematic Generation of Abstract User Interfaces

Vi Tran[1], Jean Vanderdonckt[1], Ricardo Tesoriero[1,2], and François Beuvens[1]

[1]Université catholique de Louvain, Louvain School of Management

Louvain Interaction Laboratory, Place des Doyens, 1 – B-1348 Louvain-la-Neuve (Belgium)

[2]University of Castilla-La Mancha, Albacete (Spain)

{vi.tran, jean.vanderdonckt, ricardo.tesoriero, francois.beuvens}@uclouvain.be, ricardo.tesoriero@uclm.es

ABSTRACT

An abstract user interface is defined according the Cameleon Reference Framework as a user interface supporting an interactive task abstracted from its implementation, independently of any target computing platform and interaction modality. While an abstract user interface could be specified in isolation, it could also be produced from various models such as a task model, a domain model, or a combination of both, possibly based on information describing the context of use (i.e., the user, the platform, and the environment). This paper presents a general-purpose algorithm that systematically generates all potential abstract user interfaces from a task model as candidates that could then be refined in two ways: removing irrelevant candidates based on constraints imposed by the temporal operators and grouping or ungrouping candidates according to constraints imposed by the context of use. A model-driven engineering environment has been developed that applies this general-purpose algorithm with multiple levels of refinement ranging from no contextual consideration to full-context consideration. This algorithm is exemplified on a some sample interactive application to be executed in various contexts of use, such as different categories of users using different platforms for the same task.

Categories and subject descriptors

D.2.2 [**Software Engineering**]: Design tools and techniques – *User Interfaces*. H.5.2 [**Information Interfaces and Presentation**]: User Interfaces – *Graphical User Interfaces*. I.7.2 [**Document and text processing**]: Document preparation – *Markup languages*.

General Terms

Algorithms, Human Factors.

Keywords

Abstract User Interface, Concrete User Interface, Graphical User Interface, Model-based User Interface Design, Model-Driven Engineering, User Interface Description Language, User Interface eXtensible Markup Language.

INTRODUCTION

The Cameleon Reference Framework (CRF) [3] is a conceptual and methodological framework that structures the

User Interface (UI) development life-cycle according to four levels: task and domain, abstract user interface, concrete user interface, and final user interface. In this CRF, an *Abstract User Interface* (AUI) is defined as a UI supporting an interactive task that is specified in a way that does not refer to any peculiarity belonging to the implementation world. The AUI is specified independently of any target computing platform and interaction modality that could be used for such a UI. More recently, the final report of the W3C Incubator Group on Model-Based User Interface Design [4] agreed upon the following definition:

"The Abstract User Interface (AUI) (corresponding to the Platform-Independent Model– PIM– in Model-Driven Engineering) is an expression of the UI in terms of interaction spaces (or presentation units [1]), independently of which interactors are available and even independently of the modality of interaction (e.g., graphical, vocal, haptic …). An interaction space is a grouping unit that supports the execution of a set of logically connected tasks." [19]

In order to adhere to this standard definition, UsiXML V2.1 [19] instantiates this definition by defining an AUI as a hierarchy of *Abstract Interaction Units* (AIUs), each AIU expressing the input/output required to conduct a particular task or set of semantically related sub-tasks of a task over a given domain of discourse. For this purpose, different types of AIUs are defined and may contain any AIU type.

When interested in generating a AUI from a task model and a domain model, we are generally confronted with a dilemma: on the one hand, the AUI definition should remain independent of any platform and interaction modality in order to preserve this property of independence (otherwise, the AUI is no longer called abstract); on the other hand, a general trend consists in trying to optimize the definition of potential AUIs having already in mind the constraints imposed by the target platform and interaction modality. For instance, when one desires to produce an AUI for a smartphone, consciously or unconsciously, the AUI being defined is already taking into account the constraints imposed by the target computing platform (e.g., a particular operating system on a mobile phone having a specific screen resolution) and/or the intended interaction modalities (e.g., a graphical user interface equipped with bi-touch capabilities). When the target computing platform is already decided, going through the AUI step is no longer required. Therefore, the phase of defining an AUI could be skipped. However, it may still be interesting to identify all potential AUIs that could result from a task model and then decide by progressive refinement which ones could be the most suitable for a certain context of use for a given development environment.

This paper addresses the problem of systematic generation of abstract user interfaces: first, an algorithm is provided that automatically generates all potential AUIs from a same task model; then, only AUIs relevant for a given context of use could be kept by comparing different candidates against various criteria constrained by the context of use.

Section 2 reviews the work related to the problem of identifying AUIs from a task model. Section 3 defines the three meta-models that will govern the process of systematic generation of AUIs; the task meta-model as a starting point, perhaps with the domain meta-model, and the AUI meta-model as a target point. The process of systematic generation of AUIs is detailed in Section 4, first at the outline level, then at a detailed level. The software tool that supports this process is described in Section 5. Section 6 concludes this work by summarizing the main aspects of this process and by presenting some avenues of this work.

RELATED WORK

The problem of automatically generating a UI from one or many models has been addressed extensively by many different approaches [5,7,11,13,16,17], but the problem of determining AUIs [1,8,10,12,15,18] from one or many initial models so as to initiate this process has been partially addressed. In *forward engineering*, significant work has been produced to generate one or many UIs from initial models for multiple contexts of use. Only a few of them go through the AUI level: IKnowU [8] fires rules for generating AUIs for different platforms based on task, domain, and context models. In *reverse engineering*, significant work has been produced to recover a CUI model from code (e.g., from HTML). Few of them goes until the AUI level: ReversiXML proceeds with the abstraction process until the AUI level. The observation is similar for UI retargeting, UI adaptation, etc. [20]

Bogdan *et al.* [2,7] take benefit of a discourse model to generate different AUIs for different target devices such as mobile phone, PC or PDA. However, these abstract user interfaces are completely independent of the programming languages such as Java Swing, AWT, or Windows-Forms. Discourse models are created based on human communication theories, in other words they are used to describe the human communicative acts. This approach generates UIs for multiple devices, but unfortunately its determination of the control types is not detailed. For example, one communicative act can be mapped to many control types such as a *Closed Question* communicative act mapped to a radio buttons, or a check box, or a menu.

ROAM [5] automatically generates UIs for heterogeneous platforms classified based on their capabilities such as processors, memory, screen size, and software libraries. It allows the user to migrate a UI from a specified platform to another one, provided that ROAM is installed on both.

SUPPLE [9] automatically generates a UI that is adapted to a person's devices, task, preference and abilities. This system uses various input materials to generate UIs including: user, device and task models. Moreover, it also uses a *rendering and optimization algorithm* to search the space of possible interface objects to adapt its container once the container's size has been changed by the user; and uses the *cost function* to generate styles of final user interfaces based on different parameters. Supple considers both user and device models and use well the optimization algorithms to generate user interface addressing user's subjective preferences and device capabilities.

Most approaches discussed above attempt generating a complete and executable UI for multiple platforms by using different algorithms from simple ones such as in Desktop-to-Mobile [13] or ROAM [5] to complex ones such as in SUPPLE [9]. ROAM requires that the UI designer provides various implementations for multi-platforms. In order to generate the UIs for different platforms, the UI designer has to create the different layout structures; one layout structure created is suitable to a device. Then she has to link these layout structures to the task model manually. Most steps of the UI generation process in the Supple system are performed automatically but it has also some limits e.g., this system directly generates CUIs instead of AUIs.

TOPCASED AUI [14] is an Eclipse-based modelling editor enabling designers to specify AUIs directly, without necessarily taking a task model as a starting point. This freedom has a cost: there is no analysis of the quality of AUIs resulting from this manual process.

In some aforementioned works, the use of temporal operators to link the tasks at the same abstract level has not been discussed yet. For example, in [8], the containers are specified based on the groups of tasks, but these tasks are grouped together without checking the operators between them; in practice, tasks that can also exclude each other so they cannot be grouped together. The ROAM system does not exploit the semantics of temporal operators in the generation process.

META-MODELS

This section describes the main models used in this paper including task, domain and AUI models. These models are defined within the UsiXML V2.1 framework [19].

Task Meta-Model

The task meta-model (Figure 1) represents the task decomposition view of the application in the Tasks & Concepts layer of the UsiXML framework. Inspired by the Hierarchical Task Approach (HTA), the task decomposition is defined for the tasks that can be performed independently of the situation in which a task is performed. The temporal relationship is also provided in this model. However, more information to the relationship can be added by a context model. Thus, the temporal relationship among tasks depends on the context and varies according to the context situation in which a task is performed.

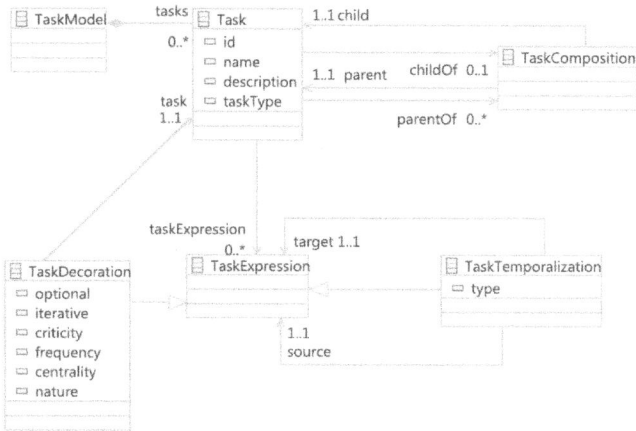

Figure 1: Task meta-model overview.

Domain Meta-Model

The UsiXML domain model describes the various entities manipulated by a user while interacting with the system. This model specifies the main concepts of a User Interface by identifying the relationships among all the entities within the scope of the User Interface, their attributes and the methods encapsulated within the entities. The UsiXML domain model uses the UML V2.0 class diagram to describe the different entities manipulated by a UI. A UML class diagram is a type of static structure diagram which provides a rich expressiveness to describe the structure of a system by using the classes, their attributes, and the relationships between the classes.

Abstract User Interface Meta-Model

The AUI model is aimed at specifying the end user interaction in terms of concepts that do not make any reference to any concrete platform or modality, which is done via the *Concrete User Interface* (CUI) [3,11,12]. Usually, AUIs are specified independently of platform and devices so that the various CUIs can be created from a single AUI. The AUI meta-model used in this paper is depicted in Figure 2 [19]. The AUI, corresponding to the Platform-Independent Model (PIM) in Model-Driven Engineering (MDE) is an expression of the UI in terms of interaction spaces (or presentation units), independently from interaction units available and from the interaction modality (e.g., graphical, vocal, haptic). An interaction unit is a grouping unit that supports the execution of a set of logically connected tasks.

ABSTRACT USER INTERFACE GENERATION

This section describes the AUI systematic generation process from task and domain models at the outline and detailed levels. At the outline level, we discuss the engineering process, the role of its components and the resources used in this process in order to identify the responsibilities to be taken for ensuring this step. At the detailed level, the main steps of the process will be overviewed as well as the mapping rules and the algorithms used so as to identify the actions that will be needed by the responsible entities of the outline level.

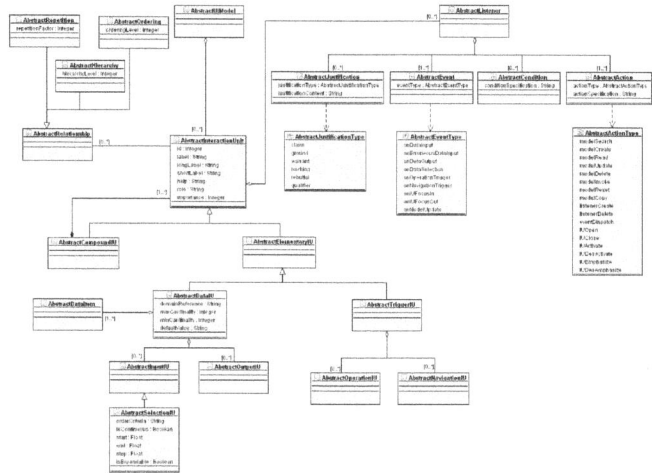

Figure 2: AUI meta-model.

Process at the Outline Level

AUI generation process and its main components are presented with respect to the UML profile for SPEM V2.0 (Software & Systems Process Engineering Metamodel specification - http://www.omg.org/spec/SPEM/2.0/). After describing components of the AUI generation process (drawn as a package), a workflow is presented and specified that details package activities and work-products.

AUI Generation

Figure 3 shows the principal components of the AUI generation process including three process-roles and six work-products. These work-products are the three UsiXML models (i.e., task model, domain model and AUI model) and three text documents (i.e., mapping rules, platform information and algorithm document).

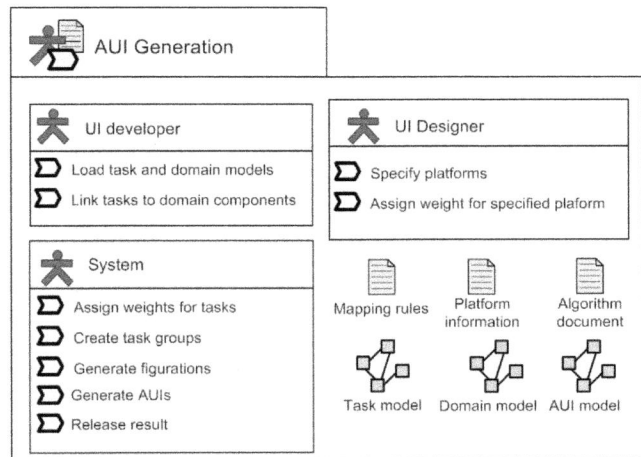

Figure 3: AUI generation and its principal components.

Workflow

Our process for generating the abstract user interface is depicted in Figure 4. This process stars with loading the task and domain models and finishes with returning the AUI model stored in terms of UsiXML specifications. The activities of the AUIs generation are depicted in order of their performance. These activities are described in Table 1. Table 2 describes the work-products used in our process.

Process at the Detailed Level

In this section, we discuss the engineering process and its main steps for the generation of AUIs from task and domain models. There are five steps namely: link tasks to domain components, assign weights for the tasks, create task groups, specify configuration and generate AUIs. In order to demonstrate the steps in this process, we use *Contact* task of eHealth application. *Contact* task describes how the information of a contact is displayed to the user and how the user can add a new contact and modify an existing one. This task has three sub-tasks: *View a contact, Search contact,* and *change phone number* (Figure 5).

Step 1: Link tasks to domain components and relation between the task and domain models

As discussed above, AUIs are generated based on the task and domain models. These models are considered for the following reasons:

- *The task model constraint the AUI.* It expresses how the UI provides information to the user and how the actions that users and system perform can be sequenced. This expression is intended to be independent of any particular implementation or technology. This explains why a same model or set of models could initiate several different UIs, whether they are abstract or concrete. However, the amount of possible AUIs that could be generated from a same task model depending on its configuration is not infinite.

- *The domain model provides the special features needed for creating a user interface.* These features are the attributes of the objects in the domain model, the relationships between these objects and prototype of the generic application functions. The domain model is used to specify the control of this user interface – at this level the user interface is specified more in details.

Two these models are related to each other. The relationship between the task and domain models can be described like the connections between the domain components and the tasks themselves that enable the user to perform operations on the domain objects. These operations are creating, deleting, modifying or selecting the objects in domain model. The UI is specified by selecting the elements of a domain model for the relevant tasks [19]. Before generating different abstract user interfaces for the different platforms, the tasks in task model will be linked to the components in domain model by the developer. The leaf tasks are linked to the components in domain model; these components maybe attributes, classes, and operations (Figure 6).

Task type	Weight	Description
1	0	Unknown task
2	1	Action task
3	2	Application task
4	3	Interaction task

Table 3: Weight of tasks

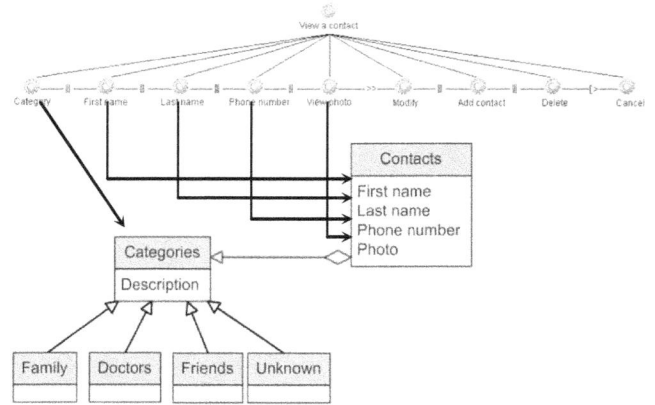

Figure 6: An example of linking tasks to domain components.

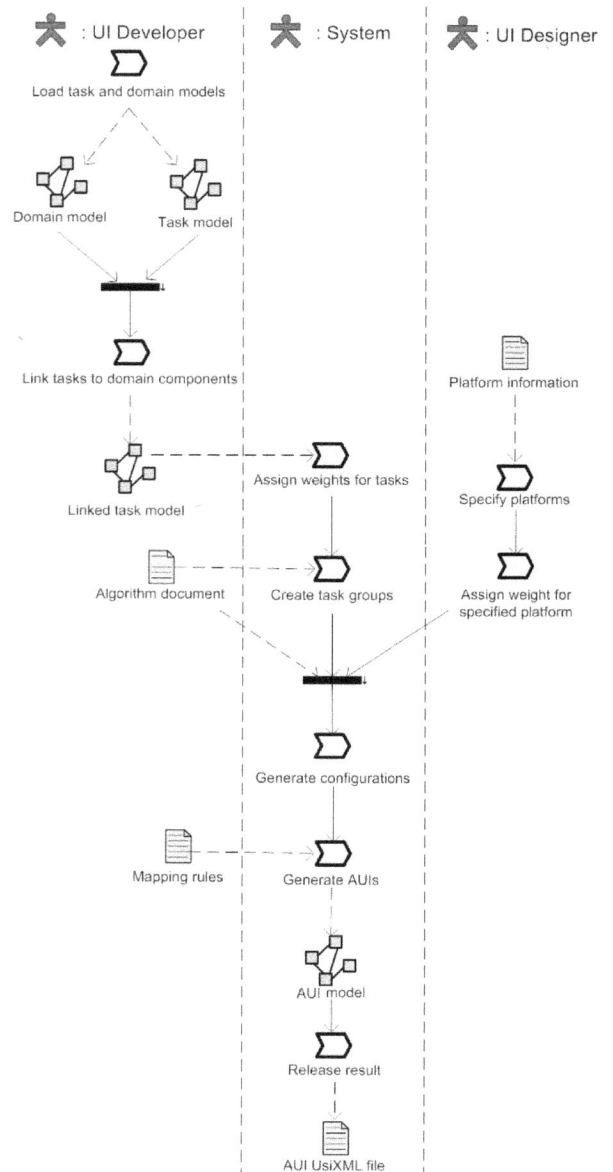

Figure 4: AUI generation workflow.

104

No	Activity name	Goal	Process role	Input	Output
1	Load task and domain models	The goal of this activity is to load task model and domain model from XML files. These files are created by UsiXML tool.	UI Developer	XML files	Task and domain models
2	Link tasks to domain components	Once task and domain models have been loaded, the tasks in task model are linked to the components in the domain model by the UI developer.	UI Developer	Task and domain models	Linked task model
3	Specify platforms	The platform on which generated user interfaces will be run is specified based on a text document. The aim of this activity is to provide the platform information such as screen size, type, …	UI Designer	Text document	
4	Assign weight for specified platform	The different platforms are assigned different weights by the UI designer.	UI Designer		
5	Assign weights for tasks	The tasks in task model will be assigned weights based on the task types. For example the weight of an action task is 1 and the one of an application task is 2.	System		
6	Create task groups	Tasks will be grouped together to create all possible combinations.	System	Linked task model	Task groups
7	Generate configurations	Once the tasks have been grouped and the platform specified, the system generates configurations suitable to this platform by selecting task groups created during the previous activity.	System		
8	Generate AUIs	AUIs are generated automatically based on the configurations and the mapping rules.	System		AUIs model
9	Release result	The AUI is stored in terms of UsiXML specifications.	System		XML files

Table 2: Work-products description.

Work-product name	Type	Description
Task model	UsiXML model	The task model is a model structured in Figure 1. This model is used to describe the user's tasks.
Domain model	UsiXML model	The domain model is a model structured in Figure 2. This model is used to describe data objects and the associations between these objects
AUI model	UsiXML model	The AUI model describes the AUIs defined by UsiXML.
Mapping rules	Text document	The mapping rule list describes the rules that are used for specifying the AUI's types.
Platform information	Text document	The platform information describes the platform's parameters.
Algorithm document	Text document	The algorithm document describes all algorithms used in AUI generation process.

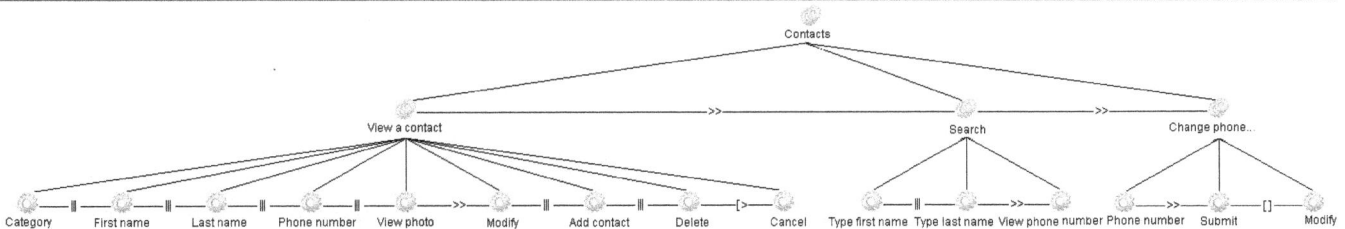

Figure 5: Contacts task model.

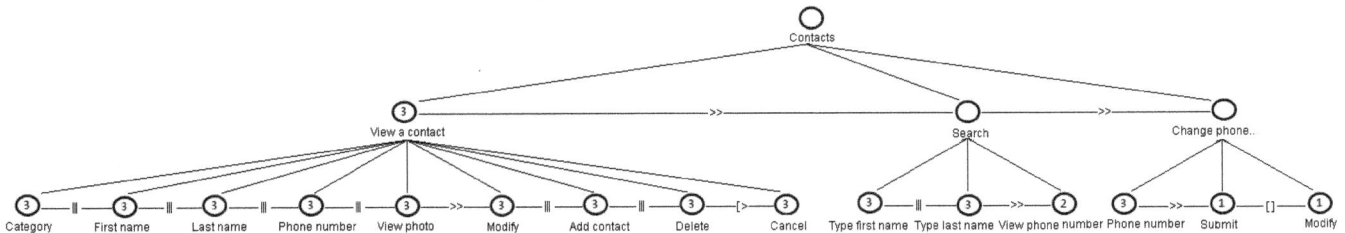

Figure 7: Tasks in task tree are assigned weights based on the task types (See Table 3).

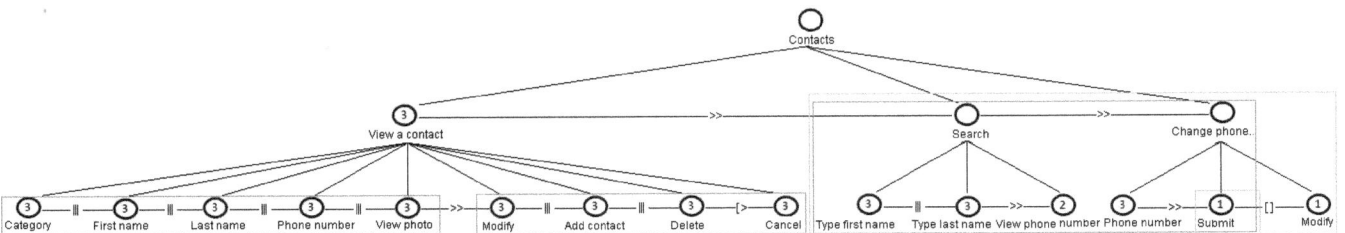

Figure 10: The configuration is based on the task weight and device weight.

105

The algorithm for specifying task weights is depicted as follows:

```
FOR each task of task model
   IF task type is action task THEN
      SET task weight to 1
   ELSE IF task type is application task THEN
      SET task weight to 2
   ELSE IF task type is interaction task THEN
      SET task weight to 3
   ELSE
      SET task weight to 0
   END IF
END FOR
```

Figure 7 depicts the result of running the algorithm with the task tree from Figure 6.

Step 3: Create task groups
This phase is decomposed in two sub-steps. The first one tries to find all of the possible groups of tasks without examining operators between these tasks (Figure 8). The second one will reject the unsuitable task groups from the ones created in the first sub-step (Figure 9). These are the ones that contain at least two adjacent tasks that the operator placed between these tasks is not suitable to the original task mode.

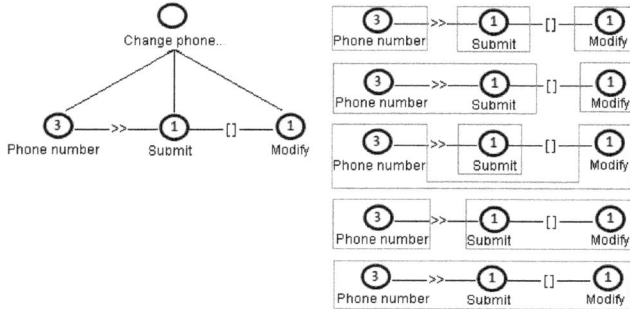

Figure 8: An example of task grouping.

The algorithm for creating task groups is depicted as follows:

```
RESET Vector taskGroups
INITIALIZE numOfTasks
FOR N = 1 to numOfTasks
   CALL Create_Group_N_Tasks(N)
END FOR
CREATE FUNCTION Create_Group_N_Tasks(number N)
   INITIALIZE taskGroup[N]
   CALL Combination(0 ,0 ,N)
END FUNCTION
CREATE FUNCTION Combination(number startIndex,
number currentIndex, number numOfTasksInGroup )
   FOR j = startIndex TO numOfTasks - numOf-
TasksInGroup + currentIndex - 1
      SET taskGroup[currentIndex] as taskList[j]
      IF currentIndex is equal to N - 1
         taskGroups.Add(taskGroup)
      ELSE
         Combination(j+1, currentIndex + 1, N)
      END IF
   END FOR
END FUNCTION
```

The main part of the source code in Java could be implemented as follows;

```
private void Combination(int startIndex, int
                currentIndex, int numOf-
                TasksInGroup){
```

```
   for(int j = startIndex; j <= numOfTasks -
      numOfTasksInGroup + currentIndex; j++){
      taskGroup[currentIndex] = taskList[j];
      if(currentIndex == numOfTasksInGroup - 1)
         taskGroups.Add(taskGroup)
      else
         Combination (j + 1, currentIndex + 1);
   }
}
```

One example for combination function is:

```
Vector taskGroups = new Vector ();
int numOfTasks = 3;
int[] taskList = {1, 2, 3};
private void Create_Group_N_Tasks (int N){
   int[]taskGroup = new int[N];
   Combination(0, 0, N);
}
for(int N = 0; N <=; N++)
   Create_Group_N_Tasks(N);
```

The result of this program is a combination of tasks 1, 2 and 3: {1, 2, 3, 12, 13, 23, 123}

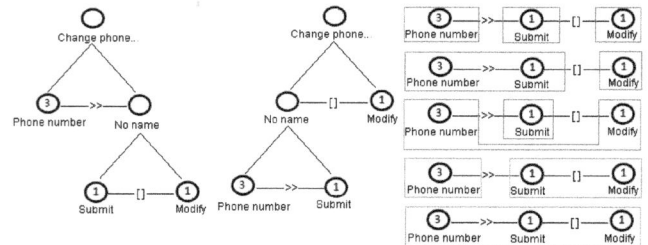

Figure 9: An example of operator check.

In order to generate valid sequences of tasks, we have formalized the definition of the task model using the Haskell programming language; which is based on lambda-calculus [6]. Lambda-calculus formalizes the function definition, application and recursion employing *Beta reduction*. Thus, we have defined a TaskExpression (TaskExp) as:

```
data TaskExp a = At a
   | En (TaskExp a) (TaskExp  a)
   | Ch (TaskExp a) (TaskExp  a)
   | Di (TaskExp a) (TaskExp  a)
   | Co (TaskExp a) (TaskExp  a)
   | Oi (TaskExp a) (TaskExp  a)
   | Su (TaskExp a) (TaskExp  a)
   | C (TaskExp  a) a
```

where a task expression is defined as an atomic task (At), a compose task (C) or any temporal relationship between temporal operations between task expressions: Enabling (En), Choice (Ch), Disabling (Di), Concurrency (Co), Order independence (Oi) and Suspend-Resume (Su). Thus, the "Change phone..." task can be expressed as:

```
C (En (At "Phone Number") (Ch (At "Submit") (At
          "Modify"))) "Change Phone"
```

To find out the valid sequences (traces) of tasks for this expression we employ the "trace" function. The following code represents part of its definition:

```
trace :: TaskExp a -> [[a]]
trace (At a)   = [[a]]
trace (C x a)  = trace x
trace (Ch x y) = trace x ++  trace y
trace (En x y) = [a ++ b |
             a<-(trace x), b <- (trace y)]
```

```
trace (Co x y) = foldr (++) []
                 [interleaving xs ys |
                    xs <- trace x, ys <- trace y]
trace (Oi x y) =
    flatten (map bt (perms (lot (Oi x y))))
```

The "trace" function takes a task expression as input parameter, and returns a list of lists of atomic task names. Each list of atomic task names represents a valid trace of tasks. The definition of the trace function is trivial for the following expressions: At, C, Ch and En. However, the rest of them require auxiliary functions, such as, "perms", "between", "interleaving", "lot", "bt". The "perms" function returns the permutation of a list of atomic task names as a list of atomic task name lists. It is defined as follows:

```
perms [] = [ [] ]
perms (x:xs) = concat (map (between x) (perms
               xs))
```

To perform the permutation, the "between" function is defined to generate all traces resulting from the insertion of an atomic task at any position of an already defined trace.

```
between e [] = [ [e] ]
between e (y:ys) = (e:y:ys) : map (y:) (between
                   e ys)
```

The "interleaving" function is linked to the concurrency operation. It takes two traces as input parameters to return a list of traces representing the concurrent execution of both traces.

```
interleaving :: [a]->[a]->[[a]]
interleaving (x:xs) [] = [x:xs]
interleaving [] (y:ys) = [y:ys]
interleaving (x:xs) (y:ys) = map (y:) (inter-
             leaving (x:xs) (ys)) ++ map (x:)
             (interleaving (xs) (y:ys))
```

The "lot" function takes a task expression, and returns the list of list of traces that represent the "composed traces" derived from the task expression passed as parameter.

```
lot:: TaskExp a -> [[[a]]]

lot (Oi x y) = lot x ++ lot y
lot t = trace t :[]
```

To generate the trace resulting from the order independence temporal operator, we apply the "bt" function on each of the list of traces generated from the result of applying the "lot" function. The "bt" function is defined as follows:

```
bt::[[[a]]]->[[a]]
bt (xss:[]) = xss
bt (xss:xsss) = [a ++ b | a<-xss, b<-(bt xsss)]
```

The result of applying the trace function to the "Change Phone..." task is: `[["Phone Number","Submit"], ["Phone Number","Modify"]]`; which reveals the valid traces only for the temporal expression. Note that "["and "]" denote a list and "," denote sequence in this case.

Step 4: Configuration is specified automatically.

Once the task groups have been created, the system automatically specifies the configurations by selecting one or more task groups. The system generates the different configurations for the different platforms based on characteristics such as screen size, processors, memory of devices. In order to do that, each platform will be assigned a max-

imum weight by the UI designer. Usually, this maximum weight is in direct ratio to the screen's size, the power of processor and memory, screen type ... The maximum weight is used to specify the number of task groups which are suitable to determined platform. The formulas for selecting task groups based on weight of task group and maximum weight are as follows:

```
Weight of a task group = ∑ Weight of its tasks
Maximum weight >= ∑ Weight of selected task
groups
```

The algorithm for selecting task groups based on the task weight and device weight is defined as follows:

```
SET current weight to 0
SET maximum weight to 15
SET current group to null
WHILE current weight is less than maximum weight
      AND group count is more than 0
   FOR each group in taskGroups
      IF current weight + group weight is less
         than or equal maximum weight AND group
         weight is less than current group
         weight
         SET current group weight to group
weight
         STORE current group as group
      END IF
   END FOR
   IF current group is NOT NULL
      COMPUTE current weight as current weight +
         group weight
      FOR each task in current group
         FOR each group in taskGroups
            IF group contains task
               REMOVE this group from taskGroups
            END IF
         END FOR
      END FOR
   ELSE
      BREAK WHILE
   END IF
END WHILE
```

Figure 10 depicts the configuration of *contacts* for a task model with a device weight of 15. In this configuration, two choices for creating the container are possible: the first one that contains: Type first name, Type last name, View phone number, Phone number and Submit; the other one that contains: Type first name, Type last name, View phone number, Phone number, and Modify

Step 5: Generating abstract user interface from task and domain models

AUIs are generated based on the mapping rules and the task groups specified manually by the developer or automatically by the system. For each created group, the system generates an AbstractCompoundIU; this AbstractCompoundIU will contain all of AUIs generated for the tasks belonging to this group. The rules for determining the AUI type are:

- **Rule1:** An AbstractSelectionUI is considered when a task derives from an attribute of a domain class which is not the edited class and the relationships between the edited class and another one is '1-1' or 'n-1'and .

- **Rule2:** An AbstractInputUI is considered when a task derives from the attributes of the classes that these classes are the edited classes.

- **Rule3:** An AbstractOutputUI is considered when an abstract user interaction has been created and its label is the task name of the task related to this abstract user interaction.
- **Rule4:** An AbstractDataItemUI is considered when a task derives from the attributes of the classes.
- **Rule5:** An AbstractTriggerUI is considered when a task derives from an operation of a class. For example. Once the tasks have been grouped by the developer based on the screen size of devices, the AUIs are generated automatically by system.

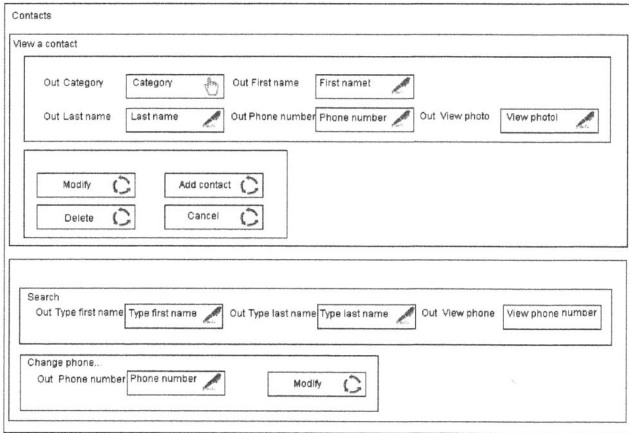

Figure 11: AUI is generated from configuration specified in Figure 10.

One of the AUI specifications generated from the configuration above is shown in Figure 11. The abstract user interface units are specified based on the following algorithm:

```
FOR each task in task list
    IF task has sub tasks
        CREATE an AbstractCompoundIU
    ELSE
        IF task type is action task OR task is
            linked to operation of class
            CREATE an AbstractTriggerIU
        ELSE IF task type is application task
            CREATE an AbstractOutputIU
        ELSE IF task type is interaction task
            IF task is linked to attributes of
class
                CREATE an AbstractInputIU
            ELSE IF task is linked to class
                CREATE an AbstractSelectionIU
            ELSE
                CREATE an AbstractInputIU
            END IF
        ELSE
            CREATE an AbstractInputIU
        END IF
    END IF
END FOR
```

SOFTWARE SUPPORT
Integrated software

The software developed to support the aforementioned process and that implements the algorithms outlined in the discussion all at once has been implemented in Java. The main purpose of the tool is to help designers to generate AUIs from the task and domain models.

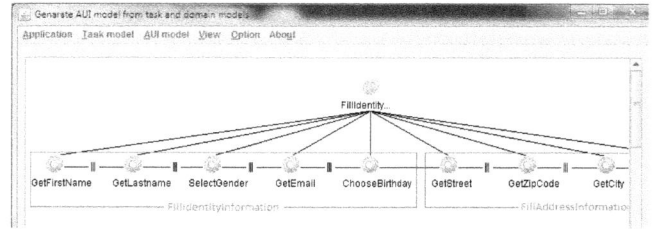

Figure 12: Task model editor.

The task model is loaded from a UsiXML file (Figure 12). Once tasks contained in the task model have been loaded, they are collected into the different groups by the designer depending on the concrete platform. The number of tasks in our task model is unlimited. There are two ways to group the tasks; the first one is that the tasks are grouped manually by the designer; and the second one is that they are grouped automatically based on the device selected by designer (Figure 13). With this tool, the designer can manipulate tasks easily with the mouse buttons and Ctrl key. In order to observe task model easily and clearly, the designer can decide which task attributes to display in the task model by using *Task model view* dialog (Figure 14).

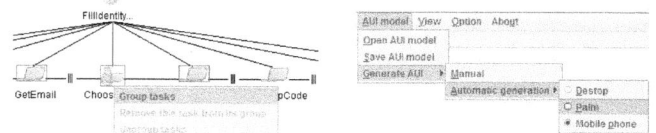

Figure 13: Grouping tasks.

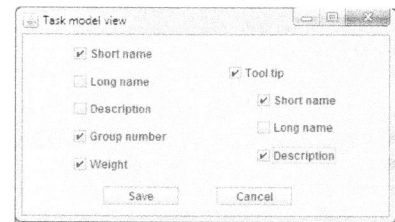

Figure 14: Selecting task attributes

The number of tasks in our task model is unlimited. In this current version, the tasks are manually linked to the components of domain model by the designer. Abstract user interfaces are automatically generated based on grouped tasks and the attributes of domain's components. Generated AUIs are stored in terms of UsiXML specification. In this version, the designer cannot directly modify automatically generated AUIs in order to preserve the rules that have been fired to obtain these results. Indeed, it the resulting AUIs are modified manually, they will no longer be consistent with the rules that were used for this generation. If the designer wants to change the AUIs, she has to modify the task group or the relation between tasks and domain's components. Our generated AUIs are depicted in Figure 15.

AUI Generation as service

The systematic generation of AUIs from a task model could be also invoked as a service from any other UsiXML compatible software.

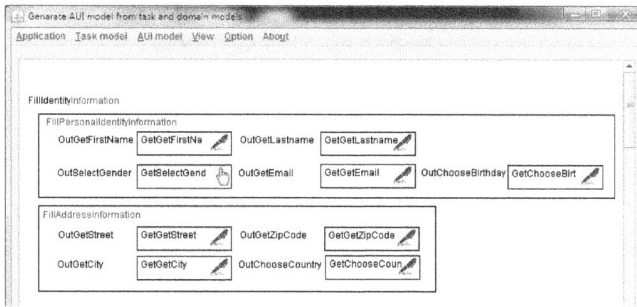

Figure 15: An example of AUI generated by our software.

For instance, Figure 16 reproduces an Eclipse-based task model editor specifying tasks according to the UsiXML V2.1 meta-model outlined in Figure 1. In this example, a simple car rental task model is depicted, with more detailed information about the sub-task FillIdentityInformation. Figure 17 details the first AUI candidates for this task by decreasing order of amount of interaction units contained and complexity, while Figure 18 shows some rendering in the integrated software.

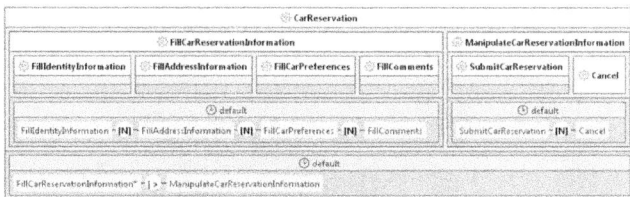

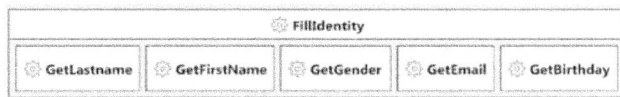

Figure 15: Task model in Eclipse-based task model editor.

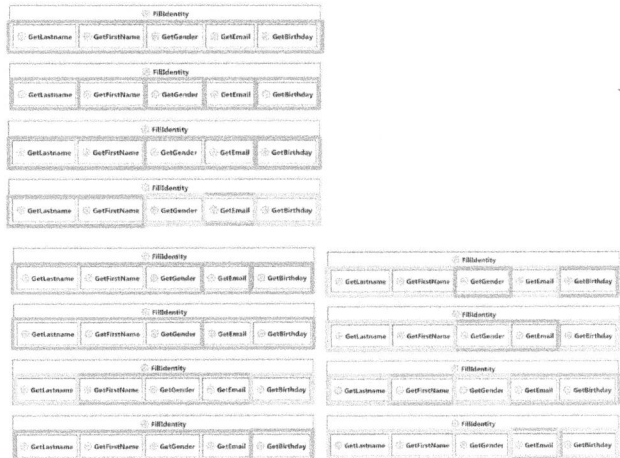

Figure 16: AUI candidates from the same task model.

CONCLUSION

In this paper, we have presented an algorithm for systematically generating all potential abstract user interfaces from a task model. Our AUI generation process has been discussed at the comprehensive and detailed levels. At the comprehensive level, we have discussed its main tasks and the resources used in the process. At the detailed level, the process is represented step by step with the rules

for specifying the abstract user interaction types and the algorithms used in each step. More specially, this paper has provided a number of necessary algorithms for an AUI generation process. In order to explore these algorithms, an editor tool has been implemented to evaluate the cost and performance of this method.

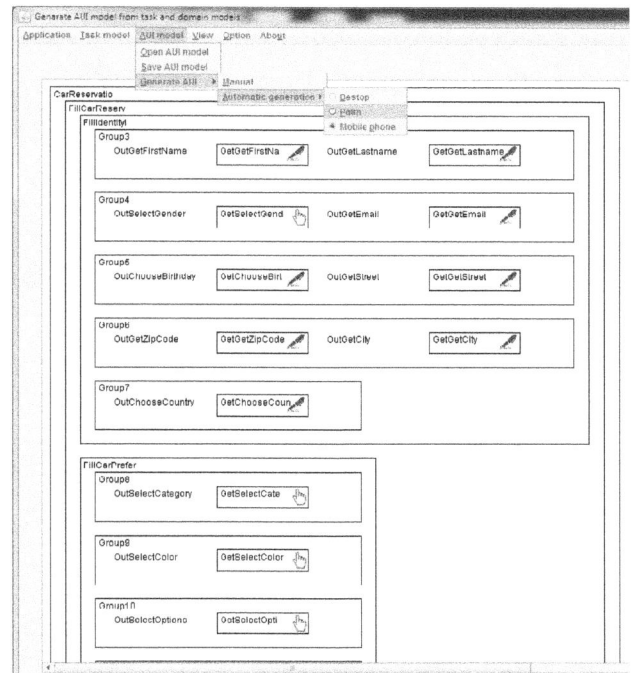

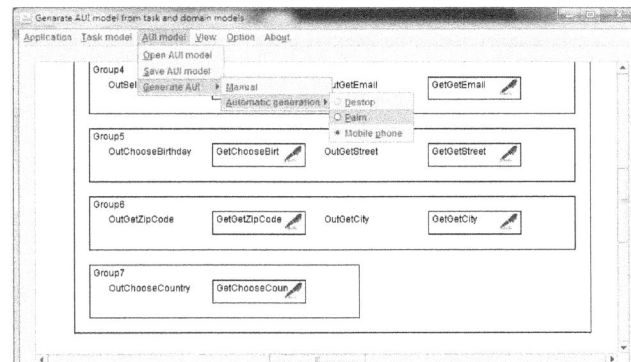

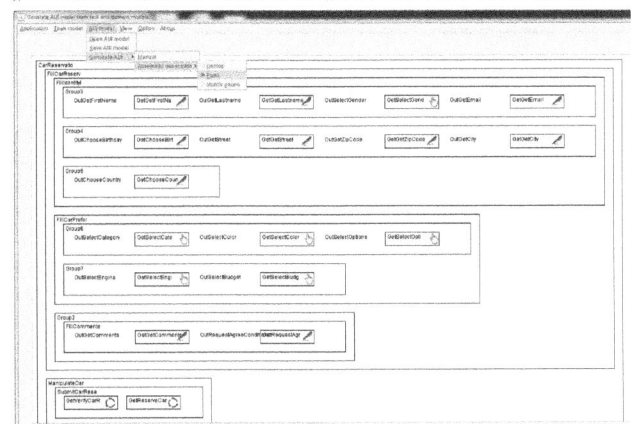

Figure 17: AUI rendered in the integrated software.

109

ACKNOWLEDGMENTS

The authors would like to acknowledge the support of the FEDER eHealth project and the ITEA2-Call3-2008026 UsiXML European project (User Interface eXtensible markup language – http://www.usixml.eu, http://www.usixml.org) and its support by Région Wallonne DGO6.

REFERENCES

1. Bodart, F., Hennebert, A.-M., Leheureux, J.-M., Provot, I., and Vanderdonckt, J. Computer-aided window identification in TRIDENT, in *Proc. of IFIP TC13 Int. Conf. on Human-Computer Interaction Interact'95* (Lillehammer, June 27-29, 1995). Chapman & Hall, London, 1995, 331–336.

2. Bogdan, C., Falb, J., Kaindl, H., Kavaldjian, S., Popp, R., Horacek, H., Arnautovic, E., and Szep, A. Generating an Abstract User Interface from a Discourse Model Inspired by Human Communication, in *Proc. of the 41st Annual Hawaii Int. Conf. on System Sciences HICSS'2008*. IEEE Computer Society, Los Alamitos, 2008, 1–10.

3. Calvary, G., Coutaz, J., Thevenin, D., Limbourg, Q., Bouillon, L., and Vanderdonckt, J. A unifying reference framework for multi-target user interfaces. *Interacting with Computers 15*, 3 (2003), 289–308.

4. Cantera Fonseca, J.M., González Calleros, J.M., Meixner, G., Paternò, F., Pullmann, J., Raggett, D., Schwabe, D., and Vanderdonckt, J. Model-Based User Interface Incubator Group, Final Report. 4 May 2010. Available at http://www.w3.org/2005/Incubator/model-based-ui/XGR-mbui/.

5. Chu, H., Song, H., Wong, C., Kurakake, S., and Katagiri, M. Roam, a seamless application framework. *J. of Systems and Software 69*, 3 (2004), 209–226.

6. Church, A. A set of postulates for the foundation of logic. *Annals of Mathematics 39*, 2 (1932), 346-366.

7. Falb, J., Popp, R., Röck, T., Jelinek, H., Arnautovic, E. and Kaindl, H. Fully-automatic generation of user interfaces for multiple devices from a high-level model based on communicative acts, in *Proc. of the 40th Annual Hawaii Int. Conf. on System Sciences HICSS-40* (Waikoloa, 3-6 January 2007). IEEE Computer Society, Los Alamitos, 2007, Track 26.

8. Furtado, E., Furtado, V., Sousa, K., Vanderdonckt, J., and Limbourg, Q. KnowiXML: A Knowledge-Based System Generating Multiple Abstract User Interfaces in UsiXML, in *Proc. of 3rd Int. Workshop on Task Models and Diagrams for User Interface Design-Tamodia'2004* (Prague, November 15-16, 2004). ACM Press, New York, 2004, 121–128.

9. Gajos, K.Z., Weld, D.S., and Wobbrock, J.O. Automatically generating personalized user interfaces with Supple. *Artificial Intelligence 174*, 12-13 (2010), 910–950.

10. González Calleros, J.M., Stanciulescu, A., Vanderdonckt, J., Delacre, J.P., and Winckler, M. A Comparative Analysis of Transformation Engines for User Interface Development, in *Proc. of 4th Int. Workshop on Model-Driven Web Engineering MDWE'2008* (Toulouse, 1 October 2008). N. Koch, G.-J. Houben, A. Vallecillo (Eds.), CEUR Workshop Proceedings, Vol. 389, 2008, 16–30.

11. Luyten, K., Clerckx, T., Coninx, K., Vanderdonckt, J. Derivation of a Dialog Model from a Task Model by Activity Chain Extraction, in *Proc. of 10th Int. Workshop on Design, Specification, and Verification of Interactive Systems DSV-IS'2003* (Funchal, June 11-13, 2003). Lecture Notes in Computer Science, Vol. 2844. Springer, Berlin, 2003, 203–217.

12. Martínez-Ruiz, F. J., Vanderdonckt, J., and Arteaga, J. M. Web User Interface Generation for Multiple Platforms, in *Proc. of 7th Int. Workshop on Web-Oriented Software Technologies IWWOST'2008* (Yorktown Heights, July 14, 2008). L. Olsina, O. Pastor, D. Schwabe, G. Rossi, M. Winckler (Eds.), CEUR Workshop Proceedings, Vol. 445, 2008, 63–68.

13. Paternò, F. and Zichittella, G. Desktop-to-Mobile Web Adaptation through Customizable Two-Dimensional Semantic Redesign, in *Proc. of 3rd Int. IFIP Conf. on Human-Centred Software Engineering HCSE'2010* (Reykjavik, October 14-15, 2010). Lecture Notes in Computer Science, Vol. 6409. Springer, Berlin, 2010, 79–94.

14. Perico, E., TopCased User Interface generator, Atos origin, 4 May 2005. http://www.topcased.org/index.php?id_projet_pere=114

15. Plomp, C. and Mayora-Ibarra, O. A generic widget vocabulary for the generation of graphical and speech-driven user interfaces. *International Journal of Speech Technology 5* (2002) 39–47.

16. Pribeanu, C. An Approach to Task Modeling for User Interface Design, in *Proc. of World Enformatika Conf. WEC'2005* (Istanbul, April 27-29, 2005). C. Ardil (Ed.). *Enformatika 5*, 2005. 5–8.

17. Schneider, K.A. and Cordy, J. Abstract User interfaces: A model and notation to support plasticity in interactive systems, in *Proc. of the 8th Int. Workshop of Design, Specification and Verification of Interactive Systems DSV-IS'2001*. Springer, Berlin, 2001, 40–58.

18. Van den Bergh, J., Luyten, K., and Coninx, K. CAP3: Context-Sensitive Abstract User Interface Specification, in *Proc. of ACM Symposium on Engineering Interactive Systems EICS'2011* (Pisa, June 13-16, 2011). ACM Press, New York, 2011, 31–40.

19. Vanderdonckt, J., Tesoriero, R., Beuvens, F., and Melchior, J. Towards a Fifth-Generation User Interface Description Language with UsiXML V2.1. Submitted to *Science of Computer Programming*, June 2012.

20. Vanderdonckt, J. Model-Driven Engineering of User Interfaces: Promises, Successes, and Failures, in *Proc. of 5th Annual Romanian Conf. on Human-Computer Interaction ROCHI'2008* (Iasi, September 18-19, 2008). Matrix ROM, Bucharest, 2008, 1–10.

Engineering Animations in User Interfaces

Thomas Mirlacher[1, 2], Philippe Palanque[2], Regina Bernhaupt[1, 2]

[1] ruwido, Köstendorferstraße 8, A-5020 Neumarkt, Austria

[2] ICS-IRIT, University of Toulouse, 118 Route de Narbonne, F-31062, Toulouse, France

thomas.mirlacher@ruwido.com, palanque@irit.fr, regina.bernhaupt@ruwido.com

ABSTRACT

Graphical User Interfaces used to be static, graphically representing one software state after the other. However, animated transitions between these static states are an integral part in modern user interfaces and processes for both their design and implementation remain a challenge for designers and developers.

This paper proposes a Petri net model-based approach to support the design, implementation and validation of animated user interfaces by providing a complete and unambiguous description of the entire user interface including animations. A process for designing interactive systems focusing on animations is presented, along with a framework for the definition and implementation of animation in user interfaces. The framework proposes a two levels approach for defining a high-level view of an animation (focusing on animated objects, their properties to be animated and on the composition of animations) and a low-level one dealing with detailed aspects of animations such as timing and optimization. A case study (in the domain of interactive Television) elaborating the application of the presented process and framework exemplifies the contribution.

Author Keywords

Animation; Interaction Design; Software Engineering Methods and Processes; User Interface Design.

ACM Classification Keywords

D.2.2 [Software] Design Tools and Techniques - Computer-aided software engineering (CASE), H.5.2 [Information Interfaces and Presentation]: User Interfaces - Interaction styles.

INTRODUCTION

While today most parts of a graphical user interface are static, animations are being increasingly used. This increase of use, especially for areas away from desktop applications, can be attributed to the fact that resources remain available after the system's main functions are executed. Areas where animations can be found include domains such as education [5,33], representation of life-like behavior on simulated objects [8,29] or support understanding of dynamic systems (e.g. programs) [17,31] and for GUIs [1].

Using animations in these application domains can decrease cognitive load [12] and increase usability, as they visually support the users in understanding the system's behavior and evolution from the current state to the future one. With animations, user interface evolutions can be represented in a "natural" way (similar to state changes occurring in an animated and continuous way in real life) possibly conveying additional information pertinent for the users' tasks.

While animations might increase usability, they also increase the complexity both for the specification and implementation of the software part of interactive systems, and therefore the probability of occurrence of faulty or undesired behaviors. For instance, the time-based nature of animations makes them hard to specify and hard to define and assess the detailed temporal behavior prior to implementation.

This paper proposes a Petri net model-based approach to bridge the gap between a multidisciplinary team responsible for the design, implementation and validation of animated user interfaces by providing a complete and unambiguous description language for defining animated interfaces. The connection of the animated behavior with the rest of the user interface is presented, making it possible to embed animations in a seamless way.

The following section starts with an overview of the engineering process representing explicit phases dealing with animation design and prototyping. It describes the engineering process from the requirements gathering to a fully animated user interface running on a dedicated execution platform. Section 2 contains an introduction of animations and classifies animations according to their type and goals and describes the properties that can be manipulated when designing and implementing animations. Section 3 together with Section 4 present the low and high fidelity prototyping of animations. Section 5 is dedicated to the motivation for modeling as well as the the formal modeling of animations. It presents the description technique used and how to handle the modeling of every component of the framework. Section 6 describes the application of the approach with a real-size case study from the Interactive Television (iTV) domain. The last section concludes the paper emphasizing the advantages and limitations of the approach and outlines future work.

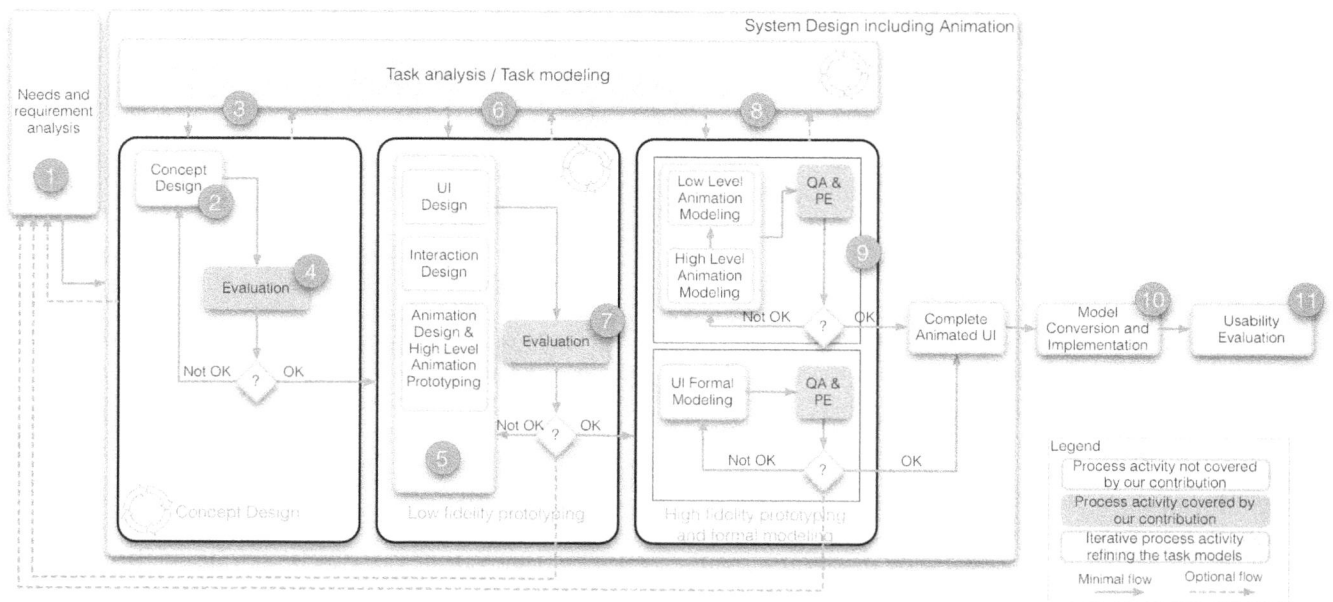

Figure 1: Development model for designing systems including animation

ENGINEERING PROCESS

Design and development of interactive animated systems is a rather complex development process (see Figure 1) involving stakeholders from multiple disciplines. When developing an interactive system, one of the first activities is a *needs and requirements analysis* ① that serves as a foundation of an iterative activity called concept design ②. In the concept design phase, the matching between design ideas and the tasks a user has to perform with the system is achieved ③. The *concept design phase* is iterative, meaning that, based on a series of (user-oriented) evaluations ④, the concept design is refined and enhanced. The result of the concept design activity is a number of mock-ups or sketches providing the groundwork for the second phase called *low fidelity prototyping phase*. The mock-ups and sketches generated in the previous phase are refined and lead to a definition of the user interface design as well as the interaction design and the interface animations. For standard software, the design of a user interface might simply consist of a selection of predefined user interface components (already having the interaction design and animation integrated), while for other software (e.g. in the area of interactive TV), this phase ⑤, ⑦ results in several iterations for designing and defining interaction as well as animation. Refinement of the design in this step will also lead to a refinement of the task models ⑥ as the artifact alters usage as described in the task-artifact cycle [7]. The *high fidelity prototyping and formal modeling* phase consists in the user interface modeling part [26] and the special iterative activity of animation modeling composed of high level and low-level animation modeling. The animation modeling can be enhanced based on a general consistency check with the refined task models ⑧. Based on quantitative analysis and performance evaluation on the prototypes ⑨, animation modeling is optimized. Animation

modeling together with the user interface formal modeling, describes the *complete animated user interface* with the foundation for *model conversion and implementation* ⑩ as well as any following process activities like *usability evaluation*.

The model conversion phase is of critical importance when the target platform might have lower capabilities than the development one. For instance, both in the area of interactive aircraft cockpits and interactive television the underlying hardware systems have strong constraints imposing additional constraints (such as CPU performance, memory limitations…) that have to be enforced in the design. The following section provides a generic introduction of animations and continues to provide a description of the sub-processes relevant for designing and defining animations in user interfaces.

ANIMATION

Animation is the illusion of movement created by displaying a series of changing pictures (or frames) in rapid sequence [30]. Each depicted frame contains only a small change, and if the frames are reproduced in a high enough frequency, the human visual system fills in the details and produces an illusion of a smooth and continuous movement, rather than a transition between discrete states.

For computer animations, two broad categories can be distinguished: computer-assisted animation and computer-generated animation. In computer-assisted animation, a classical animation is computerized and the computer provides additional support by adding effects to the animation. Computer generated animation however denotes an animation which is entirely generated by a computer system. These computer-generated animations define a time-based evolution of a sequence of images (frames).

Predefined Sequences of Images

The simplest approach to produce an animation is to use a set of predefined frames, which are computed in advance and displayed at the right point in time, for the right period of time. These frames consist of a rectangular area defined by color pixels and not moving objects [9].

Early cartoons used this stop-motion approach to create an animation. This animation is achieved by creating a sequence of still frames and by replaying them in a high enough speed so that an illusion of fluid movement emerges. Usually, if the difference between one frame and the next one is rather small and the display rate is high enough then the impression of animation is guaranteed.

Figure 2 depicts the frames of an animation of a moving ball. It shows the ball's position for each frame, which when played will generate the illusion of a ball moving from the top to the bottom and from the left to the right of the frame.

Figure 2: Linear Sequence of Images.

The restrictions for this approach are two-fold: on one hand, it is hard to alter properties of the images and thus usually all the images need to have the same size, shape, color.... On the other hand it is very difficult to adjust the animation behavior once the images are created [9].

The most time consuming part with this approach is that each frame has to be defined and (hand-)drawn (by the designer). This shows that efficient animation design requires computer support in the production of images and using keyframes together with interpolation [9].

Keyframes and Interpolation (tweening)

Keyframes [18] are frames, which define the starting and end points of a transition. These frames usually consist of objects, which are moved and or transformed from one keyframe to the next. The objects' position and appearance from one keyframe to the next, is interpolated by the computer, which is also called "inbetweening" [34] or short "tweening" and defines the means of the continuous smooth transition.

Interpolation between keyframes in the context of computer animation is an operation not performed between fully hand-drawn frames but on objects. This provides tremendous benefits in terms of efficiency when effort and time of designers are considered. Tweening can be used to interpolate the position of an object only requiring from the designer to produce the images at start and endpoint, and define the behavior in-between these keyframes. Such example is presented shown in Figure 3 (three frames between keyframes are interpolated by the system).

Figure 3: Interpolated sequence of images.

Moreover, tweening can also be used to change other properties than only the position of an object such as color and shape. This shape-changing is called morphing and represents a unique case of interpolation, which is often used for special effects and gives the impression that one object is transformed into another different one. Tweening between frames is traditionally performed by linear interpolation but can also follow non-linear (easing) rules, as defined by the tweening parameters.

LOW FIDELITY PROTOTYPING OF ANIMATIONS

When designing an animation, a designer typically starts with a design of the static representation of a user interface. This representation is usually state-based and provides a set of screens that have to be presented when the adequate event is generated by the system (typically a temporal event) or triggered by the user acting on the input devices.

To define the animation of a user interface, the stage where the animation takes place is defined first (background color/image, and elements on screen) followed by the initialization part specifying the initial position of the objects (on the stage) to be animated and their final position.

Using this information as a starting-point, the animation itself is described e.g. that a ball starts in the upper left corner of the stage and within a specified timeframe moves towards the lower left corner and slows down before it finally reaches the end-point.

Besides changing the coordinates or the position of an object (typical animation), there are a variety of other properties that can be altered to make the user perceive an animation, like opacity, color, pattern, etc.

These properties describe presentation characteristics of each object and have different sets of attributes that can be altered. For instance, animating an object using the opacity property will consist in defining the temporal evolution of an integer value ranging from 0 to 100 (usually corresponding to percentage of transparency). Similarly, altering the color of an object consists in modifying the color component parameters: R, G, and B. After being identified as animation targets, these properties are refined in the high fidelity prototyping step.

HIGH FIDELITY PROTOTYPING OF ANIMATIONS

In order to fit the needs of the designers as well as the developers, a process for defining animations at a high-level and another process for the low-level aspects of animations are presented. High-level views of animations allow the definition of an animation in an abstract way in terms of objects, events, relationships between events and global temporal constraints while low-level views of animations describes the composition of commands changing properties of objects. Despite this dichotomy which corresponds to two different sets of activities to be performed at the high fidelity animation prototyping phase (presented on the right-hand side of Figure 1), this section presents how these processes can be combined and how they are merged in order to design and implement complex animations.

Designing High-level Aspects of Animations

Figure 4 presents the five steps to be performed for defining high-level aspects of an animation. The first task is to *identify the objects to animate*. Once these objects are identified, they have to be drawn and created which corresponds to step *define graphical aspects of an object*. Once the graphical objects are in existence, an interaction designer needs to *identify the properties to animate*. These properties can include position, rotation, color, opacity and others, depending on what the animation has to present and on its purpose. After identifying the relevant properties, it is necessary to specify how these properties evolve under which temporal constraints. This definition is done during the step called *define behavior* of properties which includes also the definition of the values of each property at the beginning and at the end of the animation.

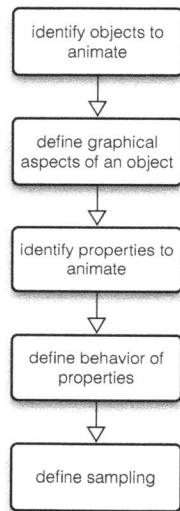

Figure 4: Five steps for defining an animation involving one object and properties of the object

The last step (*define sampling*) of this process connects the definition of the animation description to the actual presentation of the object on the screen. This binding specifies how often each property of each object is updated and displayed on the screen. This last aspect is critical when the connections between the application and the hardware capabilities are made. As explained above this is a very important step to ensure desired perception of the animation and has not been addressed in the literature. For instance dynamically changing this sampling according to CPU or GPU load (as this is explained in detail in the next section) is the only way to degrade gracefully animations.

Composing High-Level Aspects of Animations

Animations are usually more complex than the one shown in Figure 3 and involve more than one object. Animating multiple objects at a given time is common and is not covered by the process presented in Figure 4. To make animations more attractive and more meaningful multiple properties of an object might also be changed in parallel. Finally, several animations of the same object can be defined and organized temporally. An example for such an animation is depicted in Figure 5. This animation depicts two objects (a red ball and a green rectangle) being animated. The red ball is moving from the top left of a screen to the bottom left. At the same time, a green rectangle is moving from the bottom right to the top left, while rotating in parallel.

Figure 5: Animating multiple objects and multiple properties in parallel.

To be able to define this animation, the process presented in Figure 4 needs to be adjusted. The adjustment consists in combining in several ways the process of Figure 4. The result for the description of the animation described in Figure 5 is presented in Figure 6.

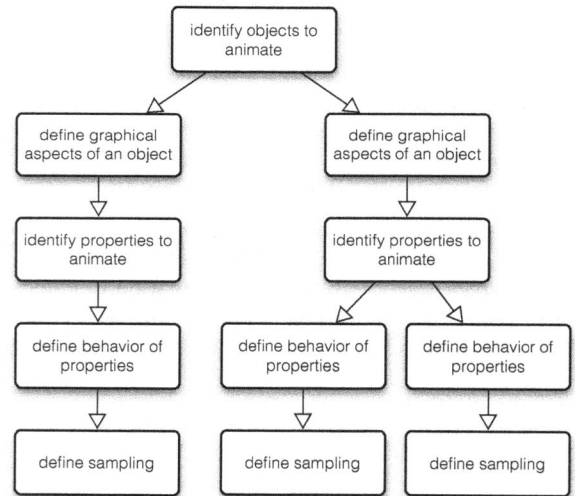

Figure 6. Combination of steps for defining animations involving several properties and several objects

The left-hand side of Figure 6 corresponds to the animation of the ball (which is exactly the same as the one in Figure 4) while the right-hand side corresponds to the animation of the rectangle. The two branches *defining behavior* and *define sampling* are duplicated meaning that both translation and rotation have to occur in parallel. If animations were to be performed in sequence, the two paths would have been represented one below the other one.

While the chaining and temporal organization between animations can be easily represented using this framework, it is not sufficient for describing low-level aspects of the animations including fine-grained temporal evolutions. A generic way to deal with this low-level animation description is described in the following section.

Definition of Atomic Components of Animations
The high-level description from above is refined into a low-level one adding detailed description of time-based evolution of properties of graphical objects as presented in Figure 7. It is important to note that the description of this low-level behavior is generic and parameterized in order to support the description of such low-level behaviors in a reusable way by only altering the parameters. Indeed, this generic description is able to handle any of the properties of an animation even though this description will have to be tuned and parameterized according to the intrinsic characteristic of each property.

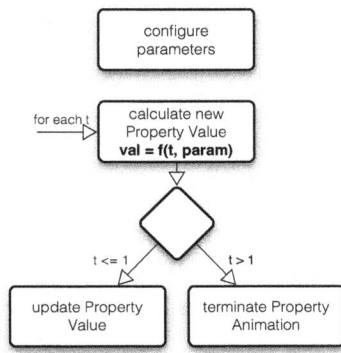

Figure 7: Principle functions of a low-level property update block.

The first block called *configure parameters* is the first step of the low-level animation and corresponds to the connection point with the high-level process presented above. In fact, it corresponds to a refinement of the step *define behavior of properties* in Figure 4 making this description more precise.

The second part of the process of Figure 7 describes the actual structure of the low-level behavior of the animation. While the animation is executed, a new value for the property is calculated at each time step (t). This calculation is based on both the time that has elapsed and the previous value of the property. The behavior of function f connects the designer-defined animation properties and the computer-generated part of the animation. This function performs the calculation of the behavior of a property over time (tweening parameters), defining the temporal pacing of an animation (such as acceleration, slow-in, slow-out or elastic/bouncing effects). After a new value for the property has been computed, either the property itself can be updated (which is performed by *update Property Value*, or if termination-condition has been reached (usually the end of the defined time-span), the update is not performed and this part of the animation of the object is terminated.

Supervising and Composing of Animations from Atomic Components
While the above description handles intra-objects changes over time, there is a need for describing inter-object animations (e.g. collisions between objects). Such descriptions require accessing information about all the objects involved but also influencing the evolution of each object in order to enforce the defined animation. For being able to oversee the global changes, a *supervisor* has been introduced. This supervisor handles inter-object constraints (as defined above), as well as detection of performance bottlenecks during runtime. Such issues have been studied in detail in the area of software engineering and are known under the term of feature interactions [6], which means that the introduction of two (or more) animations would alter one or both of them.

Performance bottlenecks occur during runtime when the system is not capable of providing enough resources to present a new frame of an animation in the timeframe that has been allocated to it. When a bottleneck is detected several strategies can be modeled in the supervisor in order to scale down the animation (for instance by dropping some frames, changing animations attributes, as well as using different animations altogether (behavior-switching) and thus to keep up with time. Such dynamic behavior is rather complex and has to be defined manually i.e. no generic patterns are available. Indeed, in order for an animation degradation to be graceful, it has to be performed according to the type of object, the type of property and above all the entire structure of the stage in which the animation takes place. Indeed, degradation might be acceptable for some objects (for instance in the background) while unacceptable for other ones (for instance the ones being the focus of attention of the user or conveying relevant information for the performance of the current user task). This leads to the last concern of the supervision, which is that above all the animation is meant to support the users in performing their tasks. Tasks must thus be gathered and represented and additionally made available to the supervisor at runtime so that the degradation can be performed taking into account the current state of the tasks performed by the user. We have presented in previous work how such tasks and interactive systems can be integrated and made available by the set of tools called PetShop and Hamsters [2].

Due to space constraints the detailed behavioral aspects of this supervisor are not presented in this paper. Beyond this space constraints aspect, the supervisor behavior heavily depends on the semantics of the interactive application in which the animation is deployed and such aspects are beyond the scope of the paper even though the case study section below will outline how these connections are made.

FORMAL MODELING OF ANIMATIONS
The generic process presented in previous sections provides a useful framework for breaking down the complexity of animation description into manageable reasonable size bricks. However, more refinements have to be performed in order to provide a complete and unambiguous description

of the animations and in order to bridge the gap between design/description and implementation [21].

This section first introduces the potential benefits of using models for describing animated interactive systems. It then proposes extensions to an existing model-based approach (called ICOs [24]) for refining the processes above in such a way that the final models will be executable making it possible to run, test and debug the animations.

The Need for Models

Model-based approaches such as [32], provide means for handling animations and related constraints and offer several benefits listed hereafter. Describing, modifying and tuning an animation with the help of a model allows one to precisely capture its requirements and describe all behavioral aspects including the connection to the rendering on the UI. An example of such an approach can be found in [10] and [12] where a visual informal language is proposed for describing time-based animations.

Modeling animations is helpful to analyze how interactive applications designers currently design animations. Presently, mockups are practical but they only convey a small amount of the complexity of animations [10], leaving a huge portion of the design to the implementation level. The modeling provides a way to describe animations at a higher abstraction level making it possible to describe states and state changes as well as rendering of these states and state changes on the GUI.

Analyzing the animation description enables developers to verify properties (on the animation and on the interactive system as a whole), to be able to conduct performance evaluations and possibly to execute the description itself, in order to avoid implementation errors while going from the description to the actual code. This is particularly important when building applications for critical interactive systems.

Another argument for using models is that the animation can be described independently from the implementation language, so that peculiarities do not jeopardize the migration to different exploitation platforms. This supports the development of user interfaces on various platforms, especially in areas like home entertainment where, for instance, users want to watch the same movie not only on TV, but also on laptops, smart phones or tablets targeting at the same objectives as the ones presented in [22].

The use of models enables developers to handle performance aspects by providing alternatives. Indeed, even if everything would be specified correctly, things might go wrong. A system might reach the limit of its available processing power or available memory, ... thus loosing (due to contingency issues) the expected benefit of adding an animation to the application behavior. Therefore, descriptions of animations have to be designed for default operation as well as for a system exhibiting performance degradation, which might be due to feature interactions [6] as aforementioned.

Beyond these descriptive aspects, some formal modeling techniques allow the prediction of the performance required in terms of time, CPU cycles, and presentation [28] but have not been applied so far to interactive systems yet. A related notation has been used to build more reliable interactions recovering from failures by switching models (for instance through models reconfigurations [23]).

If an adequate formal description technique is used, specifying, simulating and verifying an animation will allow one to produce dependable implementations of animated user interfaces, and will provide a tool for handling the added complexity in a systematic way (with respect to interactive software without animations).

To be able to model animations, the formal description technique must be able to handle the complexity that stems from animations. It is necessary to deal explicitly with quantitative temporal aspects as animations evolve according to time. One of the few notations able to handle concurrency, large state space and quantitative time are Petri nets. In addition to properties verification [16] they also allow designers to utilize performance evaluations on the models [19].

A specific dialect of Petri nets called ICOs [25] has already been proposed to describe the behavior of interactive systems. Our proposal is to build upon that formal description technique and extend it to additionally handle animations.

Informal description of ICOs

The Interactive Cooperative Objects (ICO) [25] formalism is a formal description technique designed to the specification, modeling and implementation of interactive systems [24]. It uses concepts borrowed from the object-oriented approach (i.e. dynamic instantiation, classification, encapsulation, inheritance, and client/server relationships) to describe the structural or static aspects of systems, and uses high-level Petri nets [14] to describe their dynamics or behavioral aspects.

In the ICO formalism, an object is an entity featuring five components: a cooperative object (CO), an available function, a presentation part and two functions (the activation function and the rendering function) that correspond to the link between the cooperative object and the presentation part [4].

The Cooperative Object (CO) models the behavior of an ICO. It states (by means of a high-level Petri net) how the object reacts to external stimuli according to its inner state. As the tokens can hold values (such as references to other objects in the system), the Petri model used in the ICO formalism is called a high-level Petri Net. A Cooperative Object offers two kinds of services. The first one is called system devices and concerns to services offered to other objects of the system, while the second, event services, is related to services offered to a user (producing events) or to other component in the system but only through event-based communication. The availability of all the services in a CO (which depends on the internal state of the objects) is fully stated by the high-level Petri net.

The presentation part describes the external appearance of the ICOs. It is a set of widgets embedded into a set of windows. Each widget can be used for interacting with the interactive system (user interaction → system) and/or as a way to display information about the internal state of the object (system → user interaction).

The activation function (user inputs: user interaction → system) links users' actions on the presentation part (for instance, a click using a mouse on a button) to event services. The rendering function (system outputs: system → user interaction) maintains the consistency between the internal state of the system and its external appearance by reflecting system states changes through functions calls.

Additionally, an availability function is provided to link a service to its corresponding transitions in the ICO, i.e., a service offered by an object will only be avail-able if one of its related transitions in the Petri net is available.

An ICO model is fully executable, which gives the possibility to prototype and test an application before it is fully implemented [3]. The models can also be validated using analysis and proof tools developed within the Petri nets community and extended in order to take into account the specifications of the Petri net dialect used in the ICO formal description technique.

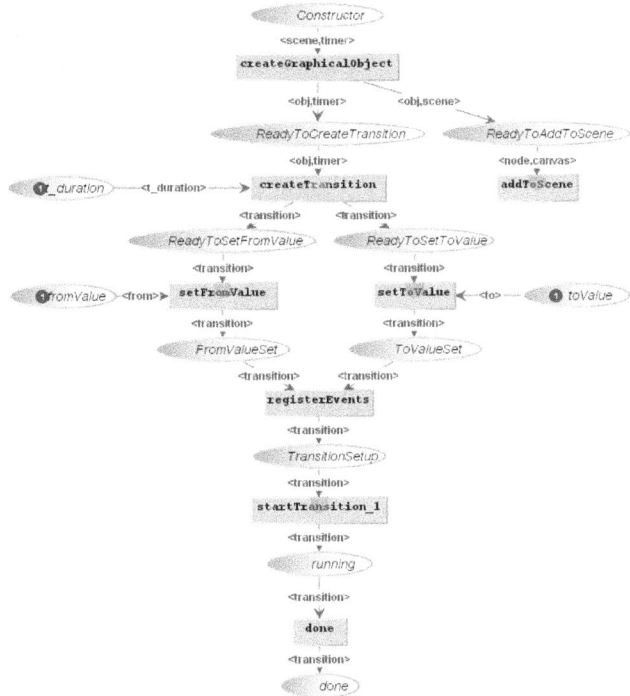

Figure 8: ICO model of the generic high-level animation behavior

However, ICOs have never been used to describe animations. Indeed, the limited attempts to embed them in interactive systems modeled using ICOs have ended up in

adding too much complexity in the models reducing this way their readability and their modifiability.

ICO modeling of the architecture components

This section presents how the ICO description technique can be used to bridge the gap between the stepwise processes described above and the implementation and simulation of animations.

This refinement takes advantage of the object oriented underpinning the ICOs notation. Each object described in the previous processes is directly translated into an ICO model and the references between the models make it possible to transfer information from one model to another one, to call methods between models and to trigger events in one model that will be received and processed by its set of listeners.

Figure 8 presents the ICO model corresponding to the process described in Figure 4 demonstrating the fact that ICO models are not meant to design animations but, on the opposite, to exhaustively describe and to run animations previously designed. This is the reason why this ICO model is less generic than the process of Figure 4 and currently re-fed into the process for executing a translation animation. More precisely that model initialize the animation, sends the parameters of the animation to the low-level ICO model (as the one in Figure 9) that are then stored in places *toValue* and *fromValue*. The tokens in these places hold the initial value of the opacity (*fromValue*) of the object and the value at the end of the animation (*toValue*).

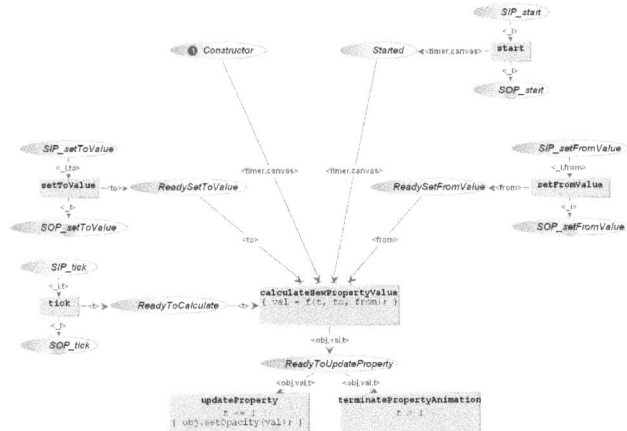

Figure 9: ICO model of the generic low-level animation behavior for Opacity property

The duration of the animation is stored in place *t_Duration* and its value is also sent to the low-level model. When the initialization is finalized a token is set in place *Running* representing the fact that the animation is currently executed. When the time has elapsed, the animation is terminated and a token is set in place *Done*.

Figure 9 presents an example of a low-level model connected to the high-level model presented in Figure 8. It describes in detail the behavior of the animation of the opacity property. The ICO services (there are four in the model) correspond to methods that are called by the high-level model: *SIP_start* (to launch the animation) and *SIP_setFromValue* and *SIP_setToValue* (to set the initial and final values of opacity). *SIP_tick* is called by the stage supervisor and corresponds to the occurrence of the temporal event triggering the calculation of the next graphical presentation of the object for the animation. Occurrence ticks triggers the execution of the transition *calculateNewPropertyValue*, which holds the code in charge of the effective calculation of the transformation. This is where interpolation and temporal pacing take place. When the calculation is performed, the resulting new value of opacity is deposited in place *readyToUpdateProperty* and is processed by transition *updateProperty*, which performs the graphical rendering. If the time has elapsed, transition *terminatePropertyAnimation* is triggered which terminates the animation of this property as well as the model itself.

Animation of other properties (e.g. movement) is modeled in a similar way, reusing the same functional approach as shown in Figure 9. The only difference is the property to be changed by the model and of course the code inside the transition called *calculateNewPropertyValue*.

A SMALL CASE STUDY

Interactive TV provides people with a new TV viewing experience, not only by enhancing the audiovisual experience of the viewer, but by introducing interactivity [11]. This interactivity allows users to actively engage in front of the TV by offering (TV related) information as well as additional services like electronic program guides, video on demand services, live interactive TV games and more. Interactivity in iTV can simply be defined as anything that takes the user beyond the passive experience of watching and that lets the user make choices and take actions [13]. Most iTV definitions have in common that iTV combines traditional TV viewing with a back channel, e.g. via the Internet.

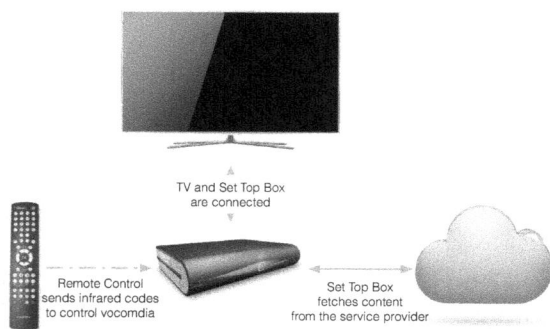

Figure 10: Schematic view of an interactive TV set-up including the vocomedia concept.

A standard setup of an interactive TV environment includes a TV, a set-top box connected to the TV screen and the user controlling this setup via a (infra-red based) remote control.

Informal presentation of the case study

vocomedia is a user interaction concept developed in a user-centered way to meet the current demands of new forms of interactive TV (iTV) and Internet Protocol TV (IPTV). The goal of the design of vocomedia was to make it easy to use in terms of efficiency and effectiveness. To reduce the cognitive effort of the user to a minimum (when interacting with the iTV system) and to minimize error, the system builds on a six-button interaction mechanism (up/down, left/right, ok, back) and a three-level navigation concept. Figure 11 shows the navigation concept that is built upon a horizontal and vertical navigation bar forming a cross. The intersection of the cross is highlighted by a "look there" field [20] being the only place in the interface where the user can select an action. To support the user in understanding system changes, a set of animations is used.

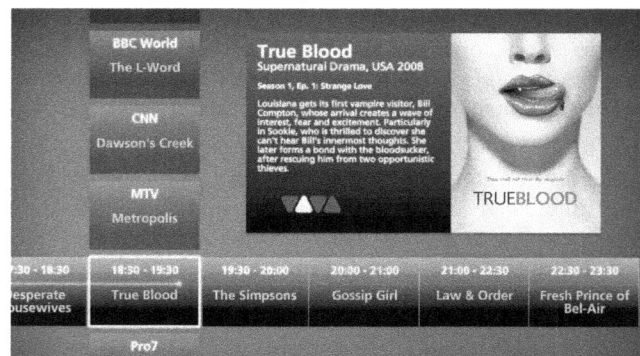

Figure 11: Screenshot of the "look there" concept: EPG with TV program and time of the day for a given channel

Figure 11 presents an electronic program guide (EPG) in which interaction takes place by means of user actions on the remote control. For instance, if the user presses button "go to right" on the remote control, it results in an animation moving the horizontal bar to the left. The animation looks like if all the elements on that bar are shifted to the left. At the end of the animation, the label "Big Shots" and the time 20:30 - 21:00 are displayed in the "look there" field (currently displaying information about "Lost" in Figure 11. The same type of animation is used when the user is pressing "go to left", using a similar translation animation to move the content to the right. For going up and down, the animation used is more complex. If the user presses button "go up" on the remote control, the horizontal bar fades out, and the vertical bar is shifted down. After this movement animation has been performed, a new horizontal bar is moved in from the right, until the horizontal line is filled again with new elements describing the program for the NBC channel.

Connecting the case study to the modeling framework

This case study has been developed following the process shown in Figure 1, bringing together designers and developers with the final target of designing and implementing an iTV system with animations.

For high fidelity prototyping of animations, we define the animations of the EPG, following the five steps to define an animation as depicted in Figure 4: (1) For the standard navigation of the graphical user interface the following two graphical objects are identified: a vertical bar (displaying main category items), and a horizontal bar (holding sub-category items related to the selected main category). All other elements in the main interface are static. (2) The graphical aspects of the objects are defined (size of the bars, colors, positioning of the content such as time information). (3) The properties to animate are position and opacity. (4) In terms of behavior, the identified objects (horizontal and vertical bar) should be animated by changing the position property (move left/right or up/down respectively), and the opacity property (fade out the bar - change opacity to fully opaque (zero)). (5) The time-based update of the properties position and opacity is performed, following the generic approach described in Figure 7.

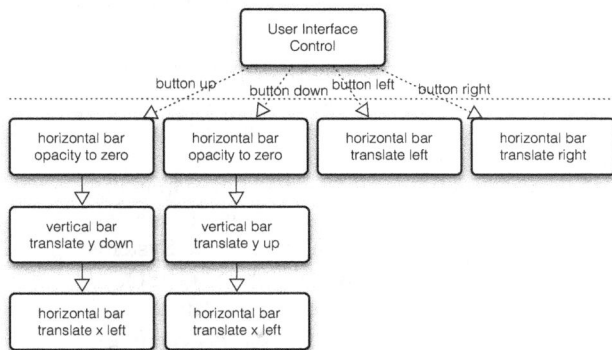

Figure 12: Overview on animations used in the case study.

Figure 12 provides an overview of the high-level description of animations (and therefore changes of the defined properties) according to the user triggered events through the input device (button press up/down and left/right) as described previously informally. When button "up" is pressed, a sequence of three animations is performed. First for the horizontal bar the property opacity is changed (fade-out), next for the vertical bar the property position is changed (move down), and finally for the horizontal bar the position is changed (move left). In this case study all the animations are triggered by user events on the input device (i.e. the remote control). The case study exhibits the connection between the animations and the behavior of the application. In this case, the connection between user events and animations is made explicit. As using the ICO modeling the application behavior is described using Petri nets, the representation at the top of Figure 12 corresponds to connections between the ICO model in charge of the behavior of the application and the ICO model in charge of the animations.

CONCLUSIONS AND FUTURE WORK

This paper has presented a framework for the design and implementation of animations in user interfaces following a two levels process. The high-level view of an animation focuses on animated objects, on their properties that are animated and on the composition of animations. This composition can take place at the object level as well as

amongst several objects. The low-level description provides very low details of animations and precisely the temporal aspects, the possible use of tweening/interpolation and the connection to the hardware rendering.

One important aspect of the contribution lies in the generality of the processes of these two levels as well as in their easy reification into tuned models for each graphical object property manipulated by an animation. The approach is introduced with a formal description technique called ICOs making it possible to refine the models in a way, so they become executable allowing designers and developers to execute and test their animations (using the CASE tool PetShop). However, it is important to note that the two levels process is not necessarily bound to ICOs and can easily be replaced by a programming language such as Flex even though abstract description, models verification and performance evaluations would be dropped.

The paper has not presented in detail (due to space constraints) how the animations are embedded in a description of a complete user interface. Indeed, it is most likely that the animations modeled will be triggered by user actions on the graphical objects of the user interface or directly by the interactive system when internal state changes occur (similarly to automation as presented in [27]). Beyond that, we only introduced the role of supervisor that has been also modeled using ICOs. This model can be rather complicated as it has to handle both inter-objects animations and the orchestration of the animations altering animations when performance is not what was expected. Designing for potential degradation adds also to the burden of designer who has to clearly identify how animations can be degraded.

Future work aims at providing an integrated framework within PetShop for seamlessly embedding the animations presented in this paper into large-scale applications such as interactive cockpits or fully animated multimedia applications like vocomedia which has been presented here.

ACKNOWLEDGMENTS
This work is partly funded by ruwido under contract 08-8RM-050 and R&T CNES (French Space Studies Center) Tortuga R-S81/BS-0003-029.

REFERENCES
1. Baecker, R.M., Small, I., and Mander, R. Bringing icons to life. *Proceedings of CHI 1991*, Myers (1991), 1-6.
2. Barboni, E., Ladry, J.-F., Navarre, D., Palanque, P., and Winckler, M. Beyond Modelling : An Integrated Environment Supporting Co-Execution of Tasks and Systems Models. *Proceedings of EICS 2010*, (2010), 165-174.
3. Bastide, R., Navarre, D., and Palanque, P. A Model-Based Tool for Interactive Prototyping of Highly Interactive Applications. *Proceedings of CHI 2002 (Extended Abstracts)*, (2002), 516-517.
4. Bastide, R., Palanque, P., Le, D.-Hoa, Muñoz, J., and Frogis, L.I.S. Integrating rendering specifications into a formalism for the design of interactive systems. *Design*

Specification and Verification of Interactive Systems 98, Springer (1998), 171-191.

5. Byrne, M.D. Evaluating animations as student aids in learning computer algorithms. *Computers & Education 33,* 4 (1999), 253-278.

6. Calder M., Kolberg M., Magill E. H., R.-M.S. Feature interaction: a critical review and considered forecast. *Computer Networks,* 41 (2002), 115–141.

7. Carroll, J.M., Kellogg, W.A., and Rosson, M.B. The Task-Artifact Cycle. In J.M. Carroll, ed., *Designing Interaction: Psychology at the Human-Computer Interface.* Cambridge University Press, 1991.

8. Chang, B.-W. and Ungar, D. Animation: from cartoons to the user interface. *Sun Microsystems, Inc. Mountain View, CA, USA,* March (1995), 1-18.

9. Chapman, N. and Chapman, J. *Digital Multimedia.* Wiley, 2009.

10. Chatty, S. Defining the Dynamic Behaviour of Animated Interfaces. *Proceedings of EHCI 1992,* (1992), 95.

11. Eronen, L. User Centered Research for Interactive Television. *Children,* (2003), 5-12.

12. Esteban, O., Chatty, S., and Palanque, P. Whizz'Ed: a visual environment for building highly interactive software. *Proceedings of INTERACT 1995,* (1995), 121-136.

13. Gawlinsky, M. *Interactive Television Production.* Focal Press, Oxford, 2003.

14. Genrich, H.J. Predicate/Transition Nets. In W. Brauer, W. Reisig and G. Rozenberg, eds., *Advances in Petri Nets 1986 Part I.* Springer-Verlag, 1987, 207-247.

15. Heer, J. and Robertson, G.G. Animated transitions in statistical data graphics. *IEEE Trans. on Visualization and Computer Graphics 13,* 6 (2007), 1240-7.

16. Jensen, K. *Coloured Petri Nets - Modelling and Validation of Concurrent Systems.* Springer, 2009.

17. Karavirta, V., Korhonen, A., Malmi, L., and Naps, T. A comprehensive taxonomy of algorithm animation languages. *Journal of Visual Languages & Computing 21,* 1 (2010), 1-22.

18. Kim, S., Coffin, C., and Tobias, H. Relocalization Using Virtual Keyframes For Online Environment Map Construction. *Work 1,* 212 (2009), 127-134.

19. Marsan, M.A., Bobbio, A., and Donatelli, S. Petri Nets in Performance Analysis: an Introduction. In G. Rozenberg and W. Reisig, eds., *Lectures on Petri Nets I: Basic Models.* Springer Verlag, Berlin, 1998.

20. Mirlacher, T., Pirker, M., Bernhaupt, R., et al. Interactive Simplicity for iTV: Minimizing Keys for Navigating Content. *Proceedings of euroITV 2010,* (2010).

21. Mirlacher, T. Modeling animations for dependable interactive applications. *Proceedings of EICS 2011,* ACM (2011), 319–322.

22. Mori G., Paternò F., S.C. Design and Development of Multidevice User Interfaces through Multiple Logical Descriptions. *IEEE Trans. Software Engineering 30,* 8 (2004), 507-520.

23. Navarre, D., Palanque, P., and Basnyat, S. A formal approach for user interaction reconfiguration of safety critical interactive systems. *Safety, Reliability, and Security,* (2008), 373-386.

24. Navarre, D., Palanque, P., Bastide, R., and Sy, O. A model-based tool for interactive prototyping of highly interactive applications. *Proceedings of RSP 2001,* (2001), 136-141.

25. Navarre, D., Palanque, P., Ladry, J.-F., and Barboni, E. ICOs: A Model-Based User Interface Description Technique dedicated to Interactive Systems Addressing Usability, Reliability and Scalability. *ACM Trans. on Computer-Human Interaction (TOCHI) 16,* 4 (2009), 1-56.

26. Palanque, P., Ladry, J.-F., Navarre, D., Barboni, E., Paul, U., and Toulouse, S. High-Fidelity Prototyping of Interactive Systems Can Be Formal Too. *Proceedings of EHCI 2009,* (2009), 667-676.

27. Palanque P., Bernhaupt R., M.F. Integrating Gaming Research and Practice in the Design of User Interfaces of (partly)-Autonomous Safety-Critical Systems. *Proceedings of ATACCS 2011,* ACM (2011), 134-143.

28. Sénac P. and Diaz M. Time Stream Petri Nets: A model for timed multimedia information. *Proceedings of Application and Theory of Petri Nets,* Springer (1994), 219-238.

29. Thomas, B.H. and Calder, P. Applying cartoon animation techniques to graphical user interfaces. *ACM Trans. on Computer-Human Interaction (TOCHI) 8,* 3 (2001), 198-222.

30. Thomas, F. and Johnston, O. *Disney Animation: The Illusion of Life.* Abbeville Press, New York, USA, 1981.

31. Urquiza-Fuentes, J., Angel, J., Azquez-Iturbide, V.E.L., Rey, U., and Carlos, J. A Survey of Successful Evaluations of Program Visualization and Algorithm Animation Systems. *Computing 9,* 2 (2009), 1-21.

32. Vodislav, D. A visual programming model for user interface animation. *Proceedings. 1997 IEEE Symposium on Visual Languages (Cat. No.97TB100180),* (1997), 344-351.

33. Wang, P.-Y. The Impact of Animation Interactivity on Novices' Learning of Introductory Statistics. *Design,* 2010.

34. Xu, H.-Y., Li, D., and Wang, J. Implicit curve oriented inbetweening for motion animation. *Computer graphics and interactive techniques in Australasia and South East Asia,* (2006).

Modelling User Manuals of Modal Medical Devices and Learning from the Experience

Judy Bowen
The University of Waikato
Hamilton, New Zealand
jbowen@cs.waikato.ac.nz

Steve Reeves
The University of Waikato
Hamilton, New Zealand
stever@cs.waikato.ac.nz

ABSTRACT

Ensuring that users can successfully interact with software and hardware devices is a critical part of software engineering. There are many approaches taken to ensure successful interaction, *e.g.* the use of user-centred design, usability studies, training and education *etc*. In this paper we consider how the users of modal medical devices, such as syringe pumps, are supported (or not) post-training by documentation such as user manuals. Our intention is to show that modelling such documents is a useful component in the software engineering process, allowing us to discover inconsistencies between devices and manuals as well as uncovering potentially undesirable properties of the devices being modelled.

Author Keywords

Formal models; interactive medical devices; manuals; Z; ProB

ACM Classification Keywords

D.2.4 Software Engineering: Formal Methods

INTRODUCTION

Medical devices such as infusion and syringe pumps, which deliver set amounts of medication to a patient over a fixed period of time, are now commonplace devices in hospitals, clinics, respite-care facilities and hospices throughout the world. These devices typically have a small hardware interface consisting of soft-keys and some sort of display. The behaviour of the soft-keys is dependent on the mode of the device and so a small syringe pump with eight soft-keys, a display and fifteen different modes is inherently very complex due to the combination of possible interactions for a user to understand and remember. In addition, there is a requirement on the user to understand how to move between modes and recognise the current mode of the device. Adding to the complexity is the fact that these are safety-critical devices (an error on the part of the user can lead to incorrect doses of medication being delivered which may be life-threatening or even fatal) which are used in high-stress environments.

In previous work we have used a particular set of models, presentation models and presentation interaction models (PIMs) [1], to model interactive software systems. These models are lightweight and easy to use with an underlying formal theory which enables them to be linked with a formal specification of a system's functionality. In this paper we show that these models are also suitable for describing modal devices, such as interactive medical devices, as well as for modelling the user manuals of such devices.

We first model the user manual of the chosen device, which is provided by the pump's manufacturer. We do this by treating each description of how to perform a task as a description of some behaviour of the actual device. We then model the pump itself by way of a manual discovery process (*i.e.* attempting to interact with it to explore all possible functions in all modes). In this example where we are reverse-engineering an existing device we must necessarily use a manual process. For both the user manual and the pump we model the interactive components using presentation models and the underlying functionality as a Z specification [6, 7, 13]. We expect that the model of the manuals will be (necessarily) incomplete, as the level of detail given is typically less than a thorough description of total functionality of the device. This is to be expected as the manual serves as an aid to a user in performing particular tasks rather than as a complete technical specification. However, the models should be consistent with each other in that there should be a refinement relation [4, 13] between the two models, which is to say that the pump should "implement" the manual. If this is not the case then either there are inaccuracies in the manual, or the device does not operate as intended or expected, or perhaps both.

The contributions of this paper are threefold: firstly we show that presentation models, which were initially designed to describe interactive software systems, can successfully be used to model modal interactive devices such as medical devices; secondly that we can use the same models for the user manuals of these devices, which enables us to formally compare user manuals with their corresponding devices to discover inconsistencies; and thirdly we show how the development and examination of such models can uncover undocumented properties and potentially undesirable behaviours of the devices themselves.

RELATED WORK

Understanding the behaviour and interactive aspects of medical devices is growing in importance as a research area as both the number of such devices and their use and sophistication increases. The CHI+MED research project [5] is undertaking a considerable amount of research in this area, and part of our motivation comes from considering the outcomes of that project so far. This includes discussions we have had with participants of that project around common interests.

In particular, Campos and Harrison's use of formal models to describe an infusion pump [3] suggested to us that the models we use in our own research for describing interactive systems could be similarly used. Blandford *et al.* have looked at user manuals of infusion pumps [11] in a comparison between manuals (in general) and the practices of medical staff. Their aim was to identify mismatches between procedures given in the manual and what medical staff are trained to do, so as to discover mismatches which might prove dangerous. They use a graph-based notation to model and understand workflows. In contrast, we aim to show where the manual and device it describes are inconsistent (although this, of course, could lead to the sort of mismatches identified in [11]).

Another approach taken to combining formal methods and modelling with user manuals is seen in the works of Thimbleby and Ladkin [12] who look at deriving manuals from specifications. Although the intention here is different (the manuals already exist for the devices we are considering) there is a common theme of modelling, or specifying, the system as the basis for understanding the requirements of the manual.

THE DEVICE
The medical device we use as the example in this paper is a syringe pump. These devices are designed to deliver the contents of a syringe to a patient in a controlled manner at a specified rate. The pump can hold a variety of different makes and sizes of syringe and contains sensors which help to detect which is being used. There are many different makes of these pumps available, and in use, in this paper we focus on the Niki T34 syringe pump which is a device commonly used throughout New Zealand in hospitals and respite care facilities. However, in general, syringe pumps are similar in terms of functionality and usage (although actual interactions and interactive elements may differ) and therefore our work can be generalised to any of these devices (and is also equally applicable to any other modal interactive device, including those outside of the medical domain). That is, we can easily apply the same process we describe here to any such device.

The T34 syringe pump is easy to describe (which suits the purposes of this paper) whilst remaining complex enough to provide a non-trivial example. It is, of course, also a safety-critical device, which makes the use of "expensive" formal methods easily affordable when the costs of not doing so are taken into account in the lifecycle (design, development, maintenance and safe use) of such a device. Further motivation for our techniques might also come from legal requirements in some jurisdictions.

In addition to the functionality which enables set-up and delivery of a prescribed dosage of medication, the pump also has safety features such as a "program" lock that prevents unauthorized changes to the programme of treatment, alarm sensors and an event log which records the previous 512 pump events. In this paper we focus on the core clinical functionality of medication delivery only and abstract away details relating to program locks, post-infusion keep-vein-open operations, event logs *etc.*

THE MANUAL
The manufacturers of the pump provide an instruction manual with the device [2], and it is this manual we describe and model in this paper. Although this is not the sole instructional information provided to practitioners (training and additional written instructions are provided by the distributors and some medical institutions provide their own material), the introduction to the manual states:
"This manual will ensure the Healthcare Provider will be able to:-

1. Identify the features of the pump and understand their use

2. Correctly load a syringe into the pump

3. Program the pump to deliver the contents of a syringe . ."

As such we believe it is a reasonable expectation that all behaviour described in the manual accurately reflects the behaviour exhibited by the pump and that it is presented in a manner that clearly explains that behaviour.

THE MODELS
Presentation Models and PIMs
Presentation models (PMs) and presentation interaction models (PIMs) [1] were developed to describe feature-rich graphical user interfaces (GUIs) of software applications. They enable us to capture all relevant behaviour of GUIs and GUI designs (abstracting away issues such as display and layout properties of the widgets) by way of the presentation model and then the navigational possibilities are described using a PIM.

The PIM is a state transition system (written as a μ-chart) [10] where "state explosion" is avoided by having a state for each distinct window or dialogue of the GUI, so each state collects together many widgets. Each such state is itself, therefore, associated with a PM that describes the relevant widgets and can be thought of as an abstraction of its associated presentation model.

So, whereas many transition models of GUIs have a state/transition pair for every possible behaviour, our models are much smaller, having a state/transition pair for each navigational possibility between distinct windows (since each of our states is associated with a PM, which is itself a collection of widgets).

This approach works well for applications where each distinct window or dialogue is modal (*i.e.* interaction can only occur with a single window or dialogue at any time) as in the best case scenario there will be a single state for each of the windows, leading to a small PIM which can be easily read and understood. So, for example, a software application with four distinct windows/dialogues will have four PMs, each describing the widgets and behaviours of one of the windows.

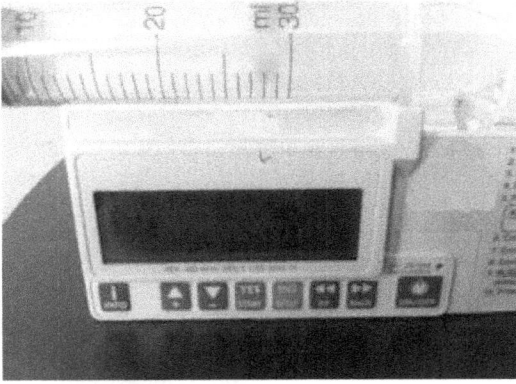

Figure 1. Niki T34 Syringe pump

The PIM will then have four states, where each state corresponds to one of the PMs and as such is an abstraction of the detail given by the PM.

As well as software GUIs there is a category of modal devices (hardware devices with mixed software/hardware interfaces) for which presentation models and PIMs can be successfully used. Such devices have a fixed set of hardware widgets, which are modally dependent, coupled with a software UI providing both functionality and feedback. A good example of such a device is the sort of medical syringe pump that we consider in this paper (shown in figure 1), which is designed to enable easy setting of volume and time limits for the infusion of medication to a patient via an intravenous line.

The ability to model devices such as these in a simple and straightforward way is an important contribution to design and safety of these devices, providing as it does the ability to communicate formally derived information to biotechnicians, medical practitioners and hardware manufacturers *etc.* who are not likely to be familiar with formal software notations and languages. In addition, these models enable a wider consideration of correctness than traditional formal methods since they include human factors, enabling us to link formal models with human requirements.

As described above, for the GUIs of software applications we describe each window/dialogue as a separate presentation model and then use the PIM to show how the user navigates between these windows. In a similar manner, for modal devices we describe each mode as a presentation model and again use a PIM to show how a user navigates between the different modes. The main difference is that the fixed set of soft-keys will be present in each of the presentation models (whereas typically in a software GUI we have a different set of widgets for each window or dialogue, and hence for each presentation model). However, the *behaviour* of these soft-keys will differ depending on the mode, and the presentation model will vary in the information it gives in providing the mode/behaviour relation.

For example, if we consider again the syringe pump shown in figure 1 we see that there are eight soft-keys and a display. These are fixed and are present irrespective of the mode the pump is in (obviously, since the physical configuration of the interface does not change, even when the pump is turned off!). Each presentation model (describing a single mode) will then have the same structure as it contains the same set of widgets. However, of course, the *behaviour* of widgets may (indeed, is likely to) differ between PMs (remember each mode is modelled by a PM). So, for example, when our pump is first turned on it is in the *LoadSyringe* mode. In this mode the *Up/Plus* button has no behaviour and so is modelled as:

(UpPlus, ActionControl, ())

We give the button a name, *UpPlus* and categorise it as an *ActionControl* - which simply means it is capable of causing some behavior to occur when interacted with, and in the final set of parentheses we name the actual behaviour (or behaviours), which in this case is none. However, if the pump is in the *DurationSet mode*, then the same soft-key is modelled as:

(UpPlus, ActionControl, (S_IncreaseDuration))

So now we have a behaviour called *S_IncreaseDuration* associated with the widget which in the simple form of the PM indicates that there is some behaviour which occurs when the button is interacted with. This is because in this mode the key is used to change the system state via the system behaviour *S_IncreaseDuration*, by incrementing some value in the state that records duration We call such behaviours S-behaviours and they are given meaning via Z operation schemas (as in the next section). So for each mode of the pump there is a single presentation model and each of these presentation models contain descriptions of the same set of widgets (the soft-keys and display) but with different behaviours.

Z

We use Z [6, 7, 13] to specify the functionality (rather than the interface) of the pump as understood from the manual also. We follow the usual Z format for a specification-we give a collection of operations (essentially one for each S-behaviour) together with a state over which the operations work. Following is a fragment of the specification:

$$
\begin{array}{|l}
\hline
\_IncreaseDuration \rule{0pt}{0pt} \\
\Delta PumpState \\
\hline
systemReady = no \\
minutesduration \leq 58 \Rightarrow \\
\quad (minutesduration' = minutesduration + 1 \wedge \\
\quad hoursduration' = hoursduration) \\
minutesduration = 59 \Rightarrow \\
\quad (minutesduration' = 0 \wedge ((hoursduration' \leq 23 \\
\quad \Rightarrow hoursduration' = hoursduration + 1) \wedge \\
\quad (hoursduration = 24 \Rightarrow hoursduration' = 0)) \\
\quad secondsduration' = secondsduration \\
\Xi BatteryState \\
\Xi Syringe \\
\Xi KeyPad \\
\Xi TechMenu \\
\Xi Program \\
\Xi VTBI \\
\Xi InfusionRate \\
systemReady' = no \\
\hline
\end{array}
$$

This describes a single operation of the system called *IncreaseDuration*. The top line states that the operation may change the *PumpState* (denoted by the Δ symbol) and below the line are the predicates which will be satisfied upon completion of the operation, for example it gives the necessary conditions of how the system observations of minutes and hours will change. The use of the Ξ symbol before several parts of the state indicate that these remain unchanged by the operation. Since the PIM is written as a μ-chart, and since a μ-chart's semantics is given in Z, we also have a Z specification that models the PIM (a tool, ZOOM, automatically provides the Z semantics from a given μ-chart). The whole model is available from www.cs.waikato.ac.nz/ stever/pump_complete_model.pdf.

PMR

We finally have to link the two parts (interactive and functional) of the model together, and that is done by relating S-behaviours to the Z operations that give them their meaning. We use a simple relation, each element of which associates an S-behaviour with an operation schema. An excerpt from this relation (which we call the PMR, for Presentation Model Relation) for the manual is:

$$S\_CalculateVTBI \mapsto InitialiseSyringe$$
$$S\_IncreaseVTBI \mapsto IncreaseVTBI$$
$$S\_DecreaseVTBI \mapsto DecreaseVTBI$$
$$S\_ShowDuration \mapsto ConfirmVTBI$$
$$S\_IncreaseDuration \mapsto IncreaseDuration$$
$$S\_DecreaseDuration \mapsto DecreaseDuration$$
$$S\_SelfTest \mapsto SelfTest$$
$$S\_ScrollSyringeListUp \mapsto SyringeScrollUp$$
$$S\_ScrollSyringeListDown \mapsto SyringeScrollDown$$
$$S\_BatteryLevel \mapsto BatteryTest$$
$$S\_DurationWarning \mapsto DurationWarning$$

So, for example, we can see that the S-behaviour *S_IncreaseDuration* in the example above is given meaning via the Z operation *IncreaseDuration* shown in the Z schema above. Once we have all these components (the Z models for functionality and the PIM, the various PMs and the PMR) we have a model of the complete device as understood via the manual.

Note that some of the operations are specified as "skip" operations, that is they do not change the state (in Z terms these are modelled by Ξ-schemas, defined by convention), because at this level of abstraction they, typically, do things like give information to the UI for displaying on the device's screen. For example *S_ScrollSyringeListUp* has *SyringeScrollUp* as its meaning:

$$\begin{array}{|l}\hline SyringeScrollUp \\ \Xi PumpState \\\hline \end{array}$$

It does not change the underlying state of the device and, at this level of abstraction (because we are not interested in the detail of what is displayed or how it is displayed) there is no output observable. This is fine, however, as a modelling step since this operation can be refined to an one that, for example, outputs some information as data for the display, and since

refinement preserves meaning, any system that has this more refined operation in place of the simple one we have used here will still be a model of the manual and have all the properties of the original model.

The same technique is used for many of the information operations in order to, at this level, simplify the model. Even operations that, we would assume, "do more", like the self-test operation (which is in fact undefined in the manual, so should be undefined in this model!) can be left as skips for now. As long as they are refined to operations which, in their entirety, cause no change of state then the meaning of the model is preserved correctly.

We use ProB [9] to animate and validate the specification. The typical way of working is to have two invocations of ProB running, one for the functionality and one for the PIM, and we also display the PIM (as a chart), the PMs for each mode and the PMR. This allows us to animate the whole device (*i.e.* UI and functionality), thus validating the whole model as ProB animations. Of course, ProB supports a variety of different specification languages so although we use Z in this paper modelling can be done in many languages and the methods we describe will still work. A screenshot of the Z specification in ProB during an animation session is given in figure 2.

MODELLING THE INSTRUCTION MANUAL

The manual is divided into 21 sections. Some of these sections relate to hardware considerations (such as changing the battery, connecting the infusion set *etc.*), which are outside of the scope of this paper. Other sections describe the initial set-up of the device before it is released for general use, or functions, such as setting the program lock, that we are not currently considering (as described earlier).

From the "features" section we can identify the soft-keys and display features of the device. The soft-keys (as mentioned earlier) are the fixed set of hardware buttons common to each of the component presentation models whose behaviour will be dependent on the current mode of the pump. The single display will contain different data items, also depending on the mode. The soft-keys and display (which we refer to collectively as the widgets of the pump) are as follows:

- On/Off button
- Display
- No/Stop key
- Yes/Start key
- Down/Minus key
- Up/Plus key
- Info key
- Left/FF key
- Right/Back key

Figure 2. ProB animation of functional specification

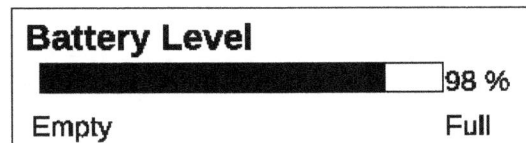

Figure 3. Battery level indicator

As an example of how we created a model from the manual, the first behaviour of one mode of the pump is described in a "batteries" section, which outlines how to perform a check on the current battery level. The instructions given are as follows:

- Switch the pump ON

- Press INFO key

- Select BATTERY LIFE from the menu and press YES to confirm

- Verify sufficient battery charge is available to complete the current program. If not, change the battery.

Beneath the text is a diagram similar to that given in figure 3 indicating how the battery level will be shown on the display. From this we can begin the first part of our model. We note that the pump is in a particular state when it is turned on (which we call *LoadSyringe*) and that pressing the INFO key changes it to a state where a menu of information is displayed (which we call *Info*).

In the *Info* state the display acts as a menu where items can be selected for expansion (at this stage we only know about the battery life option). We can then create two component presentation models called *LoadSyringe* and *Info* and pro-

125

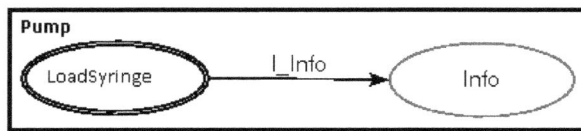

Figure 4. PIM showing deadlock

vide a small amount of behaviour (that which we currently know, much more will be added as we work further through the manual) for the soft-keys as well as the usage of the display as a selection menu. These models are (at this stage) as follows:

LoadSyringe is
      (OnOffButton, ActionControl, ()),
      (Display, MValResponder, ()),
      (NoStopSK, ActionControl, ()),
      (YesStartSK, ActionControl, ()),
      (DownMinusSK, ActionControl, ()),
      (UpPlusSK, ActionControl, ()),
      (InfoSK, ActionControl, (I_Info)),
      (LeftFFSK, ActionControl, ()),
      (RightBackSK, ActionControl, ())

Info is
      (OnOffButton, ActionControl, ()),
      (Display ,MValResponder (S_ShowInfoList)),
      (NoStopSK, ActionControl, ()),
      (YesStartSK, ActionControl, (I_BatteryLevel)),
      (DownMinusSK, ActionControl, ()),
      (UpPlusSK, ActionControl, ()),
      (InfoSK, ActionControl, ()),
      (LeftFFSK, ActionControl, ()),
      (RightBackSK, ActionControl, ())

In the *LoadSyringe* model, the only widget we can give behaviour to (at this point) is the *InfoSK* widget (the soft-key labelled INFO on the pump) as the manual tells us that this changes the mode of the pump from *LoadSyringe* to *Info*. We show that the behaviour is one that changes the mode of the pump (rather than one which changes the internal state of the pump) by prefixing it with I_. Similarly, in the *Info* model we can only show the behaviour of the *YesStartSK* widget that changes the mode to that of the battery level display. We cannot model the selection of the battery level item from the list as the manual is not explicit about how this occurs.

Our model is therefore already under-defined. The manual states that the user should "Select BATTERY LIFE from the menu and press YES to confirm", but no information is provided as to how the user makes the selection. Similarly no information is given as to how the user returns from displaying this information to the previous mode. If we create the PIM for these two states, as shown in figure 4, it implies a deadlock once the mode change has been made. We can also see this deadlock directly if we look at the ProB animation for the PIM since ProB colours operations that lead to deadlock orange.

Also worth noting here is point four of the instructions that

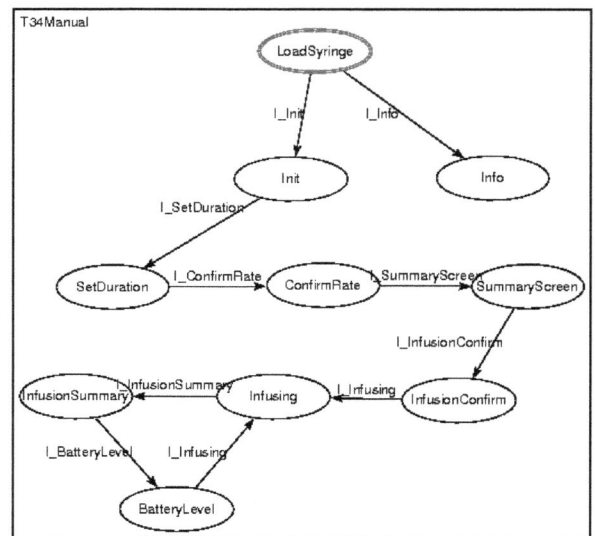

Figure 5. PIM of pump via instruction manual

require the user to "verify sufficient battery charge is available to complete the current program" as there is no indication given as to how they should determine this. The battery level graphic provides a percent value for the current level, but in no way indicates what this provides by way of timed activity. Therefore if a user encounters a battery level of *e.g.* 40% and has a planned dosage programme which will take several hours there is no way of knowing from this current information whether or not the battery level is sufficient to complete the infusion. We identify this as a potentially undesirable property. The manual should more usefully provide an estimate of the correlation between battery life and pump activity time.

We continue through the manual in a similar way. Each time a description of a mode is given we create a new presentation model for that mode containing the known (fixed) set of widgets (soft-keys and display) and add behaviours to these widgets as appropriate. Once all relevant descriptions in the manual have been considered we have a model containing ten PMs and therefore ten modes. These then become associated with unique states in the PIM, shown in figure 5. In general no information is provided about widget behaviour other than the widget of interest. So, for example, in the *LoadSyringe* mode we are told that pressing the INFO soft-key takes us to the *Info* mode (as denoted in the previous PM by the *I_Info* behaviour) but we are not told what happens if the ON/OFF soft-key is pressed. In building the presentation model we therefore assume that these widgets have no behaviour and so their behaviour sets are left empty. This turns out to be an important difference when we come to compare the model of the manual with the model of the pump.

MODELLING THE PUMP

The pump is modelled in the same manner as the manual, by identifying the modes and widget behaviours within those modes and describing them in presentation models. In order to discover the necessary information the behaviour of every widget is investigated in every mode. Therefore, unlike the model of the manual, if a widget is shown as having no behaviour in a given mode it is because it actually does nothing in that mode. We referred to the manual as necessary to understand how to achieve particular tasks. We ran into problems almost immediately when we began to interact with the pump. Loading a syringe can require moving an actuator arm (achieved by pressing the Fwd and Back soft-keys according to the manual) so that it is in the correct place with respect to the plunger arm of the syringe, which may be in different positions (further in or out) for a given syringe. A section of the manual deals with pre-loading and syringe placement and lists 23 steps in this procedure. Step 3 states:

"Load the syringe into the Pump prior to connecting the syringe to the patient"

and step 5 states:

"If the actuator is not in the correct position to accommodate the syringe leave the barrel clamp arm down and use the FF or BACK buttons on the keypad to move the actuator to the required position..."

This, however, did not seem to work as pressing either of these buttons did not move the actuator (or cause anything to happen). After several attempts we returned to the manual. As we read on we found that step 6 states:

"Lift the barrel clamp arm and load the syringe into the Pump..."

In fact step 3 is a general warning relating to connecting the pump to a patient and should not be read as an instruction to load the syringe at this point. This was not at all clear to us from our first reading of the manual. Once we had removed the syringe we were able to move the actuator an proceed as described.

One of the first things we discovered as we started the modeling process was that the pump has a timeout facility. If it is left unattended in some modes an alarm sounds and the display shows a warning message. We include this in the presentation model by declaring an additional widget called 'Timeout' for those modes that responds to a system timeout event. This is not unusual as the models are intended to describe all methods of interaction and as such we can define audio interaction in the same way as any other widget (so a widget does not need to be "materially" instantiated).

The most unexpected behaviour we discovered while modelling the pump was in relation to the ON/OFF button. A safety feature ensures that the pump cannot be easily turned off by single button press. In order to turn the pump off the ON/OFF button must be held down for the required number of seconds. This is communicated to the user by way of a progress bar, similar to that shown in figure 6, so that they can see they must continue to hold the button down if they really wish to turn the pump off. If turning the pump off is not the user's intention and they release the button before the progress bar has reached the end the pump does not turn off.

We expected that in such cases the pump would return to the mode it was in prior to the ON/OFF button being pressed. However, this is not the case. Irrespective of the mode of the pump prior to the button being pressed once it is released the

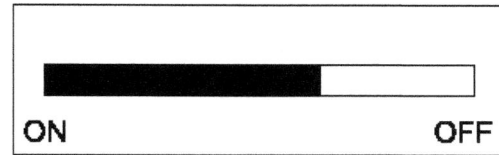

Figure 6. Off progress bar

pump returns to the Init mode. Figure 7 shows the final PIM for the pump which highlights the effect of this behaviour (all states being linked to the *Init* mode state). This makes the PIM much more complex than that of the manual (which gives no indication of the behaviour). The effect on the user is that they may be forced to repeat several steps of the setup procedures in order to return to the state they had reached prior to the button press, as values that are entered prior to the 'confirm rate' step are not saved. This means that after this accidental return to *Init* the values default to the previous saved values.

The only mode in which the ON/OFF button does not exhibit this behaviour is the *Infusion* mode. It is not possible to turn the pump off while an infusion is running so the button has no behaviour in this mode. However, if the infusion is paused and then the ON/OFF button is pressed it does once again return to the *Init* mode. Although in this case the settings are all saved as they were prior to the interruption (so time passed and amount already infused is remembered) the user is still required to repeat several steps and check this information prior to restarting the infusion. We identify this as an undesirable behaviour of the pump as it could have an impact on the length of time required to set up an infusion and also affect a running infusion.

Note that what has been happening as we build the model of the physical pump (rather than the pump-as-in-the-manual) is that we have been forced, because we are trying to discover all the ways of interaction in order to get a complete model, to consider many sequences of interaction that the manual did not cover. So, even the process of building the model from the pump itself is an important enterprise. That observation, that building models is, of itself, a valuable enterprise, is of course not new, and applies to all design and implementation endeavours.

VALIDATING THE MODELS

To ensure we have correctly built the models we must validate them. The presentation models are created using the PIMed tool [8], which also has the ability to automatically generate a set of abstract tests from a model. These tests are given in first-order logic and then exported in an XML format, and describe conditions on each of the modes with respect to the defined behaviours. Once the tests are generated from a model (either the model built from the manual or the one built from inspecting the pump) we manually instantiate them and check that the manual or the pump (depending on which model the test relates to) is able to pass the tests. If any test is not passed it is an indication that there is an error in the

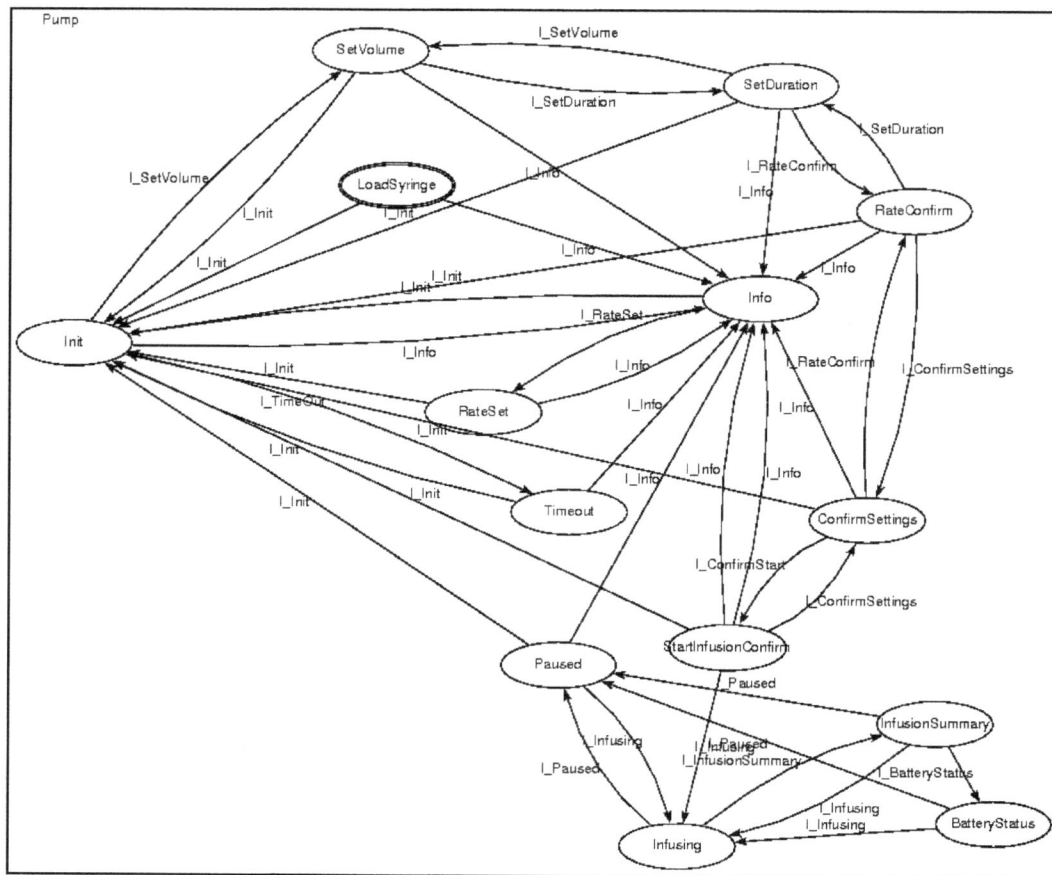

Figure 7. PIM of pump via experimentation

associated model. For example, one of the abstract tests relating to a particular I-behaviour of both the models is described (in XML) as follows:

$< ibtest >$
$< ibstate > LoadSyringe < /ibstate >$
$< ibwname > InfoSK < /ibwname >$
$< ibehaviour > I\_Info < /ibehaviour >$
$< /ibtest >$

This tells us that when the device is in the *LoadSyringe state* the InfoSK widget should exhibit the *I_Info* behaviour. Generally we can deduce the meaning of *I_Info* (as changes to the *Info* state) but if we are not sure of the meaning we can refer to the PIM for clarity. In order to pass this test the pump should exhibit this behaviour and the manual describe it. Several errors were discovered in our initial model, these were fixed and a new set of tests generated for validation. The process of testing also highlighted some issues which had not been fully explored. In particular more examination was needed of the *ResumeInfusion* mode which should occur after loading a syringe if a prior infusion has been interrupted. In order to fully test this under all conditions a further set of tests were developed. Conventional validation and testing methods can be also be used on the Z functionality model to make sure that it too is valid.

COMPARING THE MODELS

The final stage was to compare the models of the manual with the models of the pump. This can be done in several ways. We can compare the individual models (presentation models, PIMs, PMR and specification) to ensure consistency of the different elements (navigation, functional behaviour, behaviour in modes *etc.*) We can also use the sets of abstract tests generated from the models as a source of comparison. A third approach is to use the ProB animations for comparison. Finally we could also use the μ-charttrace refinement procedure defined in [10], however this final approach is beyond the scope (and size limit) of this paper.

Comparing the PIMs

The PIMs of the manual and pump are small enough to perform a manual inspection (ten states and fourteen states respectively). Before we can check them to ensure that any states and transitions in the PIM of the manual (which describe how a user navigates between modes of the pump) are also described in the PIM of the pump we need to rename some of the states and transitions to normalize the models. For example when modelling the pump we used *LoadSyringe* as the name of a mode which is concerned only with the physical insertion of the syringe into the pump and then *Init* as the mode where syringe selection takes place, but in the model of the manual we have described these as a single mode called

LoadSyringe. Once we had performed this step we then compared the models and found that they were inconsistent (for the reasons highlighted previously) and so we can state that not all descriptions in the manual which relate to how a user changes between modes of the pump correctly describe how the pump behaves (there are of course many additional transitions in the pump not described in the manual).

We are also interested in any states of the PIM exhibiting deadlock. There is a state in the PIM of the manual that has no outgoing transitions, but when we compare this to the corresponding state in the PIM of the pump there is no such deadlock. The pump's PIM is deadlock free (which we would expect as deadlock would be an adverse condition) and so in this respect the manual is under-defined. We suggest it is advisable to, in the manual, provide users with necessary information about how to leave any mode of the pump if a description of how to enter that mode is given.

Comparing the Sets of Tests

The tests describe each mode from the presentation models and the requirements on behaviours available within those modes. As we have already considered the navigational behaviours (or I-behaviours) by way of the PIM and we know that non-behavioural widgets will be different (as described earlier) we use this comparison to consider the functional behaviours (or S-behaviours). There are two requirements to check. Firstly, that any S-behaviour test for the manual is also an S-behaviour test for the pump, and secondly the detail of that behaviour (from the specifications) is the same.

While we found that all of the S-behaviour tests from the model of the manual were present in the tests from the model of the pump, there were differences in their specifications. This was mainly in relation to operations which used the UP and DOWN keys to change values (for example when changing rate or volume to be infused *etc.*) The UP and DOWN keys can actually be interacted with in two different ways, either by a single press or a continuous holding down of the button and the way the values change in response differs depending on which of these is used, this is not described in the manual. Also, whilst the manual states that the VTBI can be similarly adjusted up or down using these same buttons. In fact when this mode is first entered the VTBI can be reduced by way of the DOWN key, but cannot be increased by way of the UP key as a maximum limit is calculated based on the size of the loaded syringe and the position of the actuator. If the VTBI is reduced it can then subsequently be increased (but only up to this calculated maximum level).

CONCLUSIONS

Our main conclusion is that the manual and the device itself are not consistent. Anecdotally we know that the biomedical technicians who manage these devices at our local hospital are aware of this and do not provide the manual directly to users (instead providing both their own and the pump distributor's instructions). We have picked out a few of the ways that this inconsistency manifests itself above, and there are others. In this paper (as we planned) we have not even had to go into more detailed and mathematical techniques of looking for failures of a refinement relationship between the two models; the inconsistencies were evident without resorting to more formal means. The more formal approach would, of course, be needed were we to want to prove consistency for this safety-critical system-but that is a story for a further paper.

The methods we have described here not only show the inconsistency, but they show us, more or less, where to look in the models if we want to repair the differences.

One of the useful results of this work is the ability to model several pieces of documentation about a device (manufacturer's instructions, in-house documentation, training material *etc.*) and ensure that they are all consistent, not only with each other but also with the device. The comparison is more than just an *ad hoc* examination of the manual and then examination of the pump, it follows a systematic approach that ensures that both are fully considered in the same way. The resulting formal models mean that we have a uniform way of recording results that allows us to use tools to support reasoning. As the number of such devices increases in a medical setting it becomes critical to ensure that there is no confusion about how they are used to perform the necessary tasks and this is one step in helping to achieve this.

Another use for this technique, when designing a new device, would be to develop (and test, validate, usability test *etc.*) the model first, and then derive both the documentation and the device itself from the one single model. Consistency between manual and device is then assured.

Once a model for a manual is satisfactory, derivation of training materials can be carried out, and again these can be consistent with the manual by construction, or they can be written, modeled and checked for consistency in ways similar to those described in this paper.

FUTURE WORK

The next step for this project is to perform interviews with actual users of this pump to discover how they have (or have not) been affected by any of the issues we outline in this paper. We are also interested in discovering what sort of information they find useful in training material and investigate how much of this can be inferred from the models we have produced (*i.e.* can be use the models to derive a 'better' manual). We also intend to use ProB's visualization facility to make animation and validation more effective.

ACKNOWLEDGMENTS

We would like to thank Rex Edge and Murray McGovern from the Waikato District Health Board for access to the pump used in this research, and for useful discussions relating to this work.

REFERENCES

1. Bowen, J., and Reeves, S. Formal models for informal GUI designs. In *1st International Workshop on Formal Methods for Interactive Systems, Macau SAR China, 31 October 2006*, vol. 183, Electronic Notes in Theoretical Computer Science, Elsevier (2006), 57–72.

2. Caesarea Medical Electronics. Niki T34 syringe pump instruction manual. *ref. 100-090SS Edition* (2008).

3. Campos, J., and Harrison, M. Modelling and analysing the interactive behaviour of an infusion pump. *ECEASST 11* (2001).

4. Derrick, J., and Boiten, E. *Refinement in Z and Object-Z: Foundations and Advanced Applications.* Formal Approaches to Computing and Information Technology. Springer, May 2001.

5. Engineering and Physical Sciences Research Council. CHI+MED: Multidisciplinary computer-human interaction research for the design and safe use of interactive medical devices, epsrc reference: Ep/g059063/1, 2011.

6. Henson, M. C., Deutsch, M., and Reeves, S. *Z Logic and Its Applications.* Springer: Monographs in Theoretical Computer Science. An EATCS Series, 2008, 489–596.

7. ISO/IEC 13568. *Information Technology—Z Formal Specification Notation—Syntax, Type System and Semantics*, first ed. Prentice-Hall International series in computer science. ISO/IEC, 2002.

8. PIMed, http://sourceforge.net/projects/pims1/?source=directory.

9. ProB, http://www.stups.uni-dusseldorf.de/prob, 2012.

10. Reeve, G. *A Refinement Theory for μCharts.* PhD thesis, The University of Waikato, 2005.

11. Thimbleby, H., Blandford, A., Cauchi, A., Curzon, P., Eslambolchilar, P., Furniss, D., Gimblett, A., Huang, H., Lee, P., Li, Y., Masci, P., Oladimeji, P., Rjakomar, A., and Rukšėnas, R. Comparing actual practice and user manuals: A case study based on programmable infusion pumps. In *Proceedings ACM SIGCHI Symposium on Engineering Interactive Computing Systems (EICS): Engineering Interactive Computing Systems for Medicine and Health Care*, ACM (2011), 59–64.

12. Thimbleby, H., and Ladkin, P. From logic to manuals again. *IEE Proceedings - Software 144*, 3 (1997), 185–192.

13. Woodcock, J., and Davies, J. *Using Z: Specification, Refinement and Proof.* Prentice Hall, 1996.

Formal Analysis of Ubiquitous Computing Environments through the APEX Framework

José Luís Silva[1], José Creissac Campos[1], and Michael D. Harrison[2]

[1]Departamento de Informática/Universidade do Minho & HASLab/INESC TEC
{jlsilva, jose.campos}@di.uminho.pt

[2]School of Electrical Engineering and Computer Science, Queen Mary University of London
michael.harrison@eecs.qmul.ac.uk

ABSTRACT

Ubiquitous computing (ubicomp) systems involve complex interactions between multiple devices and users. This complexity makes it difficult to establish whether: (1) observations made about use are truly representative of all possible interactions; (2) desirable characteristics of the system are true in all possible scenarios. To address these issues, techniques are needed that support an exhaustive analysis of a system's design. This paper demonstrates one such exhaustive analysis technique that supports the early evaluation of alternative designs for ubiquitous computing environments. The technique combines models of behavior within the environment with a virtual world that allows its simulation. The models support checking of properties based on patterns. These patterns help the analyst to generate and verify relevant properties. Where these properties fail then scenarios suggested by the failure provide an important aid to redesign. The proposed technique uses APEX, a framework for rapid prototyping of ubiquitous environments based on Petri nets. The approach is illustrated through a smart library example. Its benefits and limitations are discussed.

Author Keywords

Ubiquitous and Context-Aware Computing; Analysis; Modeling; Prototyping; 3D virtual environments.

ACM Classification Keywords

F.3.1 [Logics and meanings of programs]: Specifying and Verifying and Reasoning about Programs -Mechanical verification; H.5.2 [Information Interfaces and Presentation]: User Interfaces - Prototyping; D.2.m [Software Engineering]: Miscellaneous – Rapid prototyping.

INTRODUCTION

The design and engineering of ubiquitous computing environments (i.e., electronically enriched environments that are able to sense and respond to the presence of people) present new challenges. Designing a ubiquitous computing

environment entails integrating a number of embedded devices and sensors into a meaningful whole, capable of adequately responding to multiple users and their own devices. Given the potential complexity of the interaction between all these elements, it is difficult to analyze a design thoroughly early in its development. This is further complicated by the critical role that the physical environment plays in these systems. It is not always feasible to deploy early versions of the system within a target environment because of restrictions of cost or availability.

Given this situation prototypes have a particular relevance. Indeed, using prototypes to understand an envisaged design has become a principal research approach in Ubiquitous computing [5]. We are particularly interested in the role of prototypes in evaluating the user experience of a target environment, and have been developing the APEX framework as a solution to this problem.

Previous papers have discussed use of the APEX tool as a model driven approach to the development of prototypes based on virtual environments [16, 17]. One important step in the development of a rapid prototype in APEX is to create a virtual environment that is close enough to the physical target system to provide an adequate and realistic experience for users. This environment is created for the user or users by means of a viewer in Opensimulator[1]. The simulation of the ubiquitous system can be achieved within virtual environment by using a colored Petri net (CPN) model to describe its behavior. By this means it is possible not only to interact with objects within the virtual environment but also with real users (via the viewers), simulated autonomous users that are also modeled in CPN, virtual interaction devices such as PDAs and sensors, and real interaction devices. These environments become prototypes of the envisaged systems, which can be used for evaluation.

As a result of the complex interactions arising from the combination of multiple sensors, devices and users in a physical space, observation of episodic use of the prototype alone is not sufficient to guarantee that some particular feature of the system is a property of the design. It becomes difficult to establish whether observations made about use

---

[1] http://opensimulator.org (last accessed January 20, 2012)

are truly representative of all possible interactions or whether certain characteristics of the system are true in all possible scenarios.

The fact that the behavior is driven by a CPN model makes it possible to analyze the behavior of the prototype systematically and exhaustively using CPN Tools [7]. It is this analysis of interactive systems that forms the discussion of the paper. The application of special purpose heuristics to the design of the ubiquitous system is the basis of the discussion. The next section discusses previous research. The paper then moves from a description of the approach to an example of its application.

The paper makes two of contributions.

- It introduces a method of evaluating ubicomp environments through exhaustive analysis, applying and adapting heuristics chosen from other areas of software engineering and HCI. This evaluation is complemented with an analysis of a simulation in 3D.

- It identifies property patterns in the identification and verification of properties.

The stages of analysis using these property patterns are demonstrated through an example.

BACKGROUND

A number of techniques within HCI support the analysis of the usability of an interactive system from early in its design. These techniques range from paper prototyping and Wizard of Oz, to the development of versions of the systems that can be used during user testing. Other techniques that do not require explicit user testing include the use of expert evaluation techniques such as Heuristic Evaluation and Cognitive Walkthrough.

Ubicomp environments present challenging usability evaluation problems. Because they are embedded within physical environments interactions with them differ from the styles of more traditional systems [8]. Interaction within the environment may be *explicit* and the devices used for interaction with the system subject to standard usability heuristics for small devices, or it may be *implicit* and arise simply as a result of the user changing their context (for example moving in or out of a room). In both cases each user's context plays an important role.

A number of evaluation techniques have been developed for dealing with implicit interactions within ubicomp environments. Kim et al. [8], for example, have presented several ubicomp case studies where evaluation has involved making use of physical space. Other evaluation approaches have aimed to provide early evaluation of a partially functional system by using Wizard-of-Oz techniques. Even these more limited approaches involve large resource investments: in the one case building real space for the ubicomp system, and in the other developing the system to a partially working level. These costs could be reduced by the application of heuristics to a ubicomp application as

explored by Mankoff et al. [10] in the context of ambient displays.

Scholtz et al. [18,13] have developed a framework for evaluating ubiquitous computing applications. They developed a set of sample metrics measures based on ubiquitous computing evaluation to assess whether adequate design principles are satisfied and if the design produces the desired user experience. This framework does not provide an exhaustive means of analyzing a developed prototype. Instead the focus is to identify key areas of evaluation and to identify metrics and design guidelines to improve user experience in ubiquitous systems.

Ubiquitous systems prototyping research is mostly concerned with the development of prototypes of isolated devices (e.g. Topiary [9]). Some approaches like 3DSim [15] and VARU [6] develop simulations of actual environments like APEX. The benefit of APEX is that modeling and associated analytical approaches can be combined with simulations. Additionally APEX supports a multilayered development approach: simulation layer (Opensimulator); a modeling layer (using CPN Tools) and a physical layer (using external devices and real users).

Scholtz et al. [14] argue the need to develop interdisciplinary evaluation techniques to address ubicomp properties at early stages in design. Assessment techniques are required to evaluate alternative solutions before deploying the system. The complexity of a physical environment where a number of devices are situated, and the added complexity of real world activities, means that it is hard to assess which observations are representative of the use of the system. Likewise it is difficult to assess informally whether characteristics of the system, assessed against specific heuristics, hold across all possible usage scenarios.

The experience of exploring ubicomp environments depends on individual preferences. However some characteristics of user experience can be expressed as properties of the environment. These properties can complement an understanding of experience based on empirical evaluation of the use of a prototype and should be seen as part of a toolset for evaluating a design. We argue that systematic and exhaustive techniques need to be part of an interdisciplinary approach. We follow Mankoff et al. [10] by developing property patterns from existing heuristics. Property patterns have two roles: i) helping identify interesting properties and ii) helping verify existing properties. For example a property of the *system* requires that there should be feedback for any user of the environment who carries out a particular kind of transaction. This can be expressed as a typical property that takes a standard form. This property pattern would provide the form and would complement evaluation techniques by offering exhaustive analysis of whether a property is true. This would not be feasible by exploring all possible user behaviors through observation.

APPROACH

Usability heuristics [11] are a starting point for analysis using the APEX system. In this approach the analyst is encouraged to explore how well a particular design supports general properties that encourage ease of use. The analyst or team of analysts bring their expertise in human factors or their understanding of the domain to decide where there are issues (for example in relation to ease of recovery or the visibility of the effect of explicit or implicit actions) in the design and propose design improvements.

Tool Support

To achieve a systematic and exhaustive analysis of the CPN model of the behavior of the system, the verification capabilities of CPN Tools are used. These tools provide a modeling and verification environment for Colored Petri Nets. Particularly relevant here is the State Space (SS) tool. The tool generates a *reachability* graph that defines the states that can be reached from some starting state. Each node of the graph represents an execution state. Arcs represent the binding of particular values (e.g. actions) from one state to a new one. Figure 1 illustrates part of one of these graphs. The whole graph represents all possible executions of a ubicomp system showing which actions can be executed in each system state. Each node is numbered and labeled with its number of input/output arcs. Arc and node labels are hidden by default in the tool, but can be checked interactively (e.g. arc caption in Figure 1).

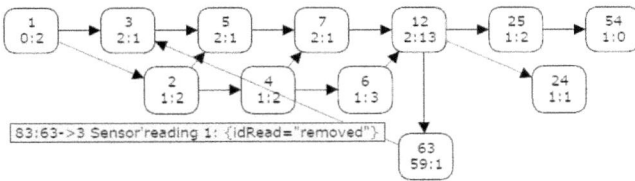

Figure 1- Reachability graph

The process of verification of a property involves applying a predicate to relevant states in the reachability graph. The returned result is either that the predicate is true of all relevant states or that the predicate fails to be true, in which case the path to the failing state is indicated. This path can then be used to explore a situation that may be of interest from the perspective of the design of the ubiquitous system.

Patterns

The approach uses verification patterns adapted from properties that are based on usability heuristics as well as a broader range of properties used in other fields [4]. Of particular interest is a set of property patterns provided by the IVY tool [2]. This tool is a model-based environment for the analysis of interactive systems that is used here as a starting point. In IVY patterns define *property templates*, expressed in temporal logic, which must be instantiated to the particular details of the system and property under consideration. This instantiation process creates a temporal formula that can be verified. Analysis based on the formula is then performed automatically by a model checker.

Applying the patterns in the context of APEX raises a number of challenges. A first challenge is how the property template defined within the pattern relates to the verification process. As explained above verification is achieved using the SS tool by writing predicates over the reachability graph. Hence, the pattern, instead of defining a temporal logic template, must define how the reachability graph is to be explored (in particular defining which predicates are needed) so that verification can be performed. Other challenges concern the interpretation of the patterns, and in particular:

- Who are the users? IVY patterns assume interaction between a user and the device. In APEX the interaction context is richer, involving spaces where several *users* might be present. Hence, when considering user actions and system responses it is necessary to consider how different users affect each other, e.g., an action by one user might trigger a system response directed to a different user. It becomes relevant to consider therefore who carried out an action or caused some change in the system state.

- What are the actions? In a ubicomp setting implicit interaction becomes relevant as well as explicit user action. The system might be responding to conditions arising through implicit user action or changes to the environment. These conditions are typically monitored indirectly through sensors, e.g., a user entering or leaving a room. Hence, rather than actions, *situations* of interest may require characterization.

- What is being analyzed? A general problem not specific to this context is whether the property is addressing the design of the system or the model itself, i.e., whether the property is being used to reason about features of the system's design, or is being used to validate the model itself. This affects the interpretation of the reachability graph. Indeed, while some nodes correspond to states of the ubiquitous system, others correspond to intermediate execution states of the model.

Setting Up the Analysis

The approach is illustrated in the next sections using a smart library context. The example illustrates the choice of property patterns and how these patterns are instantiated in the case of the example and then checked within the APEX framework.

As a brief indication of the process consider the following specific property that concerns the illumination of a book light. The light turns off depending on the user action (user taking the book or moving away) but also depends on the actions of other users (taking the book) and also of the state of the system (light already turned off). This property is an instance of a particular pattern, namely the feedback pattern. It requires that in all paths through the environment, and for all states in the paths, it is true that if the light is on for the book that the user wants and the user takes this book then in every next state the book light is turned off. This property relates to a specific user who takes the book, the one who has reserved it. The system would leave the light on in the book if the wrong person takes it, hence indicating that they are taking the book without reserving it.

For the property to be verified, the model must be converted to a form that will allow CPN Tools to check the truth of the property. CPN Tools require that the model be deterministic and "small" so as to reduce the search space used during analysis. The SS tool (part of CPN Tools) uses brute force to bind each variable to each of its possible known values, creating the reachability graph. Because in normal conditions the model exchanges information with the virtual world simulation and/or actual physical external devices, the model can in principle be of unlimited size. This large open model must therefore be translated into a closed one, so that it is tractable within the SS tool.

Closing the model means isolating it from external components. This is achieved by defining finite sets of possible values for all the variables in the model that previously held values acquired externally. CPN Tools defines a set of up to one hundred elements as *a small color set*. APEXi, a component of APEX, is used to initialize *small color sets* semi-automatically. The tool provides an interface (see Figure 5) to enable analysts to supply or select desired values that can be used to populate as tokens the relevant places of the CPN model as represented by a chosen scenario.

Property patterns are explored in APEX in the next section. They are represented formally and then instantiated for the example ubicomp environment.

PROPERTY SPECIFICATION PATTERNS FOR UBICOMP ENVIRONMENTS

Patterns provide a basis for analysis serving two roles: they aid the process of elicitation of appropriate properties; they help the analyst use CPN Tools to perform the analysis of the instantiated property. A number of relevant property patterns are now described. These patterns are adapted from those supported by the IVY tool [2] to the ubicomp context.

In [3] patterns are expressed as CTL templates to be instantiated to concrete actions and predicates. We express the patterns as predicates over the CPN model's reachability graph where actions are represented as transitions and effects as predicates over states. States are defined by the values of the attributes in the model and capture relevant configurations/conditions of the system.

The Consistency Pattern

Justification: Consistency is a heuristic that has widespread relevance, including in the Ubicomp area [10].

Intuition: The consistency pattern defined in [3] captures the requirement that a given event Q always causes a defined effect R (expressed as a predicate over the states before and after Q). There is optionally an additional predi-

cate (a guard) that constrains when the system behaves consistently.

In the ubicomp context: the event (Q) is either an explicit or an implicit action by the user which might change the environment or the state of the system. Implicit actions and environment changes are expressed in terms of the values read by the sensors in the system. The effect of the action (R) is a change in the state of the system as a whole. Whether users perceive the change in environment is an important element of the effect. Context plays an important role. If an action by some user is being analyzed then the presence of other users might also influence the response. Hence, the gate in the library may not close when a user leaves its neighborhood because of the presence of another user. These various dimensions add to the texture in which the pattern can be used beyond providing values for Q and R. The context of the analyzed environment is described by the tokens defined by *small color sets* initialized by the APEXi tool.

The algorithm: The algorithm to be followed is presented in Figure 2. For simplicity sake this algorithm assumes that the given effect happens in response to the particular event(s)/state(s) being considered only (this can be checked with the Precedence pattern below). The functions in the figure are used to identify, in the reachability graph, counter examples for the property being verified. The *counterExampleNodes* function identifies the nodes of the counter example by firstly identifying relevant nodes (corresponding to the effect R – *identifyRelevantNodes* function). Nodes correspond to states of the reachability graph. From the identified relevant nodes (returned by the *identifyRelevantNodes* function) the algorithm attempts to identify alternative paths were the desired effect is not verified. The *counterExampleNodes* function is applied to the set of relevant values of the selected scenario (using *map*) and the resulting list of nodes is held in the *CONSISTENCY* variable. If the list is empty, the property holds. The underlined pieces in Figure 2 are the parts that need to be instantiated. They identify the places in the Petri net that are relevant for the property being verified. A concrete instantiation of this algorithm is presented in Figure 6.

The Feedback Pattern

Feedback is a particular use of the consistency pattern where a user action Q always causes a perceivable effect R. In the ubicomp context the action (R) represents a change that is observable in the environment though it should be noted that the person causing the system's response might not necessarily be the same as the person who observes the response. Even if it is the same person, the fact that the response might be triggered by an implicit interaction or an environment change begs the question of whether the response will be salient enough. At this stage issues such as salience are not being considered, rather the concern is to guarantee that feedback is always provided. It is likely that evaluating the salience of a particular feedback will require input from the simulation (an example of synergy between the formal and empirical analysis - but see [12] for a formal treatment of salience).

```
fun identifyRelevantNodes obj =
  PredAllNodes (fn n => cf(obj,Mark.MODULE'PLACE 1 n) > 0)
--------------------------------------------------------------------------
fun counterExampleNodes u =
 let
  val nodes = identifyRelevantNodes u
 in
  let
   val predecessorsNodes =
   SearchNodes (nodes, fn _ => true, NoLimit, fn n => InNodes n, [], op ^^)
  in
   let
    val nodesPredecessorsNodesWith2orMoreSucessors =
    SearchNodes (remdupl(predecessorsNodes), fn n => not(contains nodes  [n])
                andalso length( OutNodes n) >= 2, NoLimit, fn n => n, [], op ::)
   in
    SearchNodes (remdupl(nodesPredecessorsNodesWith2orMoreSucessors),
              fn n => not( contains (map (fn x=> Reachable(n,x) andalso
              length(NodesInPath (n,x))>2) nodes) [true]), NoLimit,
              fn n => n, [], op ::)
   end
  end
 end
--------------------------------------------------------------------------
val CONSISTENCY =
  map(fn u => counterExampleNodes u) (UpperMultiSet (Mark.MODULE'PLACE 1)
```

Figure 2 - The consistency/feedback pattern algorithm

The Reachability Pattern
Justification: reachability is a basic property over which other properties are derived (e.g. precedence, completeness). It can be used to demonstrate that the system can reach a specific state or situation.

Intuition: The reachability pattern captures the requirement that the system can always evolve from one specific state S to another state Q.

In the ubicomp context: environmental situations are represented as states based on particular distinguishing features, for example, a book being illuminated, or a user being at a given location. Some features of the state are likely to be directly controlled by the system (the light on the book), while others are observed (the user's position), although the observed features might be indirectly influenced by the system (e.g., the gate, when it opens, enables the user to move inside the library). Depending on the complexity of the system, establishing how these influences work will not be easy and can be aided by formal verification.

The algorithm: uses the reachability graph and identifies desired states with identifying attributes. For each identified state S the algorithm checks whether it is possible to reach a new state Q with the desired environment attributes. An instance of the algorithm can be found in Figure 7.

The Precedence Pattern
Justification: The precedence pattern describes relationships between a pair of events/states where the occurrence of the first is a necessary pre-condition for the occurrence of the second.

Intuition: This pattern captures the requirement that a state or event S precedes another state or event P. The occurrence of the second is enabled by the occurrence of the first.

In the ubicomp context: This property can be used to verify that some event or state does not occur without the satisfaction of a pre-condition. Consider for example the property concerned with illuminating the book. The first state (S), triggered by a user action (for example, as the user approaches the book), is a pre-condition for the occurrence of the second state (P – book light turned on). The property requires that the light will never turn on without a relevant user approaching the book. Note that this does not guarantee that the light will always turn on when a relevant user as would be required by a consistency property.

The algorithm: identifies the second states (P) of the reachability graph based on attributes of the environment and then identifies each predecessor. The presence of state S characterized by specified attributes is verified.

Other Patterns
Several other patterns were also adapted, for example: Reversibility (the effect of a given action can eventually be undone); Possibility (some event or state is always possible throughout the execution of the system); Universality (some condition always holds); or Eventuality (some event or condition must eventually hold at some point).

DEVELOPING A MODEL FOR ANALYSIS OF A SMART LIBRARY
The patterns are now applied to an example. The analysis process requires an initial setup before property patterns can be instantiated.

Introduction to the Example
A "smart library" identifies books stored on bookshelves using Radio Frequency Identification (RFID) tags. Screens provide context sensitive information to library users. A registered library user is allowed entry or exit via gates. When a registered user arrives at the entry gate, a screen displays which books have already been requested by them (using a web interface at their desktop for example) and opens the entry gate.

The system recognizes the users' position in real-time by means of presence sensors. The users are guided to required books by further screens. As the user approaches the book's location a light with a distinctive color is turned on allowing several users looking for books in nearby locations to distinguish their own request. When the book is removed, the light on the book is turned off. As the user returns to the exit gate a personalized list of requested and returned books is displayed on a screen by the gate. The gate is then opened so that the user can leave.

While the example is not based on any specific existing system, similar systems could be used to support dispatch in relation to e-shopping or for guiding people inside a building (e.g. hospital or airport). Indeed, a method and system for localizing objects among a set of stacked objects equipped with improved RFID tags has been patented [1] suggesting the feasibility of the physical implementation of the system.

The Model

An APEX prototype of the library example is described more fully in [16]. Here the process of using it for verification is now illustrated.

Creating the prototype involves creating the virtual environment and extending the APEX CPN *base model*. The *base model* underpins the behavioral model of the ubiquitous system. Specific behavior relating to the library system is added to the *base model* and this animates the environment so that it is appropriate for evaluation based on user exploration of the virtual space as well as being a basis for verification.

A number of modules are added that simulate the behavior of gates, books, PDAs and displays. The Gate module is described using CPN in Figure 3 and holds information about the users, the devices and the sensors present in the environment. The purpose of the gates module is to open a gate when a user with appropriate "entering" permission is in the proximity of a presence sensor associated with the gate. The Gate module consists of a transition to open a gate and another one to close it. Whether the module will open or close the gate is based on information held by a number of places: *Dynamic Objects* (e.g. gates, screens), *Users* and *P_sensors* (presence sensors).

The opened or closed state of the gates is recognized through two places: the *Dynamic Object* place (holds tokens for closed gates) and the *gates opened* place (holds tokens for opened gates).

A function is used to identify the type of the objects that are being dealt with in the *Dynamic Objects* place. A particular concern is to identify the gates because the *Dynamic Object* place holds objects other than gates. The *is* function is designed to receive a dynamic object and a string as arguments and to compare the type of the object against the string to check whether there is a correspondence. In the case of the gate further information is required to decide whether to open or close the gate. This information includes whether: (i) a user is near a presence sensor; (ii) the presence sensor affects the gate; (iii)nobody is near the presence sensor.

Three functions are used to capture these conditions: *userNearPresenceSensor*, *objAfectedByPresenceSensor* and *nobodyNearPresenceSensor*.

A further module, responsible for providing directions to users, is presented in Figure 4. The module uses the positions of the requested book and the user to send information to the relevant PDA about which direction should be followed. The means of getting the direction and sending it to the appropriate PDA is associated with the *show direction* transition. In particular the *sendUserInfo* function is used to send information to a specified user. The identifier of the sensor used to obtain the direction is forwarded by the module to the *PDAs with the new direction info* place to be used to decide when to display default information (*show default* transition).

This combination of modules (along with others which pick up books and notify relevant users) can now be analyzed.

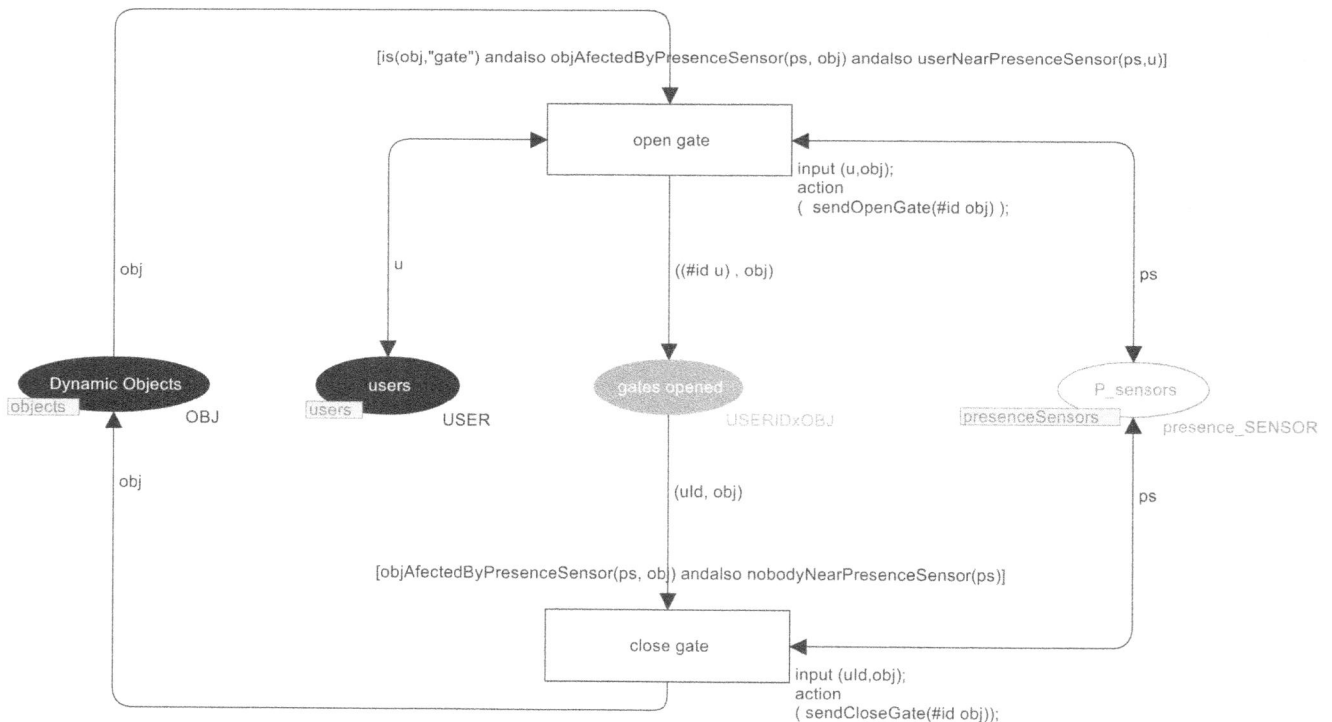

Figure 3 - Gates module

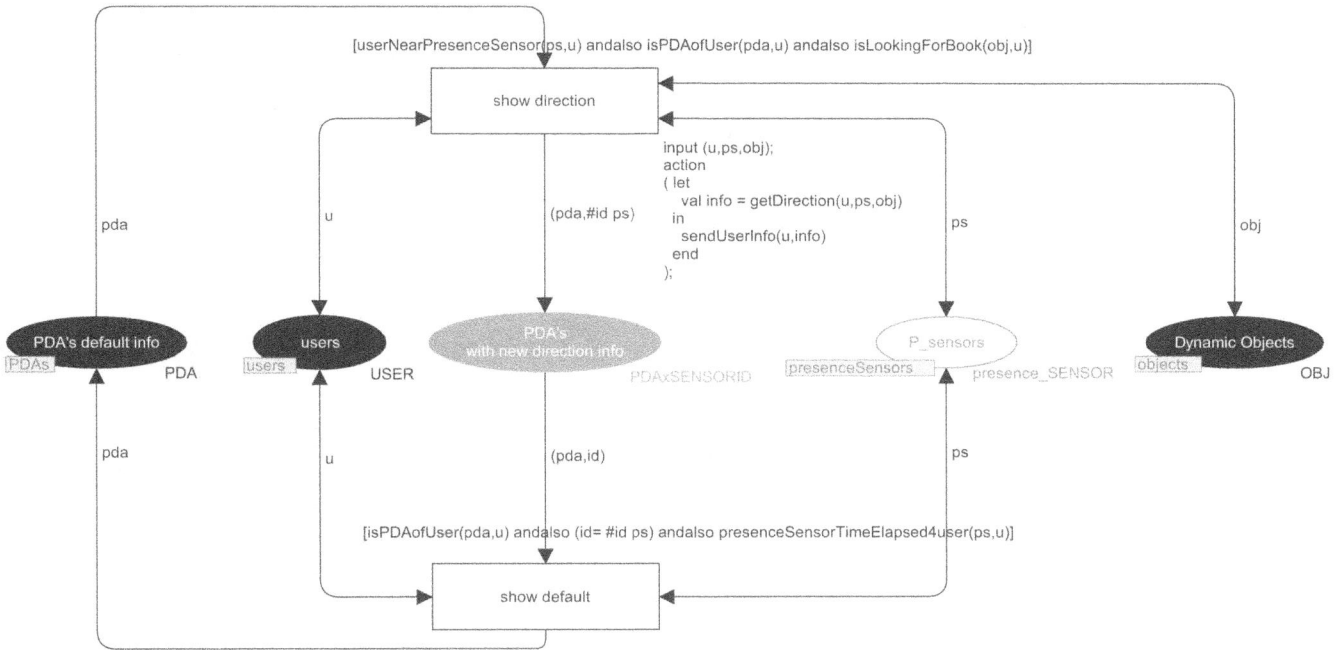

Figure 4 - User's PDA book direction module (open version)

Setting Up the Model for Analysis

The model must be transformed into a closed model containing *small color sets* in order to reduce the state space for analysis using the SS tool. This is achieved by removing the non-deterministic elements of the model, isolating it from external components using scenarios that limit the behavior of the open elements.

The APEXi tool has been designed to ease scenario creation. Values associated with instances of behavior and dynamic objects are automatically inserted into *small color sets*. Figure 5 shows values provided to APEXi as follows:

- one user (Test User - *UsersIDs* field) desiring the book with identifier 1 (*values* field);

- two presence sensors, one at the entrance and the other close to the bookshelf (*Sfeatures* field);

- two books with identifiers 1 and 2 (*ObjIDs* and *OBJfeatures* fields);

- one gate with identifier 3 (*ObjIDs* and *OBJfeatures* fields).

These values set up a scenario where the feedback property is going to be analyzed. Once external library services have been related to gates, book lights and behaviors as determined by user position and user requests for selected values. The model becomes adequate for analysis. A number of similar scenarios should be selected with the help of human factors or domain specialists to complete the analysis. For instance it does not make sense to analyze gate behaviors without users.

INSTANTIATING PROPERTY TEMPLATES

Having developed an appropriate model for analysis and selected a scenario, it is now possible to proceed. Analysts may know which property they want to prove (e.g., by observing real users as they interact with the simulation), but they can also have difficulties in their identification. The templates help them in this task. By capturing (and thus guiding the analysis towards) potentially relevant features of a design, they help the analyst discover appropriate properties.

Additionally, using property templates makes it easier to verify properties because algorithms to verify each of the property patterns can be reused.

Three property templates are considered in relation to this example: feedback, reachability and precedence. The other templates mentioned in the paper have similar application.

Feedback

Parameters for property templates are instantiated with user interactions, environment changes and features or states of the environment. An instance of the feedback pattern is whether the books always respond to relevant approaching users. The feedback pattern parameters are instantiated with the following values: action Q is defined as the implicit action occurring when the user approaches the bookshelf (the proximity of the user to the bookshelf is detected by presence sensors in the environment); effect R is defined as changing the environment so that the relevant light is switched on; guard S is defined as stating that the light must initially be off for this property to hold.

This pattern identifies a relevant feedback property: *"when a user approaches the appropriate bookshelf the book lights up (unless it is already on)"*.

137

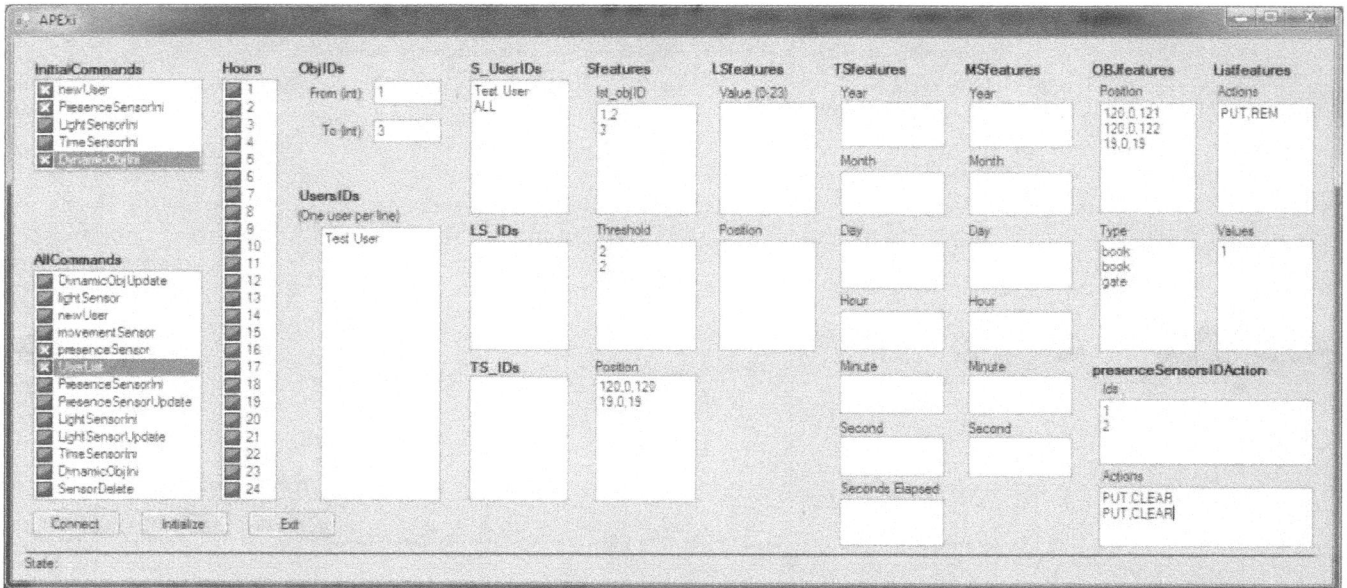

Figure 5 - APEXi tool with selected value used to analyze the feedback property pattern

Reachability

The reachability template can be instantiated similarly: state Q is the situation where a book that a user is looking for is picked up by another person (stops being available); state S is the situation when the user is notified.

This example instantiation identifies the property: "*If a book that a user is looking for is picked up by another person (stops being available), the user is notified*".

Precedence

The precedence template can be instantiated: state S corresponds to the relevant user being near the bookshelf; state P to the light being turned on.

This identifies "*the light does not turn on while the relevant user is not near the bookshelf*".

For analysis it is also necessary to know how many users this property will be applied to as well as which actions are considered (implicit or explicit), what is going to be analyzed, the environment or the mode itself. The selection of adequate scenarios for analysis is critical to the results obtained.

CHECKING THE MODEL USING THE SS TOOL

Checking the properties of the model is considered in this section. This process uses the APEX tools, specifying and instantiating the algorithms in CPN Tools as specified by the appropriate pattern.

Feedback

To verify the first property "*when a user approaches their requested book the book's light turns on*" we use and instantiate the algorithm of the feedback pattern (see Figure 6). The *identifyRelevantNodes* function of the algorithm is instantiated with the place where the search (i.e. *Books'LightedBooks*) starts to identify the relevant nodes. This function identifies those nodes of the reachability

graph where there are books with lights switched on. The other generic part of the algorithm is also instantiated, with place *AnimationSetup'Dynamic_Objects* used to identify the nodes used in the analysis.

```
fun identifyRelevantNodes obj =
PredAllNodes (fn n => cf(obj,Mark.Books'LightedBooks 1 n) > 0)
----------------------------------------------------------------
fun counterExampleNodes u =
let
  val nodes = identifyRelevantNodes u
in
let
  val predecessorsNodes =
  SearchNodes (nodes, fn _ => true, NoLimit, fn n => InNodes n, [], op ^^)
in
  let
    val nodesPredecessorsNodesWith2orMoreSucessors =
    SearchNodes (remdupl(predecessorsNodes), fn n => not(contains nodes [n])
      andalso length( OutNodes n) >= 2, NoLimit, fn n => n, [], op ::)
  in
    SearchNodes (remdupl(nodesPredecessorsNodesWith2orMoreSucessors),
      fn n => not( contains (map (fn x=> Reachable(n,x) andalso
        length(NodesInPath (n,x))>2) nodes) [true]), NoLimit, fn n => n, [], op ::)
  end
end
end
----------------------------------------------------------------
val FEEDBACK =
      map(fn u => counterExampleNodes u)
          (UpperMultiSet (Mark.AnimationSetup'Dynamic_Objects 1))
```

Figure 6 - Book's light behavior property (feedback)

After being instantiated, this concrete algorithm identifies, in this case, those nodes where the user is near the desired book and the book's light has not turned on (*FEEDBACK* variable in Figure 6). The algorithm identifies firstly the nodes in the reachability graph where the user is already detected near the bookshelf, but the system is still to react. From these nodes the system can either turn the book's light on, or alternatively choose to process some other relevant event. Selecting the second alternative (doing something else), creates the executions from which a node with the book's light on is not reached (*counterExampleNodes* function). The resulting list of nodes is empty. This means that for the analyzed scenario (considering the values provided) there is no system execution containing a node where the light should be turned on but was not.

Summing up, the feedback property algorithm was used to verify the property template. As stated the instantiation is simply accomplished, in this case, by indicating the places where the relevant nodes used by the algorithm should be reached.

Reachability

The second property, "*if a book a user is looking for is picked up by another person (stops being available), the user is notified*" is now addressed. This property is a reachability property, and its verification follows the pattern. Reachability properties demonstrate whether it is possible, from one state, to reach the other state (reachability between two nodes of the reachability graph). This is translated in the stated property as if, for every user looking for the same book and every picked up book state, a user notification state is reachable. The property pattern followed describes how the algorithm can be instantiated to check reachability properties.

This property is again executed using a specific scenario. Properties are parameterized using the selected values from the *small color sets* specified in APEXi. For example, in the property verification algorithm (Figure 7), the user *Silva* and the book with id equal to 1 (*userIDxOBJ* and *book* variables) are used because these are elements that compose the new selected scenario for analysis (APEXi selected values). Obviously this scenario should have at least two users looking for the same book.

The idea behind the demonstration of this property is to identify states from which a user picks up a book and the system is not able to reach a notification state for users looking for this book. In other words the aim is to find counter examples where the system does not have the required properties. Figure 7 shows the instantiation of the reachability pattern algorithm. This is achieved by instantiating the *targetNodes* and *originalNodes* functions to identify the relevant nodes (see underlined pieces in Figure 7). The places used to identify the nodes to be used in the analysis (i.e. *BookPickUp'User_Notified* and *BookPickUp'OBJ_deleted*) and concrete tokens to be identified in these places (i.e. *userIDxOBJ* and *book*) are provided. By this means the desired property can be verified.

The execution of this concrete algorithm identifies firstly all notification nodes (returned by the *targetNodes* function). When these have been identified, all nodes at which the book is picked up are identified (returned by the *originalNodes* function). The final stage is to identify any node in which the book is picked up and from which no notification can be made, i.e. no notification node is reachable (hold in the *REACHABILITY* variable). Checking this property using the algorithm (with each of the three users of the selected scenario as parameter) returns no nodes (*REACHABILITY* variable value) which means that for the

selected scenario (three users looking for the same book) whenever a user picks up a book it is possible to notify all users looking for the book.

```
val userIDxOBJ =
("Silva",{id="1",objType="book",position={x=120,y=0,z=121}}) : USERIDxOBJ

fun targetNodes obj
= PredAllNodes (fn n => cf(obj,Mark.BookPickUp'Users_Notified 1 n) > 0)

val TS = targetNodes userIDxOBJ
---------------------------------------------------------------------------
val book =
{id="1",objType="book",position={x=120,y=0,z=121}} : OBJ

fun originalNodes obj
= PredAllNodes (fn n => cf(obj,Mark.BookPickUp'OBJ_deleted 1 n) > 0)

val OS = originalNodes book
---------------------------------------------------------------------------
val REACHABILITY =
  SearchNodes (OS,
  fn n =>  not ( contains (map (fn x=> Reachable(n,x)) TS)) [true] ),
  NoLimit, fn n => n, [], op ::)
```

Figure 7 - Notification property (reachability)

Precedence

The third property "*the light does not turn on while the relevant user is not near the bookshelf*" follows the precedence property pattern. To reach a state where the light is on, a relevant user must be near the bookshelf. The precedence algorithm consists in firstly identifying the nodes where the light is on and secondly analyzing their predecessors to check the presence of a user close to a bookshelf. The return of zero nodes means that for the selected scenario the property is always true.

Patterns help developers to verify identified properties and then use relevant algorithms for checking the properties.

DISCUSSION

Evaluating a ubicomp environment by analyzing its behavior exhaustively does not guarantee that the proposed design solution provides an adequate experience. As seen with the feedback property pattern, a system satisfying this property could mean that at some level the system provides feedback but nevertheless the crucial elements in the environment that are actually required for feedback are missing from the analysis. Is the feedback provided salient? Can the feedback be actually seen by the user? What will the feedback look like physically? These are issues raised through analysis at the modeling layer. The value of the APEX framework with its multilayered prototyping approach is that these broader questions can be addressed. Each layer supports a specific type of evaluation: observation of virtual objects' behavior, and user reaction to them, within a virtual world (in the simulation layer); analysis of the model (in the modeling layer); observation of real objects (e.g. actual smart phones) connected to the virtual world, and users reaction to them (in the physical layer).

The framework supports a development process in which virtual, physical or mixed elements are explored depending on the availability of these components. The initial stages of development can be achieved entirely in terms of a CPN model. Further development can be moved into the virtual world before moving wholly or partially into the physical world. In summary it is possible to explore the design from a variety of perspectives.

CONCLUSIONS

This paper introduces a method of evaluating ubicomp environments through exhaustive analysis, applying and adapting heuristics chosen from other areas of software engineering and HCI. Ubicomp environments pose new challenges when compared with traditional interactive systems. The introduced approach enables the successful exhaustive analysis of ubicomp environments through property patterns. These patterns were instantiated in a variety of ways in the context of ubicomp environments leading to the identification of procedures to verify different property templates. The proposed property templates aim to help developers match properties and then to write predicates over the reachability graph making easier the demonstration of properties using APEX. More property patterns (algorithms) emerged through the analysis with the stated property templates. Due to space limitations only some of them have been presented.

APEX through CPN provides a way to analyze exhaustively and formally every portion of the system behavior for selected scenarios and to demonstrate properties on it. The APEX multilayer approach complements this analysis.

ACKNOWLEDGMENTS

This work is financed by the ERDF – European Regional Development Fund through the COMPETE Programme (Operational Programme for Competitiveness) and by the Portuguese Government through FCT – Portuguese Foundation for Science and Technology, within project ref. PTDC/EIA-EIA/116069/2009 (APEX project). José L Silva is further funded by the Portuguese Government, through FCT, under grant SFRH/BD/41179/2007. Michael Harrison is supported by the UK EPSRC (EP/G059063/1) funded CHI+MED project.

REFERENCES

1. Bauchot, F., Clement, J.-Y., Marmigere, G., Picon, J. Method and structure for localizing objects using daisy chained RFID tags. 2007. United States Patent Application Publication Pub. No. US 2007/0257799 A1.

2. Campos, J. and Harrison, M. Systematic analysis of control panel interfaces using formal tools. *Interactive Systems. Design, Specification, and Verification*, (2008), Springer LNCS 5136, 72–85.

3. Campos, J. and Harrison, M.D. Interaction engineering using the IVY tool. *Proceedings of the 1st ACM SIGCHI symposium on Engineering interactive computing systems*, ACM (2009), 35–44.

4. Dwyer, M. and Avrunin, G. Patterns in property specifications for finite-state verification. *, ICSE Proceedings*, IEEE (1999), 411-420.

5. Gellersen, H., Kortuem, G., and Schmidt, A. Physical prototyping with smart-its. Pervasive Computing, 3, 3 (2004), 74–82.

6. Irawati, S., Ahn, S., Kim, J., and Ko, H. Varu framework: Enabling rapid prototyping of VR, AR and ubiquitous applications. Virtual Reality Conference, 2008. VR'08. IEEE, IEEE (2008), 201–208.

7. Jensen, K., Kristensen, L.M., and Wells, L. Coloured Petri Nets and CPN Tools for modelling and validation of concurrent systems. International Journal on Software Tools for Technology Transfer 9, 3-4 (2007), 213-254.

8. Kim, SH., Kim, SW., Park, HM. Usability Challenges in Ubicomp Environment, In the Proceeding of International Ergonomics Association (IEA'03) (Seoul, Korea, Aug 24-29, 2003)

9. Li, Y. and Hong, J.I. Topiary: a tool for prototyping location-enhanced applications. Proc. 17th annual User Interface Software and Technology ACM 6, 2 (2004), 217–226.

10. Mankoff, J., Dey, A., Hsieh, G., and Kientz, J. Heuristic evaluation of ambient displays. Proceedings of the SIGCHI conference on Human factors in computing systems, ACM (2003), 169-176.

11. Nielsen, J. Enhancing the explanatory power of usability heuristics. Proceedings of the SIGCHI conference on Human factors in computing systems, ACM (1994), 152–158.

12. Rukšenas, R., Back, J., Curzon, P., and Blandford, A. Formal modelling of salience and cognitive load. Proc. 2nd Int. Workshop on Formal Methods for Interactive Systems: FMIS, (2007), 57–75.

13. Scholtz, J. and Consolvo, S. Toward a framework for evaluating ubiquitous computing applications. Pervasive Computing, IEEE 3, 2 (2004), 82–88.

14. Scholtz, J., Arnstein, L., Kim, M., Kindberg, T., and Consolvo, S. User-Centered Evaluations of Ubicomp Applications User-centered Evaluations of Ubicomp Applications. Intel Corporation 10, May (2002).

15. Shirehjini, A.N. 3DSim: rapid prototyping ambient intelligence. Smart objects and ambient intelligence, October (2005), 303–307.

16. Silva, J., Ribeiro, Ó., Fernandes, J., Campos, J., and Harrison, M. The APEX framework: prototyping of ubiquitous environments based on Petri nets. Proc. Human-Centred Software Engineering, Springer LNCS 6409 (2010), 6–21.

17. Silva, J.L., Campos, J.C., and Harrison, M.D. An infrastructure for experience centered agile prototyping of ambient intelligence. Proceedings of the 1st ACM SIGCHI symposium on Engineering interactive computing systems, ACM (2009), 79–84.

18. Theofanos, M. and Scholtz, J. A Framework for Evaluation of Ubicomp Applications. First International Workshop on Social Implications of Ubiquitous Computing, CHI, (2005), 1-5.

Collaborative Web Browsing: Multiple Users, Multiple Pages, Concurrent Access, One Display

Oliver Schmid
University of Fribourg
Blvd de Pérolles 90
Fribourg, Switzerland
oliver.schmid@unifr.ch

Agnes Lisowska Masson
University of Fribourg
Blvd de Pérolles 90
Fribourg, Switzerland
agnes.lisowska@unifr.ch

Béat Hirsbrunner
University of Fribourg
Blvd de Pérolles 90
Fribourg, Switzerland
beat.hirsbrunner@unifr.ch

ABSTRACT

Situations where users want to engage in collaborative web browsing are becoming increasingly common. However, current web technologies aren't designed to allow multiple users to browse the web simultaneously within a single common browser or application since they are unable to handle issues such as simultaneous access by multiple pointers, and multiple simultaneous points of focus within an application. The web-based solution that we propose is an implementation of a forward proxy that injects third-party web pages with specialized JavaScript that provides the aforementioned functionalities transparently, without affecting the original third-party web pages, and thus effectively extending them for collaborative web browsing scenarios. Moreover, our solution provides functionalities for cloning web screens to encourage awareness of the browsing activities of collaborators, and does not require any configuration or software installation on web-enabled client devices, allowing for easy walk-up-and-use interaction.

Author Keywords

Simultaneous multi-user web browsing; collaboration; web proxy.

ACM Classification Keywords

D.2.2 [Design Tools and Techniques]: Software libraries, User interfaces; D.2.11 [Software Architecture]: Patterns; H.4.1 [Office Automation]: Groupware; H.5.2 [User Interface]: Input devices and strategies; H.5.3 [Group and Organization Interfaces]: Collaborative computing, Computer-supported cooperative work, Web-based interaction; H.5.4 [Hypertext/Hypermedia]: User issues.

INTRODUCTION

Many of us have come to rely on the web as the go-to source for seeking information on a vast variety of topics, and have become increasingly accustomed to being able to connect to the web using a number of different personal devices including mobile phones, tablets and laptops. At the same time, and perhaps due in part to the ubiquity of web access, the number of situations in which we might want to browse the web collaboratively in small groups is also increasing. Examples of such situations include travel planning, shopping, social planning and more general information seeking tasks [9, 10]. Currently, scenarios requiring collaborative web browsing, and in particular synchronous web browsing where all group members participate in the browsing at the same time, are made difficult by three inter-related factors.

The first is the size of the device displays, which are often too small for even a small number of people to view the information displayed comfortably. The second is that the devices are designed to be used by one user at a time, and therefore offer only one set of input tools, limiting the number of users who can contribute simultaneously to the task or activity the group is pursuing. Finally, and closely related to the previous factor, is that web technologies themselves, independent of the device on which they are run, were also conceived for single person use [9] and are therefore not equipped to handle issues such as simultaneous access to a single browser by multiple pointers (for example pointers coming from a group of users who each have access to an input device), and multiple simultaneous points of focus within a browser (i.e. if multiple users want to simultaneously fill in the fields of an online form).

To get around the problems posed by these three factors, users have developed a number of different strategies to perform collaborative web browsing. In [9] Morris cites three in particular that appear to be used most commonly – divide-and-conquer, brute force and backseat driver. In the case of divide and conquer, group members plan in advance how to solve a task and divide the work accordingly, specifying which group member is responsible for which sub-tasks. The brute force strategy, on the other hand, involves each group member performing search and browsing related to the task on their own and then sharing their findings at a later stage. Both of these strategies involve each group member working independently on their own device, while the third strategy, that of the backseat driver, involves all group members sharing access to a single device. In this case, one group member, the 'driver' is usually responsible for providing input to the device, while the other group members give suggestions about how to proceed.

As several authors point out, each of these strategies comes with drawbacks that can influence the effectiveness of the collaboration [1, 8, 9]. For example, with the divide and conquer strategy there is less opportunity to share the results and deviate from the assigned tasks in pursuit of other interesting, relevant and perhaps ultimately fruitful avenues. In the case of brute force, the lack of awareness of what other group members are doing can lead to duplication of effort and less opportunity to immediately share information and inspire ideas in others, since information is shared only at the end, rather than throughout the browsing processes. Moreover, with both of these strategies, a loss of group coherency can be expected since for all intents and purposes, the group members are for the most part working independently.

While the backseat driver strategy (where a single display is shared by all group members) alleviates some of the above problems, the fact that only one person at a time has control over input can cause frustration among the group members. The frustration can stem from members not having their ideas or suggestions followed quickly enough, which could mean that they are lost altogether or taken out of context, not all ideas being explored due to a lack of time or resources, group members having different reading speeds, making it harder to maintain a fluid activity flow, and group members having differing search and browsing strategies. Finally, the person who is in control of the input might feel overwhelmed by the quantity of suggestions from other group members, leading to elevated levels of stress, or might selectively pick and choose which ideas to explore based on their own preferences.

In this paper, we propose a solution that attempts to resolve the existing difficulties for synchronous collaborative web browsing – single-user input limitations at both the hardware and software levels and limited screen size – by leveraging the increasing availability of large displays in private and semi-private settings such as educational institutions and businesses and the ubiquity of web access on personal devices.

In the sections that follow we will give a brief overview of related work, both in terms of existing web browsing applications and the different approaches that have been taken to implement them and motivate our own solution by presenting the requirements and use cases that are specific to the context of our work. We will then present the technical details of our solution including how we solve the problems of multi-pointer access and the availability of multiple points of focus on a web page, and various additional features that we feel are useful for collaborative web browsing applications. Finally, we present the results of a preliminary evaluation and discuss planned future work.

RELATED WORK

Much of the research that has been done in the area of collaborative web browsing and web search is relatively new. In this section, we discuss work that provides motivations and guidelines for creating collaborative web browsing applications, discuss a number of existing approaches and applications, and finally mention work that is directly related to the technical approach that we take in our solution, specifically, a web-based proxy server.

The Need for Collaborative Web Search

In exploratory studies on the topic of collaborative web search Morris [9, 10] highlights the need for collaborative web search applications in a variety of different settings including information-oriented workplaces and educational and casual settings. Notably, the results showed that over half of the respondents surveyed in [9] had participated in collaborative web search, and that almost half of those who said they had not participated in it said that had wanted to in the past. The same studies showed that users had a 'desire to parallelize task without unnecessary duplication of effort', 'difficulty in helping remote collaborators to navigate to the same content for shared context/focus' and 'not realizing the need to share the results of a search until after it is finished'. Based on her findings, Morris argues that creating interfaces that specifically support collaborative web search can improve the user experience by providing 'better coverage of the space of relevant, high-quality sites', 'higher user confidence in the completeness and/or correctness of the search' and 'increased productivity due to a decrease in redundant information seeking'. While her work focuses more specifically on the problem of collaborative web search, as opposed to collaborative web browsing, we believe that her findings can also be applied to a large extent to the browsing scenario, which in our view subsumes web search.

Collaborative Web Search Applications

In recent years, a number of applications have been developed that allow users to search/browse the web collaboratively, taking different approaches to addressing some of the problems mentioned in the introduction and in the previous section.

One approach is to distribute parts of a single web page onto a number of different devices, enabling each group member to accomplish part of the collaborative task, while maintaining some degree of awareness of where the others are, since the 'where' is constrained to the content of a single shared page [5, 7].

Another approach has been to develop purpose-built applications. For example, CoSearch [1] allows multiple mice to access a single dedicated application, giving all collaborators control over the browser in the sense that any one of them can open links in the browser window. Selected links are opened in tabs, colour-coded to indicate which user opened a particular tab. However, since only one tab is visible on the display at a time, users are free to open links on the tab that is currently in view but the results of their actions cannot be viewed immediately. This effectively slows down the search and browsing process since new avenues can only be pursued in a linear manner and negotiation is necessary about which tabs to open next etc. An additional impediment to interaction is that text input can only be provided by a single shared keyboard. A mobile phone based version of CoSearch, called CoSearchMobile [1], solves the problems of shared input and limited access to tabs that an individual user opened. In the mobile version, text queries can be sent to the dedicated application using text messaging, and links that a user selects are opened as tabs on the mobile phone to allow more detailed browsing. Since web pages opened on the mobile phone are also added as tabs to the shared application, some awareness of what other group members are doing 'off-screen' is provided. However, group awareness is still limited since the details of multiple individual interactions can only be viewed in a linear manner on the shared display.

Another purpose-built application is SearchTogether [8], which allows multiple users to perform collaborative web search both synchronously and asynchronously using a PC, and provides novel solutions for addressing issues of awareness, persistence and division of labour (splitting a larger search task into smaller subtasks that are assigned to the different group members). However, the system lacks a means of performing concurrent interaction on a single page - users can only 'see' what others are doing and looking at and make suggestions, much as in the backseat driver scenario.

Each of these applications provides an interesting solution to the problems that it is trying to address, and takes important steps toward addressing the problems with collaborative web browsing that we have outlined. However, perhaps due to the fact that these applications were designed with a PC screen as the shared display, none of them seems to provide a completely satisfactory solution. Moreover, we feel that the need to install or run specialized software, and to learn how to use the different features proposed by the applications may also be seen as a drawback or impediment to use by users.

Use of Web Technologies for Collaboration
One reason for which collaborative software applications intended for synchronous use, such as those mentioned above, have been implemented as rich client solutions could be the restrictions present in web technologies. One such restriction is in terms of performance. Restricted performance can be due to the fact that the communication protocols available in web technologies are designed for short request-based communication rather than for continuous information exchange, which means that in cases where continuous information needs to be sent, more network overhead is generated, thus affecting performance. Additionally, the fact that web technologies are based on an interpreted script language (JavaScript) means that their processing times are inherently slower than those of cases of pre-compiled code. However, a lot of effort has been invested in increasing the speed of JavaScript interpreting engines and HTML renderers in newer browsers, thus increasing their performance capabilities.

Finally, upcoming standards (such as WebSockets) bring new possibilities in terms of communication channels to web technologies. Gutwin et al. [4] have shown that these new features in next generation web browsers, as well as advancements in the standardization process of web standards, enable solutions that make the web an interesting platform for the development of synchronous collaborative applications.

Web Browsing by Proxy
The concept of using proxy technology to enable collaboration was proposed as early as 1999 by Cabri et al. [3], who used a (reverse) proxy server to collect information about URLs that clients were currently visiting, and provided a message broker for a small chatting system that allowed users to communicate by exchanging text messages. However, the use of a reverse proxy either forces the users to collaborate only in preconfigured environments or to configure their web browser to make use of the reverse proxy server. The use of Java applets for their chatting system also reduces the set of devices that can run the application to those that have a Java runtime installed. Finally, a point which is particularly relevant to our work is that this solution does not offer multiple users full interaction with the same web resource (or even on the same screen).

DESIGN CONSIDERATIONS
Our work is currently focused on creating interactive collaborative environments in semi-private settings, such as educational institutions or businesses. Since many of these settings are equipped with large displays, we decided to use this fact to our advantage and assume that any shared collaborative applications that are used in these environments will be shown on the large display. This assumption helps us avoid, to a large extent, the problem of small display size that is apparent when only personal devices such as laptops or even desktop computers are used during collaboration.

Another assumption in our work is that people will come into these interactive collaborative environments with their own personal devices, and will prefer to use their own devices to interact with the collaborative application. Since the range of possible devices (and the platforms that they run) is quite large, our solution would need to be as device independent as possible.

Furthermore, one of the key goals of our interactive environment is that the people in it should be able to concurrently access and use any shared application. This implies that our solution should be able to handle the fact that multiple elements on the screen can have focus at the same time, and that text input should be possible using methods other than a single external keyboard.

Finally, we wanted our collaborative environment to be as much as possible walk-up-and-use, which means that our solution should not require the user to download any additional applications, pay for any proprietary software, or register with any services on their personal devices in order to interact in it.

EXAMPLE USE CASES

While developing applications to test the capabilities of our environment, we came across many tasks and applications that required some degree of collaborative web browsing, a finding that is confirmed by Morris' study [9]. While our solution is flexible enough to handle additional use cases and device/display configurations, the three use cases that follow illustrate the basic types of interactions and capabilities that we wanted to accomplish. In each of the cases, a group of 3 coworkers - Ann, Bob and Charlie - are meeting to plan a business trip that they have to take together in a few weeks. They use a large display available at their workplace as the shared display, and each of them brings a personal device with them as well - Ann brings her laptop, Bob brings his smartphone and Charlie brings his tablet to the meeting.

Use Case 1: Multi-user Interaction with a Single Page

In the simplest case, which is similar to the multi-user scenarios described in [1], a single shared web browser is open on the large display, and each of the three coworkers connects to the browser using the personal device only as an input device (Figure 1). When devices are in input-only mode, the display surfaces of touch-based personal devices act the same way as trackpads on a laptop do, allowing the user to control a pointer on the large shared display with their finger. In this mode, the display of the personal device shows a blank screen, colour coded to correspond to the colour of each users' pointer on the shared large display. For example the display of Bob's phone will be blue, and so will his pointer on the shared display. If he wants to input text, he can toggle to the text mode that will call the device's native soft keyboard, which he can then use to provide text input to the large display.

In Figure 1, the 3 co-workers are looking at an airline booking site to select the flights. Any of the 3 can provide input into the online form, and they can do it at the same time - Ann can fill in the 'To' and 'From' fields while Bob selects the number of passengers from a menu and Charlie views new routes on the map.

In this case, when any one of them clicks on a link or a button, for example the 'search' button to launch the search for possible flight routes, the browser will react accordingly and change or update the page on the shared display.

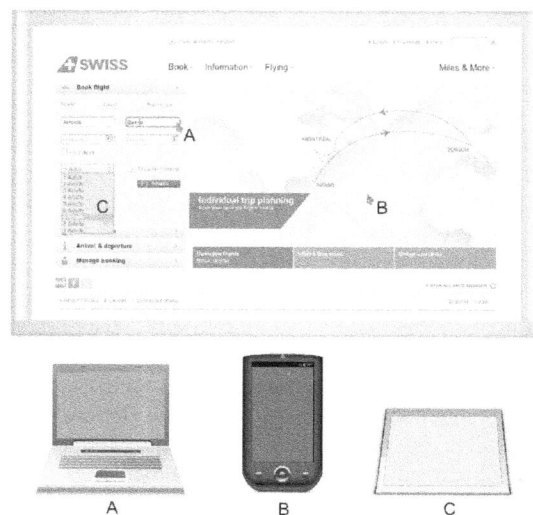

Figure 1: Concurrent multi-user interaction with a single webpage.¹

Use Case 2: Multi-user Interaction with Individual Pages

In this case, the shared display shows 3 separate browser frames - one for Ann, one for Bob, and one for Charlie – and the personal devices are used as input devices in the same way as in the first use case.

Figure 2: Concurrent multi-user interaction with several individual web browsers.

In this configuration (Figure 2), Ann is looking at possibilities for flights (upper left). Bob can see that Ann is searching for connections between Toronto and Zurich, so

---

¹ Figures 1, 2, 3 and 4 include images of devices created by Oxygen Icons and licensed by Creative Commons (CC BY-SA 3.0), and screen captures of one or more of the following websites: www.swiss.com, www.google.com, www.sbb.ch

144

he uses his browser (lower left) to search for train connections between Zurich and Bern, their final destination. In the meantime, Charlie knows that they'll have a couple of days before and after their meetings, so he's started to look at pictures of the area to get some ideas for things to do or see (right side of display).

Since the environment is fully multi-pointer, Charlie can also interact with Ann's browser (upper left) and help her fill in the form. When Bob is done checking the train schedules, he becomes interested in some of the pictures that Charlie has found. He clicks on a link in Charlie's browser, and the link opens in Bob's browser, leaving Charlie's browser unchanged. He also wants to browse the collection of photos that Charlie has found, but Charlie has his browser set up so that only he can scroll. So, Bob copies the URL of the web page that Charlie is looking at, and opens it as a new tab in his own browser.

Use Case 3: Shared Display Showing Personal Devices

In this case, Ann, Bob and Charlie each use the web browsers on their personal devices to search for different aspects of the trip - Bob is using his mobile phone to search for information about the city of Bern, Ann is using the laptop to search for train connections between Bern and various other cities they might fly into or want to visit, and Charlie is using his tablet to search for flight possibilities. Since they're all also connected using our solution, they use the large shared display to show what they're doing on their devices (Figure 3).

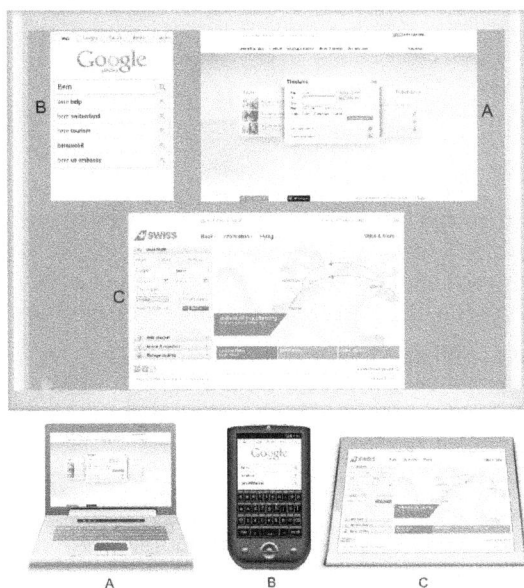

Figure 3: Concurrent multi-user interaction with multiple pages viewed on personal devices.

This way, Ann and Charlie can clearly see what Bob is searching for on his phone, even though they can't see the display of the phone itself. The large display shows what's on the display of each of the personal devices in exactly the same format as on the device itself. Since Bob is using his mobile phone to search with Google, the large shared display shows the Google mobile web page rather than the classic Google web page. This makes discussion easier, as all of the coworkers see exactly the same thing, independent of the device on which they are seeing it.

Charlie wants to access the same page that Ann is looking at, but wants to run a different search. He switches his tablet to input-only mode, which will turn it into an input device on the large display (like in the first two use cases), copies the URL of the web page Ann is using, switches back to his normal tablet mode, and then pastes the URL in his own browser. As he's doing this, Charlie's pointer can be seen on the shared display copying the URL in Ann's browser, but Ann does not see his pointer on her laptop display.

THE PROXY BROWSING SOLUTION

Since the existing solutions discussed in the related work did not meet the requirements of our particular collaborative environment, we needed to find an alternative solution that would take into account the above-mentioned requirements.

As almost all of the possible personal devices that we mentioned have wifi capabilities and are equipped with web browsers, and as Gutwin et al. [4] have pointed out web technologies are quickly becoming an interesting and suitable platform for the creation of synchronous collaborative applications, we chose to base our solution on web technologies.

In our context, an important aspect of collaborative web browsing is that multiple users can interact simultaneously and concurrently with specific content, in this case a single web page. Since most applications and environments are not designed to be multi-pointer aware, this is not a trivial problem.

Enabling Multi-pointer Interaction in Web Pages

In [2], Bowie et al. present a framework that allows developers to write multi-pointer aware web applications. Their framework implements a technology stack managed by the operating system that enables interaction using multiple mouse pointers on a single device. This solution works well for new applications that are developed within their framework. In our case however, we need to be able to support browsing of legacy and third party web pages, and not only those that are developed within a specific framework.

Being able to add the functionality of multi-pointer access and multi-focus elements to a third party web page requires taking (legal) control of the content of that web page. One way to do this is to manipulate the web browser itself, for example by using plug-ins. However, if a browser requires a particular set of additional functionalities, which may be the case in collaborative environments, separate plug-ins would have to be written for each individual case. Since we would like our solution to be easily extendible for a large number of possible applications, a more flexible solution would be preferable.

Another possibility is to include additional code segments within those web pages. This can be achieved by exploiting so-called "cross site script" (XSS) vulnerabilities, which require security leaks to be present on the specific website. Since web pages generally don't have this type of vulnerability and the application of XSS is illegal in any case, this is also not an option.

A third possibility is to use a proxy-based approach. In this case, a web page is not directly accessed by the client, but rather through a proxy web server that accesses the web page on behalf of the client. The proxy can therefore manipulate the structure of the original content of the web page and inject code segments into it before returning a response to the client. In our case, we could extend the functionality of the web page to allow for multi-pointer access and multi-focus capability by having the proxy sever inject the code segments that provide those functionalities. Moreover, since the proxy server can be accessed through any web browser that is installed on a personal device, this solution does not require the installation of any applications or plug-ins on the client devices.

Controlling the Web with a Forward Proxy

Proxy servers are commonly used in a number of different situations. Most of the time they are used as a security barrier to restrict access to specified web servers (for example by verifying user permissions or by offering access to hosts based on filter lists), but they can also be used to anonymize network traffic and hide the origin of client requests. Proxy servers can act in either a forward or reverse manner.

When a reverse proxy server is used, the client is not necessarily aware that the communication is mediated and that an intermediate server processes the response, since the server behaves in exactly the same way as if it were the server requested through the original URL of the web page being viewed. This means that if a reverse proxy server is used to control access to the web, either the clients themselves or the network they are connected to have to be configured to redirect requests to the proxy server instead of sending them directly to the original server. Given that one of our requirements is minimal configuration, the use of a reverse proxy is not ideal.

Forward proxy servers, on the other hand, take the URL requested by the client as a parameter, resulting in a request targeted to something like http://www. proxy.com/http://www.google.com and thus do not require any configuration of the client or infrastructure. We therefore decided to adopt a forward proxy server approach.

Figure 4 shows how this works in our solution. The client requests a web page (1) from the proxy server by accessing the URL http://www.proxy.com/http://www.google.com. The proxy server forwards the request to the original host

http://www.google.com (2). Due to transparent forwarding of the request headers, the original server returns the requested web page (optimized for the device that made the request) to the forward proxy server (3). This page is manipulated, injected with additional JavaScript logic (4) and returned to the requesting client (5).

Our solution also allows injection of additional JavaScript logic to handle specific cases. For example, in Figure 4A one type of logic updates the screen representation on a shared display, and in Figure 4B a different type extends existing web page elements to be able to handle multiple mouse pointers on a shared display controlled by different input devices.

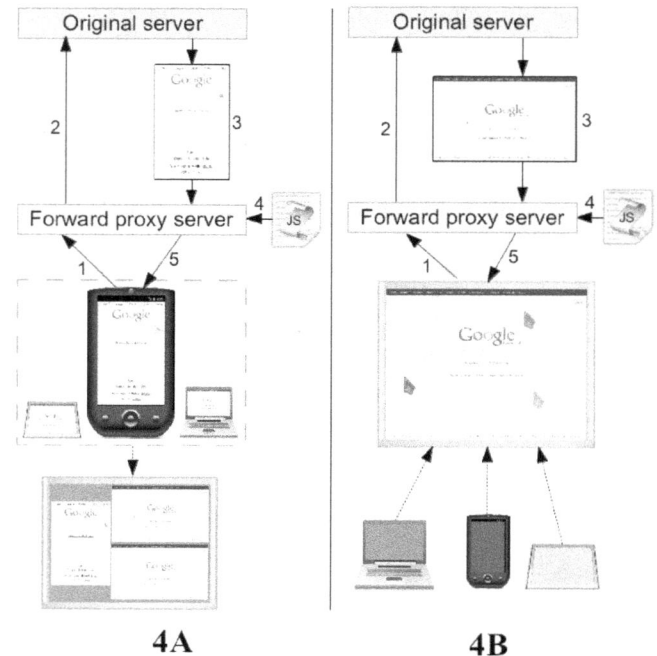

4A   **4B**

Figure 4: The forward proxy process flow in our solution. Examples – 4A personal device interaction shared on a large display, 4B personal device interaction with a single shared page on a large display.

Problems Related to Forward Proxy Servers

Although forward proxy servers are very comfortable for users since they do not require any configuration on client devices, they have two main disadvantages that are relevant to the web browsing scenario.

Loss of context

Since a client device connecting to the forward proxy server sees the server simply as a web resource delivering the (enriched) content of another web resource (for example a web page), a user browsing on their client device can easily navigate away from a URL that is mediated by the proxy server, (e.g. http://www.proxy.com/http://www.google.com) to one that is not mediated, (http://www.unifr.ch), by clicking on a hyperlink. To prevent this from happening, the proxy server has to ensure the rewriting of absolute references within the web page being viewed, so that the hyperlink in the above example points to http://www.proxy.com/http://www.unifr.ch instead.

While the manipulation of statically defined URLs is rather simple and is achieved by the identification and the adaptation of corresponding textual patterns in the response processing phase on the forward proxy, a current trend in web development is to use asynchronous requests to the server and dynamic composition of web pages with JavaScript (AJAX), which increases the complexity of URL manipulation substantially. To prevent dynamically created URL references from pointing to pages which are not under the control of the proxy server, our proxy server injects additional JavaScript that we have implemented which listens and reacts to DOM changes originating from other (third party) JavaScripts.

Inter frame communication and implications for web security
In a collaborative environment such as the one we propose, users might want to all access a single web page simultaneously, or they may want to each be able to access a different web page, all within a single browser. In this case, multiple frames in a single web page might be used, where each frame would contain a separate instance of a web site (Figure 2). Depending on the collaborative application in question, these frames may need to communicate with each other, exchange data about current use, send input data from one frame to the other etc. Web browsers usually prevent frames from communicating with one another if their origin (their host name) differs ("same origin policy"). This is done to prevent frames from spying on actions in a foreign page.

With the use of a forward proxy server, this mechanism can be worked around, since two different web pages are seen by the client web browser as sub-pages of the proxy server (both http://www.proxy.com/http://www.google.com and http://www.proxy.com/http://www.unifr.ch have the same host name). Frames under the control of the forward proxy server are therefore not restricted by this security policy and are able to access the DOM structure of other frames and invoke JavaScript in them, which allows the creation of communication interfaces between web pages in different frames. While this functionality is very useful from a technical perspective it also has some risks since it works around a security mechanism.

In addition to the same origin policy issues discussed above, transport security mechanisms are also affected by vulnerabilities when using proxy servers. Specifically, the standard transport SSL encryption only protects data en route to and from the server, but not on the server itself. Since the server is now represented by the proxy server, this data is decrypted by the proxy server, and then re-encrypted and forwarded to the original server. Since the proxy server decrypts the data, it would be possible to read or use the data. This implies that either the user has to trust that the proxy server does not do any harm to the data or

that no sensitive information is processed through the proxy server mechanism (e.g. electronic banking, e-mail checking, etc.). To make users aware of such vulnerabilities, notifications can be added to proxy-managed frames, especially in cases where users try to access pages with transport security (e.g. https).

Although these problems exist, the authors are convinced that they will have only a minor impact in the case of collaborative web browsing applications. We believe that the need to perform security sensitive activities such as e-banking or to access personal data within a collaborative environment will be rather rare and can, if necessary, be handled in an additional "private" frame that is not managed by the proxy server but rather points directly to the original web page URL. In this type of private frame all foreseen security measures would be applied since the client would communicate in the standard way with the original server. Moreover, since such private frames would not be accessible by other frames (due to the same origin policy) they would therefore no longer be vulnerable to the above mentioned security issues.

With the forward proxy server approach, it is easily possible to have private frames running alongside shared frames, or even to switch the mode of a frame on demand by simple adaptation of the URL.

MANAGING MULTI-USER INTERACTION
In the previous sections we presented a solution that allows us to take control of third party web pages and extend them with additional functionalities to make them multi-pointer and multi-focus aware. However, up to this point, we have not discusses some of the concrete problems that multi-user interaction in a shared application (in our case a shared browser) presents. Such problems include the handling of conflicts between users who want to access the same elements on the screen, visual feedback to provide awareness of cursor ownership, handling of complex pointer actions (in particular drag-and-drop), and the management of navigation history. In this section we discuss how our solution addresses these problems.

Concurrency and Conflict Handling
Given that multiple users will be interacting with the elements on the screen at the same time, our solution needs to provide built-in ways to handle conflicts between users who want to access the same page element (text field, toolbox button etc) or section (frame) of the web page at the same time. Although more complex locking mechanisms exist (see [11] for examples) in our current implementation we propose 4 basic ways to handle such conflicts:

- Full element locking – where an element can only be accessed by a single user.
- Partial element locking – where an element can only be accessed by a small subset of users.

- Frame locking – where only one user can access the content of a frame at a time.

- Full share – where all frames and screen elements are freely accessible to all users.

Since, as Munson and Dewan point out, the most appropriate way to resolve conflicts will depend on the task being done [11], we have implemented all four strategies and allow users (or application developers) to select a conflict resolution strategy depending on the needs of the particular application or task.

Visual Feedback

In multi-user scenarios each user has to be able to easily recognize his or her pointer and actions on the shared display. To this end, we propose that each pointer in the application be assigned a different colour, and that the user is always made aware of which colour their pointer is, for example by representing that colour on the display of their personal device. User-specific feedback (e.g. the user's text cursor position in an input field) could be represented in the same colour as the pointer to allow the user to distinguish the location of their current working context from that of anther user. Similar concepts exist in other applications (e.g. Google Docs).

Drag-and-drop

Drag-and-drop interaction has become increasingly common in today's web applications and has even been assigned its own attributes in some tags in the new HTML5 standard. Since drag-and-drop actions take place over a longer period of time than for example a simple selection action, they are strongly affected by issues originating from multiple pointers. The reason for this is that in normal cases, actions in a browser are recognized sequentially, but in multi-pointer scenarios sequential actions may not originate from the same pointer. An example of this is the case where one user starts a dragging action, and while that user is dragging another user moves a different pointer on the screen. In the normal case, the object being dragged by the first user will jump to the location of the pointer of the second user, since it assumes that that location is the target of the dragging action. In the multi-pointer case however, we want the dragging action of the first user to remain undisturbed by the actions of the second user. Native drag-and-drop therefore has to be replaced with a JavaScript implementation that is aware of multiple pointers and which ignores movements of pointers that are not currently involved in a particular dragging process. We have implemented this type of multi-pointer drag-and-drop functionality (which interprets the extended mouse events of the multi-pointer browser proposed in [2]) as part of our solution and tested it in multiple proof-of-concept applications.

Navigation History Management

When a single user interacts with multiple frames in a browser, the navigation history can easily be recorded sequentially and provided as a reference when functionalities such as 'back' and 'forward' are needed. However, in the case of multiple user interaction, keeping track of navigation history in a sequential manner is not useful since a "back" request could affect the current browsing state of the frame of another user. Our solution handles navigation history on a "per frame" basis, including back and forward buttons per frame instead of as a global functionality provided by the web browser.

ADDITIONAL FEATURES

The forward proxy server solution we have presented allows us to provide the basic functionalities needed for multi-pointer and multi-focus awareness in web browsers and to address some of the general problems of managing multi-user interaction for collaborative web browsing. It is also flexible enough to allow us to add a number of additional functionalities that serve the particular needs of our own collaborative environment.

Cloned Web Screens

One of the key elements necessary for effective collaboration is an awareness of what the people with whom you are collaborating are doing. Given that in the type of collaborative environments that we are working with we assume that the group will have access to a large shared display, we decided to use this fact to our advantage to help promote awareness. We therefore decided to implement a functionality that allows an integrated view of the browsers displayed on individual devices to be shown on the large shared display at the same time, as proposed in Use Case 3.

Depending on the number of collaborators, the size of the shared display, the device on which the actual browsing will be done and the computational power available, the awareness information could be displayed in different ways:

- as a fully functional browser window that can be accessed and interacted with on the shared display.

- as static snapshots of browser windows running on client devices that are taken at set intervals or when changes in the browser window occur.

- as meta information such as the search engine being used and the search terms that were entered, or the URL of the page currently being viewed.

The appropriateness of each solution would likely depend on the task being done, the number of people involved in the collaboration, and the physical and/or geographical proximity of the collaborators.

Expiring Pointers

In her exploratory study [9], Morris found that users expected to collaborate most often in groups of two, but also in groups of 3 or 4. However, the users in the study were asked to base their estimates on current experience, which involved collaborative work around a desktop or laptop computer. As it is quite difficult for more than 4 users to comfortably see and read the content of a regular computer display, this may have influenced the answers given by the users. Since our collaborative environment involves a large shared display, we believe that we could comfortably accommodate a larger number of users.

However, a study by Lalanne and Lisowska Masson [6] found that in multi-pointer environments, user performance drops when there are approximately seven or more pointers moving on the screen at the same time. Their study was done on a simple pointing task, where users only had to locate and select a specific coloured box on a shared display. We believe that for more cognitively complex tasks such as collaborative work, this finding would not only hold, but would in fact have a much stronger impact on the quality of the interaction and collaboration. As a result, we decided to limit the number of pointers that are visible on the shared display at any given time to six. In other words, the shared display is allocated a pool of six pointers, which are assigned to different clients on demand.

However, two issues still remain. The first is that pointers that are not being moved create visual clutter and might even block users from seeing content that is underneath them. The second is that this solution limits the number of people who could participate in the browsing activity to six. To address these issues, we implemented the expiring pointers feature: when a pointer is not moved for more than 5 seconds, it 'expires' and disappears from the shared display, so as not to become visual clutter. When a pointer is reactivated, it appears on the screen in the same place that it disappeared. Moreover, the pointer can either be reactivated by the user to whom it belonged before it expired (reassigned to the same client), or it can be reactivated by another user (assigned to another client), effectively allowing more than six users to participate in the browsing activity.

Pointer Sharing

We can also imagine cases where users might want to share a single pointer over multiple devices. For example, two users could implicitly or explicitly share a pointer. This solution might be useful if both users are working on the same task and act as a single user, or when a user has multiple devices and wants to control a single pointer from different devices, depending on the specific task that they are doing at a given moment (for example text entry on a tablet and pointer movement on a mobile phone).

PRELIMINARY EVALUATIONS

We have tested our forward proxy server implementation with major web portals such as Google, Yahoo, and Wikipedia, as well as with a small sample of lesser known web pages and found that the server and client-side URL-rewriting mechanism works quite well, even within very dynamic third party web pages.

We also carried out a preliminary evaluation of the multi-pointer access functionality using 6 devices: one Android-based HTC mobile phone, one iPhone (3rd generation), two iPads (one 1st generation, one 2nd generation), and two

MacBook Pro laptops. All of these devices were simultaneously connected to our proxy server, which was running on a virtual machine on a standard computer, and were used to control the movement of 6 different pointers on the computer's screen.

The pointers followed the expiring pointers solution, and would disappear if no movement was detected after 5 seconds. We noted that the pointers could easily be reactivated after expiration, and that none of the devices were 'dropped'. Moreover, we did not notice any drops in performance in the different devices as the number of connected devices increased.

In the coming months we will be carrying out experiments that will allow us to further test the robustness and performance of our solution in real-use scenarios.

FUTURE WORK

The solution that we have presented in the previous sections provides us with a set of tools that we can use to develop different types of collaborative web browsing applications. One of the main orientations of our future work will be to carry out a number of user-centered evaluations to explore how collaboration occurs in the type of multi-user multi-device environment that we have described in the Design Considerations and Example Use Cases sections. In particular, we want to explore issues of which type of browser representation is best in which contexts to best improve the collaborative experience, and the degree to which collaborative web browsing of the type we propose improves the collaborative process when compared to collaborative browsing using more traditional means and methods such as the 'backseat driver' or divide-and-conquer. Since, as we have mentioned early in the paper, many of the tasks done in such collaborative environments involve web search, these evaluations will be an excellent opportunity to test the robustness of the solution and determine whether additional functionalities are necessary.

As successful collaboration will also depend on how multi-user interaction is managed, we would also like to explore extending the current locking strategies and visual feedback mechanisms, and the effectiveness of some of the additional features that we mentioned, such as the expiring pointers, for smooth collaboration.

Additionally, since JavaScript engines will not have the same performance on all devices, we expect a need for adoption in the communication between the clients and the server (network latency would also need to be considered). We would therefore like to include a self-calibrating mechanism which would adapt the number of events passed between the devices and the server depending on the power and resources of the devices.

Finally, we would like to integrate the multi-pointer web browsing functionality into a more advanced toolkit for computer supported collaboration in distributed environments including advanced event synchronization mechanisms and security awareness [12].

CONCLUSIONS

In this paper we presented a solution based on forward proxy servers that enables collaborative web browsing in environments where multiple users can interact concurrently with a web page shared on a large display using personal devices such as mobile phones, tablets or laptops. Our solution addresses the problem of multi-pointer access to a web page, provides multi-focus capabilities, and handles a number of problems related to managing multi-user interactions. We also show how the solution can be extended to incorporate additional features into a collaborative web browsing scenario. Preliminary evaluations of our implementation are encouraging and support the appropriateness of the technical choices we made. In future work we hope to not only build on the implementation, but also to validate it through a number of real-use evaluations.

ACKNOWLEDGMENTS

We would like to thank Dr. Michèle Courant, as well as the reviewers, for their helpful comments and feedback on this work.

REFERENCES

1. Amershi, S. and Morris, M.R. CoSearch: a system for co-located collaborative web search. In *Proc. CHI 2008*. ACM Press (2008), 1647-1656.

2. Bowie, M., Schmid, O., Lisowska Masson, A. and Hirsbrunner, B. Web-Based Multipointer Interaction on Shared Displays. In *Proc. CSCW 2011*. ACM Press (2011), 609-612.

3. Cabri, G., Leonardi, L. and Zambonelli, F. Supporting cooperative WWW browsing: a proxy-based approach. In *Proc. PDP 1999*, 138-145.

4. Gutwin, C. A., Lippold, M. and Graham, T. C. N. Real-time groupware in the browser: testing the performance of web-based networking. In *Proc. CSCW 2011*. ACM Press (2011), 167-176.

5. Han R., Perret V. and Naghshineh M. WebSplitter: a unified XML framework for multi-device collaborative Web browsing. In *Proc. CSCW 2000*. ACM Press (2000), 221-230.

6. Lalanne, D. and Lisowska Masson, A. A Fitt of distraction: measuring the impact of distracters and multi-users on pointing efficiency. In *Proc. CHI EA 2011*. ACM Press (2011), 2125-2130.

7. Maekawa, T., Hara, T. and Nishio, S. A collaborative Web browsing system for multiple mobile users. In *Proc. PerCom 2006*. 12-35.

8. Morris, M.R. and Horvitz, E. SearchTogether: an interface for collaborative web search. In *Proc. UIST 2007*. ACM Press (2007), 3-12.

9. Morris, M. R. A survey of collaborative web search practices. In *Proc. CHI 2008*. ACM Press (2008), 1657-1660.

10. Morris, M.R. Interfaces for Collaborative Exploratory Web Search: Motivations and Directions for Multi-User Designs. In *CHI 2007 Workshop on Exploratory Search and HCI*.

11. Munson, J. and Dewan, P. A Concurrency Control Framework for Collaborative Systems. In *Proc. CSCW 1996*. ACM Press (1996), 278-287.

12. Schmid, O. and Hirsbrunner, B. Middleware for distributed collaborative ad-hoc environments. In *Workshop Proc. PerCom 2012*.

Weighted Faceted Browsing for Characteristics-Based Visualization Selection through End Users

Martin Voigt, Artur Werstler, Jan Polowinski, and Klaus Meißner
TU Dresden
01062, Dresden, Germany
{martin.voigt, artur.werstler, jan.polowinski, klaus.meissner}@tu-dresden.de

ABSTRACT

Faceted browsing is a widely spread, intuitive, and interactive search paradigm for information collections based on the metadata of its items. However, it has the problem that every selected criterion is mandatory so that less important ones may reduce the result set and interesting items may be removed unintentionally. On the other hand, choosing only very few facets yields to an unmanageable set of items wherein the best ones do not become obvious. In this paper, we propose *weighted faceted browsing*, which seamlessly extends the existing faceted browsing paradigm. Besides basic filtering capabilities, it provides a sophisticated relevance ranking of the result set based on the distinction between mandatory and weighted optional search criteria. Further, we show its practicability within an information visualization workbench to facilitate the end user's search for visualization components based on their characteristics.

Author Keywords

faceted browsing; query building; weighted search; filtering; visual analysis; end user

ACM Classification Keywords

H.5.2 Information Interface and Presentation: Graphical user interfaces (GUI); H.4.3 Communications Applications: Information browsers

INTRODUCTION

Today, information search is a crucial task in people's life, thus, new search algorithms but also user interfaces (UI) are evolving continuously [6]. In this context, faceted browsing – or faceted search – evolved as a highly usable paradigm to filter and navigate information collections based on the characteristics of its items [22]. For example, e-commerce platforms like amazon or eBay successfully implemented faceted browsing to allow for a flexible and uncomplicated product search also for novices.

Also the procedure of information visualization (InfoVis) is a search process which aims at finding the best presentation for a data set. This is especially challenging for end-users, as their lack of InfoVis knowledge leads to unsatisfying visualizations [5]. In order to assist the visual mapping, systems should suggest appropriate visualizations based on data attributes and other characteristics like the kind of graphic representation or the representation goal. The following two examples which emphasize different kinds of characteristics illustrate users thoughts on finding visual representations: "I'd like to visualize music events – *preferably* taking place in my home town – using a map." or "I'd like to compare interactively the number of performers according their genre, *at best* using a bar chart or – *less preferred* – a scatter plot."

Faceted browsing is a suitable approach to assist end-users in searching for visual representations for two reasons: First, users filter the collection by selecting only from existing characteristics of the remaining items. This is easier to handle than a free, textual query specification but foremost it assures not to deliver an empty result set. Second, InfoVis novices often create partial query specifications [5], e. g., by choosing one data attribute after the other to see the result. Thus, they immediately need feedback to refine their query iteratively.

Within our project VizBoard we strive for a semantics-based, end-user-centered InfoVis process [21]. As a first step, we have already developed and validated an algorithm that recommends appropriate visualization components for arbitrary Semantic Web data [20]. Unfortunately, a suitable, intuitive UI which would allow for an easy creation of search queries to "feed" the algorithm is missing. Hence, the faceted browsing paradigm comes into play.

However, with regard to the example queries mentioned above, there are problems for implementing them with existing faceted browsers. First, it is not possible to assign priorities to facets within a search query. Second, every selected facet is a mandatory search criterion. This is crucial, because facets, which are meant to be optional, strip down the result set to a great extent to maybe less relevant items. On the other hand, specifying only a few criteria causes a broad, confusing result set, where the most interesting items are not obvious to the user. In this case, ranking criteria provided by the user would be helpful but existing approaches are limited to basic sorting like the alphabetical one.

Targeting the outlined problems, the contributions of this paper are twofold: First, we propose a seamless extension of the faceted browsing paradigm, the so-called *weighted faceted browsing* (WFB). It supports the well-known filtering capabilities but adds a sophisticated ranking mechanism using facets in combination with a weight. Further, these concepts are applied to an intuitive UI. Second, we demonstrate the practicability of WFB for visualization selection within an InfoVis workbench which allows for iterative query specification using mandatory and optional weighted search criteria.

RELATED WORK

The weighted faceted browser presented in this paper builds on previous work in the three different research areas (1) faceted and (2) weighted search as well as (3) approaches to search for visualizations. We will now discuss the state of the art in these three areas.

Faceted Browsing

Faceted browsing [22] is a widely applied search paradigm, e. g., in e-commerce (amazon or eBay) or document collections (ACM digital library or IEEE Xplore), based on the characteristics of the items within a collection. In general, a faceted browser consists of three parts: a list of widgets, presenting the facets, a visualization of the result set, and the representation of the query. Existing research in this domain concentrated on providing more sophisticated facet widgets [3, 15] or more efficient browser layouts [19, 8]. However, improvements with regard to the representation of the result set have been neglected so far. Indeed, a user may specify a grouping or sorting for the items. But this is limited to single, basic, and predefined attributes like the alphabetical order. Sorting based on combinations of item characteristics or assigning a relevance to each item is not possible.

Weighted Search

Weighted search is a matured approach [16] especially in the area of multimedia database systems [18] to allow for – in contrast to weights assigned during indexing – a user driven relevance ranking. Besides the explicit specification of quantitative or relative weightings it is possible to define them implicitly [18]. For example, the high-performance search engine Lucene [1] allows for an explicit, quantitative query term weighting using its *boost* factor, e. g., event^5 map^5 place^1. However, it is currently not possible to distinguish between mandatory and optional criteria.

As outlined in the section above, faceted browsing does not support relevance ranking of the result set using the facets. An approach towards this direction illustrates the online radio service Musicovery comprising the mood pad [2]. The latter allows for choosing the mood of songs – from energetic to calm as well as from dark to positive, in a Cartesian coordinate system. By picking a point in the reference system, the user starts a new search and assigns a weight to the two mood scales implicitly. Nevertheless, it is not possible to weight other or additional characteristics of the items.

Visualization Selection for End Users

InfoVis tools provide different levels of user support to find appropriate visualizations [4]. One of the most sophisticated is Tableau, comprising the "Show Me" mechanism which suggests graphic representations for the selected data variables [12]. However, it is not possible to search visualizations based on their characteristics and representation goals or to distinguish between mandatory and optional data variables.

Further, many online galleries like visualcomplexity.com or visual.ly emerged in the last years, providing huge collections of graphic representations. Unfortunately, here the items can only be filtered and sorted using categories or basic attributes like "most viewed". [11] proposes a characteristics-based classification for visualization using the metaphor of the periodic table, but an interactive tool implementing this approach is missing. The gap of interactive filtering visualizations based on their attributes is partly bridged by DelViz [10]. Compared to DelViz, we additionally provide features for relevance ranking as well as an integration within a visualization workbench.

WEIGHTED FACETED BROWSING

In this section, we describe the general functionality of weighted faceted browsing, including the division into mandatory criteria and weighted optional criteria, the relevance ranking based on them, and finally, the interactive UI of the weighted faceted browser.

Mandatory and Weighted Optional Criteria

In order to integrate sophisticated relevance ranking seamlessly with the faceted browsing paradigm, the query which constraints the result set, is still created by incrementally selecting facet values. But now, the user can choose between mandatory and optional criteria. To narrow the results, a facet value needs to be added to the set M where all criteria are linked conjunctively – which is the standard behavior of a faceted browser. In contrast, optional facets, which are combined disjunctively within a set O, do not constrain but rank the results. Thus, the more optional criteria an item satisfies the higher is its rank.

However, if some items meet the same number of optional criteria, their ranking would be the same. Further, our second example stating that "*bar charts* are preferred to *scatter plots*" emphasizes that users also need to define priorities between single facets. To achieve this, two distinct approaches could be used. First, the weight could be set relatively to other facet values, e. g., $f_1 < f_2 \leq f_3$, where the system needs to assign quantitative values implicitly at query interpretation. As it would be complicated – especially in the UI – to define long criteria chains or the distance between two criteria, we applied a second strategy and added an explicit weight to every criterion using a quantitative scale between 1 and 100. We neglect 0 as this could suggest that the facet could be omitted. Further, mandatory criteria are not weighted as they need to be fully satisfied and not only partly.

The complete query can be represented by means of the following formula. Taking into account that the optional criteria should not constrain the result set if no item satisfies any criterion, we add a ε to O so that this set will always be *true*. This behavior could simply be skipped by removing ε again.

$$Q = \bigwedge_x \wedge \bigvee_{(y,w) \vee \varepsilon} |\forall x \in M, \forall y \in O, \forall w \in [1, 100]$$

The seamless integration of weighted, optional criteria with faceted browsing requires transforming mandatory criteria to optional ones and vice versa. In the first case, the criterion does not restrict the result set anymore but may affect its order. This navigation step, called a *zoom-out* in regular faceted browsing [17], is especially interesting in combination with a high weight. In this case, the facet value has a high impact on the ranking but does not result in items being hidden that are good candidates with respect to other criteria. For the opposite direction, moving a facet from the set O to M, being a *zoom-in* navigation step, narrows the result set and may outrange selected optional criteria as no item complies with them. As the feature is crucial for a comprehensible interaction, our compromise is to give the user visual feedback whether a facet is supported or not.

Result Ranking

The input for calculating the result set is a query in terms of the formula proposed above. While the mandatory part simply constraints the set by removing all items not supporting a chosen facet value, the relevance ranking using multiple optional facets is more complicated. To solve the multiple-criteria optimization, we can rely on an extensive set of related work, e. g., the survey proposed in [13]. Our ranking problem can be categorized as "a priori" because the user already chose the goals and weights. In this field, we can basically distinguish two opposed strategies to interpret the optional, weighted criteria:

1. The user strives for a result which satisfies all goals as much as possible. Hence, the weighting method (or weighted sum model) is applicable.

2. The criterion with the highest weight is the users primary goal and is to be preferred to others. This strategy is implemented by the *lexicographic ordering*.

We employ *both* strategies, which is a common use case [13], in an iterative way. We are optimizing by using the weighting method at first. This method considers items comprising more but possibly less important criteria and, thus, does not neglect the low weighted facets the user has selected. Afterwards, if some items share the same weight, we apply the lexicographic ordering. Finally, we order elements alphabetically if they still have the same weight.

User Interface for Weighted Faceted Browsing

After having discussed the background concepts of weighted faceted browsing, in the following, we will introduce the UI and interaction concept. Its implementation is illustrated in Fig. 1. Basically, the layout corresponds to classical faceted browsing and is split into three main areas: facet widgets at the top part ① ②, the query visualization, called *querycloud*,

in the middle ③, and the results view at the bottom part ④ ⑤. To create a query, the user simply needs to drag a desired facet value and drop it at the querycloud. The result set visualization ④ updates subsequently. By selecting an item from the list, detailed information are displayed in ⑤. In the following, we will outline these parts in more detail.

Facet Widgets

The purpose of the facet widgets is twofold: they represent the characteristics of the items per facet and offer these facet values for selection. For this purpose, the browser can dynamically integrate the widgets, usually list widgets, defined in a declarative configuration file. Further, we distinguish direct and indirect facets, similar to [7]. Whereas the first are directly associated with the items metadata, indirect facets are characteristics which are calculated or referred to based on semantic links. In our scenario of searching appropriate visualization components, the indirect data facet ① is calculated at runtime using the algorithm proposed in [20].

In order to present the semantic data in a appropriate way for users, who may not have prior semantic web knowledge, we rely on the simple but well-known indented list metaphor [9]. Therefore, we display the classes, which can be expanded to show datatype properties, at the top level. These properties are linking literals, e. g., *performer* or *genre label* in Fig. 1, and could be dragged to the querycloud. Object properties are visualized implicitly using hierarchies and its associated class, e. g., an *event* is linked to a *location* and *time*.

The widgets provide different kinds of visual feedback to assist the user. First, a number behind every datatype property and facet value shows the number of items corresponding to this characteristic and is updated after every interaction. Second, after applying a facet value to the querycloud, its color adapts to orange (mandatory) or blue (optional). Third, if a facet value is not applicable due to restrictions on the result set, i. e., its item number is zero, the facet value is removed from the widget to raise the clearness.

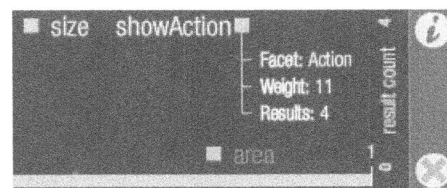

Figure 2. Details of the querycloud

Querycloud

The key capabilities of the querycloud ③ are the query configuration and its visualization. As we distinguish between mandatory and optional criteria, the cloud is split into two areas where the user can drop the chosen facet values. Within the *hot area* (orange), all must-have criteria are simple visualized as a list using the order the user dropped them. The capabilities of the cold area (blue), which represents the optional criteria, are more advanced. While dropping a facet, the horizontal position is used to assign a weight to the facet. Instead of defining a value explicitly, e. g., by using an input field, we consider that this behavior is precise enough

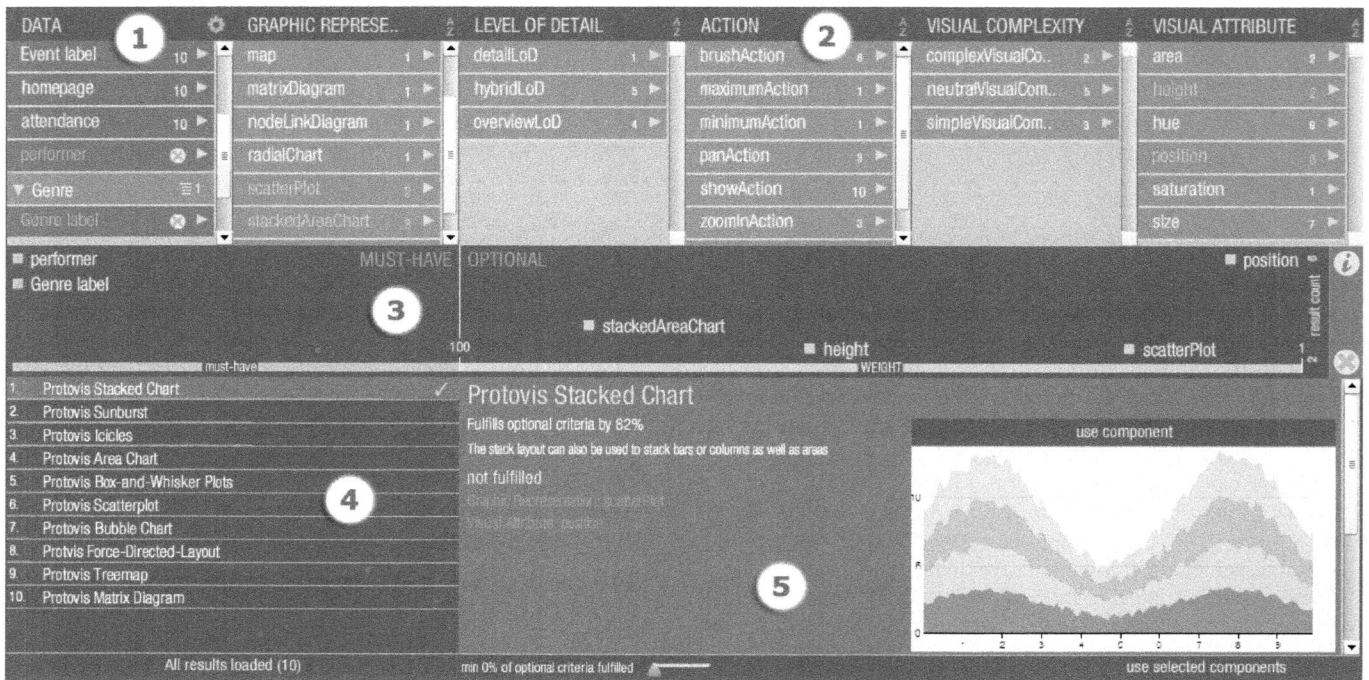

Figure 1. Overview of the weighted faceted browser

while being more uncomplicated and intuitive. The weight can be adjusted by moving the facet value on the axis. To remove any facet, the user simply needs to drop them out of the querycloud.

The vertical axis in the cold area is used to show the number of items comprising the facet value. The range is represented at the right of the area (Fig. 2). Further, as Fig. 2 illustrates for "showAction", detailed information of a criterion is given on hovering any criterion in the querycloud. This includes its facet, the assigned weight, and the number of items using the characteristic.

As discussed above, the browser needs to support the transformation of mandatory criteria to optional and vice versa. For this reason, the user may also drag and drop values between both areas of the query cloud. On dropping, all facets widgets as well as the position of the optional criteria are updated subsequently. By turning an optional criterion into a mandatory, other optionals may not be comprised by any item of the result set any longer. Hence, these facets are marked red, like the "area" facet in Fig. 2, to call the users attention.

Result Set
The result set visualization at the bottom part is split as well: ④ comprises a ranked list of items whereas ⑤ provides detailed information of the selected item. To visually emphasize the relevance and to allow for a comparison of the items at first sight, the labels are underlined using colored lines. The ranking value is mapped to the color – from green (high) to red (low) – and redundantly to the length of the lines. The representation of the detail view depends at most on the metadata provided by the items. In our case, visualization components metadata like a screenshot and a textual description

are shown. Additionally, the view represents the percentage of fulfilling the optional criteria as well as a list of optional facets which the item does not comprise.

VISUALIZATION SELECTION AS EVALUATION DOMAIN
In the following, we outline an implementation of WFB. Its integration into our InfoVis workbench VizBoard is the foundation of a preliminary user study whose results are discussed afterwards.

Implementation
The weighted faceted browsing concept was realized as essential part of the VizBoard InfoVis workbench [21] which relies on the CRUISe mashup platform [14]. Fig. 3 gives a brief architectural overview of its integration. The WFB is divided into a backend service (Fig. 3-4) and a frontend mashup component (Fig. 3-5) to counter performance issues during filtering or facet calculation. The latter, which is implemented using Adobe Flex and JavaScript, is dynamically integrated at runtime and provides the UI introduced above. The facets, its direct or indirect nature, and their appearance and layout within the browser is described declaratively to foster an easy adaptation, e. g., for other domains.

A REST-based web service interface enables the frontend to retrieve the data, e. g., the facets and their values, from the backend as well as to send the query created by the user. The WFB backend, implemented using Java and Jersey for the web service communication, handles a series of tasks. At first, it retrieves the Semantic Web data – narrowed in a forgoing pre-selection step [21] – from the data repository (Fig. 3-1) to construct the indirect data facet (Fig. 1-1). Subsequently, it initially calls the component repository (Fig. 3-2) using the

154

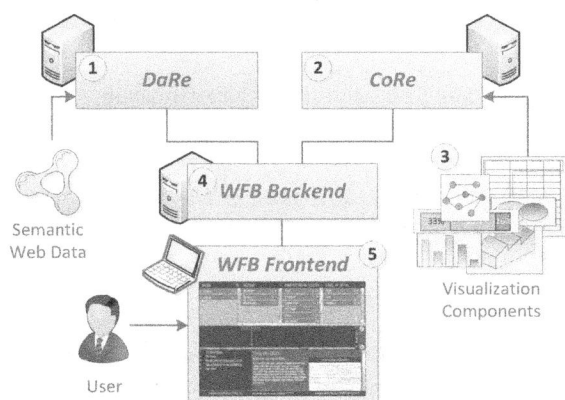

Figure 3. Overview of the software architecture and its integration into VizBoard

data to get a list of suitable visualization components (Fig. 3-3) including their metadata. The recommendation algorithm proposed in [20] determines the components which are able to visualize at least one data variable of the data set. Thereafter, the backend creates the direct facets and its values based on the metadata (Fig. 1-2). After the user has modified the query, the backend recalculates the facets as well as the result set. If the query comprises values from the data facet, again the recommendation algorithm is called to narrow the component list. Otherwise, the backend can directly process the direct facet values.

A screencast as well as a stand-alone live demo is available on `http://cruisedemos.dyndns.org/wfb/`.

Evaluation

We conducted a preliminary user study, consisting of three parts, to prove our novel concept of weighted faceted browsing in the area of visualization selection. Five students, who are familiar with faceted browsing, InfoVis tools like MS Excel or Tableau but never worked with Semantic Web data, participated. In the first part, we familiarized the users with the scenario and WFB by providing a screencast illustrating the main functionalities. Next, they got 2 minutes to explore the browser individually. In the second part, the user had to handle five basic tasks like selecting or removing facets. But, more interestingly, they had to solve five more advanced search tasks – similar to the examples mentioned in the introduction – to find appropriate visualization components. In the third part, we asked some questions related to usability issues.

The subjects answered all questions correctly. Whereas the basic tasks were solved without any help, we needed to give some assistance at solving the advanced issues. This was mostly caused by the missing understanding of the data set and the metadata of the visualization components within the facet widgets. Exemplary questions were: "Why is the *genre* shown twice?" or "What does *neutral visual complexity* mean?". Thus, we need to improve the data widget and should provide additional information for the facet values.

Further, the users stated they enjoyed the intuitive approach of the querycloud. Assigning a weight or transforming criteria from mandatory to optional and vice versa seems to be convenient. Two users suggested to give a live preview of the weight while dragging a facet over the "cold" area. Further, the participants comprehended the result view as well. On asking why they choose two particular components, they answered: "They are the first and had a great distance to the next results.".

CONCLUSION AND FURTHER WORK

This paper presents a seamless extension of the well-known faceted browsing paradigm which allows for sophisticated but intuitive relevance ranking of the result set. This is – amongst others – worthwhile if a vast quantity of items in the result set hinders to identify an appropriate one. We achieved this objective by 1) distinguishing between mandatory and optional criteria, 2) assigning priorities to optional criteria, 3) implementing a ranking method, and 4) developing a self-explanatory UI.

Furthermore, we successfully implemented our approach and proved its practicability within the InfoVis workbench VizBoard in order to facilitate end users in searching for visualization components based on their characteristics. A preliminary user study suggests that users are confident with the weighted faceted browsing and are able to express advanced search queries.

As one result of our evaluation, we are currently working on the indirect facet widget to represent the relations of the small Semantic Web dataset in a more comprehensible way. Further, we are currently discussing how to foster the understanding of single facet values by using additional visuals without losing clarity. Finally, we will verify the WFP including the relevance ranking strategy within other domains, e. g., news and media search.

ACKNOWLEDGMENTS

Work on this paper is funded within the Mefisto project by the German Federal Ministry of Education and Research under promotional reference number 01IA09001-C and also received financial support from the European Social Fond / Free State of Saxony, contract no. 80937064.

REFERENCES

1. Apache Software Foundation. Apache Lucene, 2012.

2. Castaignet, V., and Vavrille, F. Musicovery.com, 2012.

3. Dachselt, R., Frisch, M., and Weiland, M. Facetzoom: a continuous multi-scale widget for navigating hierarchical metadata. In *Proc. of the 26th conf. on Human factors in computing systems (CHI'08)* (2008), 1353–1356.

4. Gilson, O., Silva, N., Grant, P., and Chen, M. From web data to visualization via ontology mapping. In *Computer Graphics Forum*, vol. 27 (2008), 959–966.

5. Grammel, L., Tory, M., and Storey, M.-A. How information visualization novices construct visualizations. In *Proc. InfoVis 2010* (2010).

6. Hearst, M. A. *Search User Interfaces*. Cambridge University Press, 2009.

7. Heim, P., Ertl, T., and Ziegler, J. Facet graphs: Complex semantic querying made easy. In *The Semantic Web: Research and Applications*, vol. 6088. 2010, 288–302.

8. Huynh, D., and Karger, D. Parallax and companion: set-based browsing for the dataweb, 2009.

9. Katifori, A., Halatsis, C., Lepouras, G., Vassilakis, C., and Giannopoulou, E. Ontology visualization methods - a survey. *ACM Comput. Surv. 39* (2007), 10.

10. Keck, M., Kammer, D., Iwan, R., Taranko, S., and Groh, R. Delviz: Exploration of tagged information visualizations. In *Informatik 2011 - Interaktion und Visualisierung im Daten-Web* (Berlin, 2011).

11. Lengler, R., and Eppler, M. J. Towards a periodic table of visualization methods for management. In *Proc. of the Conf. on Graphics and Visualization in Engineering (GVE 2007)* (2007), 1–6.

12. Mackinlay, J., Hanrahan, P., and Stolte, C. Show me: Automatic presentation for visual analysis. *IEEE Transactions on Visualization and Computer Graphics 13*, 6 (Nov. 2007), 1137–1144.

13. Miettinen, K. Some methods for nonlinear multi-objective optimization. In *Evolutionary Multi-Criterion Optimization*, vol. 1993. 2001, 1–20.

14. Pietschmann, S., Nestler, T., and Daniel, F. Application composition at the presentation layer: Alternatives and open issues. In *Proc. of the 12th Intl. Conf. on Information Integration and Web-based Applications & Services (iiWAS 2010)*, ACM (2010).

15. Polowinski, J. Widgets for faceted browsing. In *Human Interface and the Management of Information.*

Designing Information Environments, vol. 5617. 2009, 601–610.

16. Robertson, S. E., and Jones, K. S. Relevance weighting of search terms. *Journal of the American Society for Information Science 27*, 3 (1976), 129–146.

17. Sacco, G. M., and Tzitzikas, Y. *Dynamic Taxonomies and Faceted Search: Theory, Practice, and Experience.* Springer, New York, 2009.

18. Schmitt, I., Schulz, N., and Saake, G. Multi-level weighting in multimedia retrieval systems. In *XML-Based Data Management and Multimedia Engineering EDBT 2002 Workshops*, vol. 2490. 2002, 524–528.

19. Tvarožek, M., and Bieliková, M. Collaborative multi-paradigm exploratory search. In *Proc. of the Hypertext 2008 workshop on Collaboration and collective intelligence* (2008), 29–33.

20. Voigt, M., Pietschmann, S., Grammel, L., and Meißner, K. Context-aware recommendation of visualization components. In *Proc. of the 4th Intern. Conf. on Information, Process, and Knowledge Management (eKNOW '12)* (2012).

21. Voigt, M., Pietschmann, S., and Meißner, K. Towards a semantics-based, end-user-centered information visualization process. In *Proc. of the 3rd Intern. Workshop on Semantic Models for Adaptive Interacive Systems (SEMAIS '12)* (2012).

22. Yee, K.-P., Swearingen, K., Li, K., and Hearst, M. Faceted metadata for image search and browsing. In *Proc. of the Conf. on Human factors in computing systems (CHI '03)* (2003), 401–408.

Interactive Construction of Semantic Widgets for Visualizing Semantic Web Data

Timo Stegemann   **Juergen Ziegler**   **Tim Hussein**   **Werner Gaulke**

University of Duisburg-Essen
Lotharstr. 65, 47057 Duisburg, Germany
{firstname.lastname}@uni-due.de

ABSTRACT

The rapidly growing amount of semantically represented data on the Web creates the need for more intuitive methods and tools to interact with these data and to use them in standard Web applications. We present a method how users can interactively define personalized views of large semantic data spaces. Specifically, we propose X3S as a technique and format for specifying 'semantic widgets' that integrate querying and filtering of semantic data with defining their layout and presentation style. In addition, an editor has been developed that allows to create X3S templates in a direct manipulation style. The editor and the underlying format are evaluated against existing approaches by comparing their functional capabilities as well as in an initial user study.

ACM Classification Keywords

H.3.3; H.5

Keywords

Semantic Web; Data Exploration; Data Visualization; Semantic Widgets; Semantic Stylesheets

INTRODUCTION

In the course of the decade which has passed since the vision of a Semantic Web was first articulated by Berners-Lee [3], the amount of data on the Web represented with semantic techniques has increased enormously. In contrast to the conventional Web, which links web pages as complete documents, the Semantic Web links data based on a uniform data model. This model consists of elementary statements in 'subject-predicate-object' form, expressed with RDF (Resource Description Framework), and uses shared vocabularies defined as ontologies by means of RDFS (RDF-Schema) and OWL (Web Ontology Language) [7]. Linking the individual statements results in a single, huge data graph. This is often referred to as the Web of Data.

Improved techniques for automatically translating existing datasets into semantic formats have brought about a significantly accelerated growth, leveraging large existing information pools such as encyclopedias (e.g. DBPedia which is extracted from Wikipedia [1]), geographical

databases, bibliographies, product data (for an overview see, e.g. [6]) and many others. The LOD (Linking Open Data) initiative has invested considerable effort in interconnecting different datasets, resulting in the LOD Cloud with around 295 connected datasets and 31 billion triples (as of fall 2011).

While the original objectives of the Semantic Web were mainly directed at making Web information machine-processable, it is increasingly recognized that linked open data and other semantic data pools are valuable information sources that can be used interactively by end users. This creates a need for methods and tools that allow users to interact with Semantic Web data directly, rather than through a web application that integrates and delivers data in standard web pages.

In contrast to conventional Web front ends, user interfaces and search tools for Semantic Web data can exploit the semantics of the underlying data structure to let users explore the data under different perspectives and formulate more targeted and complex queries. The potential for making semantic data explorable has been demonstrated by a variety of tools that use the different semantic relations for creating search facets, allowing users to flexibly filter the data. Visual techniques for formulating complex queries have been developed, for instance, in prior work of ours [8]. In addition to providing improved search and exploration capabilities, however, semantic representations can also enable users to construct their own views of a semantic data pool, which can either be used for exploring the data in some user-defined visual configuration or for presenting (and potentially editing) a more or less complex cut-out of the large RDF based data graph. With the development described in this paper, we aim at providing a solution for the latter problem by offering users a technique for composing complex, reusable query and presentation patterns ('semantic widgets'), that show a coherent part of a data graph in a user-defined format.

In this paper, we propose a novel technique for interactively defining reusable templates for querying and presenting semantic data. We call this technique X3S which stands for 'XSL-transformed SPARQL results and Semantic Stylesheets'. In contrast to CSS (Cascading Style Sheets), known from web design, X3S includes directives for filtering data by using SPARQL (SPARQL Protocol And RDF Query Language) as well as for presenting and decorating them (by using XSL (Extensible Stylesheet Language) transformations and CSS). For creating X3S files, we developed an editor enabling the user to create complex templates for querying and presenting semantic data in an intuitive, direct manipulation-style manner.

X3S and the associated editor targets user groups who have some knowledge of Semantic Web concepts and data structures but who may not be familiar with specific formats or query languages. Apart from exploring semantic data directly, a main purpose of the technique is to define reusable views that can be published in standard Web pages. A potential user may thus be, for example, a shop developer or administrator who needs an easy to use method for publishing semantically represented product data.

The rest of this paper is organized as follows: First, we review existing work specifically related to the X3S technique, the semantic stylesheet format proposed, and identify areas for improvement. The X3S technique and format are presented in the next section, followed by a description of an editor implementing the technique. Finally, we analytically compare it against related developments with respect to a set of requirements.

RELATED WORK

A number of tools for browsing the Semantic Web and for presenting RDF based data have been developed so far. Most of these developments either fall into the class of Semantic Web browsers or semantic data integration/mash-up tools [10]. While the latter aim at integrating different Semantic Web data sources, Semantic Web browsers serve a similar purpose for semantic data as conventional Web browsers do for HTML data.

These tools enable users to explore large corpora of data in an associative manner. However, the presentation of the data is mostly limited to tabular listings of all instances, properties, and property values. Examples of such tools are Tabulator[1] [4] and Disco[2]. While these tools are capable of providing overviews of data sets, they do not support filtering of instances or producing specific layouts and styles. These limitations prevent a more rich interaction with semantic data, which is our target. There are currently only few projects with a similar focus. We will describe them in the following paragraphs.

The Xenon project [12] has introduced an ontology described as 'RDF stylesheet language'. The goal of Xenon is to display semantic data in a human usable way and facilitate changing the representation according to the user's needs. Based on the concept of XSLT, the authors created a RDF-based stylesheet, which defines methods for transforming RDF-data. This includes concepts such as *lenses* and *views*. The purpose of lenses is to select items from instance sets, whereas views describe the visualization of data elements.

The RDF vocabulary Fresnel was developed as a successor of Xenon. Fresnel also uses lenses to select data but dropped

the views concept and with it the possibility to embed visual markup such as HTML [11]. As a replacement, the *formats* concept is introduced. It is used for formatting data and to enrich the data with additional information for rendering. For example, a format defines whether the selected lens data should be handled as a link, an image, or as a text. This additional information is used by the browser for creating the final visualization. The data might be presented, for instance, as a table or graph, depending on the decision of the browser. To select data, lenses can use a special Fresnel Selector Language (FSL) or standard SPARQL queries.

With OWL-PL [6], a language for transforming RDF/OWL data into (X)HTML is introduced. The language is strongly inspired by XLST and has the main goal of providing a simple transformation language for semantic data. OWL-PL allows the combination of transformational and representational markup. Stylesheets are converted into HTML by means of a server-side Java application.

LESS [2] supports a complete workflow, ranging from creating and processing templates to sharing templates between users. The declarative template language LeTL (LESS template language) is based on the Smarty Template Engine[3], which simplifies the separation of data and presentation of PHP-projects. It can process and transform semantic data from RDF documents or data requested by SPARQL queries. LESS provides an editor for creating LeTL templates. The editor shows available properties of the RDF data or of the SPARQL result. The properties can be directly used in LeTL code and combined with HTML markup to generate the final HTML output. The created LESS template is saved on the LESS server.

In contrast to the other approaches introduced in this section, Dido (Data-Interactive DOcument) [9], does not process semantic data in RDF format, but provides means for direct manipulation and creation of data as well as for including presentation directives. The embedded data are saved as key-value pairs in JSON (JavaScript-Object Notation). Selection and visualization are defined with lenses and views similar to Xenon. In the editor, the user can directly choose how the selected data should be presented, for example, as a list or table.

All approaches reviewed so far have in common that they define their own templating languages for handling semantic data. Only Dido and LESS include editors for creating new stylesheets. These editors, however, still require a considerable level of knowledge in semantic technologies. Editors for the other formats have not been developed so far.

Having their benefits in the respective use cases, these approaches are hard to re-implement and the editors are not very user friendly. This created the motivation for our own development. X3S provides a standards-based open format for reusable semantic stylesheets and can be used with arbitrary RDF-based data sources. The reference implementation provides an easy to use editor enabling non-

---

[1] http:www.w3.org/2005/ajar/tab

[2] http://www.wiwiss.fu-berlin.de/bizer/ng4j/disco

[3] http://www.smarty.net/

158

experts to intuitively explore semantic data visually and to define personalized templates.

Based on the analysis of the limitations of existing tools we derived a set of requirements for our own development. One important requirement is the possibility to select arbitrary properties from a specified resource, instead of receiving and displaying all available data. The technique should further allow filtering the data in a flexible manner. One of the strengths of semantic data is the possibility to define one resource as a property of another resource. The technique should therefore also provide means for nesting several properties.

DEFINING SEMANTIC WIDGETS WITH X3S

In order to construct reusable views on some set of semantic data, several steps need to be performed in a workflow-like fashion. The running example used throughout this article is based on RDF data about universities in Germany and related information. Assume a user wants to explore this information space to learn more about some of these universities and the cities, in which they are located. The user first searches for 'university' as a concept to define an entry point into the RDF data graph, then adds various descriptive (data) properties and related concepts by following object properties such as the study programs offered, the city where the university is located and cultural attractions in that city. The user then applies a visual style to this data configuration and stores the complete configuration as a reusable semantic widget. This widget can then be applied to every instance of a German university in the graph and simplifies the comparison of returned information.

X3S is a technique for describing these different steps in a single template. It also provides a format for serializing and storing templates for future reuse.

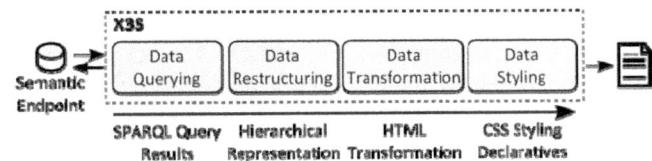

Figure 1: X3S workflow to transform semantic data into a HTML document.

Internally, X3S comprises a workflow consisting of four steps: querying, restructuring, transforming, and styling, as illustrated in Figure 1. While established formats and technologies can be used for most of these steps, a new technique for restructuring the query results was needed to allow a consistent, redundancy-free presentation. The complete workflow is finally stored as an XML document.

Querying

The first part of a X3S document contains a SPARQL encoded query. Any SPARQL compliant data source can be used. The SPARQL server handles the processing of different RDF formats and provides a standardized interface to the RDF data. With X3S, a single SPARQL query, which can request arbitrary properties, is defined. The result of this SPARQL query is a set of property-value pairs that are

formatted in a W3C (World Wide Web Consortium) conform XML representation. Figure 2 gives an example for such a query and its result.

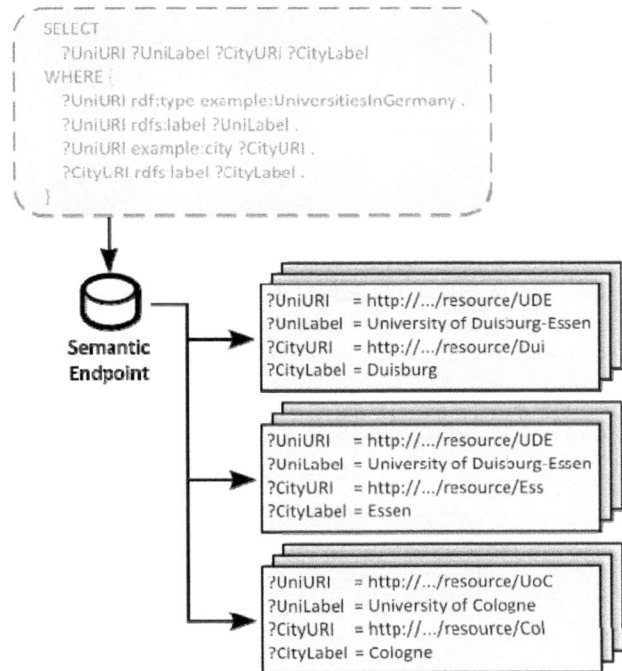

Figure 2: A SPARQL server returns several result sets for a single query.

In our example, we might request the resource URI (Uniform Resource Identifier) and label for each university and the respective city, where the university is located in. The SPARQL server returns a list of result sets, where every set contains values for one university URI, university label, city URI and city label. The URIs are particularly relevant as they represent the resource itself. Properties can be filtered, limited or ordered by SPARQL commands, which are similar to common SQL commands. By requesting the data from a SPARQL endpoint, the problem of different RDF formats and non-unique serializations can be solved.

Restructuring

The SPARQL results are returned as a list of flat result sets, without any hierarchical structure. To allow straightforward processing of the data, it should be re-structured into a hierarchical form. As the SPARQL results may contain redundancies, several result sets must also be merged. The university example provides a case, where two result sets have to be merged. Because the university of Duisburg-Essen is located in two cities (Duisburg and Essen), two result sets with partially redundant information are returned. Both result sets contain information about the university but one contains information about the city of Duisburg, the other about the city of Essen. This behavior occurs in every case where a single property provides more than one value.

To handle this behavior and to simplify the retrieval of the SPARQL query's hierarchy, an additional XML structure is used. All SPARQL results are mapped onto this structure. It is defined by the hierarchy of the previously created SPARQL query. For the XML structure, every property from the query is represented by an XML element. The root-element as well as all object properties contains their properties as child nodes. The SPARQL query and the XML structure are associated through the variable names defined in the query. These variable names are used in the XML structure as attribute values.

In our example, the XML element, representing the university URI is the root element. The elements that represent the university label and the city URI are child elements. The city URI element is a parent element of the city label element. Finally, all result sets are aggregated into a single XML structure that contains all values as attributes of XML nodes. Figure 3 shows this restructuring process.

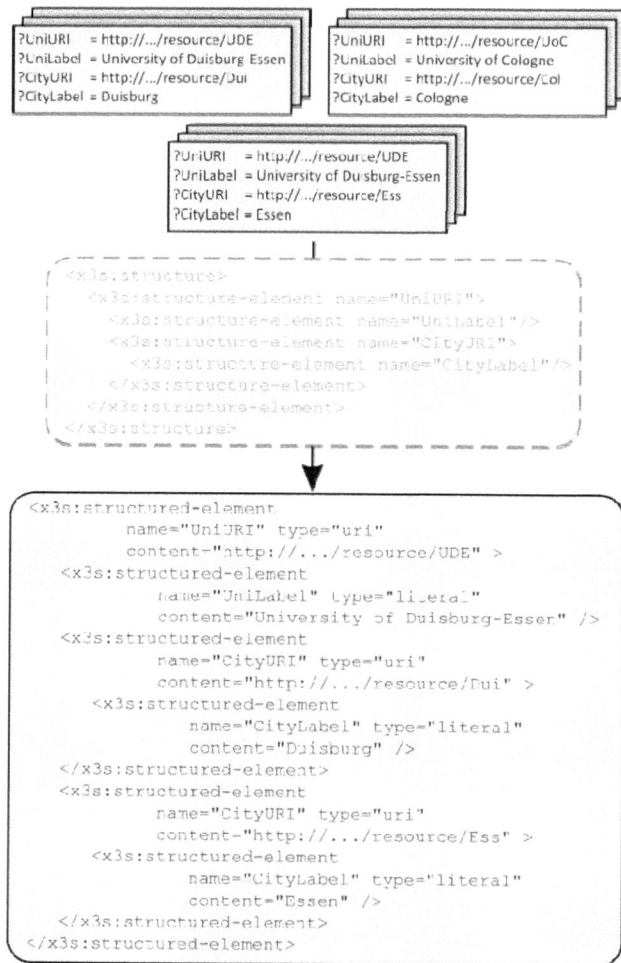

Figure 3: SPARQL results with redundancies are mapped onto a predefined hierarchical XML structure that meets the hierarchy of the primary SPARQL request. All values are saved in the node's attributes.

Direct processing of partially redundant data via XSLT, which is used in the next process step, would require grouping mechanisms that are possible but become very complex when nesting more than one object into another. Therefore all result sets are mapped onto a predefined

hierarchical XML structure that meets the hierarchy of the SPARQL request without redundancies.

The restructuring process is the only step in the X3S workflow that is not based on common techniques.

Transformation
We use XSLT 1.0 for transforming the resulting XML trees or fragments into HTML, including CSS classes and IDs that can later be used to decorate the HTML (see Figure 4).

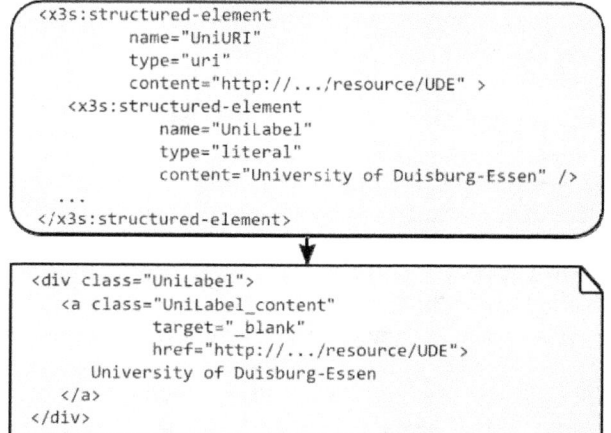

Figure 4: The restructured Data is transformed via XSLT into an HTML document.

The restriction to XSLT 1.0 instead of higher version was made to facilitate the implementation of an X3S viewer with nearly every system or programming language. The support for more recent XSLT standards is still not satisfying.

The function of the XSL transformation is to transform the restructured results into HTML code that can be put into the body-tag of a HTML document. One possibility is to keep the hierarchical structure and transform the restructured query results into nested div-tags. This is the option, we have chosen for our reference implementation. Another possibility would be to display the data as a table. Furthermore in this step, our implementation converts URLs into clickable links or displayable images. Also proper CSS class names are inserted into HTML elements for a latter styling via CSS.

Styling
In order to control the appearance of the documents, CSS can be specified. All CSS declaratives will be embedded into to the final HTML documents header. There is no further linking or other complex processing of information in this last step. The previous transformation step is responsible to ensure that the HTML and CSS code are fitting together.

AN EDITOR FOR SEMANTIC STYLESHEETS
To support users who are not experts in semantic technologies or in the template creation process we developed an editor as a rich internet application based on Adobe Flex. The editor runs in any web browser with Flash capabilities and can make use of existing semantic data repositories that provide a SPARQL interface. The editor enables users to explore the content of the repository in a visual manner and persistently store the properties of interest

in X3S format as *semantic widgets* or *stylesheets*. These widgets can later be used as templates for exploring similar data. The editor is available online[4].

Figure 5 shows the main window of the editor. We use point-and-click interactions instead of complex text-based directives: Drag-and-drop is used for selecting properties from a list of all possible attributes for the particular RDF class (Figure 5 A). The properties can be filtered and sorted by type, relevance[5], or in alphabetic order. In order to provide visual cues, datatype and object properties are displayed with different icons. We chose a visualization based on a file editor metaphor, where object properties, which contain again other properties as values, are displayed as folders and datatype properties, which contain only literals, are displayed as files. From this information the user can directly derive how properties can be nested.

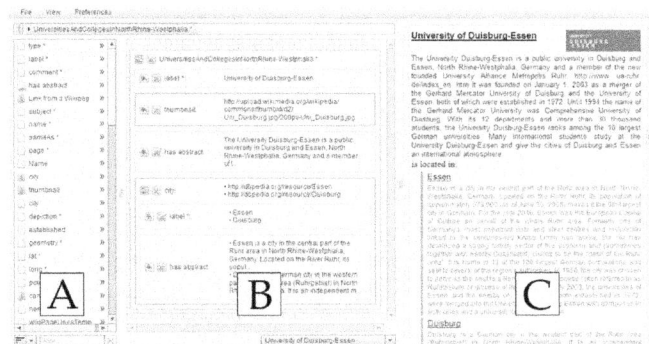

Figure 5: X3S editor while creating a semantic stylesheet, working with data from DBpedia.

The fictitious user in our example wants to select the set of all German universities as a starting point for her or his constructive exploration. The respective SPARQL query returns a list of values for each university. The semantic data corpus holds a large amount of information related to these universities. The user can drag elements from the list into the template located in the central workspace (Figure 5 B). A live preview of the resulting HTML document is displayed on the right side (Figure 5 C).

When adding datatype properties to the template, an appropriate display format can be selected (for instance showing the value of an URI as an image instead of the URI itself). The editor also tries to detect several properties automatically. As an additional feature, dynamic filters can be created based on datatype properties. This may be useful, if only a subset of all possible entities should be displayed (for instance, universities located in cities with a population between 500 000 and 1 000 000). Depending on the type of datatype property (String, Boolean, integer, etc.), widgets such as sliders for those filters are created dynamically.

---

[4] http://x3s.demos.interactivesystems.info/

[5] Relevance is measured by the frequency of occurrence of this property among all instances of the class.

The templates can finally be decorated by using standardized CSS. The editor supports the user by directly offering graphical shortcuts to common CSS declaratives such as font size. Elements can have defined borders or margins, images can be adjusted in width and height, etc.

FUNCTIONAL ASSESSMENT AND INITIAL EVALUATION

	X3S	Xenon	Fresnel	OWL-PL	LESS	Dido
Separation of Concerns	●	●	●	●	●	○
SPARQL-Endpoint Support	●			●		
Property Selection	●	●	●	●	●	●
Filtering	●	●	●	●	●	●
Styling	●	●		●	●	○
Nested Object-Properties	●	○	○	●	○	
Templating	●	●	●	●	●	●

Table 1: Comparison of the approaches: ● support, ○ partial support, no entry: no support.

We compared X3S to the other approaches described in the related work section (see Table 1). In terms of 'Separation of Concerns', all tools but Dido access their data from a source saved separately. Only X3S and LESS have a 'SPARQL-Endpoint Support' and are able to request their data directly from an external semantic database. All approaches provide means for 'Property Selection', so only a subset of the data can be selected for presentation. 'Filtering' of entries with regard to particular data values is also possible. 'Styling' of the data cannot be specified freely with Fresnel. All other candidates convert the data into HTML and can style them with CSS. It is simple with X3S and OWL-PL to display 'Nested Object-Properties' that are completely integrated into a single stylesheet. With the other procedures, a stylesheet author has to build a separate stylesheet that must be embedded into the primary one. All candidates are able to reuse the stylesheets by a 'Templating' mechanism.

We conducted an initial user study to determine the effectiveness, efficiency and user-friendliness of the X3S editor in comparison to the LESS editor. We chose LESS as a reference point because, in our review, it turned out to be the most closely related system in terms of functionality. The evaluation was designed as a user study in which ten participants had to solve five tasks with both editors (within subject design). All five tasks combined created a semantic widget, where each task covered an essential step of the overall creation process – property selection, data styling, adding static data, filtering, and nesting further objects. No Participant had previous experience of using the evaluated tools.

Using the X3S editor, the participants could immediately solve more than 80% of the tasks. Using the LESS editor instead, only 40% of the tasks could be solved without any assistance.

Across all five tasks, participants needed 7:26 minutes on average to create the whole widget with the X3S editor. With 16:36 minutes on average, it took more than twice as long to do the same work with the LESS editor.

In a finally completed questionnaire, the participants subjectively rated the X3S editor as intuitive to use for the given tasks but felt inadequately supported by the LESS editor.

DISCUSSION

The ongoing growth of the Semantic Web as an extension and complement of the conventional World Wide Web poses the problem of enabling non-expert users to interact with semantic data in an intuitive, yet flexible and powerful manner. In this paper, we have presented a method how users can define personalized views into the large semantic data space. As our main technical contribution, we have presented X3S as a technique and format for specifying 'semantic widgets'. Semantic widgets combine the querying and filtering of large semantic data sets with defining the layout and presentation style of the data. Semantic relationship between data elements can be transformed into suitable presentation structures.

To support the specification of semantic widgets, an editor has been developed that allows the creation of templates for data exploration and visualization based on the X3S specification. X3S supports the separation of data and layout as well as arbitrary filtering of data and visualization via CSS.

The technique presented supports a variety of ways of using semantic information in a wide range of web application scenarios. For example, predefined X3S templates in different configurations can be used for searching product information in the Web of data. Due to the intuitive direct manipulation style of defining semantic widgets, they are suitable for quickly building interfaces both in single-user as well as in collaborative situations, for instance, when teams are exploring data in front of large interactive surfaces.

Future work will firstly focus on optimizing the functionality developed so far. Especially, the combination of dynamically retrieved semantic data and statically added text can be improved. Furthermore, we aim at integrating data from different sources, extending the X3S technique to cover typical mash-up functions. A challenging future extension of the work would be to support transferring a semantic widget defined on some specific configuration of concepts and properties to other data graphs that are similarly structured but have different concept and object property types. This would require techniques for automatically analyzing the content of the new concepts and relations, extending the semantic widget concept towards more intelligent behavior.

REFERENCES

1. Auer, S., Bizer, C., Kobilarov, G., Lehmann, J., Cyganiak, R., and Ives, Z. DBpedia: A Nucleus for a Web of Open Data. In K. Aberer, K.-S. Choi, N. Noy, et al., eds., The Semantic Web. Springer Berlin Heidelberg, Berlin, Heidelberg, 2007, 722-735.

2. Auer, S., Doehring, R., and Dietzold, S. LESS – Template-Based Syndication and Presentation of Linked Data. In ESWC '10: Proceedings of the 7th Extended Semantic Web Conference, number 6089 in Lecture Notes in Computer Science, pages 211 – 224. Springer, 2010.

3. Berners-Lee, T., Hendler, J., and Lassila, O. The Semantic Web. Scientific American, May 2001.

4. Berners-Lee, T., Hollenbach, J., Lu, K., Presbrey, J., Prud'ommeaux, E. and Schraefel, m.c. Tabulator Redux: Browsing and writing Linked Data. In Proc. WWW 2008 Workshop: LDOW, (2008).

5. Brophy, M. OWL-PL: A Presentation Language for Displaying Semantic Data on the Web. Master's thesis, Lehigh University, 2010.

6. Feigenbaum, L., Herman, I., Hongsermeier, T., Neumann, E., and Stephens, S. The Semantic Web in Action. Scientific American 297, Dec. 2007 (2007), 90-97.

7. Heath, T., and Bizer, C. Linked Data - Evolving the Web into a Global Data Space. Morgan & Claypool Publishers, 2011.

8. Heim, P., Ertl, T., and Ziegler, J. Facet Graphs: Complex semantic querying made easy. In ESWC '10: Proceedings of the 7th Extended Semantic Web Conference, number 6088 in Lecture Notes in Computer Science, pages 288 – 302. Springer, 2010.

9. Karger, D. R., Ostler, S., and Lee, R. The Web Page as a WYSIWYG End-User Customizable Database-Backed Information Management Application. In UIST'09: Proceedings of the 22nd Annual ACM Symposium on User interface Software and Technology, pages 257–260, New York, NY, USA, 2009. ACM.

10. Le-Phuoc, D., Polleres, A., Hauswirth, M., Tummarello, G., and Morbidoni, C. 2009. Rapid prototyping of semantic mash-ups through semantic web pipes. In *Proceedings of the 18th international conference on World wide web* (WWW '09). ACM, New York, NY, USA, 581-590.

11. Pietriga, E., Bizer, C., Karger, D. R., and Lee, R. Fresnel: A Browser-Independent Presentation Vocabulary for RDF. In ISWC '06: Proceedings of the 5th International Semantic Web Conference, volume 4273 of Lecture Notes in Computer Science, pages 158–171. Springer, 2006.

12. Quan, D. and Karger, D. R. Xenon: An RDF Stylesheet Ontology. In WWW '05: Proceedings of the 14th International World Wide Web Conference, 2005.

Extraction and Interactive Exploration of Knowledge from Aggregated News and Social Media Content

Arno Scharl,[1] Alexander Hubmann-Haidvogel,[1] Albert Weichselbraun,[2]
Gerhard Wohlgenannt,[3] Heinz-Peter Lang,[1] Marta Sabou[1]

[1] MODUL University
Vienna, Department of New
Media Technology
Am Kahlenberg 1
1190 Vienna, Austria
+43 1 3203555 301
{scharl, hubmann-haidvogel,
lang, sabou}@modul.ac.at

[2] University of Applied
Sciences Chur, Faculty of Information Science
Pulvermuehlestrasse 57
7004 Chur, Switzerland
+41 812863 727
albert.weichselbraun@
htwchur.ch

[3] Vienna University of
Economics and Business,
Institute for Information Business, Augasse 2-6
1090 Vienna, Austria
+43 1 31336 5228
gerhard.wohlgenannt@ wu.ac.at

ABSTRACT

The *webLyzard* media monitoring and Web intelligence platform (www.webLyzard.com) presented in this paper is a flexible tool for assessing the positioning of an organization and the effectiveness of its communications. The platform aggregates large archives of digital content from multiple stakeholders. Each week it processes millions of documents and user comments from news media, blogs, Web 2.0 platforms such as Facebook, Twitter and YouTube, and the Web sites of companies and NGOs. An interactive dashboard with trend charts and complex map projections shows how often and where information is published. It also provides a real-time account of topics that stakeholders associate with an organization. Positive or negative sentiment is computed automatically, which reflects the impact of public relations and marketing campaigns.

Author Keywords

Interactive exploration of information spaces; social media monitoring tools; Web intelligence; visual analytics.

ACM Classification Keywords

H.5.2 [Information Interfaces and Presentation]: User Interfaces – Interaction styles.

INTRODUCTION

Interactive computing systems have been designed for analyzing social media streams across various domains including sports (Marcus et al., 2011), politics (Diakopoulos et al., 2010; Shamma et al., 2010) and climate change (Hubmann-Haidvogel et al., 2009), focusing on specific aspects like (sub-)event detection (Adams et al., 2011),

classification (Hubmann-Haidvogel et al., 2009), and the analysis of video broadcasts (Diakopoulos et al., 2010). Such media monitoring tools shed light on stakeholder perceptions, reveal flows of relevant information, and provide timely feedback for marketing and public outreach activities. Developers of such tools draw upon expertise from several disciplines including human-computer interaction, information visualization, natural language processing, and semantic systems in order to address two major challenges: (i) collect, analyze and structure very large document collections originating from sources that are heterogeneous in terms of their authorship, formatting, style (e.g., news article versus tweets), and update frequency (weekly, daily or minute-based); (ii) provide an interactive interface not only to select a relevant subset of the information space, but also to analyze and manipulate the extracted data.

The context-sensitive environment presented in this paper allows to analyze and manipulate the extracted knowledge, and to navigate the information space along multiple dimensions. Such an environment, in line with the challenges described above, requires scalable information extraction algorithms, and a rapid synchronization of multiple coordinated views. The webLyzard platform provides accurate annotation services to enrich documents with geospatial, semantic and temporal tags. Such annotations describe complex relations, which are best understood in graphical form. For this purpose, the system synchronizes geographic maps, tag clouds, keyword graphs as well as two- and three-dimensional information landscapes. These visualizations help users to understand the context of the extracted knowledge – e.g. processing search queries and showing the most relevant documents in a regional context, or comparing the online coverage by different stakeholders.

The remainder of this paper is structured into three parts: (i) the introduction of *Media Watch on Climate Change*, a public Web portal that aggregates environmental information from a variety of online sources including news media, blogs and other social media such as Twitter, YouTube and Facebook (www.ecoresearch.net/climate); (ii) a generic overview of the user interface design including the main interface elements and the synchronization mechanism employed to continuously update them; and (iii) a detailed description of the portal features including topic management, visualizations, and data services.

ENVIRONMENTAL USE CASE

Acquiring, managing and applying knowledge are crucial steps in addressing environmental issues effectively, and ensuring that change is conceived and implemented on both regional and society-wide scales (Bowman, 2008). Climate change is a good example, characterized by diverse opinions of stakeholders with different backgrounds and expertise. Understanding the reach of topics discussed and the opinions voiced by various parties is a complex task that requires knowledge on how topics and stakeholders relate to each other. The *Media Watch on Climate Change* (www.ecoresearch.net/climate; Figure 1 addresses this task. It provides analytical and visual methods to support different types of information seeking behavior such as browsing, search, trend monitoring and visual analytics.

The platform detects and tracks the evolution of *topics* that are frequently mentioned in a given data sample (typically, a collection of Web *documents* crawled from relevant sources). The advanced data mining techniques underlying the platform extract a variety of contextual features from the document space. A portfolio of synchronized visualizations allows both an overall insight into the evolution of the data set along the dimensions defined by these contextual features (temporal, geographic, semantic, and attitudinal), and subsequent drill-down functionalities to analyze details of the data itself. A key strength of the interface is that it relies on the *multiple coordinated views* metaphor, also known as linked or tightly coupled views in the literature (Hubmann-Haidvogel et al., 2009), where a change in one of the views triggers an immediate update of the others (e.g., when a new document is viewed, the maps pan and zoom to the most relevant areas for this document).

The *Media Watch on Climate Change* currently harvests data from a range of relevant sources including 150 Anglo-American news media sites, blogs, Web 2.0 platforms (Twitter, Youtube, Facebook), scientific outlets, and the Web sites of environmental organizations and Fortune 1000 companies. At any given time, only a subset of the vast document space is displayed, depending on the selected source, time interval and affective value (e.g., positive news media articles published in the first quarter of 2012).

The system automatically extracts the dominant issues that are discussed in conjunction with a selected topic – e.g. COP17 in Durban as shown in Figure 1 – and displays them through a set of charts that show the frequency and sentiment of a topic, as well as the observable level of disagreement among stakeholders.

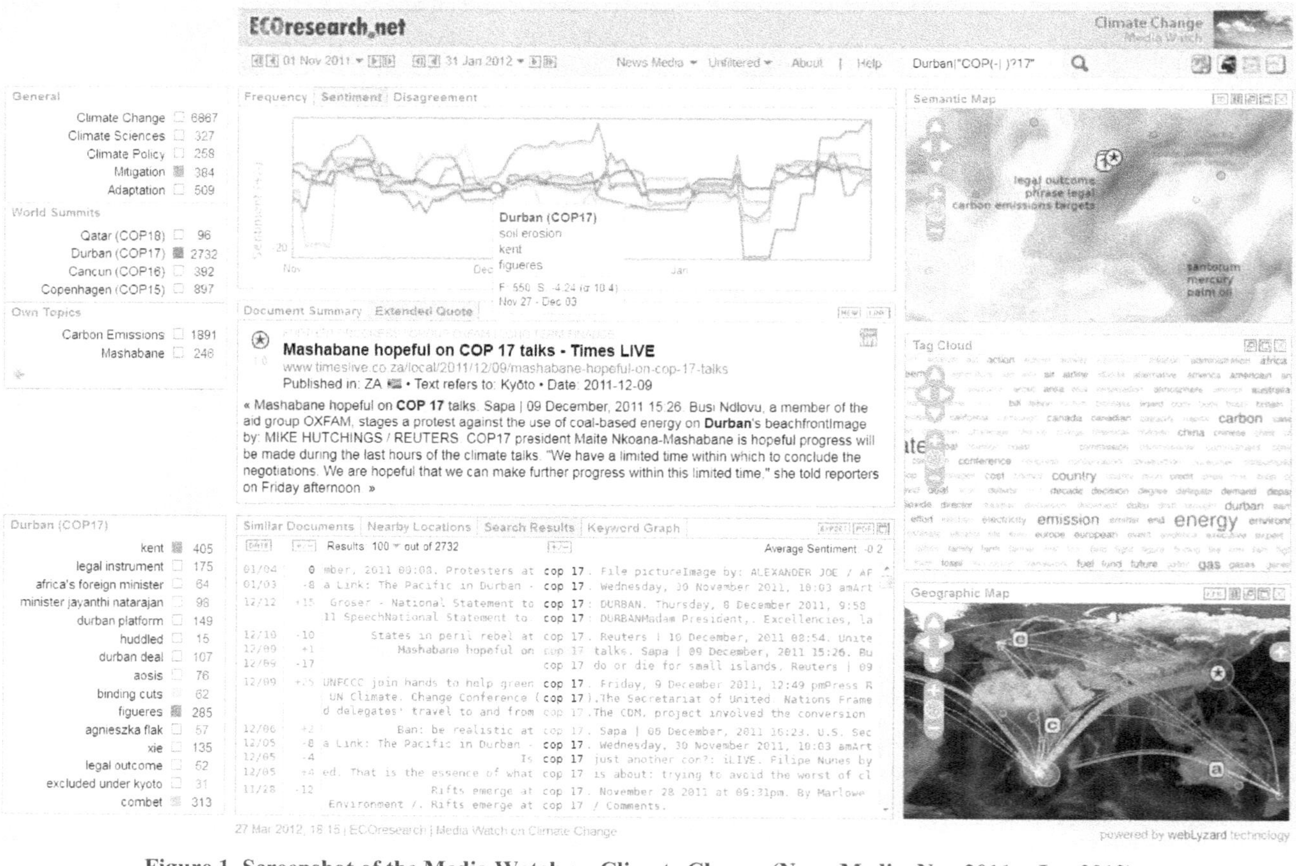

Figure 1. Screenshot of the Media Watch on Climate Change (News Media, Nov 2011 – Jan 2012)

The search results are also mapped on geographic and semantic maps to show the geographic distribution of the coverage (e.g., which places are the most talked about?), as well as its semantic content (e.g., how many documents talk about a specific issue?).

While the Media Watch on Climate Change focuses on environmental issues, the same technology is currently being used for other domains as well, including Web intelligence platforms for NOAA, the National Oceanic and Atmospheric Administration (www.noaa.gov) and the Vienna Chamber of Commerce (www.wkw.at).

In the next sections, we detail the generic aspects of our technology that support the development of interactive computing applications in various subject domains.

USER INTERFACE DESIGN

Following an evolutionary systems development approach (Scharl, 2000), rapid feedback cycles and agile software development (Dönmez and Grote, 2011) have been instrumental in the conceptualization and implementation of the Media Watch on Climate Change. For this purpose, ongoing usability inspections have been conducted to analyze and assess the system. This low-overhead, heuristic approach asks a team of experts to investigate the interface design against recognized usability principles. The evaluation has been performed periodically during the design and implementation phases, and improvements were integrated into the prototype early in the development cycle. A summative usability evaluation will be conducted in the third quarter of 2012 (see "Summary and Conclusion" section).

The webLyzard information exploration and retrieval interface (="dashboard") helps users to interactively identify, track and analyze topics across stakeholders and sources. It builds upon a comprehensive content repository structured along geospatial, semantic and temporal dimensions. The dashboard is divided into six main content areas, shown in Figure 2 and described in the following.

Overview of the webLyzard Dashboard

1. *Sources and Settings:* Drop-down elements in the upper menu let users choose the relevant constraints that are relevant for their exploration, including (i) time interval, (ii) document source, and (iii) global sentiment filter (unfiltered, positive, negative). In conjunction with full-text search capabilities and the resulting keyword graph (showing a network of co-occurring terms extracted in real time from the selected data source), the global sentiment filter is an effective means to investigate stakeholders' associations with a topic of interest.

2. *Topics:* The upper left window of the dashboard contains the topic management and content navigation. On mouse-over, users have the following options: (a) click on a term to trigger the full-text search; (b) use topic markers (= small rectangles) to select the topics to be shown in the charts; (c) compute related

terms to update the associations window ('arrow down' symbol); (d) add/modify topics and email alerts with the topic editor ('settings' symbol).

3. *Trend Charts:* Interactive charts show the frequency of selected topics in the specified time interval (default: two months), as well as the observed sentiment and disagreement regarding these topics.

4. *Content View:* The content view below shows the active document including keywords, publication date, place of publication (source geography), and primary location that is being referenced (target geography).

5. *Search Results:* The lower third of the dashboard displays the list of terms associated with a selected topic, as well as search results ranked by similar topic or nearby location (on either the document or sentence level).

6. *Visualizations:* To reveal complex and often hidden relations within the document repository, webLyzard integrates geographic maps, ontology graphs, tag clouds, and information landscapes to visualize semantic context. Maps are re-sized automatically and can be repositioned using drag-and-drop operations (see below for a detailed description of the synchronization mechanism).

Figure 2. Main elements of the webLyzard dashboard

Temporal Controls

Users can adjust the time interval and access historic data by selecting "from" and "to" dates using the two calendar elements. This is a global setting that not only affects the trend chart, as outlined in the next section, but also limits search queries and dynamic visualizations to the chosen time interval. Dates can be selected by navigating one day or week into the past or future by using the provided back and forward buttons, respectively, or by selecting a specific date using the drop-down calendar. Selecting a new "to" date automatically updates the trend charts, the active document, as well as the semantic map in case the new date belongs to a different weekly snapshot.

Real-Time Map Synchronization

The maps on the right side of the dashboard facilitate access to the underlying knowledge base. Clicking on the 'maximize' button increases the size of the maps; clicking on the 'popup' button opens the map in a separate browser window (which allows using the system in multiple-screen configurations). Maps can be rearranged by dragging them to the desired position, and switched on and off using the buttons in the top bar.

The various windows are tightly coupled – user actions in one window trigger an immediate update of all other displays – thus supporting an interactive exploration of the information space (Hubmann-Haidvogel et al., 2009; Scharl, 2006). As an alternative to entering query terms to find specific documents, users can click on any position in the maps (not only on the markers) to retrieve articles related to that particular location, topic or domain concept.

Hovering above a map previews the document closest to the current position of the mouse pointer, but does not activate it. When previewing documents, the other visualizations on the right side automatically adjust to show the immediate context of the previewed documents. Users who want to focus on a particular region can disable this default setting and "freeze" the currently displayed part of the map by pressing the pause button.

TOPIC MANAGEMENT
Registered users can add and modify topics through the topic editor, which also provides the option to set customized email alerts. The mouse-over 'settings' symbol to activate the editor is available in the topic management section.

Topic Editor
Each topic is represented as a list of regular expressions; i.e., a term list with optional wildcards for matching arbitrary character strings. For computing the charts and ranking search results, a document is considered relevant to the topic if it contains at least one of the stated terms. The topic label (= the name to be displayed in the topic management section) itself is not considered in the matching process.

Sentiment Detection
Measures of bias in news and social media coverage are essential when investigating trends and differing perceptions of interest groups (Scharl and Weichselbraun, 2008). A significant portion of news and social media coverage contains opinions with clear economic relevance: customer and travel reviews, for example, or articles of well-known and respected bloggers who influence purchase decisions. Analyzing and acting upon user-generated content is becoming imperative for decision makers aiming to engage large user communities.

The ever increasing amount of articles and the limits of human cognition require automated approaches to analyzing the sentiment expressed in user-generated content. As part of opinion mining, sentiment detection identifies and aggregates polar opinions – i.e., positive or negative statements about facts. For achieving accurate results, one needs

to deal with the inherent ambiguities of human languages. webLyzard's method to determine sentiment automatically has continually been optimized since 2003, directing particular attention to the context of opinionated terms when resolving such ambiguities (Gindl et al., 2010).

webLyzard not only uses sentiment information to enrich visualizations such as tag clouds, geographic maps and information landscapes, but also offers high-performance data services (see below) for tagging third-party content.

Trend Chart
Showing the rise and decay of topics over the last two months (default value, which can be changed using the date selector), the trend chart provides the following time series:

- *Frequency* (total, positive and negative) represents the number of occurrences in the last seven days. Selecting positive or negative coverage through the global sentiment filter affects the data displayed in the chart. Once activated, the footer of the portal also shows the current filter status.

- *Sentiment* shows the average sentiment towards the selected topic for the selected source and interval.

- *Disagreement* computed as standard deviation of the sentiment distribution reflects how contested a particular topic is (the term 'oil spill', for example, tends to have a low standard deviation since everyone agrees on its negative connotation).

Display Features. The vertical axis is rescaled automatically, a feature that is particularly useful if one keyword dominates the coverage and therefore obscures the distributions of the other keywords. Hovering above a data point displays the associated keywords and daily statistics (frequency, mean and standard deviation of sentiment). This mouse-over effect identifies topical trends and shows their impact on the individual peaks in the chart. Clicking on a data point triggers a search for this particular topic cluster in the preceding week.

MAP VISUALIZATIONS
The dashboard offers a suite of visualizations that display information along two main contextual dimensions: semantic and geographic. The *Geographic Map* allows users to interact with the information space in terms of the geographic locations relevant for the documents (i.e., both that of the author and the target of the document). The semantic dimension of the information space is exposed by three different views that leverage increasingly complex semantics: the *tag cloud* is derived from the most frequently mentioned keywords in the information space, the *information landscape* displays clusters of topically related documents thus depicting intrinsic semantic relations between documents, and, finally, the *ontology graph* displays an a-priori constructed semantic model of the domain and assigns each document to the best-matching concept.

Geographic Map

The geographic map shows the locations of documents based on analyzing their textual content – a process typically referred to as "geo-tagging" (Amitay et al., 2004). The Active Document is highlighted by a yellow asterisk, and the letters [a-e] represent the five highest-ranking documents in the Similar Topics view. If interested in a specific location rather than a topic, users can click anywhere on the map to activate the closest document (hovering above the map previews the document, but does not activate it).

After entering a search term, the set of results is visualized in the geographic map. Circular markers show the target geography of the found articles. The diameter of the marker represents the number of matching documents for a given location, its color the average sentiment of these matches. Using a color range from yellow to either green or red, trajectories link the source and target geography of an article (source geography = location of the publisher; target geography = main location referenced in the document). The little '+' symbol on the right side of the window allows users choosing alternative base maps (e.g. NASA Blue Marble, Political Borders, Google Terrain, etc.), as well as deactivating the circular markers or trajectories.

Tag Cloud

The tag cloud visualizes the most relevant keywords identified in recent online publications of a stakeholder group. Terms are arranged alphabetically; size and opacity are proportional to their importance - i.e., their relative frequency in the text archive (more frequent terms are rendered in darker shades, using a larger font, less frequent terms using a smaller font and lower opacity settings).

The color of terms indicates their sentiment (positive = green; neutral = black; negative = red). This allows investigating the "spin" across sources; e.g. typically balanced news media coverage compared to the very positive slant characteristic for corporate publications found on the Web sites of Fortune 1000 companies.

Information Landscape

Reflecting topical relatedness in large document repositories, information landscapes cluster and visualize massive amounts of textual data (Krishnan et al., 2007). They implement the concept of 'location' in an innovative way that transcends the traditional geographic interpretation. The information landscape resembles a geographic map at first sight. Instead of geographic proximity, however, it represents semantic similarity between documents. At the time of map generation, its topography is determined by the content of the knowledge base. The peaks of the virtual landscape indicate abundant coverage on a particular topic, whereas valleys represent sparsely populated parts of the information space. The visualization provides the following interface elements mapped onto the underlying topography (Sabol and Scharl, 2008; Sabol et al., 2010):

- *Captions.* The keywords for each peak are calculated automatically, based on the content of surrounding documents.

- *Document Markers.* The markers [1-5] show the position of the documents from the *Nearby Locations* window, thus allowing a cross-interrogation along both semantic and geographic dimensions by showing topics and document clusters that are being discussed in conjunction with neighboring locations

- *Document Selection.* Hovering above any location in the map shows a preview of the closest matching document in the active document window, clicking selects this document (each of the small gray dots, which become visible after zooming in, represents one document).

Ontology Graph

The ontology graph displays a clickable domain model that matches documents and concepts to help users determine their current location in the information space. The ontology graph depicts hierarchical relations as arrows. The currently active document is highlighted by a yellow asterisk, and the letters [1-5] represent the classification of the five highest-ranking documents in the similar locations view. Clicking on a concept activates the highest-ranking document for this particular concept.

SEMANTIC SEARCH

The search box is located in the top bar of the portal. The system supports the usual wildcard characters – while the asterisk (*) symbol represents any number of unknown characters, for example, the question mark (?) represents exactly one character. The results are displayed either on the sentence or the document level:

- **Sentence Level.** Upon entering a search query, the system lists all sentences containing the search term and groups them by document. The column headers show publication date, document sentiment, currently selected and total number of matches, and average sentiment of the displayed search results. Users can sort the results by their date of publication as well as the sentiment on both the document level and the sentence level (the color of the term reflects sentence-level sentiment).

- **Document Level.** Two just-in-time information retrieval agents list documents referring to similar topics and nearby locations relative to the Active Document (the term 'nearby locations' referring to the five documents with the closest target geography). The document markers (a-e, 1-5) are also used in the various maps to indicate the position of this document. The value underneath the markers represents document sentiment. Clicking on the text block extends the quote, clicking on the circular marker on the left activates that particular document. Back and forward buttons enable the user to browse the list of related documents. RSS links provide a continuously updated list of documents related to the query.

A full-text query not only returns the search results, but also updates other views including associations, similar topics, keyword graph, various maps as well as the content view, which summarizes the highest-ranking document including source and target geography. *Advanced query options* extend the capabilities of the simple search. They enable users to filter the search results by specifying restrictions based on document metadata (title, source, date, location, etc.).

SUMMARY AND CONCLUSION

This paper described the development of the *Media Watch on Climate Change* (www.ecoresarch.net/climate), a complex interactive computing system to extract actionable knowledge from unstructured and heterogeneous environmental resources. Addressing the inherent ambiguities of natural languages, the interactive process comprises document sample selection, query definition, and the configuration of filtering options and output services.

The extraction and interactive exploration of knowledge has significant commercial potential from market research and business intelligence to campaign management, product development, and monitoring the effectiveness of outreach programs. The gathered information creates feedback loops and shows how well an organization's communication is received, understood, and remembered. By uncovering patterns and trends in online media coverage and making them available through an interactive dashboard, the webLyzard platform (www.weblyzard.com) and its portfolio of semantic technologies helps to allocate communications resources and reach target audiences effectively.

Future research will involve a summative usability evaluation utilizing the eye tracking facilities of the *University of Applied Sciences Chur* (www.cheval-lab.ch). Formal experiments with test users will collect quantitative performance measurements (e.g., time required to successfully complete a given task) and analyze the collected data to optimize the interface structure and guide future development efforts.

ACKNOWLEDGMENTS

The data integration, annotation and visualization methods presented in this paper were developed as part of DIVINE (www.weblyzard.com/divine), a research project funded by *FIT-IT Semantic Systems* of the *Austrian Research Promotion Agency* (www.ffg.at) and the *Federal Ministry for Transport, Innovation and Technology* (www.bmvit.gv.at).

REFERENCES

1. Adams, B., Phung, D. and Venkatesh, S. (2011). Eventscapes: Visualizing Events Ever Times with Emotive Facets. *19th ACM International Conference on Multimedia (MM-2011).* Scottsdale, USA: 1477-1480.

2. Amitay, E., Har'El, N., Sivan, R. and Soffer, A. (2004). "Web-a-Where: Geotagging Web Content", *27th Annual International ACM SIGIR Conference on Research and Development in Information Retrieval.* Sheffield, UK: ACM Press. 273-280.

3. Bowman, T. (2008). *Summary Report: A Meeting to Assess Public Attitudes about Climate Change.* Silver Springs: National Oceanic and Atmospheric Administration (NOAA), George Mason University.

4. Diakopoulos, N., Naaman, M. and Kivran-Swaine, F. (2010). Diamonds in the Rough: Social Media Visual Analytics for Journalistic Inquiry. *IEEE Symposium on Visual Analytics Science and Technology (VAST-2010).* Salt Lake City, USA: IEEE: 115-122

5. Dönmez, D. and Grote, G. (2011). "Managing Uncertainty in Software Development Projects", *Agile Processes in Software Engineering & Extreme Programming.* Ed. A. Sillitti. Berlin: Springer. 326-328.

6. Gindl, S., Weichselbraun, A. and Scharl, A. (2010). Cross-Domain Contextualisation of Sentiment Lexicons. *19th European Conference on Artificial Intelligence.* H. Coelho et al. Lisbon, Portugal: IOS Press: 771-776.

7. Hubmann-Haidvogel, A., Scharl, A. and Weichselbraun, A. (2009). "Multiple Coordinated Views for Searching and Navigating Web Content Repositories", *Information Sciences,* 179(12): 1813-1821.

8. Krishnan, M., Bohn, S., et al. (2007). "Scalable Visual Analytics of Massive Textual Datasets", *21st IEEE International Parallel & Distributed Processing Symposium.* Long Beach, USA: IEEE Computer Society.

9. Marcus, A., Bernstein, M.S., et al. (2011). Twitinfo: Aggregating & Visualizing Microblogs for Event Exploration. *Annual Conference on Human Factors in Computing Systems.* Vancouver, Canada: ACM: 227-236.

10. Sabol, V. and Scharl, A. (2008). "Visualizing Temporal-Semantic Relations in Dynamic Information Landscapes", *11th International Conference on Geographic Information Science (AGILE-2008).* Girona, Spain: AGILE Council.

11. Sabol, V., Syed, K.A.A., et al. (2010). Incremental Computation of Information Landscapes for Dynamic Web Interfaces. *10th Brazilian Symposium on Human Factors in Computer Systems (IHC-2010).* M.S. Silveira et al. Belo Horizonte, Brazil: BCS: 205-208.

12. Scharl, A. (2000). *Evolutionary Web Development.* London: Springer.

13. Scharl, A. (2006). "Tightly Coupled Geospatial Interfaces for Collaborative Systems and Just-in-Time Information Retrieval Agents", *Research in Computing Science,* 25: 3-18.

14. Scharl, A. and Weichselbraun, A. (2008). "An Automated Approach to Investigating the Online Media Coverage of US Presidential Elections", *Journal of Information Technology & Politics,* 5(1): 121-132.

15. Shamma, D.A., Kennedy, L. and Churchill, E.F. (2010). Tweetgeist: Can the Twitter Timeline Reveal the Structure of Broadcast Events? *ACM Conference on Computer Supported Cooperative Work.* Savannah, USA.

Specifying and Running Rich Graphical Components with Loa

Olivier Beaudoux[1], Mickael Clavreul[1], Arnaud Blouin[2],
Mengqiang Yang[1], Olivier Barais[2], Jean-Marc Jezequel [2]

[1]ESEO, TRAME Team
LUNAM University
Angers, France
[first-name].[last-name]@eseo.fr

[2]University of Rennes 1
IRISA, Triskell Team
Rennes, France
[last-name]@irisa.fr

ABSTRACT

Interactive system designs often require the use of rich graphical components whose capabilities go beyond the set of widgets provided by GUI toolkits. The implementation of such rich graphical components require a high programming effort that GUI toolkits do not alleviate. In this paper, we propose the Loa framework that allows both the specification of rich graphical components and their integration within running interactive applications. We illustrate the specification and integration with the Loa framework as part of a global process for the design of interactive systems.

ACM Classification Keywords

D.2.2 Software Engineering: Design Tools and Techniques—*Computer-aided software engineering (CASE), User interfaces*

Author Keywords

Graphical components; Graphical User Interface (GUI); Domain Specific Language (DSL); Active Operations

INTRODUCTION

Building Rich Interactive Applications (RIA) often leads to the design of new graphical components. Recent interactive systems such as smart-phones and tablets well illustrate such a purpose. The design of complex graphical components that goes beyond the composition of existing widgets requires implementation effort and prevents reuse or capitalization. While recent GUI toolkits, such as GWT [26], WPF [22] and Flex [14], target the implementation of RIAs, the design of rich graphical components is still a time-consuming activity.

Providing the right methodologies, models and tools that facilitate the design and the implementation of such rich graphical components is thus an important challenge.

Standard GUI toolkits are centered on a *low level* implementation of graphical components and are based on primitive drawing functions. This statement applies to proven toolkits such as Swing [9] and remains for recent standards such as HTML 5 [10]. This situation leads to interoperability and synchronization issues between the graphical design made by the designers and its implementation written by the programmers. Current RIA environments solve this issue by proposing tools that integrate (or link) both the design and the programming environments. For instance, FlexBuilder is both a designing and programming environment dedicated to Flex applications; Expression Blend is a designer environment that produces XAML documents that can be directly used within VisualStudio, a programming environment.

Integrating design and programming environments provides interoperability and synchronization to some extent. But in this case the specification of new graphical components requires a significant implementation effort. Effort includes the definition of components, the implementation of the associated interactions and the related actions performed on the domain data, and their integration within the final application.

In this paper, we propose the Loa framework that allows both the specification of rich graphical components and their integration within running interactive applications. This framework homogenizes the process of extending and integrating previous works on data binding [3, 4], graphical templates [13, 27, 2], and interactors [19, 1, 6]. The paper focuses on the specification and integration with the Loa framework as part of a global *process* for the design of interactive systems.

The remainder the paper is structured as follows. Next section presents a global overview of the Loa framework that includes a DSL (Domain Specific Language), a development process, and a supporting tool implementation. Sections "Step 1" to "Step 6" detail each step of the process through the concrete example of building a planner application. We discuss this work and evaluate Loa with regard to existing GUI toolkits in Sections "Related Works" and "Evaluation". Last section concludes this work and proposes perspectives.

OVERVIEW OF THE LOA FRAMEWORK

A Scala-based DSL

The Loa framework is based on the Scala language [20]. This choice is motivated by the following facts: 1) Scala is an OO language fully compatible with Java, thus allowing the reuse of the numerous Java API and tools, especially GUI ones; 2) Scala embeds the imperative the functional and the object-oriented programming paradigms in a way that greatly facilitates the implementation of the framework; 3) Scala is a self-extensible language that enables the construction of new DSLs[1] while reusing the infrastructure and tools (*i.e.*, IDEs and compilers) of the Scala language for these DSLs.

The Loa[2] DSL is thus built as an extension of the Scala language that defines the very language of the framework.

With this short introduction in mind, the Loa DSL allows designers to capture the problem domain of GUI engineering within a precise, concise and dedicated language. This paper focuses on the *usage* of the Loa framework supported by the Loa DSL in the process of building new graphical components for interactive systems. Details on the Loa DSL are thus out of the scope of the paper; the DSL is rather explained through a concrete example.

The development process

The Loa framework splits the development process of interactive systems into six steps as illustrated in Figure 1. Using the usual concept of classes, application designers specify the *domain data* (step ①). Graphical designers sketch new graphical components using a graphical design tool such as Illustrator or Inkscape (step ②) that produces an XML document. Sketches are then formalized into *graphical templates* (step ③) that both define the graphical parts of the components in XML and their parameters. While steps ①, ②, and ③ require interaction between application and graphical designers, they can be executed in parallel. Application designers specify the *data binding* (step ④) using the data binding capabilities of active operations [3, 4]. Data binding consists in linking the domain data to the graphical templates. Application designers specify the *interactors* (step ⑤) using the data binding capabilities provided by the framework and an interaction model inspired from Malai [6]. The specifications that result from steps ①, ③, ④ and ⑤ are finally integrated together in a sole executable application. While the execution of the resulting application requires the whole set of specifications, each specification can be tested independently. For instance, a given graphical template can be tested while the specification of domain data or interactors are not yet provided.

---
[1] A DSL is a programming language that targets a specific problem. It contains the syntax and semantics of the language concepts at the same level of abstraction that the problem domain offers.
[2] French acronym that stands for Language for Active Operations

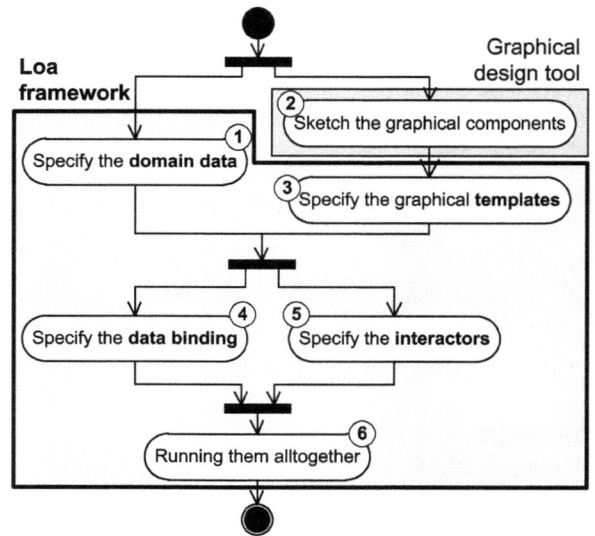

Figure 1. The development process

While the process is proposed for building new graphical components, the use of existing widgets provided by GUI toolkits fits in. In such a case, step ② relies on GUI design tools, such as Adobe FlexBuilder, Microsoft Expression Blend or Google WindowBuilder. Step ③ and ⑤ thus consists in reusing the Loa model of these widgets. Steps ①, ④ and ⑥ remain unchanged.

As one may note, the process focuses on the idea of *specification*. The ability to run a specification without requiring a hand-written implementation of the specification is an essential contribution that we summarize as:

> *"Specifying GUIs rather than implementing them"*

However, the process is *not* a methodology for the development of interactive systems. It is rather a process that formalizes the use of the Loa framework; it can be used jointly to well-known methodologies such as user's task analysis [21].

The implementation

The implementation of the Loa framework consists in an API that bridges the three main concepts of data bindings, of graphical templates, and of interactors with existing GUI toolkits.

The current *implementation* provides a bridge to *Swing widgets* as well as *Batik* for the definition of graphical templates based on the SVG standard. The case study that we present in the paper use the latter. The case study has been built using Inkscape for sketching the graphical templates, using Google WindowBuilder for designing the Swing UI in a WYSIWYG manner, and using the Eclipse workbench with Scala support for the edition and the compilation of the code written in Loa.

STEP 1: SPECIFY THE DOMAIN DATA

Figure 2 gives the class diagram that represents the domain data of the academic planning: *Planning* of a given year is composed of 0 to 52 *weeks*; a teaching *Week* is composed of 0 to 5 *days*; and each *Day* defines its *teachings*. A *Teaching* can span among multiple *TimeSlots*: the first element of relation *timeSlots* defines the starting time-slot, while the second element gives the ending time-slot. A *Teaching* also references a *topic*, a *teacher*, and *a room*.

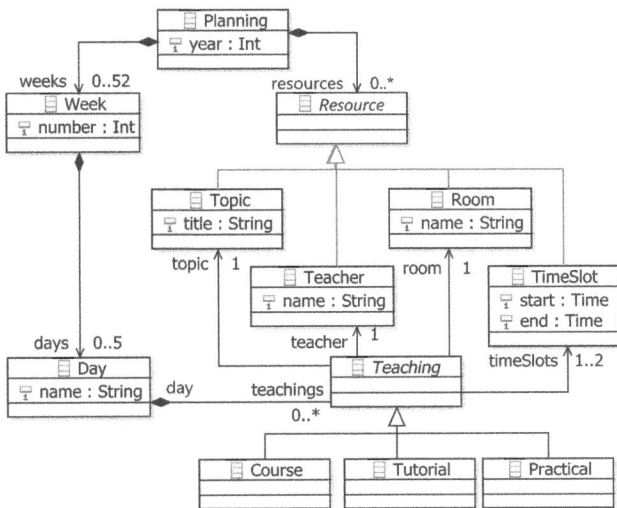

Figure 2. Class diagram of an academic planning

The Loa *data model* provides a textual representation of classes based on the use of six kinds of Loa *container*. This data model is used for specifying the domain data, the graphical templates, as well as the interactors. The following listing illustrates the specification of the class *Planning* from the domain data using the three Loa containers *One*, *OSet* and *Set*:

```
class Planning {
  val year = One(2012)
  val weeks = OSet[Week]()
  val resources = Set[Resource]()
}
```

Attribute *year* is represented as an integer boxed into a container with initial value *2012*. Relation *weeks* is represented as an initially empty ordered set of *Week* instances, and relation *resources* as a set of *Resource* instances.

	Cardinality	Uniqueness	Order
Opt	0..1		
One	1..1		
Bag	0..*		
Seq	0..*		√
Set	0..*	√	
OSet	0..*	√	√

Table 1. Loa container kinds

Table 1 lists the six kinds of container: the four last kinds are equivalent to the OCL collections [29] and are supplemented by the two kinds *Opt* and *One*. These six kinds of container differ by three properties: cardinality, uniqueness and order.

Container contents can be modified using assignment operators. Operator := is used for *Opt* and *One* containers, and operators += and -= are used for the four collection containers, as follows:

```
val p = Planning()
p.year := 2012
p.weeks += Week()
```

All the six kinds of container implement an observability mechanism that allows each change (addition, removal or update) to be captured. Observability is an important feature for graphical components, data bindings and interactors.

Finally, methods written in Scala define the application logic that is integrated in the classes of the system.

STEP 2: SKETCH THE GRAPHICAL COMPONENTS

Figure 3 gives a screen-shot of the *Academic Planning Application* that displays a weekly view of the academic planning, as introduced in the previous section; each teaching is presented to users through a *stamp* graphical component. Menu *File* allows loading and saving XML documents that contain planning data related to a specific academic year. Menu *Edit* allows editing planning resources (*e.g.,* rooms, topics), and allows duplicating or clearing the week contents. The combo-box at the top allows selecting a specific week within a year (from 1 to 52). The canvas allows direct manipulation of the selected week. Undo and redo buttons allow undoing and redoing past actions. Finally, the tab *Tree* displays the tree of the graphical scene for debugging purpose.

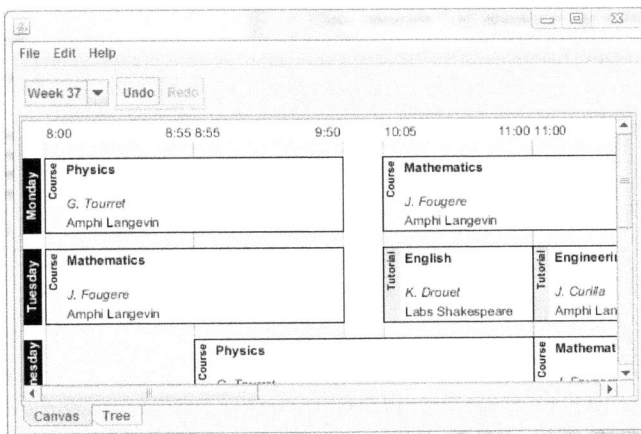

Figure 3. The Academic Planning Application

Based on the application requirements, the graphical designer sketches the necessary graphical components exported by the tool as XML representations. The following code illustrates an excerpt of a *stamp* component that uses the SVG format for its XML representation:

```
1   <g transform="translate(10,10)">
2     <!-- background -->
3     <rect width="170" height="70" fill="white"/>
4     <!-- type bar -->
5     <rect width="15" height="70" fill="yellow"/>
6     <text x="-5" y="11" transform="rotate(-90)" ...>
7       Course
8     </text>
9     <g transform="translate(20,15)">
10      <!-- labels -->
11      <text font-weight="bold">Mathematics</text>
12      <text y="20" font-style="italic">J. Fougere</text>
13      <text y="50">Amphi Langevin</text>
14    </g>
15    <!-- border -->
16    <rect width="170" height="70" fill="none"
17      stroke="black"/>
18  </g>
```

The *stamp* is an SVG group composed of: a white background (line 3); a type bar representing the *stamp* type with a text (lines 6 to 8) and a yellow background (line 5); a group of labels displaying the event description (lines 11 to 13); and a black stroke defining the stamp border (line 16 and 17).

Since SVG does not support the parametrization of symbols, the code of the *stamp* graphical component includes hard-coded value. Step ③ addresses such parametrization issues.

STEP 3: SPECIFY THE GRAPHICAL TEMPLATES

Loa formalizes sketches of graphical components (step ②) as the combination of a Loa data model and templates. In the following subsections, we present the specification of such templates with Loa and we explain how templates are transformed into an executable form.

Specification of templates

Figure 4 shows the class diagram which contains the *template classes* that formalize the sketched graphical components used by the planning application. The root template class *Calendar* represents the weekly presentation of a planning.

The presentation of a calendar is a grid that is composed of *dayLabels* and *timeAreas*. Its contents is displayed by *stamps*, each *Stamp* including a *typeBar* (*i.e.*, the type of the displayed event) and *labels*.

A template class is specified using both the Loa data model and the specification of its *template*. Template class *Stamp* specifies attributes *x*, *y*, *width* and *height* and relations *typeBar* and *dayLabels* as follows:

```
1   class Stamp extends Fragment {
2     val x = One(0)    val width = One(300)
3     val y = One(0)    val height = One(100)
4     val typeBar = One(TypeBar())
```

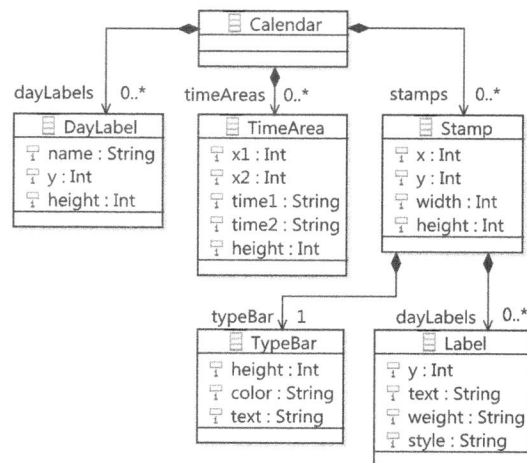

Figure 4. Class diagram of the planning templates

```
5   val dayLabels = OSet[Label]()
6
7   template {
8     <g transform="translate($x,$y)">
9       <rect width="$width" height="$height"
10        fill ="white"/>
11      $typeBar
12      <g transform="translate(20,15)">
13        $dayLabels
14      </g>
15      <rect width="$width" height="$height"
16        fill ="none" stroke="black"/>
17    </g>
18  }
19 }
```

Loa introduces the keyword *template* defined by class *Fragment* (term fragment is explained in the next subsection). Parametrization of a template is carried out by the concept of *anchor*: an anchor is bound to a container that defines the anchor contents and the anchor location within the template through symbol *$*. In the *Stamp* example, anchors *$x*, *$y*, *$width* and *$height* (lines 8 and 9) receive the contents of their associated containers *x*, *y*, *width* and *height* (lines 2 and 3); anchor *$typeBar* (line 11) receives the associated *TypeBar* instance contained in *typeBar* (line 4); anchor *$dayLabels* (line 13) will receive multiple *DayLabel* instances subsequently added into the ordered set *dayLabels* (line 5).

Instantiation of templates

Instantiation of a Loa template into a fragment consists of creating a DOM fragment with an initial content defined by the template itself, and binding the anchors of the templates within the DOM fragment. The interlacing between fragments and anchors allows the incremental construction of the final graphical components. The interlacing approach has been borrowed from eXAcT [2]. Since the mechanism is quite complex, we provide an overview of the core principles. Figure 5 illustrates the instantiation of the template *Stamp* into a fragment. For the sake of clarity, Figure 5 only contains the *$width*, *$height* and *$dayLabels* anchors.

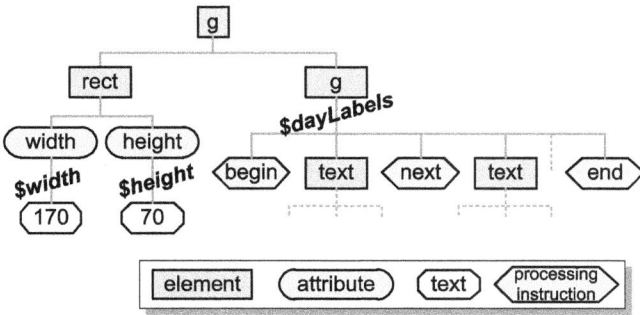

Figure 5. A subset of an instance of fragment *Stamp*

Instantiation of the template *Stamp* consists of creating a DOM fragment containing a root *<g>* element and all its nested nodes until an anchor specification is reached. For instance, when attribute *width* of element *<rect>* is reached, an anchor is created. This anchor observes the value of its associated container *width* defined in the enclosing fragment class. Similarly, when child *<g>* element is reached, an anchor is created. The content of this anchor is delimited by two processing instruction *<?begin ?>* and *<?end?>* that reflects the container *dayLabels*: adding a new instance of class *DayLabel* to the relation *dayLabels* triggers the corresponding template (containing element *<text>*). The corresponding template is thus instantiated and the resulting child fragment is inserted in between the delimiters. Separation of subsequent *DayLabel* fragments is represented by the processing instruction *<?next?>*.

STEP 4: SPECIFY THE DATA BINDING
Besides the fact that Loa containers are observable, the Loa data model allows binding two containers so that their contents remains the same. Loa introduces the assignment operator *::=* so that expression $a ::= b$ means that container a receives the same contents as container b. When used concurrently with operations available in the Loa DSL (*e.g. apply*), the assignment operator makes possible to bind multiple containers, as illustrated by the following example:

```
1  val a = Seq[Int]()
2  val b ::= a.apply{e => e.toString()}
3  a += 123
```

This example binds the sequence of integers a to the sequence of strings b. Line 2 means that b contains the string representation of integers contained in a. Since a is initially empty, b is also initially empty. When the sequence a is modified on line 3, the sequence b is updated by the execution of operation *apply* accordingly, such that b finally contains "123". The implementation

of the function *apply* is based on the observation of sequence a and on the execution of the anonymous function $e => e.toString()$ in an appropriate manner. More details on the implementation of complex functions such as *select* and *sort*, is detailed in [3].

Binding containers allows the specification and execution of complex data bindings that bind the domain data to graphical components [4]. The instantiation of templates is thus driven by the changes performed on the domain data. As an illustration, the following function *P2C* is a Loa specification that represents the data binding between a planning p loaded from menu *File*, a combo-box *ws* for selecting the current week, and a calendar c that gives a weekly presentation of p to users (see Figure 3):

```
1  def P2C(p: Planning, ws: ComboBox, c: Calendar) = {
2    c.dayLabels  ::= Seq(0 to 4).apply(DN2DL)
3    c.timeAreas  ::= p.timeSlots.map(TS2TA)
4    ws.items     ::= p.weeks.map(W2I)
5    c.stamps     ::= ws.selectedItem.rmap(W2I)
6      .days.teachings.map(T2S)
7  }
```

From a static sequence of day numbers (0 to 4), the binding function *DN2DL* creates the fragments of anchor *dayLabels* (line 2). Line 3 defines the contents of anchor *timeAreas* using the binding function *TS2TA* on *timeSlots*. Line 4 populates the *ws* combo-box with the planning weeks by calling the mapping function *W2I*: the selected item of *ws* drives the creation of *Stamp* fragments within anchor *stamps* retrieves the selected week (function *rmap*, line 5) and applies the mapping function *T2S* to all teachings of this week.

The contents of mapping functions *DN2DL*, *TS2TA*, *W2I* and *T2S* follows the same constructs as *P2C*. This example shows that we use equivalent mapping constructs for both existing widgets (*e.g.*, Swing combo-box), or specific graphical components (*e.g.*, an SVG graphics).

STEP 5: SPECIFY THE INTERACTORS
The Loa interactors are based on Malai [6]. An interactor transforms an interaction into an action on the target object. Within Loa, the target object can be either a domain data or a fragment.

Figure 6 illustrates the *life-cycle* of the *action* of any Loa interactor as *a generic* state-machine. For a mouse-based interactor, each transition corresponds to a mouse event as follows: *begin* = mouse button pressed, *do* = mouse dragged, *abort* = escape key pressed, *end* = mouse button released. If the interactor defines undo/redo data, these data are *saved* into the undo-redo stack. An interactor, such as a key or button, can request an *undo* or a *redo*, as illustrated at the end of this section. Finally, when the undo-redo stack reaches its maximal capacity, the undo/redo data are *deleted*.

Figure 7 shows a subset of the Loa interactor classes. Base class *Interactor* defines the attribute *canDo* that

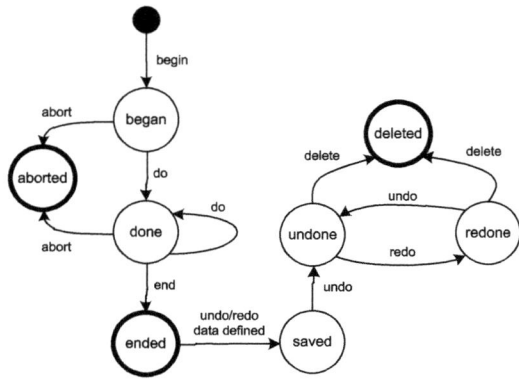

Figure 6. Action life-cycle

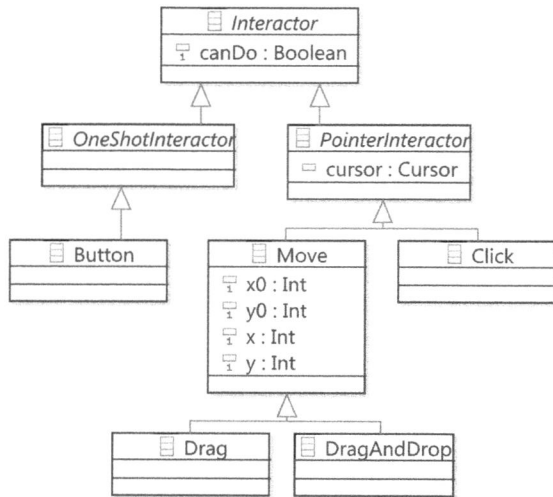

Figure 7. Loa interactors

indicates if the action associated with this interaction can be started or not. Class *OneShotInteractor* represents interactors with a state *began* that is immediately followed by a state *end* (*e.g.*, *Button* and *MenuItem*). Conversely, class *PointerInteractor* represents interactors with a complex action life-cycle (*e.g.*, *Move* and *Click*). Class *Move* defines properties $(x0,y0)$ and (x,y) that represent respectively the starting mouse location and the current mouse location.

Class *Interactor* defines a Scala *when block* that allows designers to specify actions for each possible transition of the interactor, as follows:

```
when {
  case Begin =>
  case End =>
  case Abort =>
  case Undo =>
  case Redo =>
}
```

Each *case* corresponds to a transition and triggering a transition invokes the corresponding *case block*. The

specification of actions for states depends on the kind of interactor. *OneShotInteractor* interactors only rely on the definition of either case block *Begin* or *End*. *PointerInteractor* interactors rely on case blocks *Begin* and *End*, and an optional case block *Abort* if the action needs to be aborted. Case blocks *Undo* and *Redo* provide undo/redo capabilities for *OneShotInteractor* and *PointerInteractor* interactors.

The following *Hand* interactor specifies how the user can move a stamp to another location:

```
 1  object Hand extends Drag {
 2    when {
 3      case Begin(s: Stamp) =>
 4        cursor := Cursor.Move
 5        calendar.stamps += s // put s on the top
 6        val t = s.rmap(T2S)
 7        t.day ::= y.apply(y2Day)
 8        t.start ::= x.apply(x2TimeSlot)
 9        t.end ::= (s.width + s.x − x).apply(x2TimeSlot)
10        undoData += (t, t.day, t.start, t.end)
11      case End(s: Stamp) =>
12        cursor := None
13        val t = s.rmap(T2S)
14        redoData += (t, t.day, t.start, t.end)
15      case Undo(t: Teaching, d: Day,
16          s: TimeSlot, e: TimeSlot) =>
17        t.day := d
18        t.start := s
19        t.end := e
20    }
21  }
```

Stamp s is given as a parameter in case blocks *Begin* and *End*, and corresponds to the stamp picked at location (x,y). Line 6 retrieves the teaching t that has been previously mapped to stamp s with the mapping function *T2S*, thanks to the reverse mapping operation *rmap*. Lines 7 to 9 define the new location of the picked teaching t by using layout functions that convert location (x,y) to *Day* and *TimeSlot* instances. The three properties *day*, *start* and *end* are bounded to the interactor location using operator ::=, thus meaning that these three locations will be updated while the drag interaction continues. Case block *Begin* ends with saving undo data. Case block *End* terminates the action by resetting the cursor to its default value (line 12), then by saving the undo/redo data into the Loa undo stack (line 13 and 14). Based on the undo stack, case block *Undo* restores the saved state of teaching t when necessary (line 17 to 19).

We voluntary omit case block *Redo*, since the undo/redo actions are based on the same data. Similarly, case block *Abort(s: Stamp)* has been omitted for simplification purpose.

Button *undoButton* (see figure 3) [3] specifies its action in a simpler manner, as follows:

---

[3]Button *redoButton* is defined similarly.

	Data model ①		Data binding ④			Gr. templates ②③		Interaction model ⑤		
	obs. prop.	obs. coll.	prop.	coll.	lang.	simple	nesting	events	action	interactor
Swing	H	L	L	L				H	L	
JFace	H	H	H	L				H	L	
ObjectEditor	H	H	H	M	L			H	H	
Garnet	H		H		L			H		H
Amulet	H		H			M		H	H	H
Malai			H	M	M			**H**	**H**	**H**
JavaFX 2.0	H	H	H	L		L		H		
Flex	H	H	H	L	L	M		H	L	
JavaFX 1.3	H	H	H	L	M	M	L	H		
WPF	H	H	H	M	L	H		H	L	
Ext GWT	H	H	H	M	L	H		H	L	
Hayaku			L	L	L	H	H	H		
incXSLT	M	M	H	H	M	H	H			
sXBL	M	M	H	M	L	H	H	H		
eXAcT	M	M	H	H		**H**	**H**	H		
Definitive pr.	H	H	H	L	M					
Active op.	**H**	**H**	**H**	**H**	**H**					
Loa	H	H	H	H	H	H	H	H	H	H

Table 2. Synthetic View of Related Works

undoButton.**when** { **case End** => UndoStack.undo() }

Global object *UndoStack* represents the undo/redo stack used by interactors to store undo/redo data. Button *undoButton* binds its *canDo* attribute as follows:

undoButton.canDo ::= UndoStack.canUndo

The *UndoStack* object defines attribute *canUndo* that specifies whether the undo/redo stack contains undo data or not. This attribute is bound to the *canDo* attribute of the undo button, thus resulting in disabling or enabling the button depending on the stack state.

STEP 6: RUNNING THEM ALL TOGETHER

The following Scala code defines the main entry point of the application:

```
1  object Application extends Frame {
2    def main(args: Array[String]) {
3      val calendar = Calendar()
4      val svg = SVGScene(calendar, 1400, 600)
5      val canvas = SVGCanvas(svg)
6      val planning = Planning()
7      planning.load("Planning 2011-12.xml")
8      P2C(planning, weekSelector, calendar)
9      canvas.interactors += Hand
10     canvasScrollPane.setViewportView(canvas)
11     treeScrollPane.setViewportView(DOMTreeView(svg))
12     setVisible(true)
13   }
14 }
```

The main window of the application is represented by a Java class *Frame* created with Google WindowBuilder. Since the integration of Scala code with Java is smooth, we may define a singleton class *Application* that extends *Frame*. Fragment *calendar* (line 3) is the root fragment of scene *svg* (line 4), which is rendered by the object

canvas (lines 5 and 10) and displayed as a DOM tree view (line 11). Instance *planning* is loaded from an XML file (lines 6 and 7), and then bound to instance *calendar* with the application of function *P2C* (line 8). Combo-box *weekSelector* allows a user to select a week to edit (see Figure 3), and is thus involved in *P2C*. The creation of an *Application* ends (lines 9 to 12) with the association of an interactor *Hand* with *canvas*, followed by the display of the *canvas* and its components.

RELATED WORKS AND DISCUSSION

Table 2 gives a synthetic comparison of related works for each of the four domains related to steps ① to ⑤: the *data model*, the *data binding*, the *graphical templates* and the *interaction model*. Each domain is then evaluated against two or three criteria indicating whether: *i)* the data model allows the definition of *observable properties* and/or *observable collections*; *ii)* the data bindings can be defined for *properties*, *collections* using a dedicated *language* or not; *iii)* the graphical templates allow the definition of *simple* components (*e.g.*, a *TimeArea*, a *TypeBar* - see Figure 4) and/or *nesting* components (*e.g.*, a *Calendar*, a *Stamp* - see Figure 4); *iv)* the interaction model provides an *event*-based interaction model, an *action* model, and/or an *interactor*-based model. Values for criteria are: high (H), medium (M), low (L), and none (empty cell). Concepts of the related works that we reuse within Loa are in bold.

The table splits the related works in the following five categories (from top to bottom): Java-based toolkits, interactor-based toolkits, RIA toolkits, template-based systems, and data binding languages. The following sections discuss these categories with regard to the four proposed criteria. Readers must be aware that the values presented in the table are all subject to discussion according to the subjectivity of the selected criteria. However, we think they well represent the overall tendency of each category.

Java-based toolkits

Swing [9] is based on the MVC pattern rather than on the data binding concept. Consequently, the definition of bindings requires a significant programming effort for implementing interfaces. Creating a new component is a time-consuming task that requires a full implementation from scratch. As for all GUI toolkits, the interaction model listens to predefined events. The concept of action is minimalist and does not integrate *undo/redo* features. JFace [12] explicitly uses data binding between observable properties, and allows binding observable collections with some predefined widgets. ObjectEditor [8] allows the definition of data bindings on properties and on collections, and enhances the action model with *undo/redo* capabilities. Since ObjectEditor is based on extending the JavaBean syntax, it might be considered as a language. We observe that the category "Java-based toolkits" both lacks mechanisms for the definition of *graphical templates* and of *interaction model*, and globally lacks dedicated languages for *data binding*. These issues are answered by the dedicated toolkits presented in the next sections.

Interactor-based toolkits

Garnet [17] and Amulet [18] explicitly introduce the concept of interactor to facilitate the use of predefined interactions. Amulet provides a high level action model with *undo/redo/repeat* features, as well as the ability to define simple graphical components easily. Garnet and Amulet allow the definition of constraints for binding properties with no support for collections. Malai [6] formalizes the instrumental interaction [1] into a well polished conceptual framework. Malai allows binding collections but does not support complex computation on collections. Malai interaction model has been reused and adapted to fit in the Loa data model. We observe that while "Interactor-based toolkits" support a high level interaction model with several limitations about data binding, *graphical templates* are out of their scope.

RIA Toolkits

RIA toolkits, such as JavaFX 2.0 [30], Flex [14], JavaFX 1.3 [24], WPF [22] and Ext GWT [26], provide better data binding capabilities than the two previous categories. Data bindings are often specified as string values within XML files representing the interface (*e.g.*, MXML for Flex or XAML for WPF). An alternative is to use a programming language, such as JavaFX script for JavaFX 1.3. WPF and Ext GWT use their own template model to represent simple graphical components (*e.g.*, items of a list), but this model does not allow the definition of new nesting components. Java FX 2.0 uses a hand-written representation of the scene that describes the contents of the template. JavaFX 1.3 provides a bind statement for loops on collection that allows the definition of nesting components. As a summary, RIA

toolkits support a large range of *data binding* capabilities but propose poor *interaction models* and do not support *nesting graphical templates*.

Template-based systems

As far as we know, Hayaku [23] is the only toolkit that specifically tackles the definition of post-WIMP graphical components. Using abstract representations, Hayaku ends up with good expressiveness and good overall performances. However, Hayaku does not specifically focuses on data binding except for linking the template to its data. Hayaku interaction model provides the mandatory picking capabilities. Within the selected tools that are not specific to GUI engineering, incXSLT [27], sXBL [28] and eXAcT [2] all work with a data model based on XML that we consider as a limitation here. incXSLT is an incremental XSLT processor that allows the incremental transformation of an XML document with the limitation that it does not cover the whole XSLT 1.0 language. We can use incXSLT to define graphical templates as standard *<template name>* XSLT elements. The SVG's XML Binding Language (sXBL) supports the parametrization of SVG symbols natively.; However, it offers limited data binding capabilities. eXAcT is an incremental/active Java-based transformation processor that offers good data binding capabilities. Loa uses the concept of fragment and anchor as defined by eXAcT while leveraging the inherent complexity of eXAcT transformations.

"Template-based systems" are relevant approaches for the definition of *graphical templates*. However they provide poor support for the integration of an *interaction model* and of a *data model*.

Data binding languages

Definitive principles and notations [5] proposes a novel approach for the programmatic evaluation of functions. For instance, instead of calling $y=f(x)$ each time x changes, definitive notations represent $y=f(x)$ as a constraint f that binds x and y. This works well for property bindings but there are limitations for collection bindings. Notations are defined within a dedicated language, not close to Object Oriented Programming (OOP) usage. Active operations are based on a similar principle [3] but allows the definition of data bindings using a classic OOP approach and standard operations on collections [29]. [4] demonstrates that active operations allow the definition of complex data bindings that cannot be expressed with RIA toolkit without *ad hoc* coding. Loa is based on the concept of active operations implemented as a Scala internal DSL. "Data binding languages" propose languages that support simple and complex *data bindings*. *Graphical templates* and *interaction models* are however not in the scope of these techniques.

Conclusion

This preliminary evaluation shows that GUI toolkits (*i.e.*, Java-based, interactor-based and RIA) have little to no support for the definition of nesting templates and interactor models, and limited support for data binding. The integration of relevant approaches that are not dedicated to GUI, such as XSLT templates and active operations, provides new functionalities that overcome these limitations. Loa has been designed for this very purpose: the successful integration of the various concerns of interactive systems in a unique DSL. Next section provides evaluation and discussion on the Loa language.

EVALUATION

In this section, we propose to evaluate Loa and its supporting process against the Cognitive Dimensions of Notation proposed by Green [11]. We discuss the dimensions of abstraction, hidden complexity, closeness of mappings, viscosity and progressive evaluation and support our claims with van Deursen's observations [25] about the benefits of using DSLs.

Abstraction / Hidden Complexity

Providing a good level of abstraction is essential for the designer to be productive in the design of new graphical components. Since DSLs are concise in general [16], we consider that Loa proposes a representative set of constructs with precise semantics that allows designers to focus on each specific concern of the domain rather than on the complexity of the implementation or of the development artifacts.

The use of an homogeneous representation (*i.e.*, the Loa DSL) across five of the six steps of the development process for new graphical components is a very valuable asset towards reliability and maintainability [7, 15] of the final application. The Loa DSL is also provided with a concrete syntax as a textual notation. The textual notation allows designers to set the links between the development artifacts (*i.e.*, data model, data binding, graphical templates and interaction model) that was not cover by Hayaku [23].

Closeness of Mappings

The second step of the Loa development process allows application designers and graphical designers to agree on a design that is close to the final product. From an initial sketch of the graphical component, the production of the component may be realized in parallel: the graphical designer works towards a final version of the visuals while the application designers takes care of the implementation and integration of the component into the final application.

Viscosity

Resistance to changes is a challenging activity in any process of development. While this paper does not focus on the activity of maintaining consistence as changes occurs, every step of the process is based on an homogeneous representation (*i.e.*, Loa). Homogeneity is one solution to get confidence in the consistency of the various development artifacts instead of manipulating multiple representations.

Since Loa is an internal Scala DSL, we benefit from the existing Scala and Java tooling to detect the side effects of changes at design time. As a matter of fact, the manual propagation of changes is limited to the synchronization of the data model with the data binding, and of the data model with the interaction model.

Progressive Evaluation

The development process that supports Loa covers the various specifications (*i.e.*, from the graphical design to its implementation) required to build a fully functional graphical component. However, testing a new graphical component does not require for all steps to be completed. For instance, the design of a new graphical component can be tested against its static properties while the behavior is not yet implemented. This allows designers to design components incrementally.

CONCLUSION

This paper presents the Loa framework dedicated to the engineering of interactive systems. Switching from implementation to specification, the Loa framework focuses on the definition of specifications that are executable within a final application. The framework integrates previous works on data binding, graphical templates and interactors. The Loa framework provides: 1) a dedicated DSL based on the Scala language; 2) a six-step development process that provides guidance in the use of the framework; and 3) an implementation that currently bridges the Swing toolkit and allows the definition of graphical components in SVG.

Perspectives of the framework target the implementation of bridges to other Java toolkits, such as JGraph and SWT/JFace, as well as bridges to other platforms such as .NET and Web-oriented technologies. Long term perspectives will target the integration of other concerns specific to UI design such as groupware and constraint management.

REFERENCES

1. M. Beaudouin-Lafon. Instrumental interaction: An interaction model for designing post-wimp interfaces. In *Proc. of CHI'00*, volume 2, pages 446–453. ACM Press, 2000.

2. O. Beaudoux. XML active transformation (eXAcT): Transforming documents within interactive systems. In *Proc. of DocEng'05*, pages 146–148. ACM, 2005.

3. O. Beaudoux, A. Blouin, O. Barais, and J. M. Jezequel. Active operations on collections. In *Proc. of MoDELS '10*, pages 91–105. Springer, 2010.

4. O. Beaudoux, A. Blouin, O. Barais, and J.-M. Jézéquel. Specifying and implementing ui data bindings with active operations. In *Proc. of EICS'11*, pages 127–136. ACM, 2011.

5. W. Beynon. Definitive principles for interactive graphics. *NATO ASI Series F*, 40(3):1083–1097, 1988.

6. A. Blouin and O. Beaudoux. Improving modularity and usability of interactive systems with malai. In *Proc. of EICS'10*, pages 115–124. ACM, 2010.

7. A. V. Deursen and P. Klint. Little languages: little maintenance? *Journal of Software Maintenance: Research and Practice*, 10(2):75–92, 1998.

8. P. Dewan. Increasing the automation of a toolkit without reducing its abstraction and user-interface flexibility. In *Proc. of EICS '10*, pages 47–56. ACM, 2010.

9. R. Eckstein, M. Loy, and D. Wood. *Java Swing*. O'Reilly, 2002.

10. S. Fulton and J. Fulton. *HTML5 Canvas*. O'Reilly Media, 2011.

11. T. R. G. Green. Cognitive dimensions of notations. In *People and Computers V*, pages 443–460. Cambridge University Press, 1989.

12. R. Harris and R. Warner. The definitive guide to swt and jface, 2004.

13. M. Kay. *XSLT 2.0 and XPath 2.0 Programmer's Reference*. Wrox, 2008.

14. C. Kazoun and J. Lott. *Programming Flex 2*. O'Reilly, 2007.

15. R. B. Kieburtz, L. McKinney, J. M. Bell, J. Hook, A. Kotov, J. Lewis, D. P. Oliva, T. Sheard, I. Smith, and L. Walton. A software engineering experiment in software component generation. In *Proc. of ICSE '96*, pages 542–552. IEEE Computer Society, 1996.

16. D. A. Ladd and J. C. Ramming. Two application languages in software production. In *Proc. of USENIX 1994*, pages 1–9. USENIX Association, 1994.

17. B. Myers, D. Giuse, R. Dannenberg, B. Zanden, D. Kosbie, E. Pervin, A. Mickish, and P. Marchal. Garnet: comprehensive support for graphical, highly interactive user interfaces. *Computer*, 23(11):71–85, 1990.

18. B. Myers, R. McDaniel, R. Miller, A. Ferrency, A. Faulring, B. Kyle, A. Mickish, A. Klimovitski, and P. Doane. The Amulet environment: new models for effective user interface software development. *IEEE Transactions on Software Engineering*, 23(6):347–365, 1997.

19. B. A. Myers. A new model for handling input. *ACM Transaction on Information Systems*, 8(3):289–320, 1990.

20. M. Odersky, L. Spoon, and B. Venners. *Programming in Scala*. Artima, 2010.

21. J. Redish and J. T. Hackos. *User and Task Analysis for Interface Design*. John Wiley & Sons, 1998.

22. C. Sells and I. Griffiths. *Programming Windows Presentation Foundation*. O'Reilly, 2005.

23. B. Tissoires and S. Conversy. Hayaku: designing and optimizing finely tuned and portable interactive graphics with a graphical compiler. In *Proc. of EICS'11*, pages 117–126. ACM, 2011.

24. K. Topley. *JavaFX Developer's Guide*. Addison-Wesley, 2010.

25. A. van Deursen, P. Klint, and J. Visser. Domain-specific languages: an annotated bibliography. *SIGPLAN Not.*, 35(6):26–36, June 2000.

26. D. Vaughan. *Ext GWT 2.0*. Packt Publishing, 2010.

27. L. Villard and N. Layaida. An incremental XSLT transformation processor for XML document manipulation. In *Proc. of WWW'02*, pages 474–485. ACM, 2002.

28. W3C. Svg's xml binding language (sxbl). Technical report, W3C, 2005.

29. J. B. Warmer and A. G. Kleppe. *The object constraint language: getting your models ready for MDA*. Addison-Wesley.

30. J. Weaver, W. Gao, S. Chin, and D. Iverson. *Pro JavaFX 2 Platform*. Apress, 2011.

Unify Localization using User Interface Description Languages and a Navigation Context-Aware Translation Tool

Michael Tschernuth
University of Applied Sciences
Upper Austria
Softwarepark 11
4232 Hagenberg, Austria
michael.tschernuth@fh-
hagenberg.at

Michael Lettner
University of Applied Sciences
Upper Austria
Softwarepark 11
4232 Hagenberg, Austria
michael.lettner@fh-
hagenberg.at

Rene Mayrhofer
University of Applied Sciences
Upper Austria
Softwarepark 11
4232 Hagenberg, Austria
rene.mayrhofer@fh-
hagenberg.at

ABSTRACT

The past few years have shown a tendency from desktop software development towards mobile application development due to the increasing amount of smartphone users and available devices. Compared to traditional desktop applications, requirements are different in the mobile world. Due to the massive amount of mobile applications it is important to bring a new idea to the market very quickly and concurrently target a large number of users all over the world. The aspect of localization is crucial if the product should be usable in different countries. The term localization in this context refers to the process of adapting a software to different regions by changing the language, image resources, reading direction or other regional requirements. The proposed solution covers the aspect of string translation, with a focus on devices where the screen area is limited. Translating a software poses a challenge since the text can have several meanings on the one hand and has to match the available screen space on the other hand.

Knowing the context and area where a string appears in the user interface can improve the quality and accuracy of the translation. Besides that it reduces efforts for layout implementation and testing. This paper refers to that feature as navigation context-aware. A Context-Aware Translation Tool (CATT) including this feature is presented. As an input for the tool a user interface description language (UIDL) is used which contributes platform independence to the tool. To increase the applicability of the tool to a number of description languages, a meta-model was created which specifies crucial compatibility requirements. An evaluation of existing languages regarding their compatibility to the proposed model and a discussion of limitations is included.

Author Keywords

User Interface Description; Translation; Localization

ACM Classification Keywords

H.5.2 Information Interfaces and Presentation: User Interfaces—*Evaluation/methodology*; D.2.2 Design Tools and Techniques: User Interfaces

INTRODUCTION

The goal of this paper is to unify translation for several platforms based on an abstract view of the user interface. Modern software techniques, like the model driven architecture (MDA), try to introduce abstraction to have a platform independent view on a software application which increases portability and reuseability among others [18]. Tools which are built upon an abstract layer are generic and therefore do not need to be adapted for a specific platform. A user interface description language is a possibility to create an abstract description of the user interface [5]. Tools building upon a platform independent description are not limited to one platform and have a wider area of application. Although the languages are numerous with different areas of application, some user interface description languages (UIDLs) support similar concepts and share common features. To identify the relevant features for the approach, a meta-model was developed which covers the basic elements that are important to represent the user interface content (user interface elements) and the connection between the several screens (structure).

A navigation Context-Aware Translation Tool (CATT) based on a meta-model-compatible UIDL is shown which supports the developer during the localization process, providing navigation context awareness for translations which is beneficial in case the screen size is limited due to hardware and software restrictions. Navigation context means that for example a button which is responsible to switch to another screen (e.g., *BACK-button*) is aware of the screen that is shown after it has been clicked. CATT is also able to localize images and audio resources but only the aspect of translating strings is investigated further in this paper. Localization is an issue if software applications target a larger market and therefore resources have to be adapted to a specific area by translating strings or adapting images. For the text translation part, collaborative tools or automatic translation tools may not be the perfect solution [3], hence translations still have to be done or at least double checked manually to get them right by trusted experts.

Another challenge of localizing text strings is that it implies additional development tasks for the developer. On the one hand there is the content that has to be adapted and on the other hand there is the graphical representation of the content which is influenced for example by the reading direction of the language [7]. Ideally the graphical representation should be no concern to the person translating the text in an alternative language. This issue should be handled by the designer which holds true for the desktop environment where the visual design is more flexible due to bigger screens and variable fonts. If the target platform is an embedded device, the screen and font size is limited which also affects the available screen space for a translation. One example might be the translation of a title for an embedded device where the font size is fixed and scrolling is not an option.

These issues appear on a number of embedded device platforms with different operating systems, therefore a user interface description may be beneficial to unify the localization process across those platforms. As user interface descriptions have different capabilities the focus of this work is to extract mandatory requirements of the user interface descriptions (UIDs) in order to be compatible with CATT. Metrics regarding the quality of the translations are outside the scope of this work. A study concerning this issue will be conducted as a future work. Discussed contributions regarding the translation process are as follows:

- *Extension of available UIDLs with translation features:* The main contribution is that existing description languages, in case they are found compatible, are utilizes with the proposed generic translation tool which also covers the navigation context.

- *Evaluation of UIDLs:* A compatibility evaluation of existing UIDLs based on the compatibility requirements of the evaluation section has been conducted, focused on whether and how the translatable content and navigation context is described in order to work with the extension approach to translate the UIDL with CATT.

- *Evaluation of related work:* An evaluation of related translation tools has been conducted based on the identified requirements for a translation tool which are explained in the related work section.

- *Translation tool:* CATT has been developed which takes content and structure of the user interface into account.

The remainder is structured as follows. First an overview is given over available translation approaches and to what extent they cover the identified requirements. Then the most promising approach is investigated in detail, leading to CATT which is based on this approach. An evaluation of possible input languages for CATT and a discussion of limits and future work concludes the paper.

EVALUATION OF THE RELATED WORK
This section describes existing methods and tools for translating a software. Besides that cross-platform solutions for the mobile application development which offer the possibility for a platform independent translation are shown, following

an approach where the translation is based on a generic UID. The related approaches are classified regarding the following identified requirements:

- R0 - Abstraction of the UI: The strings to translate should not be embedded in the code. Translation file and source code should be separated to provide translation possibilities for non-programmers.

- R1 - Platform Independence: The translation process should not be bound to a specific programming platform. It should be built upon an abstract view of the software and reusable for other platforms (e.g., Android and IPhone).

- R2 - Completeness: All translation relevant resources should be covered by the translation process.

- R3 - Navigation Context: Taking navigation context into account, the translation might be more concise which has a positive effect on the user interface usability especially if the display size is limited.

Translation Tools
There are several types of localization tools, some are tightly integrated with the development environment while others support more than one platform. This section analysis the different kinds of localization techniques—especially from the aspect of translating strings—with regard of their features and platform generic usage.

Translating the software automatically is not as concise and correct as letting native speakers translate it [15], thus these mechanisms are not analysed any further.

Approaches for translating strings to several languages manually are explained next.

Community-Based Translation Tools
One possibility to localize software are collaborative translation tools. A developer can load the strings that should be translated to a web platform and make them accessible to a large crowd of translators and developers which provide support throughout the translation process. The advantage of such tools is that a developer is able to localize software cost effectively and to different areas in a short period of time. Examples for community based web translations are: *Crowdin*[1], *Pootle*[2] or *GetLocalization*[3]. These tools often support different software platforms—for example, *Crowdin* supports all relevant mobile platforms[4].

The main disadvantages of these tools are that it might be difficult to choose the correct translation if one is not aware of space limitations and the context in which the string appears in the menu. Further there is no guarantee that the translations are correct which depends on the expertise of the actual translator.

---

[1] http://crowdin.net/
[2] http://translate.sourceforge.net/
[3] http://www.getlocalization.com/
[4] http://crowdin.net/page/supported-formats

Cross-Platform Translation Tools

Especially for mobile applications a variety of cross-platform solutions exist (e.g., *RhoMobile*[5], *Titanium*[6], *WidgedPad*[7], *PhoneGap*[8], *MoSync*[9]) which are used to develop one application and deploy it to a variety of platforms. Translation needs to be done only once for every application.

Some cross platform software development kits offer translation possibilities themselves. For example *Qt linguist*[10], which supports the developer during the translation process for Qt applications. Although these technology specific tools might offer collaborative and automatic translation mechanisms, their applicability is still limited to one development platform, although each vendor pursues similar design concepts all based on a separation of the graphical user interface design and the code.

Opposed to this technologies the proposed approach of this paper tries to enhance existing solutions with the functionality of a generic translation tool and not to create a new cross-platform tool or a technology specific translation tool.

Although these solutions are interesting, the translation method is specific to each solution and not generic enough to be used as a general platform independent approach.

Translation based on a Universal UIDL Format

A possibility to increase the reuse of a translation technique or tool is to create a generic description of the user interface and build tools upon such a description. Efforts have been made to create a universal format for UIDLs. The user interface markup language (UIML) is one outcome. It is a meta language to create a language independent description of the UI based on containers and parts [5] and is evaluated in detail in the evaluation section.

The intention of the solution proposed in this paper is not to create another universal description language. The idea is to find commonalities of existing user interface description techniques and compare their translation capabilities to offer one tool for a set of description languages which share similar concepts. Compatible UIDLs can still utilize their own features, the idea is to enhance the language with a navigation context-aware translation tool.

A description of a user interface can be created with a variety of concepts—for example on paper or with visual prototypes [11]. The next section describes dedicated languages for the specification of user interfaces which are used in a number of software projects.

Conclusion

Based on the requirements (R0-R3) the several existing approaches have been analysed resulting in Table 1. The option

---

[5]RhoMobile: `http://rhomobile.com/`

[6]Titanium: `http://www.appcelerator.com/`

[7]WidgetPad: `http://widgetpad.com/`

[8]PhoneGap: `http://www.phonegap.com/`

[9]MoSync: `http://www.mosync.com/`

[10]`http://code.google.com/p/qtlinguistdownload/`

Type	R0	R1	R2	R3
Community-Based Tools	Yes	Yes	Yes	No
Cross-Platform Tools	Y/N	Yes	Yes	No
UIDL	Yes	Yes	Yes	Y/N

Table 1. Overview of the translation tools.

Name	Platform	Source
XUL	Platform Ind.	Mozilla
PUC	Platform Ind.	IBM Research Center
UIML	Platform Ind.	Harmonia
UsiXML	Platform Ind.	UsiXML consortium
Android	Mobile Platform	Open Handset Alliance
iOS	Mobile Platform	Apple
XAML	Mobile/Desktop Pf	Microsoft

Table 2. Evaluated UIDL.

Y/N indicates that it depends on the used tool or on the features of the used UIDL whether the requirement is fulfilled and does not hold true for all tools of a given type.

The crucial requirement R3 can only be fulfilled if the translation is based on a UIDL and if that UIDL includes navigation context. Based on that only the option of localizing the software based on a UIDL is investigated further.

In the following, existing UIDLs are evaluated regarding their translation capabilities and their capabilities of including the navigation context (R3).

USER INTERFACE DESCRIPTION LANGUAGES

This section shows an overview over candidates that profit from the proposed solution and analysis them regarding their translation and structural characteristic. Reviews of a set of XML-based declarative user interface descriptions have been made in 2003 [19] and 2009 [4]. Throughout the descriptions presented in the following subsections, the eXtensible Markup Language (XML) has been established as a useful container format. XML comes with the advantage that there are tools to parse, translate and generate XML files in form of libraries for lots of development environments which reduces the implementation costs. Additionally a meta-model for XML languages can be created by the use of an XML schema. Therefore only XML based UIDLs are evaluated.

A compatible example description language, which is discussed in the next section, was created as an example and a proof of concept for the approach. In the evaluation section, four UIDLs which are utilized in practical projects for desktop software applications and are still actively reviewed and enhanced are investigated. Additionally three wide adopted approaches from the application development of smartphones are evaluated as well. All candidates are listed in Table 2.

Requirements

In order to be used with CATT, the language description has to fulfill certain requirements. Crucial is the possibility to specify the user interface structure as a graph. User interface structure in this context means the connection of the different screens. The graph is allowed to have input edges for the same screen (e.g., a screen which purpose is to give feedback about the success of an operation, might exist only once but is called from different parts of the program.). The second important requirement is that localization relevant elements like icons and strings have to be contained in the description as well, to be accessible by the translation tool.

An analysis of the description languages regarding their possibility to describe the user interface in a graph structure *(structure)* and their translation support for the text strings *(content)* is shown in the following section. It extends an existing coarse analysis which focus area was purely on smartphone development and did not include the translation features of the technologies [20].

XML-based User Interface Language (XUL)
XUL is used as a platform independent description of a user interface and was created by Mozilla[11] [14].

Content and Structure
The UI elements can be declared using XUL but the hierarchy is not visible in the description. For example, a button press which is responsible for a transition to a different screen does not explicitly contain the link of the target screen in the XML description. Instead, a command is specified where the screen transition is induced. The screen to which the button is connected cannot be retrieved from the XUL description.

Translation
XUL supports translation by offering the possibility to use variables instead of fixed strings. The actual values are defined in a *Document Type Declaration* (DTD) file. To switch languages, only the DTD file has to be replaced, whereas the rest of the description remains unchanged. e.g.:

```
"*.xul"
<button value="&var"/>

"english.dtd"
<!ENTITY var "Yes">

"german.dtd"
<!ENTITY var "Ja">
```

XUL provides an attribute (*dir*) to indicate the reading direction of the text which can either be *rtl* for right to left or *ltr* for left to right.

Personal Universal Controller (PUC) UIDL
An XML description language for PUCs was developed by Jeffrey Nichols and Brad A. Myers [13]. Its purpose is to describe the UI of appliances like TVs and VCRs in a declarative way.

Content and Structure
The elements on the screen can be defined and grouped together. The actual visibility of elements is handled via the tag *active-if*, which indicates when an interface element should be shown, for example only if the power of an appliance is turned on. Other than that no hierarchy can be extracted.

Translation
PUC does not support translation to date, as it is designed to define the control structure behind the UI rather than its representation and localizable text resources. This circumstance excludes this language from the list of relevant candidates for the generic translation tool.

User Interface Markup Language (UIML)
UIML is a meta language, used to describe the user interface independently of the target environment [5]. Currently UIML 4.0 is under specification by the *Organization for the Advancement of Structured Information Standards (OASIS)*[12]. UIML defines the user interface with platform independent tags. On another layer these tags are mapped to target specific elements.

Content and Structure
UIML can be used to describe the user interface content via *parts and properties*, where the elements of a UI are called parts, and for each part corresponding properties can be defined. Properties can be used for specifying presentation attributes and for adding navigational information, e.g. part x has a property called *following screen* where the name of the screen which is next can be specified. Since UIML is a meta language, a generic structure of a user interface can be created. The actual implementation for a target programming language is an additional step. This increases the reuse of a once developed description but requires transformations to generate the description of the final user interface.

Translation
In UIML variables can be used as placeholders for constants. These variables are set to the correct locale in language specific files as the following example shows.

```
<structure id="GUI">
<part class="button" id="var"/>
</structure>

<style>
<property part-name="var" name="label">
<reference constant-name="varLabel"/>
</property>
</style>

<content id="English">
<constant id="varLabel" value="Yes"/>
</content>

<content id="German">
<constant id="varLabel" value="Ja"/>
</content>
```

USer Interface eXtensible Markup Language (UsiXML)
UsiXML[13] offers the possibility to model the user interface from different contexts of use. UsiXML is the most comprehensive user interface language description technique in the

---

[11] `https://developer.mozilla.org/en/`

[12] `http://www.oasis-open.org/`
[13] `http://www.usixml.org/`

evaluation [9]. There are numerous tools which utilize the features of the language [22].

Content and Structure
UsiXML offers the possibility to build a concrete user interface model (cuiModel) [21]. This model provides concrete user interaction objects, for instance *date picker*, *graphical-Containment* and so forth. It is possible to group the concrete individual components into containers and define connections between them. So it is possible to create a compatible user interface structure and specify content.

Translation
For the purpose of translation UsiXML provides a resource model [6, 21]. It contains the definitions of resources attached to interaction objects which can be different depending on the specific location. The tool GrafiXML is a graphical user interface builder for creating a user interface description in UsiXML which offers tool support for the translation [12].

UI Description in Android
Although Android uses a description language for the user interface it is more integrated into the platform than the candidates from the desktop environment. Android uses an XML based layout file to define the user interface. The description is hierarchically organized, so every element (e.g., a Button) or *View* needs a corresponding layout type (*ViewGroup*) where it is embedded. One *ViewGroup* (Container) can contain multiple *View* objects (UI elements). During runtime the layout is loaded by the Android class that it was built for [1].

Content and Structure
User interface elements are stored in the XML description file but the connection of several screens is done in source code. In detail this means that every UI element has its callback function where it reacts to user events and could transition to other screens.

Translation
Android solves this issue with resource files[14] . For every translatable string a string resource can be added to the *string.xml* file in the *values* folder. During runtime Android looks up the correct value for the string in this file.

For every translation a new folder has to be created, named *values-xx* (xx stands for the two letter country code according to ISO 639-1), containing also a *string.xml* file. Within this file the values of the string resources should be adapted to the corresponding language. If the locale is changed in the Android system, the application uses the folder with the correct country code if available. In case the string resource is not found there, Android uses the original folder and loads the value for the string resource from there. An example for that *string.xml* file is shown below.

```
"values-en\string.xml"
<resources>
<string name="var">Yes</string>
</resources>
```

---

[14]`http://developer.android.com/reference/java/util/`
`Locale.html`

```
"values-de\string.xml"
<resources>
<string name="var">Ja</string>
</resources>
```

UI Description of iOS
Also the iOS environment tightly integrates the user interface description language with the source code. The *Interface Builder* is used for user interface creation which leads to a description file following the iOS specific XIB syntax [10].

Content and Structure
Same approach as Android.

Translation
Also similar to Android it is done via resource files. With the slight difference that the resource files are distinguished by name and the format the strings are stored in (Android uses XML, iOS uses key value pairs) e.g.:

```
"Localizable.string/en"
"var" = "Yes";

"Localizable.string/de"
"var" = "Ja";
```

XAML - Windows Phone 7
The description language used for Windows Phone 7 (WP7) is the *Extensible Application Markup Language (XAML)*. The difference to the other XML descriptions is that each XAML element is a representation of a .NET object, and therefore limited to the Microsoft platform [16].

Content and Structure
All .NET user interface elements can be defined in the description file. Regarding the hierarchy the typical way to implement screen changes is to manipulate the action code which is connected to a UI element (e.g., a Button) and set the target XAML file in source code. However it is possible—although not common—to create links between several XAML files in the XAML file itself.

Translation
There are two possibilities to translate text resources in WP7, XAML-based and Resx-based which are explained in detail in [17]. Using XAML resources and LocBaml to localize content is an interesting approach especially for the developer as translation can be done separately from the user interface description. After the XAML description of the user interface is finished and a binary (BAML) file is created, the LocBaml tool parses all data relevant for translation from the binary and stores it in a csv file. The developer has to localize these exported elements. Afterwards they are merged back into the binary.

PROPOSED SOLUTION
In this section the criteria and the properties for a translation tool compatible UIDL are discussed. Furthermore, it is shown how the relevant data is formalized in an XML schema on which grounds the UIDLs are evaluated.

As the analysed UIDLs share similar concepts it is possible to create a translation tool which supports a group of user interface description languages.

The idea is to have a universal user interface description language format to be supported by the translation tool (CATT) introduced in the next section which simplifies or at least unifies translation. The difference to UIML which can also be seen as a universal format for user interface descriptions is, that the proposed meta-model is not intended to create a variety of new description languages. Its purpose is to provide a set of constraints, elements and attributes existing languages have to contain, in order to be compatible with the approach.

For a UIDL to be compatible with this concept, it must contain **information about the localizable content** of the user interface and the **connection of the screens**.

While retrieving the strings from any of the mentioned XML descriptions can be done by parsing the XML source, it takes more effort acquiring the user interface structure.

To formalize these basic requirements, a meta-model in form of an XML schema is proposed to which the user interface description language has to conform to in order to be compatible with CATT. The basic components are shown in Figure 1 and Figure 2 (schema figures and definition have been created with XMLSpy[15]) and are explained in detail in the upcoming sections.

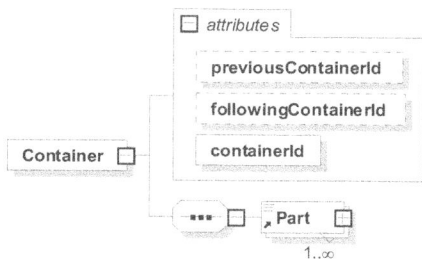

Figure 1. Schema of the container.

Container

The structure of a generic container is illustrated in Figure 1. A container comprises a set of elements (Parts) and must have a unique identifier. It is not visible itself, but can contain elements that are visible. It can also contain a reference to a following or a previous container by itself. This is a valuable reference because in case no element with a following container is available a hierarchy can still be created. Description of the attributes:

1. previousContainerId: optional definition of a previous container.

2. followingContainerId: optional definition of the following container. Unless it is the last leaf container one part or the container itself has to have a followingContainerId to be able to build the navigation graph.

[15]XMLSpy: `http://www.altova.com/de/xmlspy.html`

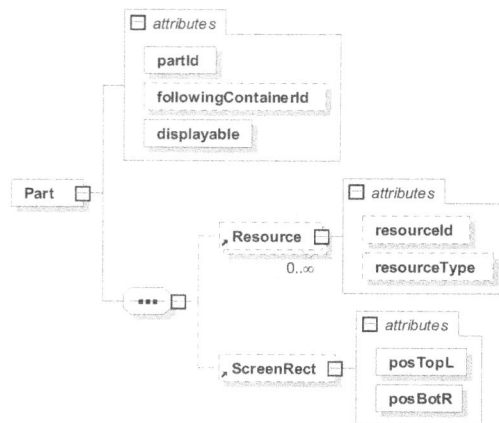

Figure 2. Schema of the part.

3. containerId: unique identifier of the container.

4. Part: an unbound number of child parts.

Part

Parts are the actual user interface elements on the current screen. These elements can either be visible (*Displayable*) or invisible. Every *Part* can contain a reference to a *followingContainer* and has a unique identifier (UID). Additionally, each part can include a screen space constraint in form of a rectangle, a resource is allowed to occupy. An unbound amount of resources can be added to a part, for example an id of a picture and an underlying id of a text. This is the essential part as these resources can be localized. Figure 2 shows how the structure of a part looks like. CATT displays the resource IDs for strings and the user can then translate it into several languages. The different localized versions of the resource are stored in a separate file.

1. partId: unique identifier of the part.

2. followingContainerId: parts are called *navigable* if this attribute has a value.

3. displayable: indicates whether the part can be rendered on the screen.

4. Resource: a part can have the link to a resource consisting of resourceId and resourceType. These are the elements which can be localized.

5. ScreenRect: a screen area rectangle which defines the area a translation is allowed to occupy.

Navigation elements

Crucial for the structure of the user interface are the *previous* and *followingContainer* attributes. As soon as a part or a container is annotated with a reference to a different container it is called **navigable**.

Constraints

In order to have a full structure of the user interface every container must at least have (a) one part that has a *followingContainerId* attribute or (b) a *followingContainerId* itself.

The only exception is the last leaf container where no following container has to be specified. The translator logic handles that case.

The *previousContainerId* attribute is not mandatory because stepping up the graph can also be done in the program logic (e.g., by maintaining a navigation history). This attribute can be used if jumps in the graph should be performed. Figure 3 shows how such a graph might look like.

```
state_mainMenu
  MI_SmsMenu (state_sms)
    MI_WriteSms (state_writeSms)
      state_sendSms
      Popup (state_smsWriteNextPopup)
    MI_ReceivedSMS (state_receivedSms)
    MI_SentSms (state_sentSms)
    line
  state_sliderClosed
  state_numberEntry
  state_startup
```

Figure 3. User Interface navigation graph.

Section Summary

This section presented a meta-model in form of an XML schema which contains crucial features a UIDL has to support in order to be compatible with the tool presented later. Finding commonalities is the first step for a unification of the translation process.

The next section will show how a new user interface description language can be built by using the elements of the schema as a basis. Following that, the translation tool will be explained taking a user interface created with the created UIDL as input data. Afterwards an evaluation of the analysed XML-based UIDLs will show which language can also take advantage of CATT or where compatibility issues exist.

Example UIDL

As a practical example a UIDL was created according to the proposed meta-model which is simlar to a language used in a project for a feature phone [8]. It consists of the elements in Table 3, which cover all relevant user interface elements for that particular purpose. Since it is based on the schema file it is possible to create a user interface structure and specify its content. One container element and one part element are described next.

Container - State

State is an instantiation of the *container* element. The relevant attributes for the CATT are:

- stateId: unique ID of the state.
- type: represents the type of the state.
- softkeySet: the reference to the active softkey set (softkeySetId)

Name	Type	Navigable	Displayable
State	Container	yes	no
Popup	Container	yes	no
MenuItem	Part	yes	yes
Icon	Part	no	yes
Label	Part	no	yes
Title	Part	no	yes
Softkey	Part	yes	yes
Timeout	Part	yes	no
Button	Part	yes	yes

Table 3. Table of elements contained in the created UIDL.

- backButtonState: the state that should be navigated to if the back-button is pressed

Part - MenuItem

As an example for a *part* a menu item element is discussed. This element represents a click/touchable menu item in a list. It is a navigable element which means that a container—in this case a state—can be attached to it. Relevant attributes:

- langId: ID of the string to display
- position: the index of the menuitem in the menu-list
- followingState: the next state to go to if the user selects it
- sofkeyRef: ID of the SoftkeySet which is active when the user has selected this specific item

Example

Figure 4 shows a snippet of a user interface description using the proposed elements, to address the content definition. Figure 5 represents an example of the structure aspect.

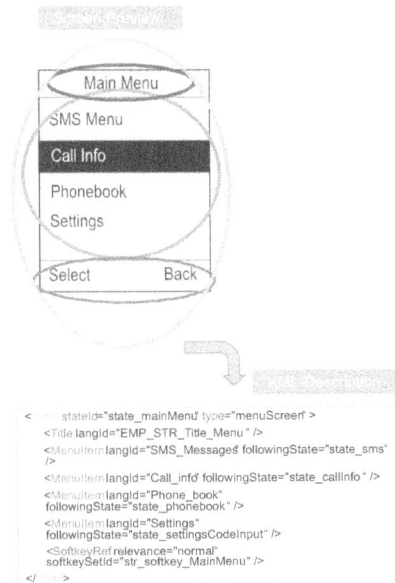

```
< ... stateId="state_mainMenu" type="menuScreen" >
  <Title langId="EMP_STR_Title_Menu" />
  <MenuItem langId="SMS_Messages" followingState="state_sms" />
  <MenuItem langId="Call_info" followingState="state_callInfo" />
  <MenuItem langId="Phone_book"
    followingState="state_phonebook" />
  <MenuItem langId="Settings"
    followingState="state_settingsCodeInput" />
  <SoftkeyRef relevance="normal"
    softkeySetId="str_softkey_MainMenu" />
</ ... >
```

Figure 4. User Interface content description example.

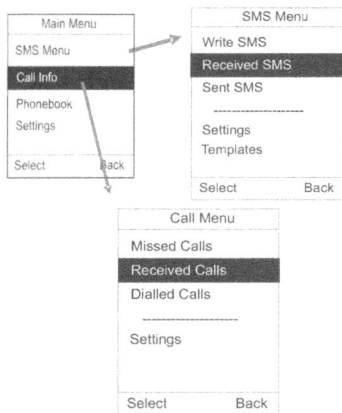

Figure 5. User Interface structure example.

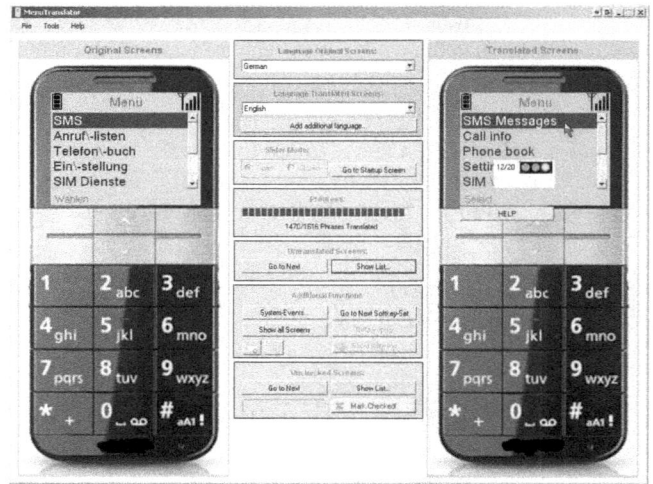

Figure 6. CATT Screenshot.

TRANSLATION TOOL - CATT

CATT (Figure 6) uses an XML based description language as an input. Currently only the UIDL described in the previous section is used as an input.

This section explains the functionalities of the translation tool and presents an evaluation of related UIDLs regarding their compatibility to work as an input for CATT.

Input Data

Basically all UIDLs which are built according to or are compatible to the proposed meta-model can be adapted to work as input data for the translation tool. The language from the case study provides the possibility to create a user interface hierarchy and a content description and can therefore be used as a basis for the translation.

Features

This subsection gives a short introduction of the features of the translation tool.

Space-aware translation

A maximum text size can be defined for every string. This attribute is checked after entering a translation and a feedback is given if the text fits or not. This is an optional feature and is only available if the description language offers a maximum text size attribute by setting the *ScreenRect* attribute and if the size of a resource (e.g., character size,...) is available.

Navigation context-aware - R3

CATT offers the possibility to navigate up and down the user interface structure by the use of the navigation keys of the keypad. This is an advantage because the user is always aware in which context a string appears and can use the most appropriate translation for the string. The user is however not bound to the navigation structure for navigation, it is also possible to jump to the next untranslated string in line directly, or jump to specific screens.

Translation count

A progress bar indicates the total amount of strings to translate and the amount which is already translated.

Completeness - R2

In case one UIDL misses some connection between screens and the screens are just loosely available in the source file, they can still be translated as the user has the possibility to jump to the untranslated screens. However this is not intended and reduces the benefit of CATT, as context information is lost. Also other resource types like images or audio are covered by the tool.

Abstraction and platform independence (R0,R1)

These two criteria are covered by the underlying UIDL which already provides those features.

Output

The export functionality is currently limited to an annotated XML format for the case study. Due to the fact that all the translated strings are stored in XML it is possible to transform the resulting translations into a platform specific output format (e.g., XUL, UIML, Android,...).

EVALUATION OF THE UIDLS

This section evaluates the mentioned candidates on basis of the requirements and summarizes the outcome in Table 4.

Given the analysis of the different UIDLs from the related work section there are three levels of compatibility:

Name	Compatibility
XUL	2
PUC	2
UIML	3
UsiXML	2
Android	1
iOS	1
XAML	3
UIDL from the case study	4

Table 4. Overview of the evaluation.

1. Not Compatible because of structural features: The language cannot be transformed to a compatible format because user interface elements which are required to build the structure are missing.

2. Not Compatible because of translation features: The language cannot be transformed to a compatible format because the UIDL does not support translation.

3. Partly Compatible: The user interface description language can be compatible, but only if the user enhances an existing UIDL with the mandatory attributes from the meta-model. For instance, UIML can be compatible if the property for a part is set with the following container.

4. Fully Compatible: The UIDL is fully compatible because the elements are derived from the meta-model directly and the constraints for the attributes are considered.

Table 4 shows the evaluation outcome of the investigated UIDLs and their applicability to the schema.

The most promising candidates are UIML and XAML. As UIML is a meta language itself it is able to specify compatible user interface descriptions, whereas XAML is also able to cover the relevant compatibility requirements.

Being compatible to the meta-model does not automatically mean it is supported by CATT. Although all relevant information is available in the language, the syntax is different and an interpreter has to be developed to be able to import these languages. Typically as the languages are XML based this can be done via Extensible Stylesheet Language Transformations (XSLT).

All languages which have compatibility level **three** and above can be used as an input for CATT if the required elements are set. The support for level **one** and **two** languages can only be handled if more than the description file is analysed. For example, if Android should be supported, the source code of the event handlers has to be analysed to find out which user interface element links to which new screen.

DISCUSSION AND LIMITATIONS

The tool is currently used in an industry project based on the UIDL described in the proposed solution section. To adapt CATT to a level-3 compatible UIDL all required attributes have to be set in the description language and the XML-format has to be adapted which is merely an engineering issue.

UIML for instance has generic properties which can be used to store structural information which is required for the tool to utilize its advantages. The variety of user interfaces that can be covered by the tool are tied to the used UIDL. If a user interface description language can be created with a supported UIDL it is as well suitable for the CATT.

CONCLUSION AND FUTURE WORK

The paper showed an idea how the translation of text resources can be unified using user interface description languages. To analyse the compatibility with existing UIDLs a meta-model was created which includes all elements and attributes required for CATT. UIDLs derived from that meta-model are considered compatible.

Desktop UIDLs and declarative concepts for mobile applications have been evaluated based on the meta-model to discover their applicability to work with CATT. CATT itself offers the user the possibility to create more accurate translations due to the fact that the navigation hierarchy is available. Further, screen size constraints can be included in the description which is valuable for embedded devices with limited screen space. To date, only the custom UIDL derived from the meta-model is fully supported.

A contribution of the paper is the approach to unify the translation for several UIDLs using one tool. Whether and to what extent CATT improves the actual translation process compared to the presented existing approaches will be analysed as a future task. Possible evaluation metrics can be the duration of the translation process or some usability criteria derived from [2]. An additional future task is to increase the support for localizing images and audio. To date a resource can be set for each locale, but screen requirements are only checked for the text strings.

For each supported description language an export function has to be developed to provide the localized resources in the language specific format which will also be part of future improvements.

REFERENCES

1. M. P. Arno Becker. *Android 2*. dpunkt, 2010.

2. L. J. Bass, G. D. Abowd, and R. Kazman. Issues in the Evaluation of User Interface Tools. In *ICSE Workshop on SE-HCI'94*, pages 17–27, 1994.

3. J.-L. Doumont. Translation 101: Myths and Realities. In *Professional Communication Conference, 2002. IPCC 2002. Proc.. IEEE International*, pages 46–50, 2002.

4. J. Guerrero-Garcia, J. M. Gonzalez-Calleros, J. Vanderdonckt, and J. Munoz-Arteaga. A Theoretical Survey of User Interface Description Languages: Preliminary Results. In *2009 Latin American Web Congress, Joint LA-WEB/CLIHC Conference, Merida, Yucatan, Mexico, 9-11 November 2009*, pages 36–43. IEEE Computer Society, 2009.

5. J. Helms, R. Schaefer, K. Luyten, J. Vermeulen, M. Abrams, A. Coyette, and J. Vanderdonckt. Human-Centered Engineering with the User Interface

Markup Language. In *Human-Centered Software Engineering - Software Engineering Models, Patterns and Architectures for HCI*, Human-Computer Interaction Series. Springer, London, 2009.

6. I. Khaddam and J. Vanderdonckt. Adapting UsiXML User Interfaces to Cultural Background. In *Proc. of 1st Int. Workshop on User Interface eXtensible Markup Language UsiXML'2010*, pages 163–170. Thales Research and Technology France, Paris, Berlin, 2010.

7. I. Khaddam and J. Vanderdonckt. Flippable User Interfaces for Internationalization. In *Proc. of the 3rd ACM SIGCHI symposium on Engineering interactive computing systems - EICS '11*, page 223. ACM Press, 2011.

8. M. Lettner and M. Tschernuth. Applied MDA for Embedded Devices: Software Design and Code Generation for a Low-Cost Mobile Phone. In *Computer Software and Applications Conference Workshops (COMPSACW), 2010 IEEE 34th Annual*, pages 63–68, 2010.

9. Q. Limbourg, J. Vanderdonckt, B. Michotte, L. Bouillon, and V. López-Jaquero. USIXML: A Language Supporting Multi-path Development of User Interfaces Engineering Human Computer Interaction and Interactive Systems. volume 3425 of *Lecture Notes in Computer Science*, pages 134–135. Springer Berlin / Heidelberg, Berlin and Heidelberg, 2005.

10. D. Mark and J. LaMarche. *Beginning iPhone development: exploring the iPhone SDK*. Apress Series. Apress, 2008.

11. T. Memmel, F. Gundelsweiler, and H. Reiterer. Prototyping Corporate User Interfaces: Towards a Visual Specification of Interactive Systems. In *Proc. of the Second IASTED International Conference on Human Computer Interaction*, IASTED-HCI '07, pages 177–182, Anaheim and CA and USA, 2007. ACTA Press.

12. B. Michotte and J. Vanderdonckt. GrafiXML, a Multi-target User Interface Builder Based on UsiXML. In *Fourth International Conference on Autonomic and Autonomous Systems (ICAS'08)*, pages 15–22. IEEE, 2008.

13. J. Nichols and B. A. Myers. Creating a lightweight user interface description language: An overview and analysis of the personal universal controller project. *ACM Trans. Comput.-Hum. Interact*, 16:17:1–17:37, 2009.

14. Open XUL Alliance. Open XUL Alliance - Creating A Rich Internet For Everyone.

15. M. Perez-Quinones, O. Padilla-Falto, and K. McDevitt. Automatic Language Translation for User Interfaces. In *TAPIA '05 Proc. of the 2005 conference on Diversity in computing*, pages 60–63, 2005.

16. Petzold Charles. *Programming WP 7*. Microsoft Press, 2010.

17. Rick Strahl and Michele Leroux. WPF Localization Guidance, 2009.

18. B. Selic. The Pragmatics of Model-Driven Development. *Software, IEEE, The pragmatics of model-driven development*, 20(5):19–25, 2003.

19. N. Souchon and J. Vanderdonckt. A Review of XML-compliant User Interface Description Languages. In *Interactive Systems. Design, Specification, and Verification, 10th International Workshop, DSV-IS 2003, Funchal, Madeira Island, Portugal, June 11-13, 2003, Revised Papers*, volume 2844 of *Lecture Notes in Computer Science*, pages 377–391. Springer, 2003.

20. M. Tschernuth, M. Lettner, and R. Mayrhofer. Evaluation of Methodologies for a Descriptive User Interface. In *Proc. EUROCAST 2011: 13th International Conference on Computer Aided Systems Theory*, LNCS. Springer-Verlag, February 2011.

21. UsiXML Consortium. Usixml v1.8-referencemanual, 22.02.2007.

22. J. Vanderdonckt. A MDA-Compliant Environment for Developing User Interfaces of Information Systems. In *Advanced Information Systems Engineering, 17th International Conference, CAiSE 2005, Porto, Portugal, June 13-17, 2005, Proc.*, volume 3520 of *Lecture Notes in Computer Science*, pages 16–31. Springer, Berlin, 2005.

What can Model-Based UI Design offer to End-User Software Engineering?

Anke Dittmar[1], **Alfonso García Frey**[2], **Sophie Dupuy-Chessa**[3]

Dept. of Computer Science, University of Rostock[1], University of Grenoble[2], UJF[2], UPMF[3], LIG[2,3]

Germany[1], France[2,3]

Anke.Dittmar@uni-rostock.de, {Alfonso.Garcia-Frey, Sophie.Dupuy}@imag.fr

ABSTRACT

End-User Programming enables end users to create their own programs. This can be accomplished in different ways, where one of them is by appropriation or reconfiguration of existing software. However, there is a trade-off between end users' 'situated design' and quality design which is addressed in End-User Software Engineering. This paper investigates how methods and techniques from Model-Based UI Design can contribute to End-User Software Engineering. Applying the concept of Extra-UI, the paper describes a Model-Based approach that allows to extend core applications in a way that some of the underlying models and assumptions become manipulable by end users. The approach is discussed through a running example.

Author Keywords

End-User Software Engineering, End-User Programming, Model-Based UI design, Human-Computer Interaction.

ACM Classification Keywords

H.5.2 Information Interfaces and Presentation: User Interfaces – theory and methods.: D.2.2.Software Engineering: Design Tools and Techniques – user interfaces.

INTRODUCTION

The term 'End-User Programming' (EUP) has been developed in response to an existing gap between design and use of interactive applications. For a long time, 'designers' were seen as the experts in developing software artefacts. They acquired the right skills and followed the right processes to do so[1]. 'Users' were mainly seen as experts in their domains who have to learn to use the software that was built for them. Today, the number of people who do programming at work or in their leisure time is many times higher than the number of professional programmers as pointed out by [9] and others. Designing for end-user programming has supported this tendency and opened the design space for (end) users. However,

---

[1]Obviously, this is an oversimplification. Software Engineering is still in its infancy.

"the problem with end-user programming is that end users' programs are all too often turning out to be of too low quality for the purposes for which they were created" [1]. There is a trade-off between 'situated design' and quality design. End-User Software Engineering addresses this problem [1].

In this paper, we investigate how methods and techniques that have been developed in Model-Based UI Design (MBD) can contribute to End-User Software Engineering (EUSE). MBD is an engineering approach that applies conceptual knowledge about the users' tasks and domains as well as ergonomic and technical knowledge about human-computer interaction to design user interfaces in a systematic way. In particular, we show how meta-models and the concept of Extra-UIs can help to put meta-design [6] into practice. In our approach, UI-designers become 'meta-designers' by adding Extra-UIs to their application under design. This offers design spaces for end users according to their main interests. They can explore possible uses of the user interface that are not necessarily intended by the designer.

The paper is organized as follows. Basic ideas and trends in End-User Software Engineering are first examined to position our own approach. The next two sections introduce MBD in more detail and illustrate one specific method and corresponding techniques through an example. This example application does not support end-user programming yet, but has to be enriched by an Extra-UI. How this can be done is shown in the following section to illustrate the overall idea of our approach that is explained at the beginning of that section. The paper concludes with a discussion of possible implications and future work.

BACKGROUND I: END-USER PROGRAMMERS AND EUSE

We first need to understand the concept 'end-user programmer' in order to understand what EUSE is about. An indirect description may be given in the definition of End-User Development (EUD)[2] in [11] as a "set of methods, techniques, and tools that allow users of software systems, who are acting as non-professional software developers, at some point to create, modify or extend a software artefact". According to [11], there are two types of EUP activities. Parameterization and customization allow the end user to choose between predefined options. Program creation and modification (e.g. by programming by example) allow them to change a program beyond the intentions of the 'professional developer'. In this paper, we are interested in supporting activities of the second type.

---

[2]EUSE and EUD are not distinguished in this paper.

A more precise view on the end-user programmer concept is given in [9]. Basically, it is seen as "a role and a state of mind". A person acts in this role if the manipulated program is not the primary outcome of their work but serves as a (often temporary) means to an end. "Traditional" software engineering assumes that developers are responsible for supplying quality products in terms of reliability, maintainability, usability etc., but that they often are not the users of their products. Personas and scenarios are well-known means for developers to understand and imagine contexts of use. In contrast, EUSE has to assume that developers modify a program for 'situated use', but may have less interest in or understanding of quality criteria and the role of abstraction in the application. Additionally, requirements and design activities are more intertwined in EUSE because end users tend to explore possible uses (appropriation). Two approaches to cope with these challenges are mentioned in [9]: dictating proper design practices, and injecting good design decisions into existing user practices. A technique that supports the latter approach, and that is also applied in this paper, is the combination of constraints and generation mechanisms. The end user can design or modify certain aspects only and the final code is generated automatically.

Above explanation reveals the weak boundaries between 'professional' programmers and end users and between related processes. Fischer et al. show how ideas of End-User Development extends the traditional notion of system development. In their meta-design approach they suggest to include users as active co-developers throughout the entire existence of the system. This includes periods of unplanned evolution and periods of deliberate (re)structuring and enhancement [6].

BACKGROUND II: MODEL-BASED UI DESIGN

MBD is a software engineering approach that uses models capturing knowledge about different aspects of human-computer interaction as a basis for producing code of user interfaces (UI) in a structured way [12]. Typically, domain-dependent Concepts and Task models serve as starting point for producing Abstract UI models (AUI). From AUIs models Final UIs (FUI) are derived via an intermediate step - the Concrete UI models (CUI) [2]. Lower-level models are produced from higher-level descriptions by transformations. They can be performed by the application of transformation rules in an automated or semi-automated way or by the designer making explicit design decisions. Just to mention two examples: enabled task sets and heuristics are used in TERESA to transform task models automatically into AUI models [13]. A manual but tool-supported transformation of task and domain knowledge into dialog models is preferred in [3]. Transformations help to consider usability criteria during the design process [14, 8]. If they are applied on lower-level models to get higher-level ones they support re-engineering activities. Mappings are used to link elements from different models and, in some approaches, to keep track of the transformations from source to target elements. For example, each task of a task model and the concepts involved to achieve the task are mapped to a set of interactors in the CUI model in [14].

In MBD approaches, models can be re-used across different

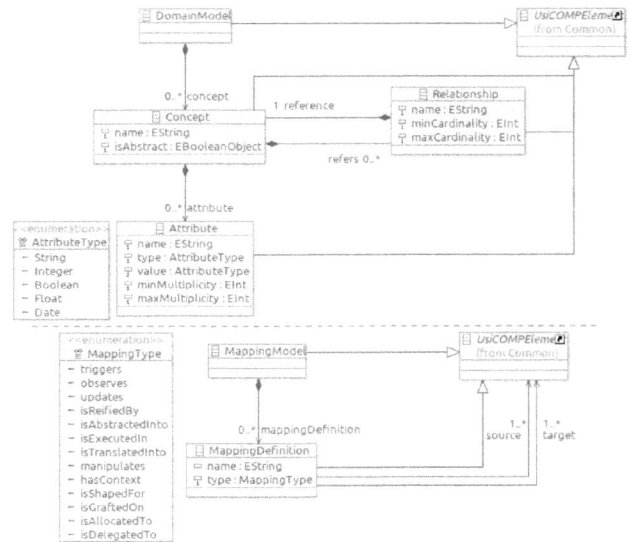

Figure 1. Ecore representations of the Domain meta-model (top) and Mapping meta-model (bottom) that are applied in the case study.

platforms and programming languages. Design decisions are made and described at conceptual levels. MBD also supports a more consistent development of UIs for different contexts [2]. However, there are still open questions concerning the link between UIs and functional cores in MBD. Limitations that arise from assumptions made in task descriptions are discussed e.g. in [4]. We will argue later that a view of UI designers as meta-designers and of (end) users as co-developers (as suggested in [6]) can change MBD practices and alleviate some of these limitations.

Meta-Models in MBD

What makes MBD possible at all is the assumption that different task/domain/AUI/... models have common underlying structures that can be described by their corresponding meta-models. Figure 1 shows parts of ecore class diagrams of meta-models that will be used in the case study later on. Like in most MBD approaches, hierarchical task structures are assumed that include temporal constraints between sub-tasks. Domain models are described by concepts with attributes and relationships to other concepts. AUI/CUI models specify interactors in a platform independent/dependent way.

An obvious use of meta-models is in the specification of transformation rules to reason about models and to find appropriate mappings (see Code 1 for an example). Mappings themselves are often organized by a meta-model if they need to be maintained for traceability and for model changes at run time. This is required e.g. for UI plasticity [15] and, generally, in all approaches defining user interfaces on the basis of other UI models. In the suggested approach to support EUSE the concept of Extra-UIs is applied. An Extra-UI is a UI that represents and provides control over a UI [15]. Later in this paper, we will show how Extra-UIs can be used to allow users (re)configuring the application from a EUSE perspective.

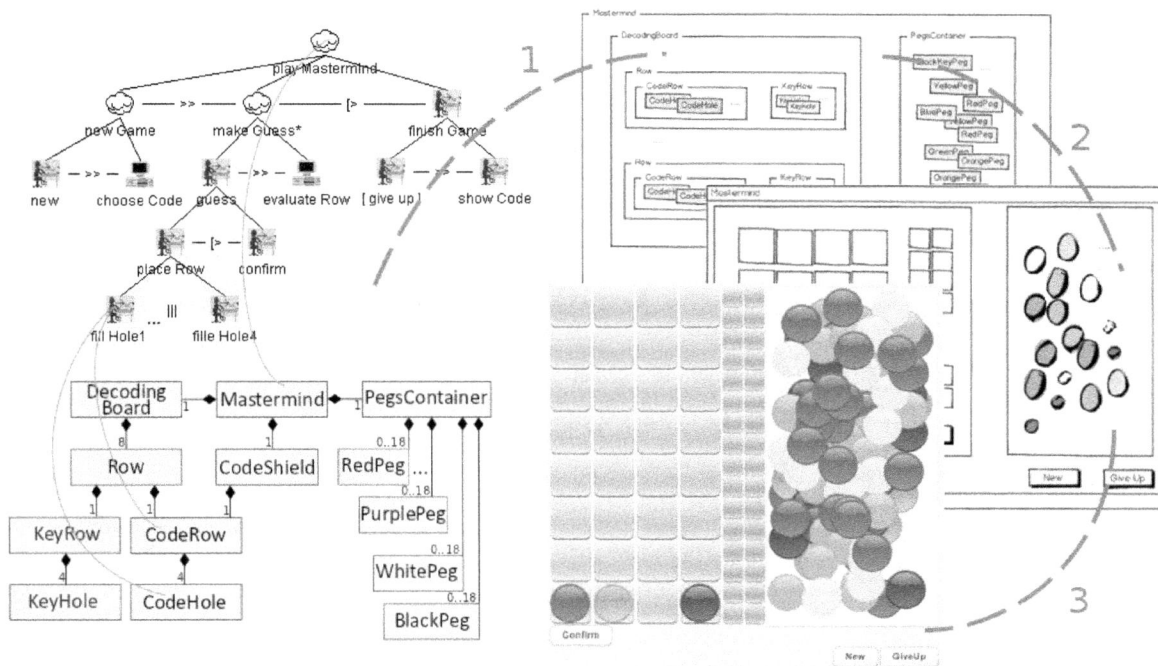

Figure 2. Models in the mastermind example. Tasks in the task model (top left) are mapped (light, curved lines) to concepts from the Domain model (bottom left). The AUI -represented by containers (white background boxes) and units (grey background boxes)- is obtained by transformation of these models in 1. The CUI is produced from the AUI in 2 before the FUI is generated in 3.

INTRODUCTION OF THE CASE STUDY

This section demonstrates above mentioned ideas by illustrating the development of a user interface for the mastermind game[3]. The applied MBD approach is similar to [2]. The example was chosen for several reasons. First, it has a reasonable complexity and the domain is easy to understand. Second, its extension in the second part of the paper shows our contribution to EUSE. Third, it is useful to illustrate 'tinkering' activities of hobbyists who form one particular end-user group. They like to explore ways "to reconfigure and personalize technology with no definite end in mind" [9].

The example is designed by using the UsiComp tool [7]. The designer needs to create the following input models using the tool: the task model, the domain and the mapping model. The mapping model indicates what concepts from the domain are manipulated by each task. The AUI is automatically produced from these models by using transformation rules. An excerpt of one of these rules is shown in Code 1. The CUI is derived semi-automatically from the AUI, i.e., the designer specifies what predefined rules are applied to each element of the AUI model. Finally, a last automatic transformation generates the java code of the UI from the CUI model (see figure 2).

In the context of this paper, sketchy illustrations of models are often used for reasons of brevity and clarity. They focus on important aspects and avoid less well-known notations. They may also help to show the generality of the approach.

[3]http://en.wikipedia.org/wiki/Mastermind_(board_game)

```
1  rule Task2DataIU {
2      from s : CTTE!Task (
3          not thisModule.manipulates(s) and
4          s.compositions—>size() = 0 and
5          s.Category = #Interaction)
6      to t : AUI!AbstractDataIU (
7          name <— s.Name),
8      m : Mapping!MappingDefinition (
9          name <— s.Name,
10         type <— #isReifiedBy,
11         source <— s,
12         target <— t)
13 }
```

Code 1. Excerpt of an ATL transformation.

MODEL-BASED UI DESIGN FOR EUSE

We consider a user interface that allows for end-user programming (EUP UI) as consisting of two parts: a) UI of the actual application (core UI), and b) UI for modifications by end users that are not considered in the description of the core tasks. Both parts are developed by the designers within the model-based paradigm and require their own functional core. The latter part can be considered an Extra-UI because the separation makes possible that its design is informed by models that were developed during the design process of the core UI (core models). As a side effect, an opportunity is provided to reflect those core models and underlying modeling assumptions. This in turn is necessary to decide about the design space that the EUP UI should offer to end-user programmers. For example, the models in figure 2 describe a core UI that is designed to play mastermind with a four-pegs code. It would be reasonable to constrain EUP activities in such a way that

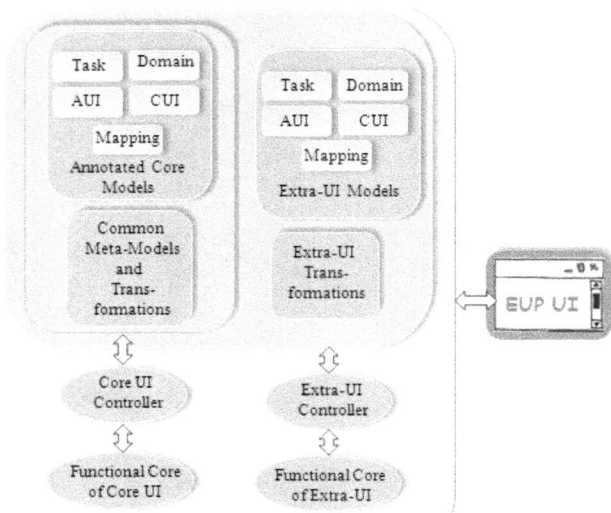

Figure 3. Generic architecture for model-based EUP UI.

the resulting UIs still include a board and some kinds of pegs. The functional core of the Extra UI implements the manipulation of core models at run time and the generation of modified core UIs that still preserve some original design decisions. In other words, an Extra UI opens a 'window' for the end user to underlying mechanisms and assumptions in the design. Figure 3 shows a generic architecture supporting these ideas. The coupling of elements of the core UI and the Extra-UI that is described later in this section (including figure 5) shows another perspective on how to develop the final EUP UI.

Design Methodology

A four steps design methodology is suggested. It certainly needs to be integrated into a more holistic approach as it will be briefly discussed in the implications section.

1. Design of core UI,
2. Specification of design space constraints for end users,
3. Design of Extra-UI,
4. Coupling of core UI and Extra-UI to the final EUP UI.

In the first step, the UI of the core application is designed using a classical MBD approach as described above. Steps 2 and 3 deal with scope and complexity of the Extra-UI. People who act as end-user programmers are focused on their domain and have no primary interest in the models and techniques used in MBD. They should have the opportunity to change conceptual aspects and their representations in the UI within the scope of the domain, but without being confronted with all model details and notations in use (as e.g. in [15]). It is a design problem in itself to find a good representation of those UI parts end users can manipulate[4]. In the following, steps 2-4 will be explained in more detail. The example study (see figure 2) will be continued for illustration.

---

[4]A good description of the problem is given in [5]: "When creating means for users to modify their environment there is often a temptation to try to do everything - the spectre of Turing equivalence rises and before long a simple end-user customisation tool becomes a full-blown and complex programming language."

Specification of design space constraints

In this step designers constrain the possible design space for end-user programmers. This is done by model annotation (but other approaches are possible). In the case study, model elements have two additional attributes *fixed:boolean* and *manipulable:boolean*. The first attribute serves to specify key elements in the core task and core domain model that cannot be deleted because they are considered as essential to the problem domain. The second attribute specifies elements that are not manipulable by the end user. Let us assume that in the core models of figure 2 tasks *playMastermind*, *makeGuess*, *startGame*, *finishGame*, *fillHole1* as well as concepts *Mastermind*, *CodeHole* and *RedPeg* are specified as fixed and their representations cannot be removed from the UI.

Design of Extra-UI

The Extra-UI needs to be constructed following the same MBD approach as used for the core UI. Moreover, models from both UIs must conform to the same meta-models to allow for a coupling in the next step. Tasks in the task model of the Extra-UI describe possible manipulations of core models and need to be mapped to corresponding parts in the Extra-UI domain model (nothing is new). The domain model again consists of the annotated core models (including all mappings) that are represented according to the meta-models in use (see figure 1). As a consequence, the designer's view on what can be manipulated by the end user is strongly influenced by the meta-models. Of course, this is both a limitation and an advantage. Typical tasks the designer identifies may be restricted to the deletion, duplication, and renaming of tasks and concepts, the modification of their presentation in the UI and so on. On the other hand, meta-models make possible the description of design patterns for Extra-UIs.

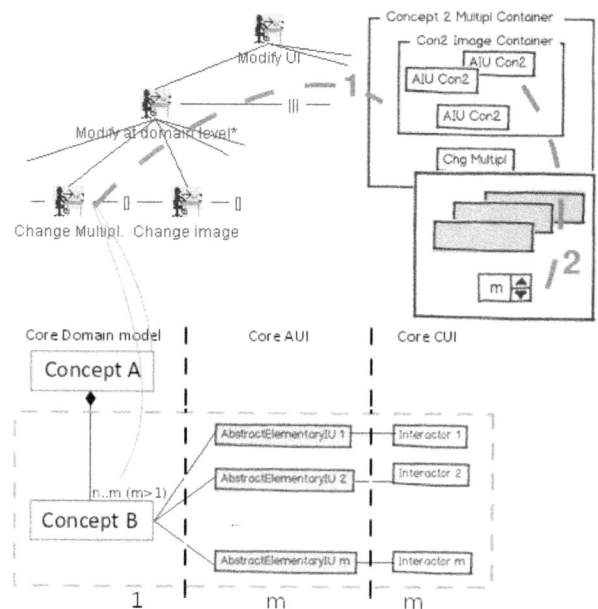

Figure 4. A 1-m-m design pattern for Extra-UIs.

Such patterns suggest representations of certain parts of annotated models in a core UI design that allow end users to modify these parts in a familiar notation. An important characteristic of design patterns for Extra-UIs is that they ensure consistency across core models. That means that the new core UI can be re-generated from modified core models. Figure 4 depicts a pattern that describes situations for applying the (Extra-UI) task *Change Multiplicity*. On the top of the left hand side, parts of the Extra-UI task model are to be seen. The bottom part of the figure describes in a generic way which parts of the core domain model, AUI and CUI model are involved. Corresponding mappings between task *Change Multiplicity* and domain concepts are indicated by light, curved lines as in figure 2. On the right hand side a transformation into an AUI and then CUI presentation for Extra-UIs is suggested that does not expect end users to be familiar with UML diagrams and the like.

Coupling of core UI and Extra-UI

If the core and Extra-UI are designed they need to be coupled into the final application. Again, involved design models can be used to support a coupling at different levels of abstraction. Model composition is not in the focus of this paper, but it is discussed by many authors in MBD (e.g. [10]). Figure 5 indicates the coupling at the task and domain level that is used in our case study. Here, task models of the core UI and Extra-UI are integral parts of the overall task model.

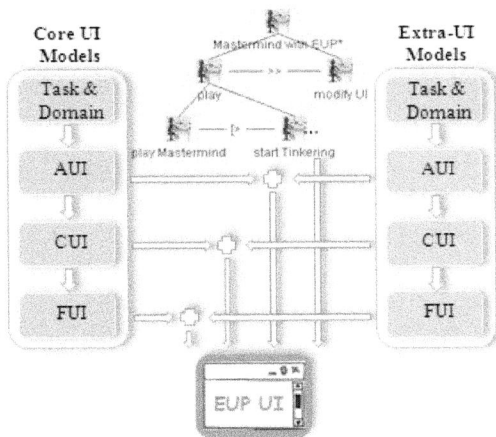

Figure 5. A coupling of core UI and Extra-UI is possible at different levels of abstraction (here illustrated at the task & domain level).

Extra-UI for the mastermind game

Figure 6 shows an Extra-UI design for the running example. The above mentioned pattern was applied several times in transformation steps (partly recursively). Two other Extra-UI design patterns were used. First, a concept can be renamed within its final presentation if there is a 1:1:1 mapping between concept, AUI element, and CUI element. Additionally, there must be inverse rules for the transformation rules. In the example, the concept *Mastermind* can be renamed (see the text entry at the top container). Second, leaf tasks that are not fixed can be deleted. This includes the removal of all mappings to domain concepts and AUI elements. If it results in

concepts with no mappings to tasks anymore the representations of the concepts are disabled in the Extra-UI and they are not represented in the modified core UI (similarly with AUI elements). In the screenshot, tasks *Evaluate Row* and *Give Up* are deleted which implies disabling the representation of the feedback part of the board and the "Give Up" button.

FINALLY: USING THE EXAMPLE EUP UI (AND SHARE)

One advantage of appropriation is the sense of ownership and empowerment it engenders. A sense of control is important for well being, and the act of tinkering gives this, whether to improve the user interface for its original purposes, or make it do something completely novel. [5]

The provided Extra-UI lets end users produce different variations of the mastermind or even new peg based games. Please take a look at figure 6 and use your imagination to modify the original game on the left hand side. One possible example of a new game is a tic-tac-toe. A human-vs-human version of this game does not require the "confirm" button, responsible for linking the evaluation function from the functional core with the UI. For a human-vs-computer game, the "share" button must be used for asking the programmers to re-implement this evaluation function.

IMPLICATIONS FOR MBD

Fischer et al. [6] encourage designers to conceptualize their activity as meta-design. In contrast to conventional design, meta-designers do not aim at the development of complete systems. Their task is to supply tools to users that empower them "to engage actively in the continuous development of systems rather than being restricted to the use of existing systems" [6]. Underdesign is suggested as a technique of meta-designers to create such design spaces for end users. The approach to MBD that is introduced in this paper supports the idea of underdesign. The separation between core UI and Extra-UI invites designers to reflect explicitly about their design assumptions that are incorporated in the core models. In a second design step, some of these assumptions are made modifiable by the user. The example illustrated that modifications of the core application by the end user can lead to new functional requirements. They need to be shared with the (meta-)designers to initiate extensions of the system, and possibly re-design steps. According to [4], MBD designers focus on the production of consistent and complete system specifications and, as a consequence, often consider task models as complete descriptions of the users' tasks. The proposed approach alleviates this problem by accepting design as an open and continuous co-operative process to find a better balance between 'too specific' and 'too universal' interactive applications.

CONCLUSIONS AND FUTURE WORK

This paper investigates how methods and techniques from Model-Based UI Design can contribute to End-User Software Engineering through three main contributions. Firstly, the concept of Extra-UI is revisited from the EUP perspective. Secondly, a four steps methodology explains how to apply this concept to create an EUP UI. And finally, we discuss some interesting annotations on the core models that help to

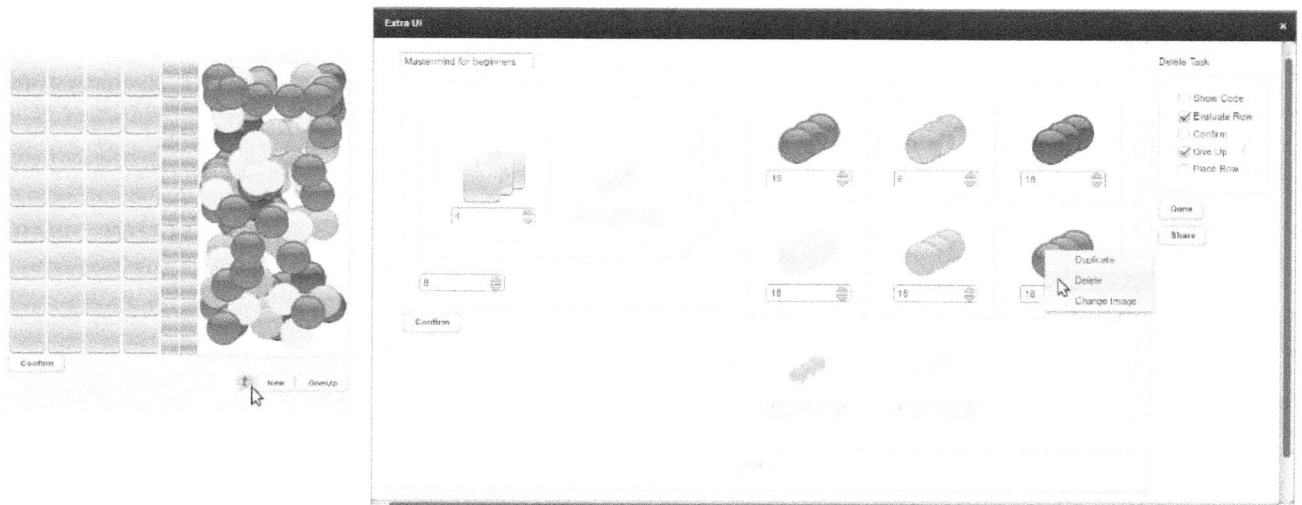

Figure 6. An EUP UI for mastermind: the game was interrupted by pressing the "tinker" button (core UI on the left) to use the Extra-UI (on the right).

decide about the design space for end users and some Extra-UI design patterns to support appropriate representations of this design space. The contributions are discussed and illustrated through a running example in which a mastermind game can be (re)programmed into a tic-tac-toe game. This example demonstrates the practicality of the method. Further work aims to make it more systematic. In addition, we want to consider sets of Extra-UIs for different groups of end-users who approach a system under design with different interests and background knowledge.

ACKNOWLEDGMENTS

We are grateful to UPMF for their fincancial support to the collaboration between the authors. The second author is supported by the European ITEA UsiXML project, the third author by the ANR MOANO.

REFERENCES

1. Burnett, M. What is end-user software engineering and why does it matter? In *Proc. of IS-EUD'09*, IS-EUD '09, Springer-Verlag (2009), 15–28.

2. Calvary, G., Coutaz, J., Thevenin, D., Limbourg, Q., Bouillon, L., and Vanderdonckt, J. A unifying reference framework for multi-target user interfaces. *Interacting with Computers 15*, 3 (2003), 289–308.

3. Dittmar, A., and Forbrig, P. The influence of improved task models on dialogues. In *Proc. of CADUI '04*, Kluwer (2004), 1–14.

4. Dittmar, A., and Forbrig, P. Task-based design revisited. In *Proc. of EICS '09*, ACM (2009), 111–116.

5. Dix, A. Opening the Box - Meta-level Interfaces Needs and Solutions. In *Proc. of Interfaces : SUI'11 Workshop at EICS'11* (2011).

6. Fischer, G., Giaccardi, E., Ye, Y., Sutcliffe, A. G., and Mehandjiev, N. Meta-design: a manifesto for end-user development. *Commun. ACM 47*, 9 (2004), 33–37.

7. García Frey, A., Ceret, E., Dupuy-Chessa, S., Calvary, G., and Gabillon, Y. UsiComp: an extensible model-driven composer. In *Proc. of EICS2012*, ACM Press (2012).

8. García Frey, A., Ceret, E., Dupuy-Chessa, S., and Calvary, G. C. QUIMERA: a quality metamodel to improve design rationale. In *Proc. of EICS2011*, ACM Press (2011), 265–270.

9. Ko, A. J., Abraham, R., Beckwith, L., Blackwell, A., Burnett, M., Erwig, M., Scaffidi, C., Lawrance, J., Lieberman, H., Myers, B., Rosson, M. B., Rothermel, G., Shaw, M., and Wiedenbeck, S. The state of the art in end-user software engineering. *ACM Comput. Surv. 43*, 3 (2011), 21:1–21:44.

10. Lewandowski, A., Lepreux, S., and Bourguin, G. Tasks models merging for high-level component composition. In *Proc. of HCI'07*, Springer-Verlag (Berlin, Heidelberg, 2007), 1129–1138.

11. Lieberman, H., Paterno, F., and Wulf, V., Eds. *End-User Development*. Kluwer/ Springer, 2006.

12. Limbourg, Q., and Vanderdonckt, J. Addressing the mapping problem in user interface design with usixml. In *Proc. of TAMODIA '04* (2004), 155–163.

13. Paternò, F., and Santoro, C. One model, many interfaces. In *Proc. of CADUI '02*, Kluwer (2002), 143–154.

14. Sottet, J.-S., Calvary, G., Coutaz, J., and Favre, J.-M. A model-driven engineering approach for the usability of plastic user interfaces. In *Proc. of EIS '08*, Springer-Verlag (2008), 140–157.

15. Sottet, J.-S., Calvary, G., Favre, J.-M., and Coutaz, J. Megamodeling and metamodel-driven engineering for plastic user interfaces: Mega-ui. In *Human-Centered Software Engineering*. 2009, 173–200.

Modeling Task Transitions to Help Designing for Better Situation Awareness

Thomas Villaren[1,2], Gilles Coppin[1], and Angélica Leal[2]

[1] Institut Mines-Télécom – Télécom Bretagne
UMR CNRS 3192 Lab-STICC
Brest, France
firstname.lastname@telecom-bretagne.eu

[2] Bertin Technologies
10bis, avenue Ampère
78053 St-Quentin-en-Yvelines, France
lastname@bertin.fr

ABSTRACT

In complex systems such as cockpits or unmanned systems, operators manage a set of tasks with high temporal dynamics. Frequent changes of situation within the same mission can sometimes induce a loss of operators' Situation Awareness.

In this paper, we introduce a methodology for design of Human-Computer Interfaces in dynamic systems taking into account the situation elements constituting operators' activity. We follow a user-centered approach; end-users and domain experts are included along the different steps of this model-based design process.

The complete methodology is presented here, from initial task & situation modeling, through transition analysis, to the final recommendations on interface design, applied to an illustrative example.

Author Keywords

Methodology; Human Factors; Situation Awareness; model-based design; interfaces; task switch; interruption.

ACM Classification Keywords

H.5.2 [User Interfaces]: Theory and methods;

INTRODUCTION

Operators of complex systems such as aircraft cockpits, air traffic control centers or unmanned aerial systems (UAS) are dealing with a set of highly dynamic tasks. Their mission usually involves switching between different tasks, each associated with a different mission context. These frequent changes may impact operators' Situation Awareness, defined by Endsley [9] as their *"perception of elements in the environment within a volume of time and space, the comprehension of their meaning and the projection of their status in the near future"*.

When switching from a task T1 to a task T2, the mission context associated with each task evolves, new situational

elements can be brought to the operator's attention, and others might become irrelevant in the light of the new task. This idea is conceptualized on Figure 1: both tasks are represented as Venn diagrams; each one corresponds to a set of situation elements. During the transition from T1 to T2, some of these elements remain relevant while others fade away (in T1) or appear (in T2).

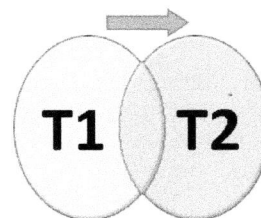

Figure 1: Venn diagrams of a "simple" transition, both tasks are overlapping, some Situation elements are shared while other are not.

Other types of transitions, such as task addition or removal, task interruption or retrieval, can also induce changes in context. These switches, particularly when they are frequent, may impact operators at different levels, and induce a decrease of their Situation Awareness (SA) (for accounts of such issues, see for instance [6,13]).

Transitions in the Literature

In the literature, transitions between tasks have been approached with different angles.

Studies on *Task Switching* have been led in the field of Cognitive Psychology for almost two decades [1,2,18,22]. This research examines the cognitive impacts of switching between low-level tasks (Stroop-like tasks [15] such as identifying and naming a color, a shape, reading a word or classifying a digit as odd or even), particularly the switch time (or "cost"). Although the transitions studied in these works are of interest, we consider tasks of higher level such "piloting a drone in manual mode".

Other works have dealt with a specific type of task transition: *Interruptions* [16,17]. These studies focus on different aspects of interruptions such as: coordinating human-computer interactions in order to interrupt operators at the most appropriate time [17], integrating interruptions in the design phase [11] or helping to recover the context after an interruption [26]. However, we identified certain types of transitions between tasks that were not addressed in the literature. For instance, "basic" transitions where a task T2 substitutes a task T1 (as in Figure 1) or when a second task is added to the first one.

Goal

In this article, we present a methodology for Human-Computer Interface (HCI) design which takes into account these context-switching situations through a model-based and user-centered approach. The goal of this methodology is two-fold:

- We aim first at ensuring operators' **cognitive continuity & compatibility,** i.e. the ability for operators to correctly perceive and interpret the same concepts in both tasks (similar definitions have been proposed in different domains: Augmented Reality (AR) systems [8], Mixed Reality (MR) systems or multiplatform systems [10]). In other words, the resulting interfaces should help minimizing, or at least reducing, the loss of Situation Awareness resulting from a transition between tasks.

- We also aim at ensuring **task functional continuity,** i.e. the ability for operators to execute the new tasks in continuity with the previous ones, with no or little adaptation (see also [10]).

The point of view adopted in our approach is a model-driven engineering one: rather than focusing on the perception aspects of the transitions (such as [5,25] for instance which could be seen as a potential answer to our analysis process), we model operators' tasks and required Situation Awareness elements as a starting point for the methodology, attaching our methodology to the Task Analysis approach [4]. We also tackle the Human Factors issues raised by such transitions through a user-centered approach, including end-users and Subject Matter Experts (SME) throughout the design process (interviews, expert validation of models and user tests of final interfaces).

The following section introduces this new methodology and describes the two models used to define the tasks and situation elements considered. Then, we discuss in detail the question of task similarity and its consequences on task analysis. Finally, we provide an example of application for this methodology.

METHODOLOGY

In order to address the issues raised in the introduction, we propose a 4-step methodology presented in Figure 2.

- During the first step, two models are built: operators' activity is described in a *Task Model* and Situation Awareness elements corresponding to their activity are described in a *SA Model*.

- Secondly, each task of the Task Model is associated with a set of SA elements from the SA Model according to the SA requirements for this specific task.

- Once all the tasks have been covered by the *Task/SA elements association* process, starts the *Transition Analysis* step: tasks are compared two by two in order to categorize the transitions that link them. Thanks to the use of adequate comparison methods, this analysis allows to detect task/SA elements associations that can raise cognitive issues in transition because of a major dissimilarity or, on the other hand, couples of tasks that transition smoothly and easily.

- Finally, the design expert emits recommendations based on the previous analysis and defines the impacts these transitions might have on HCI design, relying mainly upon his/her own expertise.

The next subsections are devoted to describing the three first steps of this methodology.

Task Modeling Phase (Step 1a)

One of the two first concomitant modeling phases of the methodology is the modeling of operators' attended tasks.

This phase requires information on operators' everyday activity. This knowledge is elicited through interviews with operators and SMEs [4] but also extracted from other sources, such as expert reports and literature reviews.

All this data is then compiled and structured into a task tree. We rely on the ConcurTaskTrees (CTT) notation [20,21] to build this task model. This notation combines the description of tasks hierarchical linking (on a downward-

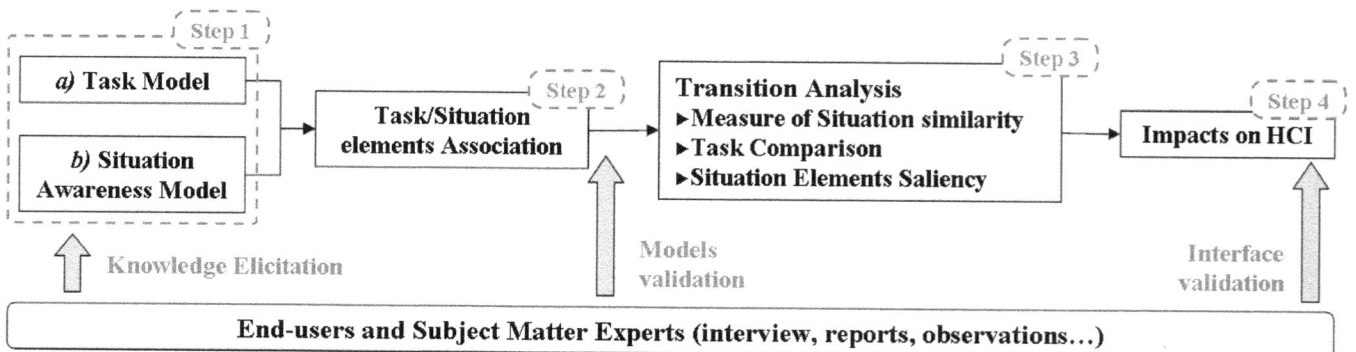

Figure 2: our 4-step methodology and its relationship with end-users & SMEs.

oriented vertical axis) with the temporal relationships between tasks of a same abstraction level (on a rightward-oriented horizontal axis).

On the vertical axis, the CTT notation allows the description of tasks at different levels of granularity, from the higher abstraction levels down to the interaction level. While the lower levels describe precisely the interaction means and provide design indications, the higher ones only explicit the main tasks performed in operators' activity. As our goal in this step is not to describe the whole interface and interaction means, but only to describe the main tasks and subtasks attended by operators, we limit ourselves to higher abstraction levels.

The horizontal axis holds the temporal relationships between the tasks of a same abstraction level. At each level, subtasks of a same parent task are linked with CTT temporal operators (inherited from the LOTOS formal description technique [12]). The extent of CTT temporal operator makes it a natural choice when modeling the transitions between tasks.

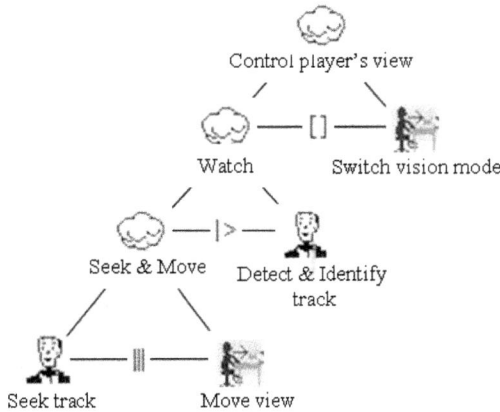

Figure 3: CTT notation applied to the control of a videogame player's view.

The left-to-right temporal orientation of CTT trees makes sense only in the case of sequencing tasks. If two sibling tasks are meant to exist in parallel or exclusively from each other, their horizontal position does not matter. The CTT notation proposes [20] to prevent reading ambiguities by either using the priority order defined in LOTOS standard (choice & parallel operators have the priority over sequence ones) or introducing new *dummy* tasks that act as "factoring" tasks and dissociate groups of sequencing tasks from groups of parallel ones. We prefer relying on the *dummy* tasks solution, which improves trees readability (see Figure 3). The ConcurTaskTrees notation is supported by the CTTE tool [19].

Figure 3 presents an extract of a player's CTT tree in the videogame Battlefield 3™: the First Person Shooter multiplayer game will serve as example throughout this article. We focus here on the *Control Player's View* task. Two exclusive tasks are present at the top of this tree: the

iterative *Watch* task and the interactive *Switch vision mode* task (the player can switch between a normal mode and a night vision mode when playing). The *Watch* task is divided into two tasks: the first, *Seek & Move*, is iterative and can be interrupted by the *Detect & Identify track* task. The bottom of this tree pictures two concomitant tasks: a user task, *Seek*, and an interactive one, *Move view*. The *Seek & Move* is an example of a dummy task: it helps disambiguate the transition from between the *Move view* and *Seek* tasks interrupted the *Detect & Identify track* one.

Situation Modeling Phase (Step 1b)
The second concomitant modeling phase consists in building a Situation Awareness Model. Amongst the wide range of models existing in the literature (see [23,24] for reviews of existing models), we selected Stanton et al.'s *Distributed Situation Awareness* (DSA) model [27,28].

In this model, SA is depicted as a system-level state-oriented phenomenon, distributed between the different operators of a complex system (each operator being in charge of a specific task). In order to describe the SA requirements for a specific system, the DSA model relies on the schema theory, supported by propositional networks representing the links between the "knowledge objects" (which can be viewed as SA requirements elements).

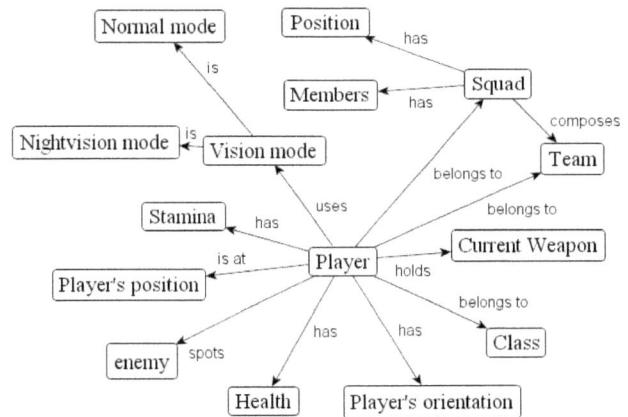

Figure 4: extract of the DSA graph of a videogame.

During the construction process proposed by Stanton et al., each operator (each managing one task) is interviewed and their knowledge is elicited in order to build a partial graph depicting the SA elements required for this task. The resulting set of graphs (one graph per operator) is then merged into a single graph picturing the overall Situation Awareness elements for the system. In order to retain the link between operator's task and their corresponding SA elements, color-coding of graph nodes is used: it indicates *"in a simple, visual manner the relationship between specific agents and specific objects over the course of the mission"* [28].

For the purpose of our methodology, we transposed the multi-operator / single-task paradigm adopted by Stanton et al. into a single-operator / multi-task paradigm. The construction of the SA network relies on the same inputs as the definition of the task tree: we build a network of SA elements describing the system's SA requirements upon the feedbacks from interviewed operators & SMEs as well as domain-specific knowledge. As in Stanton et al.'s construction method [27], we compile each operators' graph (qualified as a "*phenotype*") into a single graph (the "*genotype*"). The resulting graph is a system-specific compilation of SA requirements, gathered in a unique graph.

Figure 4 presents an extract of a DSA graph for the First Person Shooter (FPS) videogame Battlefield 3™ with a purposely reduced number of SA elements represented. Propositional networks are built upon ‹subject›‹relation› ‹object› relationships (e.g. "*Player has stamina*"). These relationships can be extracted from the transcripts of interviews as they correspond. If necessary, the relationships extracted from different sources can be adapted and merge into one triplet expressing the same relationship.

Associating Task with Situation Awareness Elements (Step 2)

Stanton et al. define DSA as "*activated knowledge for a specific task within a system*" [28]. Following this definition, and as an analogy with the color-coding of the knowledge network produced in their elicitation process, the second step of our methodology links the different tasks modeled in the first step with subsets of the overall SA elements graph.

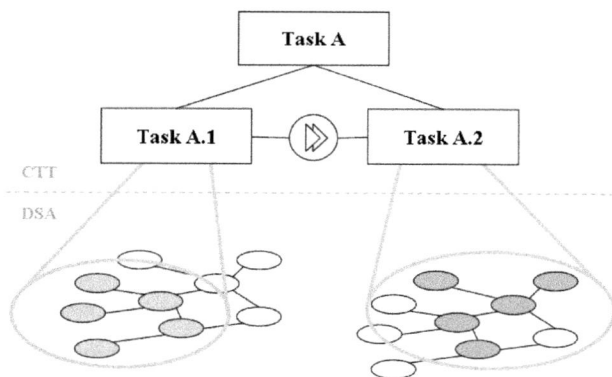

Figure 5: illustration of the Task/SA elements association process.

This "Task/SA Elements association" process is straightforward: to each *relevant* task of the CTT tree is associated a subset of the overall DSA graph nodes (a subgraph of the main graph), corresponding to the SA requirements for the task. Certain tasks can be considered as *irrelevant* during this association process, particularly *dummy* tasks (as defined earlier) which are only present for clarity sake and do not add any relevant information in terms of operators' activity. There is no association for these tasks.

The schema on Figure 5 illustrates the association process where two sequencing tasks are each associated with a different subset of the overall network (in our example, this network contains only 9 nodes). The highlight brought by the color-coding allows a fast identification of the SA requirements for each specific task.

Models built in the first step and associations defined through this second step are then refined and validated through discussions with experts. CTT and DSA notations use visual representations which make them descriptive enough to be easily understood.

TRANSITION ANALYSIS (STEP 3)

Once the two models are linked, we can start working on the third step of the methodology which consists in analyzing & categorizing the different transitions between tasks. The principle of this step is to provide different means to compare the SA contexts for two tasks and qualify the transition which links these tasks.

In the domain of *Interruption*, McFarlane and Latorella [16] propose a taxonomy of Human Interruptions in HCI. Their taxonomy uses qualitative factors (such as source of interruption, mean of interruption, characteristics of the operator, or effects of interruption…) as different viewpoints for discussing User Interface (UI) design supporting these interruptions.

Step 3 and 4 of our methodology are inspired by this two-step process, classification of an interruption followed by UI recommendations. Thus, we propose to use different qualification processes in order to categorize the transitions studied. Our focus being the impact of a transition on operators' SA, we provide different solutions to measure the similarity and differences in terms of SA between two tasks encompassing a transition.

Task comparison relies on quantitative measures (Tversky's similarity ratio model, graph matching, and extraction of salient elements) and more qualitative observations (addition of metadata to characterize SA elements).

Tversky's Similarity Ratio Model

In his work, Tversky [29] proposes different similarity models based to measure the common and distinctive features of two items. We use the *ratio model*, which provides a normalized similarity measure ($0 \le S \le 1$).

Equation (1) defines this ratio:

$$S(t_i, t_j) = \frac{f(T_i \cap T_j)}{f(T_i \cap T_j) + \alpha . f(T_i \setminus T_j) + \beta . f(T_j \setminus T_i)} \quad (1)$$

- f is the counting function. It counts common or distinctive elements between two tasks (noted T_i and T_j). In our study, counted elements are the different SA elements of the DSA graph associated to each task.

→ $f(T_i \cap T_j)$ represents the number of SA elements associated with *both* tasks T_i and T_j.

→ $f(T_i \setminus T_j)$ represents the number of SA elements associated to T_i *only* and inversely for $f(T_j \setminus T_i)$.

- In Tversky's definition α and β are positive or null coefficients. Setting them to non-null values will increase the importance of elements associated only to one task.

The scale extremities define two interesting values:

- · $S = 0$ if and only if both tasks are unconnected (they do not have any common SA elements).

- $S = 1$ if and only if both tasks are exactly associated to the same common SA elements (the case $\alpha = \beta = 0$ we do not considered relevant).

All other values of S are defined within these boundaries. The scale S can be used as a first classification method for transition categorization.

Graph Matching

In propositional networks, absence or presence of edges between nodes holds as much information as the nodes themselves. When comparing two subgraphs associated with two tasks, seeking which SA elements are common to both tasks is the first logical way to measure similarity. We propose to improve this simple comparison process by seeking the largest common subgraph (LCSG): the idea is to find sets of nodes linked together (clusters) common to both graphs which could carry a specific meaning.

Graph matching is a complex domain and many algorithms exist, particularly in the area of image analysis (see [3] for instances). These algorithms typically try to match two supposedly *independent* graphs built on data extracted from two images and which might, or not, have common features (e.g. face detection algorithms). In our case, the subgraphs compared are both extracted from the same main DSA graph (each subgraph corresponds to a highlight defined by its associated task), thus making them *dependent*. This dependency lowers the complexity of matching both subgraphs: one needs only to find the largest common subset of nodes between the subgraphs (the edges linking these nodes will be the same).

We can use the common subgraphs detected as an input for discussions for UI design.

Extraction of SA Elements' Salience

We propose another method to highlight salient elements in a transition. This method also relies on Stanton et al.'s work [28] that identifies the most pertinent information tokens of a network as "*those knowledge objects that serve as a central hub to other knowledge objects (i.e., have five or more links to other knowledge objects)*". This extraction is done on the overall network (without any color-coding from a task) and highlights the central objects of the system.

If they are involved in a transition, these central objects might need additional attention as they represent salient SA elements in the system. Particularly, if one SA element is associated to one task of the transition and not to the other one, this may have an impact on UI design.

SA Elements Tagging

In order to compare SA elements associated to transitioning tasks, we propose to add metadata describing and qualifying the state of these elements, when pertinent.

This *tagging* process would be performed during the "Task/SA elements association step" (step 2), and be based on qualitative information elicited from interviewees. Added tags can address a wide range of information such as elements dynamics, importance, relevance or representation and directly transcribe operators' specific requests on certain elements. As such, they may directly impact UI design. For instance, depending on the task, certain SA elements are best perceived by operators if displayed as a numerical value (as a number on the screen) or in a more graphical way (as a vector, a gauge...).

Unlike the previous comparison means (Tversky's ratio model, graph matching, extraction of salience), the use of metadata to qualify each SA elements is hardly automatable but it provides qualitative information on each SA elements and thus can be used as input for UI design discussions.

APPLICATION

In order to illustrate the modeling and association process presented in this article, this section presents an application of this methodology to the First Person Shooter videogame Battlefield 3™. We first introduce the videogame context, and then present an extract of the task tree and SA graph built upon it with a focus on a specific task encountered by players during their game.

Context presentation

Battlefield 3™ is a videogame published by Electronic Arts (EA) and developed by EA Digital Illusions Creative Entertainment (DICE). Released in October 2011, it runs within different Operating Systems: Microsoft Windows, Playstation 3 and Xbox 360.

This example focuses on the multiplayer mode: settled in a modern warfare environment, several game modes are proposed. We chose the *Conquest* mode, where two teams (up to 32 players on each team) are fighting for the capture of control points. When the game starts, the player needs to select a character class (*Assault, Support, Engineer, Recon*) which gives access to a specific set of weapons and items. Each player has also access to different vehicles (jeeps, tanks, aircrafts...) scattered on the battlefield at predefined positions.

Modeling process

The models presented in this section have been built upon interviews with two frequent players and additional data

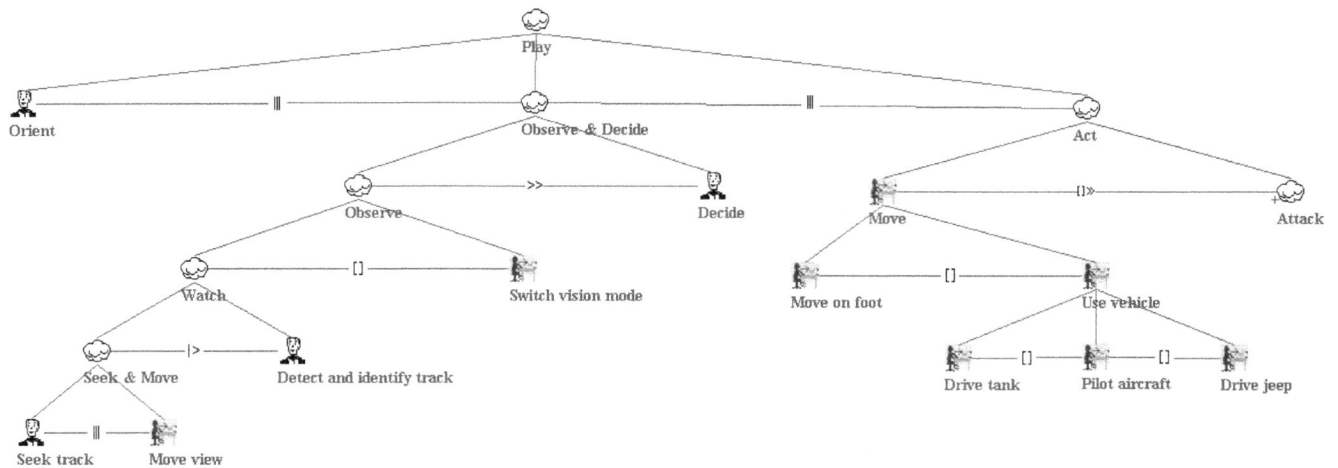

Figure 6: portion of the CTT tree for a Battlefield 3™ player in Conquest mode.

extracted from the official website (available on http://www.battlefield.com/battlefield3/).

The transition addressed in this example concerns the task of moving "on foot" in the environment to the task of driving a vehicle, and particularly a tank. Although this transition is triggered by the player, the two tasks are quite different and the switch might impact the player's SA.

Task Model
The CTT tree presented in Figure 6 describes the tasks that can be attained by the player. We purposely collapsed the *Attack* task for space sake, our focus being on the *Move on foot* and *Drive tank* tasks. The first is a subtask of the *Move* task while *Drive tank* is a sub-subtask of *Move*. The fact that these tasks don't belong to the same level is not an issue: the *Drive tank* task is a particularization of the *Use vehicle* one (which is a sibling of *Move on foot*).

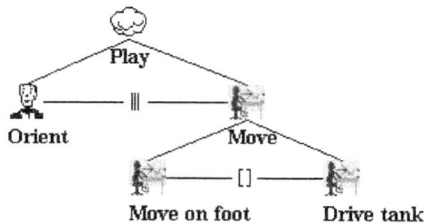

Figure 7: schematization of the switch between walking and driving the tank.

During the entire playing task, in parallel with the different tasks of the action branch, the *Orient* task is executed by the player. It consists of observing the environment with a focus on the landmarks and paths and is not goal-directed as would be the *Seek & Move* task.

In order to understand what tasks are active during the transition, we schematized it with the CTT notation on Figure 7. This simplified tree shows that the *Orient* task is always present in the background while moving (whichever moving mean is used).

Situation Awareness Model
We built a SA model composed of 57 nodes and 77 edges as shown on Figure 8. In order to illustrate the principle of the methodology, we focused on the SA elements required for the completion of the two transitioning tasks and elements relative to other tasks are not all represented here.

Task/SA Elements Association
The association step combines the SA model with the simplified CTT tree corresponding to our transition (Figure 7). Figure 8 displays this association step:

- elements colored in salmon are associated with the *Move on foot* task;
- elements colored in green (white labels) are associated with the *Drive tank* task;
- elements shared between both of *Move*'s subtasks are colored with a green and salmon gradient background;
- elements colored in purple (white labels) are associated with the *Orient* task.

During the transition, the *Orient* task is distributed to both transitioning tasks as it occurs concomitantly with these tasks. In terms of SA graphs, the SA elements corresponding to this task (the purple ones) are thus present in both graphs associated with the *Move*'s subtasks. Elements associated with both task during the transition have a dot-and-dash border.

Transition Analysis
During the switch between the two moving tasks, several changes on SA requirements occur, which may impact the player's SA.

While the *Move on foot* task requires a few elements of its own, the *Drive tank* task adds a number of new elements related to the tank that the player needs to be aware of (such as its role in the tank crew for instance). Figure 9 presents two screenshots of the videogame interface before and after the transition (the player enters the tank).

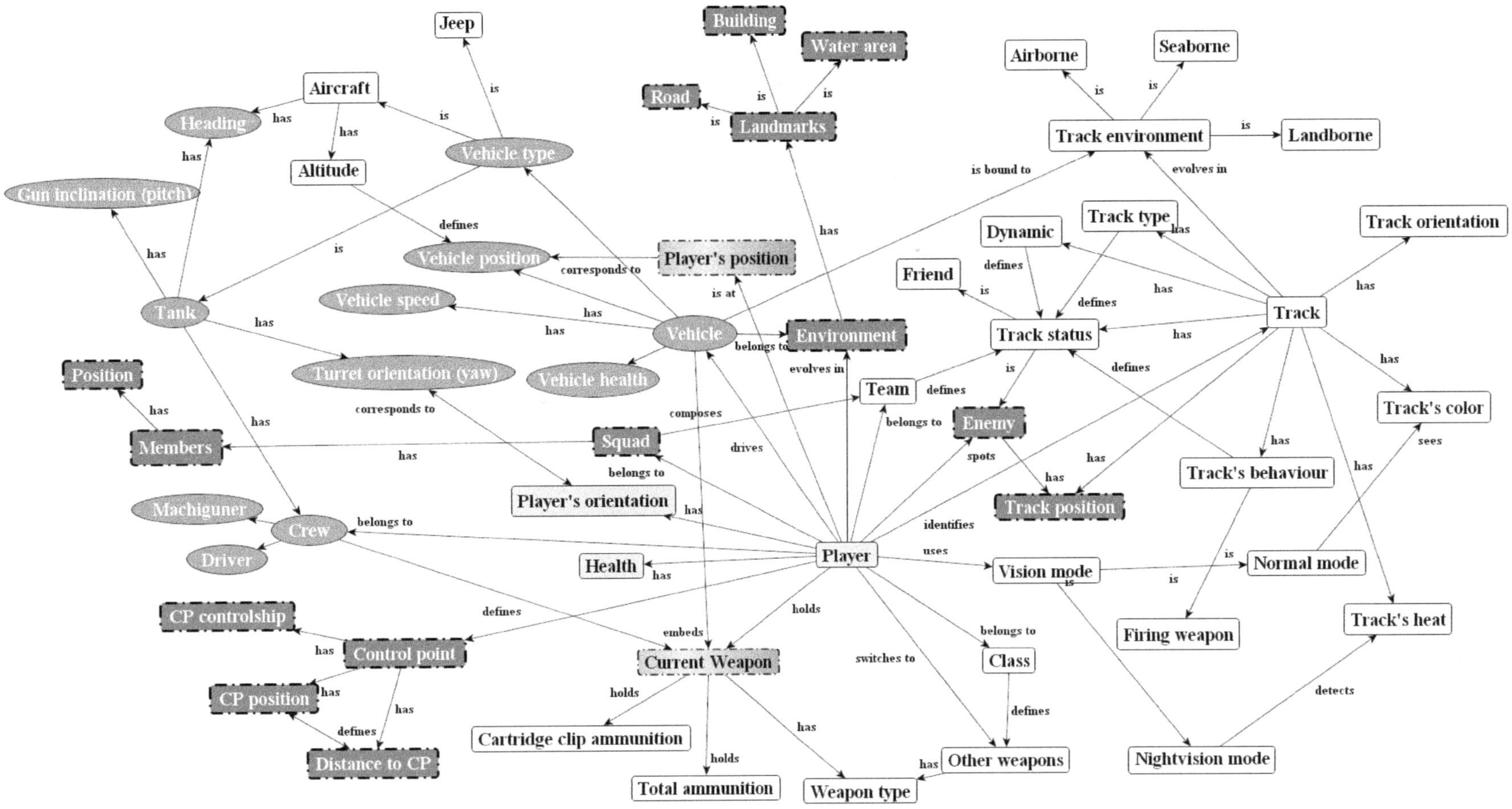

Figure 8: portion of the DSA graph for a Battlefield 3™ player in Conquest mode.

Legend:

Player — Elements associated with the *Move on foot* task

Crew — Elements associated with the *Drive tank* task

Road — Elements associated with the *Orient* task

Notes:

Elements common to the *Move on foot* and *Drive tank* tasks have a salmon & green gradient background color.

Elements with a dot-and-dash border are associated to both tasks during the transition: the *Orient* is concomitant to these tasks, thus always shared.

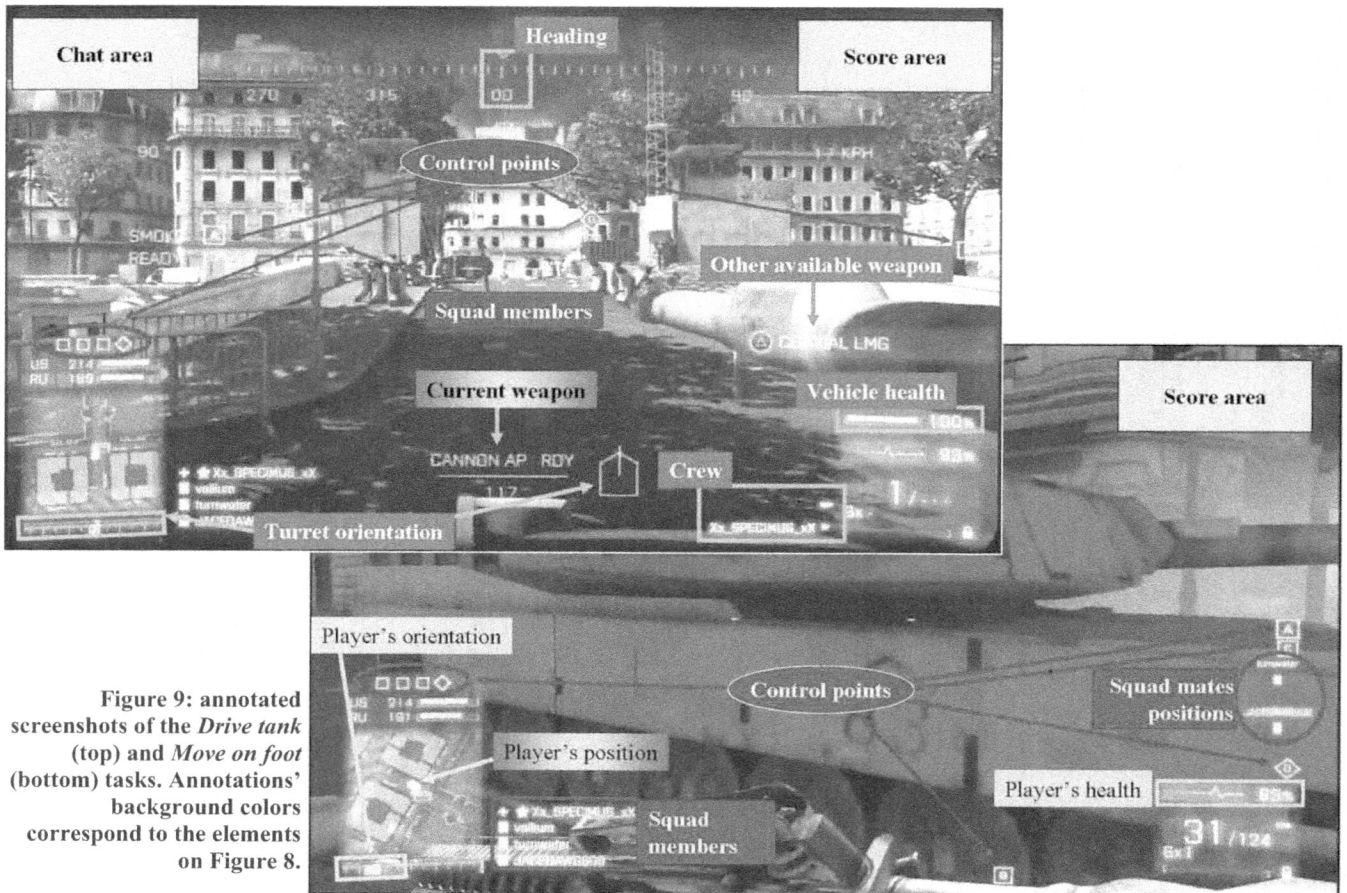

Figure 9: annotated screenshots of the *Drive tank* (top) and *Move on foot* (bottom) tasks. Annotations' background colors correspond to the elements on Figure 8.

Tversky Ratio

Amongst the 57 nodes, 3 are specific the *Move on foot* task, 12 to the *Drive tank* one, 2 are shared between those two tasks and 14 are common to the two contexts as they are associated with the *Orient* task. Tversky ratio for the transition is 0.52 if we set α and β to 1 (both tasks are considered of equal importance). This similarity score doesn't provide strong information about the type of transition studied.

Largest Common Subgraphs

When looking for the Largest Common Subgraphs to both tasks (amongst dot-and-dashed elements), we found four independent subgraphs:

- The "environment" subgraph regroups the different elements related to the landmarks and corresponds to information available on the minimap.

- The "control point" subgraph regroups the elements related to the different mission objectives (points to capture). They are displayed on the interface through "floating" pictograms.

- The "squad" subgraph relates to squad information. The members are listed on the bottom-left corner of the

interface and are visible through "floating" blue pictograms when in the field of view.

- The last subgraph is a 2-node subgraph, related to spotted enemies. These enemies are marked on the interface (with a "floating" pictogram and a mark on the minimap).

From this analysis, the Human Factors expert can express different suggestions: grouping elements from one subgraph on the interface, and accompanying the evolution of certain elements during the transition. The subgraphs extracted here all correspond to "geographical" information which are displayed graphically and will be impacted if the tank doesn't have the same orientation as the player.

Instances of recommendations may be to accompany the switch with a *third-to-first person* point of view, displaying the tank from outside for a few seconds with the same angle as the player's before entering, thus providing awareness about the change in object's position relatively to the new orientation.

Extraction of Salience

The common subgraphs are associated with the *Orient* task. Amongst the two shared elements between the moving tasks, *Player's position* and *Current weapon*, only the latter is impacted by the transition. Indeed, the player's position doesn't change when entering the tank. However, the player switches weapon.

The *Current weapon* node has 6 edges linked to it, making it a salient element. When entering a tank, the role taken by the player in the crew (driver/gunner versus machine-gunner) defines the weapons they can use. In order to enhance the awareness about the weapon switch, we can display a temporary message indicating what weapon is now equipped. This temporary piece of information would strengthen the other elements displayed (weapon image, quantity of ammunition available, crew membership status…).

New Elements

12 new SA elements are introduced with the *Drive Tank* task. Five are directly linked to elements associated with the *Move on foot* task (*Player's position, Current weapon, Crew, Vehicle* and *Turret orientation*). We addressed the 2 first in the previous sections, and the *Crew* and *Vehicle* elements are linked to the previous ones. However, the *Turret orientation*, which can be different from the tank's body orientation, is signaled through a pictogram (at the bottom of the screen), but additional SA could be provided through a third-to-first-person-view animation [7].

Expert's recommendations may be assessed with end-users through user tests based on mock-ups or prototypes resulting from these recommendations.

CONCLUSION AND FUTURE WORK

In this article, we have presented a methodology for design of complex systems' Human-Computer Interfaces. This methodology adopts a model-based approach in order to capture and formalize operators' activity and relies on these models to lessen impact of task transitions on operators' Situation Awareness.

To detect and tackle the issues raised by the different transitions, we proposed a set of quantitative and qualitative comparison methods which highlight the common and distinctive features between two tasks composing a transition. An illustrative example has been provided applying the methodology to a popular First Person Shooter videogame (Battlefield 3™), with a focus on a player entering a tank in multiplayer mode.

The methodology presented in this article is currently being applied in the context of an industrial study on Unmanned Aerial Vehicles (UAV) [30]. The data collected in this study (through operators' interviews and expert reports) will feed the Task and SA models and serve as a first empirical validation step for our methodology.

In addition to this empirical validation, we are developing an applicative tool supporting the three first steps of our methodology. The tool will allow fast and easy modeling of operators' activity, support task/SA elements association and provide support for the different task analysis means

proposed in this article. We designed the tool to be used as a mobile application: it will serve as a basis for dialogue with system operators (during the elicitation and validation phases), and could be used as a support for discussions. We plan to use this tool in the context of other industrial projects in order to assess, validate and/or tweak the methodology.

From a more theoretical point of view, some perspectives are also being addressed:

- We would like to assess the effect of transition on operators' Situation Awareness in relationship with the similar/distinctive features associated with each task. This study could feed the fourth and last step of the methodology as recommendations on UI design.

- In this article, we approach the issues raised through the *design* angle. But we believe that this methodology can be used as an *evaluation* tool for improvement of existing complex systems and will study this possibility in our future works.

- Finally, in order to address collaborative and multi-modal systems, we may study the use of CTT extensions such as COMM [14].

ACKNOWLEDGMENTS

The work presented is partly funded by the French Procurement Agency (DGA) as a Ph.D. Thesis grant. The authors would like also to thank the anonymous reviewers.

REFERENCES

1. Allport, A., Styles, E.A., and Hsieh, S. Shifting Intentional Set: Exploring the Dynamic Control of Tasks. *Attention and Performance 15*, 3 (1994), 421-452.

2. Altmann, E.M. Advance Preparation in Task Switching: What Work is Being Done? *Psychological Science 15*, 9 (2004), 616-622.

3. Bengoetxea, E. Inexact Graph Matching Using Estimation of Distribution Algorithms. 2002, Ph.D. Thesis.

4. Crandall, B., Klein, G.A., and Hoffman, R.R. *Working minds: A Practitioner's Guide to Cognitive Task Analysis*. The MIT Press, 2006.

5. Dessart, C.-E., Genaro Motti, V., and Vanderdonckt, J. Showing User Interface Adaptivity by Animated Transitions. *Proc. EICS*, ACM Press (2011), 95-104.

6. Dismukes, K., Young, G., and Sumwalt, R. Cockpit Interruptions and Distractions. *ASRS Directive*, 10 (1998), 4-9.

7. Draper, M.H., Calhoun, G., Ruff, H., et al. Transition Display Aid for Changing Camera Views in UAV Operations. *Proc. HUMOUS*, Télécom Bretagne (2008), 67-78.

8. Dubois, E., Nigay, L., and Troccaz, J. Assessing continuity and compatibility in augmented reality systems. *Universal Access in the Information 1*, 4 (2002), 263-273.

9. Endsley, M.R. Toward a Theory of Situation Awareness in Dynamic Systems. *Human Factors 37*, 1 (1995), 32-64.

10. Florins, M., Trevisan, D.G., and Vanderdonckt, J. The Continuity Property in Mixed Reality and Multiplatform systems: a Comparative Study. *Proc. CADUI*, Springer (2005), 323–334.

11. Godbole, A. and Smari, W.W. A Methodology and Design Process for System Generated User Interruption based on Context, Preferences, and Situation Awareness. *IEEE International Conference on Information Reuse & Integration*, (2006), 608-616.

12. ISO, #8807. LOTOS - A Formal Description Technique Based on the Temporal Ordering of Observational Behaviour. 1989.

13. Jones, D.G. and Endsley, M.R. Sources of Situation Awareness Errors in Aviation. *Aviation, Space, and Environmental Medicine 67*, 6 (1996), 507–512.

14. Jourde, F., Laurillau, Y., and Nigay, L. COMM Notation for Specifying Collaborative and Multimodal Interactive systems. *Proc. EICS*, ACM Press (2010), 125-134.

15. MacLeod, C.M. Half a Century of Research on the Stroop Effect: an Integrative Review. *Psychological Bulletin 109*, 2 (1991), 163-203.

16. McFarlane, D.C. and Latorella, K.A. The Scope and Importance of Human Interruption in Human-Computer Interaction Design. *Human-Computer Interaction 17*, 1 (2002), 1-61.

17. McFarlane, D.C. Comparison of Four Primary Methods for Coordinating the Interruption of People in Human-Computer Interaction. *Human-Computer Interaction 17*, 1 (2002), 63-139.

18. Monsell, S. Task Switching. *Trends in Cognitive Sciences 7*, 3 (2003), 134-140.

19. Mori, G., Paternò, F., and Santoro, C. CTTE: Support for Developing and Analyzing Task Models for Interactive System Design. *IEEE Transactions on Software Engineering 28*, 8 (2002), 797-813.

20. Paternò, F., Mancini, C., and Meniconi, S. ConcurTaskTrees: A Diagrammatic Notation for Specifying Task Models. *Proc. of the IFIP TC13 International Conference on HCI*, (1997), 362–369.

21. Paternò, F. ConcurTaskTrees: An Engineered Approach for Task Models. In *The Handbook of Task Analysis for Human-Computer Interaction*. Lawrence Erlbaum Associates Publishers, 2004, 483-500.

22. Rogers, R.D. and Monsell, S. Costs of a Predictable Switch between Simple Cognitive Tasks. *Journal of Experimental Psychology 124*, 2 (1995), 207-231.

23. Rousseau, R., Tremblay, S., and Breton, R. Defining and Modeling Situation Awareness: A Critical Review. In S. Banbury and S. Tremblay, eds., *A Cognitive Approach To Situation Awareness: Theory And Application*. Ashgate, 2004, 3-21.

24. Salmon, P.M., Stanton, N.A., Jenkins, D.P., Walker, G.H., Young, M.S., and Aujla, A. What really is going on? Review, Critique and Extension of Situation Awareness Theory. *Engineering Psychology and Cognitive Ergonomics LNCS*, 4562 (2007), 407–416.

25. Schlienger, C., Conversy, S., Chatty, S., Mertz, C., and Anquetil, M. Improving Users' Comprehension of Changes with Animation and Sound: An Empirical Assessment. *Proc. of the 11th IFIP TC 13 International Conference on HCI*, (2007), 207–220.

26. Scott, S.D., Mercier, S., Cummings, M.L., and Wang, E. Assisting Interruption Recovery in Supervisory Control of Multiple UAVs. *Proc. HFES Annual Meeting 50*, 5 (2006), 699-703.

27. Stanton, N.A., Salmon, P.M., Walker, G.H., and Jenkins, D. Genotype and Phenotype Schemata as Models of Situation Awareness in Dynamic Command and Control Teams. *International Journal of Industrial Ergonomics 39*, 3 (2009), 480-489.

28. Stanton, N.A., Stewart, R., Harris, D., et al. Distributed situation awareness in dynamic systems: theoretical development and application of an ergonomics methodology. *Ergonomics 49*, 12-13 (2006), 1288-1311.

29. Tversky, A. Features of Similarity. *Psychological Review 84*, 4 (1977), 327-352.

30. Villaren, T., Madier, C., Legras, F., Leal, A., Kovacs, B., and Coppin, G. Towards a Method for Context-Dependent Allocation of Functions. *Proc. of HUMOUS*, ONERA-ISAE (2010).

Exploring Design Principles of Task Elicitation Systems for Unrestricted Natural Language Documents

Hendrik Meth, Alexander Maedche, Maximilian Einoeder
Chair of Information Systems IV and Institute for Enterprise Systems
University of Mannheim
Mannheim, Germany
{meth, maedche, einoeder}@eris.uni-mannheim.de

ABSTRACT

During the design of interactive systems, user tasks need to be identified within natural language documents (like interview transcripts, support messages or workshop memos) and be transformed into task models. This time-consuming and error-prone analysis process demands for automation, however corresponding software support is still sparse. This paper describes a Design Science Research project, which explores design principles for a system aiming to close this gap. To evaluate the principles, they are instantiated in an innovative artifact called REMINER which combines Information Retrieval, Natural Language Processing and Annotation technology. The artifact can be used to semi-automatically identify user tasks from unrestricted natural language documents and to organize them into task models. Results of two extensive evaluations of the artifact show, that it considerably addresses the underlying problem areas of this process.

Author Keywords

Task Elicitation; Requirements Elicitation; Design Science.

ACM Classification Keywords

D.2.1 [**Software Engineering**]: Requirements / Specifications – *Tools*.

INTRODUCTION

Approximately 80% of software requirements are recorded in natural language [12]. Using analysis methods like contextual inquiries or focus groups, results in unrestricted natural language documents, as interview transcripts, or workshop memos instead of formal models or notations. In contrast to already processed texts like narrative scenarios, these documents do not use a controlled (or restricted) natural language. Controlled natural languages are well-defined subsets of natural languages that have beenrestricted with respect to their grammar and lexicon to produce less complex and less ambiguous texts [16]. To be able to proceed with subsequent design activities (e.g. visualize the interaction or create mockups), these texts need to be analyzed to identify single user tasks and create corresponding task models.

Over the course of a software development project, with a growing amount of these requirements documents, more and more information becomes available. Consequently, the analysis becomes time-consuming, error-prone and dull, especially if it is repeated multiple times, whenever updates to previously existing documents become available [2, 7]. In a study about current requirements analysis practice, Mich et al. [12] asked more than 150 software developers to name the two things in their job they would like to do more efficiently. The activity which was named most frequently (46%) was 'identify user requirements' [12]. In the same study participants have been asked about the most useful thing to improve general day-to-day efficiency of this task: The majority (69%) chose the option 'automation'. However, as illustrated in the next section, existing systems only partially fulfill this requirement.

Consequently, this paper describes a design science research project, which aims at deriving design principles of an accordant system and evaluating the principles based on a corresponding prototype. The prototype can be used to semi-automatically identify tasks from unrestricted natural language documents and to organize these requirements into task models providing a handover to subsequent UI design activities.

The remainder of the paper is organized in the following sections: The first section summarizes the state of the art in task elicitation systems and includes an identification of the research gap and the research question. This is followed by an overview of the overall methodology used in this research project. Subsequently the conceptualization and implementation of the artifact is described and the results of a first expert evaluation of the prototype are summarized. The last section concludes with the discussion of the results and next steps of our project.

RELATED WORK

Various attempts have been made to improve task elicitation based on documents written in natural language both in the field of Human Computer Interaction [4, 9, 18] as well as in the field of Requirements Engineering [1, 2].

In the **Human Computer Interaction** domain, Tam et al. [18] developed a user-task elicitation system named U-TEL that enables designers to transform passages of a textual scenario into elements of three models: action names

EICS'12, June 25–26, 2012, Copenhagen, Denmark.
Copyright 2012 ACM 978-1-4503-1168-7/12/06...$10.00.

(relevant for task models), user classes (relevant for user models), and objects names (relevant for domain models). The allocation can be conducted either manually or automatically. Brasser & vander Linden [4] propose the use of natural language parsing to automatically extract task information from written task narratives. Their system extracts two kinds of information: domain information (i.e., actors and objects) and procedural information (e.g., "when the user saves a file,..."). Lemaigre et al. [9] developed a tool for model elicitation from textual scenarios for the purpose of conducting model-driven engineering of user interfaces. Their artifact employs manual classification, dictionary-based classification, and nearly natural language understanding based on semantic tagging and chunk extraction. It uses a more detailed classification scheme than former works.

In the **Requirements Engineering** domain, Abrams et al. [1] introduce an Eclipse-based tool called Architects' Workbench (AWB), which can be used to create consistent requirements and design models and (hyper)link them with source data (e.g. in form of workshop memos). A similar functionality is offered by the descriptive module of IBM Rational Doors[1]. Ambriola & Gervasi [2] present CIRCE, an environment supporting requirements modeling and analysis by parsing requirements expressed in natural language. Users can access different views on the requirements and the system automatically models requirements in UML or provides other views on them.

Our artifact addresses several shortcomings of these works:

Restricted automation: To support the previously depicted time-consuming and error-prone analysis task, there should be at least a partial automation. However, both the AWB and the descriptive module of IBM Rational Doors only provide functionality for manual task elicitation.

Limitation to restricted natural language: All works mentioned focus on the processing of textual scenarios or other text documents that already contain a certain level of formalization and a controlled vocabulary. This requires a human pre-processing of the initially collected data like interview transcripts, support messages or workshop memos.

Restricted usage of domain knowledge: To enable automated task elicitation, a knowledge base with relevant terms is required. These terms can be either domain-independent (e.g. the verb "select") or domain-specific (e.g. the noun "travel destination"). However, only in the works presented by Ambriola & Gervasi [2] and Lemaigre et al. [9] domain knowledge is used to support the automatic elicitation process. This leaves the identification of domain-specific task elements to be a manual activity, requiring users to have significant domain expertise and spend additional time.

Large knowledge building efforts: All depicted works require building up a knowledge base in a separate, explicit process. The explicit creation of a knowledge base can be very time-consuming and therefore put the added value of the automatism into question.

In summary, no existing artifact was identified, that (partially) automates both task elicitation and the creation of (domain-specific) knowledge and could be applied to unrestricted natural language documents. This gap shall be closed by answering the following research question:

Which design principles need to be followed to support the elicitation of task models from unrestricted natural language documents?

METHODOLOGY
To be able to shape and evaluate the design principles, which were addressed in the research question, an instantiation of these principles in an artifact is proposed. We therefore follow a Design Science approach, as suggested by Hevner et al. [8], with multiple iterations and continuous user feedback. In the following, the methods used in each of the two development cycles are depicted in more detail.

Cycle 1
The first cycle of the research project was started by conducting an intensive literature review and expert interviews to create problem awareness. Based on the joint results of these activities, preliminary design principles were derived. Following these design principles, usage scenarios and personas for the artifact were specified. Building upon these first requirements a second literature study led to different design alternatives addressing the preliminary principles. Based on these alternatives, design decisions were made in a first conceptualization. This comprised a module structure describing the main functionality of the artifact and a visualization with static mockups using the mockup software Balsamiq Mockups[2]. In a next step, an interactive Powerpoint-based prototype was developed, illustrating the entire functionality of the artifact for the first implementation cycle, which was then evaluated.

In the evaluation, expert interviews were conducted, focusing on formative feedback to the artifact. To accomplish this, seven workshops were organized, each consisting of one to four requirements experts and two researchers (an overall number of 11 evaluators participated). All of the participants had extensive experience in Requirements Engineering (on average 9.7 years). The workshops lasted for about 1.5 hours and consisted of three parts: A pre-questionnaire, the presentation of the prototype and the evaluation. Each of the feedback items was then traced back to the related design decision and design principle in order to adapt the preliminary design principles.

As the evaluation based on a click-through with limited interactivity and the interaction was not done by the experts themselves but by the researcher, the focus of the evaluation was the artifact's perceived usefulness. Based on the collected feedback, the preliminary design principles were adapted for the next design cycle.

---

[1] www.ibm.com/software/awdtools/doors/productline/

[2] http://www.balsamiq.com/

Cycle 2

In the recently finished second iteration, the initial conceptualization was adapted, based on the received expert feedback and the adjusted design principles. In general, the adaption led to a leaner, more focused functional coverage of the artifact. For example social networking functionality, which was initially planned to be incorporated into the artifact, was neglected, as this functionality (against our first assumptions) added no direct benefit to the main use cases of the artifact. In contrast, the specific annotation functionality was detailed with additional features (e.g. to speed up the process).

Unlike the artifact version of the first cycle, the current version of the artifact is based on a programmed, running prototype. Whereas the first qualitative evaluation focused on the artifact's usefulness, the qualitative evaluation in the second design cycle concentrated on the artifact's ease of use. Accordingly, the artifact was evaluated by usability experts. We included usability consultants and HCI professors (additionally to requirements experts from software vendors) and conducted an overall number of five sessions with 9 experts. Again, the sample consisted of experienced participants (on average 4.7 years experience in usability engineering). The workshops were carried out in November and December 2011, lasting for about 1.5 hours. The evaluation was organized analogical to the first evaluations, except for an additional quantitative evaluation of the experts' attitude towards the design principles and their perceived implementation quality in the prototype.

CONCEPTUALIZATON AND IMPLEMENTATION

As previously described, we derived initial design principles for the prototype based on a thorough literature analysis and adapted these principles on the basis of the evaluation results of the first design cycle

Deduction of design principles

The design principles and the reasoning that motivates them are presented in the following.

Semi-automatic Task Elicitation

During the development of interactive systems, methods which produce large text documents containing uncontrolled natural language (e.g. interview memos, transcripts or meeting notes) are of particular importance [10, 14]. In contrast, subsequent development activities (like the design of the user interface) create structured artifacts (e.g. mockups), sometimes even based on abstract models (e.g. essential use cases or UML interaction diagrams) [5, 15]. The identification of tasks, which is necessary to build an abstract model or design artifact, can be error-prone and laborious and should be automated where possible [2, 7], therefore

DP1: Task Elicitation Systems should provide functionality to elicit tasks from unrestricted natural language documents in a semi-automatic mode.

Knowledge Usage and Creation

The automation of task elicitation requires a knowledge base containing both domain-independent and domain-specific knowledge [9]. To increase overall productivity, the creation of this knowledge base should require minimal additional efforts.

DP2: Task Elicitation Systems should support the usage of both domain-independent and domain-specific knowledge and require minimal efforts to build up this knowledge.

Context Traceability

To be able to build applications matching the original tasks, traceability is an important prerequisite [13]. When designing interactive systems, the incorporation of the context of use is of additional importance, resulting in a need for **context** traceability [3]. This becomes especially important when the context description is spread over multiple natural language documents, therefore

*DP3: Task Elicitation Systems should enable the user to trace back requirements to the original requestor **and** the context of use (e.g. described in multiple passages of different text documents)*

UI-Design Integration

Interaction Design projects design the user interface in an early phase, sometimes directly after the task elicitation [6, 17]. Therefore it is important to enable a seamless transition between requirements determination and UI design, to allow users a proper validation of their requirements [11]. The usage of software to connect both phases can improve re-use and consistency of the results and avoids double efforts, therefore

DP4: Task Elicitation Systems should enable a seamless transition from requirements determination to UI Design

Mapping of design principles to design decisions

During the conceptualization of the artifact, the identified design principles were mapped to design decisions. Design decisions are generic concepts which represent actual artifact capabilities and features to satisfy design principles. The results of the mapping process are depicted in table 1.

DP	Design decisions
DP1	• Semi-automatic task category highlighting • Usage of advanced Natural Language Processing and Information Retrieval algorithms to process uncontrolled natural language
DP2	• Usage of domain-specific and domain-independent knowledge items • Inclusion of manually highlighted words in knowledge base
DP3	• Visualization of requirements in original, sequential order within one document / scenario during creation of interaction flows • Linkage of design elements / requirements to individual text passages within requirements document
DP4	• Organization of extracted requirements into interaction flows, describing the sequence of interaction between system/UI and user

Table 1: Mapping of design decisions to design principles

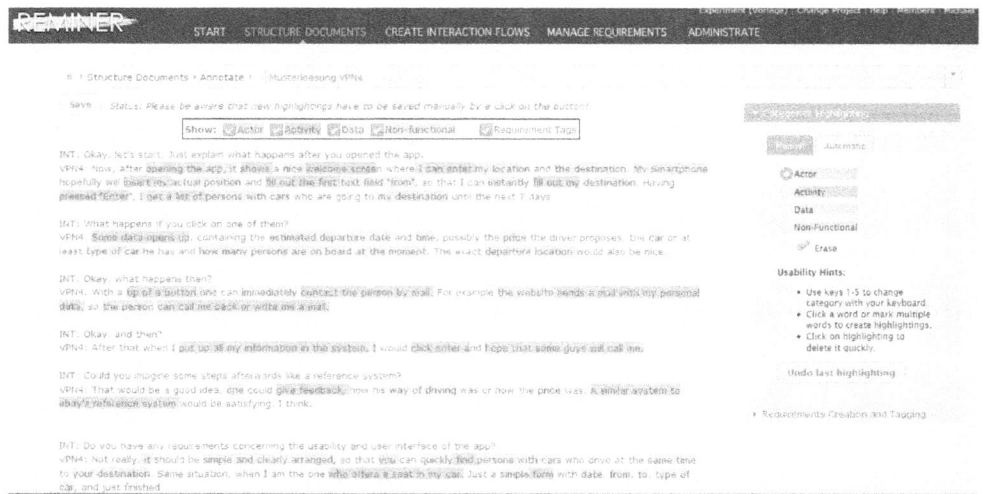

Figure 1: REMINER user interface for Category Highlighting

As described earlier, each design decision was translated into corresponding artifact characteristics, structured into two modules: 1) **Category Highlighting:** A module to semi-automatically structure natural language documents by highlighting different text passages according to their task category 2) **Interaction Flow Creation:** A module to organize the identified task elements into specific task models (called interaction flows), which represent an abstract, simplified and technology-agnostic description of the user interaction. Each of the modules is presented in detail in the following.

Category Highlighting

A common way to structure large, physical documents is the usage of text markers or highlighters while reading the document. We incorporated this metaphor into the prototype as a means to highlight different categories of tasks in previously collected documents like interview transcripts or workshop memos.

Task categories like actor, data/object and activity are represented by different highlighter colors in our prototype, following the idea to make the document structuring as intuitive as possible.

Figure 1 shows a screenshot of the corresponding REMINER user interface. The text (in this case an interview) contains highlightings, marking single words or entire text passages with the highlighter color of a specific requirements category. Two highlighting functionalities are provided, automatic and manual highlighting. In case of **automatic highlighting**, the system suggests highlightings based on three sub-processes. First, a preprocessing pipe prepares all input data for further usage. T hen, the knowledge to be used by the automatism is either uploaded to the system or retrieved from documents within the system. Finally, the highlighting suggestions are created

based on probabilistic similarity measures between unknown text elements and the previously created task knowledge. To be able to manually improve the results of the automatism, the suggestions can be altered or complemented with manual highlightings. During **manual highlighting**, the user can choose a highlighter color with a radio-button (or alternatively by pressing a key shortcut) and highlight words or text passages by clicking or marking the text on the left part of the UI (as depicted in figure 1).

Interaction Flow Creation

In the second step of our process, the identified task elements can be combined to interaction flows, a specific form of task models. Interaction flows are based on the idea of essential use cases to provide an abstract, simplified and technology-agnostic description of one interaction or task [5]. In contrast to essential use cases, interaction flows provide further structuring of each interaction step, using the previously indentified task elements.

As depicted in figure 2, **task elements** can be added to an interaction flow by selecting them from the tree structure on the right and dropping them into a grid, which represents the interaction flow. The tree structure contains all **task**

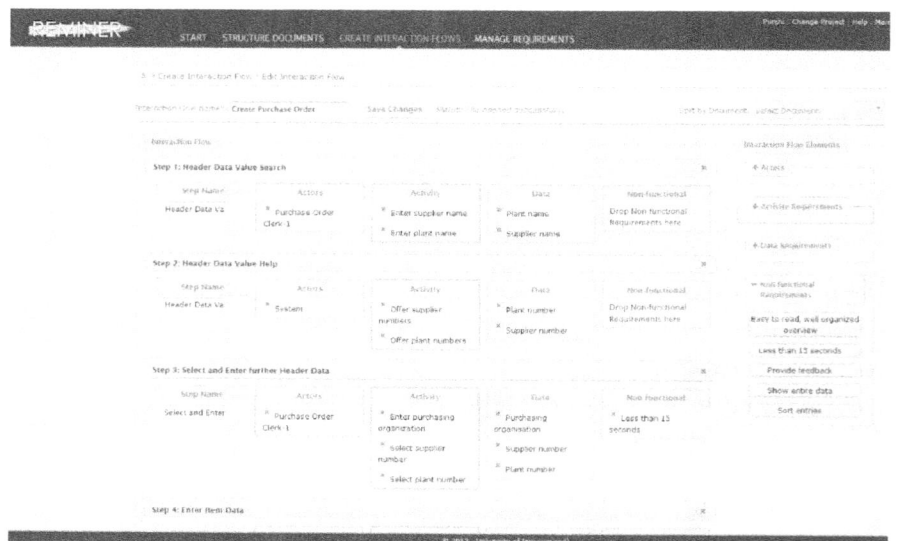

Figure 2: REMINER user interface for Interaction Flow Creation

208

elements identified in the project. Alternatively, a single document can be selected to display only the tasks coming from one document in their original order. The resulting interaction flow can be used in the subsequent design phase to inform UI designers about the interaction to be supported by the user interface.

EVALUATION

An overall number of 197 feedback items were collected during the evaluation workshops, some of which will be presented in the following.

Functional Evaluation (Cycle1)

Concerning the **highlighting** functionality, requirements experts from the software implementation sample pointed out, that for ERP implementations, during the highlighting of data elements, it would be helpful to compare requested data fields with existing data fields of the ERP system. This feedback was incorporated in the second design cycle, by providing a functionality to extend the corresponding knowledge base not only with extracted knowledge (from manual highlighting activities) but also with existing knowledge.

To improve the presented **interaction flows**, several evaluators requested a stronger linkage between process context and the resulting interaction flows, being indispensable information for the UI designer who shall create the resulting user interface. This will be incorporated into the prototype by showing the document context of a task (represented by the original phrases surrounding the highlighting in the source document) whenever it is clicked within the interaction flow.

Usability Evaluation (Cycle 2)

Multiple usability improvements addressing the **highlighting functionality** were identified during the evaluations. For example, the number of highlighting categories was reduced to avoid cognitive overload and the highlighting of single words was enabled by single-clicking on them (likewise for efficiency reasons).

Similarly, to improve the usability of **interaction flows**, it was suggested to use the same color-coding for requirements like during the highlighting, re-arrange and re-size various screen elements and incorporate features to reduce space consumption of the grid holding the interaction flow elements. All of these recommendations will be included in the upcoming, third cycle.

Overall Evaluation

Figure 3 shows the average results of the pre-questionnaire and post-questionnaire questions concerning the underlying design principles of the artifact. Concerning the attitude of the evaluators toward the design principles, the numbers show an overall medium to high accordance (values between 4.1 and 5.9), meaning that the principles targeted for the prototype are assessed as generally important for task elicitation systems. The value for "Knowledge Usage and Creation" is comparatively low, providing evidence, that this design principle might need to be revisited before the next design cycle is conceptualized.

The evaluation of the design principle implementation in the prototype itself shows comparably high values for "Semi-automatic Task Elicitation", "Knowledge Usage and Creation" and "Context Traceability" and an average value for "UI-Design Integration", which can serve as an additional indicator for improvement potential in the next design cycle (in combination with the qualitative feedback).

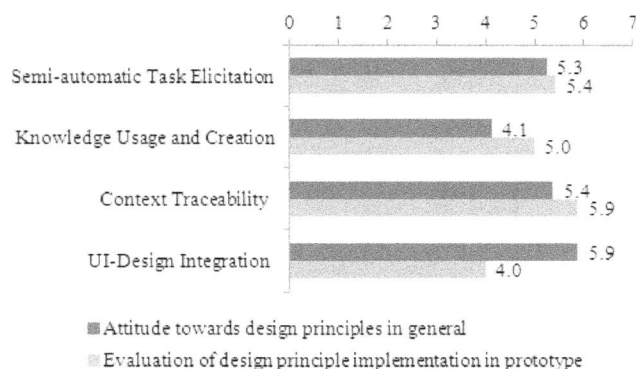

Figure 3: Evaluation of and attitude towards design principles

DISCUSSION

The presented work shows how artifact support for task elicitation can be improved. Extensive qualitative feedback was collected which was and will be the basis for further artifact refinements and evaluations. The evaluations resulted in a positive overall assessment of the prototype and its underlying design principles. Nevertheless, we are aware of several limitations of our work and issues that need to be addressed in future work.

The small sample size of our evaluations was sufficient for the primarily qualitative feedback which should be collected, but allow only limited generalization of the quantitative results. Additionally, the sampling of the study focused on large, German companies to keep the sample homogenous. Generalizations for smaller companies might therefore not be possible. Furthermore, as the conducted evaluations reflect expert opinions, only the **perceived** usefulness and the **perceived** ease of use of the artifact could be evaluated.

Our results are not restricted to the IS domain, but could be transferred to other engineering-related domains following a similar transformation process from unstructured to structured information to be able to model interaction (e.g. building machines with interaction capabilities). Consequently, from a theoretical point of view our study contributes to the design theory body of knowledge, deriving design principles which inform the development of IT systems that support task elicitation. From a practical point of view, results of our work can be used to improve existing commercial or non-commercial Task Elicitation and Requirements Engineering software packages by providing guidelines how to effectively support the task elicitation process.

In our next research activities, feedback from the second cycle, especially concerning the usability of the artifact, will be incorporated into the artifact to further improve it. Complementary to the primarily qualitative evaluations depicted in this paper, the resulting artifact will be quantitatively evaluated based on a lab experiment, measuring the initial results of the algorithm and the final results after the tool has been used by master IS students. The students will be trained in the principles of task elicitation and the usage of the artifact first. Then, based on given text documents, task elicitation productivity will be measured using our artifact in comparison to a comparison tool, which does not implement our design principles.

REFERENCES

1. Abrams, S. et al. Architectural thinking and modeling with the Architects' Workbench, *IBM Systems Journal 45*, 3 (2006), 481-500.

2. Ambriola, V. and Gervasi, V. On the Systematic Analysis of Natural Language Requirements with CIRCE, *Automated Software Engineering 13*, 1 (2006), 107–167.

3. Beyer, H. and Holtzblatt, K. *Contextual design: defining customer-centered systems.* Morgan Kaufmann Pub, 1998.

4. Brasser, M. and Vander Linden, K. Automatically eliciting task models from written task narratives, in *Proc., 4th International Conference on Computer-Aided Design of User Interfaces*(2002), 83-90.

5. Constantine, L. L. and Lockwood, L. A. D. Structure and style in use cases for user interface design, *Object Modeling and User Interface Design.* Addison-Wesley, Boston, 245–280, 2001.

6. Ferreira, J., Noble, J., and Biddle, R. Up-front interaction design in agile development, *Agile Processes in Software Engineering and Extreme Programming*, 2007, 9–16.

7. Hayes, J. H., Dekhtyar, A., and Sundaram, S. Text mining for software engineering: how analyst feedback impacts final results, in *ACM SIGSOFT Software Engineering Notes,* 30 (2005), 1–5.

8. Hevner, A.R., March, S. T., Park, J., and Ram, S. Design science in information systems research, *MIS Quarterly, 28,* 1 (2004), 75–105.

9. Lemaigre, C., Garcia, J. and Vanderdonckt, J. Interface Model Elicitation from Textual Scenarios, in *Proceedings of the Human-Computer Interaction Symposium* (2008), 53-66

10. Mao, J. Y., Vredenburg, K., Smith, P. W., and Carey, T. The state of user-centered design practice, *Communications of the ACM 48,* 3 (2005), 105–109.

11. Martinez, A., Estrada, H., Sánchez, J., and Pastor, O. From early requirements to user interface prototyping: A methodological approach, in *Proceedings of the 17th IEEE International Conference on Automated Software Engineering* (2002), 257–260.

12. Mich, L., Franch, M., and Novi Inverardi, P. L. Market research for requirements analysis using linguistic tools, *Requirements Engineering 9,* 1 (2004), 40-56.

13. Pohl, K. *Requirements Engineering: Fundamentals, Principles, and Techniques.* Springer Publishing Company, Incorporated, 2010.

14. Robertson, S. and Robertson, J. *Mastering the requirements process*, Addison-Wesley Professional, 2006.

15. Rumbaugh, J., Jacobson, I., and Booch, G. *The unified modeling language reference manual.* Addison Wesley, 1999.

16. Schwitter, R., Ljungberg, A. and Hood, D. Ecole: A look-ahead editor for a controlled language, in *Proceedings of the EAMT-CLAW03* (2003), 141-150

17. Sharp, H., Rogers, Y., and Preece, J. *Interaction design: beyond human-computer interaction.* Wiley, 2007.

18. Tam, R., Maulsby, D., and Puerta, A.R. U-TEL: A tool for eliciting user task models from domain experts, in *Proceedings of the 3rd international conference on Intelligent user interfaces*(1998), 77-80.

Reusable Decision Space for Mashup Tool Design

Saeed Aghaee
Faculty of Informatics,
University of Lugano (USI)
via Buffi 13, 6900 Lugano,
Switzerland
saeed.aghaee@usi.ch

Marcin Nowak
Faculty of Informatics,
University of Lugano (USI)
via Buffi 13, 6900 Lugano,
Switzerland
marcin.nowak@usi.ch

Cesare Pautasso
Faculty of Informatics,
University of Lugano (USI)
via Buffi 13, 6900 Lugano,
Switzerland
c.pautasso@ieee.org

ABSTRACT

Mashup tools are a class of integrated development environments that enable rapid, on-the-fly development of mashups—a type of lightweight Web applications mixing content and services provided through the Web. In the past few years there have been growing number of projects, both from academia and industry, aimed at the development of innovative mashup tools. From the software architecture perspective, the massive effort behind the development of these tools creates a large pool of reusable architectural decisions from which the design of future mashup tools can derive considerable benefits. In this paper, focusing on the design of mashup tools, we explore a design space of decisions comprised of design issues and alternatives. The design space knowledge not only is broad enough to explain the variability of existing tools, but also provides a road-map towards the design of next generation mashup tools.

Author Keywords

Mashup tools; software architecture; design rationale;

ACM Classification Keywords

D.2.2 Software Engineering: Design

INTRODUCTION

Mashup tools are interactive systems which target the needs of end-users developing a specific kind of Web applications, built of the reuse and composition of multiple Web data sources and Web services [5]. The past few years have witnessed a rapid growth of many interactive Mashup tools, both from research and industry, offering a broad range of characteristics and affordances. Some are based on visual composition languages [30], others feature a high degree of automation and liveness [47], many support collaborative development [20], engaging public and private online communities.

The challenges faced by mashup tools designers include the need for defining a high level descriptions of computations and integration logic to be combined with suitable abstractions to represent Web widgets, distributed Web services and

Web data sources as reusable components [14]. Mashups can be and are built by programmers using traditional Web technologies and tools [1], as shown on ProgrammableWeb[1], a directory listing thousands of mashups and Web APIs. The goal of most mashup tools is to enable non-programmers to build mashups, by making it easy [8] to quickly [29] reuse and reassemble whatever content, services, APIs and data sources can be found on the Web.

Architectural knowledge management [3] advocates the extraction of design knowledge from successful software projects in order to accumulate best practices [6], design patterns [7] and reusable architectural decisions. In this paper we survey the existing mashup tooling landscape with the goal of harvesting reusable architectural design decisions. The goal is to take a conscious approach to explicit design decisions, which is intended to result in higher quality software architectures. The decisions are structured into a design space, which (1) helps to classify and explain the heterogeneity of existing mashup tools; and (2) by enumerating relevant design issues and their dependencies, provides a valuable guidance model to mashup tool designers.

The rest of this paper is structured as follows: in the next section we describe the methodology we applied to extract the design issues and alternatives as well as to conduct our survey of mashup tools based on them. Next, we present the core of this paper consisting of the issues and alternatives that arise in the design of a selection of 22 mashup tools. Afterwards, we discuss how the issues and alternatives relate to each other in the context of the design of existing tools. Finally, the presentation of the related work is followed by the conclusions.

METHODOLOGY

In order to give a clear structure to the content collected in this paper, we have constructed a model (Figure 1) conforming to a simple, yet powerful decision metamodel proposed in [43] and used the corresponding tool[2] to gather and process the knowledge. The metamodel is comprised of design issues and, related to them, design alternatives. The design issues represent a design problem, while each design alternative serves as a potential solution.

Our model was constructed based on the knowledge gained from using/reading about existing mashup tools. In the surveyed literature, there are more than 60 mashup tools, from which we picked 22 tools based on their availability and their

---

[1] http://www.programmableweb.com/
[2] http://saw.inf.unisi.ch

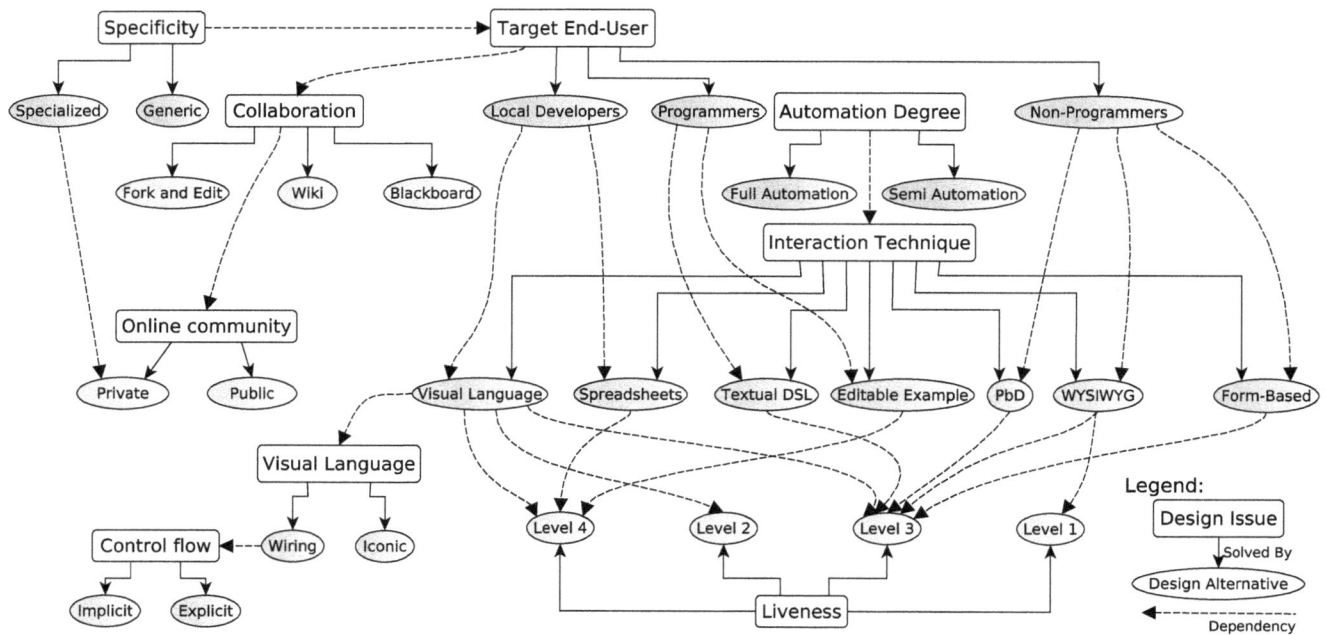

Figure 1. Mashup tool design dpace overview

representativeness to ensure that at least a concrete example corresponds to each design alternative. We further refined the knowledge into design decisions by eliminating overlapping issues and alternatives and dividing them into groups. The validation was conducted by checking whether the decision space covered all the issues found in the selected mashup tools. We prioritized those design issues with the most impact on the usability of mashup tools, seen as a specific class of interactive systems.

For the sake of readability, we classified the 9 design issues and 27 alternatives in three different groups (as shown colored in Figure 1): (1) Strategic (red), grouping the top level criteria regarding the user community where a mashup tool is supposed to be deployed; (2) Environment-specific (orange), collecting issues on the development environment where users are provided with facilities to develop and possibly execute and debug mashups; (3) Language (blue), concerning the design of mashup composition languages.

STRATEGIC DESIGN ISSUES FOR MASHUP TOOLS

Design Issue: Specificity

Mashups have gained a broad range of applications ranging from daily utilities of Web users to narrowly specialized domains. Soi and Baez [46], therefore, distinguish between specialized and generic mashup tools.

Alternative: Generic

The main characteristic of generic mashup tools is that they do not target any specific group of end-users or any particular application domain, but rather focus on addressing the daily needs of end-users. Generic mashup tools take advantage of publicly available Web resources. The growing number and

big diversity of these resources enable the creation of innovative mashups that can be published, discovered and used by other end-users.

Benefits: A generic tool has the potential to reach a wide range of end-users and become popular on the Web. Depending on the architecture of the tool, it can be further tailored to fit a particular domain or application [46].

Challenges: Due to the diversity and sheer number of end-users on the Web, it is a non-trivial task to assess and support the needs and abilities (i.e., programming skills) of all.

Example: *FeedRinse*[3] exemplifies a generic mashup tool. With the use of this tool, users can filter and combine multiple RSS feeds, and republish the results in a single RSS feed.

Alternative: Specialized

Recently, investigating the applications of mashups in different specialized domains has gained momentum. Examples of the use of mashups in specialized domains include enterprise computing [29], e-learning [16], bioinformatics [21], and telecom [4]. Specialized mashup tools support the development of mashups suited for these domains by mixing domain-related resources that can be either free or proprietary. One example of such domain-related resources could be a private enterprise database.

Benefits: The end-users targeted by specialized tools are often limited in number, homogeneous in terms of technical skills, and geared towards the same task. These factors help assess, evaluate, and improve the usability of the tool.

Challenges: Designing a mashup tool for a specialized domain requires an advanced, in-depth knowledge about that

---

[3]http://feedrinse.com/

domain. The specific functional and non-functional requirements for mashups within the domain (e.g., secure data access for enterprise data fusion) need to be extracted so that a suitable tool for domain-specific mashups can be designed.
Example: *Kapow Katalyst*[4], and the tool presented by Capuano et. al. [10] exemplify two specialized mashup tools targeting, respectively, telecom and e-learning domains.

Design Issue: Target End-user
As described by Nardi [41, p. 104], in terms of technical and programming skills, there is a spectrum of end-users, ranging from non-programmers to experienced programmers. In the middle of this spectrum lie professional end-users without programming skills but interests in computer and programming, who are referred to by Nardi as "local developers". Determining which group of end-users is targeted by a mashup tool is a design issue, as the tool should provide different affordances for a different group of end-users.

Alternative: Non-Programmers
Non-programmer do not have programming skills. Yet, they are interested in creating mashup as long as that does not require them to learn and use a programming language.

Benefits: A mashup tool created for non-programmers is designed to suit those with minimum technical skills. As a result, it will be usable and applicable to not only non-programmers, which constitute the majority of Web users, but also both local developers and programmers.
Challenges: Non-programmers should be provided with tools that limit their involvement in the development process to small customizations of predefined mashup templates, or execution of parametrized mashups.
Example: *Dapper*[5] is designed for non-programmers. It provides a set of easy-to-use toolchains to visually scrape content from a website and integrate it with Web feeds, without the need to get involved in the development process.

Alternative: Local Developers
Local developers are those non-programmers who usually have advanced knowledge in computer tools [41, p. 104]. They are willing to explore and harvest all the functionality of a mashup tool tailored for their abilities.

Benefits: Tools targeting local developers can provide composition functionality, where mashups can be assembled from scratch by composing predefined components or by customizing and changing existing examples and templates.
Challenges: Mashup tools for local developers must provide a very high level of abstraction that ideally hides all the underlying technical complexity of the mashup development. However, such a high level of abstraction usually comes at the price of sacrificing the expressive power of the tool. The challenge is thus to find a proper balance between them.
Example: *JOpera* [45] offers a high expressive power to create various types of mashups. Despite the visual language and the level of abstraction provided by the tool, creation of some complex mashups may still involve a small amount of coding in JavaScript and HTML.

---

[4]http://kapowsoftware.com/
[5]http://open.dapper.net/

Alternative: Programmers
Programmers have adequate programming skills and experience to develop mashups using programming and scripting languages (e.g., JavaScript and PHP).

Benefits: Programmers can produce high quality, feature-rich, and useful mashups, which can be later reused by non-programmers. Tools targeting programmers can provide both composition and component development features. Components can be then provided to local developers and non-programmers for reassembly and customization.
Challenges: The expressive power of the tool should not be compromised when compared to existing general-purpose programming and Web scripting languages for developing mashups.
Example: *Swashup* [36] is a Web-based development environment for a textual Domain-Specific Language (DSL) based on the Ruby on Rails framework (RoR).

Design Issue: Automation Degree
A mashup tool needs to leverage automation to lower the barriers of and enable on-the-fly mashup development. The automation degree of a mashup tool, hence, refers to how much of the development process can be undertaken by the tool on behalf of its users, and can be broken down into *semi-automation* and *full automation*.

Alternative: Full Automation
Full automation of mashup development eliminates the need for direct involvement of users in the development process. Instead, the users will gain a supervisory role with the opportunity to provide input (i.e., requirements), intervene in the development process, and validate the final result.

Benefits: Since the development process is carried out by the tool, the burden of learning is considerably lifted from the users. Also, if designed properly, it can significantly decrease the effort of mashup development.
Challenges: A common challenge is not to deviate from the user's needs by producing irrelevant mashups. The tool can allow users to iteratively validate the resulting mashup and in case of deviation to intervene in the development process. Even though this may partially address the challenge, users might encounter the risk of experiencing many iterations.
Example: *Piggy Bank* [27] uses semantic technologies to automate the extraction and mixing of content from different websites. It falls back to visual screen scraping techniques, in case the target website does not expose RDF data.

Alternative: Semi Automation
Semi-automatic tools partially automate mashup development by providing guidance and assistance. Still, their users are involved in the development process.

Benefits: Due to the direct involvement of the user in the development process, there is a lower probability of deviation from his/her needs, compared to automatic tools.
Challenges: The users should go through a relatively longer learning curve to be able to create their desired mashups. This presents a challenge to motivate and encourage end-users to learn how to use the tool.

Example: The majority of mashup tools are semi-automatic. RoofTop [25] automates and abstracts many complex aspects of mashup development. Yet, users need to actively select and connect widgets to create a mashup with it.

ENVIRONMENT-SPECIFIC DESIGN ISSUES

Design Issue: Liveness

In the context of visual languages, Tanimoto proposed the concept of *liveness* [47], according to which four levels of liveness are distinguished. We believe that the applicability of the concept can be found in the domain of mashups as well.

Alternative: Level 1. Flowchart as ancillary description

At the first level, a tool is just used to create prototype mashups that are not directly connected to any kind of run-time system. A prototype mashup usually only has the final user interface without underlying functionality.

Benefits: The main benefit is the relative simplicity of these tools. They are only used to create prototype mashups by allowing to design their user interfaces in a visual manner.

Challenges: The goal of the majority of mashup tools is to provide a development environment for creating executable mashups. However, tools supporting liveness level 1 only help to create non-executable prototype mashups.

Example: Microsoft Visio enables the creation of prototype mashups. The resulting prototypes can be fed with data and executed by Microsoft Excel [52].

Alternative: Level 2. Executable flowchart

The second level of liveness is characterized by the fact that the mashup design blueprint carries sufficient details to give it an executable semantics.

Benefits: A primary benefit of having (indirectly) executable blueprints is that its consistency (logical, semantical, or syntactical) can be verified. Another advantage is that such blueprint is self-contained in terms of documentation, hence can serve as reference for users and developers.

Challenges: The fact that design blueprints can be automatically transformed into executable mashups implies that they might need to carry on some amount of low-level technical design details, which may make them difficult to interpret by non-programmers.

Example: *Petals BPM*[6] is a Business Process Modeling Notation (BPMN) modeler that offers features such as validation, and allows the created diagrams to be exported to WS-BPEL format for the sake of execution using a different tool.

Alternative: Level 3. Edit triggered updates

Mashups characterized by the third level of liveness can be rapidly deployed into operation. Deployment in this case can be triggered for example by each edit-change or by an explicit action executed by the developer.

Benefits: Thanks to this feature, mashup designers and developers are released from the burden of going through a potentially time-consuming manual deployment process.

Challenges: Users need to be aware in which mode (design-time editor or run-time execution monitor) they are operating the mashup tool. Users may be unsure whether the design and runtime environments are in sync with each other, unless they manually press the "run" button, or make use of any other means to trigger the automatic redeployment of the mashup.

Example: A good example of a mashup tool of liveness level three is *JackBe Presto*[7]. In the tool design environment, there is a "run" button which automatically executes a mashup and switches the screen to the runtime environment used for debugging and monitoring purposes.

Alternative: Level 4. Stream-driven updates

The fourth level of mashup liveness is obtained by the tools that support live modification of the mashup code, while it is being executed.

Benefits: Designers are allowed to tinker with mashup code in the real time. In turn, changes are (almost) instantly observable, and therefore, quick adaptation is possible. As a result, the development cycle is very rapid.

Challenges: High design agility comes with the risk that uncontrolled changes to an operational system could make it fail. The same danger applies in case of live collaboration on mashup development that can potentially leave the system inconsistent. Finally, a challenge which designers need to face is that highly responsive environments can result in high costs of running the mashup, as – for example – remote Web services need to be invoked every time a change is done on the mashup code.

Example: *DashMash* [9] supports liveness at level 4 by merging the mashup design and runtime environments, and proving a mechanism to keep both of them synchronized.

Design Issue: Online Community

Online communities are an important resource in assisting end-users to program [41]. They can potentially support technical discussion as well as collaborative mashup categorization, sharing, rating, and recommendation [22]. An online community can take the form of a blog, a newsgroup, a chat room, or even a social network, depending on the role it is supposed to fulfill. From a security and privacy point of view, currently available online communities for mashup tools fall into two distinct types: *public*, and *private*.

Alternative: Public

The content published in public communities are accessible by any user on the Web who wishes to join them. This, however, does not imply that these communities do not require registration prior to accessing them.

Benefits: The added value of a public community lies in its great potential for growth, ultimately resulting in the increased number of the tool users.

Challenges: As the content shared in the community is public, users may refuse or refrain from sharing certain details.

Example: *Yahoo! Pipes*[8] maintains one of the largest public communities of mashup developers. Members of the community can share, discuss, reuse, and categorize mashups created with the Yahoo! Pipes tool.

---

[6] http://research.petalslink.org/display/petalsbpm/

[7] http://www.jackbe.com/enterprise-mashup/
[8] http://pipes.yahoo.com/

Alternative: Private

The authority to join a private or a gated community is granted on the basis of compliance with some special criteria. These criteria can be having an invitation or being a registered member of a certain organization. Private communities are usually small in number of users.

Benefits: The content stored in private communities is inaccessible to non-members, resulting in a higher level of confidence for users to discuss issues related to their organization.

Challenges: Private communities require much more effort to start. Content should be mostly created by the community staff, since with a small number of users, there will not be much user-generated content initially.

Example: *IBM Mashup Center*[9] allows enterprises to build their own private community, organized around a centralized catalogue. Users can publish mashups to this catalogue so that other users can discover and reuse them.

Design Issue: Collaboration

From a software development methodology point of view, mashup development is a form of agile development [26], which is characterized by a high degree of collaboration between the involved actors. Mashup development can also be performed in a collaborative manner [15], provided that it is supported by the mashup tool. To this end the availability of on online community is both essential and beneficial. To date, this support has came in different forms which we refer to as *fork and edit*, *wiki*, and *blackboard*.

Alternative: Fork and Edit

Fork and edit is a common method for enabling collaborative mashup development that is typically based on online communities. The method relies on a scenario, where a user creates and shares a mashup within the tool community that is later found by another user, who then edits a copy of it or reuses it inside a new mashup, and finally shares the resulting mashup back to the same community so that it can be further modified and recursively embedded into other mashups.

Benefits: This method encourages reuse and sharing amongst users. It also eliminates any chance of version or instance conflicts, due to the fact that each different instance derived from the same mashup is associated with a different user.

Challenges: Mashup instance duplication, i.e., storing multiple copies of the same mashup associated to different users, should be prevented. Another challenge is that fork and edit-based system inherently do not provide a straightforward way to merge two or more mashups originated from the same mashup into a single one.

Example: *Yahoo! Pipes* is an example of a collaborative tool following the fork and edit/reuse method. The tools is equipped with a large online community that offers mashup sharing, search, and cloning features.

Alternative: Wiki

Collaborative mashup development can be enabled with the use and adaptation of the wiki method, whose main features include versioning, multi-author editing, and changelogs.

Benefits: The working copy of a mashup is always writeable because all changes are local until committed. Moreover, commits are atomic, i.e., either all or no changes are committed. Another clear benefit is the version history allowing a user to track changes and revert back to earlier versions.

Challenges: Storing and keeping track of different versions of a mashup created by a tool may require lots of space. The challenge concerning users is that they may find it difficult to avoid and resolve editing conflicts.

Example: *Lively Wiki* [33] is a collaborative mashup tool based on the wiki method. It combines the wiki principles with a direct-manipulation user interface, through which users can create and edit mashups.

Alternative: Blackboard

A blackboard-based environment manages collaborative development in a realtime basis. All the involved users can observe changes to the mashup at the time they happen.

Benefits: The overall collaborative development process is much faster, since changes made by users take effect immediately without requiring any intermediate action (e.g., commit, or publish). As a result, conflicts are not encountered.

Challenges: The consistency and validity of the mashup need to be ensured. It can be addressed by providing versioning and history tracking. Another technical challenge is also to minimize the communication latency amongst the participants so as to ensure a real-time experience.

Example: *Sqwelch* [20] is a semantically-enabled mashup tool that allows blackboard-like collaboration amongst its users to create mashups. This mashup tool does not support versioning and history tracking.

LANGUAGE-LEVEL DESIGN ISSUES

Design Issue: Interaction Technique

There have been a number of interaction techniques through the use of which the barriers of programming can be lifted from end-users [39]. We list below some representative techniques which have been used by mashup tools. Some tools are known for using multiple techniques in combination.

Alternative: Textual DSL

Domain Specific Languages (DSL [19]) are languages targeted to address specific problems in a particular domain. Textual DSLs define textual syntax, that may or may not resemble an existing general-purpose programming language.

Benefits: DSLs, particularly those built internally on top of a general purpose programming language, usually offer a high expressive power.

Challenges: In terms of learning barriers, textual DSLs are similar to programming languages.

Example: *Swashup* [36] is a textual DSL for the mashup domain built on top of the Ruby on Rails framework.

Alternative: Visual Language

A visual programming language, as opposed to a textual programming language, is any programming language that uses visual symbols, syntax, and semantics [38].

Benefits: If designed properly, a visual language offers a high level of abstraction, thus better targeting the needs of end-users. One of their strengths is their ability to support more than one view at the same time [37], e.g. showing both the design and runtime environments in the same screen.

Challenges: A potential challenge is to make the most of the available screen space (i.e., visual scalability), as the ability to layout diagrams in two dimensions can be outweighed by the complexity and the size of the diagrams.

Example: SABRE [35] is based on a visual language corresponding to Reo [2], a coordination language that is used to define the logic of the mashup.

Alternative: What-You-See-Is-What-You-Get

In the context of mashups, WYSIWYG (What You See Is What You Get) enables users to create and modify a mashup on a graphical user interface which is similar to the one that will appear when the mashup runs.

Benefits: Since users always see the resulting mashup, the whole development process might be streamlined. Another potential benefit is the increase of the tool directness. Users place visual objects exactly in the places where they are meant to be during the runtime.

Challenges: The application logic of a mashup such as data filtering and conversion happens in the backend where is not visible in the graphical user interface, and therefore is not directly accessible for modification using a WYSIWYG tool.

Example: ServFace Builder [42] is a WYSIWYG tool. End-users can drag-drop-and-connect a set of boxes (widgets) whose current visual positions are the same both in the design time and runtime.

Alternative: Programming by Demonstration

As opposed to direct programming, PbD (Programming by Demonstration) suggests to teach a computer by example how to accomplish a particular task [11].

Benefits: This is a powerful technique that helps remove much of programming barriers. Users demonstrate what is the mashup they want without worrying about how it should be programmatically implemented.

Challenges: Termination conditions and branches are two important artifacts in the design of a mashup control flow graph—a graph that defines the execution order of components and statements. These artifacts are not, however, feasible to be directly articulated by PbD technique [41].

Example: Karma [49] allows users to create data mashups interactively by providing examples demonstrating the integration of data from different websites.

Alternative: Programming by Example Modification

Another powerful technique to remove the burden of programming is to let users modify and change the behavior of existing examples, instead of programming from scratch [34].

Benefits: Provided that adequate mashup examples are available, in most cases the modification of a mashup example or the customization of a predefined mashup template requires a small effort.

Challenges: Searching for appropriate example as a suitable starting point for the work is a challenging task for non-programmers, as they are not familiar with any programming languages. With the ever increasing number of Web APIs, providing adequate mashup examples derived from all possible combinations of these APIs is not feasible.

Example: d.mix [23] allows users to sample elements of a website, and then generates the corresponding source code producing the selected elements. These source codes are stored in a repository, where they can be discovered and edited.

Alternative: Spreadsheets

Spreadsheets are one of the most popular and widely used end-user programming approaches to store, manipulate, and display complex data.

Benefits: Since the majority of mashups are about data integration, manipulation and visualization, spreadsheets can potentially be used as a natural approach to this end.

Challenges: Spreadsheets can not be used to design the user interface of a mashup.

Example: Husky[10] is a spreadsheet-based service composition and mashup development tool. Each cell in the spreadsheet represents a service or data source.

Alternative: Form-based

In form-based interaction, users are asked to fill out a form to create a new or change the behavior of an existing object.

Benefits: Filling out online forms has nowadays become an ordinary task for end-users on the Web. This can be interpreted as a proof for "naturalness" of form-based tools [48].

Challenges: Form-based tools cannot handle complex composition patterns for mashups [28].

Example: FeedRinse provides a form-based mechanism to filter and aggregate Web feeds.

Design Issue: Visual Language

Visual programming languages proposed by existing mashup tools fall into two main classes. The first class contains the tools that are based on a *visual wiring language*. The second consists of those incorporating *an iconic visual language*.

Alternative: Wiring

In a visual wiring language for mashups, activities are visualized as solid or form-based boxes that can be wired to each other. Each activity can represent a mashup component or a predefined operation like filtering, sorting, and merging. Wires indicate the connection between these activities.

Benefits: In the realm of service composition, wiring languages can be considered one of the most *explicit* and popular approaches to express a composite service, due to the one-to-one relationship between the flow of control and data from one activity to another and visual boxes wired to each other.

Challenges: Wiring languages can cause readability problems, when there are multiple crossing edges, or when the visual graphs exceed the screen size. In the latter case, it is essential for a tool to provide auto-layout features.

---

[10]`http://www.husky.fer.hr/`

Example: The visual language incorporated by *MashArt* [12] represents queries and processing tasks over data sources as form-based boxes, which are able to connect to each other.

Alternative: Iconic

An iconic visual language represents objects to be handled by the language as graphical icons. Sentences are made with one or more icons that are related to each other according to a predefined syntax.

Benefits: Properly designed icons are generally easily interpreted, understood and remembered by users.

Challenges: An iconic visual language requires to invest significant effort and thought into icon design [31]. This is essential to avoid any further changes to the appearance of the icons, which causes confusion due to unexpected behavior.

Example: *VikiBuilder* [24] enables generation of visual wiki instances by combining various data sources. The tool uses iconic annotations to represent various predefined entities like adapter, data source, and semantic extractor.

Design Issue: Control Flow

In a visual programming language, just like in any other programming language, there should be a method with which the user can define the program's control flow. In case of the wiring method, this can be achieved through the use of either *explicit* methods or *implicit* methods.

Alternative: Explicit

The control flow is explicitly defined, for instance, by adding directed arrows connecting the boxes, or putting the boxes in a specific order (e.g., from left to right) that corresponds to their execution order.

Benefits: This alternative gives much more control over the development of the application logic of a mashup. Process-oriented mashups, for example, often incorporate a relatively complex application logic [50].

Challenges: Data flow and control flow graphs should be defined separately, which poses extra barriers on the development process. Additionally, representing a mashup with more than one diagram, each corresponding to either data flow graph or control flow graphs of the mashup, can impair the understandability and readability of the language.

Example: *JOpera* supports explicit design of the control flow graph. Each box in a control flow graph, represents an executable task whose incoming and outgoing edges define the control flow to and from the task.

Alternative: Implicit

In this case, the control flow of a mashup is derived from its data flow graph. For instance, in the simplest case, the flow of data/message from one activity to another suggests the same flow of control between them.

Benefits: This method is lightweight and gives users a natural way to represent parallel execution. They are only required to design the flow of data/message between components, which also declares a partial execution order between them.

Challenges: The shortcoming of this method is that it can only be used to create mashups with simple control flow patterns, such as those that do not contain branches and loops.

Example: *Proto Financial*[11] is based on a visual wiring language that allows integration of heterogeneous data sources in an enterprise setting.

DISCUSSION

Table 1 summarizes the mashup tool design space as well as the decisions made by the designers of each tool pertaining each design issues we previously defined within this decision space, which is mostly focused on the design of interactive systems. Given the table, we attempt to (1) analyze the design issues with respect to the evolution of the decisions made by different tools over the last 6 years; (2) highlight and scrutinize the most and the least frequently chosen design alternatives; and (3) present the impacts of design decisions on other issues and alternatives within the space.

Regarding the issue of specificity, the first-generation mashup tools are commonly general purpose, for instance, Yahoo! Pipes and Dapper. Interestingly, the application of mashups in various domains has resulted in an increase in the number of specialized tools, which have started to appear more recently. This, however, does not imply a trend shifting from generic tools to specialized tools. Rather, the broad and emerging application domains for mashups provide an on-going demand for the design of tailored mashup tools targeting different and specific domains of application.

Both generic and specialized mashup tools, in the majority of cases, tend to target non-programmers. This is a safe strategy especially for generic mashup tools, whose target users' population is large, unknown, and is dominated by non-programmers. Conversely, the target users of a specialized tool can be determined through a technical skills assessment process, for example.

After the end-user group targeted by a tool are assessed on technical skills, an important decision to make concerns the degree of the automation of the tool. Fully automatic tools are commonly believed to best serve non-programmers [18]. However, the problem lies in how a user is supposed to communicate the requirements for the mashup to be built with an automatic tool and also to give guidance and feedback to the tool in order to iteratively converge on the desired outcome. This may be done using an interaction technique as complicated as, or even more complicated than the one used to program a mashup with a semi-automatic tool. The risk of a fully automatic tool becoming too difficult to use has possibly led the design of most tools in our survey to abstain from choosing the full automation design alternative.

The core design issue for a mashup tool is to select suitable interaction techniques to let mashup developers communicate the mashup composition logic and, in case of a fully automatic tool, the goal and requirements of the mashup. To do so, there is a pool of available interaction techniques, which can also be combined in case of hybrid tool designs. According to the results of our survey, the majority of semi-automatic tools facilitate multiple interaction techniques. The most popular combination of interaction techniques is visual language and form-based programming, where tools typically offer a

---

[11]http://www.protosw.com/

Table 1. Summary of the mashup tool design decisions over the mashup design space

Name	Piggy Bank [27] (2005)	FeedRinse (2006)	Dapper (2006)	JackBe Presto (2006)	Swashup [36] (2007)	d.mix [23] (2007)	JOpera [45] (2007)	Yahoo! Pipes (2007)	Karma (2008)	SABRE [35] (2008)	Kapow Katalyst (2009)	MashArt [12] (2009)	Lively Wiki [33] (2009)	RoofTop [25] (2009)	IBM Mashup Center (2009)	ServFace Builder [42] (2010)	VikiBuilder [24] (2010)	Microsoft Visio [52] (2010)	Husky (2011)	DashMash [9] (2011)	Petals BPM (2011)	Sqwelch [20] (2011)
Specificity																						
Generic	+	+	+		+	+	+	+	+									+	+	+		
Specialized				+						+	+	+	+	+	+	+	+				+	+
Target End-User																						
Local Developers				+			+				+											
Non-Programmers	+	+	+			+		+	+	+		+	+	+	+	+	+	+	+	+	+	+
Programmers					+																	
Automation Degree																						
Full Automation	+																					
Semi Automation		+	+	+	+	+	+	+	+	+	+	+	+	+	+	+	+	+	+	+	+	+
Liveness																						
Level 1																			+			
Level 2																					+	
Level 3	+	+	+	+	+	+	+	+	+	+	+				+	+	+					+
Level 4													+	+				+				
Online Community																						
Private				+										+	+							
Public		+						+			+											
Collaboration																						
Blackboard																						+
Fork and Edit				+			+									+						
Wiki													+									
Interaction Technique																						
Editable Example						+																
Form-based		+		+			+	+			+	+				+	+					+
PbD			+				+															
Spreadsheets							+											+				
Textual DSL					+	+																
Visual Language				+			+	+		+	+	+		+	+		+				+	+
WYSIWYG														+	+	+	+					+
Visual Language																						
Iconic										+							+					
Wiring				+			+	+			+	+		+	+						+	+
Control Flow																						
Explicit					+						+										+	
Implicit				+				+				+		+	+					+		

visual wiring language, in which graphical boxes representing data sources, processing operators, etc. either contain or associated with a configuration form to specify and control the configuration properties associated with the box.

In spite of the popularity of visual languages based on the wiring paradigm, according to a study conducted by Namoun et. al. [40], these languages in the context of mashups are not "natural" to many non-programmers. In other words, a diagram representing the flow of data and control is more of a metaphor suitable for programmers rather than non-programmers. Thereby, forcing users to explicitly define flow of control in addition to flow of data in a mashup (i.e., explicit control flow alternative) can end up adding even more cognitive costs to learn how to interact with the mashup tool.

One of the most promising approaches to lower cognitive costs and increase motivation is to facilitate collaborative development [17]. In doing so, establishing an online community is crucial to effective collaboration as it brings together users with similar interests and common ground [51]. It should also be noted that the full potential of an online community to this end is exploited only when it is internally built upon the actual users of the tool (like in Yahoo! Pipes and JackBe Presto), not externally in the form of a technical blog or a fan page (like in FeedRinse and Kapow Katalyst). Therefore, it is important to consider collaborative development and internal communities designed for the sake of collaboration as important features to be implemented in next generation mashup tools.

Liveness is also another important issue affecting the usability of a tool. Interestingly, the vast majority of the tools already support liveness at level 3 through a "run" button that takes the users to the runtime environment where the mashup will be deployed and executed. The assumption is that users are capable to distinguish between the design-time modeling and composition environment and its run-time version, where the mashup execution occurs. A few tools (e.g., DashMash and RoofTop) have begun to remove this artificial distinction, and in the future we expect to witness the proliferation of mashup tools supporting the highest level of liveness, possibly combined with a WYSIWYG interface.

RELATED WORK

The field of mashup development has matured to a level where some frequently used patterns for mashup design have emerged (e.g., [44]). This paper makes a contribution towards a design space for mashup *tools* design, focusing on a collection of design issues which impact on usability aspects of mashup tools, seen as a class of interactive systems.

Existing surveys on mashup tools have been published focusing on different aspects, which can contribute together with this paper to build an even larger design space. For example, [18] classifies a small number of tools according to the chosen programming technique. The result is that no surveyed tool completely satisfies the needs for end-users. [13] collect examples of an a specific kind of mashup tools, performing integration at the business process level. A number of domain-specific, enterprise mashup tools have been classi-

fied in 2008. The survey published in [32] aims at classifying mashup tools according to a set of run-time deployment issues (e.g., client-side vs. server-side deployment, or user interface vs. data vs. process-level integration) which are complementary to the ones collected in this paper.

CONCLUSION

In this paper, we have collected 9 design issues and 27 reusable design alternatives covering essential aspects of the design space for mashup tools. To build this space, we have reconstructed and analyzed the design decisions taken by the creators of 22 contemporary mashup tools. The accumulated architectural knowledge is a useful reference and survey for engineering interactive systems for mashup composition. First, tool designers can use this survey to foster innovation during the design of next generation solutions. Second, the comprehensive explanation of the heterogeneity of mashup tools presented in this paper can provide researchers with a novel design-centric view over the state of the art. All in all, the goal of this survey is to promote the reuse of good design solutions, thus improving both the quality and the efficiency of the design process for next generation mashup tools.

ACKNOWLEDGEMENT

The work presented in this paper has been supported by the Swiss National Science Foundation with the SOSOA project (SINERGIA grant nr. CRSI22 127386) and CLAVOS project (Grant Nr. 125337).

REFERENCES

1. Aghaee, S., and Pautasso, C. Mashup development with html5. In *Proc. of Mashups '09/'10* (2010).

2. Arbab, F. Reo: a channel-based coordination model for component composition. *Mathematical. Structures in Comp. Sci. 14* (2004), 329–366.

3. Babar, M. A., Dingsøyr, T., Lago, P., and van Vliet, H. *Software Architecture Knowledge Management - Theory and Practice*. Springer, 2009.

4. Banerjee, N., and Dasgupta, K. Telecom mashups: enabling web 2.0 for telecom services. In *Proc. of ICUIMC 2008* (2008).

5. Benslimane, D., Dustdar, S., and Sheth, A. Services mashups: The new generation of web applications. *IEEE Internet Computing 12* (September 2008), 13–15.

6. Boehm, B., and Turner, R. *Balancing Agility and Discipline: A Guide for the Perplexed*. Addison-Wesley, 2003.

7. Borchers, J. *A Pattern Approach to Interaction Design*. Wiley, 2001.

8. Cao, J., Riche, Y., Wiedenbeck, S., Burnett, M., and Grigoreanu, V. End-user mashup programming: through the design lens. In *Proc. of CHI 2010* (2010).

9. Cappiello, C., Matera, M., Picozzi, M., Sprega, G., Barbagallo, D., and Francalanci, C. Dashmash: a mashup environment for end user development. In *Proc. of ICWE 2011* (2011).

10. Capuano, N., Pierri, A., Colace, F., Gaeta, M., and Mangione, G. R. A mash-up authoring tool for e-learning based on pedagogical templates. In *Proc. of MTDL 2009* (2009).

11. Cypher, A., Halbert, D. C., Kurlander, D., Lieberman, H., Maulsby, D., Myers, B. A., and Turransky, A., Eds. *Watch what I do: programming by demonstration*. The MIT Press, 1993.

12. Daniel, F., Casati, F., Benatallah, B., and Shan, M.-C. Hosted universal composition: Models, languages and infrastructure in mashart. In *Proc. of ER 2009* (2009).

13. Daniel, F., Koschmider, A., Nestler, T., Roy, M., and Namoun, A. Toward process mashups: key ingredients and open research challenges. In *Proc. of IWoWAaSM '09/'10* (2010).

14. Daniel, F., Yu, J., Benatallah, B., Casati, F., Matera, M., and Saint-Paul, R. Understanding ui integration: A survey of problems, technologies, and opportunities. *IEEE Internet Computing 11* (May 2007), 59–66.

15. Dewan, P., Agarwal, P., Shroff, G., and Hegde, R. Mixed-focus collaboration without compromising individual or group work. In *Proc. of EICS 2010* (2010).

16. Eisenstadt, M. Does elearning have to be so awful? (time to mashup or shutup). In *Proc. of ICALT 2007* (2007).

17. Fischer, G., Giaccardi, E., Ye, Y., Sutcliffe, A. G., and Mehandjiev, N. Meta-design: a manifesto for end-user development. *Commun. ACM 47* (2004), 33–37.

18. Fischer, T., Bakalov, F., and Nauerz, A. An overview of current approaches to mashup generation. In *Proc. of WM 2009* (2009).

19. Fowler, M., and Parsons, R. *Domain-specific languages*. Addison-Wesley, 2010.

20. Fox, R., Cooley, J., and Hauswirth, M. Collaborative development of trusted mashups. In *Proc. of iiWAS 2010* (2010).

21. Goble, C., and Stevens, R. State of the nation in data integration for bioinformatics. *J. of Biomedical Informatics 41* (2008), 687–693.

22. Grammel, L., and Storey, M.-A. An end user perspective on mashup makers. Tech. Rep. DCS-324-IR, University of Victoria, September 2008.

23. Hartmann, B., Wu, L., Collins, K., and Klemmer, S. R. Programming by a sample: rapidly creating web applications with d.mix. In *Proc. of UIST 2007* (2007).

24. Hirsch, C., Hosking, J., and Grundy, J. Vikibuilder: end-user specification and generation of visual wikis. In *Proc. of ASE 2010* (2010).

25. Hoyer, V., Gilles, F., Janner, T., and Stanoevska-Slabeva, K. Sap research rooftop marketplace: Putting a face on service-oriented architectures. In *Proc. of SERVICES 2009* (2009).

26. Hoyer, V., Stanoesvka-Slabeva, K., Janner, T., and Schroth, C. Enterprise mashups: Design principles towards the long tail of user needs. In *Proc. of SCC 2008* (2008).

27. Huynh, D., Mazzocchi, S., and Karger, D. Piggy bank: Experience the semantic web inside your web browser. *Web Semant. 5* (2007), 16–27.

28. Jeffries, R., and Rosenberg, J. Comparing a form-based and a language-based user interface for instructing a mail program. *SIGCHI Bull. 18* (1986), 261–266.

29. Jhingran, A. Enterprise information mashups: integrating information, simply. In *Proc. of VLDB 2006* (2006).

30. Jones, M. C., Churchill, E. F., and Twidale, M. B. Mashing up visual languages and web mash-ups. In *Proc. of VL/HCC 2008* (2008).

31. Korfhage, R. R., and Korfhage, M. A. Criteria for iconic languages. In *Visual languages*, Plenum Press (1986), 207–231.

32. Koschmider, A., Torres, V., and Pelechano, V. Elucidating the mashup hype: Definition, challenges, methodical guide and tools for mashups. In *Proc. of MEM 2009* (2009).

33. Krahn, R., Ingalls, D., Hirschfeld, R., Lincke, J., and Palacz, K. Lively wiki a development environment for creating and sharing active web content. In *Proc. of WikiSym 2009* (2009).

34. MacLean, A., Carter, K., Lövstrand, L., and Moran, T. User-tailorable systems: pressing the issues with buttons. In *Proc. of CHI 1990* (1990).

35. Maraikar, Z., Lazovik, A., and Arbab, F. Building mashups for the enterprise with sabre. In *Proc. of ISOC 2008* (2008).

36. Maximilien, E. M., Wilkinson, H., Desai, N., and Tai, S. A domain-specific language for web apis and services mashups. In *Proc. of ICSOC 2007* (2007).

37. Myers, B. A. Evaluation of visual programming and program visualization. In *Proc. of CHI 1989* (1989).

38. Myers, B. A. Taxonomies of visual programming and program visualization. *Journal of Visual Languages Computing 1* (1990), 97–123.

39. Myers, B. A., Ko, A. J., and Burnett, M. M. Invited research overview: end-user programming. In *Proc. of CHI EA 2006* (2006).

40. Namoun, A., Nestler, T., and Angeli, A. D. Service composition for non-programmers: Prospects, problems, and design recommendations. In *Proc. of ECOWS 2010* (2010).

41. Nardi, B. A. *A small matter of programming: perspectives on end user computing*. MIT Press, Cambridge, MA, USA, 1993.

42. Nestler, T., Feldmann, M., Hubsch, G., Preussner, A., and Jugel, U. The ServFace builder - a wysiwyg approach for building service-based applications. In *Proc. of ICWE 2010* (2010).

43. Nowak, M., and Pautasso, C. Goals, questions and metrics for architectural decision models. In *Proc. of SHARK 2011* (2011).

44. Ogrinz, M. *Mashup Patterns: Designs and Examples for the Modern Enterprise*. Addison-Wesley Professional, 2009.

45. Pautasso, C. Composing RESTful services with JOpera. In *Proc. of the International Conference on Software Composition (SC 2009)*, vol. 5634 of *LNCS*. Springer, 2009.

46. Soi, S., and Baez, M. Domain-specific mashups: from all to all you need. In *Proc. of Current trends in web engineering* (2010).

47. Tanimoto, S. L. Viva: A visual language for image processing. *J. Vis. Lang. Comput. 1*, 2 (1990), 127–139.

48. Thomas, J. C., and Gould, J. D. A psychological study of query by example. In *Proc. of AFIPS 1975* (1975).

49. Tuchinda, R., Szekely, P., and Knoblock, C. A. Building mashups by example. In *Proc. of IUI 2008* (2008).

50. Vrieze, P. d., Xu, L., Bouguettaya, A., Yang, J., and Chen, J. Process-oriented enterprise mashups. In *Proc. of GPC 2009* (2009).

51. Wenger, E. *Communities of practice: learning, meaning, and identity*. Cambridge University Press, 1998.

52. Wright, S. D., et al. Designing mashups with excel and visio. In *Expert SharePoint 2010 Practices*. Apress, 2011, 513–539.

The Design of a Hardware-software Platform for Long-term Energy Eco-feedback Research

Lucas Pereira
Madeira-ITI, University
of Madeira
Caminho da Penteada,
9020-105 Funchal,
Portugal
lucas@m-iti.org

Filipe Quintal
Madeira-ITI, University
of Madeira
Caminho da Penteada,
9020-105 Funchal,
Portugal
fquintal@m-iti.org

Nuno Jardim Nunes
Madeira-ITI, University
of Madeira
Caminho da Penteada,
9020-105 Funchal,
Portugal
njn@uma.pt

Mario Bergés
Civil and Environmental
Engineering,
Carnegie Mellon
University
Pittsburgh, PA 15213-3890
marioberges@cmu.edu

ABSTRACT

Researchers often face engineering problems, such as optimizing prototype costs and ensuring easy access to the collected data, which are not directly related to the research problems being studied. This is especially true when dealing with long-term studies in real world scenarios. This paper describes the engineering perspective of the design, development and deployment of a long-term real word study on energy eco-feedback, where a non-intrusive home energy monitor was deployed in 30 houses for 18 months. Here we report on the efforts required to implement a cost-effective non-intrusive energy monitor and, in particular, the construction of a local network to allow remote access to multiple monitors and the creation of a RESTful web-service to enable the integration of these monitors with social media and mobile software applications. We conclude with initial results from a few eco-feedback studies that were performed using this platform.

Author Keywords

Hardware-Software platform; Eco-feedback; Non-Intrusive Load Monitoring; Sustainability;

ACM Classification Keywords

H.5.2 [Information Interfaces and Presentation]: User Interfaces – Prototyping;

INTRODUCTION

The world is witnessing a change in residential energy consumption habits. For the past couple of decades, electricity emerged as the main source of residential energy consumption [1]. The factors leading to the growing consumption are well known, and are tightly coupled with economic indicators of development [2]. As more people in emerging countries have access to higher levels of comfort the impact of domestic electricity consumption will increase significantly world wide [3].

The effects of residential electrical consumption on our energy balance and carbon emissions are hard to overestimate. This effect is so relevant that increasing the energy efficiency in residential buildings is considered one of the top seven actions that may lead to large savings in carbon emissions [4]. Nevertheless, any attempt to improve building efficiency generally involves changing the lifestyles of the residents. Thus, the transition to a more sustainable future involves behavior change, which can only take place in response to peoples' changing needs, drives and motivations.

The Human-Computer Interaction (HCI) community embodies knowledge and expertise that will be crucial to address the design, interaction, and usage issues surrounding sustainable technologies and practice. Eco-feedback technology plays a central role in reducing and motivating sustainable behavior [5]. This technology is defined as that which provides feedback on individual or group behaviors with the goal of influencing future energy saving strategies thus reducing the environmental impact of the actions.

This paper presents a hardware and software platform that was developed to enable the quick deployment of long and short-term studies of eco-feedback technology and at the same time serve as a research platform for developing non-intrusive load monitoring algorithms and techniques. Here we report on more than 2 years of experience developing and improving a research platform that combines low-cost non-intrusive monitoring of energy in households and quantitative measures of user behavior. We start by reviewing the state of the art eco-feedback technologies, and then provide an overview on the work that has been done to date on Non-Intrusive Load Monitoring (NILM). Following this, we introduce the research platform that we have been developing to support research in both of these fields. Lastly, we report on a few studies that were performed using this platform and offer recommendations for future improvements.

Eco-feedback Technology

Many studies sustain that providing users with real-time energy eco-feedback is an effective way of changing consumption behaviors. Savings reported in the literature range from 5% to 10% [6]. However other studies showed that this effect is not long lasting [7, 8] and hence might compromise the long-term effectiveness of eco-feedback technology.

There are many examples of eco-feedback systems that promote behavior change. For instance Kohlenberg and colleagues in the 1970s [9] found that a simple eco-feedback mechanism that turned *on* a light bulb when the household energy was reaching 90% of peak consumption, was effective in promoting behavior change. More recently Spagnolli et al. [10] reported on a disaggregation system that gave detailed feedback information to users using pervasive technologies to decrease the energy usage and preliminary results shown that households that used their prototypes saw an energy consumption reduction of 5% over the previous year's when the prototype was not available. Similarly, Peschiera and colleagues [7] investigated how residents of a dormitory building would respond to different information regarding their consumption. The results demonstrated that providing comparisons between building occupants results in more reliable improvements in energy utilization when compared with individual feedback.

Eco-feedback is of value in itself as a learning tool and must be considered in context. The outcomes vary according to circumstances, but they can also sometimes be improved when used in conjunction with advice and information.

Sometimes people need help in interpreting eco-feedback and deciding their courses of action. This help may come from energy conservation programs such as the one promoted by the company OPower[1], which mails home energy report letters comparing the energy usage of households in similar neighborhoods and provides energy conservation tips to the residents. This program began near the end of 2009 with nearly 600.000 US households in treatment and control groups, and results show that after two years it is still possible to find average savings if feedback is consistent. For example, reports show 2.89% average savings for high consuming households receiving monthly reports, and 1.70% for low consumption households receiving only quarterly reports [11].

In fact, one concern of the effectiveness of eco-feedback is called the response-relapse behavioral pattern meaning that after a while consumption would relapse to values prior to the study, and this was also the subject of a study reported in [7] where it was possible to observe that users will gradually return to previous behaviors if feedback is no longer present or is less frequent.

Despite the need to properly assess its long-term effectiveness, the promising results of eco-feedback

---

[1] www.opower.com

technology have lead researchers to propose the expansion of this technology to other areas of consumption, in particular water, personal transportation, product purchases and garbage disposal [12]. These new areas of eco-feedback have been the central subjects of several studies. For instance Strengers and colleagues [13] explored 26 households using water and electricity meters, and came up with a set of design implications to improve user experience with eco-feedback systems. Miller and Buys [14] conducted a study with 7 families that had an energy and water consumption meter installed, and obtained guidelines in how eco-feedback systems should be built and marketed as a product. Finally in [15], Froehlich et al. explored a mobile tool for tracking and supporting green transportations habits. After a 3-week field study the results show that such tools can easily engage the user into sustainable actions, and that there is a potential to enable behavior change regarding transportation habits.

With the advent of low costs sensing technology for both energy consumption and human behavior there is a new opportunity to assess the effectiveness of eco-feedback technology beyond the small-scale, short-term studies promoted in the past. Moreover, having access to better sensing technology, promotes the low-cost capability to disaggregate power consumption, hence offering the possibility of providing users with disaggregated information regarding the consumption of house divisions or even individual appliances. The basic assumption is that people will be able to change their behavior and thus their consumption if they understand which appliances are responsible for their overall energy consumption breakdown. This was especially noticeable in [6], were Parker and its colleagues performed a pilot evaluation of two low-cost monitoring systems and found that users quickly discovered that by looking at the differences in demand from turning on and off appliances they could easily approximate the energy use of each individual appliance and better understand the consequences of their actions.

Non-Intrusive Load Monitoring

Attempts to monitor and disaggregate electric energy from a single sensing point go back to the early 1980's. Schweppe and Hart first introduced Non-Intrusive Load Monitoring (NILM) [16]. Generally a NILM system is designed to identify and monitor the energy consumption of individual appliances that co-exist in a building's electrical circuit. The main assumption of the first NILM algorithms is that every change in the total power consumption of a building happens as a response to an electric device changing its state, e.g. a television turning *on* or a hair drier going from *low* to *high*. The approach consists of applying sophisticated signal processing and statistical learning techniques to current and/or voltage measurements taken at a limited number of locations in the electric distribution system of the household [16]. In high-level terms a NILM process can be described in six consecutive steps:

1. **Data acquisition**: sensors measure the current and voltage signals flowing into the house from a single point.
2. **Data pre-processing**: previously acquired current and voltage signals are converted into traditional power metrics (e.g., real power, reactive power and power factor).
3. **Event detection**: changes in certain metrics (traditionally real power is used) are detected and flagged as events for further processing in the other modules.
4. **Feature extraction**: features are extracted from the samples surrounding the detected event. Together these features form an individual signature that presumably uniquely identifies each power event.
5. **Event classification**: previously trained machine learning algorithms are applied to unclassified event signatures to obtain a classification.
6. **Energy computation**: by keeping track of all the load events that occur and their associated power levels it is possible to estimate how much energy each appliance is using.

Much research was done is this field since the early days when Hart presented his approach that consisted of analyzing real and reactive power steady state changes at the fundamental frequency (60Hz in the US). With the improvement of sensing technology researchers saw an opportunity to explore frequency domain features of the electric signal and in particular power harmonics. For instance Laughman et al. [17] found that by using information in the 3rd and 5th spectral envelope coefficients it was possible to distinguish between loads that would otherwise overlap when using only the changes in real and reactive power. In [18] the research team used linear regression to extract features from the first seven odd power harmonics of the current signal. Different basis functions (polynomial, Gaussian, radial and Fourier) were used for the linear regression and traditional machine learning algorithms (e.g. nearest neighbor and decision tress) were used to classify the power load events based on these features. Results reported classification accuracy ranging from 67% to 100%.

Some authors achieved similar results with completely different approaches. Patel et al. [19] proposed to monitor electric noise in voltage measurements taken at electrical outlets in the home to detect and classify the behavior of most appliances. Three years later the same authors criticized their previous work mentioning problems such as the computational expense of analyzing transient noise, and presented ElectriSense [20] a system that focuses on sensing very high frequency (36-500 kHz) electromagnetic interference (EMI), which is constantly generated by switch mode power supplies (SMPS) that are present in most modern consumer electronics, as well as fluorescent

lightning. A very good summary of the work being done in this field and future directions can be found in [21].

Overall NILM represents a major change in the load-monitoring paradigm and it is definitely a low-cost alternative to traditional intrusive technology based on multiple individual sensors that are costly to install, maintain and monitor. The potential of non-intrusive sensing is growing rapidly from energy to other domains. For instance, Cohn et al. [22] developed GasSense, a single-point acoustic sensor for gas flow. A similar solution was implemented to control water usage. HydroSense [23] is a single-point pressure sensor and was presented by Froehlich and it colleagues. Their system allows the identification of any individual water feature activity, and is capable of estimating the amount of water each feature is using. The sensor is connected to a faucet in the houses' plumbing system and when a valve switches (for instance a bathroom faucet or a mechanical valve in a dishwasher), a pressure change will occur and a pressure wave is generated in the plumbing system that can be sensed anywhere in the house. The characteristics of this waveform will be different for every existing valve, what makes it possible to once again apply NILM techniques to classify events. For households sensor fusion will also enable a wider application range and accuracy of unsupervised or semi-supervised algorithms.

In the remaining sections of this paper we present and in-depth view of our low-cost implementation of a hardware and software platform for non-intrusive home energy eco-feedback research. We start by explaining how our load monitor works, and then we show how we are providing eco-feedback to the users including the management and collection of data. Finally we present our design decisions and experiences concerning the deployment of our system and finalize we some conclusions and results from eco-feedbacks studies that were done during the deployment of this research platform.

SINAIS: A HARDWARE-SOFTWARE PLATFORM FOR NON-INTRUSIVE HOME ENERGY ECO-FEEDBACK RESEARCH

Although existing studies on eco-feedback show very promising results, there are still almost no studies that assess the long-term effects of this technology. We argue that this may be because conducting long-term studies is both costly and difficult with existing sensing technology. The research platform described here is part of the Sustainable Interaction with social Networks, context Awareness and Innovative Services (SINAIS) research project, which involves a team of multidisciplinary researchers looking at using NILM, social networking and context awareness to understand and motivate people to reduce their energy consumption in the residential and transportation domains.

We were required to develop a low-cost solution that could be easily deployed in dozens of houses with very little installation and monitoring costs. The system was required to acquire data from a single point in the household and preferably also provide users with feedback about their energy consumption. Additionally, we sought to acquire usage data from the sensor related to the capability of the system do detect human-activities.

Given this set of requirements we started looking at available commercial metering solutions and soon understood that none of the existing solutions offered enough flexibility at low cost of installation and monitoring. A good review of existing hardware can be found in [24]. While some commercial systems are relatively inexpensive, they do not offer all the data needed for a NILM implementation (some only sampled current and reported average values at 1Hz). Other systems did not offer a flexible method for providing feedback to the users. As for the most expensive solutions (e.g., circuit-level meters), some offered all the required data, from instantaneous current and voltage to power factor, but were considered too expensive and difficult to install. One final problem with these commercial solutions was the fact that none offered a built-in method for inferring human activity, which was an important requirement for our study.

The failure to find a viable commercial solution led us to build the custom end-to-end NILM home energy monitor described here. To lower the cost we decided to implement the hardware / software platform using a simple netbook. We used the netbook's built-in Analog to Digital Converter (ADC) of the audio input to sample current and voltage. The mini display and the speakers provide the feedback, while the Wi-Fi card enables communication over the Internet. Additionally the built-in camera and microphone can act as low- cost sensors for human activity. With this solution we were able to come up with a compact package that could be acquired for less than 300 euros and offered the possibility of being used in future research projects.

Data acquisition and load monitoring

In our NILM solution the measurements are taken by combining current and voltage sensed at the main power feed. Selecting this sensing point enables the coverage of the whole house consumption. The measured values are then used for event detection, event classification and, ultimately, the breakdown of consumption into individual appliances. In the meantime power consumption and power event data are stored in a local database to be used by any external application to provide eco-feedback to the householders. As described previously our power metering system is a combination of both hardware (sensors and netbook) and software (power calculation and load disaggregation algorithms).

Hardware Components

In many European countries residential buildings have single-phase electric circuits fed by 230V 50Hz AC. Therefore, only two sensors are required to measure power:

one for current and the other for voltage. We use a standard split-core (clamp-on) current transformer (Figure 1, left) to measure current. The sensor costs up to 30 Euros, depending on the maximum current range. The input-end is placed around the current conductor and in the output-end there is a 3.5 mm Tip, Ring, Sleeve (TRS) connector. For the voltage sensor we opted for a custom solution that steps down 230V RMS input to 0.5V RMS that we can acquire using the line in. The sensor is a simple voltage transformer (Figure 1, center) that was tailor-made by a local company. The input-end is connected to a voltage source in the main fuse box, and we added a 3.5 mm TRS connector to the output-end that never reaches the peak 0.9 Volts, which is the maximum voltage that can be sampled by the sound card. Since both sensors have TRS connectors in the output ends it is possible to connect them to the netbook sound card using a 3.5 mm TRS splitter (Figure 1, right).

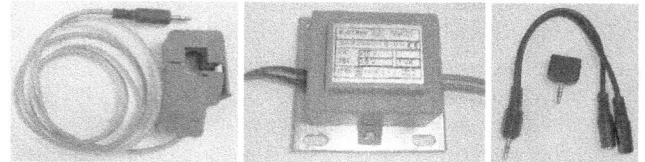

Figure 1: Hardware being used. From left to right: split-core current sensor, voltage sensor and TRS splitter connectors

Software Components

In terms of software, we designed and implemented a real-time power meter using the Java programming language, taking advantage of its sound Application Programming Interface (API) to read the data from the sensors. The system represented in Figure 2, is based on the *pipe-and-filter* software architecture. This very simple but powerful, architecture consists of any number of components (filters) that transform or filter data, before passing it on via connectors (pipes) to other components. Because all the filters are working *in parallel* this architecture is very suitable for systems where data transformations need to be done as close to real time as possible, which was clearly our case. In the following section we describe the filters that comprise our load monitor.

Data acquisition and Power Calculations

Current and voltage are continuously sensed and sent to the *data acquisition filter* to be sampled. This module is able to extract current and voltage signals from the left and right audio channels, respectively. The resulting data is then added to a queue that is connected to the next filter where the power calculations will take place. As current and voltage are sampled they are sent to the *power calculations filter*. This filter is responsible for performing the power calculations and driving the resulting data to the splitter, which is an active filter and is responsible for sending the power samples to the filters that are connected to it.

The power values (current, voltage, real power, reactive power and power factor) are computed by applying a Fast

Fourier Transform (FFT) to each period of the current and voltage waveforms, which are represented by 160 samples each (considering a sampling frequency of 8000 Hz and a 50 Hz mains frequency).

Splitter

Because our system requires multiple filters to access the same data simultaneously (e.g., one filter is storing the power in a local database while another is running an event detector algorithm), we needed to find a way to share the same data among all the filters. This is a well know pattern in software engineering (*single producer and multiple consumers problem*), and our solution was to implement a publish-and-subscribe pool where the entire customer filters (consumers) have to subscribe in order to access the power samples. The producer is then responsible for driving the power samples to each of the subscribers.

Graphical User Interface (GUI)

The GUI is a sink, and is responsible for plotting the power as it is being calculated. Initially this technical GUI was important to calibrate our system and it is still being used to improve the implemented algorithms.

Power storage

The role of the power storage filters is to store instantaneous power measurements. However, given the high rate or power samples (50 measurements per second) we opted to store average power samples instead. The average power samples are calculated based on a predefined number of samples that by default was set to 1500 (roughly 30 seconds at 50Hz). This filter is also responsible for storing and updating the power events as they are detected and classified.

Median filter

The *median filter* is used to apply a median filter to the power samples, also based on a predefined window size. The filtered samples are sent to the *power event detector* filter. This process is used as a smoothing technique and it is particularly important to improve the event detection

stage as currently the number of appliances that are running simultaneously inside a house is constantly increasing, hence resulting in noisy signals that can make the event detection harder.

Event detections and load identification

Once the power calculations are done, an event detector processes the power signal (normally the real power is used) to find the changes in the load that are generated by the working appliances. In the current system, the event detector is a modified version of the mean detector that uses a log likelihood ratio test [25]. When a change of interest is detected, this module triggers a programmable event that will be handled by the load identification filter.

The *disaggregation filter* is a composite filter that captures the events triggered by the *power event detector* It is composed of two filters that work together to disaggregate the load, the feature extractor and the event classifier.

The *feature extraction filter* extracts features from the samples that surround the power event and sends them to the classification filter to be analyzed and obtain a classification for the event. Two main features, extracted from both real and reactive power, are used in the current implementation: 1) the mean change in power when the event occurs and 2) the coefficients of a 3rd degree polynomial fitted to a fixed-window of samples around the event using a least squares curve fitting algorithm.

The *event classification filter* applies a machine learning algorithm to the event features and attempts to find the appliance whose features are a best match to any new set of features. Currently only the *k*-Nearest Neighbor (*k*-NN), a very simple instance-based learning algorithm, is implemented in the power meter. New instances are classified by observing the class label of their *k*-nearest neighbors and selecting the class that is found most frequently. The nearest neighbors are those instances on the training set that have the smallest distance (overall distance of the existing parameters) to the instance being classified.

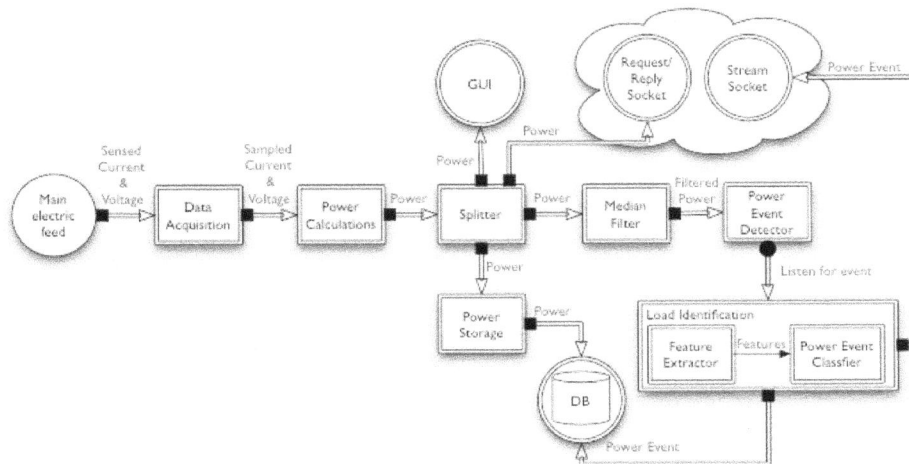

Figure 2: SINAIS Non-Intrusive Load Monitor software architecture.

Applying other machine learning algorithms is straightforward given that our system is compliant with the Java Machine Learning[2] and Weka[3] APIs that are already integrated in the system.

Communication

In order no enable real time communication between the power meter and other applications we have also added a communication layer. This implements two socket servers that are opened to external connections.

One is a simple *request / reply socket* that will send data to its connected clients upon request. The requests and reply messages must follow a pre-defined structure that is understood by both server and clients. The other is a streaming socket that is used to stream the power event data as they occur. To facility the communication between both parts the exchanged data is in a predefined XML format.

Eco-Feedback

Our system offers eco-feedback to the user using the netbook monitor. We have built two user interfaces that not only provide historic consumption data, but also connect to the energy monitor through the existing TCP sockets to get real time information for either energy consumption or power events. One of the unique features of our implementation is the possibility of inferring human activity and therefore having the chance to include quantitative measures of user attention.

Our research also aims at exploring other dimensions of eco-feedback, namely place and availability of information. The flexibility of our platform enabled the integration of a social networking and a mobile client that present consumption to the users in different ways.

Local Eco-feedback

During the design of our research platform two different user interfaces providing consumption information to the users were deployed using local eco-feedback through the netbook screen. Both interfaces are capable of recording every user interaction with the local eco-feedback system. This is achieved in two ways: one by keeping track of mouse clicks an transitions between the different visualizations, and the second inferring human presence using the built-in webcam. For that effect we have implemented motion and face detection algorithms to sense when residents were passing by or looking at the netbook. We also used the sensing to trigger and initiate some user interaction with the system. For instance, if the system detected human presence the screen would become brighter in an attempt to call the user attention.

---

[2] www.java-ml.sourceforge.net

[3] www.cs.waikato.ac.nz/ml/weka

First deployment of the eco-feedback

The first interface was design based on the feedback that we received after performing a pilot study with 5 families using commercial power meters. This interface uses mostly traditional column charts to display the consumption information. When the system detects motion nearby, it displays a "spectrum-like" graphic that represents the consumption over the last 8 hours (this representation is made through a color code: green, yellow or red depending on the consumption), it also presents the current consumption and the aggregate consumption over the day (represented in kWh and gCO_2). The users can also access detailed energy consumption. The system displays a column chart with the total energy consumption over the current day, and also the consumption of all the past days. It is also possible to compare the consumption of the current week against last week on a daily basis. In Figure 3 (top) we show an example of the daily consumption in a column chart, were each column represents one different hour of the day.

Second deployment of the eco-feedback

The second version was designed based on feedback we received from the deployment of the first version. In this interface we used a gauge analogy to display consumption information to the user. The information was displayed in two forms: the more traditional displayed the quantities in numerical format while the less traditional consisted of a color-code that would change according to the household consumption (the colors would vary from a light green when the consumption was low to a very dark read when the consumption reached abnormal levels).

The interface displays information for the hour, week, month and year's consumption and is organized in a tabbed menu. As described previously, the consumption is mapped through a color code ranging from green to dark red and if the mouse cursor hovers over the gauge it displays information about CO_2 emissions and cost associated with that time slot.

Both versions are able to display the current consumption information, but only the second one is able to display power events. These are displayed in the hour view because displaying the events in the day or month view would result in a very confusing interface (the hour view is refreshed every hour, meaning that only events for the current hour are displayed). Every time a power event is detected a small dot is added to the interface as close as possible to the time of occurrence. The size of the dot is also used to help indicate the amount of power change, and a click on it reveals the appliance that has the highest probability of triggering that event. Additionally the user can confirm or correct the system's estimate. In Figure 3 (bottom) we depict the hourly consumption with dots that represent the power events and the possibility of manually labeling them.

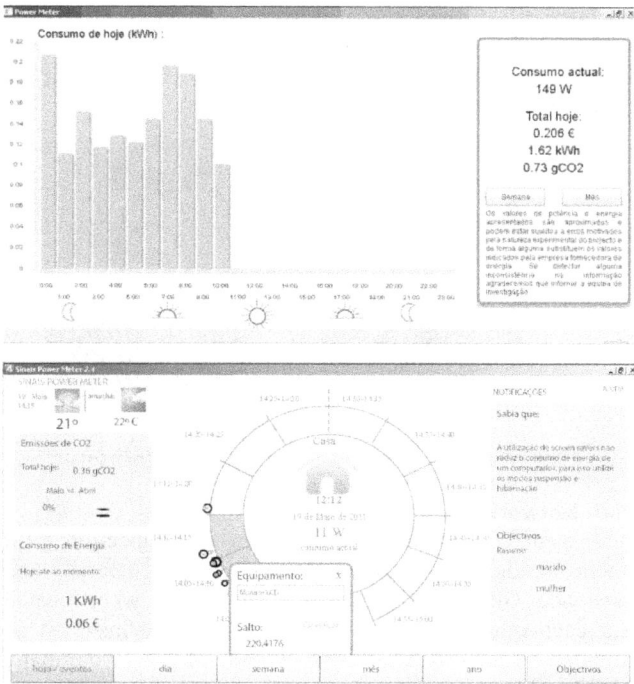

Figure 3. Different eco-feedback interfaces: first deployment (top) and second deployment (bottom).

Around the central gauge, additional information is presented, specifically: comparative information with analogous time periods, the total consumption in terms of monetary cost and CO_2 emissions and finally some generic advice regarding sustainable practices.

Social Networks Integration

In order to provide eco-feedback to the users when they are not close to the power meter, we have integrated our system with the Stepgreen.org social networking platform. Stepgreen[4] is a free service provided by the HCI Institute at Carnegie Mellon University that tries to promote sustainable behavior and constructive discussion between its users by making them commit to a set of environmentally friendly goals.

Once the integration was done, the families with power meters installed in their homes were able to see a replicated version of their local system on the social network. To accomplish this we have created flash components similar to the gauges displayed in the local meter. The consumption data is loaded on these components using web-services that we have created for this purpose. These web-services will be further explained in the following sections. Figure 4 shows what was presented to the users after they have logged-in in to the social network system.

To integrate our system with Stepgreen all the website had to be translated to our users' native language and a user

---

[4] www.stepgreen.org

account had to be created for each family. To keep the original goal of Strepgreen, our platform is also able to retrieve the user-selected goals from the Stepgreen account and show them in the local eco-feedback interfaces.

Figure 4. Stepgreen welcome screen after user logs in.

Smartphone prototype

As a showcase of our framework capabilities and as exploratory exercise for future devices, a smartphone prototype was developed (see Figure 5). The prototype was implemented for the android platform. As with the social networking system, the mobile application also accesses our web-services to load consumption data. Another feature of the mobile application is the possibility of connecting to the TCP sockets provided by the power meter hence enabling the display of the current consumption and power events in real time. Additionally, there is a possibility of providing a classification for the detected events.

DATA MANAGEMENT

Storing data in a centralized repository is very important requirement for any research platform producing impressive amounts of data. After 1 year the data warehouse form this research project holds around 15 million power events and 25 million power samples corresponding to 5 gigabytes of storage data. In our deployment, every meter stores its own data in a local SQLite database. For integration purposes, we opted to use a web-based file hosting service as this allowed us to keep all the database files synchronized in one place as long as there was an Internet connection available. The local databases are then integrated into a single data warehouse using the SQL Server Integration Services.

Web Server

In addition to the central SQL Server described previously, our framework also has an online web server. This server is running a MySQL database that is updated by our meters with consumption information every 20 min. (average consumption in W and power events information). The update process is accomplished by a simple application written in Java, executed by the task manager. A series of RESTful web-services were implemented in the server using an open source framework. With such services it is possible to easily access data aggregated in several ways. For instance the consumption average by day, the day with highest consumption or the top five houses with less consumed energy. The applications described in the section above (Stepgreen.org and the android prototype) obtain consumption information using these services.

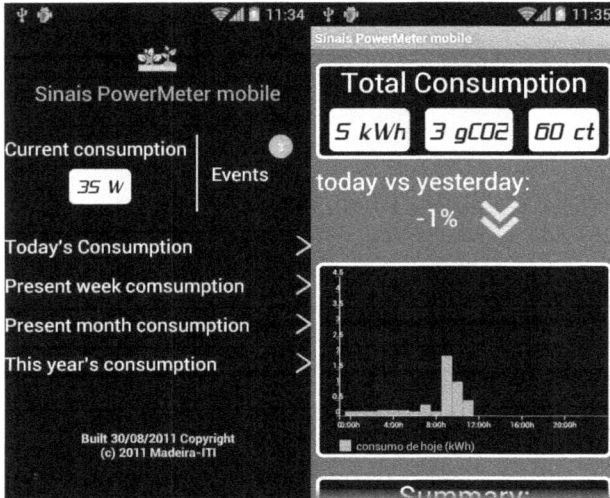

Figure 5. Android prototype: main menu (left), daily consumption (right).

SYSTEM DEPLOYMENT

Our system was used in about 30 houses during a period that lasted from several weeks in some houses to more than 1 year in steady sample of 20 houses. During that period the system was constantly monitored and perfected and several eco-feedback studies, including qualitative interviews and surveys, were conducted. In this section we discuss the issues related to the deployment of the system and in particular positioning, installation and maintenance.

Positioning

The main restriction to the positioning of our system is that the current and voltage sensors need to be connected to the main fuse box. Since both sensors were designed with very short cables we decided to attach our meter to the fuse box door with Velcro like shown in Figure 6. This solution allowed us to remove the system easily and it was proven to be secure. All of the houses in the study had the fuse box next to main door or in the kitchen, although we are aware that in some houses (mostly older ones) this box might be located in the basement or in the attic, and that in those cases the system would not work as a feedback mechanism unless the information was displayed through other means such as, for example, the smartphone prototype.

Installation

In order to install the system, the netbook power cable had to be cut, stripped and connected to both edges of a circuit breaker and to the ground source. This procedure requires specialized labor and involved the support of an electrician from the local power company. The sensors and the netbook power cables are hidden in the box cover with only 2 audio cables passing to the front.

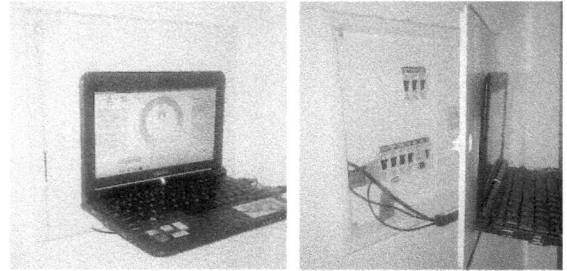

Figure 6. Netbook installed near the main fuse box.

Wi-Fi Network

Our system required an Internet connection for synchronizing the data and for remote access and assistance. Given that 75% of the households were located near each other in 3 apartment buildings, we installed an extended-range Wi-Fi network. The local power company helped with the installation, and provided long ranged access points (AP) in power poles near the buildings. An ethernet cable was extended from our lab to the closer access point, and this device was responsible for both covering the closer households and repeating the signal to the remaining AP's.

Several constraints limited the use of our network. For instance, heavy rain in the winter of 2011 damaged one AP and left 4 houses offline for 2 weeks. Also, due to the architecture of one of the buildings, 3 houses on the back of that building were not covered or had a weak connection. Those problems were solved by the goodwill of the affected users who were willing to share their personal Internet connection. During the eighteen-month-long study we managed to keep 70% of the households always online

Maintenance and Updates

When running such a long-term study it is very important that one have easy access to the deployed equipment for maintenance and update tasks. We use a proprietary software package for this purpose: Teamviewer[5]. With this software one can remotely control each deployed monitor. Additionally this software also allows file transfer, and this is very handy to upload small updates to the system.
Teamviewer was installed in every meter and also in the database server, and a partner list was created for easy access to each deployed meter.

STUDIES

During the deployment, several quantitative and qualitative studies were conducted. The first large-scale study with this

---

[5] www.teamviewer.com

research platform was made shortly after the system was first deployed and the results were presented in [8]. This study analyzed data gathered from 21 houses in the first 9 weeks of the deployment, and showed that 4 weeks after the initial deployment of the system the users started to pay less attention to the eco-feedback device. This is a very relevant result as much of the literature on HCI aspects of eco-feedback is based on deployments that last 2 or 3 weeks and will likely ignore this novelty effect. Another important result from the same study was finding that users with higher consumption had a greater interaction with the system and that during the period of the study they had an average of 6.4% decrease in consumption (as opposed to the 2.3% decrease of the users that had less interactions with the system). Again the relative long-term nature of our deployments enabled conclusions that are seldom found in the HCI literature on eco-feedback. Moreover after conducting some interviews with these users we learned that low consumers tend to interact less with the eco-feedback because they felt that they could not save any more energy than what they actually accomplished. The graph in Figure 7 represents the count of interactions with the system over the period of the first study. The bars display the sum of all interactions. And the line represents only the intended interactions (with the mouse).

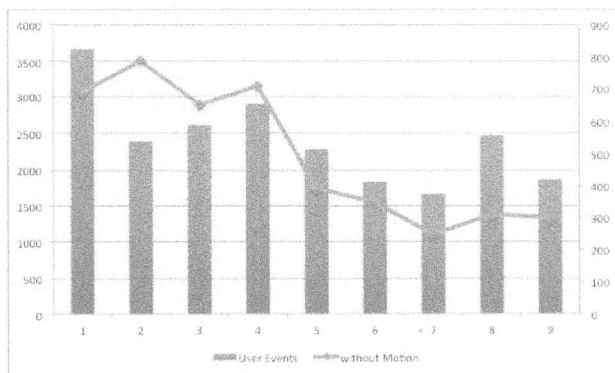

Figure 7. User interactions with the meter over the first 9 weeks.

A second study was conducted with 13 houses, one year after the first deployment and it involved the 2nd version of the eco-feedback interface. The results of this study can be found in [26], and they showed that in some houses the users stopped using the meter (some of them even closed the netbook), while others kept using it, although with less frequency (once or twice a day). This study also disclosed that even though we could find a decrease in consumption during the first 2 months of deployment, the average consumption remained virtually unchanged throughout the rest of the study.

From a qualitative perspective these studies also revealed that the system fostered discussion in the family about sustainable behaviors. For example, the father in one of the households complained that the kids always forget to close the fridge properly [27].

> *"I saw high consumption and went around to see that the fridge's door was open ... they always forget to close it properly!"* (Family 7 Father, ref 1).

Currently we are still exploring the big dataset collected during the 2 deployments. Comparisons between houses with different consumption profiles, analysis of the influence of the season in the consumption, exploring any change during the usage of appliances are all examples of future analysis.

CONCLUSIONS

In this paper we report on the efforts to build a cost-effective NILM energy consumption research platform. The HCI research literature is abundant in research results coming out of short-term research deployments of eco-feedback technology. Here we report on the requirements of the long-term research efforts comprising in the domain of sustainability. The complex hardware/software platform the research team was required to build posed many engineering challenges that are seldom reported in the literature. This paper describes in detail the problems and solutions found by the research team to develop and deploy a low-cost non-intrusive energy-monitoring research platform that combines energy and human sensing with the potential do deploy different eco-feedback visualizations.

Our system was deployed for a period of 18 months in more than 30 different houses, running 24/7 and acquiring valuable data that was used by an interdisciplinary team of researchers to monitor and understand how people react to eco-feedback technology. During this time several quantitative and qualitative studies took place. In one of the studies it was possible to see that 4 weeks after the initial deployment of the system the users started to pay significantly less attention to the eco-feedback device. The architecture of our framework allows the implementation of different eco-feedback solutions, without worrying about the complex sensing and consumption calculations.

As future work, the team is already implementing new prototypes that use avatars, or images of the local endemic forest in an attempt to create an emotional connection with the user, and to reduce the decrease of attention that was noticeable during our studies. We also plan to deploy the system in other cities and countries in an effort to better understand the cultural and international aspects of energy consumption.

REFERENCES

1. European Environment Agency: Household consumption. http://eea.europa.eu/themes/households (April 2012)

2. Enerdata: Global Energy Statistical Yearbook 2011. http://yearbook.enerdata.com (April 2012)

3. Hubacek, K., Guan, D. and Barua, A. Changing lifestyles and consumption patterns in developing countries: A scenario analysis for China and India. *Futures*, Volume 39 (9), 1084-1096. 2007.

4. Pacala, S., and Socolow, R. Stabilization wedges: solving the climate problem for the next 50 years with current technologies. *Science*, 305(5686), 968-72. 2004.

5. Froehlich, J., Findlater, L., and Landay, J., The Design of Eco-Feedback Technology. In *Proc.* CHI 2010.

6. Parker, D., Hoak, D., Meier, A., Brown, R. How Much Energy Are We Using? Potential of Residential Energy Demand Feedback Devices. *Solar Energy*, 1665-06. 2006.

7. Peschiera, G., Taylor, J. E., and Siegel, J. A. Response–relapse patterns of building occupant electricity consumption following exposure to personal, contextualized and occupant peer network utilization data. *Energy and Buildings* 42, 1329-1336. 2010.

8. Nunes, N. J., Pereira, L., Quintal, F., and Berges, M. (2011). Deploying and evaluating the effectiveness of energy eco-feedback through a low-cost NILM solution. In *Proc.* Persuasive 2011.

9. Kohlenberg, R., Phillips, T., and Proctor, W.: A behavioral analysis of peaking in residential electrical-energy consumers. *Journal of Applied Behavior Analysis*, 9(1), 31-18. 1976.

10. Spagnolli, A., Corradi, N., Gamberini, L., Hoggan, E., Jacucci, G., Katzeff, C., et al.: Eco- Feedback on the Go: Motivating Energy Awareness. *Computer*, 44 (5), 38-45. 2011.

11. Cooney, K. and Provencher, B. Evaluation Report: OPOWER MSUD Pilot Year 2. Navigant Consulting. 2011.

12. Froehlich, J., Everitt, K., Fogarty, J., Patel, S. and Landay, J. Sensing Opportunities for Personalized Feedback Technology to Reduce Consumption. In *Proc. CHI 2009 Workshop "Defining the Role of HCI in the Challenges of Sustainability."* 2009.

13. Yolande, S.: Designing eco-feedback systems for everyday life. *2011 annual conference on Human factors in computing systems* (pp. 2135-2144). 2011.

14. Miller, W. and Buys, L. Householder Experiences with Resource Monitoring Technology in Sustainable Homes. *Cities*. 2010.

15. Froehlich, J. et al. UbiGreen: investigating a mobile tool for tracking and supporting green transportation habits. In *Proc.* CHI 2009.

16. Hart, G.W.: Nonintrusive appliance load monitoring. In *Proc.* IEEE 80, 1870- 1891 (1992).

17. Laughman, C.; Kwangduk Lee; Cox, R.; Shaw, S.; Leeb, S.; Norford, L.; Armstrong, P. Power signature analysis. *Power and Energy Magazine, IEEE* , vol.1, no.2, pp. 56- 63, Mar-Apr 2003

18. Bergés, M., Soibelman, L. and Scott Matthews H. Learning Systems for Electric Consumption of Buildings. ASCE *Computing in Civil Engineering.* 2009.

19. Patel, S. N., Robertson, T., Kientz, J. A., Reynolds, M. S., & Abowd, G. D. At the flick of a switch: Detecting and classifying unique electrical events on the residential power line. In *Proc.* Ubicomp 2007.

20. Gupta, S., Reynolds, M. S., & Patel, S. N. ElectriSense: single-point sensing using EMI for electrical event detection and classification in the home. In *Proc.* Ubicomp 2010.

21. Zeifman, M. and Kurt, R. Nonintrusive Appliance Load Monitoring: Review and Outlook. *IEEE Transactions on Consumer Electronics* 57 (1) 76-84, 2011.

22. Cohn, G., Gupta, S., Froehlich, J., Larson, E., and Patel, S. N. GasSense: Appliance-Level, Single-Point Sensing of Gas Activity in the Home. *Pervasive Computing*, p. 265–282. 2010.

23. Froehlich, J.E., Larson, E., Campbell, T., Haggerty, C., Fogarty, J. and Patel, S.N. HydroSense: infrastructure-mediated single-point sensing of whole-home water activity. In *Proc* Ubicomp 2009.

24. Berges, M., Soibelman, L., Scott Matthews, H., Goldman, E. Evaluating the Electric Consumption of Residential Buildings: Current Practices and Future Prospects. In *Proc. Construction Research Congress*, 71-80, 2010.

25. Luo, D., Norford, L. K., Shaw, S. R., and Leeb, S. B. High Performance Commercial Building Systems Monitoring HVAC Equipment Electrical Loads from a Centralized United Technologies Corporation. *ASHRAE Transactions*, 108(1), 841-857, 2002.

26. Quintal, F., Pereira, L. and Nunes, N. J. A long-term study of energy eco-feedback using non-intrusive load monitoring. In *Ext. Abstracts Persuasive 2012*.

27. Barreto, M. and Karapanos, E. and Nunes, N. J. Social translucence as a theoretical framework for sustainable HCI. In *Proc. Interact 2011*, 195—203. 2011.

Considerations for Computerized In Situ Data Collection Platforms

Nikolaos Batalas
Eindhoven University of Technology
Den Dolech 2, 5600MB
Eindhoven, The Netherlands
n.batalas@tue.nl

Panos Markopoulos
Eindhoven University of Technology
Den Dolech 2, 5600MB
Eindhoven, The Netherlands
p.markopoulos@tue.nl

ABSTRACT

Computerized tools for in-situ data collection from study participants have proven invaluable in many diverse fields. The platforms developed within academic settings, eventually tend to find themselves abandoned and obsolete. Newer tools are susceptible to meeting a similar fate. We believe this is because, although most of the tools try to satisfy the same functional requirements, little attention has been paid to their development models also keeping in line. In this paper we propose an architectural model, which satisfies established requirements and also promotes extensibility, interoperability and cross-platform functionality between tools. In doing so, we aim to introduce development considerations into the larger discussion on the design of such platforms.

Author Keywords

Software Architecture and Engineering; End-User Programming; In situ data collection

ACM Classification Keywords

J.4 [Computer Applications]: Social and Behavioural Sciences; D.2.11 [Software Engineering]: Software Architectures

INTRODUCTION

Research Methods that rely on data collection from participants in situ, while their daily lives unfold, are seeing wide adoption from researchers in a variety of different fields, ranging from clinical psychology[16] to human computer interaction[7]. Methods to do so include diaries, where participants are instructed to log events, as well as the Experience Sampling Method[15] and its variants. Some of the most common reasons for using these methods are, mitigating memory biases in self reports, and making sure that observations take place within the context of interest, thus ensuring ecological validity[6].

The past decade has seen an impressive evolution of devices that are affordable, portable and networked, merging computing and sensing capabilities. PDAs in the past, and smartphones and tablet computers in the present, are prime products of this evolution. The more these devices are adopted by consumers and become instruments of communication and information handling within their daily activities, the better suited they become to in situ data collection. They are always on one's person, always functioning, multitasking, ready to serve the needs of a researcher, while still performing their primary functions.

In order to leverage the potential of these devices for data collection, the research community has built during the last decade, software tools, some of which have been made freely available[3][5][9][12]. They tend to be complex pieces of software that need to be configurable by researchers, have networking capabilities, and often feature server components. Development of these kinds of platforms is a non-trivial task. Therefore, it makes sense to have generic tools that can accommodate common data collection needs across research areas, such as the compilation and distribution by researchers, of questionnaires to be filled out at opportune moments, the capturing of photos and other media by participants that would be of use to the researcher, or the detection of the context within which events take place, through the sensors of the device.

In the academic community, efforts to build such tools have always been carried out on platforms available at the given time, targeting the functional requirements needed to implement research methods. The focus has been on the particular methods and their applications, rather than the development process. As such, development has been carried out with an end-user mindset, where the software is a means to an end, not the end itself[14]. As a result, iterations on the tools have been concerned with the evolution of the requirements that need to be satisfied and not with the iterative evolution of the software as an artifact.

Admittedly, the community that is interested in building data collection tools seems to be converging to an implicit paradigm of constituent components for the tools, as indicated by an agreement on the need for client-server components and configuration interfaces[13][8]. However, it has only been roughly outlined and has not yet been made explicit in more specific terms. We feel that the lack of discourse on this topic is hampering the software products in terms of interoperability and cross platform functionality.

In this paper we try to address this issue by introducing requirements for development in the general discussion on requirements, and by proposing a generic but also realistically implementable model for the construction of software for data collection in the field. In doing so, we aspire to promote the case for a general development platform which can be extendable and future-proof, as the basis for these tools.

In the following sections we outline the issues that data collection tools face in addressing challenges in the application of in situ research methods. Requirements gathered from previous works are then summarized, and requirements for development are proposed. Finally, a model which satisfies these requirements is detailed, and an example of its implementation is briefly discussed. We conclude by offering thoughts on the benefits of the approach.

BACKGROUND

Researchers planning to perform data collection in a computerized manner, would find significant obstacles upon choosing to employ ad hoc means. They would have to make sure that their tools are robust, perform as expected during the course of the study, and gather reliably the data intended for collection.

A preferable option is to use one of the tools that are already available, as is. Tools that have been used widely in the past, and have been extensively tested in the field[3][9], are still in use, but have aged along with the hardware they have been written for. Handheld devices become outdated at quite a fast pace. Smartphones running Windows Mobile, dominant in 2007, are no longer in the market, and PDAs are now relics of the past. To use them in the present, researchers have to get hold of legacy devices, and impose their use on their participants.

Currently modern tools do not present such problems in terms of hardware, but still need to be considered in the light of how well they can be adapted to the evolving needs of research methods. As sensor technology embedded in smartphones is growing, the potential for capturing rich data in novel modalities for studies should not be left untapped, and ways to elicit input from participants evolve as well, moving past the traditional questionnaire format, into diverse research instruments. These might involve multimedia or even functional application prototypes, as can be the case for user centered design[10]. Therefore, given pieces of software cannot universally satisfy every inquisitive requirement on the part of researchers. For them, employing alternative ways to collect data, also comes at the expense of implementing the interfaces to do so in software.

Indeed, some of these tools are available as open source software[3][9][5][12], and researchers who can develop software could theoretically adapt an open source tool to tailor its functionality to their own needs. Reuse of source code is commonly seen as a way to increase productivity and save time and effort in software development. On the other hand, several barriers to software reuse exist. A study by Agresti[1] is indicative of the barriers developers face when considering reuse of software components. It cites awareness (the devel-

oper must know of the existence of the reusable artifact) and acceptability (the reused artifact must be acceptable to the developer for use in the new project and its environment) as the two major factors that prevent one from reusing code. In the same study, the complexity of the code examined for reuse was found to be a prominent inhibitor of acceptability. Additionally, in the case of open source software developed in academic environments, as people move on to different things, projects naturally tend to lose their own leading developers, which is a cause for their presence, as viable options for reuse, to fade[4].

Conclusively, for all their merits, individual software applications for in situ data collection, have not, to our knowledge, been able to exhibit resilience against, or respond to the corrosive effects of age of their hardware and inscrutability of their codebase. Past tools have been good at the tasks they have been designed for, on the platforms they have been written for. However, they are platform specific, and their code base has not been migrated to newer platforms, nor have they had additional features added to them, and therefore are being rendered obsolete. More recent works are also susceptible to the same challenges.

The situation is aggravated by the fact that each tool stands insulated, developed in isolation from similar efforts. This has led to a very fragmented landscape of tools. However, the observation that all these tools meet familiar functional requirements gives us hope that, expanding the problem domain to include developers in the set of stakeholders, will, in a fashion similar to the functional requirements, lead to succinct, interoperable components for future development efforts to rely upon.

REQUIREMENTS

Previous efforts to build data collection tools have identified a number of requirements the software should meet with regard to the researchers and the participants. However, they have only focused on these two roles, overlooking the role of the developer. The following section lists the findings of past works, in relation with the researcher and the participant, and suggests considerations for the development of the software.

Requirements for researchers

Researchers should have the ability to *monitor the process of data collection in real time*. This gives them the ability to detect and deal with participant dropout issues, which could take place because of fatigue or device failures. Also, it allows them to better curate collected data for timely follow ups such as interviews[3][5][11][12].

In conjunction with real-time monitoring, *real-time modification of the study should also be provided*. The setup of the study could contain oversights, errors or be found to yield lower information quality than expected. Easy, remote reconfiguration of the study in real time can help salvage such situations.[5][8]

It is impossible to meet the exact needs of every researcher with regard to the interfaces that can be presented to participants for data gathering. *Domain-specific studies require cus-*

tom interfaces, up to the point of fully functional applications, that only researchers can understand, and should be able to deliver to their participants.

In the programmed behaviour of data collection software, the strict separation of studies to diary, experience sampling, context or event contigent questionnaires and all their variants, can be quite artificial. *Study protocols could benefit from mixing methods* that have been traditionally considered separately, as has been the case in [17].

Requirements for participants

Participants should not have to use mobile devices issued by the researchers. For researchers, monetary cost can be high, and the number of participants would be limited to the number of available devices. For participants, adversities related to adoption and retention of technology could apply. Rather, *use of a participant's own device should be made.* [5][11]

Also, the burden of installation or maintenance of the software's uninterrupted function should be minimal. Moreover, *the software should not stand in the way of the regular use of the device*[9][13].

Access to the study should be possible from multiple platforms. As participants move between different devices and contexts, from smartphone to tablet to desktop pc, so could access to the study follow.

Ability or desire to comply with the study's instructions might be varied from user to user. *Study designs should allow using tailored configurations for each user.*[5]

Requirements for development

In addition to the previous set of requirements, as has been proposed by previous works, this section lays out considerations that pertain to the development of the tools. Both the platform, as the product of software engineering, and the people involved in its development and use, as drivers of the engineering process, need to be considered.

A notable characteristic of the platforms for data collection in the field is that they can, and need to be, in perpetual development. Their goals need to be constantly shifting and new sets of features will always need to be added in order to take advantage of the latest hardware or to satisfy the evolving needs of researchers. To address such issues a careful layering of components with clear roles needs to be applied. Hardware-specific layers should aim to be as thin as possible. *Component layers should be isolated from one another, so that modifications to one cause minimal rippling effects to the next.*

Another distinctive property is that development of, and extensions to the platform need to accommodate a wide spectrum of developer roles. Multiple people with varying intent could potentially take on the role of developer, ranging from the social scientist to the professional programmer. They have varying levels of expertise and they target different aspects of the platform. For example, the former have little expertise in, and little patience for building low-level mobile services or

database systems. On the other hand, the latter cannot foresee or care for all the possible ways a participant might be required to interact with the system for data input, or how collected data could be visualized. To deal with this, *the platform needs to maximize the ability of problem-owners to cater to their own needs, but not require them to be concerned with greater issues.*

At the same time, stakeholders in the development process should be thought of as users, as much as developers. A programmer focusing on a client application, can be thought of as a user of the server's facilities or vice versa, while a researcher interested in the development of a specialized widget for participants to interact with, can be thought of as user of the client's facilities, and so on.

It would therefore be fair to say that the platform we should be building is faced with an interesting dichotomy. On one hand, it needs to rely on professional programming skills that can make accessible and abstract sets of features that are realized through hard to manage technologies, such as servers, databases and low-level hardware capabilities. These relate to the whole range of stakeholder interests, right down to the participant.

On the other hand our platform should accommodate more specialized end-user development intents, which relate only to small partitions of stakeholders, on a case by case basis. These could be achievable with as simple means as producing configuration specs, or with the slightly more complex customization of components, or even with regular programming. In these cases, the application of widely established practices should be allowed and the use of pre-existing knowledge should be encouraged. *Demand for domain-specific scripting and use of custom frameworks should be discouraged.*

SYSTEM DESIGN SPECIFICATIONS

Our model acknowledges two dimensions of development-related concerns. One dimension is that of developer roles, adopting the view that the distinction between end-user and professional development, is one of intent and is continuous instead of being dichotomous, as defined by Ko et al. In [14] they state,

> "as the number of intended uses of the program increases, a programmer will have to increasingly consider software engineering concerns in order to satisfy increasingly complex and diverse constraints. Second, even if a programmer does not intend for a program to be used by others, circumstances may change: the program may have broader value, and the code which was originally untested, hacked together, and full of unexercised bugs may suddenly require more rigorous software engineering attention".

This view of developers allows us to match their variable intent to specific system components, which make up the second dimension of our concerns. In this way, we aim to make explicit how the people involved in development, and make use of the platform, relate to each system layer, and offer some insight as to how concerns can be separated not only across components, but also across developers, whose aim is to take advantage of the potential for reuse.

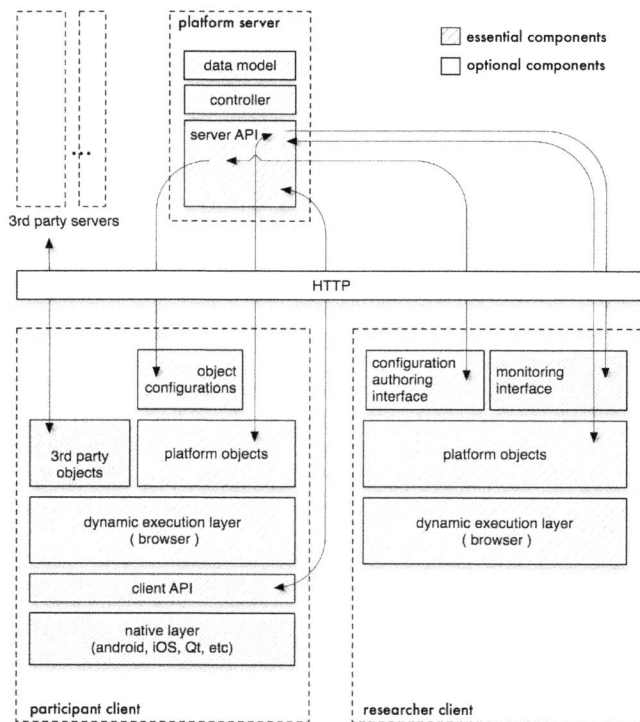

Figure 1. An overview of the system's components. Arrows indicate http requests to store or retrieve data.

This section presents a generic view of how the system is layered. Figure 1 gives an overview of the 3 main subsystems, a server and two client components, one to be used by the participant and the other by the researcher. Central to the system's composition is the dynamic execution environment that the browser has become nowadays, which is commonplace in smartphones, tablets and desktop systems. Alongside existing as a standalone application, it is also integrated in frameworks such as iOS, android and Qt, providing interfaces to lower-level system features. The javascript programming language features many capable and very actively developed frameworks, such as jQuery and jQuery mobile, which offer exemplary extensibility in the form of easy to reuse plugins. Also. the advancing scripting features of HTML5 make it a robust and rich platform which can facilitate many levels of development expertise.

This makes our system revolve around the authoring and distribution of what essentially are web applications, with the additional capacity to call system-specific features, as made available by the client API, and with the native layer substituting the server that traditional web applications need to constantly be in communication with. We agree with Anttonen et al. who state that in the future, a vast majority of software will be developed using web technologies, while binary programs will be limited to system software, and we are equally

excited about the opportunities for development, deployment and use that are opened up[2].

In Figure 1, we take the liberty of dividing the layers below the browser into optional and essential, to indicate that the essential layers are the absolute minimum for the most basic data collection study, such as a diary, to run. The more the needs of a study scale, the more essential and rich in features the 'optional' layers need to be.

By discussing the role each component plays in the platform, we hope to show how the requirements we established previously can be satisfied:

Server

The server maintains the central data store, and exposes an API,implemented in the controller, through which requests to retrieve or store data can be made. Requests can be made by both the researcher client and the participant client, providing the grounds for real-time communication between researchers and participants.

Participant client

Native layer and client API.
There are cases when the browser's features are not sufficient. The native layer serves two purposes. It integrates the platform with the rest of participant's device as a regular application. It can be launched and used in way familiar to the participant, or monitor its environment through a background process, and trigger events and make use of the server API. Its second purpose is to provide access to the client's hardware components and operating system functions. Sensors and local data stores and background processes can be accessed, encapsulated into the client API, and offered to the browser as javascript functions to be used by layers above.

Platform objects and third party objects
The platform objects, adhering to the object-oriented paradigm, are units that encapsulate javascript code and state variables, and are instantiated and executed in the browser. They can be the interface components which are expose to the user, and can be as simple or complicated as the needs of the study dictate and the developer's skills allow. They can make use of the underlying client API, as well as the server API. An example of a very simple platform object would be an html-form. More complicated ones can implement complex logic, display graphics and audio, take pictures with a smarphone's camera, or even be functional application prototypes to be evaluated by users.

If, in the set of their state variables, they make the kinds of parameters they are initialized with explicit, then object configurations can be produced for them through the authoring interface on the researcher's client.

To illustrate the things that can be made possible, the system could also afford third party objects, as custom or off-the-shelf javascript code that can be agnostic of the underlying API and extend the platform objects, with access to data and well established applications and APIs already available in the Web.

Object configurations

Object configurations, while also objects in themselves, are distinct from platform objects in that they are the system components that can be authored in the simplest possible way, even through a GUI. They contain sets of parameters meant to initialize and customize the platform objects. JSON is a format easily suited

Researcher client

Platform objects and authoring

Purely a web application, the researcher client harbours the exact same platform objects that are available to the client. Its configuration authoring interface can parse these objects and enable the production of object configurations through a GUI. Moreover, the code for additional platform objects can be submitted to the server for distribution to participant clients. Participant management, and allocation of platform objects to participants, are also handled through this module by calling the server API,

Monitoring interface

The monitoring interface is a distinct component that makes use of the server API to query the server for data that has been submitted by participant clients, and handles them locally in the browser for processing or visualization.

Implications for developer roles

Having explored the dimension of system components, in Figure 2 we offer a conceptual distribution of how each component can be mapped on development concerns, from the end-user developer role, where the product concerns a small set of the user population, to the professional developer role, whose output affects a greater body of users.

The system components that befall the end-user developers such as object configurations can only be sets of key-value pairs that can simply be produced through a GUI. Platform objects contain scripted and programmed behaviour, and the popular libraries and tools available for end-user authoring of HTML and javascript can be put to use to produce them. They are the key components to making the platform truly customizable. More complex behaviours than those that the browser allows, need to be implemented in the client API, and should more aptly be dealt with in a more professional mindset.

It should also be noted that the more volatile and easy to throw-away a component is, the easier it is to produce.

IMPLEMENTATION

The model is under progressive implementation, with the resulting application able, at the point of this writing, to support an ongoing diary study, with conditionally branching questionnaires, featuring offline data logging for android clients with limited connectivity. In the absence of a dedicated client for a participants' device, access has still been possible from a regular browser on a smartphone, tablet, or desktop, thanks to the support that the jQuery mobile library provides for a host of different devices.

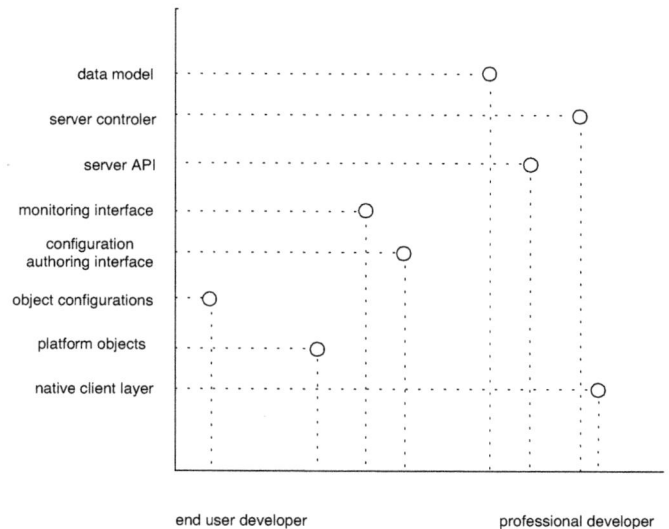

Figure 2. Estimation of how system components are distributed across development stakeholders.

The platform objects that have been implemented are configurable through a generic GUI, which produces key-value pairs in JSON, and can be customized and updated for each participant in real time. Participants' responses are also stored in JSON. They can be monitored and graphically visualized over time through a separate monitoring component which makes use of jQuery plugins to draw graphs. The researcher has been able, by observing the behaviour of participants, to modify the interfaces to better suit the inputs the participants provide. Optionally, responses can be downloaded as comma separated values for processing in packages such as Matlab or SPSS.

The researcher also has the ability to add to the pool of platform objects, produce configurations for the code and serve the new content to participants, without having to redeploy any component. For this to take place, the javascript object needs to implement two short methods and provide values for three specific members, in order to interface with the system.

In the future, the addition of an event handling component in the client API and the extension of the configuration authoring GUI with trigger specifications will allow for the implementation of experience sampling studies as well, without modification to the platform objects.

CONCLUSION

Challenges for tools for in situ data collection lie not only in how to allow participants to run applications that perform data collection, or in how to allow researchers to appropriate the tools in their studies. The need for developers to keep chasing after moving targets, such as constantly evolving hardware platforms and new design goals, without considering a general direction for the research community at large, leads to recurring reimplementation of tools, where only incremental or partial implementation is needed.

By enforcing a separation of end user development concerns

as related to system components, we have proposed a model that can be implemented on established standards that have massive support from the greater software development community, and a very exciting future.

Applying a common direction for tools such as the one suggested in this paper, provides benefits for both developers and users of the tools.

- For those interested in development of the tools, agreement on a modular approach can lead to shared client and server APIs that will promote the interoperability and reuse of components. The cost to implement new methods in software can be made lower. Also, iterations on past efforts can be allowed to focus only in areas of interest and not have to worry about the system as a whole.

- For those interested in using them to conduct studies with, access to a greater base of components to choose from will be possible, as well as mixing components from different projects, to produce a custom system that suit their needs. Additionally, having systems that are directly comparable can take us closer to consicely explicating research protocols for purposes of repetition and comparison across individual studies.

This work is not at odds with previously implemented platforms, but rather complementary to their efforts. Modern tools also apply technologies we advocate for in their implementations[12], but do so in isolation from each other. It is therefore the opportune moment to address the overarching issue of how to attain maintainable and reliable data collection tools, which can be interoperable, within the academic community. We urge academic developers and software designers who are building these tools to also consider these issues in the relevant discourse.

REFERENCES

1. Agresti, W. W. Software reuse : Developers experiences and perceptions. *Business 2010*, January 2010 (2011), 48–58.

2. Anttonen, M., Salminen, A., Mikkonen, T., and Taivalsaari, A. *Transforming the web into a real application platform*. ACM Press, 2011, 800–807.

3. Barrett, L. F., and Barrett, D. J. An introduction to computerized experience sampling in psychology. *Social Science Computer Review 19*, 2 (2001), 175–185.

4. Bezroukov, N. Open source software development as a special type of academic research (critique of vulgar raymondism). *First Monday 4*, 10 (1999), 1–16.

5. Carter, S., Mankoff, J., and Heer, J. *Momento: support for situated ubicomp experimentation*, vol. San Jose,. ACM, 2007, 125–134.

6. Carter, S., Mankoff, J., Klemmer, S., and Matthews, T. Exiting the cleanroom: On ecological validity and ubiquitous computing. *Human-Computer Interaction 23*, 1 (2008), 47–99.

7. de Sá, M., and Carriço, L. A mobile tool for in-situ prototyping. *Proceedings of the 11th International Conference on Human-Computer Interaction with Mobile Devices and Services - MobileHCI '09* (2009), 1.

8. Fischer, J. E. Experience-sampling tools : a critical review. *Journal of Youth and Adolescence 57*, 3 (2009), 1–3.

9. Froehlich, J., Chen, M. Y., Consolvo, S., Harrison, B., and Landay, J. A. *MyExperience: a system for in situ tracing and capturing of user feedback on mobile phones*, vol. San Juan,. ACM, 2007, 57–70.

10. Froehlich, J., Dillahunt, T., Klasnja, P., Mankoff, J., Consolvo, S., Harrison, B., and Landay, J. A. *UbiGreen: investigating a mobile tool for tracking and supporting green transportation habits*, vol. 09. ACM, 2009, 1043–1052.

11. Gerken, J., Dierdorf, S., Schmid, P., Sautner, A., and Reiterer, H. *Pocket Bee: a multi-modal diary for field research*. ACM, 2010, 7–10.

12. Hicks, J., Ramanathan, N., Falaki, H., Longstaff, B., Parameswaran, K., Monibi, M., Kim, D. H., Selsky, J., Jenkins, J., Tangmu, H., and Estrin, D. ohmage : An Open Mobile System for Activity and Experience Sampling. *ACM* (2011).

13. Khan, V.-j., and Eggen, B. Features for the future experience sampling tool. *Human Factors* (2009), 2–5.

14. Ko, A. J., Myers, B., Rosson, M. B., Rothermel, G., Shaw, M., Wiedenbeck, S., Abraham, R., Beckwith, L., Blackwell, A., Burnett, M., and et al. The state of the art in end-user software engineering. *ACM Computing Surveys 43*, 3 (2011), 1–44.

15. Larson, R., and Csikszentmihalyi, M. The experience sampling method. *New Directions for Methodology of Social and Behavioral Science 15*, 15 (1983), 41–56.

16. Myin-Germeys, I., Oorschot, M., Collip, D., Lataster, J., Delespaul, P., and Van Os, J. Experience sampling research in psychopathology: opening the black box of daily life. *Psychological Medicine 39*, 9 (2009), 1533–1547.

17. Khan, V.J., Ruyter, B. D., Markopoulos, P., and Eggen, B. Reconexp : A way to reduce the data loss of the experiencing sampling method. *Technology* (2008), 471–476.

Fear Therapy for Children – A Mobile Approach

Marco de Sa
Yahoo! Research
Santa Clara, CA, USA
marcodesa@acm.org

Luís Carriço
University of Lisbon
Lisboa, Portugal
lmc@di.fc.ul.pt

ABSTRACT
Mobile devices have shown to be useful tools in supporting various procedures and therapy approaches for different purposes. However, when applied to children, particular care has to be taken, considering both their abilities and their acceptance towards the used approaches. In this paper we present mobile applications, designed specifically for children and young patients, aiming at supporting fear therapy procedures. The software was developed following a user centered design approach and offers users an intuitive and metaphor based interaction paradigm that overcomes the paper-based counterpart's limitations. We describe the design process, the software and the results that we have obtained during an exploratory trial study.

Author Keywords
Mobile devices; fear and anxiety therapy; user centered design.

ACM Classification Keywords
H.5.m. [Information interfaces and presentation (e.g., HCI)]: Miscellaneous.

INTRODUCTION
The use of mobile devices within therapeutic and medical domains is not novel. In particular, they have been used to support therapists and clinicians while managing their records, accessing local or remote information and even assuming a more traditional personal assistant role [8][9]. The extension of these functionalities for patients has also been increasingly addressed by researchers and caregivers [11]. Among these, one can find simple registration (e.g., amount of cigarettes per day) diaries, short text-based tests or basic procedures and guidelines [17].

More recently, some approaches have been addressing and promoting cooperation between therapists and patients and even offering some support for personalization within the used tools [20]. However, traditionally, these require some computer usage skills, from both actors, and are usually aimed at adults or young adults. They aim at addressing

Cognitive Behavioral Therapy (CBT) [12] procedures and techniques for disorders such as depression, anxiety or even pain associated issues (e.g., thought registration, diary studies and questionnaire completion).

However, for teenagers and, most importantly, for children, who are also, frequently, in need of support, guidance and therapeutic aid, the number of existing tools is very low [5, 19]. Requirements for applications directed toward children are significantly different from those that are oriented toward adults [26] and, in a vast majority of situations, adult oriented applications are not adequate to younger patients. The small amount of existing examples, are often unsuccessful because they fail to address the following requirements: (1) lack of adequacy of its content for infants and children who are in different cognitive stages (2) inability to support younger children without reading skills (3) low adherence and (4) frequent disengagement from therapy.

These issues assume even greater importance when dealing with children who are undergoing therapy for fear (e.g., caused by traumatic experiences, bullying, phobias) and related anxiety or depression. In such situations, given the lack of available tools and software, children are often faced with paper-based artifacts [14] that can be difficult to use, hindering the process and, once again, leading to high levels of disengagement from therapy and poor end results extending, in some cases, the therapy processes for long periods of time.

In this paper we present a set of mobile applications that aim at supporting therapy procedures for children between 5 and 14 years of age, suffering from fear related disorders. The developed software takes into account the current limitations and requirements of existing approaches and was developed in cooperation with a Psychotherapy research team. The applications are composed by components that offer an easy to interact and easy to understand approach based on drawings and moveable interactive components that do not require the ability to read or previous knowledge of how to interact with mobile devices. The applications are being developed in cooperation with clinical therapists and psychotherapy researchers and consider both the requirements that the artifacts for children require in terms of development and the need to increase acceptability and engagement on the therapy process. Our major contributions over existing work are the development of specific digital applications for fear therapy that can be used in the situations where they are most needed and their adequateness to children of various ages, especially younger ones.

This paper describes our work, stressing the design process and used approach and providing detail on the developed applications and their functionalities. We present results from an exploratory evaluation process, discuss our current results and draw some future paths to follow.

FEAR THERAPY FOR CHILDREN

Children are often faced with a wide variety of frightening situations during their daily lives (e.g., bullying, school, dark places, and traumatic events). In certain cases, these situations and feelings lead to anxiety, depression and may severely affect their lives, requiring therapy even at very early ages. Therapy is usually comprised by an initial diagnosis stage where therapists try to assess the fear's origin, its intensity and how it affects the child. This diagnosis is followed by different therapy approaches in which, for most cases, children are frequently asked to assess their improvements or to indicate the amount of fear they felt in a specific situation, in order to rationalize their fear and gradually overcome it.

Currently, to achieve so, paper artifacts and self-rating questionnaires are used [14], during therapy sessions with the therapist and, if necessary, at home or at the situations that cause the child to feel fear. This ubiquitous use is most important and much more effective as the child is able quantify his/her feelings when they are easier to recollect and, at a posterior stage, assessing this information from a different and guided viewpoint.

However, this type of procedure poses several issues to both therapists and patients, especially when the latter are of young age. For therapists it is difficult to manage the gathered data and collect reliable information through the various situations that may cause problems to children. In particular, it is common for patients to provide erroneous information (e.g., usually completing their homework just before going to a therapy session and not when required by the therapist) or simply to state they forgot the annotations and filled-in questionnaires at home. For children, among others, engagement to the therapy process is reduced and, for younger patients (especially those without reading skills), the utilization of the traditional questionnaires is problematic. Moreover, some of the most used questionnaires are standard, often containing terms that are difficult to comprehend; most of the included information relates to situations that do not affect the child (e.g., pre-defined events and fear inducing situations); and offer very little customization and personalization options.

In addition, these currently used artifacts are generally inadequate to be used (e.g., fetching a paper and annotating several values) during the situations where they matter the most, whenever the stressful events take place.

RELATED WORK

The quick evolution of technology has promoted its inclusion within a wide set of our society's activities and domains. In particular, the recent burst of mobile and personal devices has allowed for the development of assistive technologies and software that provide pervasive support for patients on the go. More recently, this support has been evolving to personalized levels, matching therapies, artifacts and technology to each individual user to a level that was unavailable before. Examples of existing applications/artifacts range from simple questionnaires; digital books, diet control forms, relaxation tutorials, tests, etc., but are generally restricted to a particular type of artifact and domain. Some tools that allow the customization of digital artifacts have also started to emerge and have showed high success within their domains [20].

Following these advances, studies on how computers can improve clinicians' work [8][13][17] and the development of applications directed to support this kind of activities has been naturally gaining some momentum. Excluding expedite diagnosis solutions that have revealed strong human rejection [6], studies demonstrated the effectiveness of the computer role in the process of therapy [10][26].

However, most of the existing systems are directed towards adults and require either some knowledge of how to work with computers and access the internet or include content that is not suited to younger patients. Moreover, most examples are confined to simple descriptions of existing pathologies and are generally directed towards therapists, indicating drug dosage or providing reference information about diseases or drugs [9].

Still, applications developed for the treatment of specific pathologies, such as bulimia nervosa, had positive outcomes [16]. On a mobile strand, making use of handheld such as PDAs or TabletPCs, some self-control or relaxation procedures are also available [18]. Nevertheless, they offer no options to adjust to patients' needs, especially the possibility of including content that is suited to children such as interactive images, drawings and conveying a message that is easily comprehended by them.

Several web-based self-help applications and websites are also available [1]. Overall, in spite of the advantages inherent to this type of solutions, such as remote assistance and costs lowering, they have many disadvantages [24]. For instance, patient disengagement is frequent, as well as patient misinterpretation of the site's objectives and they usually require adult supervision or are not easily accessible by teenagers and, especially, children. In addition, they do not comply with the need to quickly collect information in during ubiquitous situations and activities.

Albeit non mobile, there are some examples of multimodal and much more interactive systems applied to therapeutic procedures, however, once again, they are very focused on specific pathologies and cannot be applied to children. For instance, in [2] the authors developed a system directed for the support of on-consultation heart stroke rehabilitation. These involve multimodal interaction methodologies (e.g., movement recognition) that were introduced in order to capture patient's biofeedback and should provide a good approach for tools that can be adjusted to support therapy procedures for children. Furthermore, they enable creation, storage and manipulation multimodal annotations [28] but, nevertheless, lack the necessary content and usability levels that are required for very young patients. In fact, most of the work found in the available literature does not address therapy support for young patients (e.g., teenagers and children), providing means for them to use the necessary tools at home, while away from the therapist and even without assistance from an adult.

DESIGN PROCESS

Given our problem's domain, sensitive subject and the end-users to which it is directed, the design approach followed during the development of our work was strongly based on a user centered design methodology. In addition, considering the sensitive topic and complexity of designing and evaluating new health care interventions [7] we followed an iterative design process as previous applied to the CBT domain [5]. This paper describes the exploratory stage of this process as defined by Campbell et al [4].

The selected techniques for this project were also developed to cope with the added challenges of mobile applications and mobile interaction [22]. They suggest a set of directives for the generation of scenarios and highlight several dimensions that affect mobile interaction within real settings in order to drive design [22]. Additionally, it introduces a set of techniques for prototyping and evaluation of user interfaces for small handheld devices.

Throughout the process, two different teams were involved, namely a computer engineering team, with four researchers, and a team composed by two senior psychology researchers and clinicians who have worked with children, for over 10 years. The design process described in this paper spanned for approximately two months. This period comprised several sessions, especially for the initial design stages, which composed the majority of this period. Once the requirements were defined and validated with an initial evaluation, the actual development of the resulting software took a shorter amount of time.

Establishing Requirements

During the initial stage of the design process, four meetings, taking 1 to 2 hours each, were held in order to establish and analyze requirements. This stage comprised around one week. Interviews and brainstorming sessions with therapists, children and their parents, were conducted in order to understand children's habits and knowledge regarding computers and handheld devices. It was also necessary to establish how their disorders affected their daily life, especially in regard to how and when they usually accomplished their tasks and chores (related to

therapy). Informal interviews were made by the therapists with colleagues and patients. Therapists also shared detail on the goals of the existing artifacts, used procedures and problems that usually affected their patients during the sessions in which they utilize these artifacts.

These studies demonstrated children feel reluctant in using the traditional paper based artifacts, as highlighted by their therapists, pointing out that disengagement is common and that patients frequently forget to register what is required. Additionally, the type of questionnaire and used approach poses, often, issues to smaller children who still lack reading abilities. Naturally, even the medium poses issues to the process as it is complicated for younger children to carry the paper questionnaires and necessary material to fill them in during the activities in which they usually face their problems (e.g., playground, kindergarten).

However, when questioned about the use of technology, children responded very positively. From a group of 15 children that were interviewed, 13 stated that they frequently used games and portable devices (e.g., portable media players, cell phones) and were very familiar with this type of technology. Even those that had less experience with technology feel very compelled and interested by computers. Parents who were also interviewed confirmed these results, especially emphasizing that sometimes they would not allow their younger children to use their computers but that most provided cell phones and mobile devices to be able to reach and keep in touch with their children. Throughout these meetings the currently used artifacts were reviewed and a set of requirements, directed towards children and the process were identified:

• Use approaches that are meaningful to children and to which they can relate to.

• Facilitate access to children who cannot read.

• Enhance the process to overcome disengagement.

• Facilitate data collection while away from the therapist.

• Facilitate data analysis by therapists.

Based on these initial requirements, a first design stage was initiated, involving mainly the psychotherapy team, followed by brainstorming sessions with both teams.

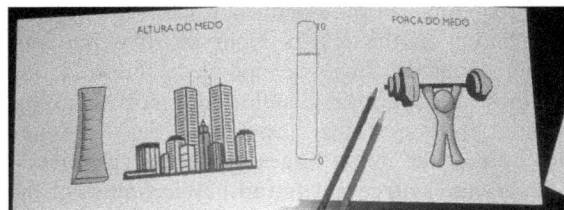

Figure 1. Image-based paper artifacts used by therapists for young patients to quantify their fear.

Figure 1 depicts the very first approach by the Psychology team to overcome some of these issues. In trying to avoid the traditional paper questionnaires, composed by multiple-choice questions and free annotation forms, the team that worked on this project tried to develop a paper sheet with an image, where the patient is usually requested to point (e.g., marking with a pen or pencil directly on the ruler – on the left side) the amount (or the height) of fear s/he feels in a certain situation. The main contribution from this new approach is that the form is based on metaphors and images, becoming more appealing to patients and easier to understand. At this point, children were not involved as therapists believed it was too early in the process and were still unsure about the outcome and its implication on the therapy process for potential participants.

For the initial tests made with these artifacts, the therapy research team commented that they were frequently inquired by their patients if, rather than marking on the ruler, they could draw a new building (on the image's city landscape) representing the height of their fear. On the right side, a second paper sheet shows a simple drawing with a gauge on the left side for patients to point the strength of the fear. These different options can be used at the beginning of the therapy process, in which therapists try to assess the most suited metaphors and artifacts to each particular child. These new artifacts were used by the therapy team with their patients and showed significant promise. In a general perspective, patients from various ages seemed to respond better to the drawings, when compared to the traditional text-based format. At least one of the used metaphors was also simple to understand by every child.

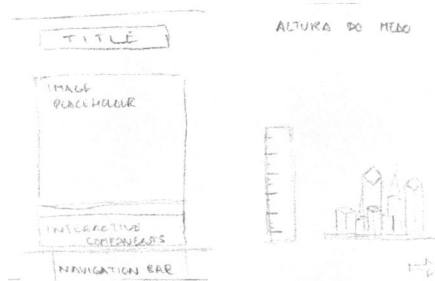

Figure 2. Wireframe and low-fidelity sketches used for the early stage evaluation.

Early Design and Prototyping
Once initial requirements were defined, a set of low-fidelity prototypes, based on the results from the two previous stages, were created. This development followed the previously mentioned specific guidelines for mobile devices (i.e., creating prototypes that provide a realistic usage experience even at the initial stages of the design process) [**Error! Reference source not found.**]. Wireframes of the user interface (see Figure 2) and respective functionalities were drawn, based on the existing artifacts, taking into account the targeted devices and their characteristics (e.g., screen size, available interaction modalities). The wireframes were shown to the involved therapists and researchers and a few think-aloud and walkthrough sessions

were conducted in order to assess the navigation and usability of the early stage prototypes.

From the initial wireframes, one layout was selected and a set of sketches, including some functionalities and content were designed, materializing the initial low-fidelity prototypes.

Early Stage Evaluation
The sketches were used together with a few rigid frames, composing physical prototypes that closely resemble actual devices (e.g., size, weight) and provide a realistic feel of the actual usage experience, which was essential to provide children with a clear idea of what would they interact with (Figure 3). As an evolution from paper-based questionnaires, it was necessary to add this physical dimension and affordance to the low-fidelity prototypes so that children could understand the differences and for the design team to detect issues that could emerge when using such devices. Nevertheless, low-fidelity prototypes were essential given the size of the design team and the age of the end-users to which the software was being designed.

To assess the prototypes and sketches, these were tested and reviewed by therapists. To properly understand how the tools would be used in real-life situations, a set of simulated therapy sessions were performed. For instance, meetings took place at a therapist's office where therapist and patients used the low-fidelity prototypes. Three young children (between 9 and 11 years old) participated on these initial studies. At this point, none of them had or were undergoing any type of therapy. Still, at this stage the main concerns were focused on usability and accessibility issues.

Some of these simulated sessions also took place at different settings within a school, emulating real-world experiences and aiming at understanding the children's behavior while using the prototypes in different settings. All these studies, involving children, were carefully planned. The goals, procedures and used equipment were explained to every participant.

The Wizard-of-Oz technique was used to allow the participants to interact with the various screens and simulate the tool's behavior according to their actions. Figure 3 shows a child interacting with a low-fi prototype, during one of the evaluation studies, while the designer is switching the various sketches/screens. Every session took less than 15 minutes and was followed by a short interview. Again, the main focus was on the usability and clarity and affordances of the user interface. No fear inducing simulations took place.

Early Results
Although the younger patients (9 years old) had some difficulties while understanding the concept behind the tools and imagining the actual application's functionality based alone on the interaction with paper-based sketches, results were very positive. In fact, their interest and

enthusiasm towards the prototypes was overwhelming, as suggested by the requests to use the final tool and to keep some of the sketches with them. Naturally, care was taken not to immediately consider this a success as children tend to be very enthusiastic with new approaches for a short period of time. Still, their acceptance of the overall layout and suggested sequences and affordances of the used components was very promising as well. Some of the new ideas that were applied on the software application were directly obtained by observing children's expectations when interacting with the paper-based sketches.

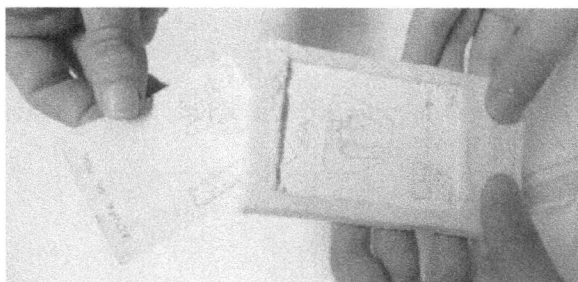

Figure 3. Child interacting with a low-fi prototype and designer acting as the Wizard-of-Oz (replacing a card).

For instance, an interesting fact observed during these tests showed that their perception of the fear's weight was clearly related to the pressure that they would put into the drawing of a scale, shown in one of the prototypes (Figures 3 and 5). Naturally, this is a dimension that can only be introduced on a digital version. Additionally, it was clear that the most used approach to interact with the various interactive components (explained to them at the beginning of each study) was direct manipulation, as children would immediately touch the device's screen and point directly on the drawing what they wanted to express.

These results were added to our initial requirements and were considered during the development process that followed this initial design stage.

THE SOFTWARE CATALOGUE
Given the positive results from the early stage evaluation, a software catalogue with three therapy applications, based on the selected sketches, was developed [21]. The following subsections provide detail on the concept and various functionalities that were included in each artifact and the overall software catalogue.

Concept and Goals
As previously mentioned, the software catalogue is the enhancement and improvement of an existing set of innovative paper-based artifacts created by one of the researchers from the psychotherapy team. These artifacts' main goals are to allow children to quantify, subjectively, their fear (towards any given subject), through a set of drawings and measures, each using a different metaphor (weight, strength, height). The child is able to navigate freely through the various drawings and, using different

interaction approaches for each metaphor, select the amount or intensity of his/her fear. These results can be discussed with the therapist during a session or can be reviewed by the therapist once all the results are stored (usually when completed at home). Accordingly, our goals with this application are to overcome the interaction issues (e.g., editing, erasing, writing, and marking the amount and intensity for requested subject), providing the existing tools on a digital format, but also to create artifacts that are presented in an enticing format that appeals to patients and increases their enthusiasm, consequentially affecting the long term commitment to their tasks and therapy procedure.

Additionally, we aim at providing the needed flexibility for therapists to quickly detected and decide which approach, and used metaphor, is most adequate to each child. At the same time, using the digital medium, we aim at including the necessary means to detect when and if the patients followed their instructions and completed their homework. To achieve so, the collection of results and logging of the various interactions that take place is automatic and time stamped. Moreover, therapists are able to configure and select which screens are shown to the child, adjusting the artifacts to the stage of the therapy or diagnosis process.

Interaction
In order to maintain coherence with the traditionally used procedures, the catalogue follows a similar organization to that used by therapists during initial sessions. Every screen is arranged sequentially and each presents a different question and option for the user to register the intensity of his/her fear. Users are also able to navigate back a forth freely, editing their results as much as necessary. However, once they reach the final screen, a congratulatory message is display and the results are stored for posterior analysis, a requirement that emerged early during the initial design stage. There are a total of 5 screens, one introductory screen, three screens/artifacts containing questions and a final screen that informs the user that s/he has reached the end, also displaying a congratulatory message.

Figure 4. Screen to quantify the fear's height.

For later stages of therapy, and based on the child's progress, therapists are able to omit or select screens, focusing more intensively on those that allow the child to better express his/her feelings/fear.

Navigation between screens is support by two buttons at the bottom of each screen (next and previous). Each button is disabled at the end or at the beginning of the application. For instance, the next button is disabled once the patient reaches the final screen.

To support an easy to use and intuitive usage experience for children of various ages, the metaphors previously used on the paper-based version were maintained. However, taking advantage of the digital medium and the devices' capabilities, especially the different interaction modalities and input channels that it supports, every screen was augmented with new interaction options.

Figure 4 depicts one of the screens in which children are requested to set the height of their fear. It is based on the paper sheet shown on figure 1 left, and on the low-fidelity prototype from figure 2. However, on the software counterpart, the intensity of the fear is not marked on top of the ruler/scale but is defined by the height of one of the buildings. The numeric scale on the left can be shown/hidden according to the therapist's decision (e.g., for younger or older patients).

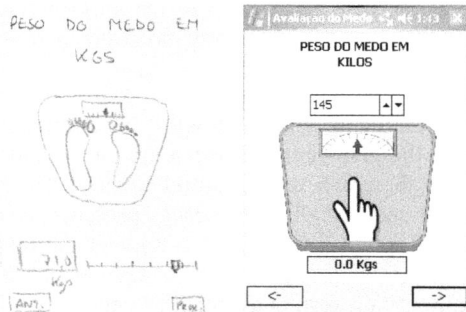

Figure 5. Left) Low-fidelity sketch of the user interface to measure the fear's weight. Right) The software user interface.

The building on the far left, with the label "Aqui!" can be stretched or shrunken directly by the user. By pressing the label and moving downwards or upwards, the child is able to manipulate the size of the building and scale his/her feelings by interacting directly with the drawing. This can be done by simply placing a finger (or the stylus) on the marked location, moving it to set the building (and fear)'s height. For devices without a touch screen, the generic keypad can also be used to increase or decrease the building's size. The first approach, of allowing patients to draw their own buildings was dropped following the suggestions of all the therapists, in order not to distract or provide too much alternatives to patients.

The screen shown in Figure 5, on the right, aims at allowing patients to quantify their fear, indicating the fear's weight. The paper based artifact, designed by therapists, shows a similar drawing of a scale and requests users to write down their fear's weight. The developed tool presents the same options. Still, it also allows the user to set his/her fear's weight through three additional approaches. As shown on top of the drawing, a counter can be used to directly type

the weight or, using the up and down arrows, increase the valued showed on the textbox. Finally, the drawing is also interactive and can be used to edit the weight value as well. By pressing and holding the drawing, as pointed by the "hand icon", children are also able to edit the values without the need to type. The weight is increased as long as the scale's drawing is pressed simulating a pressure sensor, much alike a real scale.

Naturally, some of these options are only available on devices with touch screens. Below there is a reset button that sets the weight back to zero. Overall, the three different options aim at: on the one hand allowing children without writing skills to use it but also providing more advanced modalities for older patients and; on the other hand, allowing the artifacts to be used on different devices with different characteristics and features.

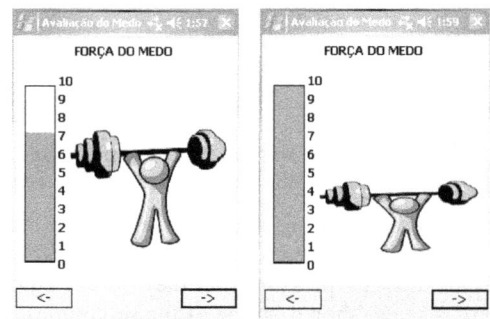

Figure 6. User interface to quantify the fear's strength.

Another example of how patients can interact with the various screens in shown in Figure 6. Here, to select the fear's strength, the user must touch the scale on the left, filling it up or emptying it according to the selected level. Additionally, in order to reinforce the used metaphor (weight of the fear) and to provide additional visual feedback to the users, the image on the right grows in a reverse proportion to the selected level. For instance, whenever the fear levels are very high, the size of the drawn human figure shrinks, simulating the effect of a very heavy weight squashing down the drawn figure.

Globally, every screen presents the same information that is contained on the paper-based artifacts but enhances it with different interaction possibilities and additional visual feedback that provides patients alternative ways to understand the actions and levels of each subject when classifying their fear.

EXPLORATORY EVALUATION AND VALIDATION

Initial Experiments

To validate the developed artifacts, an initial set of tests was conducted. These tests were performed by a team of therapists who, during several sessions, presented the software for their patients to use. These tests were conducted during a two week period at one of the therapist's office. A total of 10 children and teenagers, aged between 6 and 14 participated on the study (see Figure 7). Every child was a student, attending school from the 1st to 10th grade. Eight of them were undergoing therapy for fear, anxiety and associated issues, caused by bullying, or specific traumas related to fire accidents, dog attacks, water, etc. All the participants had varied social backgrounds. The eight oldest owned their own cell phones.

Additionally, five more therapists, not involved in the project, and four parents were also included on this trial and utilized the software.

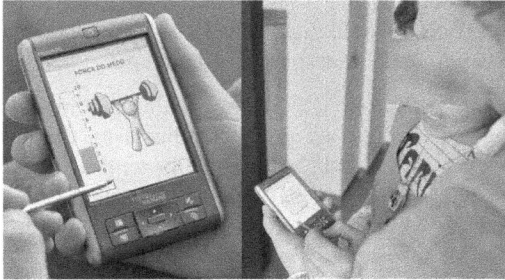

Figure 7.a) Close up of a child interacting with the tool on a PDA. b) Another child testing it accompanied by her mother.

All the participants had a short period, without any aid, to interact freely with the software. This period was monitored, at a distance, by therapists and designers/engineers. Afterwards, participants that were familiarized with therapy completed two separate tasks. One in which they had to use the software artifacts as if it was a normal therapy session, indicating their fear through the various available screens and a second task, in which they had to follow some suggestions. For the former, the goal was to assess how quickly they would detect the various interaction options that were available and how well would they be able to use the tools. This exercise also provided an initial idea on their preferred metaphors and chosen interaction modalities.

For the latter, they were asked to go through all the screens, using the several available modalities and interaction possibilities at each step, explaining what they thought of the current actions and if they felt it would be possible, or even more interesting, to interact with that user interface, or provide that some information, through a different manner. Those modalities that they had not detected were explained to them on the second task. These tasks were monitored and annotations were taken. The two youngest participants (aged 6 years old) only completed this second task accompanied by a designer and a therapist.

The studies, for each of the first eight participants, were followed by a short interview and a questionnaire that users were requested to complete.

The studies, interviews and questionnaires were controlled and managed by therapists, in order to select the appropriate timing, language, and requests to each of the patients and

provide them with a comfortable and familiar setting to which they were accustomed to.

Patients' Results and Suggestions
Results from the interviews that took place after each evaluation session, were clearly positive. Participants were asked to rate whether they enjoyed the application and its various components and whether they thought it was easy to use. Three out of the eight patients were very pleased with the tool, scoring it as a 7 on a scale from 1 to 7. Only one of the participants, the oldest one, an adolescent, scored the tool as a 3, saying it was a bit too childish, while the three remaining children scored it as a 6. Moreover, five of the eight participants thought the tool was very easy to use, scoring it as a 7 and three of the participants scored it a 6.

Figure 8 presents the results from the questionnaires that were completed by the eight patients. Globally, the questionnaire aimed at assessing the software catalogue usability wise, and to understand whether it was preferred over the previous paper-based artifacts. All the participants stated that they understood what they had to do in each of the screens, where to touch and with which components to interact, and what was expected with each drawing and question. In addition, all the participants concurred that they would be able to use the tool even when away from the therapist, by themselves, without requesting assistance. Finally, the large majority of the participants (7 out of 8) thought that it was easier to use the digital artifacts (materialized by the tool) than the traditional paper-based versions. The same was verified for their preference between the two versions. Only one of the enquired patients had no opinion while the other seven preferred to use the software version over paper.

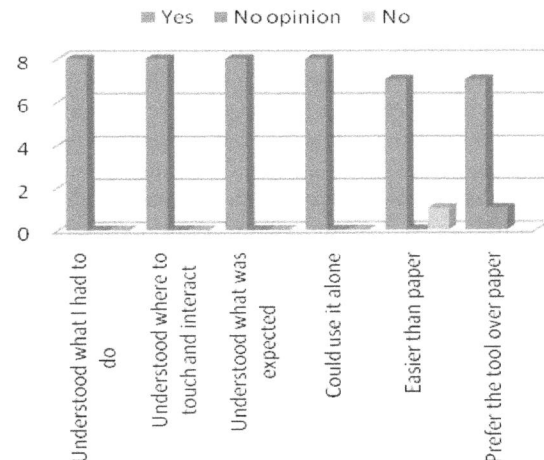

Figure 8. Results from children's questionnaires.

The questionnaire included a suggestions' item, where the participants were requested to provide suggestions for each of the screens that compose the tool. Although results from both the interviews and questionnaires were very positive, every participant had suggestions on how to improve the tool. General comments, shared by most of the participants, requested the tool to provide audio feedback as well. For instance, for the measurement of the fear's height, some children wanted to listen to a construction's noise while the building is growing and a demolition noise while reducing the building's height. For this screen, a reset button, to set the building's size to the initial height was also one of the suggestions.

For the second screen, where patients weigh their fear, suggestions included the inclusion of movement on the scale's small pointer, the inclusion of a "monster" over the scale to represent their fear and for that monster to grow proportionally to the fear's weight. On the fear's strength, the third screen, participants also wanted to see more feedback on the drawing. For instance, one suggestion mentioned the possibility of increasing the number of weights on the dumbbell or for the human figure to gain more muscles when the fear's strength was lower or even to change the figure's color also according to the fear's strength. Finally, some patients also suggested that some of the used drawings should be more directly related to fear and should be more realistic and more adult. Naturally, children's predisposition to enjoy technology and the novelty factor were taken into account for all of these questionnaires. However, these interviews and questionnaires were overseen by therapists and gathered through interviews, where some of these factors were attenuated by the used approach, the selected wording and the involved therapists' experience with children.

The two younger participants were also interviewed and observed while interacting with the software artifacts. Both were quickly able to detect all of the interactive components. When asked to explain what each screen meant, they replied very confidently and very accurately what each screen and metaphor represented, which corroborated the initial results regarding the ability all the involved patients had to understand the chosen metaphors. Additionally, none had any problems while navigating back and forth through the catalogue and understood when and how to press each button and the resulting effect of each action. Overall, the two youngest patients, who had still very limited, or in one case no reading abilities, had no trouble interacting with the catalogue and while understanding how to use it.

Therapists' and Parents' Opinions
During the trial, as previously mentioned, some of the patient's parents (3 parents) were also interviewed and requested to interact with the tool. Five therapists also participated on the study.

Globally, they all were very enthused with the selected features and with the overall usability and interactivity of the software artifacts. In particular, parents were unanimous in stating that this would probably make it much easier to convince their children to do their homework and therapy tasks while at home. Apart from the 5 therapists that participated on the trial with children, mediating and

overseeing the process, the software was also presented at a therapy for children workshop. Thirty (30) practicing therapists attended the workshop, where one of the researchers from the psychotherapy team presented the software, explaining its goal and functionalities.

All the attending therapists were very pleased with the possibility of using mobile devices with their patients, especially considering the utilization of tools that can be used by children without needing any particular computer skills and with a very short learning curve. The opinion that just by introducing the digital medium and mobile devices into the process would significantly increase their patients' enthusiasm towards therapy was unanimous.

From a short discussion, it was noticeable that in addition to the expected increase on patient enthusiasm, the ability to monitor and collect data automatically would provide very useful data. For instance, with the logging capabilities, therapists are able to see when each artifact was used and compare this information with that provided by the patient. Additionally, this also serves as means to understand whether the patient edited his/her results and, through the time of day of each log, to locate where a situation that led to using the software took place. The ability to use the metaphors and interactive approach that patients can relate to was also very well received by all the therapists. All the participating therapists showed great interest in using the software with their patients.

Exploratory Clinical Study
To continue validating our approach, and based on the early results, an exploratory clinical study also took place. The software catalogue, along with 4 PDAs was given to 3 practicing therapists (not involved in the project) for them to use with their patients. The PDAs were provided so that no bias was introduced and so that all the patients had access to the same material. The study is still taking place and 4 patients, aged between 9 and 11 are participating.

However, at the end of the fourth month, all the therapists were interviewed and provided their feedback and a brief summary of their patients' opinions, along with some of the parents' opinions as well. Patients' data and private information was not accessed at any time but the therapists summarized reports on therapy engagement. Thus far, according to the three therapists, results have been extremely positive. In particular, they highlighted the fact that patients provide much more registries. The number of registrations for each participant has increased over 200%. Additionally, these registrations are more detailed and descriptive of the situations in which they occur than previously reported by the same patients. Therapists have highlighted the additional advantages over the previous approach:

- patients cannot say they lost the paper sheet with their registrations;

- as registrations are time-stamped, the therapist is able to check when the registration was done (e.g., not just before entering the therapist's office);

- the feedback provided by the system increases patients' motivation and being able to see different events (e.g., smaller monster or weight lifter) helps them keep motivated for longer periods;

- time spent to quantify and use the system to create a registration is smaller than using pen and paper;

- because of the new approach there was much more parent involvement on the process, which is particularly important for this type of therapy;

- according to the patients, the approach is fun, opposed to the boring paper registration;

- and most importantly, patients feel more comfortable using the device, even when surrounded by friends, providing accurate information collected in-situ, after a specific event. As mentioned by one of the therapists, information is better because it is collected right after the events but also because the patient loses inhibition.

It is important to mention that the amount of registries, and the information that they contain, is one of the most important measures of success for this type of therapy. Results conveyed to us by the therapists clearly demonstrate the initial success the new approach is having by significantly increasing therapy engagement.

In addition to the positive impact that it had on patients and the therapy process, therapists are also very satisfied with the ability to collect data in a much easier way and also verify in which situations and at what moments, patients registered their thoughts or emotions.

DISCUSSION

The experiments that took place during the evaluation period have demonstrated that children responded very positively to the software approach. We believe this is a direct result from the interactive features and accessible approach, which provide an appealing and engaging way for children to assess their own feelings and express them through the use of a new medium.

In particular, the positive results from the clinical study have solidified our belief that the tool can motivate a better and more engaging therapy process. This is in accordance with the opinions of all the consulted therapists who stated that besides the clear ability that younger patients have to adapt and learn how to use technology; these devices would also emphasize their excitement and willingness to participate on the various tasks and, most importantly, that this enthusiasm is usually constant through time.

Moreover, even without considering the patients' engagement over the traditional paper-based approach, the inclusion of the automatic data collection features provide a much closer monitoring process from the therapist,

allowing him/her to adjust the therapy procedure to the patient's behavior and evolution. As stated by all the therapists that were interviewed and consulted this is in itself, a major contribution to the process.

In general, we also believe that the ability to interact and manipulate the drawings, in concert with the different types of feedback, was crucial and propelled the children's interest in using the software artifacts. Still, it is also necessary to consider that evolutions and additions to the catalogue might be necessary in order to maintain the patients' interest through longer periods of time and renewing the novelty factor that is paramount for children.

Nevertheless, when compared to the traditional paper based approach, the tools overcome most of the initial limitations that motivated this work by supporting:

(1) an easier editing process, as children can easily control the interactive components, setting values at will; and an easier and more complete analysis process for therapists;

(2) younger children to easily interact with it and quickly provide the necessary information to their therapist. This was shown not only by the two participants who were not able to read but could easily use the software, but by the remaining participants who were under the age of 10 and understood the goal of each artifact;

(3) increase children´s enthusiasm and engagement to the therapy process by providing an interactive medium that can be adjusted to them and, given the used platform (e.g., mobile devices), can be integrated into their life style;

(4) collection of more reliable information automatically, increasing the amount and frequency of gathered data, which is determinant to the success of the therapy process.

CONCLUSIONS

The use of mobile devices to support various types of therapy has shown to provide very positive results. Currently available tools offer different options that target several issues and support both therapist and patients on a set of therapeutic procedures and endeavors. However, most do not apply to the specific requirements that arise when patients are very young.

We presented a software catalogue, composed by a set of digital therapy mobile applications, which aims at supporting fear therapy procedures for young children and teenagers. The software was designed in cooperation with practicing therapists following an iterative user centered design approach, in which early stage tests, with low-fidelity prototypes, allowed children to interact and provide their input during the development process. This resulted in an interactive set of mobile applications that augments paper-based artifacts and enhances them by providing several means for users to select and measure the fear levels using different metaphors. In addition, it allows therapists to control the therapy process and collect valuable information that is unattainable otherwise.

Initial tests showed very positive results and great acceptance from the children that experimented with the software and lots of enthusiasm from parents and therapists. For patients, it was noticeable that there were no difficulties in understanding and interacting with the software artifacts. In fact, for the majority of the participants, the mobile applications were much preferred to the original paper-artifacts. A large group of therapists concurred with these results and believed it had great promise. These results were solidified by the clinical study. Although still exploratory, it was noticeable that the applications overcome the paper versions' limitations and had a significant impact on the process and on the wellbeing of the children.

FUTURE WORK

Further tests, with updated artifacts, new interaction modalities and applied to other disorders are already planned. The integration of these tools with non-intrusive physiological sensors is also being prepared.

Furthermore, the current exploratory study is still taking place and minor adjustments have been made to some of the applications. A working release, to be used for a clinical trial, will be launched soon. Finally, a collaborative version of the tool, allowing therapists to monitor patient progress in real time is being developed.

REFERENCES

1. Andersson, G., Kaldo, V., 2004. Internet-Based Cognitive Behavioural Therapy for Tinnitius. In Journal of Clinical Psychology, No.60 171-178

2. Bälter, O., et al, Wizard-of-Oz Test of ARTUR, pp. 36-43, ASSETS'05, October 9-12, 2005.

3. Boujarwah, F. A., et al. 2011.REACT: intelligent authoring of social skills instructional modules for adolescents with high-functioning Autism. SIGACCESS Access. Comput. 99 (January 2011),13-23.

4. Campbell, M., Fitzpatrick, R., Haines, A., Kinmonth, A.L., Sandercock, P. & Tyrer, P. Framework for design and evaluation of complex interventions to improve health. British Medical Journal, 2000. 321 p.694-696.

5. Coyle, D. et al. 2011. Exploratory evaluations of a computer game supporting cognitive behavioural therapy for adolescents. In Proceedings CHI '11. ACM, New York, NY, USA, 2937-2946.

6. Das, A. K., 2002. Computers in Psychiatry: A Review of Past Programs and an Analysis of Historical Trends. In Psychiatry Quarterly, No.79 (4).

7. Doherty, G. et al. 2010. Design and Evaluation Guidelines for Mental Health Technologies. Interacting with Computers, Vol. 22, Issue 4, 2010, Pages 243-252.

8. Garrard, C., 2000. Can computers improve the way doctors work? Schweitz Med Wochenschr, No. 130(42).

9. Grasso, M. A., Clinical Applications of Hand Held Computing. 17th IEEE Symposium on Computer Based Medical Systems, 141-146, 2004.

10. Hailpern, J., Encouraging Speech and Vocalization in Children with Autistic Spectrum Disorder, SIGAccess Newsletter, pp.47-52, 89, 2007.

11. Herman, S., Koran, L. (1998). In vivo measurement of obsessive-compulsive disorder symptoms using palmtop computers. Computers in Human Behaviour 14(3).

12. Mahoney, M. (2003). Constructive Psychotherapy. New York; The Guilford Press.

13. Moffatt, K., et al., The Participatory Design of a Sound and Image Enhanced Daily Planner for People with Aphasia, CHI 2004, April 24–29, 2004, Vienna, Austria.

14. Muris P, et al. (2002). What is the Revised Fear Survey Schedule for Children measuring? Behavior Research Therapy.Nov; 40 (11):1317-26.

15. Newman M. G., 2004. Technology in psychotherapy. In Journal of Clinical Psychology. No. 60 (2) pp 141-145

16. Norton, M., et al, 2003. The use of palm top computers in the treatment of bulimia nervosa. European Eating Disorders Review. 11(3), 231–242.

17. Proudfoot, J., 2004. Computer-based treatment for anxiety and depression: is it feasible? Is it effective? Neuroscience and Biobehavioral Reviews, 28, 353–363.

18. Przeworski, A., Newman, M., 2004. Palmtop computer-assisted group therapy for social phobia. Journal of Clinical Psychology. 60(2)179–188.

19. Przeworski, A. & Newman, M. G. (2006). The efficacy and utility of computer-assisted cognitive-behavioral therapy for anxiety disorders. Clinical Psychologist 10.

20. Sá, M., Carriço, L., Antunes, P., Ubiquitous Psychotherapy, Pervasive Computing, 6,1, 2007, IEEE.

21. Sá, M., et al. 2010. Designing for children: a fear therapy tool. CHI EA '10 ACM, NY, USA, 3487-3492.

22. Sá, M., Carriço, L. 2008. Lessons from early stages design of mobile applications. In Procs of MobileHCI '08. ACM, NY, USA, 127-136.

23. Serrano, M., Nigay, L., Demumieux, R., Descos, J., Losquin, P., 2006. Multimodal interaction on mobile phones. Mobile HCI'06. Vol.159, pp 129 - 136, Finland.

24. Tate, D., Zabinski, M., 2004. Computer and internet applications for psychological treatment, Journal of Clinical Psychology. No 60(2).

25. Tate, D., Zabinski, M., 2004. Computer and internet applications for psychological treatment, Journal of Clinical Psychology. No 60(2).

26. Wyeth, P. Purchase, H. C., 2003. Using developmental theories to inform the design of technology for children. In IDC '03, pp., 93–100, New York, USA, 2003. ACM.

27. Wright, J., Wright, A., 1997. Computer-assisted psychotherapy. Psychotherapy Practice. N.6 pp315–319.

28. Xu, W., et al, Real-Time Collaborative Annotation and Information Visualization in a Biofeedback System for Stroke Patient Rehabilitation. 3d Workshop Capture Archival, Retrieval of Personal Experiences, 2006.

Using Ontologies to Reason About the Usability of Interactive Medical Devices in Multiple Situations of Use

Judy Bowen
The University of Waikato
New Zealand
jbowen@cs.waikato.ac.nz

Annika Hinze
The University of Waikato
New Zealand
hinze@cs.waikato.ac.nz

ABSTRACT

Formally modelling interactive software systems and devices allows us to prove properties of correctness about such devices, and thus ensure effectiveness of their use. It also enables us to consider interaction properties such as usability and consistency between the interface and system functionality. Interactive modal devices, that have a fixed interface but whose behaviour is dependent on the mode of the device, can be similarly modelled. Such devices always behave in the same way (*i.e.* have the same functionality and interaction possibilities) irrespective of how, or where, they are used. However, a user's interaction with such devices may vary according to the physical location or environment in which they are situated (we refer to this as a system's context and usage situation). In this paper we look at a particular example of a safety-critical system, that of a modal interactive medical syringe pump, which is used in multiple situations. We consider how ontologies can be used to reason about the effects of different situations on the use of such devices.

Author Keywords

Ontologies; Formal models; Safety-critical interactive systems; Context and situation

ACM Classification Keywords

H.5.2 Information Interfaces and Presentation: Theory and Methods

INTRODUCTION

Understanding how users interact with software applications and interactive devices is a well-studied problem and forms the basis of human-computer interaction (HCI) research. In this paper we talk about devices (interactive medical devices specifically) but our work is equally applicable to software applications. Typically, we seek to discover all aspects of how a device will be used, and by whom, in order to ensure that it is designed to be easily understood by intended users with minimal errors.

The design process should include consideration of the context in which a device will be used in order to ensure usability within that context. In fact, usability is defined in ISO 9241-11 as the "extent to which a product can be used by specified users [..] with effectiveness [..] in a specified context of use" [2]. User-centred approaches aim to ensure quality of system use and contextual design [15] gathers information about the environmental context of users in the field.

Once a device has been tested and is released 'into the wild', we assume (or hope) that we have considered all intended uses and that the device will be usable in all of these situations. It may be, however, that having proven to be successful in a given context, a particular device is then used in a different environment from that which was first intended. At this stage there is no guarantee that usability will be preserved as there are new circumstances which were not examined in the initial design phase.

Naturally, one would expect that decision makers responsible for choosing to use a device in a different context would understand the implications of this and consider carefully the appropriateness of their choice. However, the context of use may seem unchanged to the device domain expert (*e.g.* a device is used by caregivers for delivery of pain relief to patients) though that may not be that case from the viewpoint of an HCI expert. It is therefore unlikely that such decision makers would have a full understanding of HCI or access to experts who could assist with such a decision.

Our work in this paper is motivated by a real-world example presented to us by our local health board. Within their hospitals a variety of different medical devices are in use which are intended to assist with patient care. These devices are interactive and consist of both hardware and software interfaces and functionality. A device may be brought into the hospital for use in a specific clinical setting, but subsequently may be considered as an appropriate tool for use within other settings. For example, a syringe pump which has been purchased to provide pain relief within a palliative care environment may be considered as a useful device to deliver pain relief within an emergency rescue helicopter or air ambulance. Prior to making this decision there are many factors to take into account and it would be helpful to have a full understanding of what the implications of this might be with respect to a user's interactions with the device.

We aim to find a solution which supports such decision making by enabling health practitioners and managers (as opposed to interactive system developers and HCI practitioners) to answer the following types of questions:

1. Should a particular device ever be used in a particular situation?

2. Is device *A* or device *B* a better choice for use in situation *S*?

3. What additional or different user training or information is required to use device *A* in situation *S*?

For small examples we can reason as humans by considering single elements of a situation and a device. For example, device *A* has a display which is not backlit, so using it in situation *S*, which has low levels of lighting, may be problematic because it will be hard for the user to read the display. These 'obvious' properties are easily identified and can be considered on a case by case basis. However, as medical devices continue to proliferate and modes of interaction diversify (voice recognition, touch screen *etc.*) and situations of use become more complex, we want to be able to provide general support across a wide range of devices and situations.

The importance of being able to fully understand these implications should not be taken lightly. Failures in healthcare settings are rarely the result of one large catastrophic event. More typically they are a combination of smaller factors in a system of moderate complexity, which on their own may appear trivial but in combination can become deadly [19]. A good examination of such a situation can be found in Thimbleby's work on hospital beds [1].

The U.S. Department of Health and Human Services Food and Drug Administration (FDA) released a report in 2000 that specifically identifies the use of medical devices in multiple contexts which are not fully understood as a potential hazard. It further states that within human factor considerations the use environment (which may include attributes such as light, noise, motion/vibration, workload and distraction) must be taken in to account in order to protect safe and effective outcomes in the use of such devices [29].

The World Health Organisation defines patient safety as "the absence of preventable harm to a patient during the process of health care" [31]. Currently, in developed countries as many as one in 10 patients is harmed while receiving hospital care. The chance of being harmed during heath care is one in 300 while the chance of being harmed during air travel is one in 1,000,000 [31]. A summary of issues of patient safety problems in the American Health Care system is given by Kohn *et al.* [17].

Our approach to addressing some of these problems is to use an ontology which allows us to capture the domain information related to multiple situations and reason about the use of multiple devices (which are often complex in their own right) within those situations. The intention is to use the structured and automated reasoning provided by ontologies (via tools such as Protégé [13] for example) to try and deduce the necessary information required to answer the sorts of questions we have posed above.

The remainder of the paper is structured as follows: First we introduce some background to our work along with our motivations. We next describe the requirements for achieving our research goals and introduce a running example which is used throughout the paper. Next we introduce ontologies and show how we develop the requirements we have outlined within such an ontology. We then widen the discussion to look at ontology use in general and in particular existing medical ontologies to show how our research can be integrated with such work. Finally we draw our conclusions and outline future work.

BACKGROUND

In previous work we have investigated the use of formal modelling for interactive devices [4, 5] and provided a framework and a set of models that enable us to describe interactive elements of software systems and model them by way of their behaviours [3]. In ongoing work we have been extending this to consider modal interactive devices, such as safety-critical medical devices, with a view to being able to test such devices against a variety of conditions. This is in the manner of work being conducted within the CHI+MED project [11] and we are motivated by works such as [6, 27, 28] which share similar considerations to our own with respect to the use of formality for interactive systems. Having formal models of both functionality and interactive possibilities (as in [5]) can provide assurances that these safety-critical devices will behave as expected and that users can interact with them successfully and effectively.

Whilst the current focus of our work is interactive medical devices, the models we use are equally applicable to interactive devices in other domains as well as software applications. As such our work can be generalised to a wider range of problems. Our initial question was whether or not we could take the formal models we have developed and somehow use them (or extend them to support that use) in wider considerations of usability within specific contexts. That is, to model identified differences in circumstances of use (which we refer to in this paper as situations) such that they can support the identification of interaction issues which may arise when particular devices are used in particular situations. Our existing models of devices provide information about component widgets of the device, the type of that widget and the behaviour associated with it. For example we may have a widget called *UpButton* with a type *ActionControl* (indicating it generates a system behaviour) and a behaviour called *S_Increase*, being the system behaviour generated when the widget is interacted with. The widget type can also be used to infer the nature of interaction depending on the granularity used in the model.

First we consider how a device may be compromised in a given situation using the widget descriptions as a starting point. It was clear to us that the different environmental factors capable of affecting device use were dependant on the nature of interaction required to use the widgets, which can be inferred from the model of that device. For example, in a noisy environment a device with only visual and haptic widgets can be used just as easily as in a quiet environment, whereas the same is not true for a device with audio widgets. With this in mind we want to represent the relationships between factors, their locations, widgets and their devices.

The domain we are working in can be described as the environment, E, which consists of multiple locations where multiple devices are in use. We identify a set of devices, D, consisting of $d_1 .. d_n$ individual devices; a set of widgets, W, consisting of $w_1 .. w_n$ individual widgets; a set of locations, L, consisting of $l_1 .. l_n$ individual locations; and a set of factors, F, consisting of $f_1 .. f_n$ individual factors.

The relationship between widgets and devices is many to many. A widget may occur on several devices (widgets are described generically so a description of an On/Off button which has the same behaviour on several devices is in some sense shared by those devices) and several widgets may occur on a single device. Similarly the relationship between factors and widgets is many to many, the same factor may affect several widgets and several factors may affect a single widget. Finally the relationship between locations and factors is also many to many, a location may exhibit several factors and several locations may exhibit the same factor. An example of a possible scenario described in this way is depicted in Figure 1.

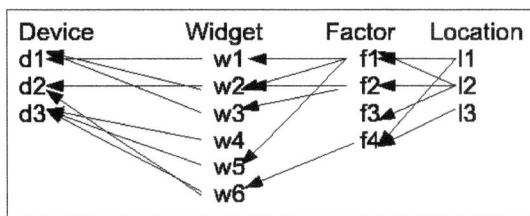

Figure 1. Relationships

The devices and widgets can be identified from the formal models of these interactive systems. In an ideal world these would exist for all interactive devices in the domain (in fact we have already developed models of several such devices). The factors (or situational factors as we will call them) must be identified for each location (or situation) as necessary. This can be done using standard ethnography or similar techniques as described next.

In this paper we focus on physical attributes of an environment such as noise levels, lighting levels *etc.* but factors may also include less tangible elements such as patient/practitioner ratio, degree of stress in a location *etc.* Extending the presentation models to include this new information, although possible, did not seem to be the best approach. Whilst the existing models provided important information about the devices which would be useful for understanding situations, the detail of the models was not central to our concerns and the sort of inferences we wished to deduce would require analysis in some formal tool. Instead we looked for a different approach that allowed us to use the information provided by the presentation models as a starting point. We decided on an approach using ontologies, and throughout the rest of this paper we discuss why we made this choice and the benefits it afforded.

REQUIREMENTS

In order to provide guidelines on whether or not certain devices are suitable for use within certain situations we need to understand how devices are interacted with, what types of factors may affect that interaction and what factors exist within the situation we are considering. What we mean by factors affecting interaction is whether they are detrimental to:

- ease of performance
- speed of performance
- cognition of performance

So, it is the user who is affected by the situation rather than the device itself. The user may have a fixed set of goals and tasks to perform which can be achieved through a particular set of interactions (*i.e.* the things the user can do with the device). In different situations the device does not change but the way in which the user interacts with that device may. If we can identify the factors which cause such changes we can not only highlight potential issues which may occur when interacting with the device in that situation we can also find ways of supporting users in different situations (through different types of training *etc.*).

A particular device may have a set of instructions or training material provided for it which enables a user to interact with it in the appropriate manner. However, in a different situation they may require different information. By capturing this formally we can ensure that the correct training is provided for each situation and also understand how to develop new instructions for any new situation of use which may arise. Understanding a situation is similar to the need to understand context, which is often part of the design process. As such, the methods used to acquire this information are well-studied, and include activities such as ethnographic studies, contextual design [15], situated actions [26] *etc.* Our aim is to use such information (gathered in one of the traditional ways) as a basis for developing new knowledge. Our focus, however, is not on new design, but rather new situations of use.

EXAMPLE SCENARIO

Throughout this paper we will use a simplified example based on the real world scenario described in the introduction. This example is small enough to easily explain and understand within the confines of this paper but contains all of the elements necessary to motivate our work. In addition it can be shown how this example can be scaled up to the real-world scenario we are addressing.

We assume we have a modal interactive medical device, such as a syringe pump. A syringe pump is a small battery powered device which delivers the contents of a syringe to a patient via an intravenous line over a set period of time. In this simplified example we assume that the pump has a single interactive element (or widget) which is an audible alarm (real syringe pumps of course have a variety of widgets including visual displays, push buttons *etc.*). We wish to consider the use of this pump within a helicopter and we assume that there is only one consideration of interest within the helicopter, which is the excessive noise. We already have a way of modelling modal interactive devices and their interaction possibilities (based on [5]) and we use this as the starting point for developing the knowledge we will store in the ontology. Our simplified example pump with its single widget can be modelled by the following presentation model:

```
Pump is
    (audibleAlarm, singleValueResponder,
                        (S_SoundAlarm))
```

where the single widget, called *audibleAlarm*, is categorised as something which responds to a behaviour of the system called *S_SoundAlarm*. We now wish to take this information and develop a way of representing the additional information required to consider situations of use for such a device.

ONTOLOGIES

Research in context-aware systems has long attempted to describe and capture situational factors or context of a system. For this, a number of context models have been explored for different applications. Strang and Linhoff in 2004 classified context modelling approaches into five approaches [25]:

- Key-Value

- Markup Scheme

- Graphical

- Object-oriented

- Logic-based

- Ontology-based

They evaluated these approaches according to six criteria (distributed composition, partial validation, richness and quality of information, incompleteness and ambiguity, level of formality, applicability to existing environments). Most of these requirements could only be fulfilled in object-oriented and ontology-based models.

Strang and Linnhoff concluded that ontologies provide the most expressive models. In particular, ontology-based models excelled in their support of providing a "shared understanding", ensuring that participating parties share the same interpretation of the data exchanged and its meaning. Due to this feature of "shared meaning", ontology-based models are semantic models. Ontologies (and logic-based models, such as the Situation Calculus [12]) further allow inference of knowledge. That means, ontology-based models support not just the capturing of contextual and situational data but also the explicit and implicit capturing of complex relationships between the captured data items. Both capturing of semantics and support of inference (reasoning) are vital for our project.

Our motivation in using ontologies stems largely from the expressiveness of the ontology model. However, it is also influenced by the availability of existing models for hospitals, health care, and medical environments. Knowledge bases such as the one we are proposing here cannot rise to their full

potential when they function in isolation. It is therefore further advantageous that some medical ontologies already exist and there is potential to incorporate our work into existing medical ontologies for wider use.

An ontology is a formal explicit description of concepts in a domain (classes), properties and attributes of each concept, and restrictions on attributes. Classes can have subclasses representing concepts that are more specific than the superclass. Developing an ontology includes the definition of classes, their arrangement into taxonomic hierarchy, definition of attributes and allowed values and filling in the values for instances. An ontology together with a set of such individual instances of classes then constitutes a knowledge base.

The next section describes the structure of our ontology for capturing of situational data; the reasoning on the ontology is described subsequently in reference to the tools we used. Related medical ontologies and the incorporation of our model into an existing system is then discussed.

PLANNING THE ONTOLOGY

The ontology will consist of classifications of elements (being the items within our domain, such as medical devices, their components, situations *etc.*) and the relationships between these classes. The level of detail and granularity required should, in general, be just enough to answer what Noy and McGuinness refer to as 'competency questions' [21]. For us this equates to the questions we have posed in the introduction to this paper and so we will build our ontology to reflect this. For example we might ask the question "can the syringe pump be used effectively in a helicopter?" We start by considering the widgets of devices and the nature of their user interaction (*i.e.* how does the user interact with a particular widget). So, for example, we might identify the following categories:

- Audio widgets

- Haptic widgets

- Visual widgets

Next, we identify the situational factors (*i.e.* the things within a situation which can affect interaction) which might include:

- Excessive noise

- Requirement for gloves to be worn

- Low levels of lighting

Within the ontology we will classify these items, so our knowledge base may contain the following distinct classes:

- Device

- Widget

- Situation

- Factor

As we expand the knowledge base to include more information we become more specific and so we create subclasses:

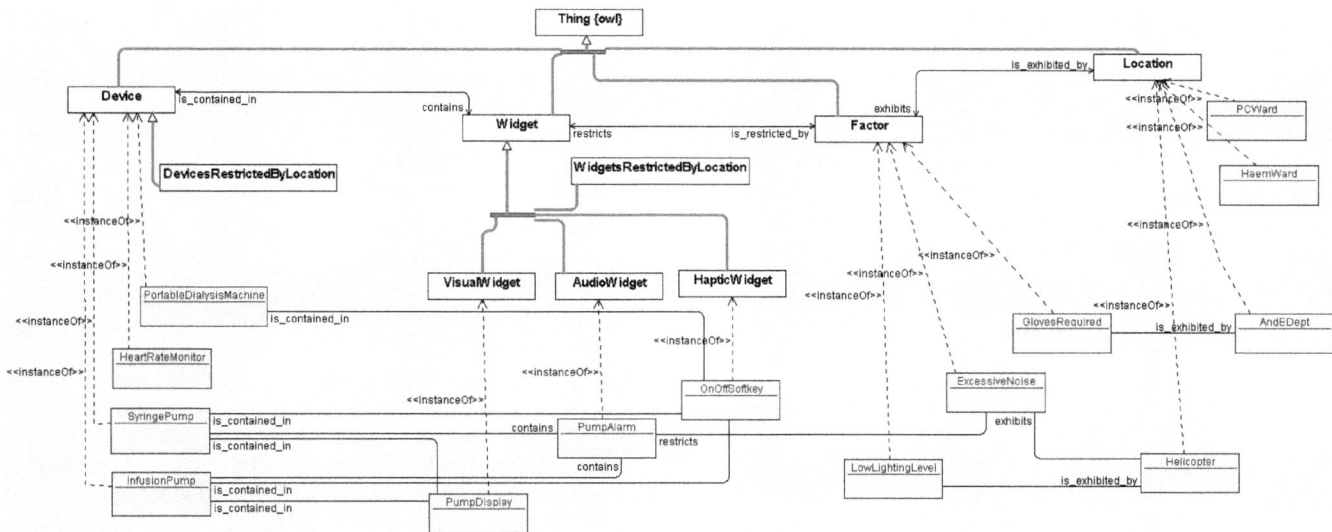

Figure 2. Ontology (example part) before reasoning

- Device

- Widget

  – AudioWidget

- Situation

- Factor

Although in the general case we have identified more than just audio widgets, we will continue our explanation based on the small world of our example scenario and only include those elements relevant to that. Finally we can create actual instances of these classes from our example:

```
Pump isA Device
AudibleAlarm isA AudioWidget
Helicopter isA Situation
ExcessiveNoise isA Factor
```

The identification of actual devices and their widgets can be taken from the existing formal models of these interactive devices described previously. The next step is to consider relationships between the classes. We want to define axioms showing the relationships which will guide the reasoning within the ontology. At a high level we might state:

```
Location exhibits Factor
Factor restricts Widget
```

which is the most general description (it is possible that any factor may restrict any widget). Then as we refine our understanding to become more specific we can apply this relationship to specific known instances of the factor and widget classes:

```
ExcessiveNoise restricts AudibleAlarm
Helicopter exhibits ExcessiveNoise
```

We can already see (informally) that there is a relationship between *Helicopter* and *AudibleAlarm*. Furthermore, if we

develop relationships between widgets and devices, for example:

```
Device contains Widget
```

we have the first step to identifying devices which may in some way be restricted when used within a given location. However, we must find a way to formalize this relationship within our ontology in order that such relationships can be inferred automatically. We discuss this next.

BUILDING THE ONTOLOGY

To model the situational data and to reason about it, we used the open-source editor Protégé 4.2[1] and its in-built reasoned HermiT 1.3.5 [24]. The ontology described in the previous section, was modeled in Protégé and visualized using OWL-GrEd[2] (UML style graphical editor for OWL). Figure 2 shows the parts of the ontology that refer to our example (the original small example with some additional instances of the defined classes) where pump alarm is affected by helicopter noise. Classes are represented as yellow rectangles (in the upper part of the figure); instances are shown in green boxes (in the lower part). The *isA* relationships from the previous section are now modelled as *OWL:InstanceOf* relationships. Relationships between classes find possible instantiations between instances.

In addition to the classes discussed previously, we defined two target classes to contain the devices and widgets that are restricted by location. Members of these classes can be inferred by describing rules to determine their members, this enables us to begin to reason about our knowledge in the desired manner.

Protégé supports the construction of OWL models and additionally allows for the definition and execution of rules using

---

[1] Available for download at
`http://protege.stanford.edu/download/protege/4.2/`
[2] Available for download at `http://owlgred.lumii.lv/`

251

SWRL (a superset of OWL-DL /Description Logic). Rules are of the form of an implication between an antecedent and consequent, in which both antecedent and consequent are conjunctions of atoms *atom, atom, ..., atom ↦ atom, atom*. Each atom is a predicate symbol with arguments, such as *pred(arg, arg)*. Predicate symbols can include OWL classes, properties or data types. Arguments can be OWL individuals or data values, or variables referring to them. For our small example, we defined the following two rules:

```
Device(?d),
contains(?d, ?w),
exhibits(Helicopter, ?f),
is_restricted_by(?w, ?f),
-> DevicesRestrictedByLocation(?d)

Widget(?w),
exhibits(Helicopter, ?f),
is_restricted_by(?w, ?f)
-> WidgetsRestrictedByLocation(?w)
```

to identify instances of the two target classes. The first rule finds all devices which contain a widget restricted by some factor which is exhibited by the Helicopter, these devices then become inferred members of the target class *DevicesRestrictedByLocation*. So if we ask the question "which devices may be affected if used in the helicopter?" the answer is found in the target class. The second rule identifies those widgets restricted by factors exhibited by the helicopter and these then become the inferred members of the *WidgetsRestrictedByLocation* class. By changing the location in the rule (from Helicopter to some other location) we identify devices and widgets similarly affected in other locations.

Within our example, the two rules above identify the *AudioWidget* as being restricted by the *Helicopter* location and the affected device as the *SyringePump* (see Figure 5). This answers the third of our initial questions "What additional or different user training is required to use a syringe pump in a helicopter?" The new knowledge is that the audio alarm cannot be relied on in the helicopter and so alternate strategies must be developed for using the syringe pump in this situation. This may also lead to answering the first question, "Should a syringe pump ever be used in a helicopter?" as the knowledge that the audio alarm will be compromised may be a contributing factor in that decision. Similarly, if we introduce a second device, *B*, we can consider the second question, "Is the syringe pump or device *B* a better choice for use in the helicopter" by considering if one, both, or neither appears in the *DevicesRestrictedByLocation* class.

THE BIGGER PICTURE: HOSPITAL ONTOLOGIES

The best use of our model for situational context will be in the wider context of a hospital model. A number of hospital-based ontologies have been proposed as well as ontologies for modelling situational context; we analyze here a selection of ontologies for use with our model.

Many ontologies have been developed for the healthcare domain to model context mainly for medical decision making. One such example is the Systematized Nomenclature of Medicine (SNOMED CT) – a classification system for medical and clinical terms, encoded as an ontology. The focus of the project is on medical terms and less on hospital and situation awareness. Moreover, it is a general terminology system that does not deal with particular individuals. It is therefore not a good match of our model. Furthermore, Heja *et al.* observed that the SNOMED CT ontology is of somewhat limited use for formal reasoning [14].

Some ontologies have been developed that address the context of continuous care. Mokkarala *et al.* proposed an ontology describing errors in healthcare to support the development prevention strategies [20]. Their errorOntology aims to be the equivalent of SNOMED for medical errors. Similar to our ontology, this project covers a range of health care settings and locations. It is, however, not geared towards recognition of potential problems, but towards classification and description of known errors. Here our model could be a helpful extension, approaching the field from the opposite end. Instead of starting from recording each MedicalerrorEvent (as done by Mokkarala *et al.*), our model is geared towards receiving a warning about potential hazards. Patterns recognized in the errorOntology could, therefore, serve as input for our model. Wilson *et al.* [23] independently developed a similar taxonomy of ambulatory medical errors, for which much the same comments apply.

The ontology for hospital scenarios (OntHOS) by Blandford *et al.* was developed to facilitate integration between domain descriptions of several independent projects [27]. It focused on describing hospital organization and processes and did not support context-aware reasoning. The applications were mostly scenario-based; care error detection or the prediction of potential interaction issues were not part of the focus. Similarly, Kataria *et al.* [16] implemented an ontology for an intelligent hospital ward to address data sharing and semantic heterogeneity. Their ontology did not incorporate context-aware reasoning. Ongenae *et al.* [22] suggest oNCS – an ontology-based nurse call management system, which provides a mobile button for each patient to create a person-oriented call system. The system takes the callers context into account when assigning a nurse to callers. The oNCS system consists of an ontology and rules for the nurse call algorithm. In addition to classes describing the hospital and staff, the ontology provides detailed information about patient requirements towards their care givers (such as language or faith) and risk factors (such as high age or recently resuscitated). With its focus on inferring factors for quality care and awareness of hospital layout and person-focused locations, the oNCS ontology would have been a good candidate for our extension. However, unfortunately the ontology was not freely available to be used.

The context-embedded intelligent Hospital Ontology (CiHo) by Yao and Liu [32] aims to define a common vocabulary for the hospital domain. It supports reasoning for ubiquitous applications in an intelligent hospital. The concepts modeled refer to personnel, patients, locations and activities executed in locations using devices and documents. CiHo has been previously used and extended within the oNCS project. The CiHo model is closely related (in its focus) to our model. Through the (simple) reasoning and rule support in CiHo, contexts of patients can be identified in a similar way that our model identifies relational context of devices. CiHo aims to fill the gap between general purpose context-aware frameworks and a healthcare domain specific ontology. Because of its general compatibility in aim and modelling technique, we next use our model in collaboration with the CiHO hospital ontology as one example of an extensible existing ontology.

USING THE ONTOLOGY

The process of linking our ontology to an existing hospital ontology shows how one can merge our model of potential error sources with an existing model of a hospital with its wards and patient-related transactions. The merging of ontologies is the act of bringing together two conceptually divergent ontologies or the instance data associated to two ontologies. This merging process can be performed in a number of ways, manually, semi automatically, or automatically. As manual merging is very labour intensive, a current research aim is for (semi) automated techniques to merge ontologies based on statistics of similarities of concepts and instances. For explicitly stating similarity between semantic concepts, OWL provides special relationships (*e.g.* "sameIndividualAs" and "equivalentClass").

In order to create the link between our ontology and the Hospital Ontology, a number of small adjustments needed to be made in the models, using Protégé. Within the two ontologies there was an overlap in some class names, namely both had device and location classes. To avoid any problems this may cause, we firstly renamed the classes in Hospital Ontology to hdevice and hlocation, respectively, and then created a link between these classes and their counterparts in our ontology to indicate their equivalence. This helps to ease the integration and ensures that pre-existing data from both ontologies will be used. Through refactoring all references to the respective classes were also renamed. To link the respective equivalent classes within each ontology we define them as *OWL:equivalentClass* (see details for h/device in Figure 3).

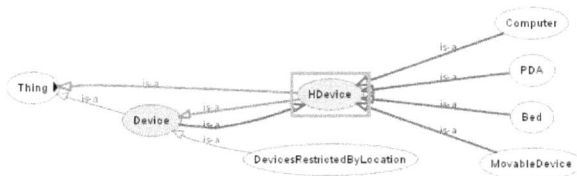

Figure 3. Equivalent classes device and hdevice

Consequently, classes from both ontologies now form the class hierarchy of the resulting ontology. Figure 4 shows the resulting class hierarchy in Protégé. The classes marked in bold are the ones from our ontology; the other ones are from the Hospital Ontology. Each of the two ontologies came with its own set of rules that originally only referred to classes and properties within its originating ontology. By definition, each set of ontology rules is still executable after the import. Once

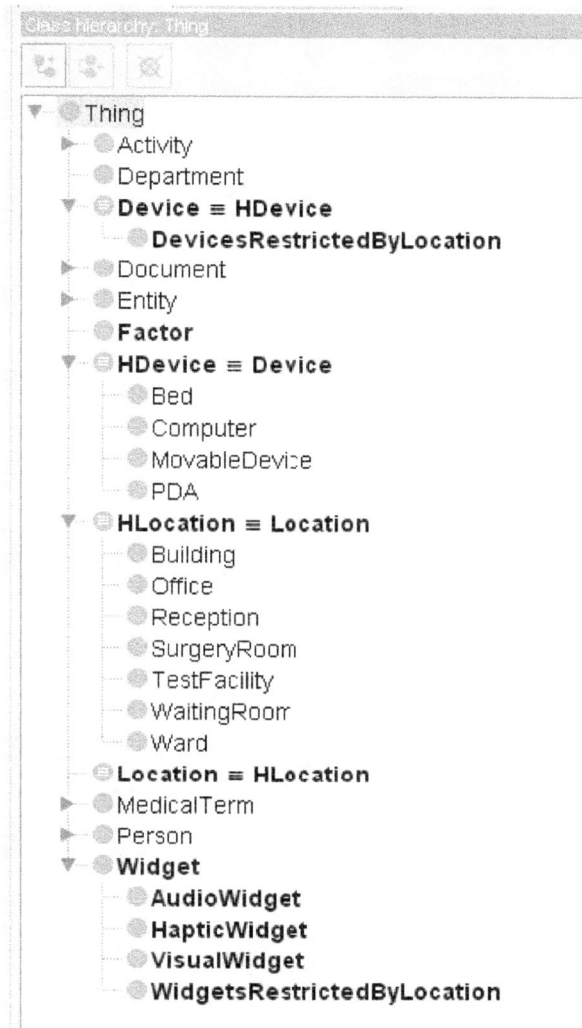

Figure 4. Class hierarchy of combined ontologies

explicit links had been made between classes and instances, our rules can also be meaningfully executed within the Hospital Ontology. In our case, the pre-existing location instances within the Hospital Ontology needed to be linked to exhibiting factors. We assigned environmental factors such as noise and lighting level to instances of wards and surgery rooms in Hospital Ontology. For example, we defined Building 5 as being close to a current building site and therefore affected by excessive noise.

After thus linking hospital locations to situational factors, our rules defined to identify potential device problems now also cover the hospital layout modelled in the Hospital Ontology. We can identify that out of the list of available devices in Building 5, it has now been inferred that both infusionPump and syringePump may be adversely affected (see Figure 5).

The merging of ontologies is the act of bringing together two conceptually divergent ontologies or the instance data associated to two ontologies. This merging process can be performed in a number of ways, manually, semi automatically,

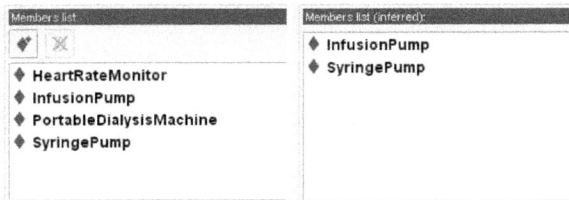

Figure 5. Available devices (left) and inferred affected devices (right) shown in Protégé

or automatically. As manual merging is very labour intensive, current research aim for (semi) automated techniques to merge ontologies based on statistics of similarities of concepts and instances. For explicitly stating similarity between semantic concepts, OWL provides special relationships (*e.g.* "sameIndividualAs" and "equivalentClass").

DISCUSSION OF RELATED SITUATION ONTOLOGIES
Existing situation ontologies have been mostly developed for context-aware and ubiquitous systems. We here describe the influence of this difference in approaches.

Most of these situation ontologies model situations as a composite of contexts, with or without temporal dimensions. One such model has been suggested by Costa *et al.* [9]. They understand context as being intrinsic or relational. Our model focuses on the relational aspects between a device and the caregiver, and their interaction with the intrinsic context of each location. In this way, our model describes situations and different types of contexts without explicitly modelling these concepts. Costa's ontology could be used as an upper ontology for our ontology.

Yau and Liu [32] similarly suggested a layered situation ontology for pervasive computing. The model has a (lower) context layer and an (upper) situation layer, aggregating contexts into situations. The principle is similar to [9] but with a clearer distinction between situation and contexts. Meissen et al. [18] use an ontology layer for modelling situations, which, in turn, are composites of contexts (collection of environmental values). They define duration-based situation patterns that are used to identify situations in pull or push mode (continuously reacting to incoming context events) [18].

Crowley [10] in his situation-based approach supports the opposing view of context being a network of situations in relation to roles. A situation is defined as a state defined by a conjunction of relations. The work identifies situation events (=relation events) context and role events. The model is a very high level abstraction following a psychological approach to human understanding. Despite differences in the modelling, their approach is fundamentally related to the one of Costa *et al.* and could serve as a generalization layer.

Although these models capture general concepts of context and situations (and support reasoning), they are not specific for the healthcare domain. They could be used as an upper generalization layer in our model, which may allow further generalization. A similar layered approach is taken by Chen and Nugent for their smart home assistant [7]: depending on

the situations recognized, reactions to events and alarms are executed. Here a situation is understood as a description of an unknown activity, which is then identified by reasoning.

The significant difference for our ontology is that its application is not intended for the expert user. Furthermore, the modelling of context and situations for context-aware systems significantly differs from our setting insofar as the devices taken into consideration are not themselves context-aware. Context modelling for context-aware systems aims to influence the system design in such a way that the best action is triggered in a given situation. However, in our healthcare setting, the design of the devices cannot necessarily be influenced.

DISCUSSION AND CONCLUSIONS
In this paper we have shown how ontologies can be used to reason about safety-critical interactive devices and their use within multiple locations within an environment. Our original intention was to find ways of reasoning about these devices in a manner which would support decision makers within the given environment to answer the sorts of questions we posed in the introduction to this paper. We believe that using ontologies in the manner described enables this. Furthermore, the existence of large-scale medical ontologies and the ability to combine our reasoning with these (as shown) means that we already have a large data set to work with removing the need to develop the entire knowledge base from scratch. As already discussed in describing linking to the Hospital Ontology [32], our ontology could be used in the context of existing ontologies. Most of these, however, are still in their fledgeling state or intended only for proprietary access. Given the current situation, we believe the most prudent way forward to ensure that the notion of errors sources in a given care environment is integrated into medical and heath care modelling would be a link to the W3C Healthcare and LifeSciences [30] in a similar manner to the work of Cheung *et al.* [8].

This ontology is a biomedical knowledge base that integrates 15 distinct data sources using currently available Semantic Web technologies. The reason for selecting this particular ontology is not necessarily the information sources that have already been incorporated into the knowledge base, but rather the aim of its creators to extend the knowledge base in depth and breadth, as well as its openness and support by the W3C.

The Semantic Web Health Care and Life Sciences Interest Group (HCLS IG) aims to develop and support the use of Semantic Web technologies across health care (as well as life sciences, clinical research and translational medicine). Our research, as well as other research in these domains, will gain from interoperability of available information.

Whilst context-aware computing is a well-researched and continually evolving area of research, one of the interesting factors within our work is precisely that the devices are not context-aware. The interactive modal devices considered here are not aware of, and do not react to, their environment, which is where the potential for usability problems arises. The contextual information we have modelled by the creation of a usability-related knowledge base is not designed to support a device being used in a context which changes during use, but rather a device which can be used within different contexts (*i.e.* context-aware knowledge instead of context-aware systems).

Medical devices, such as the syringe pump used as an example here, are ubiquitous in the healthcare environment – ubiquitous in the sense of being so prevalent and integrated into everyday environment that we lose awareness of them. This is why potential hazards and sources of errors due to changing situations and contexts of use can no longer be detected by their users. Our approach combines location-specific HCI rules with modelling of usage situations and thus provides decision makers with the means to (1) detect potentially error-prone situations, (2) select appropriate devices to be used in situations, and (3) identify the need for additional staff training and information as new situations arise. Whilst we have focused on a medical domain in this paper, our approach is equally applicable to any set of safety-critical devices in any domain.

Limitations and Future Work
Our experiences in using Protégé 4.2 – a tool widely used within the semantic web community for development of and reasoning about ontologies – has persuaded us that an important future step for this project is to investigate how best to report the inferences made within the ontology in a manner most useful to our intended users and also to consider how they might go about adding new data. It is clear to us that expecting such personnel to interact directly with the ontology through a tool such as Protégé is unlikely to prove successful. There is a steep learning curve for this tool, erratic documentation (many features present in previous versions have been removed in Protégé 4.2) and even with a firm understanding of the accepted vocabulary of ontologies no consistent relation between this and the terminology used in the tool.

An additional problem lies in the creation of the ontology. In order to successfully support decision making the ontology should fully describe all aspects of the domain, building such an ontology from scratch is a time-consuming job both in terms of the necessary background research required as well as the ontology creation. As we have stated, there are existing medical ontologies which we can use, however there are difficulties with merging ontologies which require manual processes to fix. In addition, some aspects of existing ontologies may not adequately or correctly describe all aspects of our particular domain, which again requires careful manual work to identify such issues and amend the ontology accordingly. Our next goal is therefore to investigate the development of a tool which would interact with the ontology (by enabling addition of data and reporting of results) but provide a more friendly interface and user-experience for non-technical decision makers.

Prior to this, of immediate interest is to perform some ethnographic studies within our example domain and expand the ontology with real-world information. In addition, the classes we have added to the ontology are, at present, one-dimensional in that they consist solely of the name of the class they represent. However, within an ontology it is possible to add property descriptions and values to classes allowing us to refine the knowledge. For example, a class called *Noise* may have a property reflecting an actual decibel level, by recording this we can similarly refine the reasoning to consider these properties, *e.g.*, consider only locations where the noise level is within a given range.

ACKNOWLEDGMENTS
Thanks to Rex Edge and Murray McGovern from Waikato District Health Board for helpful discussions and the inspiration for the example used in this paper.

REFERENCES
1. Acharya, C., Thimbleby, H. W., and Oladimeji, P. Human computer interaction and medical devices. In *Proceedings of BCS HCI*, T. McEwan and L. McKinnon, Eds., ACM (2010), 168–176.

2. Bevan, N. Usability is quality of use. In *Proceedings of 6th International Conference on Human Computer Interaction, July 1995*, Anzai and Ogawa, Eds., Elsevier (1995).

3. Bowen, J., and Reeves, S. Formal models for informal GUI designs. In *1st International Workshop on Formal Methods for Interactive Systems, Macau SAR China, 31 October 2006*, vol. 183, Electronic Notes in Theoretical Computer Science, Elsevier (2006), 57–72.

4. Bowen, J., and Reeves, S. Using formal models to design user interfaces, a case study. In *HCI 2007: Proceedings of the 21st BCS HCI Group Conference (HCI 2007, University of Lancaster, UK)*, vol. 1, British Computer Society (2007), 159–166.

5. Bowen, J., and Reeves, S. Formal models for user interface design artefacts. *Innovations in Systems and Software Engineering 4*, 2 (2008), 125–141.

6. Campos, J., and Harrison, M. Modelling and analysing the interactive behaviour of an infusion pump. *Electronic Communications of the EASST 11* (2001).

7. Chen, L., and Nugent, C. D. Situation aware cognitive assistance in smart homes. *Journal of Mobile Multimedia 6*, 3 (2010), 263–280.

8. Cheung, K.-H., Frost, H. R., Marshall, M. S., Prud'hommeaux, E., Samwald, M., Zhao, J., and Paschke, A. A journey to semantic web query federation in the life sciences. *BMC Bioinformatics 10*, S-10 (2009), 10.

9. Costa, P. D., Guizzardi, G., Almeida, J. P. A., Pires, L. F., and van Sinderen, M. Situations in conceptual modeling of context. In *Proceedings of EDOC Workshops*, IEEE Computer Society (2006), 6.

10. Crowley, J. L. Context aware observation of human activities. In *Proceedings of International Conference on Multimedia and Expo, ICME (1)*, IEEE (2002), 909–912.

11. Engineering and Physical Sciences Research Council. CHI+MED: Multidisciplinary computer-human

interaction research for the design and safe use of interactive medical devices, EPSRC reference: Ep/g059063/1, 2011.

12. England, D., Randles, M., and Taleb-Bendiab, A. Situation calculus for HCI design. *International Conference on Developments in eSystems Engineering* (2010), 155–159.

13. Gennari, J. H., Musen, M. A., Fergerson, R. W., Grosso, W. E., Crubézy, M., Eriksson, H., Noy, N. F., and Tu, S. W. The evolution of Protégé: an environment for knowledge-based systems development. *International Journal on Human-Computer Studies 58*, 1 (Jan. 2003), 89–123.

14. Heja, G., Surjan, G., and Varga, P. Ontological analysis of SNOMED CT. *BMC Medical Informatics and Decision Making 8*, Suppl 1 (2008), S8.

15. Holtzblatt, K., and Beyer, H. R. Contextual design: Using customer work models to drive systems design. In *CHI Extended Abstracts*, A. Edwards and S. Pemberton, Eds., ACM (1997), 184–185.

16. Kataria, P., Macfie, A., Juric, R., and Madani, K. Ontology for supporting context aware applications for the intelligent hospital ward. *Journal of Integrated Design and Process Science 12*, 3 (Aug. 2008), 35–44.

17. Kohn, L., Corrigan, J., and Donaldson, M. *To err is human: building a safer health system*. National Academy Press, Washington, 2000.

18. Meissen, U., Pfennigschmidt, S., Voisard, A., and Wahnfried, T. Context- and situation-awareness in information logistics. In *Proceedings of EDBT Workshops* (2004), 335–344.

19. Merry, A., and Webster, C. Medication error in New Zealand – time to act. *Journal of the New Zealand Medical Association 121*, 1272 (2008).

20. Mokkarala, P., Brixey, J., Johnson, T., Patel, V., Zhang, J., and Turley, J. Development of comprehensive medical error ontology. *AHRQ: advances in patient safety: new directions and alternative approaches 080034*, 1-4 (2008).

21. Natalya Fridman Noy, D. L. M. Ontology development 101: A guide to creating your first ontology. Tech. Rep. KSL-01-05, Knowledge Systems, AI Laboratory, Stanford University, 2001.

22. Ongenae, F., Myny, D., Dhaene, T., Defloor, T., Goubergen, D. V., Verhoeve, P., Decruyenaere, J., and Turck, F. D. An ontology-based nurse call management system (oNCS) with probabilistic priority assessment. *BMC Health Services Research 11*, 1 (2011), 26–28.

23. Pace, W., Fernald, D. H., Harris, D., Dickinson, L. M., Araya-Gierra, R., Staton, E. W., VanVorst, R., and Main, D. S. *Developing a Taxonomy for Coding Ambulatory Medical Errors: A Report from the ASIPS Collaborative*, vol. 2. 2005, ch. Concepts and Methodology.

24. Shearer, R., Motik, B., and Horrocks, I. Hermit: A highly-efficient owl reasoner. In *OWLED*, C. Dolbear, A. Ruttenberg, and U. Sattler, Eds., vol. 432 of *CEUR Workshop Proceedings*, CEUR-WS.org (2008).

25. Strang, T., and Linnhoff-Popien, C. A context modeling survey. In *Proceedings of Workshop on Advanced Context Modelling, Reasoning and Management, UbiComp 2004 - The Sixth International Conference on Ubiquitous Computing, Nottingham/England* (2004).

26. Suchman, L. A. *Plans and situated actions: the problem of human-machine communication*. Cambridge University Press, New York, NY, USA, 1987.

27. Thimbleby, H., Blandford, A., Buchanan, G., Furniss, D., and Curzon, P. Few are looking: Invisible problems with interactive medical devices. In *Proceedings of the ACM Workshop on Interactive Systems in Healthcare (WISH) — CHI 2010*, G. R. Hayes and D. S. Tan, Eds., ACM (2010), 9–12.

28. Thimbleby, H., Blandford, A., Pietro, G. D., Gallo, L., Gimblett, A., and Oladimeji, P. Engineering interactive computer systems for medicine and healthcare, EICS4Med. In *Proceedings ACM SIGCHI Symposium on Engineering Interactive Computing Systems — EICS2011*, ACM (2011), 341–342.

29. U.S. Department of Health and Human Services Food and Drug Administration. Medical device use-safety: Incorporating human factors engineering into risk management. *Guidance for Industry and FDA Premarket and Design Control Reviewers* (2000).

30. W3C healthcare and lifesciences ontology. available online at: `http://www.w3.org/TR/hcls-kb/`, 2007.

31. WHO patient safety factfile. available online at: `http://www.who.int/patientsafety/en`, 2012.

32. Yau, S. S., and Liu, J. Hierarchical situation modeling and reasoning for pervasive computing. In *The IEEE Workshop on Software Technologies for Future Embedded and Ubiquitous Systems, and International Workshop on Collaborative Computing, Integration, and Assurance*, IEEE Computer Society (Los Alamitos, CA, USA, 2006), 5–10.

GAMBIT: Addressing Multi-platform Collaborative Sketching with HTML5

Ugo Braga Sangiorgi
Louvain Interaction Laboratory, Université
catholique de Louvain
Pl. Place des Doyens, 1 - B-1348
Louvain-la-Neuve (Belgium)
ugo.sangiorgi@uclouvain.be

Jean Vanderdonckt
Louvain Interaction Laboratory, Université
catholique de Louvain
Pl. Place des Doyens, 1 - B-1348
Louvain-la-Neuve (Belgium)
jean.vanderdonckt@uclouvain.be

ABSTRACT

Prototypes are essential tools for design activities since they allow designers to realize and evaluate ideas in early stages of the development. Sketching is a primary tool for constructing prototypes of interactive systems and has been used in developing low-fidelity prototypes for a long time. The computational support for sketching has been receiving a recurrence of interest in the last 45 years and again nowadays within the mobile web context, where there are diverse devices to be considered.

The tool presented on this paper was built with HTML5 and Javascript in order to run on any device with browsing capabilities, for the main purpose of aiding an investigation on addressing issues of multi-platform collaborative sketching.

Author Keywords

Electronic sketching; Multi-platform systems; Collaborative design; Prototyping.

ACM Classification Keywords

H.5.2 User Interfaces: Prototyping

INTRODUCTION

A prototype is a working model built to develop and test design ideas. In User Interface design, prototypes are essential tools for fostering discussion regarding both interface and interaction with stakeholders. Techniques such as Paper Prototyping [17] became very popular due to its' low cost and efficiency, since they are made using sketches for quick generation of prototypes.

Lately, there has been a recurrence of interest on supporting electronic sketching (i.e. sketching at electronic devices and interactive surfaces), and despite sketching *recognition* to be fairly well addressed on the literature, the adoption of electronic sketching as a *design tool* is still a challenge [7].

The current popularization of touch screen devices and the multi-platform capabilities made possible by using HTML5 might pose new opportunities for researchers to explore, for instance, how designers use sketching to prototype interfaces for a target device by producing and testing them on the device itself.

When designing, people draw things in different ways, which allows them to also perceive the problem in new ways. People engage in a sort of *conversation* with their sketches in a tight cycle of drawing, understanding, and interpreting [15]. When prototyping by using the target device, other elements come into play in that conversation. Nowadays, there are many devices available for designers to sketch upon [9], with different screen sizes, weight and processing capabilities; this is a fact to be addressed in current sketching research.

We introduce GAMBIT, a multi-platform collaborative tool for User Interface design that allows the sketching and simulation of UI's on many different devices.

The tool is an essential part of a research on sketching, whose goal is to investigate electronic sketching usage in current UI design practices taking into account the multi-platform context for producing and validating interactive prototypes. The system's core contepts are:

1. Sketch-based - electronic sketching is supported as the main mode of interaction, it is used to quickly put ideas on an external medium, where they can be discussed, improved and stored for further reference [4];

2. Multi-platform - for it allows users to sketch using the device of their preference, and also allows the prototyping and testing of systems on the very device it is intented to run. The system was built with HTML5 and Javascript in order to run on any device with browsing capabilities, through a browser or embedded into a native application;

3. Collaborative - for it focus on group sessions, allowing not only designers to sketch and discuss together, but also to include end users in the process.

This paper is organized as follows: in the next section we motivate the system construction together with the related works. Section 3 presents the requirements gathered in order to support design sessions. Section 4 presents the system's architecture and we conclude on Section 5.

257

SKETCHING IN USER INTERFACE DESIGN

Sketching is considered to be a powerful tool for doing design. As the findings of [5] point out, the presence of ambiguity in early stages of design broads the spectrum of solutions that are considered and tends to deliver a design of higher quality.

As for the fundamentals of sketching, we could mention Van der Lugt's work [18] who conducted an experiment to analyze the functions of sketching in design, in which participants produced individual sketches and then presented them for the group for discussion. Three primary sketching functions were identified:

F1 Sketching stimulates a re-interpretive cycle in the individual designer's idea generation process: Schon and Wiggins [14] describe design as a cyclic process of sketching, interpreting and taking the sketches further.

F2 Sketching stimulates the designers to re-interpret each other's ideas: when sketching to also discuss (as opposed to sketch for self-interpretation), the designer invites others to interpret her drawings as well. The function of inviting re-interpretation is especially relevant for the idea generation process, as re-interpretation leads to novel directions for generating ideas [18].

F3 Sketching stimulates the use of earlier ideas by enhancing their accessibility: Since it is externalized, sketching also facilitate archiving and retrieval of design information.

UI design by sketching is recognized for several proved virtues such as, but not limited to: maintaining an informal representation to foster creativity [3, 11, 10], complementarity between paper and pencil and software [1, 18], capability to take one design idea at a time and work it out in details or consider alternative designs at a time (i.e. lateral transformation [10]), ability to reveal as much usability problems as if it was a real UI [6].

In order to support sketching into UI design, we needed to analyze the process in which UI design is included. Currently, the development life cycle of interactive applications consists of a sophisticated process that does not always proceed linearly in a predefined way. The tools available for UI development are usually not focused on UI **design**, in which designers usually explore different alternatives but in UI **modeling** as a final product, where designers must attend to formal standards and notations.

There are many tools available for both modeling and design, however practitioners are currently forced to choose formal and flexible tools. Whichever they choose, they lose the advantages of the other, with attendant loss of productivity and sometimes of traceability and quality.

As the study reported in [2] mentions, designers desire an intelligent whiteboard because it would not require hard mental operations while sketching during meetings and design sessions.

However, electronic sketching is still behind the classical sketching in paper, since the tool in use becomes too evident

[19]. Perhaps until the gap between displays and paper are minimized, (for instance with paper-like displays [16]), this distance will continue high, hindering the designer's *conversation*.

A great care must be taken to support the designer's reflection when making design software that employs sketch recognition, for instance. If the system interprets drawings too aggressively or at the wrong time, it may prevent the designer from seeing alternative meanings.

Calico [10] and DENIM [11] are good examples of "vanishing tools" since they keep out of the way between the designers and the problem at hand, and this can be useful especially during early design stages.

Therefore, fostering creativity is specially important since design is essentiallly a problem of *wicked nature*, i.e. the process of solving it is identical with the process of understanding it [12]. In wicked problems, the designer does not have a clear understanding of what to produce and has only a vague goal in mind in the beginning.

However, electronic sketching has some important advantages over classical 'pen and paper' approach. While sketches are useful to facilitate discussions on the conceptual level, computer prototypes are useful for discussing operational and interaction issues [6]. Thus, raw sketches and interactive prototypes are complementary.

One important issue with currently sketch-based systems for prototyping of user interfaces is that they are *single-platform*, since they are usually made to be used on Desktop computers [11, 10], even though the prototypes are targeted at multiple devices [8].

A designer could sketch and test interfaces for many platforms using just a single platform such as a large sketching device (e.g. Wacom, TabletPC). However, the main benefit of sketching as a prototyping technique is to allow us to 'see as' and 'see that' [15]. That benefit is hindered since only the size of the target device is being considered, while there are other significant factors such as weight, screen resolution, brigthness and interaction modes (e.g. multi-touch, WIMP).

We argue that a more complete prototyping system would allow sketching and simulation on the target device, enriching both designers' and users' experience with an interactive prototype, allowing them finally to have a richer *conversation* with the working design at hand.

REQUIREMENTS

We have observed design sessions conducted in two companies related to user interface development. The people involved on those sessions were designers, project managers, programmers and frequently stakeholders. In overall, in these companies the design sessions are usually done around a central topic, about which people discuss in order to produce some artifact, usually a report with a list of requirements, wireframes and some session log of the decisions made around the interaction. It is important to note that this report is not produced on site but after the meeting, for what

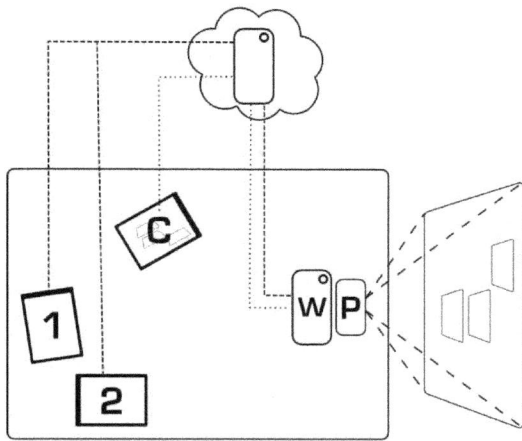

Figure 1. Physical setup of GAMBIT.

people usually take pictures for remembering and registering what was discussed. Nevertheless, the design sessions most often proceeded with three distinct phases:

1. Mental model construction and concepts: the mediator leads the task, asking the participants the essential elements of the tasks.

2. Scenario construction: the participants are usually divided into groups to focus on one scenario each. They usually do it using a big sheet of paper and use post-its. After each group agrees on its own scenario, the sheets are arranged as a storyboard on a wall for discussion.

3. Interface prototyping: the participants' sketches the user interface based on what was discussed and learned on the scenarios discussion.

Based on Van der Lugt's work [18] and on the observation of the design session, a preliminary list of requirements for a system to support collaborative sketching was constructed as follows:

R1 Support sketch production and visualization on different devices;

R2 Support session storage and retrieval;

R3 Support private/public production of sketches;

R4 Provide a broad view of the drawings (like papers arranged on a wall);

R5 Provide a fine view of a drawing;

R6 Support the UI design with different level of fidelities;

GAMBIT SYSTEM

The tool support for the investigation is the GAMBIT system, a distributed software environment designed to be physically deployed around a table, with tablets and a projector. It is multi-platform since it is essentially an embedded website, which might be used through a browser or through a native mobile application (i.e. a 'wrapper' application).

The system is currently developed as depicted on Figure 1: the many input devices (1 and 2 in the figure) can be tablets, mobile devices, large graphical tablets, etc. They are used by designers to sketch and submit drawings to the device representing the wall (W) showing the sketches as if they are real sheets of papers organized onto a real wall.

The wall is projected using a common projector (P) and can be controlled using a tablet, called 'control tablet' (C). The roles of the devices are interchangeable – a user might request the wall's control at any time, organizing and grouping the sketches. Since GAMBIT is a web-based system operating through a browser, the wall (W) might be a full-screen browser window opened on a desktop computer, a projection or a large interactive display.

Figure 1 (left) shows the deploy scheme of the system, with designers using different devices each around a projector in the middle. In the right part the wall shows the sketches being organized with the control tablet.

Figure 1 (right) shows a picture taken during a preliminary study (not to be described on this paper) with designers from one software development company. That experiment showed some indications regarding designers' preferences of device types for each one of the requirements, and it is one of the expected outcomes of the tool.

The system was developed in HTML5 in order to centralize the code for different platforms. In this sense, the system can run on any device with a browser. The sketch interface of the system is showed on Figure 2, with a drawing area that uses HTML5 <canvas> element and Javascript routines to capture the mouse/pen/touch events.

The left part shows a toolbar that can be used to switch from sketching to control functionalities. Figure 3 shows the wall with the sketches arranged like sheets of paper that can be dragged and grouped. The black background is intentionally put in order to make only the "sheets" to be projected on the wall, so as to mimic the physical storyboard mentioned during the interviews. The wall is the main part of the system, since the design session progresses around it.

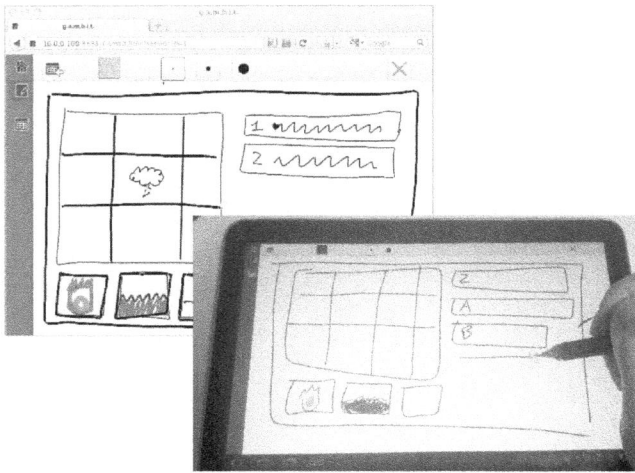

Figure 2. GAMBIT interface for sketch production respectively on a desktop and a tablet.

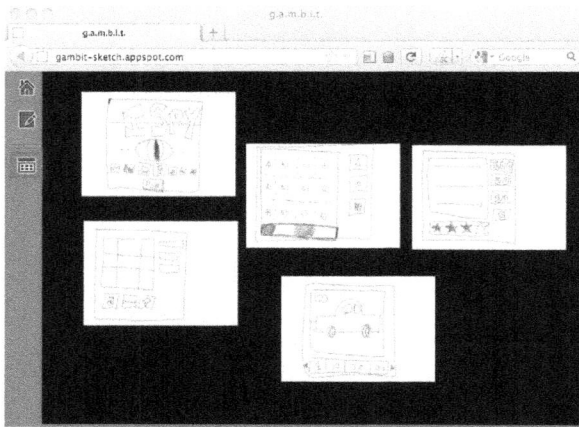

Figure 3. Interface for overview or "Wall sharing" on big displays

GAMBIT was logically designed as depicted in Figure 4, with many HTML5 clients running on tablets, smartphones and/or desktops, while being managed by a cloud-based web server. The various components of this software architecture are further explained in the next sub-sections.

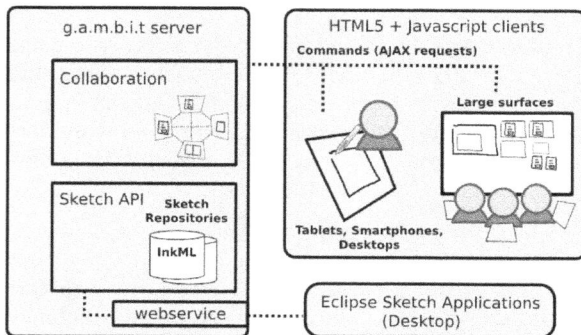

Figure 4. The logical components of GAMBIT

HTML5 + Javascript clients The clients run the same application frontend trough a browser or a wrapping application that only displays the website (without browser controls). The communication with the server is made through asynchronous requests via Javascript (AJAX). The designers might choose the device that better suit their needs, for instance, a designer might want a light device such as a tablet for a face-to-face meeting with a client in order to start a design, and a large interactive surface for online meetings or solo work.

GAMBIT server The server is responsible for managing the users, their collaborative activities and their sketches. Also, it relies on a sketch recognition API that is originally part of Eclipse Sketch project [13]– an Eclipse project created to add sketching capabilities to meta model editors built with Eclipse.

Sketch (recognition) API This component processes the sketch separately from the rest of the system, in a way referred in the literature as 'lazy or postponed recognition', which means that the sketches are not actively recognized and replaced by high-fidelity versions of what the algorithm interpreted the sketch to be. This is important in order to maintain the original look of the sketch, without stopping the designer's creativity flow and *conversation* with the sketch [7, 15]. The sketches are stored in InkML format (http://w3.org/TR/InkML).

GAMBIT is original with respect to the state of the art in that it supports user interface design by combining the following preeminent features: multiple stakeholders, multiple input devices, multiple output devices, multiple levels of fidelity, multiple ways on multiple computing platforms, thus supporting multiple configurations in a flexible way. Regarding the requirements, its current state is outlined below:

R1 *Support drawing sharing, visualization and consequently discussion*: The wall device acts as a sharing repository of sketches, aiding the discussion around a design. It is possible to send sketches to the wall, organize them, put them side-by-side for comparison, etc.

R2 *Support session storage and retrieval*: Sessions storage are supported, and can be loaded, saved and continued. History support is also planned.

R3 *Support private/public production of sketches*: Each input device is able to produce live sketches or to produce a sketch separately for later publication on the wall. Sub-group collaboration of two or more participants to produce a sketch is planned, but yet to be supported.

R4 *Provide a broad view of the drawings*: the wall was designed to serve exactly as a physical wall with 'projected sheets of paper', which are the images and sketches.

R5 *Provide a fine view of a drawing*: the input device can serve as a fine view of any sketch, and they can be re-drawn and sent once again to any other device.

R6 *Support the UI Design with different levels of fidelity*: For the moment, only low fidelity is supported.

CONCLUSION

We introduced GAMBIT (Gatherings and Meetings with Beamers and Interactive Tablets) as a system for investigating electronic sketching on a multi-platform collaborative context. It is a system aimed at constructing prototypes and will evolve to be used at design sessions in companies with a low cost of deployment, which is expected to ease the process of performing experiments.

The tool is a fundamental part of a research on sketching, whose goal is to advance the state of the art in electronic sketching, and its usage in current design practices taking into account the diverse multi-platform context.

By producing and using the prototypes directly on the target device, we expect the designers to have a richer *conversation* with the working design at hand. Experiments will be conducted comparing prototypes produced with tools such as DAMASK [8] (a single-platform tool for multi-platform prototyping) and our tool.

The system currently supports drawing and sharing in many platforms, and will evolve to allow the construction of interactive prototypes in a way similar to DENIM [11], but also including post-WIMP funcionalities, with interactive regions for touch/click events and flow connections between them.

ACKNOWLEGDEMENTS

The authors would like to acknowledge the support of the ITEA2-Call3-2008026 UsiXML (User Interface extensible Markup Language) European project and its support by Région Wallonne, Direction générale opérationnelle de l'Economie, de l'Emploi et de la Recherche (DGO6).

REFERENCES

1. Bailey, B. P., and Konstan, J. A. Are informal tools better?: comparing DEMAIS, pencil and paper, and authorware for early multimedia design. In *CHI'03: Proceedings of the SIGCHI conference on Human factors in computing systems*, ACM (New York, NY, USA, 2003), 313–320.

2. Cherubini, M., Venolia, G., DeLine, R., and Ko, A. J. Let's Go to the Whiteboard: How and Why Software Developers Use Drawings. *Proceedings of the SIGCHI conference on Human factors in computing systems - CHI '07* (2007), 557.

3. Coyette, A., and Kieffer, S. Multi-fidelity Prototyping of User Interfaces. *Ifip International Federation For Information Processing* (2007), 150–164.

4. Craft, B., and Cairns, P. Sketching sketching: outlines of a collaborative design method. In *Proceedings of the 23rd British HCI Group Annual Conference on People and Computers: Celebrating People and Technology*, British Computer Society (2009), 65–72.

5. Goel, V. "Ill-Structured Representations" for Ill-Structured Problems. In *Proceedings of the Fourteenth Annual Conference of the Cognitive Science Society*, vol. 14, Lawrence Erlbaum (1992), 130–135.

6. Johansson, M. A case study of how user interface sketches, scenarios and computer prototypes structure stakeholder meetings. *People and Computers XXI -*

HCI... but not as we know it: Proceedings of HCI '07 (2007).

7. Johnson, G., Gross, M. D., Hong, J., and Yi-Luen Do, E. Computational Support for Sketching in Design: A Review. *Foundations and Trends® in Human-Computer Interaction 2*, 1 (2008), 1–93.

8. Lin, J., Landay, J. A. J., Berkeley, U. C., and L, J. A. Damask: A tool for early-stage design and prototyping of multi-device user interfaces. In *In Proceedings of The 8th International Conference on Distributed Multimedia Systems (2002 International Workshop on Visual Computing)*, In In Proceedings of The 8th International Conference on Distributed Multimedia Systems (2002 International Workshop on Visual Computing (2002), 573–580.

9. MacLean, S., Tausky, D., Labahn, G., Lank, E., and Marzouk, M. Is the iPad useful for sketch input? A comparison with the Tablet PC. *EUROGRAPHICS Symposium on Sketch-Based Interfaces and Modeling* (2011).

10. Mangano, N., Baker, A., and van der Hoek, A. Calico: a prototype sketching tool for modeling in early design. In *MiSE '08: Proceedings of the 2008 international workshop on Models in software engineering*, ACM (New York, NY, USA, 2008), 63–68.

11. Newman, M., Lin, J., Hong, J., and Landay, J. DENIM: An informal web site design tool inspired by observations of practice. *Human-Computer Interaction 18*, 3 (2003), 259–324.

12. Rittel, H. Dilemmas in a general theory of planning. *Policy sciences 4*, 2 (1973), 155–169.

13. Sangiorgi, U., and Barbosa, S. D. J. SKETCH: Modeling Using Freehand Drawing in Eclipse Graphical Editors. In *FlexiTools: Workshop on Flexible Modeling Tools at the 32nd ACM/IEEE ICSE Intl. Conf. on Software Engineering*, (Cape Town, South Africa, 2010).

14. Schön, D. A. *The Reflective Practitioner: How Professionals Think in Action*. Basic Books, 1983.

15. Schon, D. A., and Wiggins, G. Kinds of seeing and their functions in designing. *Design Studies 13*, 2 (1992), 135–156.

16. Shah, J., and Brown, R. M. Towards electronic paper displays made from microbial cellulose. *Applied microbiology and biotechnology 66*, 4 (Jan. 2005), 352–5.

17. Snyder, C. *Paper prototyping: the fast and easy way to design and refine user interfaces*. Morgan Kaufmann, 2003.

18. van der Lugt, R. Functions of sketching in design idea generation meetings. *Proceedings of the fourth conference on Creativity cognition - CC '02* (2002), 72–79.

19. Weiser, M. The computer for the 21st century. *Scientific American* (1991).

UsiComp: an Extensible Model-Driven Composer

Alfonso García Frey[1], **Eric Céret**[2], **Sophie Dupuy-Chessa**[3],
Gaëlle Calvary[4], **Yoann Gabillon**[5]
UJF[1,2], UPMF[3], Grenoble INP[4], CNRS[1,2,3,4], LIG[1,2,3,4], UVHC[5]
41 rue des mathmatiques, 38400 Saint Martin d'Hres, France[1,2,3,4]
Univ. Lille Nord de France, F-59000 Lille, France, LAMIH, F-59313 Valenciennes, France[5]
{Alfonso.Garcia-Frey, Eric.Ceret, Sophie.Dupuy, Gaelle.Calvary}@imag.fr,
yoann.gabillon@univ-valenciennes.fr

ABSTRACT

Modern User Interfaces need to dynamically adapt to their context of use, i.e. mainly to the changes that occur in the environment or in the platform. Model-Driven Engineering offers powerful solutions to handle the design and the implementation of such UIs. However this approach requires the creation of an important amount of models and transformations, each of them in turn requiring specific knowledge and competencies. This leads to the need of an adapted tool sustaining the designers' work.

This paper introduces UsiComp, an integrated and open framework that allows designers to create models and modify them at design time as well as at runtime. UsiComp relies on a service-based architecture. It offers two modules, for design and execution. The implementation has been made using OSGi services offering dynamic possibilities for using and extending the tool. This paper describes the architecture and shows the extension capacities of the framework through two running examples.

Author Keywords

Model-Driven Engineering; User Interfaces; Design Tools.

ACM Classification Keywords

H.5.2 Information Interfaces and Presentation: User Interfaces – theory and methods.: D.2.2.Software Engineering: Design Tools and Techniques – user interfaces.

General Terms

Design, Human Factors.

PROBLEM AND MOTIVATION

With the increasing amount of platforms and devices as well as of the new expectations of users, designers need to create User Interfaces (UIs) that are able to adapt to their context of use, i.e. to the changes that occur in the environment, the platform and/or the user profile.

However, the huge amount of possible combinations of these context elements makes it no longer possible to anticipate and predefine all the eventual situations at design time. Systems have to be designed to be able to adapt themselves to their context of use while preserving usability [2]. Model Driven Engineering (MDE), which is based on the generation of applications from models, provides powerful solutions for the creation of such UIs. In this paradigm the models represent the different facets of the system to be created. These models are successively transformed and combined to finally generate the code. This opens possibilities like easier evolutions and reuse [6], dynamic adaptation to the context of use, greater quality, early detection of defects and inclusion of knowledge in executable models [11].

However, creating all the models and all the transformations for an application is a long and complicated work: the designer has to understand the underlying meta-models, write the models that conform to these meta-models and elaborate some transformations. Then, the designer needs to create a system that runs the transformations and generates the final code. This is why several studies have been driven to create frameworks to manage these stages and handle models at runtime.

This paper introduces UsiComp, a tool for creating a complete set of models (Tasks, Abstract UI, Concrete UI, Domain, Context, Mapping, Quality) and simplifying the creation of transformations. UsiComp's design and execution modules, relying on an extensible service-based architecture, include an easy graphical interface that offers an efficient way of creating models by drawing them or by combining predefined components, permitting fast prototyping possibilities. This makes it a powerful and innovative tool for designing a system with an MDE approach. This paper first relates the state of the art in the field. Then it presents UsiComp's architecture and exemplifies its extensibility on two running examples.

RELATED WORKS

Several MDE frameworks have been proposed in academic or commercial projects. For instance, UsiXML [9] offers a rich set of tools like SketchiXML [3], IdealXML [12] or

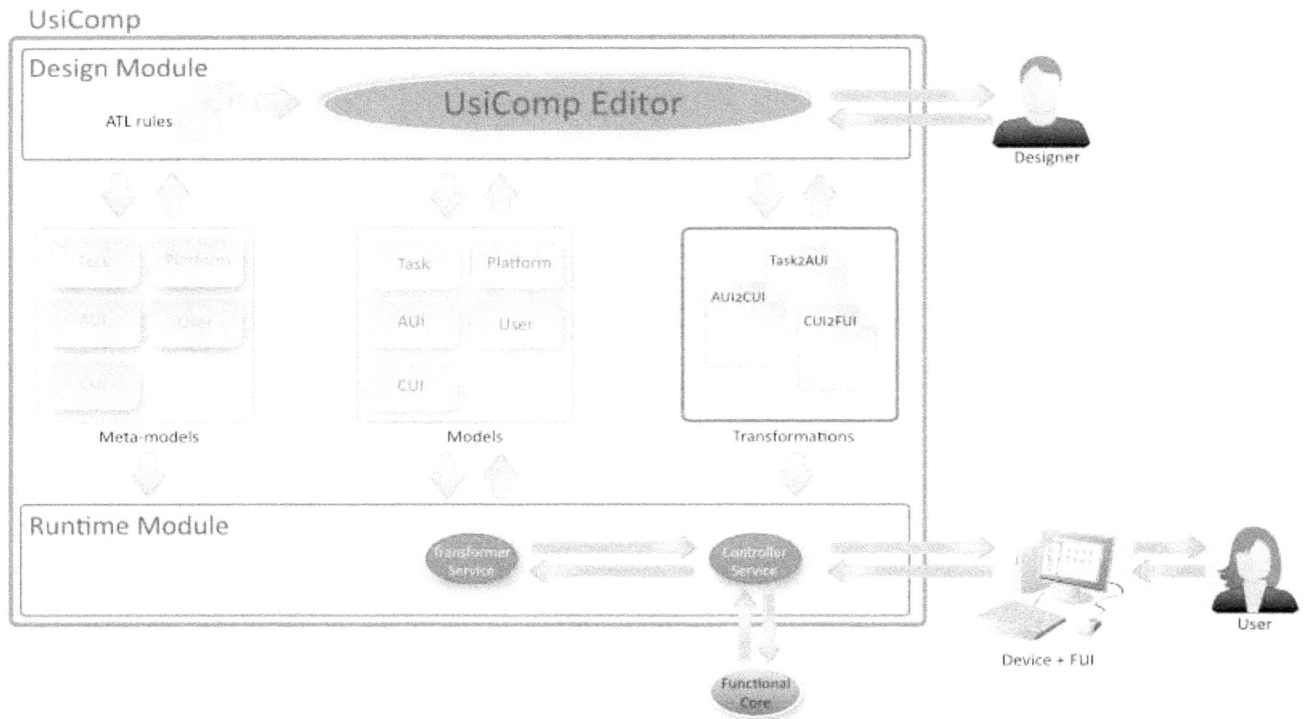

Figure 1. UsiComp software architecture: meta-models, models and transformations at the heart of both design time (IDE for designers) and runtime (FUIs for end-users).

GraphiXML [10]. This series of tools aim at covering the different phases of the development process while complying with the separation of concerns principle. Altogether, they support flexibility in the sense that they make it possible to forward and reverse engineer sketches as well as final UIs. However, in practice, effort still needs to be put on their methodological integration so that to guide the designer in selecting the right set of tools according to his needs and situation.

MARA [16] is both an architecture and a tool for managing UIs through models at runtime. Like UsiXML, MARA implements a transformation sequence starting from the Task model to successively generate the Abstract UI (AUI), Concrete UI (CUI) and Final UI (FUI). MARA supports the dynamic selection of models, meta-models and transformation. However, MARA neither includes a models editor nor does it support multiple entry points: the designer has to start with the Task model and then to implement all the predefined set of models.

Leonardi is a commercial software with two versions: a free version available on the Internet[1], and a retail version[2]. The free version requires that the designer starts from a mockup of the UI, while the full version adds the possibility of starting from a workflow. Leonardi offers a direct transformation of the UI prototype into code that is interpreted at runtime. The

two versions rely on a fixed set of models with a proprietary format.

Blumendorf et al. [1] have also proposed a framework that makes it possible to manage and to extend the calls to the services of the functional core. However, the editor is the standard Eclipse Modeling Framework which offers poor specific help for designing models and transformations. In addition, the transformation sequence starts at the Task model only.

MARIA [15] introduces a rich event manager and supports design and runtime for creating applications that use the functionalities offered by Web services. These services are annotated with hints helping the generation of UIs. However, this language (and the associated tool) does not allow the designer to extend the set of models.

SOFTWARE ARCHITECTURE

The software architecture of UsiComp relies on services. The term service refers to "a set of related software functionalities that can be reused for different purposes, together with the policies that should control its usage" [18]. These services are implemented according to the OSGi specification [13]. The main service is the Controller Service (figure 1). The Controller Service is in charge of orchestrating the whole process in which a UI is generated by successive transformations. Transformations may be reifications or abstractions [2]. Reification (respectively Abstraction) lowers (respectively increases) the level of abstraction of a model. Currently, only

---

[1]http://www.leonardi-free.org
[2]http://www.w4.eu

264

reifications have been implemented and integrated into Usi-Comp. However, the architecture is fully generic, and so capable of integrating abstractions as well.

UsiComp (figure 1) is made of two modules: one for design, another one for runtime. They share common resources: meta-models, models and transformations.

Design Module

The design module includes a visual editor (figure 2) for designing and prototyping UIs. The UsiComp editor offers the following functionalities:

- It allows designers to define all the models and transformations needed to produce a UI. The UI of the UsiComp editor is divided into three different areas (figure 2): 1) a toolbar with the most common actions, 2) the workspace presenting graphical representations of the models, and 3) the right panel which provides access to the different elements of each meta-model. Designers can create models by picking up the needed components and combining them. For instance, figure 2 shows the UsiComp editor and three models with their respective transformations. The model at the top of the figure is a task model, represented with the CTT notation [14]. This task model is transformed into an AUI model represented with blue boxes. These blue boxes show different Abstract Interaction Units and their arrangement. The AUI model is in turn transformed into a graphical CUI model that UsiComp represents with a mock-up.

- Transformations between models are composed of rules. A rule specifies how one specific set of elements of a source model is transformed into a set of target model elements. Designers can select what rules they want to apply to a given model, and the system will automatically compose the resulting transformation. These rules are represented by arrows from the source element to the target. Most common rules are already available in the system, but designers are free to add other rules if needed. Transformations and rules are written in the Atlas Transformation Language (ATL) [8].

- The UsiComp editor verifies that the designed models comply with their corresponding meta-models. For instance, a binary operator in the task model must link two different tasks. The UsiComp editor also composes and compiles the transformations and rules thanks to an integrated ATL compiler.

- The resulting Final UI, which is the code of the UI, can be directly executed from the IDE (green play button on the toolbar) giving designers the opportunity to preview the generated UI.

Runtime Module

The UsiComp runtime infrastructure is built on OSGi services [13]. It works as follows:

- Once a new device becomes available to the framework (a specific client is installed into the device for this purpose), UsiComp identifies its specific platform model containing

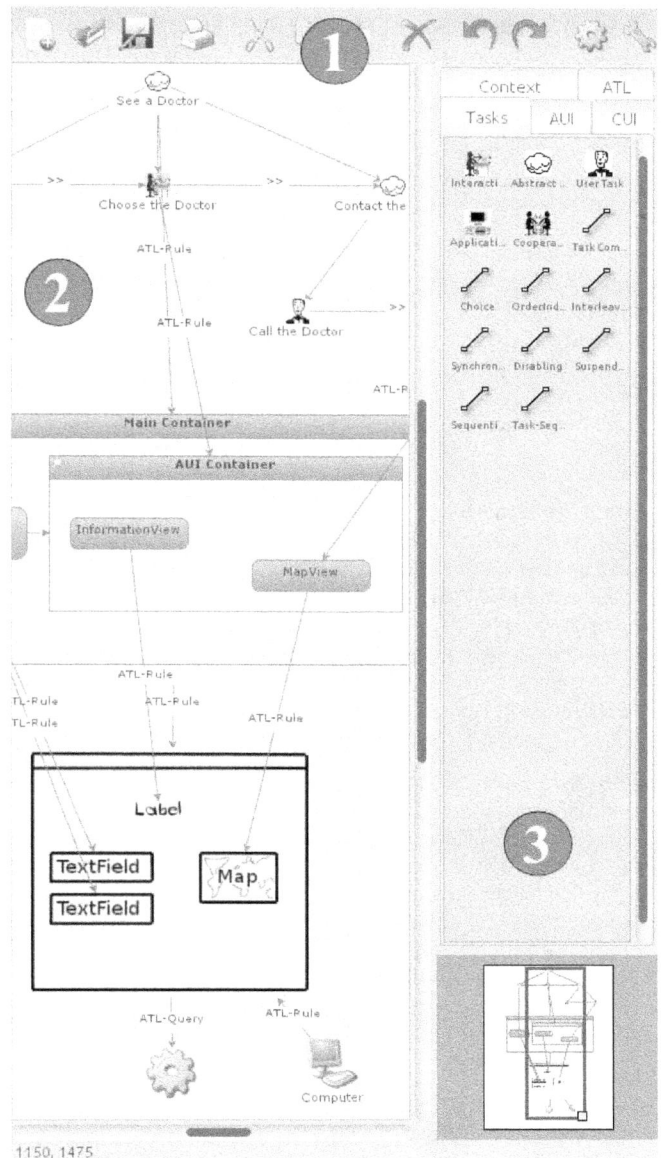

Figure 2. UsiComp Development Environment. From Top to Bottom: Task model, AUI model, CUI model. Transformations are represented by arrows.

the platform details. The current version of UsiComp contains platform models specified by hand.

- The Transformer Service (Figure 1) is a generic transformation service that can apply any transformation to any model or models, producing models or text as output.

- To produce the UI, the Controller Service manages the transformations, their order of execution and their related models and meta-models, calling to the Transformer Service as many times as needed. The platform model is considered in the transformation process to produce an adapted UI.

- In the transformation process, the Controller weaves the functional core of the application into the UI, embedding the calls from and to the UI.

The models, meta-models and transformations involved in the generation are directly accessed by the Controller Service, which is also responsible of linking the application logic from the functional core to the UI and viceversa.

UsiComp has been entirely implemented in Java, EMF [17] and ATL [8]. The development environment can be launched as a normal Desktop application or as a Web application embedded in an applet. Thanks to the OSGi services, it is possible to dynamically update the editor without stopping the application. For instance, updating a service or replacing the transformation language for another one can be dynamically achieved.

Code Generation

UsiComp currently supports the generation of Java code. The Java code is directly generated from CUI models with an ATL transformation. ATL supports not only model to model transformations, but also model to "primitive value" transformations. This last type of transformations is called queries. They can be used to generate text from models. In this particular case, the primitive value is a String data type containing all the generated code of the UI.

The code generation is directly done by transformation instead of using external tools for several reasons. First, most of the technologies that already exist focus on one language only (as for instance JaMoPP [7] for Java), or only one programming paradigm, mainly imperative in most of the cases. As the generated UI must be platform independent, the code generation cannot rely on only one specific language or paradigm. For instance, we would like to generate GTK UIs in the future for a functional language such as Haskell. Not all the languages and paradigms are supported by external generators, so integrate an external tool each time is not always possible.

Technically, the code generation is done by parsing the CUI model with a Depth First Search algorithm, i.e., translating the first element of the CUI model (at the top of the model, for instance, the main window) and exploring/transforming as far as possible along each branch before backtracking. This is possible because the CUI metamodel forces a free loops tree-like CUI models.

EXTENSION ABILITIES

UsiComp has extension abilities that are illustrated in the two following examples. Both extensions are summarized in figure 3. Figure 4 shows the classical transformation sequence and its related models and transformations, and how the examples extend UsiComp at different levels. These extensions are Compose for the task model generation and Balsamic Mockup for the CUI model generation. They are integrated at the Tasks and CUI levels respectively.

Example 1: Find a Doctor

This first example shows how to integrate an external and independent tool into UsiComp. The goal is to produce a Final

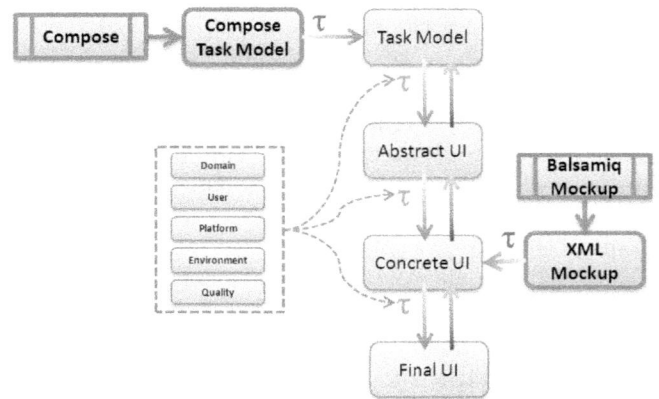

Figure 3. Two examples of the UsiComp extensibility.

UI from classical UI models in a top-down transformation process, starting from the task model and ending with the generation of the code. To show the versatility of UsiComp we extend the tool with task model generation capabilities, i.e. the task model is not created by a designer at design time as done in traditional Model-Based Design approaches, but produced with another tool called Compose. Compose [4] is a framework that generates a task model according to a specific goal. This goal can be expressed by the end-user or, as in our case, by the designer. A video showing the global process and the generation of different user interfaces from the same goal is provided with this paper and available online[3].

The generation of the task model is made by automated planning algorithms [5]. Compose relies on a set of possible abstract or concrete actions described by predicates. The combination of these predicates make the goal achievable (or not). For instance, the action "find a possible route" with the help of a map needs an Internet access (described by the predicate "internet", which is a logical condition that can be true or false). When this action is executed, the map is displayed if a map widget is available (described by the predicate "map").

The output of Compose is a task model that fulfils the goal. This task model uses a specific Compose notation. To generate a UI for this task model, we first need to integrate the model into the UsiComp transformation chain. To this end, we have written an ATL transformation rule that converts the task model produced by Compose from its specific format to the UsiXML format, which is understandable by UsiComp.

The UsiComp editor produces UIs that are adapted to different platforms. These platforms are described through a platform model, which includes platform features such as the number of screens, their resolutions, the operating system of the platform, the available technologies and their versions, etc. For instance, if we want to generate Java code for the UI we would like to know if there is a Java support on the target platform, and what the current version of the available Java

---

[3]http://youtu.be/Q_Ub3XHQxck

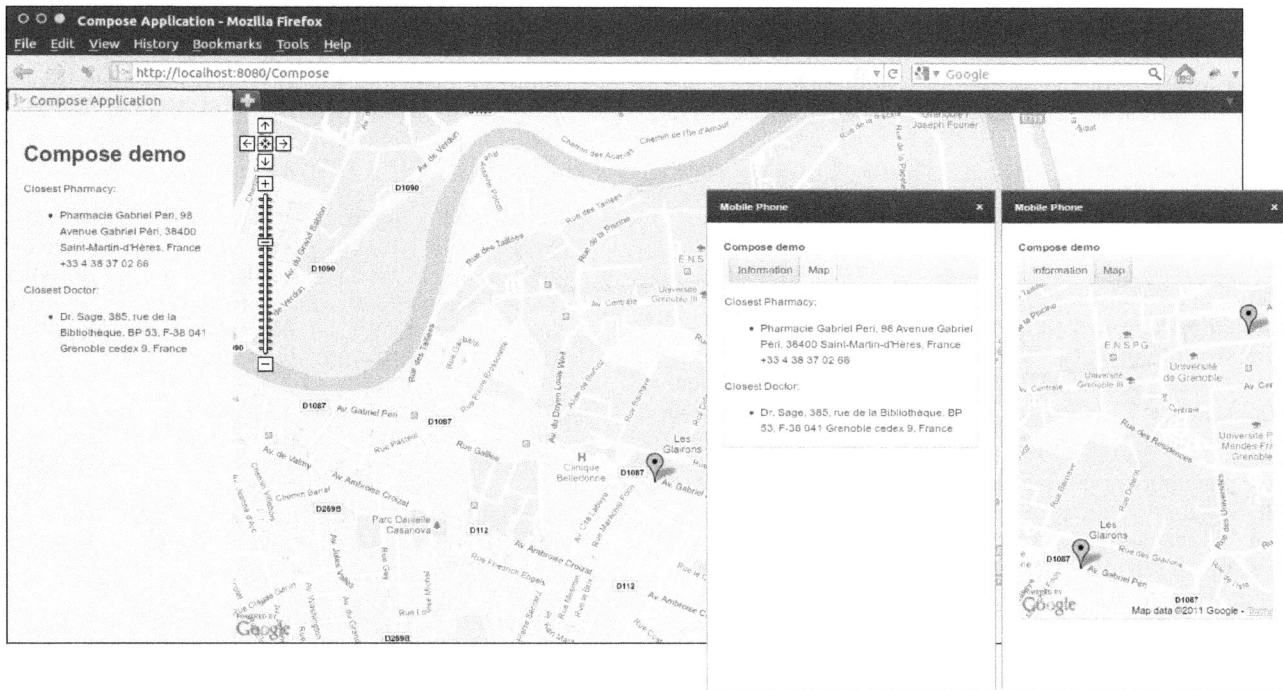

Figure 4. Two UIs generated from the same task model. The UI in the background has been generated for a PC screen with higher resolution that the UI for the mobile phone in front of the figure.

Virtual Machine is. Two different platform models are currently available in the tool, a PC platform and a mobile phone platform. The video shows how to use the editor for changing from one platform to another, and (re)generate the UI in a few clicks. Figure 4 shows the two different UIs that are produced for these two platforms. In the background, we can see the UI adapted to the screen of the PC platform. In the front, the two tabs of the generated UI for the mobile platform are shown. Some of the adaptations being performed in the process are also visible. Among others, the original screen from the PC platform has been split into two tabs due to the small resolution of the mobile phone screen. The zoom controller of the map widget has been removed as well.

Example 2: Balsamiq Mockups

The UsiComp classical transformation sequence has also been extended to integrate a UI mockup at the CUI level. This possibility refers to the situation in which a designer has a very precise idea of the UI he wants to implement. Indeed, the successive transformations do not guaranty that the resulting UI will match the precise picture of the designer. With this extension, the designer can draw a mockup of the desired UI using an external tool, like Balsamiq Mockup. Balsamiq Mockup[4] is an online tool offering a sketching service for UI prototyping. The UI produced with Balsamiq Mockup can be exported to a XML file. This file is integrated into UsiComp transformation sequence and converted into a CUI via a supplementary transformation (see Code 1 for an excerpt). In order to indicate where this CUI has to be considered in the

---

[4] http://www.balsamiq.com

transformation process, a task node is decorated to indicate that it will be defined at a more concrete level.

```
1    -- Concrete Containers
2
3    rule Control2Window {
4      from
5        s : BalsamiqModel!Control (
6            s.isAWindow()
7        )
8      to
9        t : CUI!Window (
10           Title <-- s.controlProperties.text.regexReplaceAll('%20', ' '),
11           WindowComposedOfMenuBar <-- s.WindowComposedOfMenuBar(),
12           WindowComposedOfPanels <-- s.WindowComposedOfPanels()
13       )
14   }
15
16   rule Control2MenuBar {
17     from
18       s : BalsamiqModel!Control (
19           s.isAMenuBar()
20       )
21     to t : CUI!MenuBar (
22         MenuBarComposedOfButtons <-- s.MenuBarComposedOfButtons()
23         -->collect(e | thisModule.String2Button(e))
24     )
25   }
```

Code 1. Excerpt of the ATL transformation from Balsamiq Mockup to the CUI.

CONCLUSIONS AND PERSPECTIVES

This paper presents UsiComp, a UI development and execution environment based on UsiXML. The underlying architecture is composed of a design module which includes an integrated editor for designing purposes, and a runtime

267

module, responsible for generating the UI, weaving it with the functional core, and keeping the target platform in the loop. The open architecture of UsiComp allows us to integrate new (meta-)models and transformations, such as the Compose task model. This model is integrated into the Usi-Comp generation process via a supplementary transformation.

In future work we plan to add more (meta-)models to Usi-Comp, including one Transformation meta-model so we can model transformations as well. We plan to add more transformation rules in two specific areas of UsiComp. First, enriching the current repository of transformations from the task model to AUI and from AUI to CUI will help the management of sophisticated UIs. Second, improving the code generation for supporting new languages and programming paradigms.

We are planning to evaluate UsiComp with an industrial project implementation in order to measure the usefulness, the ease of use and the completeness of the tool. The usefulness will be measured according to the possibilities for designers to produce the expected UIs. The ease of use and completeness will be evaluated with questionnaires about users' satisfaction.

ACKNOWLEDGMENTS

This work is funded by the european ITEA UsiXML project.

REFERENCES

1. Blumendorf, M., Lehmann, G., Feuerstack, S., and Albayrak, S. Executable models for human-computer interaction. In *Interactive Systems. Design, Specification, and Verification*, T. Graham and P. Palanque, Eds., vol. 5136 of *Lecture Notes in Computer Science*. Springer Berlin / Heidelberg, 2008, 238–251.

2. Calvary, G., Coutaz, J., Thevenin, D., Limbourg, Q., Bouillon, L., and Vanderdonckt, J. A unifying reference framework for multi-target user interfaces. *Interacting with Computers 15*, 3 (2003), 289–308.

3. Coyette, A., and Vanderdonckt, J. A sketching tool for designing anyuser, anyplatform, anywhere user interfaces. In *Human-Computer Interaction - INTERACT 2005*, M. Costabile and F. Patern, Eds., vol. 3585 of *Lecture Notes in Computer Science*. Springer Berlin / Heidelberg, 2005, 550–564. 10.1007/11555261_45.

4. Gabillon, Y., Petit, M., Calvary, G., and Fiorino, H. Automated planning for user interface composition. In *Proceedings of the 2nd International Workshop on Semantic Models for Adaptive Interactive Systems: SEMAIS'11 at IUI 2011 conference*, Springer HCI (2011).

5. Ghallab, M., Nau, D. S., and Traverso, P. *Automated planning - theory and practice*. Elsevier, 2004.

6. Hamid, B., Radermacher, A., Lanusse, A., Jouvray, C., Gérard, S., and Terrier, F. Designing Fault-Tolerant component based applications with a model driven approach. In *SEUS* (2008), 9–20.

7. Heidenreich, F., Johannes, J., Seifert, M., and Wende, C. Closing the gap between modelling and java. In *Software Language Engineering*, M. van den Brand, D. Gašević, and J. Gray, Eds., vol. 5969 of *Lecture Notes in Computer Science*. Springer Berlin / Heidelberg, 2010, 374–383.

8. Jouault, F., Allilaire, F., Bézivin, J., Kurtev, I., and Valduriez, P. Atl: a qvt-like transformation language. In *Companion to the 21st ACM SIGPLAN symposium on Object-oriented programming systems, languages, and applications*, OOPSLA '06, ACM (New York, NY, USA, 2006), 719–720.

9. Limbourg, Q., and Vanderdonckt, J. USIXML: a user interface description language supporting multiple levels of independence. In *ICWE Workshops* (2004), 325–338.

10. Michotte, B., and Vanderdonckt, J. GrafiXML, a multi-target user interface builder based on UsiXML. In *ICAS* (2008), 15–22.

11. Mohagheghi, P., Fernández, M. A., Martell, J. A., Fritzsche, M., and Gilani, W. *MDE Adoption in Industry: Challenges and Success Criteria*. 2008.

12. Montero, F., and López-Jaquero, V. Idealxml: An interaction design tool. In *Computer-Aided Design of User Interfaces V*, G. Calvary, C. Pribeanu, G. Santucci, and J. Vanderdonckt, Eds. Springer Netherlands, 2007, 245–252.

13. OSGi Alliance. OSGi Service Platform Release 4. [Online]. Available: http://www.osgi.org/Main/HomePage. [Accessed: Mar. 20, 2012], 2007.

14. Paterno, F., Mancini, C., and Meniconi, S. ConcurTaskTrees: A Diagrammatic Notation for Specifying Task Models. In *INTERACT '97: Proceedings of the IFIP TC13 Interantional Conference on Human-Computer Interaction*, Chapman & Hall, Ltd. (London, UK, UK, 1997), 362–369.

15. Paternò, F., Santoro, C., and Spano, L. D. Maria: A universal, declarative, multiple abstraction-level language for service-oriented applications in ubiquitous environments. *ACM Trans. Comput.-Hum. Interact. 16*, 4 (Nov. 2009), 19:1–19:30.

16. Sottet, J.-S., Calvary, G., Coutaz, J., and Favre, J.-M. A model-driven engineering approach for the usability of plastic user interfaces. In *Proc. of EIS '08*, Springer-Verlag (2008), 140–157.

17. Steinberg, D., Budinsky, F., Paternostro, M., and Merks, E. *EMF: Eclipse Modeling Framework (2nd Edition)*, 2 ed. Addison-Wesley Professional, Dec. 2008.

18. Wikipedia. Service (Systems Architecture) - Wikipedia. [Online]. Available: http://en.wikipedia.org/wiki/Service_(systems_architecture). [Accessed: Mar. 20, 2012], 2012.

The Design and Architecture of ReticularSpaces – an Activity-Based Computing Framework for Distributed and Collaborative SmartSpaces

Jakob E. Bardram, Steven Houben, Sofiane Gueddana, Søren Nielsen
The Pervasive Interaction Technology Laboratory
IT University of Copenhagen, Rued Langgaardsvej 7, DK-2300 Copenhagen, Denmark
{bardram,shou,sgue,snielsen}@itu.dk

ABSTRACT

Interactive workspaces are increasingly physically distributed, highlighting the challenge of building interfaces that support group interaction with digital documents through multiple locations and devices. This paper presents the technical implementation and user interface of *ReticularSpaces*. Based on the concepts and principles of Activity-Based Computing (ABC), *ReticularSpaces* implements a novel approach to smart space user interfaces, and supports task-based information management, mobility, and collaboration.

Author Keywords

Distributed User Interfaces, Multiple Display Environments, Smart Spaces, Activity-Based Computing

ACM Classification Keywords

H.5.2 INFORMATION INTERFACES AND PRESENTATION: User Interfaces—*User interface management systems*

INTRODUCTION

Since the pioneering work at Xerox PARC on the design of the Ubiquitous Computing technologies for meeting support [17], a significant line of research has been investigating such kind of 'smart space' technologies. 'Smart space' is an ill-defined concept, but in general the term covers research into augmenting a physical space – typically a meeting room – with computational resources. These resources often include; interactive vertical and horizontal collocated multi-touch displays of various sizes; mobile devices including laptop computers, tablet computers, and smart phones; embedded sensors and room control for sensing of people and objects in the room, and control of e.g. lighting. A core research problem – often referred to as 'Distributed User Interfaces' – is investigating how the devices and displays (fixed and mobile) can work together in a unified and interlinked way. Another research problem is how to design a smart space infrastructure for device discovery, interoperation, and information management.

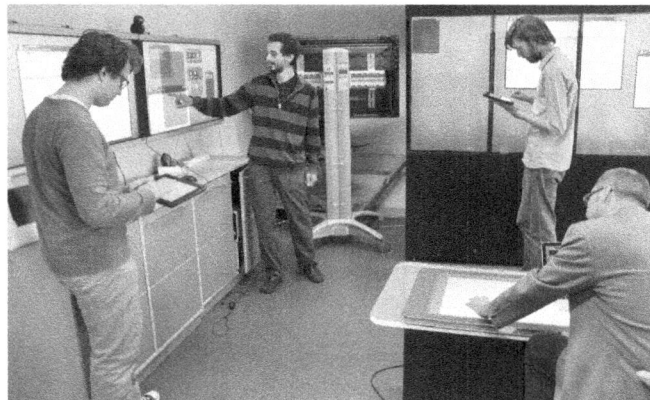

Figure 1. The RecticularSpaces smart space setup, comprising of large wall-based displays, horizontal tabletop displays, laptops, and tablet computers.

Looking at recent research into these problems, some of the important design tradeoffs in the design of smart space technologies seem to be:

- Operating System (OS) – should a smart space run on existing (primarily commercial) personal computing OSs like Windows, Linux, and Mac OS? Or is there a need for a new type of operating system for smart space technologies?

- User Interface (UI) – should smart space technology extend and build on existing user interfaces (mostly designed according to the desktop metaphor)? Or is a novel design metaphor and user interface needed?

- Information Management – does the smart space provide support for 'smart' or context-aware information management (like automatic capture and access of relevant documents for a meeting)? Or is information management left for the users to handle?

- Mobility – to what degree should a smart space support mobile or nomadic users? Does smart space support extend beyond the smart space itself? Should users be able to enter and leave the smart space?

- Devices – what sort of devices are supported by the smart space? Does it support fixed wall displays? Mobile devices? Phones? Service Devices such as printers and scanners? Embedded devices like HVAC controls, sensors, and lighting?

- Collaboration – what sort of collaboration is supported? Collocated collaboration within the smart space? Or remote collaboration with users outside the smart space?

The work done on the Ubiquitous Computing environment [17] and the iLand design of RoomWare technologies [15] took a rather fundamental approach by designing and building special-purpose hardware, displays, infrastructures, operating systems, and even furniture for smart spaces. The core argument was, that the existing approach to computing, designed according to the personal computer model with its desktop metaphor UI, was not suited for this new kind of 'Post-PC' computing environments. And hence, a new technology stack including everything from hardware to UI was needed. More recent work on smart space technologies have to a larger degree taken the existing OSs and UIs for granted, and have tried to extend these with support for smart spaces. For example, the GAIA meta-operating system [12] and the One.World framework [11] have been extending contemporary operating systems to also support features like application migration and service discovery, which are used in a smart space. Similarly, recent approaches like iRos [13], ComPUTE [6], Impromptu [8], Aris [7], and AirLift [1] focus on extending and augmenting the UI of existing personal computing operating systems with features for smart space interaction. This include graphics redirection; pointer, control, and view redirection; annexation of local displays; relocation of information across displays; and engagement of multiple users in collaboration on shared content.

Hence, prior research have investigated a wide range of issues and have provided a set of infrastructure and UI technologies for smart spaces. However, a set of the core questions listed above still seems rather unexplored. First, even though much of the recent research have taken the approach to merely extending the contemporary UI desktop metaphor, it is still questionable if a 'desk' with its icons, folders, files, and documents is the right design metaphor for a smart space. Beyond the obvious familiarity to users, this metaphor seems to provide little leverage for a smart space. Second, even though most research incorporate support for mobile devices entering and leaving a smart space, this support rarely goes beyond the room itself. But mobile and nomadic work is increasingly an important target for computer technologies and hence smart spaces. Smart spaces should not only be targeting meeting rooms in regular office buildings, but will also be use in e.g. hospitals [4] and biology laboratories [11], which has a high degree of mobile and nomadic work patterns. Third, few approaches support collaboration beyond collocated collaboration inside the smart room. But an important part of work *inside* a smart room is to be able to collaborate with users *outside* it. Finally, existing research have been addressing information management by focusing on document sharing and context-aware file management. There is little or no support for the overall tasks that users are engaged in, and the 'smart' space is often surprisingly unaware of what activities and tasks are taking place inside it.

In sum, there is still a set of challenges in the design of smart space technology, infrastructures, and interfaces that support spanning activities over a large amount of devices, better support for content and document management, while supporting collaboration amongst multiple users and across multiple locations[1].

In this paper we present *ReticularSpaces*, which is novel infrastructure and user interface for smart spaces [2]. Figure 1 shows *ReticularSpaces* in use. Compared to prior research on smart spaces, *ReticularSpaces* focuses specifically on providing answers to 4 of the questions listed above:

- **User Interface** – *ReticularSpaces* implements a completely novel UI metaphor for smart space. As such, *ReticularSpaces* does not rely or expand on existing desktop UIs, but implement a new design based on an 'Activity' metaphor. The goal is to align the UI metaphor to the activities of the users, rather than their desktop.

- **Information Management** – according to the 'Activity' metaphor, *ReticularSpaces* implements an activity-based computing approach to information and data management. Thus, in contrast to the desktop metaphor where information management is modeled according to an office (files, folders, trashcans), the goal of *ReticularSpaces* is to align information management to the activities of the users.

- **Mobility** – *ReticularSpaces* has inherent support for mobility of users as well as devices. In addition to supporting devices entering and leaving a smart room, *ReticularSpaces* supports mobility within a larger smart space, which typically spans a large geographical areas like a hospital, large factory, or a campus.

- **Collaboration** – *ReticularSpaces* has inherent support for collaboration amongst users and devices. In addition to supporting collocated collaboration by display sharing inside a room, remote collaboration across a larger site is supported.

This paper presents the technical design and implementation of the *ReticularSpaces* system infrastructure and UI management system. The overall motivation, design, and usage of *ReticularSpaces* is described in [2].

RETICULARSPACES TECHNICAL ARCHITECTURE

ReticularSpaces is the 5th generation of our research into activity-based computing (ABC) and applies a peer-to-peer (P2P) architecture illustrated in Figure 2. In contrast to the 3rd [3] and 4th [5] generation of the ABC infrastructure where the *Activity Manager* was located on a central server, each peer (client) in *ReticularSpaces* has an instance of the activity manager running. Each client can also run the user-interface client called *ReticUI* . A *ReticUI* client knows the network address (default is 'localhost') of its activity manager (connection of type C1 in Figure 2). Activity managers are constantly looking for other activity managers (using mDNS), and can thereby discover and connect to each other (C2). An *ReticUI* client can connect to any activity manager which

---

[1]This conclusion is in line with the discussion and conclusion from recent CHI workshops on the design of smart space and related systems. For example the CHI 2006 workshop on 'Information Visualization and Interaction Techniques for Collaboration across Multiple Displays' [16] and the CHI 2011 workshop on 'Distributed User Interfaces' [10]

is discovered and enlisted by its (local) Activity Manager. Hence, in Figure 2, the activity browser on *client_1* can mount and access data in activity manager on *client_2* (C3), once the activity manager of *client_2* has discovered and connected to the activity manager of *client_1* (C2).

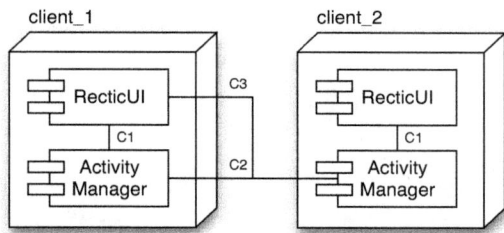

Figure 2. A schematic view of the *ReticularSpaces* P2P architecture.

A more elaborate deployment example is illustrated in Figure 3. This deployment setup is the demonstration setup illustrated in Figure 1 and used for the evaluation presented in [2]. In Figure 3 the smart room runs a dedicated smart room activity manger on a separate server machine. The *ReticUI* client of each of the displays fixed inside the smart room – such as the wall and tabletop displays – connects to this central activity manager (C1 type of connections). When a mobile device (in this case the tabletPC) enters the smart space network environment, the two activity managers will discover and connect to each others (C2). The *ReticUI* client will display available activity managers as shown in Figure 4. By clicking on the label for an activity manager, the user 'mounts' this activity manager and thereby establish connection C3.

This illustrates the technical setup in the scenario where a user enters the smart room with a tablet computer, which is discovered and displayed on a wall display. Any user can then go to the wall display, mount the activity manager, and access its data from the wall display.

Activity Manager

The core component in the ABC infrastructure is the Activity Manager. Figure 5 illustrates the overall software architecture of the activity manager. The activity manager is implemented using the Aexo framework [9] by extending the base Aexo component called `AComponent`. An Aexo component is hosted by the Aexo runtime on a host device, and uses an event-based RESTful communication interface. This allows clients to get, post, and delete data as well as subscribe to changes in data in a component, in which case the client (subscriber) will get notified if data is updated. In *ReticularSpaces* , the Aexo `ActivityManagerComponent` basically initializes itself within the Aexo runtime system, and then holds a reference to the `ActivityController`, which is responsible for all the logic in the ABC infrastructure. Using three registries, the activity manager holds references to other discovered activity managers, services (such as printers, sensors, etc.), and attached *ReticUI* clients.

Activity managers maintain information about the physical location of devices running a *ReticUI* client. In the example above, the smart room server's activity manager knows

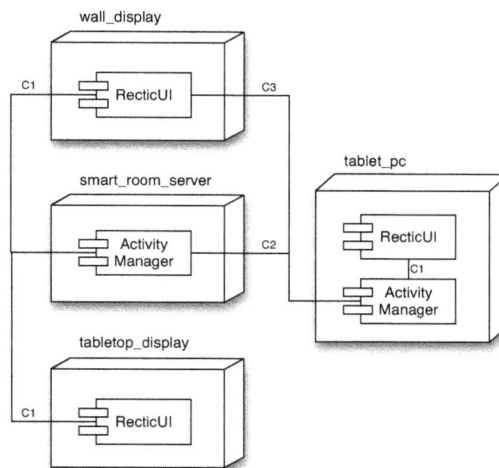

Figure 3. The deployment diagram for the setup in Figure 1.

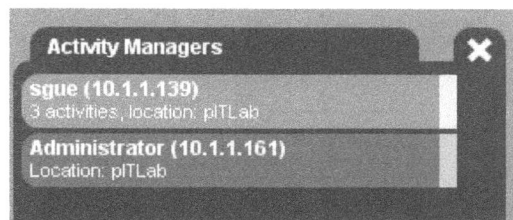

Figure 4. Details from the Activity View of *ReticUI* (Figure 8) showing a list of activity managers available in this location (the 'pITLab'). Each activity manager has a color code, which is used to identify activities from this activity manager.

the location of the wall and tabletop displays, as well as the location of the tablet computer.

Information Management

The activity manager's data model is shown in Figure 6. This model organize all documents, resources, services, etc. that are relevant for a human activity into a corresponding 'Computational Activity', or just 'Activity'. Each *activity* is composed of a set of *actions*, each again holding a set of *operations*. Each operation points to a *resource*, such as a document, a picture, html page, etc. Resources can also be external *services*, such as a device, like a printer, which can be accessed through an operation. Each activity has a list of *participants*, and only participants can access (resume/suspend) the activity, and its actions and operations. *Relationships* allows users to organize activities, actions, and operations in different workflow structures. Such structures could be simple association links showing which activities are related, as well as more complex workflow constraints specifying which activities has to be done before another activity can be resumed. Because of the overlapping properties between activities, actions and operations, they are abstracted into an *enactment*.

Dynamic Behavior

From a dynamic view, *ReticularSpaces* implements a distributed model-view-controller (dMVC) architecture. The activity manager holds the activity model, which is replicated

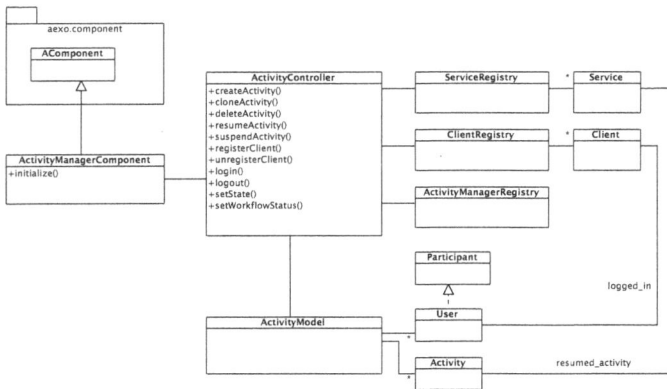

Figure 5. The Activity Manager Class Diagram.

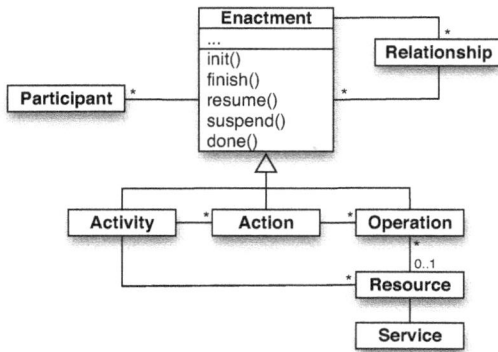

Figure 6. The ABC Ontology used in *ReticularSpaces*.

to each *ReticUI* client. On each *ReticUI* client, a standard (local) MVC patterns keeps views updated, and manages changes to the model. Data model replication and synchronization is done using the event-based system in Aexo.

When a *ReticUI* client connects to the infrastructure it can display and manipulate data elements like activities, actions, operations, resources, and services. Changes to the client's replicated data model propagate to the distributed model and updates other client models. To render resources and services, *ReticUI* clients access an URI of the service and show any data coming from that service, with a different rendering component according to the data type.

This distributed model-view-controller pattern is also used in the collaborative features of *ReticularSpaces*. Since, the layout and location of certain UI elements is part of the data stored in the data model, the distributed model-view-controller setup implies that the view of certain relevant part of the *ReticUI* user interface is synchronized in real time across multiple displays. This means that users working on different devices on the same activity will see a synchronized view similar to the WYSIWIS principle[2].

---

[2]Acronym for "What I See Is What You See", used for groupware that guarantee that users see the same thing at all times.

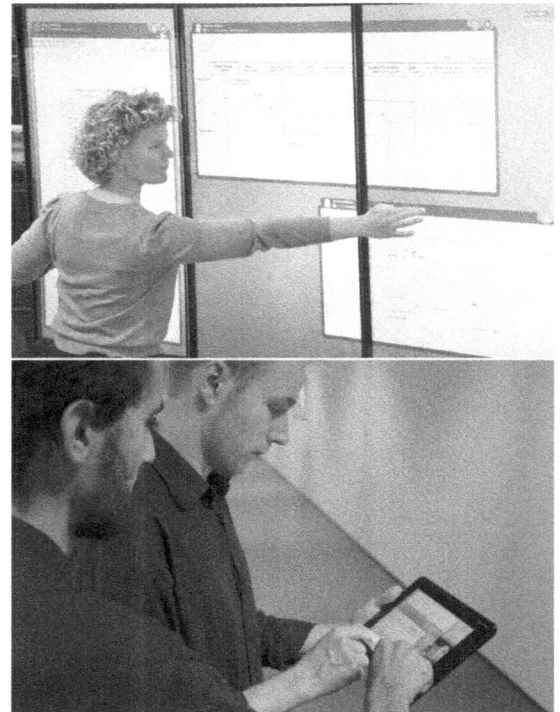

Figure 7. Use of *ReticUI* on very large wall displays (top) and on mobile devices in remote locations (bottom).

RETICULARSPACES USER INTERFACE

As described above, *ReticularSpaces* has adopted a completely new UI metaphor based on the principles of activity-based computing [2]. This UI – called *ReticUI* – is designed to run on a wide range of interactive displays, and supports different display features:

Size – *ReticUI* implements panning and zooming on an indefinite canvas, and hence scales from small tablet displays (12"), to tabletop displays (46"), to very large wall displays (120" or more) – see Figure 7. In contrast to e.g. Exposé in the Mac OS, or ScalableFabric [14], *ReticUI* widgets and components can be interacted with in any scale.

Touch modality – *ReticUI* supports both pen-based interaction, single-touch, and multi-touch. Depending on the type of touch, various gestures implements different commands, like zooming, panning, and action resume/suspend.

Video – if devices have a video camera, video connections are automatically established during activity sharing session of remotely located devices.

Commands – all commands in *ReticUI* are accessible through gestures and/or pie menus. Since *ReticUI* can run on very large displays, pie menus can be activated by clicking the background canvas in any place where the user may be located in front of the display.

The UI of *ReticUI* is shown in Figure 8 and 9. The main 'widgets' in the activity-based computing UI metaphor are; activities; actions; operations; resources; services and participants. These widgets are organized according to the activity ontology shown in Figure 6. *ReticUI* consists of two main

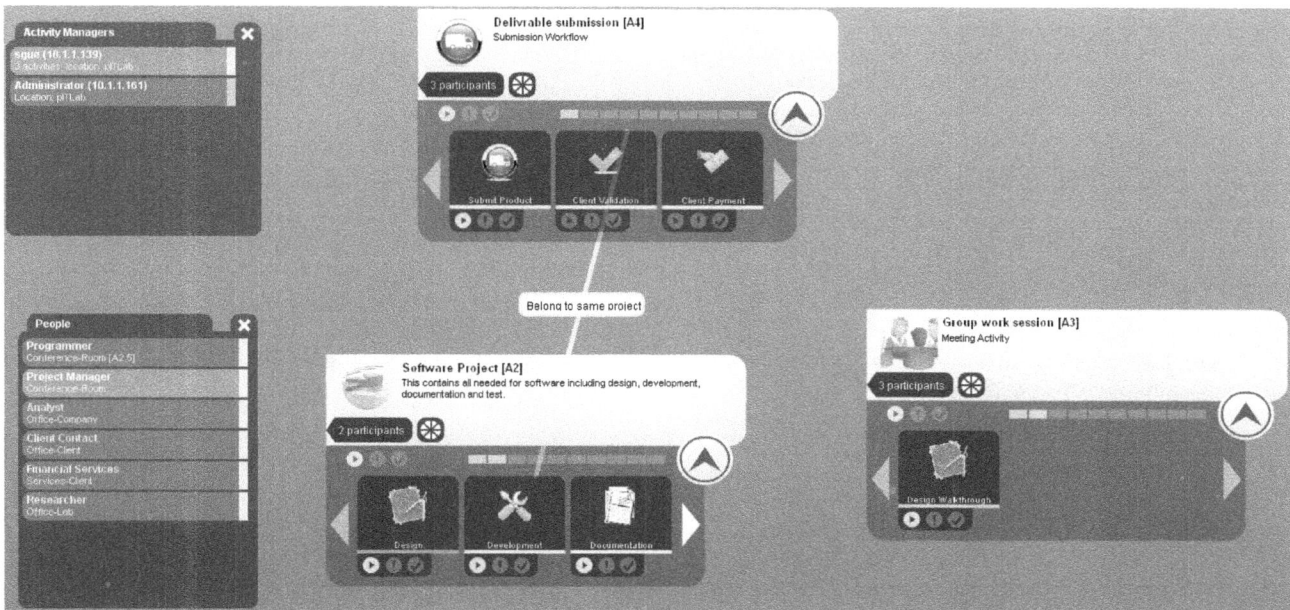

Figure 8. The *Activity View* showing a list of available activity managers, a list of users in this location, and the relevant set of activities from all mounted activity managers. Each activity (the while box) can be expanded to show its list of actions and participants. Relationships between activities are shown as lines with a text label.

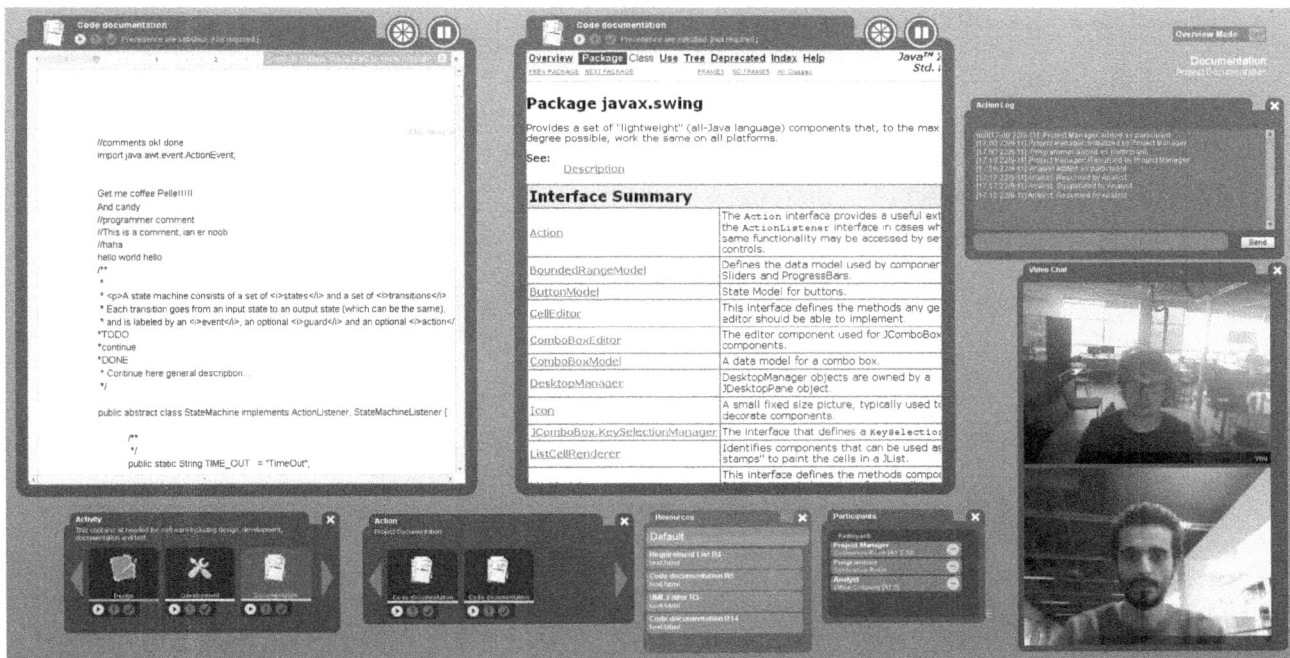

Figure 9. The *Action View* is displayed when a user resumes an action by clicking on it in the activity view. The action view shows the action's operations and the resource each operation links to; in this case a source code document and a web page showing Java documentation. The action view can show various overview panels as shown at the bottom of the view. From left to right these are overviews of; all actions in the overall activity; all operations in this action; available resources; and the participants. On the right side the collaboration windows are shown, including (from the top); the action log and the remote video feeds. Users can switch between the activity and action views by suspending and resuming an action.

views; the *Activity View* (Figure 8) and the *Action View*. The activity view provides an overview of all relevant activities from mounted activity managers, as well as contextual information about location, collocated users, and available activity managers. Each activity (the while box) can be expanded to show its list of actions and participants. Workflow relationships between activities are shown as lines with a text label. The *Action View* (Figure 9) is displayed when a user resumes an action by clicking it in the activity view. The action view shows the action's operations and the resource each operation

273

links to, such as a text document or a web page. The action view can show various overview panels as shown at the bottom of the view. From left to right these are overviews of: all actions in the overall activity; operations in this action; available resources; and the participants. On the right side the collaboration windows are shown, including (from the top); the action log (which works as a instant messaging system when users are engaged in online activity sharing) and the remote video feeds. Users can switch between the activity and action views by suspending and resuming an action.

SUMMARY

This paper has presented the software architecture and user interface technology of *ReticularSpaces*. *ReticularSpaces* is a smart space technology based on the principles of activity-based computing. The core design goal of *ReticularSpaces* was to provide a novel user interface for smart space technologies based on 'activity' as the core metaphor; to support task-based information management across several displays and locations; to support mobility inside a larger smart space such as large factories, hospitals, or a campus; and to support collaboration both collocated inside a smart room, as well as between remotely distant locations. We are currently working on improving the *ReticularSpaces* technologies. On the infrastructure level, a more robust and scalable infrastructure is being designed by leveraging cloud technologies. On the interface part, better support for learning this new UI metaphor is needed and the workflow visualizations and usage needs to be improved. The long term goal is to use *ReticularSpaces* for projects within different domains, and for real-world deployment.

REFERENCES

1. T. Bader, A. Heck, and J. Beyerer. Lift-and-drop: crossing boundaries in a multi-display environment by airlift. In *Proc. of AVI 2010*, pages 139–146. ACM, 2010.

2. J. Bardram, S. Gueddana, S. Houben, and S. Nielsen. Reticularspaces: Activity-based computing support for physically distributed and collaborative smart spaces. In *Proc. of CHI 2012*. ACM, 2012.

3. J. E. Bardram. Activity-based computing for medical work in hospitals. *ACM Transactions on Computer-Human Interaction*, 16(2):1–36, 2009.

4. J. E. Bardram, J. Bunde-Pedersen, A. Doryab, and S. Sørensen. Clinical surfaces — activity-based computing for distributed multi-display environments in hospitals. In *Proc. of INTERACT 2009*, pages 704–717. Springer-Verlag, 2009.

5. J. E. Bardram, J. Bunde-Pedersen, and M. Soegaard. Support for activity-based computing in a personal computing operating system. In *Proc. of CHI 2006*, pages 211–220, New York, NY, USA, 2006. ACM Press.

6. J. E. Bardram, C. Fuglsang, and S. C. Pedersen. Compute: a runtime infrastructure for device composition. In *Proceedings of the International Conference on Advanced Visual Interfaces*, AVI '10, pages 111–118. ACM, 2010.

7. J. T. Biehl and B. P. Bailey. Aris: an interface for application relocation in an interactive space. In *Proc. of GI 2004*, pages 107–116, 2004.

8. J. T. Biehl, W. T. Baker, B. P. Bailey, D. S. Tan, K. M. Inkpen, and M. Czerwinski. Impromptu: a new interaction framework for supporting collaboration in multiple display environments and its field evaluation for co-located software development. In *Proc. of CHI 2008*, pages 939–948. ACM, 2008.

9. J. Bunde-Pedersen. *Distributed Interaction for Activity-Based Computing*. PhD thesis, Computer Science Department, University of Aarhus, Denmark, 2009.

10. J. A. Gallud, R. Tesoriero, J. Vanderdonckt, M. Lozano, V. Penichet, and F. Botella. Distributed user interfaces. In *Proceedings of the 2011 annual conference extended abstracts on Human factors in computing systems*, CHI EA '11, pages 2429–2432. ACM, 2011.

11. R. Grimm. One.world: Experiences with a pervasive computing architecture. *IEEE Pervasive Computing*, 3(3):22–30, July 2004.

12. C. K. Hess, M. Román, and R. H. Campbell. Building applications for ubiquitous computing environments. In *Proc. of Pervasive 2002*, pages 16–29. Springer-Verlag, 2002.

13. B. Johanson, A. Fox, and T. Winograd. The interactive workspaces project: Experiences with ubiquitous computing rooms. *IEEE Pervasive Computing*, 1:67–74, April 2002.

14. G. Robertson, E. Horvitz, M. Czerwinski, P. Baudisch, D. R. Hutchings, B. Meyers, D. Robbins, and G. Smith. Scalable fabric: flexible task management. In *Proceedings of the working conference on Advanced visual interfaces*, AVI '04, pages 85–89. ACM, 2004.

15. N. A. Streitz, J. Geißler, T. Holmer, S. Konomi, C. Müller-Tomfelde, W. Reischl, P. Rexroth, P. Seitz, and R. Steinmetz. i-land: an interactive landscape for creativity and innovation. In *Proceed. of CHI 1999*, pages 120–127. ACM, 1999.

16. L. Terrenghi, R. May, P. Baudisch, W. MacKay, F. Paternò, J. Thomas, and M. Billinghurst. Information visualization and interaction techniques for collaboration across multiple displays. In *Extended Proc. of CHI 2006*, CHI '06, pages 1643–1646. ACM, 2006.

17. M. Weiser. The Computer for the 21st Century. *Scientific American*, 265(3):66–75, September 1991.

Software Architecture for Interactive Robot Teleoperation

Nader Cheaib, Mouna Essabbah, Christophe Domingues, Samir Otmane

IBISC Laboratory, University of Evry Val d'Essonne

40 Pelvoux Street, 91020 Evry, France

firstname.lastname@ibisc.fr

ABSTRACT

In this paper, we present a software architecture for interactive and collaborative underwater robot teleoperation. This work is in the context of the Digital Ocean Europe project that aims at digitalizing seafloor sites in 3D imagery using underwater robots (ROVs), and uses this information in order to edit interactive, virtually animated environments diffused online. The work presented in this paper concerns the software architecture of the interactive system in order to collaboratively teleoperate the robot, using two types of interfaces: 1) an intuitive web interface and 2) a Virtual Reality (VR) platform. The particularity of our system is the separation of the systems' functional core from its interfaces, which enables greater flexibility in teleoperating the robot. We discuss the conceptual software architecture as well as the implementation of the systems' interfaces.

Author Keywords

Interactive systems; Groupware Architecture; Virtual Reality.

ACM Classification Keywords

D.2.11 [Software Architectures]; D.4.7 [Organization and Design]: Interactive systems; H.5.3 [Group and Organization Interfaces]: Computer-supported cooperative work.

INTRODUCTION

Teleoperation consists of remotely commanding and manipulating robot systems. This type of control allows doing complex tasks in hostile environments, where some of them may be hard to accomplish by humans. The application domains of teleoperation are numerous and present in most of research fields (medical, spatial, etc.). In particular, remote operation of underwater robotic systems seems to be a growing research concern in many application domains [12, 15]. On the other hand, as the use of the internet and the services offered with it are exponantially emerging, people are in increasing need of flexible and agile applications in order to execute collaborative tasks. The emergence of collaborative work

over the internet was a solution to the high complexity of systems and the technical difficulties that arise from their use, as geographically distributed users are increasingly working together on common tasks, but using rigid and often incompatible applications. In this paper, we propose a new groupware (collaborative software) architecture to collaboratively teleoperate an underwater robot, independently of the interfaces used. Hence, people connected to the internet are able to teleoperate the robot using a PC, mobile or virtual reality platforms. This work is in the context of the Digital Ocean Europe that aims at enhancing public awareness on the ocean and increases their marine scientific literacy. Hence, the aim is to give public means to remotely operate an underwater robot online in order to to discover underwater environments.

We will proceed as follows: Firstly, we present some related work in the field of underwater robot teleoperation. Then, we define the concept of collaboration and the need for a new software architecture supporting it. Then, we present our conceptual software architecture. After that, we describe two types of interfaces that our software architecture supports for robot teleoperation: an intuitive web interface and a VR platform. We discuss the originality of our system as well as its application to robot teleoperation. Finally, we present a conclusion and perspectives in the field.

RELATED WORK

Many researchers have proposed software architectures for teleoperating underwater vehicles. The authors in [18] describe a system for long-distance remote observation of robotic operations targeted to e-learning, called AQUA. They present a software architecture that provides a uniform look-and-feel web interface presenting sensor information on the distance robot. Other work, such as in [19], present a system that facilitates interactive remote control of a high definition camera on an underwater robot, while transmitting the video feedback using web services. The aim of this system is to enable the public to control their own view of the undersea environment, independently of their location. The authors in [4] present the E-Robot project that enables users to interact with an underwater ROV (Remotely Operated Vehicle) through an Internet Browser to pilot the ROV in real time, while visualizing underwater images taken under the ice in the Arctic region. Furthermore, the authors in [13] present an Internet-operated deep-sea crawler, equipped with sensors to measure the temperature, pressure, water currents, methane and turbidity. This system, called Wally, supports a pan/tilt webcam, affording detailed views of the seafloor sediments and local sea life. The authors in [2] present GOYA, a teleoperated system for blasting applied to hull cleaning in ship maintenance. The authors followed the COMET methodology for designing the systems' classes in order to design the robots' control units. Finally, the authors in [1] present a reference architecture for robot teleoperation systems developed using the domain-engineering process and architectural patterns. This software architecture has been applied to various systems for maintenance activities in nuclear power plants, such as the ROSA, IRV and TRON systems.

In fact, a common aspect for most of these systems is their use of web interfaces for robot teleoperation. However, they do not take in consideration other types of interfaces, as well as collaborative aspects of teleoperation. For the authors in [11], user-interfaces' design for teleoperation involves a trade-off between ease of use and the capacity for complex tasks. This is a challenge for web-based interfaces as they need to support users having diverse skills. Hence, web interfaces should be designed so that novice users feel comfortable using it, while not being a constraint on expert users. Also, the authors in [16] present user interface issues to consider while designing collaborative teleoperation, such as visible navigation aids, chat channels, data presentation, etc. In this paper, we present a software architecture that tries to remedy these constraints by separating the functional core of the system from its physical interfaces. It also takes in consideration collaboration between users, by dividing the collaborative experience into communication, coordination and production spaces.

COLLABORATION AND THE 3C MODEL

In order to further understand the concept of collaboration, we base our work on the 3C functional model proposed by Ellis [8], shown in Figure 1. According to this model, a groupware system covers three domain specific functions, production/cooperation, communication and coordination. The production space designates the objects resulting from the activity of the group (ex: word document, paint etc.). For Ellis, this space is concerned with the result of common tasks to be achieved, and is the space where the production takes place. The coordination space defines the actors and their social structure, as well as different tasks to be accomplished in order to produce in the production space.

Ellis eventually completed the model with the communication space that offers to actors in the coordination space means to exchange information in which the semantics concern exclusively the actor, and where the system only acts as a messenger. In our work, we use this decomposition of groupware's functionalities in order to introduce a collaborative software architecture

supporting the functional decomposition of services that can be present in an interactive groupware system.

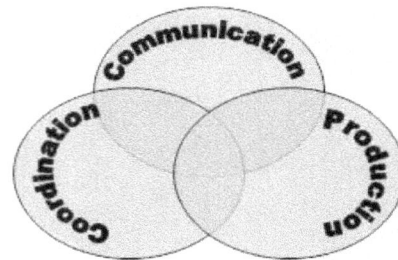

Figure 1: 3C model by Ellis

In fact, there exist some work in the literature that make use of the 3C model in order to create collaborative applications [10, 14, 17] for various application domains. The authors in [10] affirm that the understanding of communication has transformed from being vertical, where orders are passed from above and reports sent up the line, to a peer-to-peer paradigm where communication, coordination and cooperation predominate. This is due to the fact that command and control paradigm is losing effectiveness in the society. People are increasingly using tools and applications with no specific or centralized source that issues orders, but where people are collaboratively coordinating and dividing tasks between them, and eventually taking group decisions. In our work, we use the 3C model to define the three main aspects of a collaborative application. Hence, an optimal collaboration pattern is achieved when the collaborative process is initiated by communicating, and ends by a concrete realization of the task at hand.

GENERIC SOFTWARE ARCHITECTURE

We rely on the Arch model [3] that separates the physical interface (Layer 0 in Figure 2) from the Functional Core (FC) of the system (Layers N-1 and N). However, in contrast to the Arch model where the FC is a dead-end component (implements static domain functionalities), our FC is connected to the internet in order to communicate with the external world (Internet). In this paper, we discuss the FC's design (Layers N-1 and N) as well as the physical layer (Layer 0). Furthermore, we rely on Dewan's model [7], which is a generalization of the Arch model. This model structures a groupware system into a variable number of replicated and shared layers. Thus, it defines a collaboration degree between the system's components and users, where the highest layer is the most semantic one, corresponding to the FC of the system (coincides with the one of the Arch model as well as the Abstraction facet of the PAC* model [5]), and the lowest layer representing the material level (corresponds to the Arch's Physical Interaction component as well as the Presentation facet of PAC*). Note that Figure 2 representing our proposed architecture shows only the FC of the system, along with the physical interaction layer that implements interactions between users.

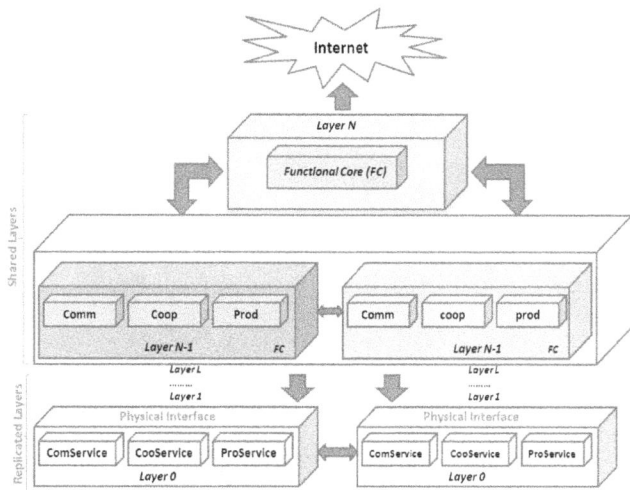

Figure 2: Conceptual software architecture

Our software architecture is constituted of a root representing shared layers among all users in the system, as well as several replicated layers for every user. The layers communicate vertically using interaction events, and horizontally through collaboration between users over the network. However, in contrast to the Clover model [14] where the functional core is also split into two layers: one private and shared, while the other is replicated and public, our functional core is represented by two layers that are both shared and constitute the root of the system.

Functional Core (FC)

The shared layers of the software architecture constituting the FC enable users to manipulate domain objects and have access to various services in the system, while the replicated layers handles the set of services and the state of the system that is private for every user in collaboration. We extend this layer abstraction as in [14] by decomposing each layer of the architecture into sub-components, each dedicated to one facet of Ellis' 3C model, while providing and managing specific services for communication, coordination and production on the layer N-1. These services can be considered as orchestrations of atomic services based on the functionalities they offer, and are exposed to users through systems' interfaces. In our work, we suppose that only the layers on the level N-1 and on the lowest level (Layer 0) satisfy these three main classifications, while we make no assumption about the decomposition of the highest layer in the software architecture, which is mainly composed of a module to synchronize data from users collaborating using the system. Further information concerning the software architecture can be found in our earlier work [6].

INTERACTIVE INTERFACES FOR ROV TELEOPERATION

We present two types of Human-Robot Interfaces (HRI) hosted on the layer 0 of our software architecture. Our first HRI enables an easy access to teleoperate the ROV via a simple web browser. In our project, we have integrated a Web interface on a submersible device called Dolphyn, shown in Figure 3, which is an aquatic PC integrating an x86 tablet running on Windows 7. This device diffuses multimedia content while using two integrated joysticks to teleoperate the ROV via Internet. It aims at visualizing underwater media while being in a swimming pool for a more realistic underwater exploration. The second HRI is based on a VR/Augmented Reality (AR) platform, which gives users a multisensory exploration of the underwater site. Hence, it enhances the feeling of presence due to stereoscopic display and haptic interfaces.

In fact, three main components are used in our system: 1) The client side application (Web or VR/AR) on the Layer 0, 2) the ROV's server and the video streaming service to control the distant ROV while capturing video images on the Layer N-1, and 3) the multiuser service on the Layer N. Recall that Layer N-1 and Layer N represent the system's FC. In our case, the user interacts with the system through its interfaces in order to visualize the content diffused by ROV's camera, while using the Dolphyn.

Figure 3: The Dolphyn

Indeed, the real-time streaming service allows bringing the video broadcast to the internet. The process involves a camera on the ROV, an encoder to digitalize the content as well as a content delivery network in order to distribute and deliver the content. The media can then be viewed by end-users in real time. For encoding the PAL signal, we have chosen the Ogg format, where we use the HTTP protocol for delivery. On the other hand, the multiuser service is used to synchronize data between users performing a collaborative virtual diving. Indeed, Layer N of our software architecture is used to accept network connections and transfer commands sent by users to the ROV. It is also used to prevent multiple and heavy connections to the ROV through the use of a priority list (First come first served).

Web HRI on the 3C Model

We present the Web HRI dedicated to ROV teleoperation on mobile or desktop computers. In fact, this interface allows sending commands to the ROV (2) as well as supervising sensors' data from the ROV (1, 3 and 5). It also enables a user to use various functionalities (Chat, various Web services, etc.) in the interface (part 4 and 6).

As mentioned, the physical layer (Layer 0) is decomposed into sub-components according to Ellis' 3C model, while providing and managing specific services for communication, coordination and production. Hence, our Web interface shown, in Figure 4, has the following structure:

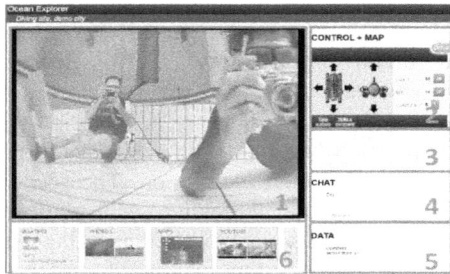

Figure 4: Web HRI for mobile devices and desktop PCs

- **Communication**: The communication space offers to users means to exchange information relative to ROV teleoperation missions. This space, represented by the region (4) of the interface, is based on a textual communication. More communication services can be added, such as audio and video services. However, in this stage of the project, an essential design constraint is to keep the interface as easy-to-use as possible, since we consider that our system will be used by the general public. Adding more functionalities in the interface can be overwhelming for systems' first use.

- **Coordination**: The coordination space (2) implements commands enabling users to create collaborative diving trajectories. It also enables allocating users to various diving paths in teleoperation sessions.

- **Production**: The production space (1) is crucial for visualizing underwater sites from the ROV's camera as video streams. Hence, this space gives users a visual feedback of their diving trajectories that are being executed by the ROV. Also, our system uses AR technologies by the reorganization of 2D real markers, as shown in Figure 5. Those markers can be used to add multimedia data (text, images, videos, fauna and flora 3D models, etc.), as well as to localize the ROV using its camera, which adds a rich interactive experience.

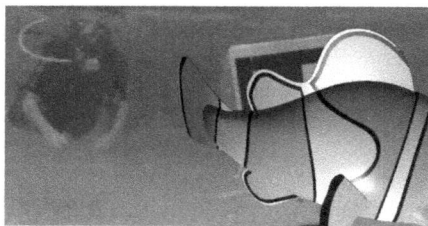

Figure 5: Augmented Reality to display 3D models

VR HRI

The second HRI we present in this paper is a VR interface. In fact, in order to effectively teleoperate a remote robot, HRIs must provide tools to perceive the remote environment, to make decisions, and to generate commands. We cite similar work such as in [12, 20] or [15] that introduces a ROV safety domain. Furthermore, we attempt to maximize information transfer while minimizing cognitive and sensorimotor workload. In our system, we used a multimodal interface that contains stereoscopic viewing as well as a haptic feedback for a more intuitive HRI. In fact, it aims to reduce training and overcome the unfamiliarity in using VR systems. This interface improves the feeling of presence and awareness among users doing a virtual seabed exploration. Furthermore, it provides two types of diving scenarios: 1) a simulated dive in a virtual environment without real control of the ROV, which enable users to learn and test a path before doing a real exploration, and 2) a dive in the Mixed Reality (MR) environment via ROV teleoperation.

VR/AR semi-immersive platform

The human scale semi-immersive platform used is composed of a large screen (3.2mX2.4m) and a DLP projector (120Hz MIRAG E4000) that provides active stereoscopy. We use stereoscopic glasses (Crystal Eyes 3) and their corresponding transmitter. The interaction is provided by a device having six degrees of freedom force feedback called SPIDAR (SPace Interface Device for Artificial Reality), shown in Figure 6 (1).

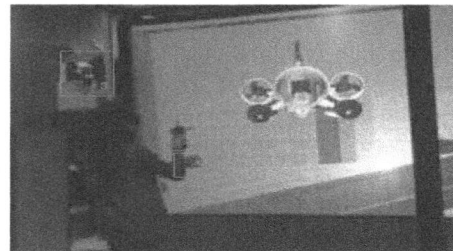

Figure 6: Semi-immersive VR/AR platform

The control system is ensured by a handheld flystick (2) that includes a set of markers for real time tracking using two infrared cameras (3) (ARTTrack1). Communication between the VR/AR platform and the ROV is made via the internet, similarly to the Web HRI.

VR teleoperation interface

A virtual environment in our system consists of simulating seabed diving sites, and the navigation task in the virtual scene is done through ROV's teleoperation. Thus, we created a virtual ROV, shown in Figure 7, in order to simulate movements of the real ROV. The navigation using the virtual ROV is done according to the marker placed on the SPIDAR's effector, which reproduces users' position movements. By manipulating the virtual ROV, the operator is actually controlling the real ROV. The system's control allows managing robot's features (camera switch, activate lights) as well as showing instructions for effective usage.

The visual modality is used to display: 1) live video stream from the ROV's camera, means to control the camera as well as a switch from virtual to real teleoperation; 2) virtual and interactive 3D environment representing the explored site; and 3) a top view 2D map of the explored site. Other information, such as sensor data, is also displayed. The force feedback can simulate collisions and increase the feeling of navigation in water (viscosity, marine current, etc.). Furthermore, audible information completes the data offered through the virtual diving interface, which is used to inform the diver of events occurring, such as the thrusters' sound (indicating the ROV's speed, as well as any troubleshooting issues).

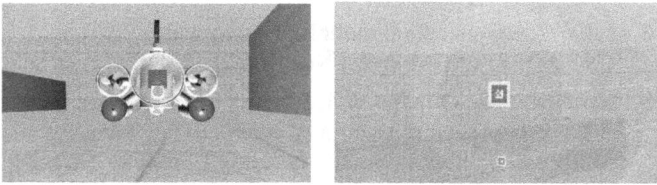

Figure 7: (a) View from a third camera in the virtual test environment (swimming pool), (b) View from the ROV's embedded camera

This multimodality is also used for 3D interaction assistance. In fact, while assembling different issues related to human, environment and teleoperation factors, we observed some technical constraints, such as loss of ROV maneuverability and transmission delays, which affect system's use (navigation precision, robot's safety and divers' spatial awareness). Hence, we applied an assistance model [9] that includes a set of guides (virtual fixtures) in order to remedy these constraints. As an example of a virtual fixture, the operator must choose a diving path that he/she must follow. To be as accurate as possible, we show a 3D curve representing this path as well as an arrow directed towards the trajectory.

In order to assist the user, our system can switch between real and virtual navigation. In fact, the user can choose to control the real ROV through its embedded video camera. In this case, we calculate the corresponding trajectory of the virtual ROV (not being visualized). The user can also control the virtual ROV through the VR interface. In this case, the real ROV will respond to the commands sent to the virtual ROV, and will execute them as well. We also changed system's autonomy through correspondence between the real and virtual ROV. In fact, the coherence between real ROV's position and the virtual one is provided by real 2D markers (shown in Figure 5). When these markers are detected by the real ROV's camera, an estimation of the camera's position is achieved. Once the position (and orientation) of the ROV is calculated according to 2D markers' positions, we calculate the position of the real ROV in its environment. As the positions of the 2D markers are known, we use them as waypoints on the diving path.

DISCUSSION
The originality of our model is the use of existing software architecture models in order to create an interactive system for collaborative robot teleoperation. Our model is inspired by the Arch and Dewan's models for separating the logic of the application from its interfaces, and thus carrying with it many essential properties such as flexibility, which is

crucial in the CSCW domain. Indeed, the two layers constituting the FC are both shared and handle exclusively the services dedicated to robot teleoperation. A functional core adaptor (not discussed in this paper) situated between the functional core and the physical layer handles users' private domain-dependent objects. Furthermore, the functional breakdown according to the 3C model contains several properties. In fact, from the implementation's perspective, it will result in a greater modularity. For example, it would be easier to add a communication service through a video stream mechanism without affecting existing services in the system. This enables the addition of independent and heterogeneous services in order to improve the distribution of features. In Figure 8, we can see the application of our software architecture for robot teleoperation. Recall that the particularity of our software architecture is the separation of the interfaces from the FC. Hence, our system gives access to various interactive interfaces to order to collaboratively teleoperate the ROV. We have implemented two HRIs that offer a rich interactive and collaborative experience for underwater exploration through ROV teleoperation. In our system, the FC is responsible for offering various teleoperation services, as well as creating an infrastructure through interactive interfaces for issuing commands to the real ROV.

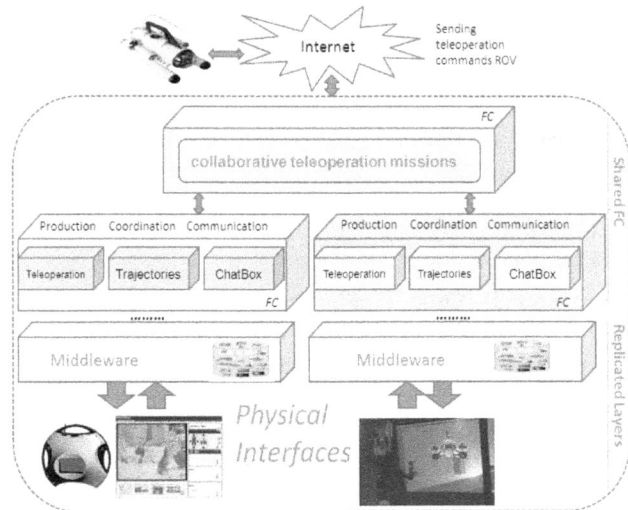

Figure 8: Software architecture applied to ROV teleoperation

CONCLUSION

In this paper, we have proposed a software architecture for interactive and collaborative teleoperation of an underwater robot using two interactive interfaces. One crucial particularity of our system is the separation of the interfaces from the system's FC, which allows a greater flexibility in teleoperating the robot. Furthermore, we have explicitly taken in consideration the collaborative aspect of the system, in order to allow multiple users to communicate and coordinate for ROV teleoperation. This fact brings a rich interactive and collaborative experience. However, robot teleoperation over the internet is, sadly, limited in communication possibilities in real time situations. Hence, an interaction between users and the distant robot is not guaranteed without any network delays. For this reason, our short-term goal is to add a Quality of Service (QoS) component in the software architecture proposed, which enables handling none-functional attributes such as bandwidth, response time, packet loss, etc. Another objective is to adapt the teleoperation interface on the VR platform according to the 3C model. Indeed, we want to optimize the collaborative experience with other users using the Web interfaces to teleoperate the robot. One possibility is to integrate an audio mechanism (3C model's communication space) in order to enhance the communication process (as the use of keyboards is not possible on the VR platform). Also, we aim at adding a visual feedback of teleoperation trajectories created using the VR platform, in order to diffuse them on the system's Web interfaces. This fact enhances the coordination and cooperation between users using both interfaces (Web and VR) simultaneously. We believe that our system constitutes a first step towards a rich interactive experience for underwater robot teleoperation, both for the general public (through web interfaces), and expert users (VR platform).

ACKNOWLEDGMENTS

This work is done in the context of the Digital Ocean Europe project funded by the European Commission (FP7).

REFERENCES

1. Alvarez, B., Iborra, A., Alonso, A. and de la Puente, J.A.Reference architecture for robot teleoperation: development details and practical use. *Journal of Control Engineering Practice*, Volume 9, Number 4, Elsevier, 395-402, 2011

2. Álvarez, B., Ortiz, F., Martínez, A., Sánchez, P., Pastor, J.A., and Iborra. A. Towards a Generic Software Architecture for a service robot controller. *In the 15th Triennial World Congress, Barcelona, Spain*, 2002

3. Bass, L. A metamodel for the runtime architecture of an interactive system, *User Interface Developers' Workshop*, SIGCHI Bull. 24(1) (1992).

4. Bruzzone, G., Bono R., Caccia M., Coletta P., Veruggio G., "Internet-based teleoperation of the Romeo ROV in the arctic region", *Manoeuvring and control of marine craft 2003 (MCMC 2003)*: 6th IFAC Conference, Elsevier Science Ltd, 2004.

5. Calvary, G., Coutaz, J. and Nigay, L. From Single-User Architectural Design to PAC*: a Generic Software Architecture Model for CSCW. *In the ACM Conference on Human Factors and Computing Systems (CHI'97)*, 1997, pages 242-249, ACM Press.

6. Cheaib, N., Otmane, S. and Mallem, M. Tailorable Groupware Design based on the 3C Model. *In the*

7. Dewan, P. Architectures for collaborative applications, *Journal of Computer Supported Cooperative Work (CSCW), Trends in Software* (John Wiley & Sons, Chichester, 1999), 169–194.

8. Ellis, C.A.Conceptual model for groupware. *Proc of CSCW 1995* (ACM Press, New York), 79-88

9. Essabbah, M., Otmane, S. Hérisson, J and Mallem, M. A New Approach to Design an Interactive System for Molecular Analysis, Lecture Notes in Computer Science (LNCS 5613), Human-Computer Interaction, (HCII 2009), pages 713-722, Springer-Verlag, 2009.

10. Fuks, H., Raposo, A.B., Gerosa, M.A and de Lucena, C.J.P. Applying the 3C model to groupware engineering. *International Journal of Cooperative Information Systems*, v.14, n. 2-3, 299-328, 2005

11. Grange, S., Fong T., Charles Baur C. Effective Vehicle Teleoperation on the World Wide Web. *In the IEEE International Conference on Robotics and Automation (ICRA 2000), San Francisco, CA*, 2007-2012, 2000.

12. Hamzah M. S. M., Zakaria M., Abd Jalil M. F. I., and Zamli K. Z. 3D virtual simulation software for underwater application. *In 2nd International Conference Underwater System Technology*, 2008.

13. Jenkyns R., "NEPTUNE Canada: Data integrity from the seafloor to your (Virtual) Door", *in IEEE OCEANS 2010*, 1-7, 2010.

14. Laurillau, Y. and Nigay, L, Clover architecture for groupware. In the Proc of CSCW, ACM, 236-245, 2002

15. Lin Q, and and Kuo, C. On applying virtual reality to underwater robot teleoperation and pilot training. *In the International Journal of Virtual Reality*, Volume 5, Number 1, 2001.

16. Monferrer, A. and Bonyuet, D. Cooperative robot teleoperation through virtual reality interfaces. *In the Sixth International Conference on Information Visualisation*, 243-248, 2002.

17. Oliveira, F.F., Antunes, J.C.P., and Guizzardi, R.S.S. Towards a collaboration ontology. *Proc. of the Brazilian Workshop on Ontologies and Metamodels for Software and Data Engineering.*

18. Rekleitis, I., Dudek, G., Schoueri, Y, Giguere, P and Sattar J. Telepresence across the Ocean. *In the 2010 Canadian Conference on Computer and Robot Vision*, 261-268, 2010.

19. Roston J., Bradley C., Cooperstock JR. Underwater window: high definition video on VENUS and NEPTUNE, *in IEEE OCEANS 2007*, 1-8, 2007

20. Santamaria, J, and Opdenbosch A. Monitoring Underwater Operations with Virtual Environments. *In Offshore Technology Conference, 2002.*

A Transformation Engine for Model-driven UI Generation

Roman Popp, Jürgen Falb, David Raneburger and Hermann Kaindl
Institute of Computer Technology
Vienna University of Technology
Gusshausstrasse 27-29, A-1040 Vienna, Austria
{popp, falb, raneburger, kaindl}@ict.tuwien.ac.at

ABSTRACT

Current engines for model-driven transformations do not sufficiently support specifics of automated generation of user interfaces (UIs). For achieving better (graphical) UIs in more specific situations (e.g., a specific small device, or a specific button), more specific rules should be supported, without having to discard the more general ones. For enabling optimization (e.g., for small devices), comparing alternatives is mandatory. Therefore, we present a new and implemented transformation engine for declarative rules specifically designed for model-driven UI generation and optimization as well as its application to various devices and applications. This engine is the basis for advanced UI generation already presented previously, including its results for automatically optimized UIs for smartphones.

Author Keywords

UI Generation; Model Transformation Engine

ACM Classification Keywords

D.2.2 Design Tool and Techniques: User Interfaces

INTRODUCTION

More and more different devices are used to interact with computer applications. Since these devices have screens, e.g., with strongly varying screen sizes, their graphical UIs (GUIs) have to be provided or adapted according to such properties.

Manually creating several UIs is expensive, and automating this process is desirable. Automated generation of especially GUIs has certainly advanced in years, especially based on model-driven approaches, but much more work has to be done. For example, we presented in [11] an approach for automatic generation of UIs and their optimization for small screens. This approach requires an extended transformation engine, since general-purpose model-transformation languages like ATL[1] or SmartQVT[2] and, in particular their

---

[1] http://www.eclipse.org/atl/

[2] http://sourceforge.net/projects/smartqvt/

transformation engines, have some limitations for use as generation engines for device-tailored UIs.

The most prominent limitation is that only one rule may match a single input model element in current declarative (or hybrid) model-transformation engines. Especially for achieving acceptable usability, it is important to provide different implementations of structurally similar input model parts depending on the context and other constraints (screen or window size, device, etc.). Thus it becomes a difficult tasks to design all rules in a mutually exclusive way, so that always only one rule matches some input element. Therefore, it is important to support the design of a rule set combining general and specific rules.

So, according to our experience, an automated model-driven UI generation approach requires two additional features of a model-transformation engine:

- An engine has to support generating different target model elements (UI elements) for the same source element. An example of such different target elements is to display information side by side on one screen, or to group the information in a tabbed pane (if there is not enough space to display all the information side by side).

- An engine has to be able to generate the best possible GUI according to given optimization objectives, constrained by device and screen properties.

The remainder of this paper is organized in the following manner. First, we present the state of the art in model transformation with a focus on GUI generation. Then we present our engine overcoming the limitations by supporting these features. This presentation starts with explaining the architecture of our engine, which is composed of two sub-engines, the Model Transformation Engine and the GUI Optimizer. Subsequently, we explain these sub-engines. Finally, we provide a brief outlook and conclusion.

STATE OF THE ART

Approaches to model-driven UI generation like [6, 8] typically use device-dependent high-level models as a starting point. They apply model-to-model transformations to refine these high-level models before finally transforming them to executable source code. These approaches typically use input models that are already constrained to a certain device and exploit further constraints (e.g., user profiles) to resolve

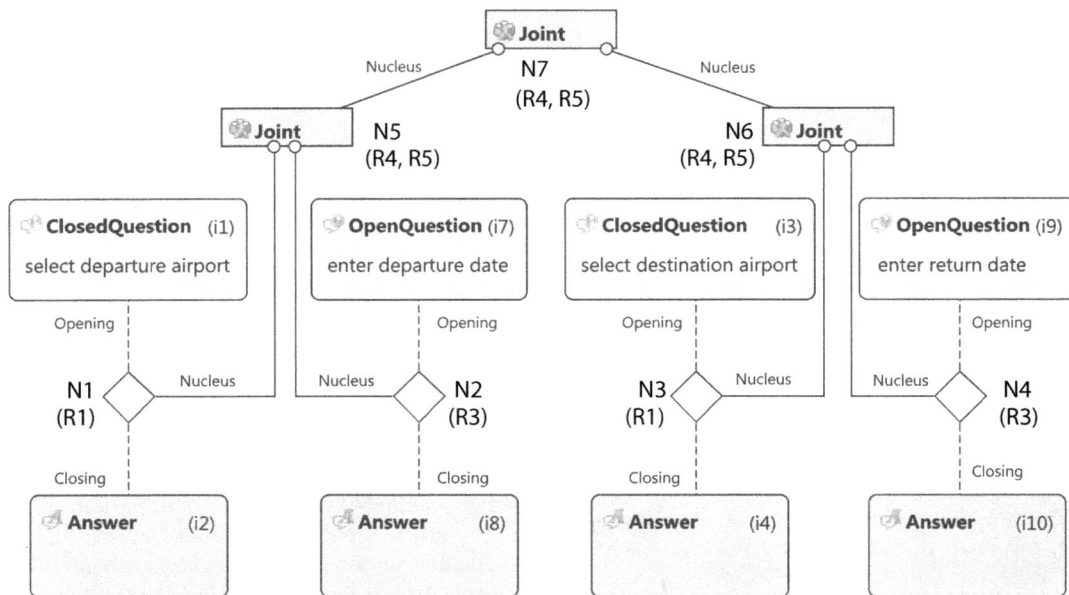

Figure 1. FlightSelection Discourse (based on [8])

conflicts during the transformation process. In this way, possible conflicts like the ones sketched above are usually resolved before the transformation, and no design space has to be explored. However, intermediate models that are created during the generation process are accessible for the designer and allow her to manually explore the design space through modifying the input model of a transformation.

A comprehensive overview and classification of 30 general-purpose approaches is given by Czarnecki and Helsen in [2]. Conflict resolution before the actual transformation is required by all of these model-transformation approaches. Wagelaar [13] et al. introduced the concept of module super-imposition, which supports overriding transformation rules. They implemented their approach by extending the Atlas Transformation Language (ATL) [4] and QVT[3]. Module superimposition requires the human designer to satisfy the UI generation requirements. General-purpose transformation engines, like the ATL or QVT transformation engine, do not support conflict resolution. Therefore, different rendering alternatives can only be explored through manual modification of the transformation rules by the designer. Additional effort is required in general-purpose engines, as the designer needs to make sure that only a single transformation rule matches a specific source pattern. Interestingly, none of these existing transformation engines provide conflict resolution like ancient tools supporting rule-based knowledge representation, such as, for example, KEE [3].

OUR COMPOSITE ENGINE FOR UI OPTIMIZATION

Our transformation engine is composed of a sub-engine for the transformations per se, and another one for optimization. The input of our composite engine is a communicative-interaction model and the output is a UI model. This in-

put model is on a high conceptual level, device-independent and on the task & concepts level of the Cameleon Reference Framework [1]. In contrast, the output UI model is tailored to a specific device and serves as the input for code generation and is on the concrete UI level.

More precisely, we use Discourse-based Communication Models [9] as the starting point for our UI generation and optimization process. These models specify high-level communicative interaction of the user with the application, primarily based on discourses in the sense of dialogues.

In order to make this paper self-contained, let us explain (part of) such a model using a simplified version of a flight-selection application. It also serves as a running example for explaining our new engine. Figure 1 shows an excerpt of the Discourse Model part of such a model for our running example. It specifies how to book a round-trip flight. For such a selection, four pieces of information are needed first, the departure airport, the departure date, the destination airport and the return date. The related questions and answers are modeled as so-called Adjacency Pairs (shown as diamonds), with opening and closing Communicative Acts (shown as yellow and green rounded rectangles). These Adjacency Pairs are related with each other through Joint Relations (shown as blue rectangles), which specify that all the information can, in principle, be entered concurrently.

For reference purposes in this paper, let us attach extra information to this figure. For each relation or Adjacency Pair an identifier (N1...N7) is shown in Figure 1, for making referencing a specific model element easy. Below the identifier of each element, the transformation rules possibly matching are written in brackets (labeled with the identifiers R1...R5). These rules are explained below.

---

[3]http://www.omg.org/spec/QVT/1.0/PDF

The two additionally required features identified above are multiple matching and optimization. According to separation of concerns we divided the engine in two sub-engines, as shown in Figure 2. The Model Transformation Engine is responsible for model transformation including multiple matching, the GUI Optimizer for optimization for a specific device.

More precisely, the Model Transformation Engine is responsible for selecting the rules, which can transform a specific element in the input model into elements in the output model. It is possible to specify a Constraint Model, which reduces the number of rules in the used rule sets according to some of the constraints in the Constraint Model. An example for such a constraint is, that a rule can only be included for matching if all widgets potentially generated by it in the output model are supported by the target device. Also the screen size of the target device is specified in the Constraint Model.

The GUI Optimizer can be configured with an Optimization Strategy and influences the model transformation in the Model Transformation Engine indicated by the feedback loop in Figure 2. It is possible to configure the GUI Optimizer with different Optimization Strategies. Such a strategy provides optimization objectives for GUIs and allows restricting the possible transformation rules for a specific element in the input model. Examples for such objectives are:

1. maximum use of available space,

2. minimum amount of navigation clicks,

3. minimum scrolling.

MODEL TRANSFORMATION ENGINE

The Model Transformation Engine transforms an interaction model according to our modeling approach to a concrete UI model. The overall transformation consists of three major steps:

1. The interaction model is transformed to a structural model of the UI.

2. The structural UI model is converted to a Screen Model [10], which defines the screens of the final UI.

3. Each screen is layouted to calculate its real-estate usage [12] and to avoid usability problems.

In this paper, we focus on the first step of our rule-based Model Transformation Engine. Details of the other two steps are not necessary for understanding the innovative aspect of matching multiple rules.

Transformation Input

Our Model Transformation Engine requires three different models for operation:

- an *input model* that usually captures the interactions and communication between the user and the machine,

- a *constraint model* that specifies the context and constraints like device constraints (e.g. screen size, screen resolution, pointing granularity, available widget set, etc.),

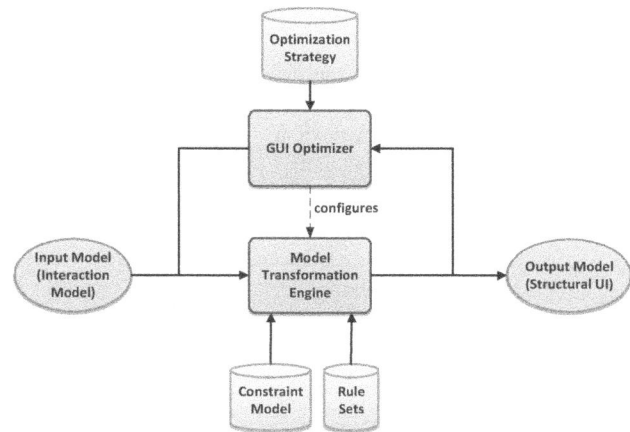

Figure 2. Architectural structure of model-driven UI Generation engine

- and a *rule set* containing declarative rules that map input model elements to output model elements and specify attributes that define the context of applicability.

For our rule-based transformation engine, we have developed our own transformation language. This transformation language combines the Discourse-based Communication Model and the UI Model languages. In principle, also an existing transformation language could have been used. Our language has a graphical syntax supported by a specific editing tool.

Figure 3 shows two examples of transformation rules. Each rule consists of a source pattern, a target pattern and optional mapping elements. The source pattern is a Discourse-based Communication Model part. The target pattern is a UI Model part on concrete UI level. Both rules in Figure 3 define the transformation of a Joint Relation to a UI element. The upper rule, shown in Figure 3(a) creates a Panel element in the UI model. The Mapping element specifies that the generated UI parts for all source model child elements, are inserted in this Panel. These child elements are related to the Joint Relation via a Link element in the Discourse-based Communication Model. This rule is labeled with R4 in the context of this paper. The second rule, shown in Figure 3(b), creates a Tabbed Pane. In this Tabbed Pane the corresponding UI parts of the source model child elements are added as separate Tabs. This rule is referenced as R5.

It is possible to constrain the application scope of such rules. An example of such a constraint is that a specific rule should not match for a device with a touch screen. The transformation engine uses the Constraint Model to evaluate such a constraint.

Transformation Process

In the first step of the transformation process, the rules are filtered according to the Constraint Model. Rules can specify any number and kind of constraints to characterize the context in which the rule can be applied. For instance, a rule can specify a "$resolutionX > 720$" constraint to indicate that this rule is preferably applied for screens with a minimum screen width of 720 pixels. (E.g., the rule could gen-

(a) Joint rule - panel (R4)

(b) Joint rule small - tabbed pane (R5)

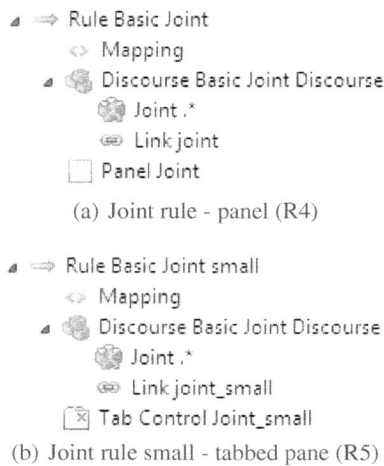

Figure 3. Joint transformation rules (R4, R5)

erate a 720p-HD movie player, which does not make sense to be included on devices with smaller screens). Rules can also inherit constraints specified for the whole rule set. These constraints are matched against the Constraint Model which, for instance, specifies a concrete device with a resolution of "320 × 480". Rules with constraints that do not fit the Constraint Model are filtered out.

In a subsequent step, the engine calculates a specialization degree for each rule. Rule constraints that match the Constraint Model get the highest weight, followed by rule constraints that are not specified in the Constraint Model. The source pattern (LHS) characterized by its size (number of pattern elements) gets the least weight. These precedencies guarantee that context-specific rules are considered first, independently of their LHS pattern size.

In the last step, the engine iterates over all input model element and matches the rules. All matching rules are sorted according to their specialization degree. Before applying the most specific rule, the engine hands over the sorted list of matching rules to the GUI Optimizer for further filtering or reordering. From the returned set of matching rules, the most specific one is applied to the input model element and leads to the creation of output widgets as specified in this rule.

In order to provide a better separation of the overall UI structure and the information to be displayed on the UI, the engine operates in a two-pass mode. This enables the designer to create transformation rules that generate the overall UI structure/layout in the first pass, and rules that transform domain elements/information in the second pass [5]. This separation of concerns also increases the reusability of the structural UI transformation rules in other UI application domains.

GUI OPTIMIZER

The GUI Optimizer is responsible for the device tailoring of the generated UI. This sub-engine selects the best GUI of all possible GUIs that can be generated according to given optimization objectives to achieve this device tailoring.

The optimization objectives can be grouped in two categories.

In the first category are objectives that can be evaluated based on the selected rules themselves. The objectives in the second category can only be evaluated on the generated UI Model. An example for the first category is the "minimum amount of navigation clicks". Each rule can be analyzed, if an additional navigation click is created. All objectives of this category can be mapped to a weighting function. An example for the second category is "minimum scrolling". This objective can only be evaluated on the generated UI Model, because also the layout of the generated UI is necessary to calculate the size of the generated UI.

For the selection of the best GUI (according to the given objectives), it is necessary to generate a set of possible GUIs. For this purpose, the Model Transformation Engine has to provide a list of matching transformation rules for each specific element in the source model. Based on the list of elements in the source model and the list of matching transformation rules, a search space can be generated. The generation can be done by generating all possible rule combinations. In general, this is an exponential problem and can lead to scalability problems. Therefore, it is possible to use an Optimization Strategy that provides a more sophisticated generation process. Some optimization strategies use some of their optimization objectives in this step, like the one presented in [11]. After the GUI search space is generated, each of the possible GUIs is rated according to the weighting function.

The best rated GUI is generated by the Model Transformation Engine by executing all three transformation steps (model transformation, Screen Model conversion, and layouting). For this purpose, the GUI Optimizer provides for each input model element the selected transformation rule to the Model Transformation Engine as sketched in the last section of this paper. Then the generated UI is evaluated according to the second category of optimization objectives. If the generated GUI fulfills these optimization objectives, this is the device-tailored GUI searched for. Note, that the ordering before is necessary to guarantee that the one found here is actually (one of) the best GUIs generated. Otherwise, this GUI is removed from the search space and the next GUI is generated. This loop is repeated until a GUI fulfills all of these optimization objectives, or no further GUI is available.

The GUI Optimizer itself is independent from the optimization objects. These objectives are provided by an Optimization Strategy. Therefore, the GUI Optimizer is configured by an Optimization Strategy. If some of the objectives can exclude possible GUIs before executing the model transformation, it is possible that the strategy reduces the search space of possible GUIs as presented in [11].

In the following, we illustrate the work of the GUI Optimizer by describing the steps for the generation of the GUI for our running example. First, the Model Transformation Engine provides a map of elements in the Discourse-based Communication Model and the possible matching rules. Out of this map the search space is generated as presented in [11]. After that, the possible rule combinations are ranked according to the two optimization objects, "minimum amount of navigation clicks" and "maximum use of available space".

Table 1. Possible rule-combinations

Rule-Combination	#Additional Navigation Clicks
(N7,R4) (N5,R4) (N6,R4)	0
(N7,R4) (N5,R4) (N6,R5)	1
(N7,R4) (N5,R5) (N6,R4)	1
(N7,R5) (N5,R4) (N6,R4)	1
(N7,R4) (N5,R5) (N6,R5)	2
(N7,R5) (N5,R5) (N6,R4)	2
(N7,R5) (N5,R4) (N6,R5)	2
(N7,R5) (N5,R5) (N6,R5)	3

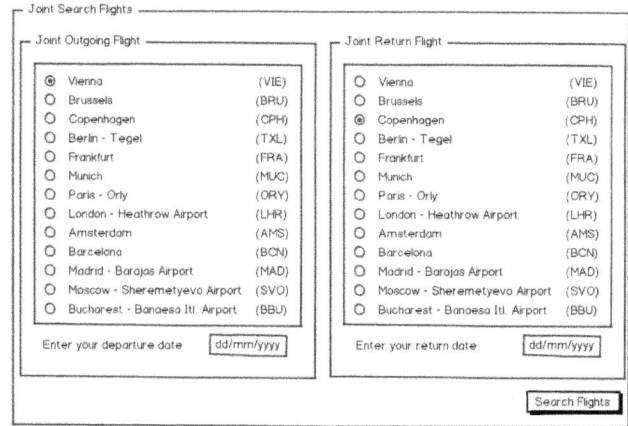

Figure 4. GUI mock-up for a tablet PC

For our example, we got eight possible rule combinations for a GUI model as illustrated in Table 1, because we have for the three Joint Relations two possible rules (R4, R5). This table includes only the elements where more than one rule can match. For each of the presented Adjacency Pairs, only one matching rule is contained in the used rule set.

The *Joint rule – tabbed pane* (R5) creates a tabbed pane, which leads to at least one additional navigation click, depending on the number of children. In our running example, we only have two children for all Joint Relations, so the number of additional navigation clicks is one. The best ranked rule combination is, that for all Joint Relations rule R4 is selected, which adds no additional navigation clicks. The next three rule combinations apply for a single Joint Relation rule R5, which leads to one additional navigation click. Then for two of the three Joint Relations the rule R5 is selected, which leads to two additional navigation clicks, and finally for all Joint Relations rule R4 is selected, which leads to three additional navigation clicks.

The optimization objective "maximum use of available space" is reflected in the rule selection for the Adjacency Pairs, so we do not have to take this objective into account. For this special Optimization Strategy, some of the possible UIs are equally ranked, i.e., they fulfill the optimization objectives on the same level. Based on the first entry of the list of ranked possible UIs, the model-transformation engine generates the GUI Model, where the third optimization objective, "minimum scrolling", is evaluated. If the GUI does not fit on the screen of the device, it is discarded and the next possible GUI is created. For a device with a bigger screen, like a tablet PC, the first created GUI may fit, be (one of) the best (because of the ordering before), and the GUI Model generation is finished. Figure 4 shows a mock-up of the generated GUI. The depicted Structural UI model is on concrete UI level. We use a mock-up for visualization of this model, because this model is independent of the used toolkit on the device and more illustrative than the final UI model.

For a device with a smaller display, like a smartphone, the generated GUI does not fit on the screen and so this GUI is discarded. Then one of three equally ranked UIs with one additional navigation click is selected. Let use assume that we select the rule combination where for the Joint N5, rule R5 is selected. For this rule combination, the GUI model is created and for the smartphone the GUI does not fit on the

screen, so it is discarded again. The next possible GUI results from the rule combination where for the Joint N7, the rule R4 is selected, and this rule combination leads to a GUI which fits on the screen of the smartphone. Fig 5 shows a mock-up of this GUI.

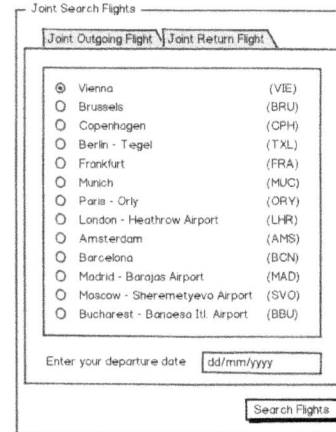

Figure 5. GUI mock-up for a smartphone

DISCUSSION & OUTLOOK

Our approach supports automated generation of optimized UIs from a given high-level model, top-down. Paternó et al. developed an approach to convert desktop UIs to mobile UIs through reengineering existing UIs [7]. Reverse engineering a final UI model into an interaction model involves inferring high-level semantics from a low level model. We did not pursue such an approach, but rather started from a given high-level model and concentrated on automating the derivation of multiple UIs, optimized for different devices. Our approach could be incorporated in Paternó's second (top-down) step — transforming an interaction model into a device-specific UI model.

So far, we used our optimization approach primarily to generate GUIs for small devices, in terms of screen estate. Surprisingly, it has turned out to be easier generating such UIs with reasonable usability than GUIs for larger devices. The counter-intuitive reason is that the smaller screens are more constraining. However, we have to compare with GUIs human designers may produce, and these face the same constraints. While our optimization search can deal with these constraints well enough, for lager screens today's approaches to automated GUI generation lack other criteria such as esthetics, which human designers obviously can deal with much better.

When we applied our approach to a very small device (i.e., 4.2", 320 × 240 display), our approach generated a tabbed pane that contained another tabbed pane [11]. In this way, the information fit, but tabs are hard to handle on a very small device. Additionally, such small devices are typically equipped with a touch screen and scrolling/swiping is quite easy on such devices in comparison to a device using a mouse. We will, therefore, extend our future investigations on other optimization strategies. As the next step, we plan to investigate different optimization objectives and develop optimization strategies that capture them.

Subsequently, we will simplify the mechanisms that support manual overriding of transformation rules, to provide a sound basis for final customizations by a human designer.

CONCLUSION

We found that the usual engines for model transformations according to MDA are insufficient for advanced generation of GUIs. Therefore, we developed our own one, which can match and fire several rules in a given situation. This supports easier adoption to specific cases for several devices. It even allows automatic optimization for specific devices and their given constraints in the course of generating the GUI. This serves as the technical basis for optimizing UIs, e.g., for current smartphones.

REFERENCES

1. G. Calvary, J. Coutaz, D. Thevenin, Q. Limbourg, L. Bouillon, and J. Vanderdonckt. A unifying reference framework for multi-target user interfaces. *Interacting with Computers*, 15(3):289 – 308, 2003. Computer-Aided Design of User Interface.

2. K. Czarnecki and S. Helsen. Feature-based survey of model transformation approaches. *IBM Systems Journal*, 45(3):621 –645, 2006.

3. R. Fikes and T. Kehler. The role of frame-based representation in reasoning. *Communications of the ACM*, 28(9):904–920, 1985.

4. F. Jouault and I. Kurtev. Transforming models with atl. In J.-M. Bruel, editor, *Satellite Events at the MoDELS 2005 Conference*, volume 3844 of *Lecture Notes in Computer Science*, pages 128–138. Springer Berlin / Heidelberg, 2006. 10.1007/11663430_14.

5. S. Kavaldjian, J. Falb, and H. Kaindl. Generating content presentation according to purpose. In *Proceedings of the 2009 IEEE International Conference on Systems, Man and Cybernetics (SMC2009)*, San Antonio, TX, USA, Oct. 2009.

6. O. Pastor, S. España, J. I. Panach, and N. Aquino. Model-driven development. *Informatik Spektrum*, 31(5):394–407, 2008.

7. F. Patern and G. Zichittella. Desktop-to-mobile web adaptation through customizable two-dimensional semantic redesign. In R. Bernhaupt, P. Forbrig, J. Gulliksen, and M. Lrusdttir, editors, *Human-Centred Software Engineering*, volume 6409 of *Lecture Notes in Computer Science*, pages 79–94. Springer Berlin / Heidelberg, 2010. 10.1007/978-3-642-16488-0_7.

8. F. Paternò, C. Santoro, and L. D. Spano. Maria: A universal, declarative, multiple abstraction-level language for service-oriented applications in ubiquitous environments. *ACM Trans. Comput.-Hum. Interact.*, 16:19:1–19:30, November 2009.

9. R. Popp and D. Raneburger. A High-Level Agent Interaction Protocol Based on a Communication Ontology. In C. Huemer, T. Setzer, W. Aalst, J. Mylopoulos, N. M. Sadeh, M. J. Shaw, and C. Szyperski, editors, *E-Commerce and Web Technologies*, volume 85 of *Lecture Notes in Business Information Processing*, pages 233–245. Springer Berlin Heidelberg, 2011. 10.1007/978-3-642-23014-1_20.

10. D. Raneburger, R. Popp, H. Kaindl, J. Falb, and D. Ertl. Automated Generation of Device-Specific WIMP UIs: Weaving of Structural and Behavioral Models. In *Proceedings of the 3rd ACM SIGCHI Symposium on Engineering Interactive Computing Systems*, EICS '11, pages 41–46, New York, NY, USA, 2011. ACM.

11. D. Raneburger, R. Popp, S. Kavaldjian, H. Kaindl, and J. Falb. Optimized GUI generation for small screens. In H. Hussmann, G. Meixner, and D. Zuehlke, editors, *Model-Driven Development of Advanced User Interfaces*, volume 340 of *Studies in Computational Intelligence*, pages 107–122. Springer Berlin / Heidelberg, 2011.

12. D. Raneburger, R. Popp, and J. Vanderdonckt. An Automated Layout Approach for Model-Driven WIMP-UI Generation. In *Proceedings of the 4th ACM SIGCHI Symposium on Engineering Interactive Computing Systems*, EICS '12, New York, NY, USA, June 2012. ACM.

13. D. Wagelaar, R. Van Der Straeten, and D. Deridder. Module superimposition: a composition technique for rule-based model transformation languages. *Software and Systems Modeling*, 9:285–309, 2010. 10.1007/s10270-009-0134-3.

A Formal Specification for Casanova, a Language for Computer Games

Giuseppe Maggiore; Alvise Spanò; Renzo Orsini; Michele Bugliesi; Mohamed Abbadi;
Enrico Steffinlongo

Università Ca' Foscari Venezia

DAIS - Computer Science

{maggiore,spano,orsini,bugliesi,mabbadi,esteffin}@dais.unive.it

ABSTRACT

In this paper we present the specification and preliminary assessment of Casanova, a newly designed computer language which integrates knowledge about many areas of game development with the aim of simplifying the process of engineering a game. Casanova is designed as a fully-fledged language, as an extension language to F#, but also as a pervasive design pattern for game development.

Categories and Subject Descriptors

D.2.2 [**Software Engineering**]: Design Tools and Techniques – *Software libraries*
D.3.3 [**Programming Languages**]: Language Constructs and Features – *abstract data types, polymorphism, control structures*
H.5 [**Information Interfaces and Presentation**]: Multimedia Information Systems – *Artificial, augmented and virtual realities*

General Terms

Performance, Experimentation, Languages.

Keywords

Game development; Casanova; databases; languages; functional programming; F#

1. INTRODUCTION

Games are a huge business [1] and a very large aspect of modern popular culture. Independent games, the need for fast prototyping gameplay mechanics [2] and the low budget available for making serious games [3] (when compared with the budget of AAA games) has created substantial interest in research on principled design techniques and on cost-effective development technologies for game architectures. We believe our proposal makes a significant step in this direction. Moreover, several teaching institutions are nowadays beginning the introduction of game development as a tool for engaging students in studying programming and better understanding computer science [4].

In this paper we will present the Casanova language and framework, which are built to simplify the creation of games while at the same time retaining the ability to build applications which are "more than toys". Casanova comes in two flavors: on

one hand there is the language itself, but on the other there is a general methodology (aided by various libraries) for making games in existing languages. In this paper we describe the current state of the Casanova project, which has moved from the design phase of [5] into specification and implementation. In particular, we describe how the mechanisms behind Casanova work, from the syntax, type and semantics of our work in Section 2, to a discussion on implementation in Section 3 and to a final comparison of Casanova with other widely adopted frameworks such as C# and XNA to assess the effectiveness of our framework in Section 4.

1.1 RELATED WORK

The two most common game engine architectures found today in commercial games are object-oriented type hierarchies and component-based systems [6], [7]. These two more traditional approaches both suffer from a noticeable shortcoming: they focus exclusively on representing single entities and their update and draw operations in isolation, rather than by cooperating with all other entities. Also, behaviors that take longer than a single tick are hard to express inside the various entities, which often end up storing explicit program counters to resume the current behavior at each tick. Moreover, these architectures simply upgrade everything in place, and offer no guarantees of the correct sequence of updates of the various entities of the game. To mitigate the difficulties of programming with this model, pre-existing game engines have been built to allow programming a game with a mixture of a visual programming language (called *editor*), plus a scripting language for further behaviors.

There are a few additional coding approaches for games that have emerged in the last few years as possible alternatives to traditional architectures: (functional) reactive programming [8], and SQL-style declarative programming [9]. FRP offers a solution to the problem of representing long-running behaviors, but it neither addresses the problem of many entities that interact with each other, nor does it address the problem of maintaining the consistency of the game world. SQL-queries for games (SGL) use a lightweight, statically compiled and optimized query engine for defining a game; SGL suffers when it comes to representing long-running behaviors, since it focuses exclusively on defining the tick function.

We have designed Casanova with all these issues in mind: the integration of the interactions between entities and long-running behaviors is seamless, and the resulting game world is always consistent. Furthermore, all the aspects of a game architecture can be integrated in a Casanova program: not just the game logic, but also rendering, networking, input management, etc.

2. ANATOMY OF A CASANOVA GAME

A Casanova program starts with the definition of the game world, that is a series of type declarations. Casanova does not require the developer to specify an update or a draw function; rather, the developer specifies a series of rules inside the various type declarations of the game entities. Rules describe how an entity (and its contents) changes value during a tick of the game loop. The update function will then consist of traversing the game state and building the new state by evaluating all the available rules. The draw function, similarly to the update function, traverses the state to fill a series of deferred batches. Whenever it encounters instances of any of the preset drawable entities (`DrawableModel`, `DrawableText`, `DrawableSprite`), the system adds each entity to its batch; each batch is then drawn with all its entities after traversal is complete.

After defining the game state, the developer defines its initial value. This initial value represents the starting state when the game is launched.

Rules are high-level, expressive constructs and being declarative they allow for many optimizations. As such, all that can be written in terms of Casanova rules should be. This said we recognize that rules sometimes can be awkward to use, and a more imperative, straightforward approach may be needed. To address this shortcoming we have built an additional scripting system to specify imperative *processes* (through coroutines), which smoothly integrate with rules. Coroutines invoke each other with the `do!` and `let!` monadic operators [10]; the former does not expect a returning value, while the latter does. When the invoked coroutine suspends itself with a `yield`, then the caller suspends as well. It is worthy of notice that our system is similar to the scripting systems based on coroutines that many games use already, even though the degree of integration of our coroutine system with the rest of the game engine is higher when compared with that of commonly used mechanisms which typically "attach" to the main engine an external scripting language with ungainly binding mechanisms [11].

The developer then defines the game scripts: the main script, plus a list of pairs of input scripts, where each pair is composed of an event detection script and an event response script. Whenever the first script detects an input event then the response is run.

Casanova supports mutable values through the type constructor `var`, and reference values which are not updated (since they are just references to values stored elsewhere in the state) through the type constructor `ref`.

2.1 SYNTAX

In the following is shown the syntax of a Casanova program: we start with the type definitions of the game state and the various game entities, each specifying the rules that define an update of the game state. Then we give the initial state, and finally we give the main and input scripts. Keep in mind that the initial state definition and the `GameState` type declaration do not show up explicitly in the grammar, as they are simply a let binding and a datatype declaration respectively and they are statically checked for existence after parsing:

```
Program   ::= (Type-decl | Let-binding)* Expr
Type-decl ::= type Id [('a, ..)] = Type-body
Type-body ::= Type
            | { Id [: Type] = Expr; .. } [with (Rule)+]
            | Uid [of Type] | ..
Rule ::= rule Id = Expr
Type ::= 'abc.. | Id [(Type, ..)]
       | Type * .. * Type | Type + Type
       | ref Type | var Type
```

```
            | script Type | table Type
Let-binding ::= let Pattern = Expr
              | let rec Id = Expr and ..
Expr ::= Lit | Id | Uid | fun Pattern ▯ Expr
       | Let-binding in Expr | Expr.Id | Expr; Expr
       | if Expr then Expr [else Expr]
       | match Expr with Pattern ▯ Expr | ..
       | { MExpr }
Pattern ::= _ | Id | Uid [Pattern] | (Pattern, ..)
          | Pattern as Id | (Pattern | Pattern)
          | Pattern : Type
Lit ::= 123.. | 12.34.. | "string.." | 'c' | ()
      | [Expr; ..] | [CExpr; ..] | { Id = Expr; .. }
      | { Expr with Id = Expr; .. }
CExpr ::= for Pattern in Expr do CExpr
        | Pattern in Expr | Expr | yield Expr
        | if Expr then Expr else Expr
MExpr ::= repeat MExpr | wait Expr | run Expr
        | return Expr | MExpr ==> MExpr
        | MExpr && MExpr | MExpr || Mexpr
        | Mexpr; Mexpr | Expr := Expr | yield
        | let! Pattern = Expr in MExpr
        | do! Expr | Let-binding in Mexpr
        | match Expr with Pattern ▯ MExpr | ..
        | if Expr then MExpr [else MExpr]
Id  ::= <any-case identifier>
Uid ::= <upper-case identifier>
```

For the sake of completeness, we included productions for all meaningful language constructs such as `let`, `if`, `fun` and in general all the terms usually found in a standard implementation of the ML language [12], from which Casanova derives strongly.

2.2 CASANOVA TYPE SYSTEM

Note: in type rules, we denote type application according to the Casanova type syntax – i.e. the Haskell-style type application syntax where `T a` denotes the application of type parameter `a` to the parameterized type `T`. In F# excerpts we will instead use the .Net notation `T<'a>`.

The Casanova type system is very similar to one of the many known type systems of similar functional languages. We will not specify the typing rules for `if`, `let`, etc., as they are well known [12]. Casanova has two specific aspects that differentiate it from its cousin languages: how mutable variables, rules and scripts work. Rules are used to describe how a field, item or constructor of type `T`, defined inside a type definition for a type named `Entity`, is updated during a tick. Rules are thus associated with a function-term that defines how the next value for the rule will be computed during a tick of the update loop; this term takes as input the current game state, the value of the entity to which the rule belongs, and the delta time between the current and previous ticks. The term has thus type:

```
(GameState * Entity * float) -> T
```

`Entity` is the name of the parent type that contains the rule itself. For example, a valid rule may increment the position of an asteroid with time and with respect to its velocity:

```
type Asteroid = {
  Position : var Vector2; Velocity : Vector2 }
with rule Position = fun (state:GameState,self:Asteroid,dt) ->
  self.Position + self.Velocity * dt
```

Record fields bound to a rule appear simply as fields of the declared type, either `var` or not. They can therefore be read or even assigned accordingly. The rule function is used internally by the generated code in the `update` loop.

Values of type `var` can of course be accessed through the dereference unary operator (`!`):`var T->T` which is typed as:

$$\frac{\Gamma \vdash x : var\ T}{\Gamma \vdash !x : T}$$

Assignment to vars are instead allowed only within scripts - Casanova in general controls effects by typing effectful computations as scripts. The typing rule for assignment is:

$$\frac{\Gamma \vdash x : var\ T,\ v : T}{\Gamma \vdash x := v : Script\ Unit}$$

As shown by the language syntax, terms of kind *MExpr* offer all effectful constructs scripts have access to. Among those that introduce effects, `yield` suspends the current script for the remainder of the current tick and resumes it at the next tick, while `wait` suspends the current script for a certain amount of time:

$$\frac{\Gamma \vdash \diamond}{\Gamma \vdash yield : Script\ Unit} \qquad \frac{\Gamma \vdash t : float}{\Gamma \vdash wait\ t : Script\ Unit}$$

Scripts are sequenced together by binding them with either `let!` or `do!`, as in [F# monads]:

$$\frac{\Gamma \vdash t_1 : Script\ T \qquad \Gamma, x : T \vdash t_2 : Script\ T'}{\Gamma \vdash let!\ x = t_1\ in\ t_2 : Script\ T'}$$

When `t1 : Script Unit` then we can use `do!` instead of `let!`. To return a value from a script we use the return operator:

$$\frac{(\Gamma \vdash x : T)}{\Gamma \vdash return\ x : Script\ Unit}$$

The remaining combinators for scripts are (`&&`) to run two scripts in parallel, (`||`) to run two scripts concurrently (stop with the first to terminate), (`==>`) runs a script when another script finished with result `Some x` for some x, and finally `repeat` keeps running a script forever. As a simple example let us consider a script which waits for a flag to be turned on, and then it moves an entity right for 10 seconds:

```
{ return a.start_moving } ==>
  (repeat (a.p.x := a.p.x + 0.1) ||
  wait_condition { return a.p.x > 10.0 })
```

2.3 SEMANTICS

The Casanova semantics is defined with two main goals in mind: consistency and performance. Consistency is needed to make sure that during each iteration of the update function the game state and all its contents represent values that belong to the same iteration; a large number of bugs in games come from manipulating a game state that is not fully updated. For example, consider an asteroids game where we wish to remove those pairs of asteroids and projectiles which are currently colliding. In this example, in-place update of the state can give undesired results when computing collisions between asteroids and projectiles:

```
[a1; a2; a3] [p1; p2] // a2, p1 collide
[a1; a3] [p1; p2]     // update asteroids
[a1; a3] [p1; p2]     // update projectiles
```

The result above should be [a1; a3] and [p2].The bug above, while simplistic, is a more general instance of all those inconsistencies that arise from updates where some of the temporal invariants of the state are broken, that is the game state contains data that is part in the present and part in the future.

Good performance is needed to ensure that the update function executes as fast as possible, in order to make the game run at an interactive frame-rate. Performance is guaranteed by avoiding a "wasteful" semantics that would perform unnecessary computations, and by including important optimizations. We have defined Casanova in terms of how its programs are translated into equivalent F# programs. First, types are translated into (possibly imperative) F# types; then Casanova rules are used to build the update function and finally scripts are compiled into F# monads

and run stepwise within the update loop. The generated F# program does not create a new game state at each tick of the update function, since this would allocate and discard too much memory (thus adding excessive overhead to the game runtime in terms of garbage collection). Still, purity makes it much easier to reason about our games, so we use a double buffering strategy for values resulting from the evaluation of rules: one slot is reserved for the value currently held by the rule (the value computed during the last tick), and the other to hold the next value, the one that is being computed during the current tick. The next value for each rule is only writable during each tick, while the current value is only readable; in effect, this gives the same result that we would have by generating a new game state, but without the overhead. Further optimizations are described in 2.3.4.

2.3.1 TYPE TRANSLATION

We define a transformation from Casanova types into F# types. The transformation mostly preserves the original structure: tuples remain tuples, records remain records, and so on. The only difference is that rules are represented with the special data-type `Rule<'a>`:

```
type Rule<'a> = { mutable Current : 'a; mutable Next : 'a }
```

When an entity is defined in terms of a rule, the `Rule` data-type is inserted into the entity together with a property that simplifies access to this field. For example when we write the following Casanova data-type:

```
type Ship = { Position : Vector2 = … } with rule Position …
```

it is turned into the F#:

```
type Ship = { _Position : Rule<Vector2> = … }
  member this.Position
    with get() = this._Position.Current
    and set p' = this._Position.Next <- p'
```

The body of the rule is ignored while generating types and it is used only to create the update function of the game.

2.3.2 RULES AND UPDATE

The `update` function is generated entirely by Casanova, and it evaluates all the rule functions associated with the game state definition and stores their result in the `Next` field of their rule. It is modeled as a polytypic function [13] (emulated through reflection and on-the-fly compilation) on the original game state; in the following we adopt the convention that T_{cnv} is the original Casanova type and $T_{F\#}$ is its transformation into F#. The `update` function simply traverses the state, and when it encounters a rule then it assigns to its `Next` field the result of evaluating the rule function. `update` is generated by a traversing the type definitions, starting from the game state and then one entity at a time. The function takes as input the type of the game state and returns a function that performs the update on its transformed F# type. In the following, we denote a type parameter as followed by the big arrow `=>`, and a regular parameter with the regular arrow `->`; a type parameter in this context can be analyzed with a switch-case:

```
update : Type_cnv => Type_F# -> float -> Unit
```

`update` uses an auxiliary generator function which takes as input the type of the game state, the type of the current entity and the type of the field in the entity that is being updated; this auxiliary function is called `update'` and has type:

```
update' : GameState_cnv => Entity_cnv => T_cnv =>
          GameState_F# -> Entity_F# -> T_F# -> float -> Unit
```

The update function simply invokes the `update'` function; since at the start of the generation of the update function the state is the entity we are processing, we invoke `update'` by passing the state three times: one as the state, one as the current entity and one as the current field. Type parameters are written between square brackets [∘]:

```
update [GameState_cnv] (s:GameState_F#) (dt:float) =
  update' [GameState_cnv] [GameState_cnv] [GameState_cnv] s s s dt
```

When we encounter a primitive or a reference value then we do nothing:

```
update' [S] [E] [P] s e v dt = ()
update' [S] [E] [ref T] s e v dt = ()
```

When we are processing a variable inside an entity E then we proceed by updating the contents of the variable. If the type parameter T of the variable is a type declaration, that is it has a name, then the processed value becomes the current entity:

```
update' [S] [E] [Var T] s e v dt =
  if T is not a type decl then update' [S] [E] [T] s e v dt
  else update' [S] [T] [T] s v dt
```

When we encounter a tuple (or, similarly, a record) then we update all its internal values:

```
update' [S] [E] [T_1 * ... * T_n] s e (v_1,...,v_n) dt =
  if T_1 is not a type decl
    update' [S] [E] [T_1] s e v_1 dt
  else
    update' [S] [T_1] [T_1] s v_1 v_1 dt
  ...
```

When we update a discriminated union then we pattern match on the updated value and update the parameter of the current constructor:

```
update' [S] [E] [T_1+T_2] s e v dt =
  match v with
  | Left v_1 ->
    if T_1 is not a type decl then
      update' [S] [E] [T_1] s e v_1 dt
    else
      update' [S] [T_1] [T_1] s v_1 v_1 dt
  | Right v_2 ->
    if T_2 is not a type decl then
      update' [S] [E] [T_2] s e v_2 dt
    else
      update' [S] [T_2] [T_2] s v_2 v_2 dt
```

Similarly, a list is updated by iterating and updating all its elements. Finally, if the update function encounters a rule, then the rule body is evaluated and its value is updated, stored in the state (since rules may be assigned in the transformed F# data-types) into Next and then the Current value is updated; we update Current rather than Next value for consistency (since Next is treated as a write-only value during a tick):

```
update' [S] [E] [rule T = term] s e v dt =
  v.Next <- term s e dt
  if T is not a type decl
    update' [S] [E] [T] s e v.Current dt
  else
    update' [S] [T] [T] s v.Current v.Current dt
```

The update function does not traverse functional terms or scripts. When the update function has finished performing its work, then it traverses the game state and swaps all the Current and Next fields of each rule, since the Next field is now fully computed and contains the latest value of the rule. The definition of the function that performs the swap of Current and Next for each rule is omitted as it is very similar to the definition of the update function seen above: this function iterates all entities recursively starting from the game state and whenever it encounters a rule it swaps its Current and Next fields.

2.3.3 SCRIPTS

Scripts are compiled into F# monads. For a more comprehensive treatment of this mechanism, see [14]. The various scripting constructs are translated with a one-by-one correspondence into our monad. Since scripts represent computations that may be suspended and resumed, we implement such a coroutine system.

The monadic data-type that we use represents a script as a function that performs a step in the computation of the script. This function, when evaluated, performs some side-effects on the state, and then it either returns the final result if the script has finished computing, or else it returns the continuation of the script:

```
type Script<'a> = Unit -> Step<'a>
and Step<'a> = Done of 'a | Next of Script<'a>
```

Returning simply encapsulates a value around the Done data constructor:

```
let return(x:'a) : Script<'a> = fun () -> Done x
```

Binding runs a script until it returns a result with Done. When this happens, the result of the first coroutine is passed to the second coroutine, which is then run until it completes:

```
let bind (p:Script<'a>, k:'a->Script<'b>)
  : Script<'b> =
  fun () ->
    match p () with
    | Done x -> k x ()
    | Next p' -> Next(this.Bind(p',k))
```

Yield suspends and then returns nothing:

```
let yield : Script<Unit,'s> = fun s -> Next(fun s -> Done ())
```

The above functions (bind, return, and yield) are a complete definition of a fully functional monad; they cover the let!, do!, return and yield constructs of the Casanova language.

At each tick of the simulation each active script is run for a single step by passing it a () value and by replacing it (for the next iteration) with its own result, that is its continuation; if the script finishes then it is removed from the list of active scripts.

2.3.4 OPTIMIZATION

A great deal of development effort in modern games is spent working on editing the game source, but rather than adding new and useful features the same code is tuned until it is efficient enough, by applying various optimizations such as visibility culling (to reduce the number of rendered models) and other techniques. One of the original design goals of Casanova is to save developers time and effort by automatically performing several of those optimizations that would otherwise be hand-written.

A lot of the effort in game optimization goes into optimizing quadratic queries [15]; many games feature lots of searches to compare two collections: collision detection, visibility, interaction, etc. Let's consider example of such a query when finding the asteroids that collide with a projectile in an asteroid shooter game; this query would be computed for each projectile, and thus its overall complexity in a naïve implementation would be $O(n_{ast} \times n_{proj}) = O(n^2)$. By using a spatial partitioning index on the asteroids, it becomes possible to evaluate this query in a much shorter time. Quadratic queries in Casanova generate optimized code by adding an appropriate index to the game state and solving predicates faster by taking advantage of this index in all related queries [16]. Another important optimization is that of avoiding completely the rule swapping routine at the end of the update function. To avoid this, we modify the rule data-type as follows:

```
type Rule<'a> = { Values : 'a[]; Index : ref<int> }
  member this.Current with get() = Values.[!Index % 2]
  member this.Next with set v' = Values.[(!Index+1)%2] <- v'
```

With this implementation, swapping the various current and next values inside all the rules of the game simply requires incrementing the `Index` reference, which is a global value shared among all rules. Collections inside rules can be optimized as well with a simple modification. Instead of constantly creating new collections at each tick of the update function, collection rules are optimized by pre-allocating two mutable collections (the F# data-type is `ResizeArray`). When computing the new value of the collection rule the `Next` collection is cleared and the values of the new collection are added to it.

The final optimization that is performed by Casanova is parallel evaluation of rules in different thread, since no two rules can write the same memory location.

2.4 CASE STUDY

As a test-bed for Casanova, we have built an actual game with a group of MSc students. The game, Galaxy Wars, is a real-time strategy game where the player conquers a star sector by building and using fleets of starships. It may be found at [17], both the sources and the latest executable. The game features more than a hundred thousand lines of code, and supports hundreds of interacting entities and up to eight players across LAN and Internet. This project has allowed us to see rules, scripts and most of Casanova in action in a much larger work than the usual smaller samples of code we have worked with [18], and from the feedback of this project many aspects of Casanova have taken their final shape. The game is also in the process of being published commercially.

3. IMPLEMENTATION

It is important to stress out that while we have designed Casanova as a fully-fledged programming language (the compiler of which is currently under construction), considering it just from this point of view is reductive. Casanova is more importantly a design methodology for making games, which covers the definition of the game state, and of the update and draw functions. At the time of writing there are two implementations of Casanova that cover the aspects of the language presented above in various manners. The first implementation is simply as an F# library. Said library contains an implementation of the scripting monad and an implementation of rules. Drawing and updating the state are done automatically through highly optimized reflection. While this library does not support everything about Casanova (for example rules require the use of specialized data-types), the fact of it being a library makes it flexible and easy to use in many contexts. We show how to use the library to implement various games in [18]. Moreover, the library takes full advantage of all the development tools built to support F#. This library is currently being used and extended organically in the Galaxy Wars research game [17] and in a series of smaller sample games [18]. The second implementation is a C++ meta-programming library which implements state traversal, updating and drawing, and coroutines with a rather articulated system of partially specialized templates. The renderer for the F# library is built in XNA, while the renderer for the C++ library is built with DirectX 10.

Both systems are still a work in progress, but they may be tested, experimented with and extended into further projects already.

4. FINAL ASSESSMENT

Assessing the quality of a programming language for a given activity is a daunting task. Programming languages, much like natural languages, have a deep relation with the existing knowledge of the user. Similarly, there exist no metrics that make it clear that a language is good for a certain job, or even to compare that a language is better than another at that job. It is with this in mind that we proceed with exposing a series of arguments in answer to our original claim that Casanova is better suited than traditional mainstream object-oriented languages such as C# (plus libraries such as XNA) for real-time game development. We have chosen C# as it is widely used in the game industry (Xbox, iOS, Windows Phone 7, Android) and because it is widely used as a "simpler" game development language when compared with the industry standard of C++. We will discuss how Casanova programs are overall much shorter than equivalent C# programs (measured excluding lines containing only parentheses such as { and } or trivial code such as property declarations and such), and we will also discuss how a series of "typical" snippets of game code taken from three different games (an asteroid shooter game, an action/adventure game and a strategy game [18]) compare between Casanova, the Casanova F# library, and idiomatic C#.

The first comparisons that we make are concerned with the surrounding infrastructure, which is all the game code that is not strictly part of the game logic or drawing, and the overall length of the various samples:

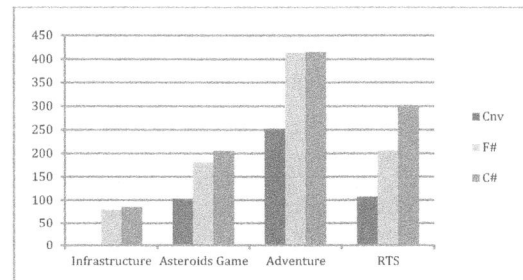

We now move to the comparison of the single snippets of game code that we have discussed in the previous section; we remark once again of the relevance of these snippets, since they can act as fundamental building blocks for a large number of games:

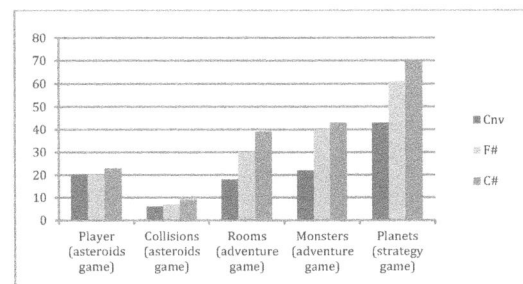

With the data just listed, we feel it's safe enough to conclude that Casanova allows to express game-related concepts with less verbosity than traditional mainstream languages; specifically, Casanova removes the need for boilerplate code, it removes the need to traverse the game world to update and draw each entity, and it allows to express the logic of the game with fitting abstractions.

We have also performed a series of benchmarks on a single game implemented in Casanova to test the gains obtained by the various types of optimizations available in term of ticks per second that the game becomes able to perform. We compare the optimized Casanova programs with their un-optimized version to assess the effectiveness of each optimization, but notice that the un-optimized Casanova version is compiled into F# code that offers roughly (within 5% in all our tests) the same performance of equivalent C# code:

Optimization	FPS	% gain
None	0.375	N/A
Fast rule swap	0.387	103%
No realloc for lists	0.387	103%
Rule threads	0.782	203%
Query	213	> 10000%
All together	233	> 10000%

As we can see, the various optimizations each offer some speedup, but parallelism and query optimization do the most. It is also important to keep in mind that these optimizations require no work on the part of the Casanova developer. The sources used for the benchmark are those of the RTS game in [18].

5. CONCLUSIONS

Games and multimedia applications are extremely widespread. Disciplined models and techniques that simplify game development have a unique chance of having a significant impact by allowing the creation of games without needing to focus on lots of complicated details that are not really related to the game itself. Casanova is a step in this direction, and the framework is shaping up as to cover the creation of a complex game logic, plus flexible input management, and drawing.

6. REFERENCES

1. Entertainment Software Association. Industry Facts. (2010).
2. Fullerton, Tracy, Swain, Christopher, and Hoffman, Steven. Game design workshop: a playcentric approach to creating innovative games. Morgan Kaufman, 2008.
3. Ritterfeld, Ute, Cody, Michael, and Vorderer, Peter. Serious Games: Mechanisms And Effects. (2009), Routledge.
4. White, Li Ty and Alice Team R and Y Pausch (head and Tommy Burnette and A. C. Capehart and Dennis Cosgrove and Rob Deline and Jim Durbin and Rich Gossweiler and Koga Jeff. A Brief Architectural Overview of Alice, a Rapid Prototyping System for Virtual Reality.
5. Giuseppe Maggiore, Alvise Spanò, Renzo Orsini, Giulia Costantini, Michele Bugliesi and Mohamed Abbadi. Designing Casanova: a language for games. In Proceedings of the 13th conference on Advances in Computer Games, ACG 13, Tilburg, 2011, Springer. In 13th Internation Conference Advances in Computer Games (ACG) (Tilburg, Netherlands 2011), Springer.
6. Ampatzoglou, Apostolos and Chatzigeorgiou, Alexander. Evaluation of object-oriented design patterns in game development. In Journal of Information and Software Technology (MA, USA 2007), Butterworth-Heinemann Newton.
7. Folmer, Eelke. Component based game development: a solution to escalating costs and expanding deadlines? In Proceedings of the 10th international conference on Component-based software engineering, CBSE (Berlin, Heidelberg 2007), Springer-Verlag.
8. Conal, Elliott and Hudak, Paul. Functional reactive animation. In International Conference on Functional Programming (ICFP) (1997), 263–273.
9. Walker White, Alan Demers, Christoph Koch, Johannes Gehrke, and Rajmohan Rajagopalan. Scaling games to epic proportions. In Proceedings of the 2007 ACM SIGMOD international conference on Management of data (SIGMOD) (New York, NY, USA 2007), ACM, 31–42.
10. 10. Costantini, Giuseppe Maggiore and Giulia. Friendly F# (fun with game programming). (Venice, Italy 2011), Smashwords.
11. Figueiredo, L. H. de, Celes, W., and Ierusalimschy, R. Programming advance control mechanisms with Lua coroutines. In Game Programming Gems 6 (2006), Mike Dickheiser (ed), Charles River Media, 357–369.
12. Pierce, Benjamin. Types and Programming Languages. MIT Press, Cambridge, Massachusetts , 2002.
13. Jeuring, Patrik Jansson and Johan. PolyP - a polytypic programming language extension. (1997), Symposium on Principles of Programming Languages (POPL).
14. Giuseppe Maggiore, Michele Bugliesi and Renzo Orsini. Monadic Scripting in F# for Computer Games. (Oslo, Norway 2011), Harnessing Theories for Tool Support in Software (TTSS).
15. Buckland, Mat. Programming Game AI by Example. (Sudbury, MA 2004), Jones & Bartlett Publishers.
16. Garcia-molina, Hector, Ullman, Jeffrey D., and Widom, Jennifer. Database System Implementation. (1999), Prentice-Hall.
17. Maggiore, Giuseppe. Galaxy Wars Project Page. In http://vsteam2010.codeplex.com, http://galaxywars.vsteam.org.
18. Maggiore, Giuseppe. Casanova project page. In http://casanova.codeplex.com/.

Tag-Exercise Creator: Towards End-user Development for Tangible Interaction in Rehabilitation Training

Ananda Hochstenbach-Waelen,
Annick A.A. Timmermans, Henk A.M. Seelen
Adelante Centre of Expertise
in Rehabilitation and Audiology
Zandbergsweg 111, 6432 CC Hoensbroek
{A.Hochstenbach,A.Timmermans,
H.Seelen}@adelante-zorggroep.nl

Daniel Tetteroo, Panos Markopoulos
Department of Industrial Design
User Centred Engineering Group
Eindhoven University of Technology
Den Dolech 2, 5612 AZ Eindhoven
{D.Tetteroo,P.Markopoulos}@tue.nl

ABSTRACT

Tangible and embodied interactive technology (TEIT) consists of tightly coupled physical devices and software, which is less the case with mainstream platforms like personal computers, smartphones, etc. Currently TEIT is manufactured by small- and medium-sized niche technology providers for whom application domain specific development can represent an excessive threshold. End-user development by domain specialists emerges as an avenue to mitigate this issue. This research has set out to enable therapists to create solutions for rehabilitation training, through the development of the *Tag-Exercise Creator* (TEC). This paper motivates the use of tangible interactive systems for this problem domain, and describes the design, implementation and initial evaluation of TEC. Our study indicates that tools like TEC can enable domain experts to perform EUD tasks and create training content. Improvements and extensions to TEC are under way to enable a field trial of the system where the feasibility of EUD as a professional practice will be evaluated.

Author Keywords

End-User Development, rehabilitation technology, tangible interaction, upper extremity, neurology.

ACM Classification Keywords

D.2.6 Programming Environments: Programmer Workbench, D.2.13 Reusable Software: Domain engineering, H.5.2 Information Interfaces and Presentation: User Interfaces

INTRODUCTION

Almost two decades since the introduction of graspable/tangible interaction [4], related technologies are gradually making the transition from research laboratories

to the market. Contrary to traditional interactive software that relies on rather standardized input/output devices, such standardization has not yet been achieved for tangible interactive systems [11]. This hampers the development of TEIT by exposing application developers to low level hardware and software issues, which are typically the tasks of specialized technology providers. For such companies, typically small and medium sized, application domain specific development can represent an excessive threshold. One approach to overcome this threshold is to enable domain experts to contribute to the development of relevant solutions, acting as end-user developers. This research explores how to enable this venture in the domain of rehabilitation technology, where the need arises for rehabilitation therapists to create training content tailored to different pathologies and even to specific patients. Specifically we examine how end-user development (EUD) can enable therapists to create solutions for rehabilitation training after stroke.

Technology For Stroke Rehabilitation

Longitudinal studies of recovery after stroke have shown that less than 50% of the stroke survivors regain a functional arm [1]. For the remaining patients permanent sensory and/or motor disability of the hand constitutes a major problem, since they experience difficulties to use the hand in activities of daily living [10]; this in turn greatly affects their social participation. Stroke incidence is on the rise [15], so a general increase in therapy demand is anticipated. Rehabilitation technology may play an important role to 1) reduce therapist time needed to provide upper limb (skill) training and 2) enable rehabilitation training at home, extending and complementing current training approaches.

TEIT may be a valuable aid to support rehabilitation training, especially where this involves manipulation of real life objects, which is key to (re)learn and optimize everyday life actions [13]. Moreover, to exploit the patient's potential for motor learning, training content has to be varied with a large number of exercises that are tailored to the needs of a particular patient [2].

A successful research prototype that supports task-oriented training for neurological patients is the Philips

Rehabilitation Exerciser. This system combines the *TagTiles* board (Serious Toys BV, Den Bosch, NL) with a sensor-enhanced feedback system [12]. A clinical trial of this system showed promising results regarding improvement of arm-hand performance in stroke patients [12]. However, this system also revealed some of the limits of the classical technologist driven approach to innovation in therapy: Participants in the clinical trial were confronted with the lack of an extended library of exercises to continuously challenge them to train and help them keep training beyond the duration of the trial (8 weeks). The need was identified for therapists to add exercises that are customized to the training needs of patients (e.g. supporting different skills and exercise variability), as well as to their proficiency level (e.g. changing the level of difficulty).

End-User Development

Currently, adding and modifying exercises requires software development knowledge, as such exercises need to be programmed into the TagTiles board. Although due effort has been made to facilitate non expert developers to program the TagTiles board through the ESPranto Software Development Kit (SDK) [16], this still presents a prohibitive threshold for therapists, who do not have the skills required to create exercises with such an SDK [7]. While ESPranto facilitates the otherwise daunting task of programming TEIT, till now mostly the task of specialized laboratories, it still requires an investment of effort and a motivation to engage in development that is not consistent with the priorities and mindset of the professional therapist [7]. Therapists are primarily motivated and paid to provide care rather than to create software. Their busy schedules can be prohibitive for extensive software development, and in all cases EUD [9] practices should be contained rather than divert therapists away from their primary activities. In addition, therapists are lacking time to (learn to) program, since time for providing therapy is prioritised and therapy time is limited.

A simple, yet versatile domain specific tool to create new and adjust existing exercises on the TagTiles board would be helpful for therapists. Therefore a software tool, called the Tag-Exercise Creator (TEC), was developed with which a therapist can both make use of, or edit programmed exercises (already available in a library of exercises), as well as add new ones that fit the patient's personal needs and proficiency level. Our longer term ambition is to enable therapists to engage in practices related to software creation and sharing, which are well known and practised in the open source software community but are still far removed from the problems and challenges facing health workers nowadays: End-users (e.g. therapists in stroke rehabilitation) should be able to create and share exercises for rehabilitation training. An online community is being developed to enable therapists to use this community as a tool for the dissemination, sharing and co-creation of software for therapy (e.g. the exercises programmed with the TEC).

In the present paper the design and usability evaluation of the first TEC prototype is described. Therapists can use the TEC for setting up a training programme of arm-hand exercises for stroke patients on the TagTiles board. The complete training system, i.e. the combination of the TagTiles board and the TEC, is called the *Tag-Trainer*.

TAG-TRAINER

The Tag-Trainer was designed to serve three main goals:

- The TEC should facilitate therapists to quickly and easily set up patient-tailored exercises for training arm-hand skills of stroke patients on the TagTiles board.

- Stroke patients should be able to train with the Tag-Trainer themselves.

- Therapists should be able to use the TEC as a tool to disseminate and share exercises with other rehabilitation experts in the WikiTherapist online community[1].

The Tag-Trainer consists of two main parts:

1. The *TagTiles board* (see Figure 1) is a programmable interactive board that consists of a checkerboard area (24 x 24 cm) of 12 by 12 squares. The board can produce sound and each square on the board can provide output through different coloured LED lights in each square. The board is able to detect where and which RFID tags are placed on the board. In this way everyday life objects (to be used for skill training) that are tagged can be recognized by the board and displacements of tagged objects may be tracked. The combination of the board and the tagged everyday life objects is to be used by stroke patients for rehabilitation training of the upper limb. A pre-production version of the board has already been used to create training solutions for children with Cerebral Palsy [3,8] and patients with stroke [12].

Figure 1. TagTiles board by Serious Toys, NL.

---

[1] See http://www.wikitherapist.nl

2. A software tool: the *Tag-Exercise Creator (TEC)*. The TEC has been developed for therapists as a tool to set up patient-tailored exercises for training arm-hand skills of stroke patients on the TagTiles board.

Below we discuss the design process, implementation, and user evaluation of TEC.

DESIGN PROCESS

Seven physiotherapists and occupational therapists working in rehabilitation at the Adelante Rehabilitation Centre (Hoensbroek, NL) were interviewed to obtain insight into criteria that technology should meet to be useful and usable in assisting arm-hand skills training in stroke patients [6]. In addition, information was obtained from previous research in the field of technology-assisted arm-hand therapy performed at Adelante [12-14]. The TEC is especially inspired by the iterative design and development of the Philips Rehabilitation Exerciser [12] which showed how stroke rehabilitation could be supported on the TagTiles board. Based on these sources, an initial set of exercises for arm-hand training were created on the board. These exercises were used to demonstrate to therapists the potential of the board and to solicit feedback regarding adaptations and modifications they would like to have or would likely need in order to use it in their practice. It was thought that this would help derive requirements for the TEC tool. Five therapists and two rehabilitation researchers provided input for designing the TEC in repeated sessions over a period of 6 months, gradually extending the capabilities of the system and adjusting its graphical interface. At the end of this process, the TEC tool was evaluated in a summative evaluation process involving final year physiotherapy students, as surrogates to practicing therapists. We discuss the various steps of this process in more detail below.

Initial Exercise Design

To familiarize with the nature of the training software that TEC should help create, and to expose therapists to it, we developed and implemented an initial set of exercises on the board. We used the T-TOAT (Technology-supported Task Oriented Arm Training) method [12,14] to define eleven sub-tasks relating to the daily life activities 'eating with knife and fork' and 'drinking from a cup', e.g., grasping, picking up, reaching out, placing an object on the board. These subtasks were programmed on the board by providing auditory and visual stimuli to the patient. The software was implemented using the ESPranto language [16].

The exercises consisted in a basic pattern of four steps:

1. A blue plane lights up on the board.
2. A tagged object is placed on the blue plane.
3. The blue plane turns into a green plane after which the green plane fades away.
4. The object is removed from its position after which the next blue plane appears.

To keep visual feedback/instructions simple and uniform for stroke patients, blue was chosen as the default colour to represent a location on which tagged objects need to be placed, while green was chosen to confirm that an object is placed correctly. To make feedback to patients possible on the number of repetitions still to be completed, each cycle of step 1 until step 4 is considered as one repetition of a movement within an exercise.

Therapist Requirements

The initial exercises were demonstrated to two experienced rehabilitation researchers and to five therapists working in stroke rehabilitation. After the demonstrations the therapists and researchers were interviewed on the usefulness of the exercises in training of stroke patients, on the usefulness of the system's features (e.g. auditory instructions and feedback, light feedback, tagging objects, selection of detection plane size) and on desired adjustable options. Participants indicated that they were content with

- The visual and auditory feedback for individual subtasks and progress feedback for the number of exercises performed.

- The possibility to tag and make use of real life objects in the exercises.

- The simple and uniform use of colours as visual feedback/instructions.

In addition they stated, among others, that they need to be able to

- Adjust exercises, auditory feedback and instructions to individual patients.

- Adjust the number of repetitions, duration (e.g. to determine the interval between picking up and putting down objects) and accuracy of object placement within an exercise.

- Create one handed as well as bimanual tasks.

- Prevent patients from simply sliding an object when they need to pick it up and displace it.

- Make use of more TagTiles boards to enlarge the movement range.

Workflow Concept

Therapists will use the TEC to *set up an exercise program* (of several exercises) tailored to the needs of an individual patient. If an already programmed exercise for one patient is not suitable for another patient (e.g. because it requires a high level of accuracy), the therapist can decide to *adjust the already existing exercise* to the specific needs of the latter patient. Therapists may also decide to *develop completely new exercises*, e.g. to match their own therapy approach or the latest developments in their field.

The TEC accommodates these three tasks in that it provides three options upon the start of the program:

1. Creating a new exercise
2. Adjusting an existing exercise, or

3. Creating a complete exercise programme for a patient.

The latter option makes it possible to select several exercises from the exercise database and start a training programme for an individual patient.

Creating And Modifying Exercises

Figure 2 shows an overview of the TEC interface that allows the creation and modification of exercises. This section discusses in detail the design of this part of the application.

Exercise set-up. As described before, the board can contribute to picking up, displacing, sliding and/or putting down everyday life objects during task training by tracking the tagged objects. Therapists should be able to set the sequence of target locations (as blue planes lighting up on the board), thereby facilitating the displacements. The basic pattern of four steps described TEC above has been abstracted into ready-made building blocks. The following building blocks can be dragged into, and deleted from, the exercise structure to compose an exercise:

1) *Sequential block* – the added block appears in sequence over time after the previous block(s).

2) *Parallel block* – two or more parallel planes will light up at the same time, which is necessary for exercises in which

two or more objects should be placed at the same time (e.g. picking up and putting down knife and fork). This block gives therapists the opportunity to program bimanual tasks.

3) *Sequence of blocks* – this block provides an abstraction mechanism for repeating a sequence of blocks (i.e. a specific order of appearance of consecutive planes). A number of repetitions can be set for a sequence in order that therapists do not need to repeatedly add identical sequences.

4) *Waiting time* – this building block can be used to postpone the lighting up of the next plane(s), which is necessary in e.g. strength training (e.g. holding objects in the air for a longer period of time). In addition it often is necessary to add a rest period for the patient to avoid fatigue.

Block settings. The building blocks can be used to create new exercises, but also to adjust existing exercises to individual patients' needs. Each block contains several settings that can be adjusted: the type of object to be placed on the blue plane, if and which auditory instruction should be provided, if feedback should be given or not, and how many times the block should be repeated. In addition, for each block a target plane can be selected on the schematic representation of the TagTiles board by clicking the individual squares. This offers the opportunity to select

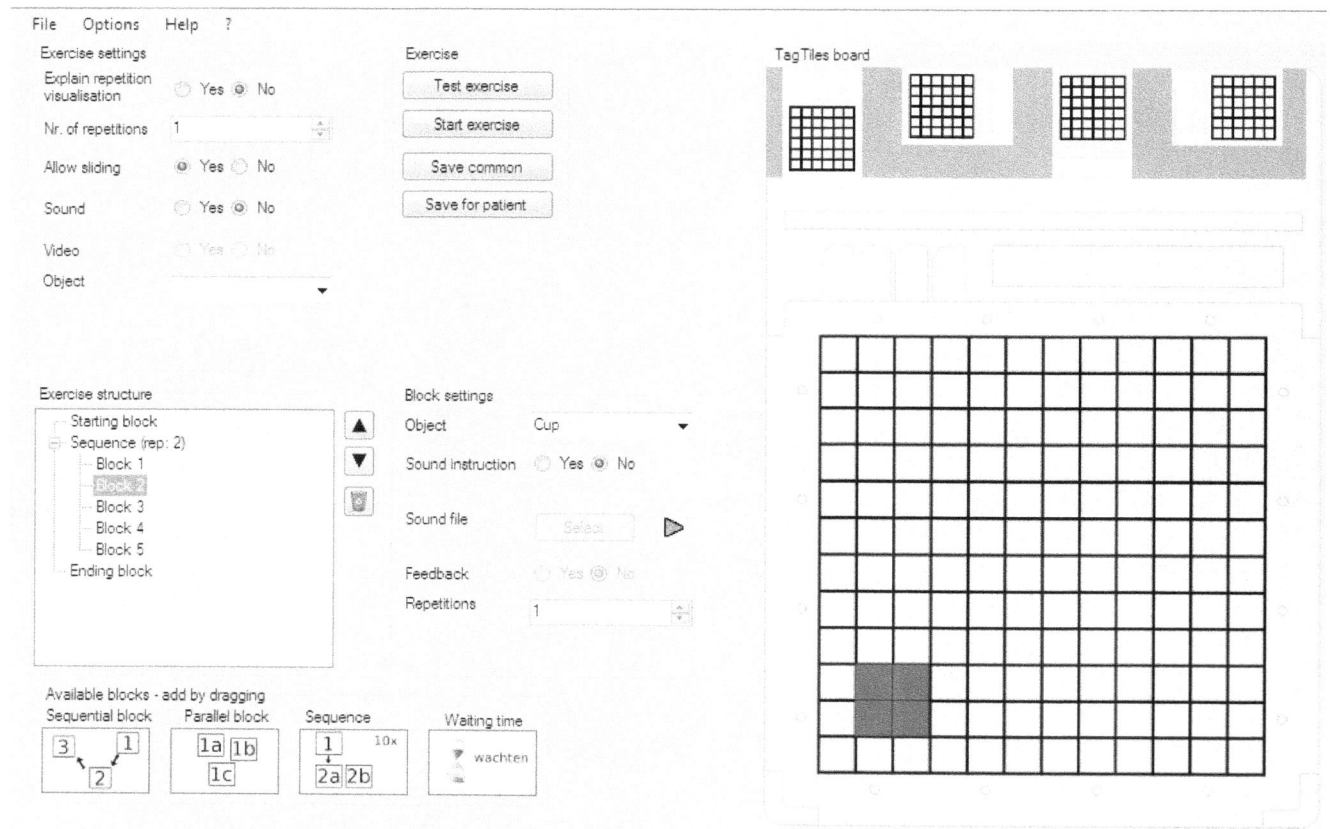

Figure 2. Overview of the TEC application part that allows creation and modification of exercises.

bigger or smaller planes to determine the accuracy of object placements, since smaller planes require a higher degree of accuracy from the patient.

Exercise settings. The 'exercise settings' offer the opportunity to select, among others, the number of repetitions of the complete exercise and whether sliding an object across the board is allowed or not. In addition, an exercise can be tested (virtually, on screen), started (physically, on the board) and saved as general or patient-tailored exercise.

TEC USABILITY EVALUATION

A small-scale (N=7) user study was performed to assess whether the tool (i.e. the TEC) is usable enough to be deployed in a larger scale field study. All participants had little or no programming experience and had at least a basic level of domain-specific knowledge on rehabilitation therapy for stroke patients.

Method

Participants received a brief explanation about the purpose of the Tag-Trainer and the role of the TEC within the Tag-Trainer. Afterwards, participants were given 5 minutes to familiarize themselves with the tool. As participants could not be expected to map directly general exercises for arm-hand training to tasks that could be done on the board, they were shown a video of a stroke patient executing one out of the initial set of exercises. Finally, the participants were given 3 time-constrained tasks expected to be typical in future use by therapists, i.e.: 1) modification of an existing exercise, 2) creation of a new exercise, and 3) compilation of a training program for an individual patient.

Participants were asked to report their thoughts and experiences while performing the tasks (i.e. think-aloud protocol was applied). Finally they were presented a questionnaire with 34 statements about using TEC, based on the Cognitive Dimensions (CD) framework [5] and the Technology Acceptance Model (TAM) [17]. Participants were asked to indicate their agreement with each statement on a 7-point Likert-scale.

Results

All users were able to complete the tasks given to them, albeit with varying levels of success. In terms of TAM-constructs, users rated TEC overall moderately easy to use (Med.=5, IQR=1.5) for the modification and construction of rehabilitation exercises. Still, a number of usability issues were detected that greatly hindered the performance of some users.

Results from the cognitive dimensions questionnaire show that although participants found it easy to modify exercises, TEC did not always prevent users from making errors (Med.=4, IQR=2.75, see Figure 3), mainly because the effects of certain operations are not always directly visible. One frequently observed user action was drawing multiple planes in a single exercise block. Only when a participant wanted to test or execute the exercise, it became clear that this behavior was not supported by the TEC.

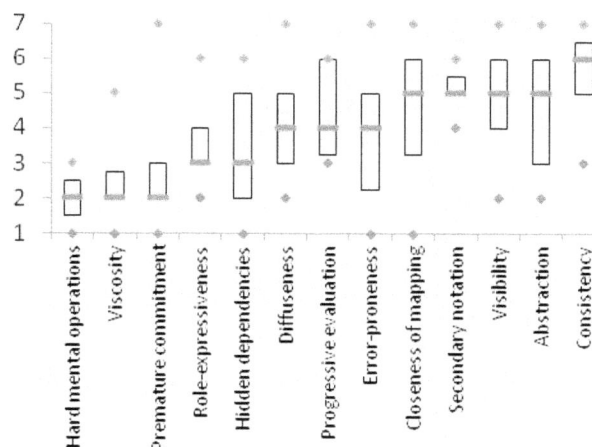

Figure 3. Questionnaire scores for Cognitive Dimensions

It is also interesting to note that, although currently the possibilities to re-use parts of exercises are very limited, participants rated the tool to feature a fairly high level of *abstraction* (Med.=5, IQR=3, see Figure 3). While the concept of 'blocks' provides an abstraction layer by integrating several steps of an exercise (lighting-up target plane, waiting for object placement, showing confirmation), the tool contains no abstraction that enables for example group wise operations on blocks themselves.

Finally, another interesting result is that participants gave a low rating for the tool's *viscosity* dimension, i.e. the effort required to make modifications with changes in one part of the program propagating to the rest (Med.=2, IQR=0.75, see Figure 3). An important goal of the tool is to enable therapists to quickly make changes in existing exercises in order to adapt them to individual patients. The low rating for viscosity is promising in this aspect, because it implies that the tool provides a quick way for tailoring training content.

CONCLUSIONS AND FUTURE WORK

This research illustrates the importance of carefully designed EUD tools, especially for highly-specialized domains such as rehabilitation therapy. The relevance for EUD in this domain is clear: Therapist time needed to provide therapy to patients may be reduced, since therapists only need to set up the patient-tailored training programme after which patients can train by themselves. However, this is only possible if therapists are able to use and modify the technology by themselves in order to create patient-tailored therapy programmes. Previous attempts to provide end-user programming tools for TEITs have been too generic in nature. We developed a domain specific end-user programming tool (TEC) to enable therapists to create and modify exercises for arm-hand rehabilitation on the TagTiles board.

The contribution of this paper is to illustrate the nature of the tools that are required to enable domain experts to perform EUD tasks. Furthermore, we show that certain aspects of such a tool, like low viscosity, low error-proneness and high abstraction facilitate therapists in their EUD tasks.

Once further improvements have been made on the usability of the tool, it will be deployed for a larger-scale field trial. This trial will focus on the acceptance of a tool like TEC, the therapists' willingness to perform EUD tasks, and organisational antecedents of acceptance in the therapy domain. In parallel to this trial, a clinical study will be performed to validate the therapeutic value of the proposed system. Finally, we want to evaluate the viability of the used approach (therapists as end-user developers) when applied to other pathologies. In this way technology-assisted therapy could play an important role in decreasing the future therapy demand on therapists

ACKNOWLEDGMENTS

We acknowledge the support of the Innovation-Oriented Research Programme 'Integral Product Creation and Realization (IOP IPCR)' of the Netherlands Ministry of Economic Affairs, Agriculture and Innovation. In addition, we thank Mark de Ronde (Hogeschool Zuyd, Heerlen, NL) for his contribution to the development of the TEC, the rehabilitation therapists of Adelante Rehabilitation Centre (Hoensbroek, NL) for sharing their valuable expertise, the physiotherapy students of Fontys (Eindhoven, NL) for participating in the usability evaluation, and Serious Toys BV (Den Bosch, NL) for providing software and advice during the creation of TEC.

REFERENCES

1. Broeks, J.G., Lankhorst, G.J., Rumping, K. and Prevo, A.J. The long-term outcome of arm function after stroke: results of a follow-up study. *Disabil Rehabil, 21*, 8 (1999), 357-364.

2. Demain, S., Wiles, R., Roberts, L. and McPherson, K. Recovery plateau following stroke: fact or fiction? *Disabil Rehabil, 28*, 13-14 (2006), 815-821.

3. Dhillon, B., Goulati, A., Politis, I., Raczewska, A. and Markopoulos, P. A set of customizable games supporting therapy of children with cerebral palsy, in *Proceedings of INTERACT 2011* (Lisbon, Portugal, 2011), Springer-Verlag, 360-361.

4. Fitzmaurice, G.W., Ishii, H. and Buxton, W. Bricks: laying the foundations for graspable user interfaces, in *Proceedings of CHI 1995* (Denver, Colorado, USA, 1995), ACM Press, 442-449.

5. Green, T.R.G. and Blackwell, A.F. Cognitive dimensions of information artifacts: a tutorial, *Tutorial presentation at BCS HCI 1998*

6. Hochstenbach-Waelen, A. and Seelen, H.A.M. Embracing change: practical and theoretical considerations for successful implementation of technology assisting upper limb training in stroke. *J Neuroeng Rehabil* (2012), Accepted for publication.

7. Kierkegaard, P. and Markopoulos, P. From Top to Bottom: End User Development, Motivation, Creativity and Organisational Support. *End User Development, Lecture Notes in Computer Science, 6654* (2011), 307-312.

8. Li, Y., Fontijn, W. and Markopoulos, P. A tangible tabletop game supporting therapy of children with Cerebral Palsy, in *Proceedings of the 2nd International Conference on Fun and Games 2008* (Eindhoven University of Technology, 2008), Springer-Verlag, 182-193.

9. Lieberman, H., Paterno, F., Klann, M. and Wulf, V. End-User Development: An Emerging Paradigm, in *End User Development*, Springer, Dordrecht, 2006, 1-8.

10. Nowak, D.A. The impact of stroke on the performance of grasping: usefulness of kinetic and kinematic motion analysis. *Neurosci Biobehav Rev, 32*, 8 (2008), 1439-1450.

11. Shaer, O. and Hornecker, E. Tangible User Interfaces: Past, Present and Future Directions. *FnT in HCI, 3*, Nr 1-2 (2010), 1-138.

12. Timmermans, A.A., Seelen, H.A., Geers, R.P., Saini, P.K., Winter, S., te Vrugt, J. and Kingma, H. Sensor-based arm skill training in chronic stroke patients: results on treatment outcome, patient motivation, and system usability. *IEEE Trans Neural Syst Rehabil Eng, 18*, 3 (2010), 284-292.

13. Timmermans, A.A., Seelen, H.A., Willmann, R.D. and Kingma, H. Technology-assisted training of arm-hand skills in stroke: concepts on reacquisition of motor control and therapist guidelines for rehabilitation technology design. *J Neuroeng Rehabil, 6* (2009), 1.

14. Timmermans, A.A.A., Geers, R.P.J., Franck, J.A., Dobbelsteijn, P., Spooren, A.I.F., Kingma, H. and Seelen, H.A.M., T-TOAT: A method of task-oriented arm training for stroke patients suitable for implementation of exercises in rehabilitation technology, in *IEEE 11th International Conference on Rehabilitation Robotics*, (Kyoto International Conference Center, Japan, 2009), 98-102.

15. Truelsen, T., Piechowski-Jozwiak, B., Bonita, R., Mathers, C., Bogousslavsky, J. and Boysen, G. Stroke incidence and prevalence in Europe: a review of available data. *Eur J Neurol, 13*, 6 (2006), 581-598.

16. Van Herk, R., Verhaegh, J. and Fontijn, W.F.J. ESPranto SDK: an adaptive programming environment for tangible applications, in *Proceedings of CHI 2009* (New York, USA, 2009), ACM, 849-858.

17. Venkatesh, V. and Davis, F.D. A Theoretical Extension of the Technology Acceptance Model: Four Longitudinal Field Studies. *Management Science, 46* ,2 (2000), 186-204.

User Interface Master Detail Pattern on Android

Thanh-Diane Nguyen, Jean Vanderdonckt

Louvain Interaction Lab., Louvain School of Management (LSM), Université catholique de Louvain, Place des Doyens, 1
B-1348 Louvain-la-Neuve (Belgium) – {thanh-diane.nguyen, jean.vanderdonckt}@uclouvain.be

ABSTRACT

The purpose of this work is to understand some existing user interface (UI) patterns and to adapt them to the constraints of mobile devices running on the Android system. We focus mainly on the Master/Detail pattern and on the surrounding patterns. The contributions are multiple: our background study consists of a brief summary of the principles of some existing user interface patterns. Based on it, we provide an adapted version of each pattern targeted to mobile phones through a framework called MandroiD. We will also present a basic case study application that takes advantage of the framework. This application is developed with Android guidelines in mind. Indeed, one of our goals is to provide the reader with some knowledge about Android applications development. Limitations of general mobile devices (e.g., the small screen) require of "reducing" homogeneous elements. MandroiD overcome theses constraints. A statistical analysis is conducted on the developed mini-application. Evaluation of it shows a general satisfaction concerning the ergonomy of the application by various users.

Author Keywords

User interface; patterns; mobile development; Android.

ACM Classification Keywords

D.2.2 [**Software Engineering**]: Design Tools and Techniques – *Modules and interfaces; user interfaces*. D.2.m [**Software Engineering**]: Miscellaneous – *Rapid Prototyping; reusable software*. H.5.2 [**Information interfaces and presentation**]: User Interfaces – *Graphical user interfaces (GUI); style guides; user-centered design*. H.5.3 [**Information interfaces and presentation**]: Group and Organization Interfaces – *Evaluation/methodology*.

General Terms

Algorithms; Design; Languages.

INTRODUCTION

As we can observe in our everyday life, mobile devices evolved with the introduction of high level development capabilities. Modern computing and interfaces design activities have to take into account the constraints of mobile devices [1,2,11], which often have a small-sized screen and no physical controller, such as a keyboard and/or mouse.

The problem of today's literature is that most of the interface descriptive and generative patterns [9] were designed for desktop environments [8,10,15] and therefore lack of support for mobile-related operations related to generative patterns. For example, the size of the screen is not a concern (nothing is said about small-sized screens with low resolutions). Ubiquitous computing is not supported by those patterns [11,14]. Design patterns can be used to capture essential problems of different "sizes". Moreover, the using of pattern for documenting design knowledge "divides a large problem area into a structured set of manageable problems" [3]. The purpose of this work is to provide adapted versions, with an evaluation, of some existing design patterns based on Object Oriented Method that can be very useful to developers and end users.

We decided to focus on Android-based mobile systems instead of iPhone devices (iOS-based). We motivate our choice by the fact that Android development is accessible and free, with a great support from the community. Furthermore, Android could not require any add-learning of specific language: Android applications are written in Java, which is a widespread programming language known by all developers. iPhone application is relied on Objective-C which can be less learned in academic classes by its material requirement. Nevertheless, the guidelines introduced in this document are valid for both systems.

Structure

This paper is organized as follows. The first part focuses on a background study of some patterns introduced in [13]. We have chosen three main patterns: the Master/Detail, the Order and the Filter patterns. This choice is motivated by the fact that there are very common patterns that are, according to our experience, generally poorly supported in mobile computing. Furthermore, some of them (e.g. the Master/Detail pattern) involve a recursive design whose conception is a very interesting challenge. In the second part, we propose a framework that could be used by programmers for implementing UIs with that kind of patterns.

Afterwards, we will take a basic application as a case study illustrating the framework. The objective is to prove that it is usable for real applications, such as a car-configurator application targeted for customers of car dealers (e.g. Audi, BMW, etc.). Finally, we present a statistical analysis which assesses the overall quality of the developed interfaces, according to some criteria that have been evaluated by external and non-technical users.

RELATED WORK

In this section, we explore some existing design patterns that need to be implemented on Android systems.

This background study is based on [12,13], which proposes a **Presentation Model**. This approach is "*a methodological guide representing the user interface in an abstract and design independent way*".

We do not explore all the patterns presented there, but we focus on a combination of some patterns which are [8, 10]: the Master/Detail, the Filter and the Order criterion against a given Population. After this exploration, we discuss some guidelines for designing user interfaces on mobile devices. Again, we restricted our study to some of the most important rules for conceiving high quality interfaces.

The definition of Filter and Order criterion patterns are obvious. **Filter pattern** is used for defining custom criteria that allow selecting some parts of a population. **Order criterion pattern** is mainly used for sorting elements of a population in ascending or descending order. In the tool built in this work, we stay generic by creating a generic filter object that could be extended according to any specific requirement, and by letting developer create any kind of ordering criteria. These auxiliary patterns are also similar to the current available collection of pattern-catalogues in the HCI domain [7, 16].

Population

A population unit is an abstraction defined for representing set of elements. Typically, populations are implemented as lists or arrays.

Master/Detail

The Master/Detail pattern is illustrated in Figure 1. It is the most interesting pattern to present because it combines the concepts defined previously: the Master part, located on the left of Figure 1, consists of a Population unit, which can also be combined with filters and ordering criterion. The Detail part, on the right, can be any graphical component required for presenting the details of the selected element of the list. In the framework presented in the next section, we still stay generic so that any user-defined component can be a member of the list: even non-trivial elements are allowed. Similarly, the detail can be any specific component, even a nested Master/Detail structure.

Android style guidelines

Developing on Android means creating and using Activities, which correspond to the "windows" of the applications on desktop computers. Although this mechanism is aimed at allowing modular designs, it should be used with parsimony because activities are *stacked* in the system. The end-user can navigate between activities by pressing the *Back* button of his device. Consequently, minimizing the amount of activities started is a main goal of our framework.

Generally, and similarly to desktop applications, we have to keep the interactions between the user and the system as clear as possible in order to not create unnecessary confusion. This property has to be enforced on Android system because devices with this operating system, OS, could have neither physical keyboard nor mouse for navigating.

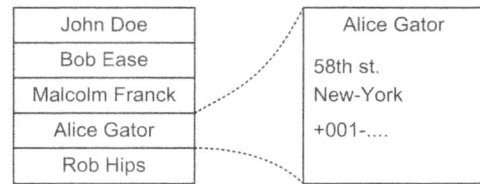

Figure 1. Master Detail.

Therefore, we try to keep the interactions limited to simple "click" actions and to predefined components (e.g. instead of entering the date manually, a widget should be used). The last guideline is more a recommendation on the Android philosophy which tends to ensure that only the essential information are shown, with the least superfluous data possible. Unlike for desktop environment, there is no free-space on the left and the right of wide screens for presenting additional and non-essential data. This observation has to be taken in consideration while conceiving graphical user interfaces.

MANDROID: A JAVA FRAMEWORK FOR IMPLEMENTING THE MASTER/DETAIL PATTERN

The purpose of this paper is not to compare different environments that generate GUIs for mobile devices, but rather to see how patterns for desktop (implementation in OlivaNova [10]) could be transferred to another system for other platform at what cost. In addition, the usability of resulting GUIs is work to be examined. Then, one result of this work is a Java framework called MandroiD. It is targeted for implementing interfaces through the Master/Detail pattern. Its name simply represents a combination of the initials of the pattern name with the android word. The architecture of the classes composing the framework is shown in Figure 2.

LayoutProvider

We start by defining an abstraction whose purpose is to declare a common behavior for displaying complex graphical object representation. We call this class `LayoutProvider` and define a method `getLayout()` that should be called by the interface creation procedure. Thanks to this class, we are able to define any kind of complex layout objects, and to reuse them in the remainder of the framework, in composite elements. A `View` is an Android object referencing graphical component. An `Activity` corresponds to a *window* of the application, it is needed because the definition of the `getLayout()` method in the subclasses generally build components that all require this reference when they are created. For instance, a user-component providing a date-chooser in a white rectangle block could be implemented as a `LayoutProvider`.

Population

The next brick of the framework is the `Population` class. It is used for representing a *list* of graphical elements to the user, and therefore it extends the `LayoutProvider` class. A list is composed of zero to many `ListElement` objects which are aimed at storing pairs of graphical elements and actions that are triggered when the element is clicked. The next brick of the framework is the `Population` class.

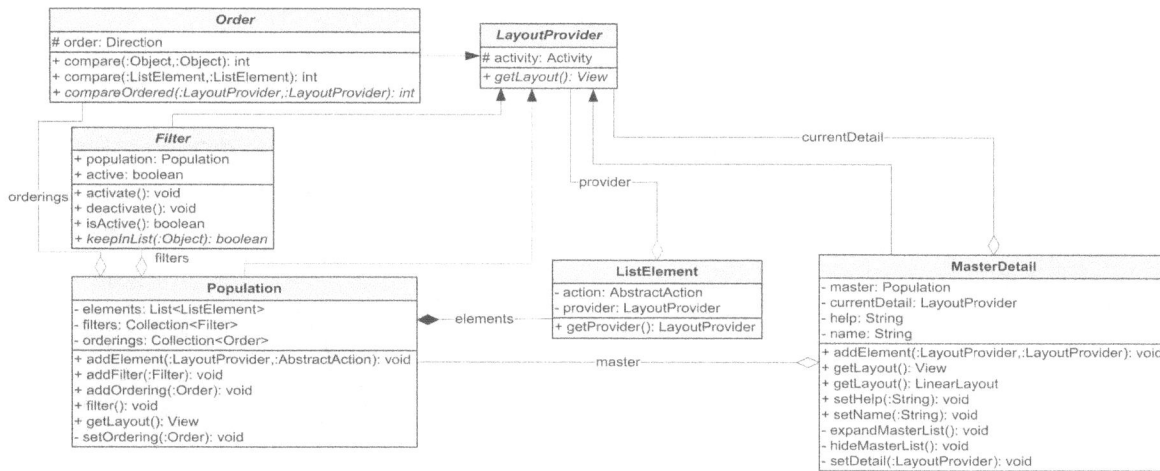

Figure 2. The UML Class Diagram of Mandoid.

It is used for representing a *list* of graphical elements to the user, and therefore it extends the `LayoutProvider` class. A list is composed of zero to many `ListElement` objects which are aimed at storing pairs of graphical elements and actions that are triggered when the element is clicked.

Filters and Orderings

Filters and ordering criteria can be attached to populations through `Filter` and `Order` objects, respectively.They both provide layouts in order to be presented to the user, for activation and deactivation They are *abstract* classes, and consequently concrete filters have to be defined according to the needs of the application. Defining a new filter means implementing the `keepInList()` method which returns `true` if the given element should stay in the list, and `false` otherwise. Defining ordering criteria can be done by extending the `Order` class and implementing the `compareOrdered()` method. Once filters and ordering critera are attached to populations with the `addFilter()` and `addOrdering()` methods, the framework manages their display, their activation (through user-input) and deactivation.

Master/Detail

The most relevant point to present is the `MasterDetail` class. This class manages the display of elements according to the Master/Detail pattern which has been described in the previous section. A `MasterDetail` is defined, among others, by a `Population` which corresponds to the *master* part, and by a `LayoutProvider` corresponding to the *detail* part. The most interesting thing comes from the type of the detail part, which can be any `LayoutProvider` object, including a nested `MasterDetail`. The framework can then handle (potentially) infinite recursion. Pairs of master elements and corresponding details can be added with the `addElement()` method which is responsible of inserting the element in the list, and of creating the event handler that will update the detail part when the element is selected by the user.

The `expandMasterList()` and `hideMasterList()` are used internally for replacing the population by an "*expand*" control, in order to avoid the graphical structure becoming

too big because of several nested master-details. In this section, we presented the internal architecture of the framework. The next section presents a case study application relying on MandroiD.

A DETAILED CAR REPOSITORY

For this case study, we built a basic application which takes advantage of our framework, MandroiD, for conceiving its graphical UI. The purpose of the application is to provide detailed information describing the configuration of each model of car of a dealer. The underlying intension is to be used by potential buyers who are interested in exploring all the details of their future car. On a strictly graphical point of view, the first screen of the application is the one asking the user to choose a dealer. Each screen contents follow general ergonomic rules [4]:

1. Elements of a window have to be align.
2. Create a screen balanced.
3. Unicity of elements provides better overview.
4. Insert regularity and harmony in the way of a set ordered elements from a central point.

The relevant patterns for this first step are the Master/Detail and the Order ones. First, the user is able to sort alphabetically the brands and, secondly, when a brand is selected, the detail (i.e. the next step of the car configuration) appears. If the user wants to sort the models in descending order, the result is in Figure 4.A.

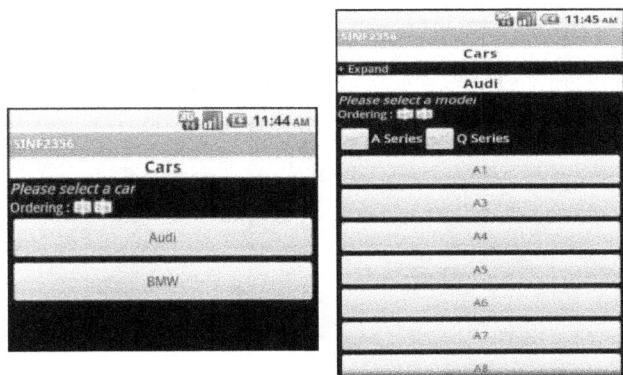

Figure 3. Dealer selection (3.A) - Model selection (3.B)

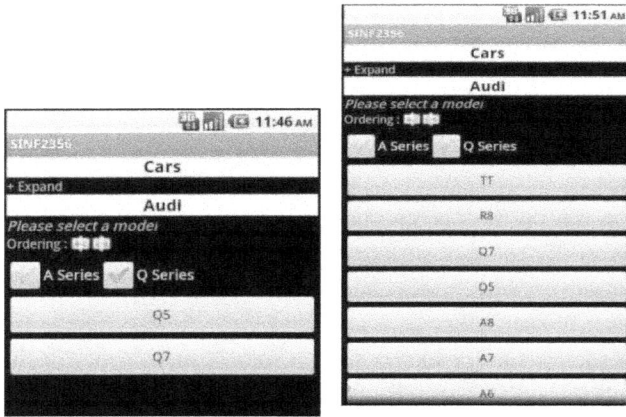

**Figure 4. Model selection: DESC order (4.A)
-filtering (4.B)**

Then, the user has to select a model of car represented by standard button of Android System. Basically, this step is implemented the same way as the previous one, using Master/Detail and ordering, but it also contains the Filter pattern. The latter is used, in this case, to keep only a specific branch among the different models (i.e. the population). For instance, if the user selects the "Q Series" checkbox (see on Figure 4.B).

Once the model is selected, the resulting detail concerns the selection of the body style of the car. This step uses a nested Master/Detail pattern. Therefore, it is not illustrated. Next, the user can specify the options and the color that s/he wants as shown on the Figure 5.A. The color and options buttons (i.e. masters) render the same kind of view (i.e. detail) when clicked. So, we only focus on the "Options" one. Typically, the detail of this button is a list of options, which, once again, use the Master/Detail pattern. When an option is selected, a screen allowing the user to select it appears.

To get back to the options list, the "+ Expand" link can be clicked. This link is present each time the Master/Detail pattern is used in order to get back to the master. Finally, a preview of the car is available.

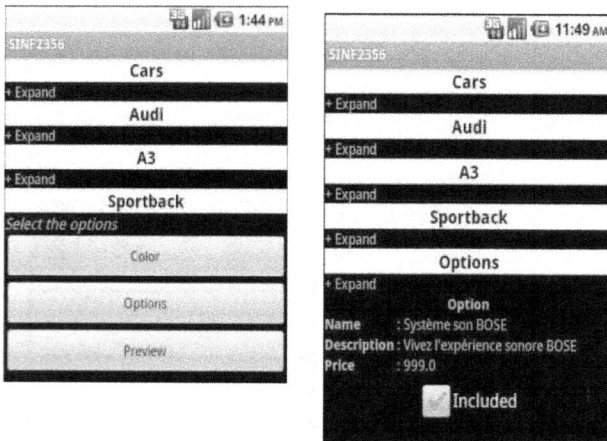

Figure 5. Options selection (5.A)-Option inclusion (5.B)

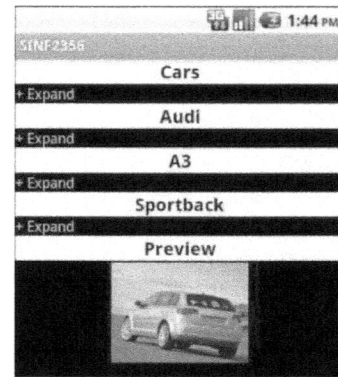

Figure 6. Preview

On a technical point of view, the filling of the application is done automatically thanks to our XML parser compatible with Android. Indeed, all packages available in standard Java are not part of the Android SDK and we had to develop a tool to help us parsing textual data in order to make the application more flexible. In this case, the missing package was *javax.xml*.

Thanks to the developed tool, the data is fetched from a XML-file and then presented on the user interface. This strategy enables to update the data about cars and even add new models and/or brands (without having to recompile the application). The idea behind the algorithm is the following: each time we meet a node in the XML-file we check its value and create the corresponding elements with the attributes specified in the XML-file. Example: a node with value "model" causes the creation of a Master element. Every node that follows and whose value is different from "model" concerns the model previously created (we go through the XML-file line by line). Then, depending on the values of the next nodes, masters and details elements are created and added to previous elements. If the value is equal to "ordering" or "filter", the corresponding patterns are initialized on the population of the appropriate master. This XML parser helped us to maintain our application clean and well structured. Those two points are very important to enforce the quality of the user interface and to efficiently work in team.

STATISTICAL ANALYSIS

This statistical analysis is based on the Post-Study System Usability Questionnaire (PSSUQ) [5]. This method provides a set of questions (see Table 1) that users have to answer after processing our case scenario [17]. Each question consists of a 5-point Likert scale [6]. The questions are grouped in 5 categories:

- Usability of the system (SYSUSE)
- Quality of the information (INFOQUAL)
- Quality of the interaction (INTERQUAL)
- Overall of the system (OVERALL)
- Ergonomy (ERGONOMY)

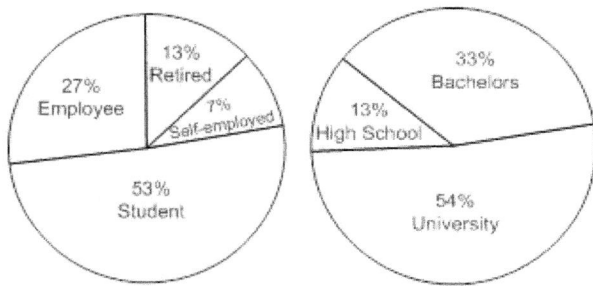

Figure 7. Occupation of testers (7.A)
- Level of studies of testers (7.B)

The scenario is the following:

1. Find the options available on Audi Q7.
2. Look at the beautiful shape of Audi A5 Sportback.
3. What is the price of the Audi TT Roadster's GPS?
4. What are the colors available of BMW serie 1?

For this analysis, we did not take all the questions of PSSUQ as-is because they were not applicable for our application. Each question has to be answered with an evaluation number from 1 to 7. 1 means: "I totally disagree" and 7 means: "I totally agree". PSSUQ is accurate because the questions it provides are suitable for scenario-based usability test. To collect the data that serve to this analysis, we create first a set of action items that users have to do, and then ask them to answer to question set. The testers we found are friends or family of us. We found 15 peoples, 53% of them are woman and 47% are man. Figure 7.A and Figure 7.B show the current occupation of testers as well as their level of education.

As a result, we can see that the set of testers are mainly student but other categories are represented as well. We can also put out that our testers have high level of study. Figure 8 shows the results of the answers of the testers.

The first observation is that the average score of every category is high. The master details pattern is interesting while programming on mobile device. Nevertheless, the standard deviation of the fourth first categories is big because our application needs to be improved with new features. The standard deviation of ERGONOMY is not high though, thus suggesting that participants are generally satisfied concerning the ergonomy of the application.

This is one of the most important observations because it shows that our implementation of nested master/details does not result in losing the user in complex hierarchies, thanks to the "expand" mechanism which keeps the "path" of his current location clearly visible at any time.

This was challenging because of the limited screen-size of the devices. The black background behind white texts may also be discussed, but that is the default configuration for applications on Android systems. This analysis showed that it did not confuse any user.

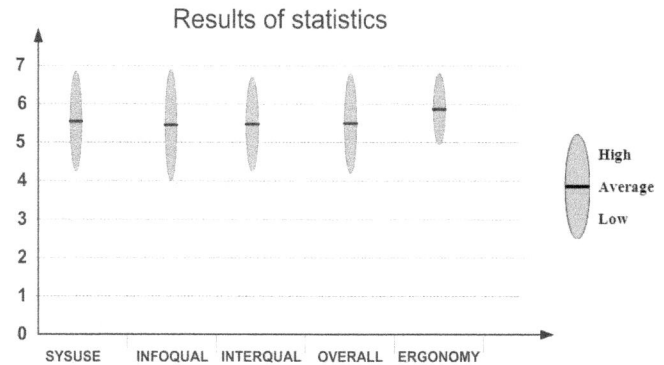

Figure 8. Results of statistics

CONCLUSION

During this work, we explored some existing design patterns and adapted them to the criteria of the mobile devices running on Android systems. This paper is aimed at determining to what extent a java framework could support automated generation of graphical UIs or mobile devices based on pattern approach.

The main contribution of this work is a framework called MandroiD, which supports generative patterns for mobile devices. It provides specific constructs for building three commonly used patterns; the most impressive is the Master/Detail because it introduces recursive structure in graphical interfaces. The underlying problem was the limitations of general mobile devices, which have a small screen on which a minimal set of information is available at any time. We achieve the goal of minimizing the accessible information set thanks to an adequate use of "reducing" and "expanding" controls of the list, so that the user keeps the focus on the part of the application s/he is using.

We also proved that the framework is usable in practice, firstly by providing an application taking advantage of it, and secondly with the interface evaluation part which shown that although some points could be improved, the implemented patterns are convenient for being used by most of the users.

The future work can be to extend the evaluation with a larger community of developers using the framework. This evaluation will show their feeling on development practices with this framework and any suggestion to improve it. Another future work can be a comparison of different other implementation approach of Mandroid on other frameworks or systems with an evaluation of their performances.

ACKNOWLEDGMENTS
The authors would like to thank L. Carlier, Y. Hanson, J. Janssens, D. Jeusette, and A. Moulai for implementing Mandroid and for testing it with various users. Our thanks also go to all the volunteers that filled in the surveys

303

Question ID	Question statement	Statistics per questions				
		Average	Median	Average of deviations	Standard deviation	Confidence
1	Overall, I am satisfied with how easy it is to use this system	5,67	6,00	0,84	1,11	0,56309217
2	It was simple to use this system.	5,40	6,00	0,91	1,12	0,567407115
3	I could effectively complete the tasks and scenarios using this system	5,20	5,00	1,15	1,47	0,745719046
4	I was able to complete the tasks and scenarios quickly using this system.	5,80	6,00	0,80	1,08	0,54772223
5	I was able to efficiently complete the tasks and scenarios using this system.	5,47	6,00	0,97	1,19	0,600812099
6	I felt comfortable using this system.	5,27	5,00	1,22	1,53	0,776168992
7	It was easy to learn to use this system.	5,80	6,00	0,69	1,01	0,513239047
8	I believe I could become productive quickly using this system.	5,47	6,00	0,97	1,19	0,600812099
9	Whenever I made a mistake using the system, I could recover easily and quickly	5,33	6,00	1,24	1,54	0,780868343
10	The information (on-line help, on-screen messages and other documentation) provided with the system was clear	5,67	6,00	0,89	1,05	0,529610677
11	It was easy to find the information I needed	5,40	6,00	0,99	1,18	0,598778888
12	The information provided for the system was easy to understand	5,13	5,00	1,21	1,51	0,761897047
13	The information was effective in helping me complete the tasks and scenarios.	5,07	5,00	1,27	1,67	0,843916033
14	The organization of information on the system screens was clear.	5,60	6,00	0,93	1,24	0,62858689
15	The interface of this system was pleasant.	5,27	5,00	0,95	1,22	0,618810449
16	I liked using the interface of this system.	5,53	5,00	1,10	1,25	0,630523989
17	This system has all the functions and capabilities I expect it to have.	5,47	5,00	0,90	1,06	0,536474169
18	Overall, I am satisfied with this system.	5,07	5,00	0,89	1,16	0,588507476
19	I always know where I am and how to go where I want	5,93	6,00	0,63	0,88	0,447213328
20	Colors are chosen in order to let information visible	5,60	6,00	0,69	0,83	0,419057927

Table 1 : Questions and scores

REFERENCES

1. Abrahão, S., Iborra, E., and Vanderdonckt, J. "Usability Evaluation of User Interfaces Generated with a Model-Driven Architecture Tool." In E. Law, E. Hvannberg, and G. Cockton (eds.), *Maturing Usability: Quality in Software, Interaction and Value*. Vol. 10, Springer, London, 2008, pp. 3-32.

2. Aquino, N., Vanderdonckt, J., Condori-Fernández, N., Dieste, Ó., and Pastor, Ó., "Usability Evaluation of Multi-Device/Platform User Interfaces Generated by Model-Driven Engineering." In *Proc. ESEM'2010*-ACM Press, New York, 2010, Article #30.

3. Erik G. Nilsson. "Design patterns for user interface for mobile applications.", *Adv. Eng. Softw.* 40, 12 (December 2009), Oslo, Norway, pp. 1318-1328.

4. Galitz, W., "The essential guide to user interface design, an introduction to GUI design principles and techniques." Wiley Computer Publishing, Indianapolis, Inc., 1997

5. Lewis, J. R. "*IBM* Computer Usability Satisfaction Questionnaires: Psychometric Evaluation and Instructions for Use." IBM, Human Factors Group, Boca Raton, FL, 1993.

6. Likert, R. "A technique for the measurement of attitudes." *Archives of Psychology 22*, 140 (1932), pp. 1–55.

7. Mobile UI Pattern (04/05/2012) http://mobile-patterns.com/

8. Molina, P.J., Meliá, S., and Pastor, O. "Just-UI: A User Interface Specification Model." In *Proc. of CADUI'2002*. Kluwer Academics, Dordrecht, 2002, pp. 63-74.

9. Molina, P.J., Meliá, S., and Pastor, O. "User Interface Conceptual Patterns." In *Proc DSV-IS'2002*. Springer-Verlag, Berlin, 2002, pp. 159-172.

10. Molina, P.J. "User interface generation with OlivaNova model execution system." In *Proc. of IUI'2004*. ACM Press, New York, 2004, pp. 358-359.

11. Mori, G., Paternò, F., Santoro, C. "Design and Development of Multidevice User Interfaces through Multiple Logical Descriptions." *IEEE Transactions on Software Engineering* IEEE Press Piscataway, NJ, USA, 30, 8 (2004), 507–520.

12. Pastor, O. "Generating User Interfaces From Conceptual Models: A Model-Transformation Based Approach." In *Proc. CADUI'2006*. Kluwer Academics, Dordrecht, 2006, pp. 1-14.

13. Pastor, O. and Molina, J.C. "MDA in Practice: a Software Production Environment Based on Conceptual Modeling." Springer-Verlag, Berlin, 2007.

14. Vanderdonckt, J. "Model-Driven Engineering of User Interfaces: Promises, Successes, and Failures." In S. Buraga and I. Juvina (eds.), *Proc. ROCHI'2008, (Iasi, 18-19 September 2008)*. Matrix ROM, Bucarest, 2008, pp. 1–10.

15. Vanderdonckt, J. and Montero, F., "Generative Pattern-Based Design of User Interfaces", *Proc.* PEICS'2010

16. Van Welie pattern catalogue (05/03/2012): http://www.welie.com/patterns/

17. Wohlin, C., Runeson, P., Host, M., Ohlsson, M.C., Regnell, B., Wesslén, A. Experimentation in Software Engineering: An Introduction. Volume 6 of International Series in Software Engineering. Springer, 2000.

A Pattern-based Approach to Support the Design of Multi-Platform User Interfaces of Information Systems

Nguyen Thanh-Diane

Université catholique de Louvain- Louvain School of Management-OIS
Louvain Interaction Laboratory, Place des Doyens 1 - Louvain la Neuve – Belgium
thanh-diane.nguyen@uclouvain.be

ABSTRACT

This PhD thesis is focused on a pattern approach for designing multi-platform user interfaces. The pattern approach is applied on the complete user interface (UI) development process. UI patterns can be used to improve the usability and cycle-life development. To achieve a good quality of software development, UI patterns related to ergonomic context can be used in unification of models to support the UI development process.

UI Patterns of the OO-Method are introduced in the whole model driven process of UI in order to obtain different UIs in the Final User Interface (FUI) level including specific platforms. In using different patterns on other devices, the thesis analyses the derivation of up-to-date UIs with the application of the built ergonomic guide and extended patterns. A comparative study of these different FUIs built in different contexts is necessary to show how difficult it is to adapt the different patterns on variety platforms.

Author Keywords

Patterns; Multi-Platform; User Interfaces.

General Terms

Human Factors; Design; Experimentation; Evaluation.

ACM Classification Keywords

D.2.2 [**Software Engineering**]: Design Tools and Techniques – *Modules and interfaces; user interfaces.*
H.5.2 [**Information interfaces and presentation**]: User Interfaces – *graphical user interfaces, user interface management system (UIMS).*

INTRODUCTION

User interfaces (UIs) with good usability must be developed to accommodate different types of users and devices in changing environments [6]. Patterns are a solution to common problems in a specified design context [9,15,16]. Indeed, patterns provide an advanced concept of reuse and a more aggregated perspective in the UI process [7]. UI pattern sets up the best design practices from distilled experience from real life [14]. Previous works used patterns in the UI development process [13] but are not focused on multi-platform and ergonomic contexts. The objective of this PhD Thesis is to develop a framework that considers in a general and systematic way the UI pattern development cycle. For this purpose, a certain level of abstraction with respect to code is desired, such as in Cameleon Framework (Figure 1) or in OMG's framework (CIM, PIM, PSM) for developing multi-target UIs [4].

General patterns with ergonomic guidelines on multi-platform context are introduced in a XML-compliant format. These guidelines are stored in a specific database and compose the ergonomic guide. They comprise two abstraction levels: a generic one (adapted on multi-platform) and a specific one (based on specific platform). Our objective is also to extend the ergonomic guide and its application in developing more different FUIs, based on the code level in Model-Driven Engineering (MDE), on a variety of devices. Therefore, this thesis also extends the conceptual model of patterns.

In generating different FUIs based on the UI pattern approach, this thesis aims at demonstrating the performances of the ergonomic guide related to multi-platform-based patterns with different users and the extension of the usability UI patterns related to information systems (ISs).

Section 2 of this paper presents the motivations; Section 3 describes the related works; Section 4 explains the contributions of this research and Section 5 describes the conclusion.

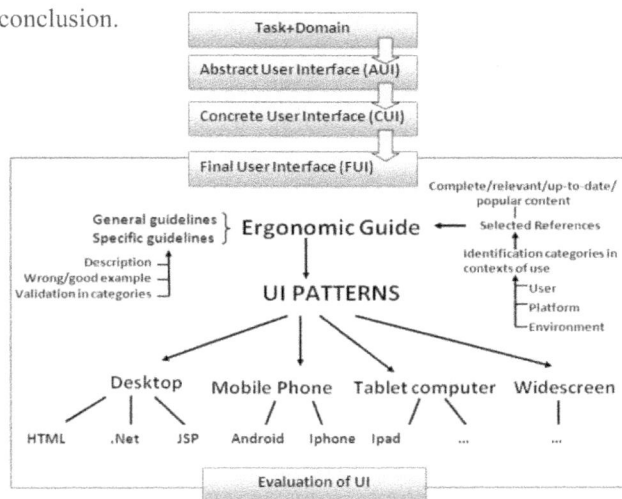

Figure 1: UI patterns in the whole UI process

MAIN MOTIVATIONS

A huge variety of platforms are currently available. The average time spent on them rises constantly. Time spent in designing UI (on average, 48% of the coding efforts are spent in interactive human-computer application and the average time spent on different phases of design and construction is estimated between 40% and 50% [2]) represents a large part in the development cycle of an application, particularly in terms of pure development and maintenance, even for application of a "traditional" single target platform.

Objectives of the interface development based on models allow to:

1. extend development environments ;
2. design contexts and the implementation of software, to improve the portability and adaptation of interfaces;
3. have a solid development cycle;
4. integrate the development of usability studies (to promote the usability of interfaces for their users and to have a performance measure of the software quality [6]);
5. specify the UI at a high level of abstraction independently of the implementation.

RELATED WORK

The first part of the thesis consists of being aware of the problem context, understanding the current highest level of development of techniques, scientific fields about the designing of UI based on pattern approach.

The emergence of new devices and services brings a new dynamic in UI development. The multitude of interaction devices has created a diversification of environment interactions and an increase of multi-profile. Furthermore, the information is extremely dynamic. Therefore, UIs have to adapt to the variation of context (users U, platforms P, and environment E). Patterns are a solution to common problems in a specified design context [9,16]. Using a pattern approach allows to design UIs by a set of models (the UI model-based development) [7] and to provide knowledge on different fields. For instance, "Using patterns to clearly and succinctly describe particular workplaces, in order to understand possible impacts of new technologies [12]."

[17] described a developed method for implementing GUI based on generative patterns . This method used the Pattern Language Markup Language (PLML) applied to support designing patterns. UI patterns extended from PLML had been represented in an UML diagram class (Figure 2). This representation implies UI patterns in a method involved models found in UI development life cycle (based on the Cameleon Framework [4]). The multi-platform and ergonomic context is limited in this content.

In [14], code generators based on usability patterns are the results of the JUST-UI concept. This approach considers the conceptual model in the Object Oriented Method, OO-Method.

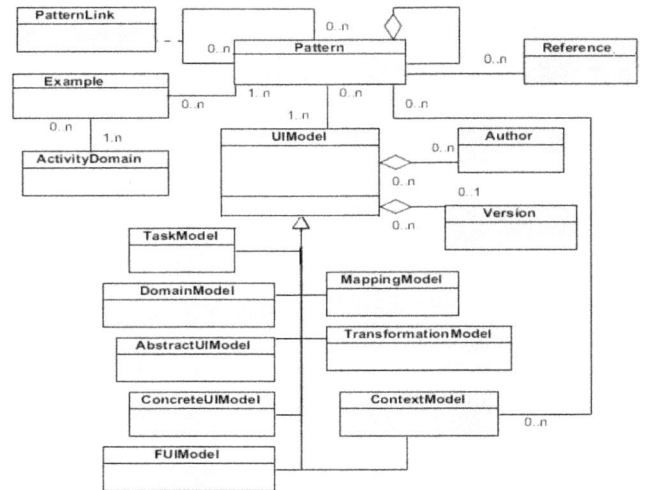

Figure 2: UI patterns extended from PLML represented in UML

The conceptual model is structured in four elements: Object Model, Dynamic Model, Functional Model and Presentation Model. This fourth component specifies the issue on how the users interact with the system. In the Presentation Model, the set of conceptual patterns are called interaction units. In addition to the execution of a service and to the manipulation of an (or a set of) object(s), these interaction units provide frequent scenarios in which we can find an interaction between the user and the system without an up-to-date ergonomic rules on variety contexts (U, P, E).

Another tool that supports the application of patterns during the IS development is demonstrated by [8]. In this work, task models with patterns and pattern-supported model transformations are described. Although, patterns are used to transform models in an interactive way, it is limited to implementation to one single platform.

To know current ergonomic context, selected guidelines were integrated using a specific template in a database integrated, DESTINE, a software-based ergonomic evaluation of websites. The approach used in this software is a language called XML-enabled GDL (Guideline Definition Language) [11]. This software evaluates web site in ergonomic conform. It adopts a methodology for evaluating the inter-usability that allows therefore to ensure the usefulness and usability of products for the benefit of simultaneous users and organizations.

COMPUTATIONAL FRAMEWORK
Shortcoming and Requirements

The literature reviews are limited for some reasons:

1. **Specialization of research**. The current works about patterns are constrained to one or some levels of the UI process and do not consider the integration of UI patterns in the entire process. Most of pattern works derivate only from the task model.

2. **Lack of conjunction and consistency.** Content information is described in model fragments.

Moreover, some links between other levels of the UI Process are missing.

3. **Lack of structure.** Current pattern catalogues are not correctly structured. They do not cover the whole domain of dependent and independent modeling and design problems.

4. **Limitation of technological space.** Some works consider only of UI patterns in only one platform.

5. **Lack of ergonomic approach.** Tools to support pattern assisted design and development exist but the ergonomic aspects should be detailed in an enough expressive way to give rise at applicability.

6. **Limitation of the context.** The context (U, P, E) is necessary to take all problems into consideration.

7. **Lack of evaluation of the pattern performance.** "Most of pattern languages/libraries have not been proved if their solutions are suitable to address the identified problems."[3]

In order to address these shortcomings, improvements are required:

1. Integration of UI patterns in the whole UI development process
2. Consolidation of methods and techniques
3. Appropriate organizational structures
4. The overall coverage of available technological space
5. Designing UI pattern within ergonomic context
6. Context-awareness to design patterns
7. Validation of UI patterns with an up-to-date ergonomic guide

The result of [3] explains how current tools on patterns are easily accessible to the developers but new evaluation methods are needed to prove the usability of patterns. This evaluation is one objective of the thesis. Indeed, in the comparative study, all extracted FUIs from patterns and ergonomic guides designing from each level of UI process based on UI descriptive language are compared. According to [1], languages based on models offer new opportunities for the validation of rules of ergonomics, as they include information not present in the final structure of UI.

INNOVATIVE APPROACH AND RELEVANCE OF TOPIC

The contribution of this thesis to its research field consists of an improvement in the IS life-cycle. The usability patterns are used to have an attractive view to end-user platforms as well as an ergonomic aspect. The objective is to have a validated model based on various quality factors (e.g., QUIMERA [9]) and resources and to optimize the schedule of developers and project managers. Therefore, the project enables the improvement of research management in IS to prevent changes, management errors and quality management of UI on different platforms and to improve time and effort of designers and developers on the life-cycle development of software.

METHODOLOGY

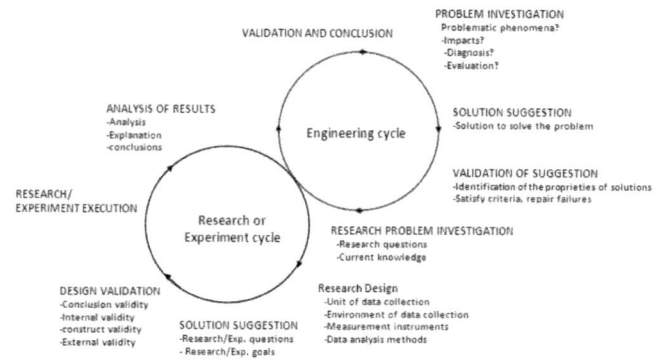

Figure 3: Engineering Methodology adapted to this thesis

The research design used in this work is based on the popular "Requirements Engineering Research Methodology" from [18]. The methodology of this thesis uses two cycles. The first one specifies the main purpose and uses a cyclic way, the engineering process, to fix objectives, to investigate, to provide feedback and continuous evaluation. The second one is more focused on the research/experiment process.

In the Engineering cycle, after the identification of the problem and the suggestion of a general solution, the investigation part consists of the identification of state of the art information, current methods and techniques of patterns in UI design and ergonomic guidelines. Relevant information on ergonomic guidelines is inserted in a specific database and constitutes the ergonomic guide, DESTINE [11]. This last element and information of patterns are necessary to develop UI patterns of the OO-Method in the whole UI process (see on Figure 1). For instance, the thesis evaluates a master/detail pattern described in Just-UI concept. On the first time, this pattern implements task and domain model merged with the patterns of [5] corresponded to problems. Then, different frameworks of patterns from AUI are created. Each AUI framework designs a CUI based on specific platform (for example, one CUI on Desktop computer and another one on Mobile Phone). Then, the Patterns based on the ergonomic guide are applied in FUI. In the FUI level, we can find several usability guidelines in the ergonomic guide aiming at helping developers to develop user interfaces with good usability and to adapt it into an explicit context.

Currently, several studies suggest a list of guidelines which may be incomplete due to a lack of illustrations, definitions, simplicity, structure or because the guidelines are not adapted to the current situation of the new devices. The ergonomic guide, inserted in a specific database, is built in order to avoid these scenarios and to provide a support to facilitate the development of interface on multi-platforms.

The properties of FUIs involved different platforms and range of possibilities still need to be validated. For example, the current technology enables the problem to be solved. The application of researches with experiments will be measured and compared with the initial suggestion of the problem, a feedback about all the engineering process will be defined at the end. The conclusion will be the identification of the pursued objectives, contribution, limitation, and future activities.

The experiment cycle begins with current works on technics and the appropriate design of experimentations. Experimentation based on the qualitative research measures the efficient of ergonomic guide and the most popular patterns by end users. The evaluation process, by using a quantitave methodology, makes sure that the building framework is in line with the UI regarding usability patterns for multi-platform interfaces.

CONCLUSION

The history of pattern applications and language is limited by its lack of up-to-date ergonomic approach and its context (U, P, E). This proposal represents UI patterns of the OO-method, supported by an up-to-date ergonomic approach involved in the UI design process based on a uniform modeling language. This language building on XML-compliant format supports the transition between different models such as task, domain, AUI, CUI, FUI, context model and mappings between them. User requirements are involved in each stages of the project in order to maximize ergonomic context and consistency. The usability of an interface determines the performance of the user. Evaluations and study cases are planned in order to depict the performance (the strength of evidence) of UI patterns contained in a variety of FUI prototypes adapted to different contexts. An evaluation of the ergonomic guide involved in the UI pattern design is also planned in the performance study.

REFERENCES

1. Atterer, R. and Schmidt, A., "Adding Usability to Web Engineering Models and Tools". *Proc. of the 5th International Conference on Web Engineering*, Springer, Sydney, Australia, July 2005. pp.36-41

2. Bayle E., Bellamy R., Casaday G., Erickson T., Fincher S., and Grinter B. "Putting it all together: towards a Pattern Language for Interaction Design." CHI'97, New York, NY, USA, vol.30, 1(1998), pp.17-24.

3. Breiner, K., Seissler, M., Meixner, G., Forbrig, P., Seffah, A., and Klöckner, K., "PEICS: towards HCI patterns into engineering of interactive systems" *Proc. of PEICS '2010*, ACM Press, July 2010

4. Calvary, G., Coutaz, J., Thevenin, D., Limbourg, Q., Bouillon, L., and Vanderdonckt, J., "A Unifying Reference Framework for Multi-Target User Interfaces", *Interacting with Computers*, 15(3), 2003, pp. 289–308.

5. Coad, P., North, D., and Mayfield, M., "Strategies and Patterns Handbook: Hypertext Edition", Version 2.1, Prentice Hall, Object International, Inc. 1997

6. Folmer E. and Bosch J., "Usability Patterns in Software Architecture", *Proc. of Workshop on SE-HCI*, Greece, 2003, pp. 61–68.

7. Forbig P. and Lämmel R., "Programming with Patterns", *Technology of Object-Oriented Languages and Systems*, 2000. *Proc.34th TOOLS 2000*, Santa Barbara, CA, USA pp.159-170

8. Forbrig,P. and Wolff, A., "Different kinds of pattern support for interactive systems", PEICS '10: *Proceedings of the 1st International Workshop on Pattern-Driven Engineering of Interactive Computing Systems*, Berlin, Germany, July 2010, pp.36-39

9. Garcia Frey, A., Céret, E., Dupuy-Chessa, S., and Calvary, G. "QUIMERA: a quality metamodel to improve design rationale." In *Proc. of the 3rd ACM SIGCHI symposium on Engineering interactive computing systems* (EICS '11). Pisa, Italy, ACM, 2011, pp.265-270.

10. Javahery H., "Usability Pattern-Oriented Design: Maximizing Reusability of Pattern Languages over the web",Faculty of Engineering and Computer Science Concordia University,(2002) http://www.cusec.net/archives/2002/javahery.pdf

11. Mariage, C., Vanderdonckt, J., Beirekdar, A., Noirhomme, M. "DESTINE: outil d'aide à l'évaluation de l'ergonomie des sites web", IHM 2004 *Proc. of the 16th conference on Association Francophone d'Interaction Homme-Machine*, Namur, Belgium, ACM, 2002

12. Myers, B. "Survey on User Interface Ace Programming." *Proc.* CHI'92, Monterey, California, Addison Wesley, 1992, pp.195-202.

13. Paterno F., "Model-based tools for pervasive usability", *Interacting with computers*, Elsevier, May 2005, vol.17, Issue 3, pp. 291-315

14. Pedro J. Molina, Santiago M., and Pastor O., "User Interface Conceptual Patterns", *Lecture Notes in Computer Science*, Springer 2002, Vol.2545/2002, pp. 159-172

15. Radeke, F. and Forbrig, P. (2008): "Patterns in Task-based Modeling of User Interfaces", Winckler, M., Johnson, H., Palanque, P. (Eds.): *Proc. of 6th International Workshop on Task Models and Diagrams for User Interface Design*, TAMODIA 2007, Toulouse, France, Springer, Berlin/Heidelberg, 4849, 2008

16. Van Welie M. and Van Der Veer, G. C., "Pattern Languages in Interaction Design: Structure and Organization", *In Proc. INTERACT '03,* Zurich, Switzerlan, 2003, pp. 527-534

17. Vanderdonckt, J. and Montero, F., "Generative Pattern-Based Design of User Interfaces", *Proc. of 1st International Workshop on Pattern-Driven Engineering of Interactive Computing*, PEICS'2010

18. Wieringa, R. "Requirements Engineering research methodology. Principles and practice." 2008, (18/10/2011), http://wwwhome.cs.utwente.nl/~roelw/DesignScienceMethodology-handout.pdf

Addressing Multi-platform Collaborative Sketching

Ugo Braga Sangiorgi
Louvain Interaction Laboratory, Universite catholique de Louvain
Pl. Place des Doyens, 1 – B-1348 Louvain-la-Neuve (Belgium)
ugo.sangiorgi@uclouvain.be

ABSTRACT

Prototypes are essential tools for design activities for they allow designers to realize and evaluate ideas in early stages of the development. Sketching is a primary tool for constructing prototypes of interactive systems and has been used in developing low-fidelity prototypes for a long time. The computational support for sketching has been receiving a recurrence of interest in the last 45 years and again nowadays within the mobile web context, where there are diverse devices to be considered.

The research reported on this paper aims at addressing issues on multi-platform collaborative sketching using a prototyping tool for user interfaces. The tool was built to aid the investigation on how designers sketch using many different devices and collaborate using their sketches during design sessions.

Author Keywords

Electronic sketching; Multi-platform systems; Collaborative design; Prototyping.

ACM Classification Keywords

H.5.2 User Interfaces: Prototyping

INTRODUCTION

A prototype is a working model built to develop and test design ideas. In User Interface design, prototypes are essential tools for fostering discussion regarding both interface and interaction with stakeholders. Techniques such as Paper Prototyping [16] became very popular due to its' low cost and efficiency, since they are made using sketches for quick generation of prototypes.

Lately, there has been a recurrence of interest on supporting electronic sketching (i.e. sketching at electronic devices and interactive surfaces), and despite sketching *recognition* to be fairly well addressed on the literature, the adoption of electronic sketching as a *design tool* is still a challenge [7]. The current popularization of touch screen devices and the multi-platform capabilities made possible by using HTML5 might pose new opportunities for researchers to explore, for instance, how designers use sketching to prototype interfaces

for a target device by producing and testing them on the device itself.

When designing, people draw things in different ways, which allows them to also perceive the problem in new ways. People engage in a sort of 'conversation' with their sketches in a tight cycle of drawing, understanding, and interpreting [14]. When prototyping by using the target device, other elements come into play in that conversation. Nowadays, there are many devices available for designers to sketch upon [9], with different screen sizes, weight and processing capabilities; this is a fact to be addressed into contemporary sketching research.

We introduce GAMBIT (Gatherings and Meetings with Beamers and Interactive Tablets), a multi-platform system for constructing prototypes that allows the construction and testing of interfaces on the very device it is intented to run. The system was built with HTML5 and Javascript in order to run on any device with browsing capabilities, aiming at addressing multi-platform sketching support in collaborative design sessions.

In this work we define an approach that is:

1. Sketch-based - electronic sketching is supported as the main mode of interaction, it is used to quickly put ideas on an external medium, where they can be discussed, improved and stored for further reference [4];

2. Multi-platform - for it allows users to sketch using the device of their preference, and also allows the prototyping and testing of systems for a device on the very device it is intented to run;

3. Collaborative - for it focus on group sessions, allowing not only designers to sketch and discuss together, but also to include end users in the process.

SKETCHING IN USER INTERFACE DESIGN

Sketching is considered to be a powerful tool for doing design. As the findings of [5] point out, the presence of ambiguity in early stages of design broads the spectrum of solutions that are considered and tends to deliver a design of higher quality.

As for the fundamentals of sketching, Van der Lugt's work [17] conducted an experiment to analyze the functions of sketching in design, in which participants produced individual sketches and then presented them for the group for discussion. Three primary sketching functions were identified:

F1 Sketching stimulates a re-interpretive cycle in the individual designer's idea generation process: Schon and Wiggins

[13] describe design as a cyclic process of sketching, interpreting and taking the sketches further.

F2 Sketching stimulates the designers to re-interpret each other's ideas: when sketching to also discuss (as opposed to sketch for self-interpretation), the designer invites others to interpret her drawings as well. The function of inviting re-interpretation is especially relevant for the idea generation process, as re-interpretation leads to novel directions for generating ideas [17].

F3 Sketching stimulates the use of earlier ideas by enhancing their accessibility: Since it is externalized, sketching also facilitate archiving and retrieval of design information.

UI design by sketching is recognized for several proved virtues such as, but not limited to: maintaining an informal representation to foster creativity [3] [11] [10], complementarity between paper and pencil and software [1] [17], capability to take one design idea at a time and work it out in details or consider alternative designs at a time (i.e. lateral transformation [10]), ability to reveal as much usability problems as if it was a real UI [6].

In order to support sketching into UI design, we needed to analyze the process in which UI design is included. Currently, the development life cycle of interactive applications consists of a sophisticated process that does not always proceed linearly in a predefined way. The tools available for UI development are usually not focused on UI **design**, in which designers usually explore different alternatives but in UI **modeling** as a final product, where designers must attend to formal standards and notations.

There are many tools available for both modeling and design, however practitioners are currently forced to choose formal and flexible tools. Whichever they choose, they lose the advantages of the other, with attendant loss of productivity and sometimes of traceability and quality.

As the study reported [2] mentions, designers desire an intelligent whiteboard because it would not require hard mental operations while sketching during meetings and design sessions.

However, electronic sketching is still behind the classical sketching in paper, since the tool in use becomes too evident [18]. Perhaps until the gap between displays and paper are minimized, (for instance with paper-like displays[15]), this distance will continue high, hindering the designer's 'conversation'.

Calico [10] and DENIM [11] are good examples of "vanishing tools" since they keep out of the way between the designers and the problem at hand, and this can be useful especially during early design stages.

Therefore, fostering creativity is specially important since design is essentiallly a problem of *wicked nature*, i.e. the process of solving it is identical with the process of understanding it [12]. In wicked problems, the designer does not have a clear understanding of what to produce and has only a vague goal in mind in the beginning.

RESEARCH AGENDA

Electronic sketching has some important advantages over classical 'pen and paper' approach. While sketches are useful to facilitate discussions on the conceptual level, computer prototypes are useful for discussing operational and interaction issues [6]. Therefore, both aspects (raw sketches and interactive prototypes) are complementary, and a sort of hybrid approach is considered to be useful since it allows designers to explore alternative solutions for the same problem [10, 5].

The goal of this research is to advance the state of the art regarding electronic sketching usage in current design practices taking into account the diverse multi-platform context. The first step of the research is the GAMBIT system itself, as an alternative tool that explores the multi-platform context.

One important issue with currently sketch-based systems for prototyping of user interfaces is that they are *single-platform*, since they are usually made to be used on Desktop computers [11, 10], even though the prototypes are targeted at multiple devices [8].

We argue that a more complete prototyping system would allow sketching and simulation on the target device, enriching both designers' and users' experience with an interactive prototype, allowing them finally to have a richer *conversation* with the working design at hand.

The main research issues to be accounted at this research are:

Electronic sketching as a tool A designer could sketch and test user interfaces for many platforms using just a single platform such as a large sketching device (e.g. Wacom, TabletPC). However, the main benefit of sketching as a tol for prototyping is to allow us to 'see as' and 'see that' [14]. That benefit is hindered since only the size of the target device is being considered, while there are other significant factors such as weight, screen resolution, brigthness and interaction modes (e.g. multi-touch, WIMP).

How the *conversation* is perceived to change from different approaches (single-platform and multi-platform sketching)? Experiments can be conducted comparing prototypes produced with tools such as DAMASK [8] (a single-platform tool for multi-platform prototyping) and our tool.

Sketching devices as a medium Among the available devices, which of them are suitable for sketching? Given that there are many differences in terms of performance according to the device type, how users perceive the different features inherent to each device, such as *lag*?

We argue that in order to start an investigation of electronic sketching on that diverse context, an acceptable **lowest limit** for sketching rendering speed needs to be properly investigated.

Sketching Recognition Considering an eventual sketching recognition mechanism, how the different inputs delivered by the different devices differ? What kind of adaptation a sketch recognition system needs to perform in order to correctly recognize inputs from the same user on different devices?

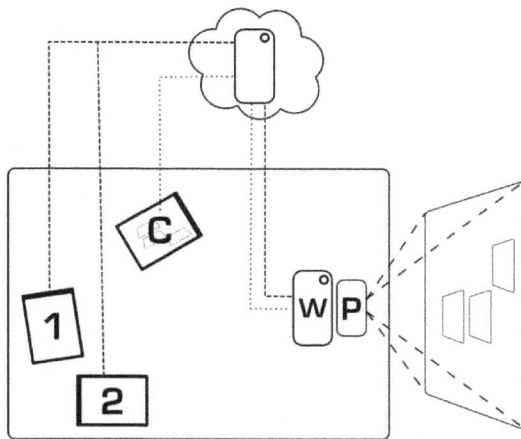

Figure 1. Physical setup of GAMBIT.

MULTI-PLATFORM SKETCHING ENVIRONMENT

The tool support for the investigation is the GAMBIT system, a distributed software environment designed to be physically deployed around a table, with tablets and a projector. It is multi-platform since it is essentially an embedded website, which might be used through a browser or through a native mobile application (i.e. a 'wrapper' application).

The system is currently developed as depicted on Figure 1: the many input devices (1 and 2 in the figure) can be tablets, mobile devices, large graphical tablets, etc. They are used by designers to sketch and submit drawings to the device representing the wall (W) showing the sketches as if they are real sheets of papers organized onto a real wall.

The wall is projected using a common projector (P) and can be controlled using a tablet, called 'control tablet' (C). The roles of the devices are interchangeable – a user might request the wall's control at any time, organizing and grouping the sketches. Since GAMBIT is a web-based system operating through a browser, the wall (W) might be a full-screen browser window opened on a desktop computer, a projection or a large interactive display.

Figure 1 (left) shows the deploy scheme of the system, with designers using different devices each around a projector in the middle. In the right part the wall shows the sketches being organized with the control tablet.

Figure 1 (right) shows a picture taken during a preliminary study with designers from one software development company. That experiment showed indications regarding designers' preferences of device types for different activities, and it is one of the expected outcomes of the tool.

The system was developed in HTML5 in order to centralize the code for different platforms. In this sense, the system can run on any device with a browser. Figure 2 (front) shows the sketching interface of the system, with a drawing area that uses HTML5 <canvas> element and Javascript routines to capture the mouse/pen/touch events.

The left part shows a toolbar that can be used to switch from

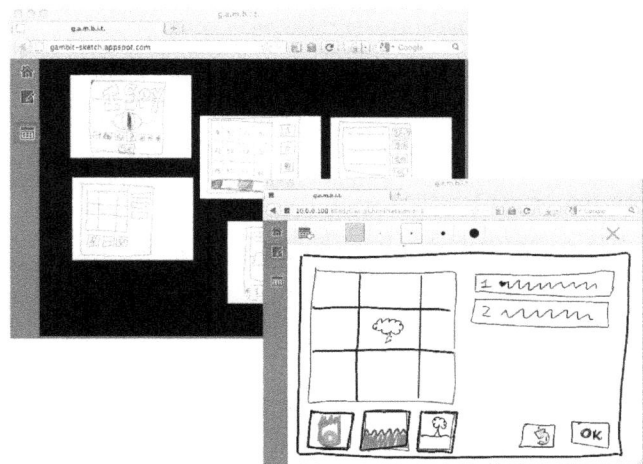

Figure 2. GAMBIT interfaces for sketch production and "Wall sharing".

sketching to control functionalities. Figure 2 (back) shows the wall being displayed, with the sketches arranged like sheets of paper that can be dragged and grouped. The black background is intentionally put in order to make only the "sheets" to be projected on the wall.

CONCLUSION

This paper introduced GAMBIT and a research agenda for investigating electronic sketching and its usage in current design practices taking into account the diverse multi-platform context.

REFERENCES

1. Bailey, B. P., and Konstan, J. A. Are informal tools better?: comparing DEMAIS, pencil and paper, and authorware for early multimedia design. In *CHI'03: Proceedings of the SIGCHI conference on Human factors in computing systems*, ACM (New York, NY, USA, 2003), 313–320.

2. Cherubini, M., Venolia, G., DeLine, R., and Ko, A. J. Let's Go to the Whiteboard: How and Why Software

Developers Use Drawings. *Proceedings of the SIGCHI conference on Human factors in computing systems - CHI '07* (2007), 557.

3. Coyette, A., and Kieffer, S. Multi-fidelity Prototyping of User Interfaces. *Ifip International Federation For Information Processing* (2007), 150–164.

4. Craft, B., and Cairns, P. Sketching sketching: outlines of a collaborative design method. In *Proceedings of the 23rd British HCI Group Annual Conference on People and Computers: Celebrating People and Technology*, British Computer Society (2009), 65–72.

5. Goel, V. "Ill-Structured Representations" for Ill-Structured Problems. In *Proceedings of the Fourteenth Annual Conference of the Cognitive Science Society*, vol. 14, Lawrence Erlbaum (1992), 130–135.

6. Johansson, M. A case study of how user interface sketches, scenarios and computer prototypes structure stakeholder meetings. *People and Computers XXI - HCI... but not as we know it: Proceedings of HCI '07* (2007).

7. Johnson, G., Gross, M. D., Hong, J., and Yi-Luen Do, E. Computational Support for Sketching in Design: A Review. *Foundations and Trends® in Human-Computer Interaction 2*, 1 (2008), 1–93.

8. Lin, J., Landay, J. A. J., Berkeley, U. C., and L, J. A. Damask: A tool for early-stage design and prototyping of multi-device user interfaces. In *In Proceedings of The 8th International Conference on Distributed Multimedia Systems (2002 International Workshop on Visual Computing)*, In In Proceedings of The 8th International Conference on Distributed Multimedia Systems (2002 International Workshop on Visual Computing (2002), 573–580.

9. MacLean, S., Tausky, D., Labahn, G., Lank, E., and Marzouk, M. Is the iPad useful for sketch input? A comparison with the Tablet PC. *EUROGRAPHICS Symposium on Sketch-Based Interfaces and Modeling* (2011).

10. Mangano, N., Baker, A., and van der Hoek, A. Calico: a prototype sketching tool for modeling in early design. In *MiSE '08: Proceedings of the 2008 international workshop on Models in software engineering*, ACM (New York, NY, USA, 2008), 63–68.

11. Newman, M., Lin, J., Hong, J., and Landay, J. DENIM: An informal web site design tool inspired by observations of practice. *Human-Computer Interaction 18*, 3 (2003), 259–324.

12. Rittel, H. Dilemmas in a general theory of planning. *Policy sciences 4*, 2 (1973), 155–169.

13. Schön, D. A. *The Reflective Practitioner: How Professionals Think in Action.* Basic Books, 1983.

14. Schon, D. A., and Wiggins, G. Kinds of seeing and their functions in designing. *Design Studies 13*, 2 (1992), 135–156.

15. Shah, J., and Brown, R. M. Towards electronic paper displays made from microbial cellulose. *Applied microbiology and biotechnology 66*, 4 (Jan. 2005), 352–5.

16. Snyder, C. *Paper prototyping: the fast and easy way to design and refine user interfaces.* Morgan Kaufmann, 2003.

17. van der Lugt, R. Functions of sketching in design idea generation meetings. *Proceedings of the fourth conference on Creativity cognition - CC '02* (2002), 72–79.

18. Weiser, M. The computer for the 21st century. *Scientific American* (1991).

Industrial Playgrounds. How Gamification Helps to Enrich Work for Elderly or Impaired Persons in Production

Oliver Korn

University of Applied Sciences Esslingen,
Kanalstr. 33, 73728 Esslingen, Germany
oliver.korn@hs-esslingen.de

ABSTRACT

This paper introduces an approach for implementing motivating mechanics from game design to production environments by integrating them in a new kind of computer-based assistive system. This process can be called "gamification". By using motion recognition, the work processes becomes transparent and can be visualized in real-time. This allows representing them as bricks in a "production game" which resembles the classic game Tetris. The aim is to achieve and sustain a mental state called "flow" resulting in increased motivation and better performance. Although the approach presented here primarily focuses on elderly and impaired workers, the enhanced assistive system or "wizard" can principally enrich work in every production environment.

Keywords

Augmented Reality; User-Centered Design; Assistive technology; Human Computer Interaction (HCI); Human Machine Interaction (HMI); Elderly; Gamification

ACM Classification Keywords

H.1.2 [**User/Machine Systems**]: Human factors, Human information processing, Software Psychology; H.5.1 [**Multimedia Information Systems**] Artificial, augmented, and virtual realities; H.5.2 [**User Interfaces**]: User-centered design; H5.m [**Miscellaneous**]: HCI; I.2.1 [**Applications and Expert Systems**] Games, Industrial automation; I.2.10 [**Vision and Scene Understanding**]: Motion; K.4.2 [**Social Issues**]: Assistive technologies for persons with disabilities

INTRODUCTION

The growing demand for highly individualized products promotes the return of human assembly work in production. At the same time the work of impaired and elderly persons in production environments becomes increasingly important [1]. In our research we have studied the requirements for assistive systems that address the needs of these two groups more aptly. We discovered three major issues that need to be addressed: (i) current systems have been focused primarily

on the control of results, while new systems need to become more process-oriented (ii) user interfaces have to be simplified and support natural interaction (iii) mechanisms that increase motivation have to be integrated. Within this larger framework, the work presented here focuses on the gamification approach. Other aspects of this new kind of assistive system in production environments (ASiPE) like motion detection and in-situ projection will be described in future work.

MOTIVATION

The ASiPE addresses two groups: Firstly elderly workers and secondly impaired or disabled workers. The motivation for focusing on these groups, as well as general developments in production supporting their growing importance, will be briefly described.

While the percentage of older employees grows in European countries, the employment rate in the population aged 55 to 64 years was 41.7% in 2003. The European Union has set a target rate at 50% by 2013 for the EU15 countries, implying an increase of 8.3% within 10 years [2: 362]. The aim of all EU countries is the prolongation of working lifetime and thus more employees working in older age. While the elderly often excel in knowledge, work expertise and commitment [3], it has been established 40 years ago that they also suffer from a gradual reduction of short term memory [4]. This results in a decrease of learning abilities [5] and an increase of human errors in manual production. As a consequence elderly workers retire more early than they had to and often more early than they want to [6]. The establishment of motivating process-oriented assistive systems in the workplace is an efficient way to meet this demographic challenge.

The market for manual production work with impaired or disabled persons becomes increasingly important. This is mainly due to two reasons: (i) Many European countries oblige companies to employ a certain percentage of disabled and impaired employees. This obligation can be met by contracting "sheltered work" organizations which focus on providing work conditions for them. (ii) The increased cost and time requirements for transport when outsourcing production processes make lean production with little storage capacity more difficult, so reasonably priced regional alternatives become more attractive.

The organizations working with disabled and impaired persons are eager to establish assistive systems empowering their employees: on the one hand they want to meet the rising customer demands and thus become more profitable and on the other hand they could provide more attractive and meaningful work.

Finally it is well-established, that the demand for customized products and thus the need for manual production tasks have both been rising in recent years [7]. Production methods like "build-to-order" and "design-to-order" led to an increasing number of product variants. This customization directly results in smaller lot sizes which in turn make manual production a more economical alternative than automation. This development makes assistive systems in production more important because they empower low skilled worker (both workers with impairments an older workers) to produce high quality components.

However, working in manual production requires the repeated performance of a series of tasks with high accuracy at a reasonable speed. Even with an attractive product at hand, the permanent repetition of a single or very few assembly sequences makes this kind of work prone to becoming dull – and reduced concentration and motivation increase the likeliness of mistakes. The direct implementation of a motivating reward structure (and other elements known from gaming) into a new process-oriented assistive system will increase the production workers' alertness and general presence of mind.

ASSISTIVE SYSTEMS IN PRODUCTION TODAY

Current computer-based assistive systems in production focus the control of work results rather than the support of the worker. If there is support, it focuses on describing the upcoming steps in the work process, often combined with images or animations on how to place or assemble a specific part (figure 1). These "classic" production assistants are purely functional systems helping to decrease the workers' cognitive load and reduce the sources of errors – they are not intended to make work more attractive. The well-established "pick-by-light" system is a good example: It simply marks the next box to pick from by a small indicator lamp or LED attached below.

Figure 1: Current assistive systems in production focus on technical aspects of the assembly

Until very recently, the idea of interfaces having an aesthetic quality stood in opposition to the purely functional

perspective applied to human machine interaction (HMI) in production environments. Even the most advanced systems using augmented reality or projections directly at the workplace are designed using "suboptimal concepts of information technology" and thus are not suited to ensure "efficient and ergonomic guidance of assembly workers" [8]. The concept of using game mechanics is completely new to this line of thought and the industry HMI traditions.

REQUIREMENTS

As pointed out above, the highly repetitive work in manual production can easily become dull, even for impaired workers who may have to retrain the task the next morning. As McGonigal puts it, underutilization leads to boredom and a feeling of lacking appreciation [9: 29]. Furthermore keeping workers focused helps to reduce the likeliness of mistakes. We argue that the implementation of motivating elements and a game-like reward structure will eventually increase the production workers' alertness and general presence of mind. Here we see a win-win situation: as the workers' fun increases, so does the quality of the assembly process.

To clarify the requirements, 134 German companies willing to use an enhanced assistive system in production have been addressed by a questionnaire, resulting in 30 valid data-sets. The questions were based on user-centered scenarios about what currently is and about what will become relevant for the industrial practice. Although it could not directly address the later users, it clarified the demands and set the stage for the approach.

The study showed that about 17% of the companies already employ more than 6% of impaired workers. All companies clearly see that the number of impaired or old workers will increase further. Although the majority still thinks of an assistive system as a means to control work results (e.g. more than 53% want to control if parts are picked correctly), almost 87% would appreciate a wizard that increases the well-being of the employees by checking ergonomic requirements like an upright body position. Furthermore above 63% would consider a system that contains motivating elements as "attractive". These results indicate that – in awareness of the demographic change –industrial companies are ready to test new approaches in human-machine interaction (HMI) like gamification.

THE CONCEPT OF GAMIFICATION

The idea of using games to promote "serious" purposes came up in pedagogy where motivating pupils to learn has always been a key issue. With the success of mobile devices, intuitive and "playful" interaction becomes common in society and spreads to other platforms, as the gesture-oriented Metro Design of Windows 8 shows. Playful designs and games have reached many parts of society and are frequently used to support elderly and impaired people [10, 11].

After "serious" and pervasive games have become a field for industry and research, the term "gamification" is the latest addition in a development of gaming technologies transcending the traditional boundaries of their medium – an "umbrella term for the use of video game elements to improve user experience and user engagement in non-game services and applications" [12]. Until today industrial applications in production have not been influenced by these developments: classical assistive systems in this domain are purely functional. Making work more attractive or introducing fun has not been a development goal. Although the idea of using gamification to create more engaging workplaces has already been described [13], so far only general business processes have been focused. Implementing assistive systems which use gamification in production environments is a completely new approach.

In the context of this paper gamification is seen as a means to achieve "flow" – a mental state in which a person feels fully immersed in an activity, experiencing energized focus and believing in the success of the activity. It is an area where high skill and adequate challenge converge, first proposed by Csíkszentmihályi in 1975. These are four conditions necessary to achieve the flow state [14]:

- One must be involved in an activity with a clear set of goals. This adds direction and structure to the task.
- One must have a good balance between the perceived challenges of the task and the own perceived skills. One must have confidence to be capable to do the task.
- The task at hand must have clear and immediate feedback. This helps negotiate changing demands and allows adjusting performance to maintain the flow state.
- The activity is intrinsically rewarding, so there is a perceived effortlessness of action.

PROPOSED GAMIFICATION APPROACH

The first step for implementing gamification in production environments was to shift from a purely result-oriented perspective to a continuous, process-oriented perspective. By using motion recognition, the work processes become transparent and can be analyzed and visualized in real-time. Since the sequence of assembly steps is predetermined, each work process can be visually represented by a brick in a puzzle game resembling Alexey Pajitnov's 1984 classic Tetris (figure 2). This method can be generalized and applied to all manual tasks in production environments.

During the work process the brick's color slowly changes from green to red. To support dual coding, this optical change can optionally be accompanied by an adequate sound sequence. The duration of this color change cycle is directly derived from the user's performance: if an assembly process which normally would take the user 10 seconds is completed in only 8 seconds, this will result in a dark green stone (while a duration of 14 seconds would result in a yellow stone). The underlying time values are derived by the user's average time, so he or she is not competing against other users but only trying to "beat the personal record".

To make this competition exciting or motivating, a maximum of transparency regarding the work performance is essential. For this reason the user's average process speed is represented by a grey brick, so he or she can check anytime how the processes completed so far compare to the personal average. This method called "shadowing" has been derived

from racing games, where drivers compete against their own best rounds or recorded best drives.

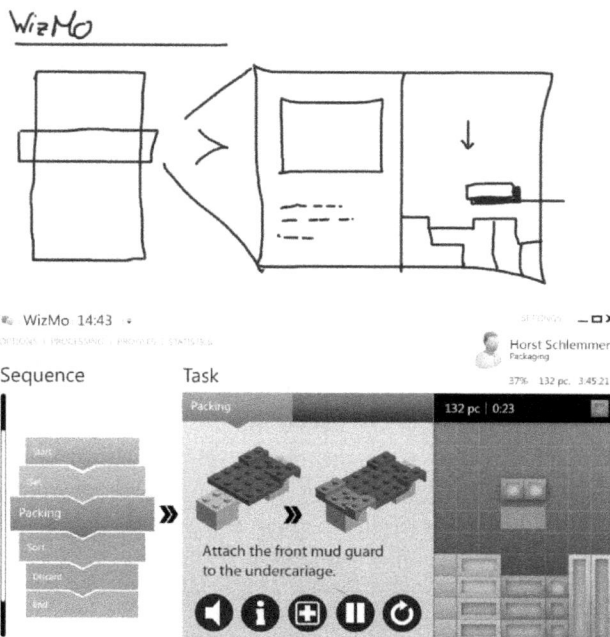

Figure 2. First Draft and current Metro-oriented Design of the gamification element "WizMo"

After a certain number of sequences are completed, the build-up brick rows disintegrate in an "explosion". Both the intensity of this visual feedback and the number of resulting points are based on the number of green bricks, i.e. the performance. If the resulting daily and weekly high scores exceed certain values for a longer period, the assistive system allows to "raise the bar" (as any game does) by reducing the underlying process durations. This change will be made transparent and has to be accepted by the worker – but since the "level-up" is a direct result of good work performance it should result in monetary or other adequate compensations.

The changes in performance and the resulting trends can also help to find hidden strengths: especially impaired workers are often assigned processes which do not adequately access their potential. Here the ASiPE increases transparency, e.g. if a certain type of work process is dark green while the others are red. Thus a hidden strength (previously unnoticeable in an average result) is revealed, helping the worker to get access to new challenges (i.e. more demanding tasks) and better wages.

Since a motivating implementation is considered essential for both user acceptance and performance improvement, the approach meticulously addresses the conditions for achieving the flow state:

Condition	Implementation
being involved in an activity with a clear set of goals	(i) macro level: complete a (flawless) assembly sequence (ii) micro level: complete the active process (brick movement) as quick (green) as possible
good balance between perceived challenges and perceived skills	(i) starting difficulty level based on average user competence (ii) adjustable process durations (e.g. shorter durations / more demanding sequences)
task must have clear and immediate feedback	(i) color changes and shadowing dual-code visual feedback (ii) (optional) sound integrates another sensory channel
the activity is intrinsically rewarding	(i) on the micro level "getting a brick down" quickly is immediately pleasing (ii) the final visually pleasing disintegration of the built brick sequence appeals to the basic human desire for order and completion

Table 1. Flow: Condition and implementation

CONCLUSION AND NEXT STEPS

Within the larger framework of ASiPE (assistive system in production environments) this paper introduces an approach for the integration of the gamification element. Motion recognition allows analyzing the work in real-time and enabled us to make the work processes transparent, visualizing them in real-time as bricks in a puzzle game. The aim is to improve motivation and work quality and performance of elderly, impaired or disabled workers.

The next step will be the evaluation of the gamification's usability as well as its impact on motivation and work process times, especially the sharing of attention between production tasks and the game panel. We will test larger groups (n>20) of both impaired and unimpaired production workers in an extensive experimental study.

ACKNOWLEDGMENTS

We thank the sheltered work organization "Beschützende Werkstätte Heilbronn" for providing valuable feedback in the user-centered design process and the company KORION for supporting the interface design.

REFERENCES

1. Brach, M. & Korn, O.: Assistive Technologies at Home and in the Workplace – A Field of Research for Exercise Science and Human Movement Science. *EURAPA (European Review of Aging and Physical Activity)*, vol. 9, 2012, DOI:10.1007/s11556-012-0099-z

2. Ilmarinen, J.: *Towards a Longer Worklife: Ageing and the Quality of Worklife in the European Union*. Finnish Institute of Occupational Health (FIOH), Helsinki: FIOH Bookstore, 2006

3. Dul, J.; Bruder, R; Buckle, P.; Carayon, P.; Falzon, P.; Marras, W. S.; Wilson, J. R.; van der Doelen, B.: A Strategy for Human Factors / Ergonomics: Developing the Discipline and Profession. *Ergonomics* 55:4, 377-395, 2012, DOI: 10.1080/00140139.2012.661087

4. Anders, T. R.; Fozard, J. L. and Lillyquist, T. D.: Effects of Age Upon Retrieval from Short-term Memory. *Developmental Psychology*, vol. 6, iss. 2, 1972, 214-217

5. Satre, D.; Knight, B. G.; David, S.: Cognitive Behavioral Interventions with Older Adults: Integrating Clinical and Gerontological research. In *Professional Psychology: Research and Practice*, (37), 2006, 489-498, http://escholarship.org/uc/item/1qg446xk

6. Steg, H.; Strese, H.; Loroff, C.; Hull, J. & Schmidt, S.: *Europe is facing a demographic challenge. Ambient assisted living offers solutions. Report compiled within the Specific Support Action "Ambient Assisted Living"*, Berlin, 2006

7. ElMaraghy, H. A. (ed.): *Enabling Manufacturing Competitiveness and Economic Sustainability: Proceedings of the 4th International Conference on Changeable, Agile, Reconfigurable and Virtual Production*, Montreal, Canada, 2011

8. Zäh, M. F.; Wiesbeck, M; Engstler, F; Friesdorf, F; Schubö, A.; Stork, S; Bannat, A; Wallhoff, F.: „Kognitive Assistenzsysteme in der manuellen Montage. Adaptive Montageführung mittels zustandsbasierter, umgebungsabhängiger Anweisungsgenerierung. *wt Werkstattstechnik online*, 2007, 644-650

9. McGonigal, J.: *Reality is Broken: Why Games Make Us Better and How They Can Change the World*, London: Random House, 2011

10. Nunes, F.; Silva, P. A.; Abrantes, F.: Human-Computer Interaction and the Older Adult: An Example Using User Research and Personas. *PETRA '10 Proceedings of the 3rd International Conference on PErvasive Technologies Related to Assistive Environments*, ACM, New York, USA, 2010

11. Brach, M.; Hauer K.; Korn O.; Konrad, R.; Göbel, S. Modern Principles of Training in Exergames for Sedentary Seniors: Requirements and Approaches for Sport and Exercise Science. *International Journal of Computer Science in Sport*, 11, 2012, 86--99

12. Deterding, S.; Sicart, M.; Nacke, L.; O'Hara, K.; Dixon, D.: Gamification: Using Game Design Elements in Non-Gaming Contexts. *Proceedings of the 2011 Annual Conference on Human Factors in Computing Systems*, ACM, New York, USA, 2011

13. Reeves, B. & Read, J. L.: *Total Engagement: Using Games and Virtual Worlds to Change the Way People Work and Businesses Compete*, New York, USA, 2009

14. Csikszentmihalyi, M.; Abuhamdeh, S.; Nakamura, J. 2005: Flow. Elliot, A. (ed.): *Handbook of Competence and Motivation*, New York, USA, 598-669

Differential Formal Analysis:
Evaluating safer 5-key number entry user interface designs

Abigail Cauchi

Future Interaction Technology Lab
Swansea University
csabi@swansea.ac.uk

ABSTRACT

Differential Formal Analysis (DFA) is an evaluation method based on stochastic simulation for evaluating safety critical user interfaces with subtle programming differences. This method enforces rigorous science by requiring two or more researchers to perform the analysis which in itself, raises important issues for discussion. This method is demonstrated through a case study on 5-key number entry systems which are a safety critical interface found in various popular commercial medical infusion pumps. The results of the case study are an important contribution of this paper since it provides device manufacturers guidelines to update their device firmware to make their 5 key number entry UIs safer, as well as a method that could be applied to other designs.

Author Keywords

Number entry, stochastic simulation, medical devices, interactive systems.

ACM Classification Keywords

H.5.2 User Interfaces: Input devices and strategies

INTRODUCTION

Safety critical and dependable applications should be designed to reduce risk to be As Low As Reasonably Practical (this is enshrined as the ALARP principle in the UK Health & Safety At Work Act, 1974).

As a concrete example, this paper will consider the task of interactive number entry. Incorrect drug doses and incorrect drug dose calculations are a significant contributory factor in unnecessary fatalities in healthcare. There are many papers on the prevalence of prescribing errors (e.g., [3]), but very few on user interaction errors, since interaction errors are harder to measure as they generally do not leave a paper record that can be easily analysed. Vicente *et al* [9] estimate the probability of fatal number-entry errors on PCA pumps (ones controlling pain, typically delivering opiates) as between 1 in 33,000 to 1 in 338,800 (the large uncertainty is due to estimating reporting rates—many errors are not reported); or in absolute

terms approximately 65–667pa in the US or (scaling by population) 155–1587pa in Europe. (Vicente *et al* warn that these are low estimates as they are based on fatalities in the US but the PCA pump is used worldwide, and hence the denominator, the number of pumps sold, used would have been too high.) By way of comparison, the probability of death from general anæsthesia is approximately 1 in 200,000–300,000.

This work is motivated by the vast interaction differences between implementations of number entry systems in popular, commercial medical infusion pumps. The 5-key number entry system (see figure 2) is gaining popularity in infusion pumps from leading manufacturers such as BBraun and Zimed and by studying these pumps we found that the same keying sequences in apparently identical number entry interfaces results in very different outcomes. Consider the starting screen of 0, if our goal is to input a dose of 950ml, we can key ◄ ▲ ▲ ▲ ▲ ▲ ◄ ▼. One commercial pump results in a display of 950 but keying in the same sequence starting from the same state on a different commercial pump results in 000.1 — a massive underdose which would leave a patient untreated, possibly resulting in harm, or even death. A resultant display of 000.1 may be unexpected, a detailed and formal description of why this happens in this particular pump may be found in [5].

We recognise that there are different interaction design choices which lead to different values on the display, we are concerned about finding the best combination of choices to make the design more resilient to human error. In our case study, we use the presented process to do this.

RELATED WORK

Keystroke-level model GOMS (Goals, Operators, Methods and Selection rules) [1] is a well-established evaluation method which is useful for obtaining a measure of time to perform a specified goal. In the design of safety critical number entry systems, the "best" design is not necessarily the fastest or most appealing to users. In safety critical domains, having a design that reduces errors is desirable, however, we highlight that design is a trade-off—in general, we aim at achieving an appropriate balance between speed and safety. In the KLM-GOMS approach, errors are not taken into consideration and it is assumed that users do not make errors. On the other hand, in our approach, human error has an integral role, making it suitable for helping evaluate safety critical designs.

Oladimeji *et al* [6] empirically compare so-called serial and incremental number entry interface styles. This research used eye tracking and uncovered some important design principles (including an explanation of why incremental interfaces are more dependable than numeric keypad interfaces for number entry). Our current work compares 5 different design features in up to 28 combinations: this scale of comparison complements this empirical work by targeting subtle variations in interface layouts which in [6] are all classed under a single "incremental" heading.

Fields [4] explores the consequences of different kinds of error being made, based on a similar classification to ours. He developed a finite state transition notation for describing task models that can be combined with a device model. Combined models were then analysed using off-the-shelf model checking technology to analyse the effect of executing tasks on the device. He also defined patterns of user error that could be introduced into the model based on a similar classification to ours (e.g., omission or repetition of action). The consequences of the introduced errors could then be investigated via model checking. An issue that arises is how to determine which errors are likely to occur in practice and so worth considering the weights of proposed design changes. Fields considers exploring underlying cognitive causes, an approach further considered by, for example, Rukšėnas et al [2]. Our work here offers a different solution—to consider sensitivity analysis.

This work complements [5], which defined the property **predictability** of a user interface in higher order logic, and explored how such a property can be verified on real systems through automated reasoning tools. The predictability property tests whether an expert user can tell what state the device is in from the perceptible output of the system, and hence accurately predict the consequences of an action from that state—normal human users can do no better. The analysis was performed on the formalisation of two real devices, and showed that devices, when closely examined, have many boundary cases where interactive functionality seems awkward. Here we explore the impact of errors, and assess in a systematic way if variations in the design of the numeric entry system can reduce harm when errors are made.

Following [7], we performed our work retrospectively by initially reverse-engineering commercial products. Had we worked in the development teams, we could have proceeded exactly as described here, except we would have been implementing devices directly from requirements or perhaps from prototypes, rather than by reverse engineering. An important aspect of our research is that it is deliberately handling design issues on a realistic scale, with realistic quirks and issues. The faithful reverse engineering ensures our systems are at the same sort of scale of complexity as commercial product features. In other words, our proposed methodology can be applied in practice to commercial development of dependable interactive products. In fact, as anticipated by [7], the discipline of reverse engineering itself uncovered numerous design questions that are important to consider in safety critical systems.

DIFFERENTIAL FORMAL ANALYSIS

The Differential Formal Analysis (DFA) process is aimed at evaluating safety critical number entry interface designs to find the design which is most resilient to human error.

The process starts by determining optional design features which are either on or off. One design is a combination of features and all the combinations make up the design space. Two or more researchers then use Stochastic Key Slip Simulation (SKSS) detailed in [8], to rank all the designs.

Put briefly, SKSS entails: generating a large number of key sequences (e.g., 10^6) which take us from one number to another (i.e., 10^6 pairs); inserting a keying error (substitution, deletion, repetition or transposition) with probability p per keystroke; if the error is beyond a certain magnitude (say, out by 10), we count the error; we rank according to the probability of out by K (where K is the magnitude) and the higher the probability of error, the lower the rank is for that design.

SKSS reveals interesting design and evaluation issues when performed by independent researchers. Our simple case study revealed that the features we described were not described formally enough and numerical disagreements raised sharp empirical questions about how people enter numbers which we would not have revealed otherwise. After discussing disagreements (if any), the features are refined, SKSS implementations are modified to reflect this and ranks are determined again. This iteration happens as many times as necessary for the researchers to converge on results.

The DFA process enforces rigorous science by ensuring that results are repeatable (4 researchers independently repeated the case study analysis), and thoroughly discussed. In effect, the important safety critical issues are well thought out and we can have more confidence in the results.

CASE STUDY: 5-KEY NUMBER ENTRY DESIGNS

As a case study we applied DFA on 5-key number entry systems to find the system which is least sensitive to human error. This type of interface (shown in figure 2) is popular in commercial medical infusion pumps and it is safety critical. The 5-key system uses a cursor and arrow keys to change digits and an OK key to submit the number.

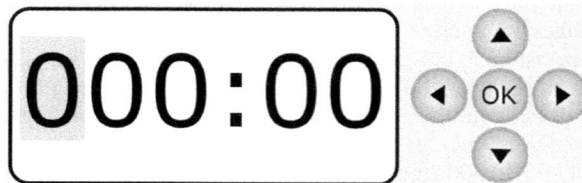

Figure 2. An example of 5-key user interface layout. Here the cursor is shown in the left-most position, and the display format is suitable for entering times, 0 minutes to 999:59 hours. Some 5-key interfaces omit the OK button as its use can be implied by the user performing any action with any non-arrow button.

From reverse engineering infusion pumps from different manufacturers we found that there are implementation variations on how the cursor works and how the independent digits

318

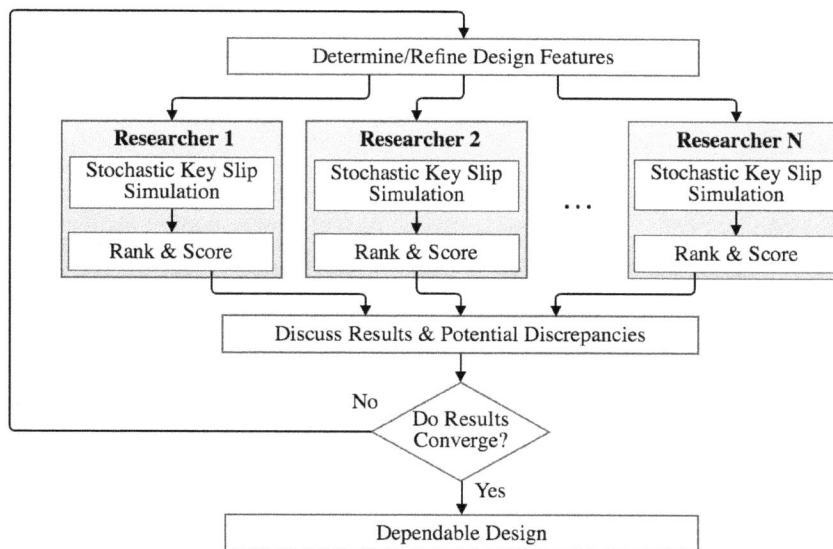

Figure 1. The Differential Formal Analysis Process

work. These make up our design features and are described here.

Wraparound — if applied to digits, if the digit is at the maximum and ▲ is pressed, the digit goes to the minimum value and vice versa for pressing ▼ on the minimum value. If wraparound is applied to the cursor, if ◄ is pressed on the leftmost position, the cursor goes to the rightmost position and vice versa.

Block errors — blocks interaction if the user tries going beyond a boundary when wraparound is not enabled.

Arithmetic — if a display show 9 and ▲ is pressed on 9, the display shows 10. Hence, when arithmetic is on, simple arithmetic operations are performed on the display through the ▲ and ▼ keys.

Cursor start position — this is the choice of what the cursor position is when the number entry interface starts.

Four independent researchers implemented SKSS for analysing 28 designs made up of all combinations of these features (28 not 32 since some features interact). The probability of out by 10 error for each design was used to determine a rank. Each researcher carried out slightly different experiments because of different understandings of the features and this raised important issues for discussion. (Implementation details and variations are described in [8]).

The main issues raised from implementing SKSS were about how users key in numbers and how the features behave at the boundaries. To simulate number entry, we considered finding the best possible path from one number to another but we found that programming solvers for the best path was complex and it is unlikely that a user enters numbers in this way. We agreed to implement realistic, simple solvers which consider shortcuts users are likely to take, however these raised

issues are worth studying empirically, especially since the domain is safety critical.

After a few iterations to improve and synchronise the SKSS implementations, the researchers converged on the results presented here. In figure 3 we see bar graphs (generated from the data) of error sensitivity depending on whether a feature is on or off. A lower bar is better and the most important feature to have is blocking errors and wraparound (cursor or digit) should be avoided.

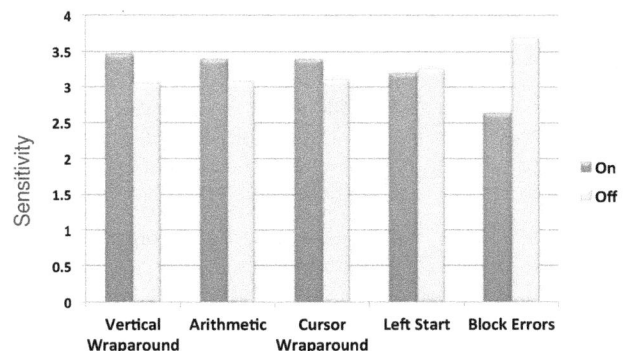

Figure 3. Summary of design feature impact analysis.

The parallel coordinates plot in figure 4 shows the relation of how the ranking scores of each different design changes depending on what type of slips we have in SKSS. The parallel lines in the diagram represents each slip error present in the experiment: all slips with equal probability of being chosen; transposition errors only; deletion errors only; repetition errors only; substitution errors only. Each design is represented by a polyline passing through each of the parallel lines and the position of each vertex on the a line corresponds to the score value of each design. This visualisation show that the

319

best designs remain best regardless of the specific mix of user errors therefore our key design recommendations do not depend on the mix of slips users make.

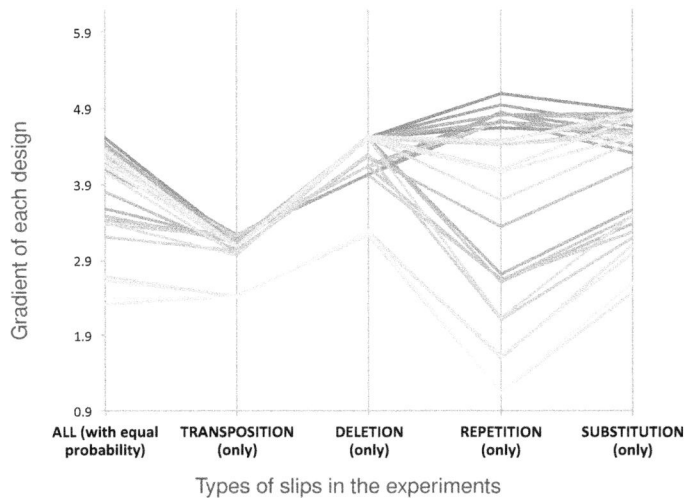

Figure 4. Parallel Coordinates visualisation showing the relation of design rankings depending on slips

DISCUSSION

The DFA process compliments empirical work nicely by encouraging rigorous engineering. DFA is useful for thorough analysis of safety critical systems and it enforces repeatable work and discussion about results — essential for a safety critical domain.

The discussion is an important part of the process because it encourages thoroughness in important safety critical issues. DFA raises sharp empirical questions which are worth researching e.g., in the case of the 5-key number entry interfaces, interesting questions were raised about how users input numbers, whether users understand the features, and whether this matters. This method is generalizable and can be easily applied to other number entry interfaces such as those which use chevrons, numeric keypad, knob, slider, and so on.

DFA is useful for studying safety critical number entry systems where error rates are very low. The process is much quicker than user studies and the results we get are rigorously founded. However, user trials should be done in conjunction with DFA for insight into whether users understand the analysed features and to give us even more confidence in our rigorously founded results.

CONCLUSIONS AND FUTURE WORK

DFA is a new methodology which should be used to complement user trials for more rigorous evaluation of safety critical number entry systems. Subtle interaction design choices in number entry lead to drastically different outcomes, it is crucial that we explore these choices and implement a design which is resilient to human error.

The issues and process presented are globally important and it is critical that we, as a community, get it right. Although these are clearly human-computer interaction issues, the presented approach which focusses on *safe* design, is not conventional and further work is necessary to bridge the gap between human-computer interaction and *safe* human-comp-uter interaction.

Acknowledgments
Special thanks goes to the author's supervisor, Harold Thimbleby and colleagues, Paolo Masci, Andy Gimblett, Paul Curzon and Michael Harrison for their input to this work. This work is funded as part of the project entitled, CHI+MED: Multidisciplinary Computer-Human Interaction research for the design and safe use of interactive medical devices, UK EPSRC Grant Number EP/G059063/1.

REFERENCES

1. S. K. Card, A. Newell, and T. P. Moran. *The Psychology of Human-Computer Interaction.* L. Erlbaum Associates Inc., Hillsdale, NJ, USA, 2000.

2. P. Curzon, R. Rukšėnas, and A. Blandford. An approach to formal verification of human-computer interaction. *Formal Aspects of Computing,* 4(19):512–550, 2007.

3. B. Dean, M. Schachter, C. Vincent, and N. Barber. Prescribing errors in hospital inpatients: their incidence and clinical significance. *Quality and Safety in Health Care,* 11(4):340–344, 2002.

4. R. E. Fields. *Analysis of erroneous actions in the design of critical systems.* DPhil thesis, University of York, 2001.

5. P. Masci, R. Rukšėnas, P. Oladimeji, A. Cauchi, A. Gimblett, Y. Li, P. Curzon, and H. Thimbleby. On formalising interactive number entry on infusion pumps. In *FMIS2011, the 4th Intl. Workshop on Formal Methods for Interactive Systems,* 2011.

6. P. Oladimeji, H. Thimbleby, and A. Cox. Number entry interfaces and their effects on error detection. In *Proceedings of the 13th IFIP TC 13 international conference on Human-computer interaction - Volume Part IV,* INTERACT'11, pages 178–185, Berlin, Heidelberg, 2011. Springer-Verlag.

7. H. Thimbleby. Interaction walkthrough: Evaluation of safety critical interactive systems. In G. Doherty and A. Blandford, editors, *Proceedings The XIII International Workshop on Design, Specification and Verification of Interactive Systems — DSVIS 2006,* volume 4323 of *Lecture Notes in Computer Science,* pages 52–66. Springer Verlag, 2007.

8. H. Thimbleby, A. Cauchi, A. Gimblett, P. Masci, and P. Curzon. Evaluating safer 5-key number entry user interface designs using differential formal analysis. Technical report, Swansea University, 2012.

9. K. J. Vicente, K. Kada-Bekhaled, G. Hillel, A. Cassano, and B. A. Orser. Programming errors contribute to death from patient-controlled analgesia: case report and estimate of probability. *Canadian Journal of Anesthesia,* 50(4):328–332, 2003.

Integrating Usability Engineering in the Software Development Lifecycle Based on International Standards

Holger Fischer
University of Paderborn, C-LAB
Fuerstenallee 11
33102 Paderborn, Germany
holger.fischer@c-lab.de

ABSTRACT

The integration of usability activities into software development lifecycles still remains to be a challenge. Most of the existing integration approaches appear to be on an operational level and cannot be transferred to other processes. Furthermore, UE standards and methods are hardly applied. How can organizations be supported in understanding and using this existing knowledge? The approach in this paper focuses on the constellation of standards to integrate UE and SE. Therefore, current development processes and standards will be analyzed and discussed to formulate recommendations for activities. In this manner, a toolset will be established to support the selection of suitable methods, the documentation and communication of intermediary results as well as the definition of competencies.

Author Keywords

Integration; usability engineering; software development; international standards; methods; competencies; recommendations; fields of activity.

ACM Classification Keywords

H.5.2 [User Interfaces]: User-centered design---integration; D.2.0 [General]: Standards

INTRODUCTION

While looking at today's industry usability has been recognized as an important quality aspect in the software development process. However, the integration of usability engineering (UE) and software engineering (SE) still remains to be a challenge in practice [13], even though implications of good usability are obvious: End-users will be able to work more effectively and efficiently with a greater satisfaction. Furthermore, usability is not an exclusive attribute of the generated product; it is also a fundamental attribute for the development process itself. Thus, a systematic human-centered design approach is needed in order to create usable products. Many large-scale

companies have this in mind and already use suitable processes and methods. Science and industry have contributed a lot to address questions and problems in such companies. Usually, such approaches focus on company's specifics and are not applicable in other companies and processes, such as small and medium-sized enterprises (SME). There is a lack of knowledge and experience regarding UE methods and UE standards [14]. Standards are helpful to define predictable and repeatable processes, to ensure a certain quality, and to communicate on a common base of knowledge. Currently, large-scaled companies use and test the added value of standard-based approaches. Current studies show that the application of UE methods in SME is up to 28 percent (sample of 2.000 participating companies), while 53 percent stated that they do not use or rarely use a method. In addition, only 15 percent of the companies indicated that they use one of the referenced standards, e.g., ISO 9241 [14]. An understanding of systematic approaches for integrating usability is not given likewise. No further studies could be found indicating why the use of UE standards and methods is low and if there is a difference between SME and larger enterprises. Hence, one hypothesis is that due to different organizational cultures the staff hierarchy is lower and more expertise as well as the quality of the results depends on a single person within a SME. Further on, there is a shortage of applicable tools regarding the manageable, efficiently and effectively use of methods and reference models for the implementation on an operational and organizational level. Thus, suitable management strategies are needed to implement the quality aspect of usability in a smooth way and to educate or help SME to use and understand UE standards and methods. Nevertheless, the research field of integrating UE is not a new one and some approaches already exist.

RELATED WORK

While looking on existing integration approaches a considerable amount can be found, which primarily take UE and SE into account. These can be organized along four general categories [11, 12]: Approaches that a) concern the concrete implementation; b) present a common specification; c) address the definition of processes and process models; and d) focuses on abstract or generic approaches.

Category a - Concrete Implementations

Activities and artifacts as well as links to existing SE activities were defined in approaches concerning the concrete implementation. As an example, Ferre [5] specified a set of 51 generic UE techniques that had been reviewed by experts following some criteria, e.g. how adaptable the techniques are to software development processes, how the applicability of the techniques is in general, how much it costs to perform the techniques and how the acceptance is in the field of human-computer interaction. The concepts and the terminology of SE have been adapted in order to ensure the relation of the techniques to SE.

Category b - Common Specifications

Further on, common specifications have been elaborated in the second category of integration approaches. For example, Juristo et al. [8] developed an approach concerning the measuring and evaluation of usability topics using architectural patterns embedded in the system architecture design, Therefore, they identified several patterns of UE and adopted them to SE.

Category c - Definition of Processes and Models

A third group of integration approaches address the definition of processes and process models distinguishing between independent UE models and SE models with integrated UE activities. For example, Düchting et al. [3] derived practice-oriented recommendations out of discussing existing agile process models (e.g., Scrum or eXtreme Programming [9]) for the implementation of UE activities.

Category d - Abstract and Generic Approaches

Other integration approaches focus on abstract or generic approaches specifying general conditions to be considered for the integration. As an example, Metzker et al. [10] present an 'Evidence-Based Computer-Aided Usability Engineering Environment (CAUSE)' for the organizational level of an organization. They developed a process meta-model supporting the selection of UE methods based on the paradigm of a situation-based decision-making.

Regarding the different types of integration approaches, Nebe [12] differentiates into three levels of abstractions:

1) 'Standards that define the overarching framework, [...]'
2) '[...] process models that describe systematic and traceable approaches [...]'
3) '[...] and the operational level in which the models are tailored to fit the specifics of an organization.'

Shown by the variety of UE and SE integration approaches, a lot of research is going on. However, it can be said that most of the approaches for integration appear to be on an operational level, which results in very specific activities or customized methods (see category a) and b)), which focus on a lightweight integration reducing the organizational or

structural change within an organization. Thus, these approaches cannot be easily transferred to any other situation in practice. Hence, it seems to be promising to investigate in a more abstract view of integration. Approaches out of category c) focus on an interrelation with existing process models. Therefore, these approaches are more transferable than approaches on the operational level. Approaches out of category d) describe general conditions, principles and paradigms as well as meta-models. They are more abstract and meet the idea of standards. The level of standards is a basis to realize a far-reaching and transferable integration approach with both internally and externally organizational aspects. Furthermore, standards are a framework to ensure and preserve consistency and quality within and outside of an organization.

Standards in UE and SE

Looking at UE and SE, different quality- and process-oriented standards exist. Essential for the development process are the following ones:

Usability Engineering:

- ISO 9241-210: Provides requirements and recommendations for human-centered design principles and activities throughout the life cycle of computer-based interactive systems.
- ISO/TR 18529: Process description for human-centered development processes.
- ISO/TS 18152: Presents a human-systems model for use in ISO/IEC 15504-conformant assessment of the maturity of an organization in performing the processes that make a system usable, healthy and safe.

Software Engineering:

- ISO/IEC 15288: Establishes a common framework for describing the life cycle of systems created by humans.
- ISO/IEC 12207: Establishes a common framework for software life cycle processes, with well-defined terminology, that can be referenced by the software industry.
- ISO/IEC 15504: Provides overall information on the concepts of process assessment and its use in the two contexts of process improvement and process capability determination. Also known as Software Process Improvement and Capability dEtermination (SPICE).

While looking on these standards, it becomes obvious that UE and SE development processes are similar to each other and that the integration on the level of standards seems to be promising [6]. First approaches on the level of standards already exist in the technical report ISO/TR 16982. The report addresses the combination of UE and SE and supports the selection of suitable UE methods for the integration in the SE process. Nevertheless, the report only defines 12 method categories, but does not focus on selecting an adequate method. Furthermore, the report does not take into account the correlation between methods within a development process. The awareness about the existence of UE methods is also prevented by the large amount of existing methods [7]. A good knowledge about their differences and applicability is needed. This is also necessary for the selection of suitable methods. The variety of the partially contrary guidelines for method selection [1] leads to uncertainty among the selecting persons or reduces the openness to use unknown methods. Thus, the effectiveness of SME may be inhibited according to their limited budget and low resources.

Based on the level of standards, integration approaches can be transferred onto given process models and finally onto the operational implementation. All mentioned advantages, like consistency, repeatability of processes, independence of organizations, quality, basis for communication, would remain. General applicable and comparable techniques are necessary to identify concrete lacks in a process. In addition, specific measures are needed to support the selection of suitable methods in the operational business.

According to limited human resources and smaller iterations in a process, the adaption of standards in SME hardly exists. Recommendations for activities and best practices are needed for the integration of UE and the use of standards. This leads us to the following objectives.

OBJECTIVES

According to the challenge of integrating UE and SE, one topic is not to focus only on people who are responsible for usability and software development, but to have also people in mind who are responsible for requirements engineering (RE), quality management (QM) and project management (PM). The hypothesis is that a kind of basic competence has to be continuously established in a project team focusing on results during a project. Roles have to be distributed in an appropriate way. The persons assuming the roles have to be qualified so that they are capable of how to reach a certain goal, how to create a specific result, how to suitably document the result and whom to communicate the result in order to embed it in the project. Hence, the qualification of the project members and their use of methods as well as the quality of the outcomes are necessary in order to establish a long-term added value of UE in the enterprise.

As mentioned above, international standards are not frequently used in enterprises. Nevertheless, standards are a written form of expert's consensus. Therefore, the knowledge aggregated in and the knowledge about existing standards has to be made accessible in order to enrich the integration of UE. This knowledge will be used to achieve the following objectives:

- Educate and help enterprises in using UE methods and standards, while making these more accessible
- Formulating recommendations to use a constellation of standards for the integration of UE in the software development lifecycle.

- Supporting usability specific roles in selecting appropriate methods to achieve a result.
- Supporting project roles in documenting and communicating the results among each other.
- Defining fields of competencies for the roles in software development projects to enable the team members in creating qualitative results.

How to approach the challenge will be presented in the next section.

METHOD

To reach the specified objectives of the PhD thesis, the following approach will be considered (see Figure 1).

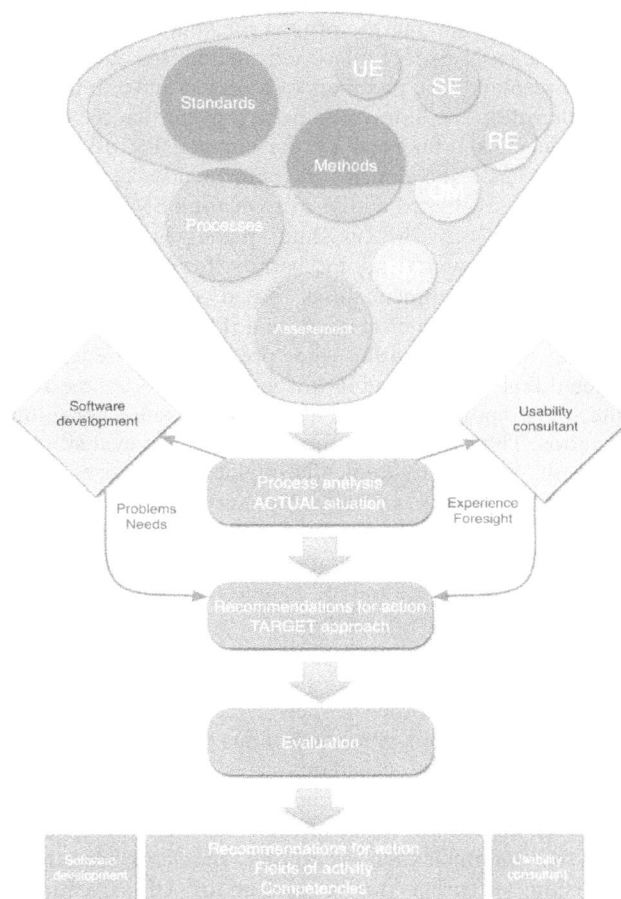

Figure 1. PhD Approach

At first, a scalable assessment method will be developed based on national and international standards (e.g. ISO 9241-210, ISO/TS 18152) as well as on different assessment approaches like the 'Usability Maturity Method: Processes (UMM-P)' [4] or the DAkkS Guidelines on Usability (DE) [2]. It will consist of activities, quality requirements and documentation guidelines. However it is still work-in-progress how this assessment will look like in detail. Using this method, the maturity of development processes out of some companies will be measured in order to identify point of weakness, problems and needs. This will be done in analyzing the processes of software developing companies and in regarding the knowledge and experience of usability consulting companies likewise. Based on the results, a study will be carried out to identify possible barriers for the use of UE standards and methods in SME in particular. Branch-specific and unspecific aspects will be identified to see which ones support or inhibit the diffusion of integrating UE.

In the next step, recommendations for activities will be formulated. These will focus on statements about using a constellation of standards to ensure the integration of UE activities as well as the quality within the processes. At the same time, the backup of intermediate results and their communication among the project members as well as the competencies in SME will be considered. On the basis of limited resources the members of a project have to perform multiple roles. The aim would be to prevent that the quality of a project is influenced by the competence of a single person. The developed recommendations will be qualitatively evaluated within a project of a SME. They will be integrated in the existing processes. It will be investigated in which way the barriers for standards can be reduced, if recommendations based on standards can support the selection of methods and if the level of usability can be increased within the process. The evaluation protocol that will be used is still in discussion. At the same time, their application will be tested in some consulting scenarios. Thus, the integration of UE and the evaluation of the results will be prototypically implemented. Based on the gained knowledge, a range of services for usability constants and project managers will be developed. This could be a kind of an assessment catalogue to support the acquisition and allocation of resources. In this way, UE activities will be integrated likewise.

CONCLUSION

The integration approach for UE into the software development lifecycle presented in this paper focuses on the level of standards. Standards are based on expert's consensus. They enable consistency, repeatability of processes, the independence of organizations, quality, and a basis for communication. Therefore, standards seem to be promising to enrich the integration of UE. Creating a constellation of standards and linking them to processes should support usability specific roles in selecting appropriate methods, documenting and communicating their results and to define fields of competencies for the roles in software development projects in order to ensure quality.

Currently, standards in the field of usability engineering, software engineering, requirements engineering, quality management and project management are gathered, categorized and linked. Thus, a basis should be created to enable the analysis of SME processes, which will be the next step.

REFERENCES

1. Bevan, N. UsabilityNet Methods for User Centered Design. In *Proceedings of HCII '03* (Crete, Greece), pp. 434-438, 2003.

2. DAkkS Leitfaden Usability, version 1.3, 2010.

3. Düchting, M., Zimmermann, D., and Nebe, K. Incorporating User Centered Requirement Engineering into Agile Software Development. In Jacko, J.A. (ed.) *HCII '07*, LNCS 4550. Springer: Berlin, Germany, 2007.

4. Earthy, J., Usability Maturity Model: Processes. INUSE/D5.1.4(p), EC INUSE (IE 2016) final deliverable (v. 0.2). London: Lloyd's Register, 1997.

5. Ferre, X. Integration of Usabiliy Techniques into the Software Development Process. In *Proc. of ICSE '03* (Portland OR, USA), pp. 28-35, 2003.

6. Fischer, H., Nebe, K., and Klompmaker, F. A Holistic Model for Integrating Usability Engineering and Software Engineering Enriched with Marketing Activities. In Kurosu, M. (ed.) *Human Centered Design*, HCII'11, LNCS 6776. Springer: Berlin, Germany, 2011.

7. Furniss, D., Blandford, A., and Curzon, P. Usability Evaluation Methods in Practice: Understanding the Context in which they are embedded. In *Proc. of ECCE'07* (London, UK), pp. 253-256, 2007.

8. Juristo, N., Lopez, M., Moreno, A.M., and Sánchez, M.I. Improving software usability through architectural patterns. In *Proc. of ICSE'03* (Portland OR, USA), pp. 12-19, 2003.

9. Kniberg, H. Scrum and XP from the Trenches. Lulu Enterprises: Raleigh NC, USA, 2007.

10. Metzker, E., and Reiterer, H. Evidence-Based Usability Engineering. In Kolski, C. et al. (eds.) *Proc. CADUI '02* (Valenciennes, France), pp. 323-336, 2002.

11. Nebe, K., and Paelke, V. Key Requirements for Integrating Usability Engineering and Software Engineering. In Kurosu, M. (ed.) *Human Centered Design*, HCII'11, LNCS 6776. Springer: Berlin, Germany, 2011.

12. Nebe, K., Zimmermann, D., and Paelke, V. Integrating Software Engineering and Usability Engineering. In Pinder, S. (ed.) *Advances in Human-Computer Interaction*, pp. 331-350. I-Tech Education and Publishing KG: Vienna, Austria, 2008.

13. Seffah, A., Desmarais, M.C., and Metzker, E. HCI, Usability and Software Engineering Integration: Present and Future. In Seffah, A. et al. (eds.) *Human-Centered Software Engineering*. Springer: Berlin, Germany, 2005.

14. Woywode, M., Mädche, A., Wallach, D., and Plach, M. Gebrauchtauglichkeit von Anwendungssoftware als Wettbewerbsfaktor für kleine und mittlere Unternehmen, 2012.

Reverse Engineering of GWT Applications

Carlos Silva
HASLab / INESC TEC
Departamento de Informática/ Universidade do Minho
Braga, Portugal
cems@di.uminho.pt

ABSTRACT

Web applications have gained significant popularity. Relevant technologies, however, are to a great extent still immature and in constant evolution. This means many current applications are subject to constant change to keep up with the technology, leading to a degradation of application quality, both from an implementation and a usage perspective.

In this context, tools that enable reasoning about the quality of the application from its source code can have a significant role. This paper reports on our preliminary work on reverse engineering the user interface layer of web applications directly from source code. Its applicability to GWT is described through two examples.

Author Keywords

User Interfaces; Reverse Engineering.

ACM Classification Keywords

H.5.2 [**Information interfaces and presentation**]: User Interfaces – graphical user interfaces.

INTRODUCTION

Internet applications have gained significant popularity over the last few years. With ongoing technological development, internet applications have evolved into a new type of applications (Rich Internet Applications – RIAs), providing a usage experience closer to that of desktop applications. Unfortunately, the fast evolution of Web applications towards the desktop paradigm also means that RIAs development is currently based on a plethora of fast evolving technologies, making it hard to develop applications according to rigorous software engineering principles [10]. This is particularly true of the user interface layer of such applications.

Building and maintaining a RIA requires a significant amount of work. This can be reduced if aided by high-level model abstractions of the system, which enable a simpler system's specification and analysis. Models are useful in order to help in the development and maintenance of interfaces. However, constant application changes and updates make it difficult to keep models and systems synchronized.

A solution to this problem is having a reverse engineering tool to expeditely abstract the system into a model. This PhD's goal is the development of tools and techniques to reverse engineer the GUI layer of web applications. This paper reports on an approach to this problem, centered on the Google Web Toolkit (GWT).

BACKGROUND AND RELATED WORK

Reverse engineering is the process of analyzing a system in order to discover its components and their interrelationships. Its main purpose is the extraction of information from already existing systems. This information is usually gathered by building or synthesizing abstractions that are less implementation-dependent. System's tendency for degradation is one of the reasons reverse engineering has been an important subject to the software industry in the last few years [7].

There are two main approaches to the realization of a reverse engineering process: static and dynamic analysis. Static analysis implies the analysis of the software system without the actual execution of the software. Dynamic analysis implies analyzing the system while running, that is, while the software system is being executed.

A number of static source code analysis reverse engineering tools aimed at user interfaces can be found in the literature. For instance, ReversiXML [2] applies derivation rules to reverse engineer an HTML web page into UsiXML [8], a modelling language for user interfaces. [6] describes a tool that performs a static control-flow analysis for JavaScript applications running in Web browsers. In the approach, a behaviour model is extracted, and, afterwards, an intrusion detection is performed from the server side. Their analysis, however, has a different focus from the one we intend to perform, as the model built is a flow graph of URLs whereas we will focus on the interface behaviour. Also worth mentioning, the same approach was successfully tested on the JavaScript code generated from a GWT application.

Dynamic analysis aims to obtain a model of a system from its run-time behaviour. Dynamic analysis has numerous implementations. For instance, [12] analyses the run-time behaviour of Java software in order to generate state diagrams. [3] uses reverse engineering to accomplish a specification-based testing of user interfaces. Users can graphically control test specifications that appear as Finite State Machines (FSM) which abstract the run-time system. [9]

describes an application called GUI Ripping which consists in a dynamic process that traverses a GUI by opening all its windows and extracting all the widgets (GUI objects) and their information. [1] uses dynamic analysis to reverse engineer finite state machines from AJAX applications.

There are also hybrid approaches such as [5] which discovers a model of an interactive system by simulating user actions using a dynamic approach that also considers the source code of the application.

GOOGLE WEB TOOLKIT

The Google Web Toolkit (GWT) is a set of Java-based tools, programming utilities, and widgets that enables the development of Ajax-based rich internet applications in Java [4]. GWT components can be split into two major groups: development tools, which include the compiler and the development mode; and class libraries, which contain the JRE emulation library and the widget library.

The widget library comprises a set of widgets to ease client-side UI development. GWT provides the most popular widgets used on Web applications. For example: the *Button* widget to create button elements, or the *Table* widget to produce table elements. Widgets are the elements responsible for the user interaction with the application, and are organized in panels. Panels (the GWT equivalent to desktop application windows) determine the widgets' arrangement on the page.

REVERSE ENGINEERING GWT

Our goal is to reverse engineer the user interface of GWT applications from source code, focusing on the behavioural aspects of the interface. Relevant aspects are the occurrences of GUI events, the triggering of system actions, and the GUI states reached as a result. To achieve this, we perform a systematic analysis based on the events which can take place in the GUI widgets present in the interface. For each event the guarding conditions, the actions that are executed, and the changes that are produced in the interface are analyzed.

To support this analysis we resort to GUIsurfer [11]. GUIsurfer defines a framework for tools capable of analyzing the source code of applications, and generating behavioural models of their user interfaces. GUIsurfer focus on being retargetable to other languages and its first version of the GUI behavioural abstraction module was developed for the Swing toolkit. Since GWT is itself a Java toolkit, ideally there would only be the need to perform the slicing step with a different set of GUI components (those of GWT instead of those from Swing).

However, a few issues arose. The first was related to the genericity of the tool, and it was due to GUIsurfer's original implementation's use of the 'addActionListener' method of Swing components to identify actions. In GWT methods are registered though the 'addClickHandler' method. Solving this problem meant parameterizing GUISurfer on the method used to register event handler in the interface.

A second issue arose related to differences in the functionality of both toolkits (Swing and GWT). Since a GWT application is a web application, the closing window (panel, in GWT) actions available in Swing are not present. Closing a web application is an unusual action, and thus there is no direct support in GWT for doing it. Nevertheless, it can be achieved by invoking native JavaScript.

A third issue occurred in detecting a change from a window/panel to another. In Swing this is achieved by invoking the 'dispose' method on a class. In GWT this is accomplished by manipulating the visibility attribute of the panels. Again, changes were introduced to address this situation by changing the method GUIsurfer analyses to the "setVisible" method.

RESULTS

Two examples illustrate the results that can be achieved. In the first, the tool is applied to a third party, open source, GWT component. In the second, the tool is applied to a small application that was developed to mimic an existing Java/Swing application. Together, these two examples illustrate applying the tool to third party code, and using the tool to compare different versions of an application. In this case, two versions developed in different technologies.

FlexTable Example

FlexTable is an example of a third party open source GWT component available on the Web. It is a widget, based on an HTML table. Its purpose is to have varying numbers of cells in each row. The component is depicted in Figure 1.

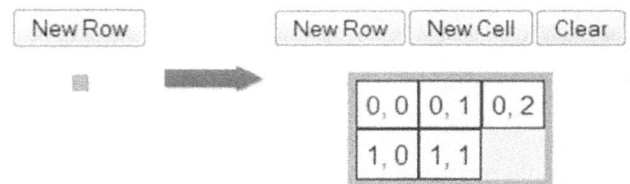

Figure 1 – FlexTable Application

It starts, as shown on the left side of the image, with an empty table, and a single button available, the *New Row* button. Every time *New Row* is clicked, a new row is added the table. When rows are available, two more buttons become visible: *New Cell* and *Clear*. The *New Cell* button adds a new cell to the table, in the last created row. Each of the table cells has the value of its respective coordinate on the table. Button *Clear*, clears the table, thus returning to the initial, empty, table state.

The created module was executed on the component's original source code (except for a few edits to make it compliant with GWT 2.0). All actions, events and conditions were discovered by the tool. However, GUIsurfer was using the enabling and disabling of widgets to identify new window states. Thus, the application buttons appearance and disappearance were not triggering state changes. To solve this issue, changes were made to the tool, allowing it to trigger new states when changes to the widgets' visibility happened. After performing these changes and executing the tool again, it produced the model depicted in Figure 2.

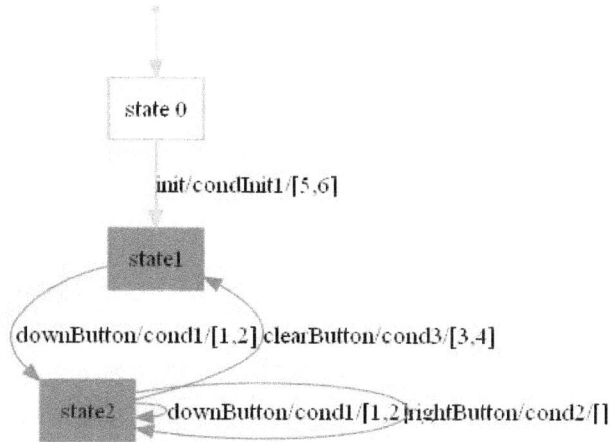

Figure 2 - FlexTable model

An analysis of the model shows that two states were identified: the state with a single button, namely the *New Row* button (*state1*) and the state with the three buttons (*state2*). It is important to emphasize the accurate definition of the two states. As there are two buttons being set to visible or invisible, the tool could have created a state for each. However, the tool correctly analyzed the application, and since the two buttons are always set visible or invisible simultaneously, only one state was considered.

Moreover, the tool properly identified the two different transitions for pressing the *New Row* button. If the table is empty, it will perform a transition to the following state, *state2*. Otherwise, it will remain in the same state. This aspect is relevant because the event handler of button *New Row* always sets the two buttons, *Clear* and *New Cell* to visible.

Furthermore, Figure 2 also depicts that there are no final states, that is, there are no "close`` or "cancel`` states. This enables us to conclude that the Flex Table application does not end. Obviously, the application not ending relates to the fact that it is always enabled on that specific Web page. Web applications can always end by changing the Web page currently being browsed.

Contacts Agenda Example
While the previous example consists of a single window, the next example considers several windows. As depicted on Figure 3, it is a simple interactive agenda of contacts, and was developed to mimic an existing Java Swing application.

The application begins with the *Login* panel (Figure 3, top-left panel), where users must fill in username and password. If the information is correct, the *Login* panel is replaced with the *Mainform* panel. This panel (Figure 3, top-right panel) is the main application panel; it has the list of the various contacts, and buttons that enable users to find or edit them. The *Exit* button allows a user to logout, therefore returning the application to the *Login* panel.

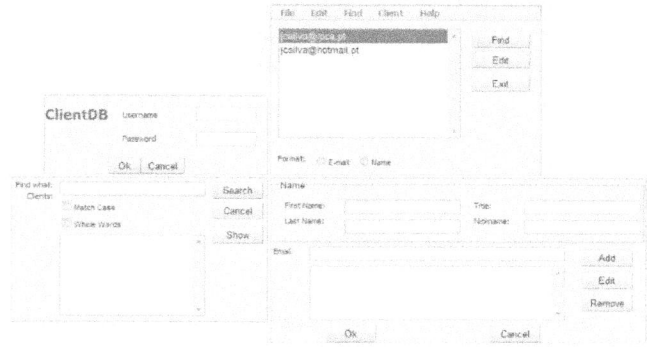

Figure 3 - GWT Contacts Agenda Application

When the *Find* button is pressed, the Find panel (Figure 3, bottom-left panel) appears. By clicking the *Edit* button, the user navigates to the *ContactEditor* panel (Figure 3, bottom-right panel). As the name implies, this panel enables changing a contact's information. Since each contact can have several e-mails, they are presented in a list. The *Add*, *Remove* and *Edit* buttons are used to modify it. If the e-mails list is empty the remove button is automatically disabled.

Figure 4, compares the FSMs generated after executing the GUIsurfer tool over the login class for both the GWT and the original Swing versions of the application. The *init* event represents the application start, and in both cases leaves the interface in *state1*.

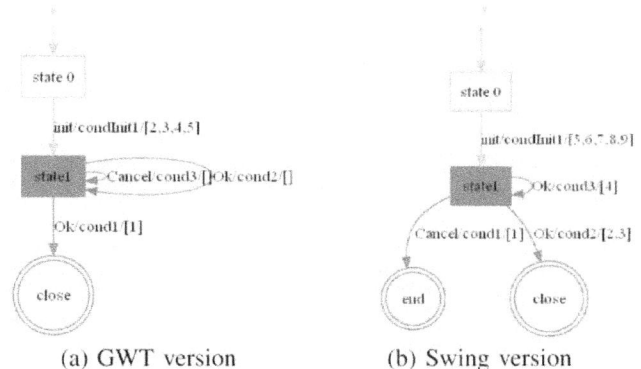

(a) GWT version   (b) Swing version

Figure 4 - Login Window FSM

Some differences are immediately noticeable. For instance, the GWT login application does not have an "end" state. In the GWT version, when the user presses the *Cancel* button, the state remains the same. In the Swing version, the application ends. In the GWT case, our approach was to design the application's login with a different functionality, when the *Cancel* button is pressed the login window textboxes, i.e., the username and password, are cleared and the login window remains active. This occurs because it does not make sense for a web application to simply close and leave the browser with a clear page. This difference in the behavioural models produced by the tool is actually highlighting differences in the user interaction supported by two versions of the application.

CONCLUSIONS AND FUTURE WORK

In its current state the tool is already capable of analyzing a range of applications, including third party source code. Configuring GUIsurfer to consider GWT applications lead us to make a number of improvements to the framework. This was the case, for example, regarding the identification of new GUI states. However, limitations were found:

- GUIsurfer makes the assumption that new states occur only when some interface widgets are enabled or disabled. There are many other interface alterations that could be recognized as new interface states, and that must be explored. Similarly, JavaScript alerts are currently not perceived as new application states.

- A number of extensions to GWT have been proposed in the guise of extended widget toolkits. Applications using one of these extensions will currently not be adequately processed. This is a further area for improvement.

- Moreover, the work is limited since a purely static approach was being used, which restraints the amount of discovered states.

- Another issue detected with our preliminary work is that using a meta-model with a specific, purpose built, DSL limits the applicability and usefulness of the reverse engineering tool.

Therefore, in future research we will try to address these limitations by focusing on the dynamic analysis of web applications also. The goal is to define a hybrid approach that will combine static and dynamic analysis in order to achieve better results. The reverse engineering of web applications through dynamic analysis normally poses challenges such as how to identify clickable elements, or how to navigate through an application interacting with the application's forms and dialogues (which typically involves filling in values at appropriate fields). Therefore, the main challenge in dynamic analysis is to see if all the application states have been correctly discovered. Our hypothesis will be to see if a hybrid approach will bring new capabilities to the analysis, thus discovering more application states.

Using an existing User Interface Description Language (UIDL) will enable the reuse of the tools already available for that UIDL, and broaden the universe of possible users of the tool. In this area, we are also researching the feasibility of using a Markup language like HTML as a Concrete User Interface model.

The envisaged outcome of the whole research program will be a browser plugin (e.g., for the Firefox browser), which automatically analyses a Web application and generates a model, supporting, for example, the adaptation of the website to different devices.

Acknowledgments

This work is funded by the ERDF through the COMPETE Programme, and by the Portuguese Government through FCT - Foundation for Science and Technology, under contracts PTDC/EIA-CCO/108995/2008 and SFRH/BD/ 71136/ 2010.

REFERENCES

1. Amalfitano, D. and Fasolino, A. R. and Tramontana, P. Reverse engineering finite state machines from rich internet applications. In Proc. of the 2008 Working Conference on Reverse Engineering, pages 69–73, Washington, DC, USA, 2008.

2. Bouillon, L and Limbourg, Q. and Vanderdonckt, J and Michotte, B. Reverse engineering of web pages based on derivations and transformations. In: Proc. of third Latin American web congress LA, 2005.

3. Chen, J and Subramaniam, S. A GUI environment to manipulate FSMs for testing GUI-based applications in Java. In HICSS '01: Proceedings of the 34th Annual Hawaii International Conference on System Sciences Volume 9, page 9061, Washington, DC, USA, 2001.

4. Dewsbury, R. Google Web Toolkit Applications. Prentice Hall, 2008.

5. Gimblett, A. and Thimbleby, H. User Interface Model Discovery: Towards a Generic Approach. EICS '10: Proc. 2nd ACM SIGCHI symposium on Engineering interactive computing systems, pp 145–154, 2010

6. Guha, A and Krishnamurthi, S. and Jim, T. Using static analysis for Ajax intrusion detection. In Proc. 18th international conference on World Wide Web, pp 561–570, New York, NY, USA, 2009.

7. Jacobson, I. and Christerson, M. and Jonsson, P. and Overgaard, G. Object-Oriented Software Engineering: A Use Case Driven Approach. Addison-Wesley, 1992.

8. Limbourg, Q and Vanderdonckt, J and Michotte, B. and Bouillon, L. and López-Jaquero, V. UsiXML: a language supporting multi-path development of user interfaces. LNCS vol. 3425, pages 200-220. 2005.

9. Memon, A. and Banerjee, I. and Nagarajan, A. GUI ripping: Reverse engineering of graphical user interfaces for testing. In WCRE '03 - Proceedings of the 10th Working Conference on Reverse Engineering, page 260, Washington, DC, USA, 2003.

10. Mikkonen, T. and Taivalsaari, A. Web applications – spaghetti code for the 21st century. In 6th International Conference on Software Engineering Research, Management and Applications, pp 319–328, 2008.

11. Silva, J. C. and Silva, C. and Gonçalo, R and Saraiva, J. and Campos, J. C. The GUISurfer tool: towards a language independent approach to reverse engineering gui code. In EICS 10: Proc. 2nd ACM SIGCHI symposium on Engineering interactive computing systems, pages 181–186, New York, NY, USA, 2010

12. Systä, T. Dynamic reverse engineering of Java software. In Proc. of the Workshop on Object-Oriented Technology, pages 174–175, London, UK, 1999.

Towards Safer Number Entry in Interactive Medical Devices

Patrick Oladimeji
Future Interaction Technology Lab.
Swansea University
p.oladimeji@swansea.ac.uk

ABSTRACT

Number entry is prevalent in the use of many interactive medical systems and number entry interfaces vary in complexity. Currently, research on number entry is focused on the numeric keypad and its different layouts. There are alternatives to the numeric keypad in use in safety critical contexts such as hospitals. I have surveyed several number entry systems and propose properties that would help compare them. My research on this topic aims to understand the characteristics of the styles of these interfaces, focusing on their effects on number entry error, the severity of such errors and exploring possible design choices that can reduce or manage the errors. This research will uncover number entry interface design trade-offs that will help designers make informed decisions about the safety and dependability of number entry systems.

Author Keywords

User interfaces; number entry; data entry; safety critical design.

ACM Classification Keywords

H.5.2 User Interfaces: Input devices and strategies

INTRODUCTION

Number entry is a ubiquitous task performed by millions of people everyday. Depending of the context of use, a variety of user interfaces can be used for entering numbers. Tasks such as performing calculations on handheld calculators, setting the timer on a microwave oven, manually tuning into a radio station or setting up a medical device such as an infusion pump could all present different user interfaces for performing a task which is fundamentally equal at a low level. All these tasks are various forms of number entry. The number entry aspects of these tasks are however usually secondary to the user's goal. For instance in setting the timer on a microwave oven, the primary task might be to warm up some food for lunch, while in the setup of an infusion pump, the primary task might be to get a drug delivered to a patient as

quickly as possible. An infusion pump is an interactive medical device used for accurate intravenous delivery of medication to patients.

Intravenous drug administration contribute to a significant portion of medication administration and they also pose a higher risk for error [12]. Various ethnographic studies have shown that error rates in intravenous drug administration range from 49% - 81% [9, 1, 5]. These errors can be in the form of a wrong rate, dose, time or volume. Number entry is a critical part of setting up an infusion.

In general, number entry is assumed to be simple, straight forward and uninteresting. Nevertheless, number entry errors occur for many different reasons and depending on context, the cost of such errors can be very high.

RESEARCH MOTIVATION AND OBJECTIVES

Number entry error types depend on the number entry interface used. A rigorous understanding of errors requires the exploration of all the types of interfaces and subsequently the types of errors they induce or support.

My research aims to build a classification of number entry interfaces and to develop a detailed understanding of the effects of interface style on number entry error and error detection. This understanding will inform safer design decisions in safety critical contexts like the design of medical devices - a valuable contribution that could reduce errors in medical device use and potentially save lives.

Due to the popularity of infusion therapies in hospitals and their higher error risks, my research focuses on interfaces found on infusion pumps. Despite this initial focus,it is my aim that the results are generalisable and would be informative to the design of new number entry systems.

CLASSIFYING NUMBER ENTRY INTERFACES

So far, I have identified three standard categories of widget based number entry interfaces.

Serial digit entry

In serial digit entry, the user enters the required number sequentially from left to right as in keyboard based text entry. There is a bijection between user input and display output. An example of serial digit entry is the numeric keypad found on telephones, ATMs or calculators. For instance entering the number '103' requires the user to press the keys $\boxed{1}$, $\boxed{0}$, $\boxed{3}$ on the keypad in exactly that order. The digits making up the

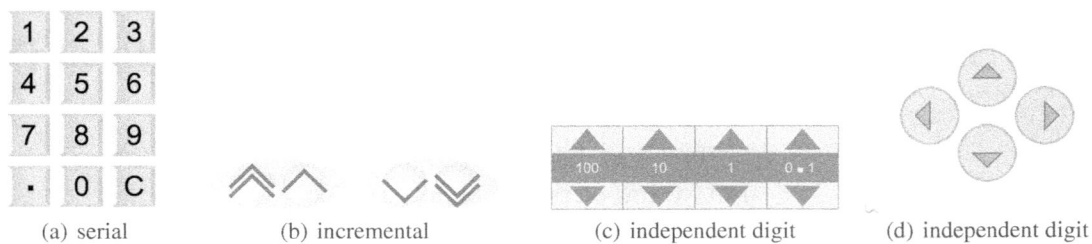

Figure 1. Sample number entry interfaces found on interactive medical devices and their corresponding classes.

number must be entered in descending order of their place value in the number.

Serial digit entry interfaces provide the user with the set of keys $\boxed{0}$ through $\boxed{9}$ and the key $\boxed{C}$, which may either be implemented to clear the screen or delete the last number entered. Providing a decimal point key is optional. When there is no decimal point key, a decimal point is inserted in a fixed position, typically giving 2 decimal digits (so keying 1234 would input 12.34). Serial entry provides the quickest method for arbitrary number entry, and its use also coincides with how numbers are spoken in many Western languages.

In serial digit entry, the two most popular layout in use are the telephone layout, which has $\boxed{1}$ $\boxed{2}$ $\boxed{3}$ at the top and the calculator layout, which has $\boxed{7}$ $\boxed{8}$ $\boxed{9}$ at the top.

Independent digit entry

In independent digit entry, the user may control the digits that make up the intended number separately (and sometimes independently of the other digits) and can choose which place value in the number they wish to edit. There is no constraint on the order for entering the digits as long as each digit ends up at the correct place value in the transcript as they were in the intended number. For instance entering the number '103' on this interface, the user might choose to first **set** the units position to '3' then **set** the hundreds position to '1'. Figures 1(d) and 1(c) are an example of this interface style.

The digit being edited is controlled with a pair of buttons: one each for increasing and decreasing the digit. The digits can be changed to any number between 0 and 9. The details of what happens between the transition between 0 and 9 gives rise to a few variations in the way the interface works. The effect may be arithmetic in nature, where a value of 1 is carried over to the digit to the left of that being edited. The digit may simply wrap around without affecting any neighbouring digit or this transition (between 9 and 0) might be forbidden [2]. A variation on this interface style uses a single button instead of a pair of buttons to cycle through the digits 0 - 9 usually in increasing order.

Incremental number entry

In incremental number entry, the user enters a number by increasing or decreasing the number. The interaction here is analogous to a user scrolling through values on the number-line. The user then has control over the speed of the scroll. This interface is commonly controlled using sliders, knobs or a pair of buttons that can be clicked as well as held down.

BACKGROUND

Given the pervasiveness of number entry interfaces, until recently, number entry errors have been hardly researched and consequently, little understood. Wiseman et al. ran an experiment to induce number entry errors in order to better understand the causes of number entry error and the types of errors. They developed a taxonomy of number entry error based on the errors reported in their study [13].

Thimbleby and Cairns have proposed methods for blocking syntax errors such as multiple decimal points in number entry which could half the probability of out by ten errors. They also suggest a general framework for parsing the input stream from a serial interface to better detect errorneous input and alert the users to any possible errors as opposed to leaving the application to guess what the user might have meant [10]. These guidelines are however only applicable to the serial digit interface as syntax errors are only possible on interfaces such as the numeric keypad.

Wang et al. have applied data mining techniques to detect number entry errors using electroencephalography (EEG) data. In their study, participants performed hear and type tasks of number entry whilst wearing an EEG cap. Their analyses of the EEG data present a strong possibility for predicting errorneous keystrokes in number entry when a serial digit interface is used [11].

Other earlier research in number entry user interface design have focused on the performance effects of different layouts of the serial interface [4, 3, 8, 6]. The general concensus on the preferred layout had been to use the telephone layout [3]. More recent research by Marteniuk et al. suggests that the placement of the $\boxed{0}$ key (i.e., at the top or bottom of the layout) is what affects number entry performance rather than the overall layout of the telephone or calculator style [6].

All these works have the same limitations as they are focused on the serial digit interface style. It is not always practical to have a full numeric keypad on an interface. In a space constrained environment such as mobile devices, an interface with fewer buttons might be necessary. Moreover, the keys on an incremental interface could be overloaded with menu navigation functionality. As a result, it is imperative to understand the tradeoffs between different classes of number entry interfaces.

EXPLORING THE TRADEOFFS IN INTERFACE CHOICES

These entry styles can be further described using properties from three groups addressing usability, safety and design is-

330

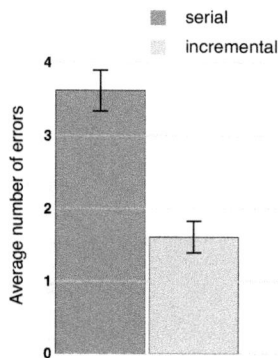

Figure 2. Average number of errors committed per participant on the serial and incremental interface

sues. Usability properties affect the end users of the interface, the safety properties affect the error tolerance of the interface and the design properties affect the space requirements of the interface and the range requirements of the numbers in the application. Using these properties, I compare examples of the three styles of number entry interfaces to show the relative trade-offs involved in chosing one of the interfaces over the other (Figure 3).

Usability properties
Speed of entry
This is how quickly a user can enter a number using the interface. This can generally be measured in terms of average time required to enter a new number using the interface.

Ease of adjusting values
This refers to the possibility of making small alterations to a number using an interface.

Independent digit edit
This refers to whether the interface allows independent control of each digit of the number on the interface.

Movable decimal point
This refers to whether the interface allows the user to control the position of the decimal point when entering a number.

Allows sequential entry
This refers to whether the interface offers controls to enter numbers sequentially from left to right.

Safety properties
Syntax error possible
This refers to the possibility of making syntax errors like entering multiple decimal points in a number.

Encourages error detection
This refers to the likelihood that an error is noticed by the user when using the interface [7].

One step error severity
This refers to the worst case deviation from the intended number caused by a one step user error e.g., clicking an extra button after the correct sequence.

Error recovery
This refers to how easily a user could correct a one step error.

Design properties
Interface space requirements
This refers to the minimum number of buttons required to implement the interface for a given range and precision of numbers and how the number of buttons grows as the range and precision grows.

Range of values covered
This refers to the minimum and maximum values that a user can enter using the interface.

Precision of values covered
This refers to the precision (i.e., the number of decimal places) to which users of the interface can enter numbers.

NUMBER ENTRY ERROR AND INTERFACE STYLE
I have run an experiment to investigate the effect of interface style on error detection [7]. This experiment compared the serial interface style (Figure 1(a)) to an incremental interface style (Figure 1(b)). The results of the experiment showed that users are more likely to notice and correct errors when using an incremental interface than when they were using a serial interface even though the latter offers faster number entry. In the experiment, I used an eye tracker to collect users' gaze and fixation on the user interfaces. The data showed that users spent most of their interaction time looking at the display when using an incremental number entry interface whereas they spent most of the interaction time looking at the input (the numeric keys) when using the serial interface.

Analyses of the types of errors that occurred in the experiment also suggested that for the serial and incremental interface tested, the interface style had an effect on the type of error committed. For instance transposition errors (where adjacent digits in the intended number are swapped) and wrong digit errors were more prominent on the incremental interface. On the other hand, the omission of the decimal point was only possible on the serial interface. Furthermore, the results show that the severity of errors (i.e., the deviation from the intended number) on the serial interface were a lot larger than those that occurred on the incremental interface.

CONCLUSIONS & FUTURE WORK
Discovering the factors, human *and* technical, that stimulate certain number entry errors would help to inform better and more resilient number entry interface design for safety critical devices.

My current experiment reports the behaviour of general users. Future experiments will use trained nurses as participants to explore any differences in behaviour given their training and safety critical background. Future experiments will include interfaces from all classes of number entry and will use a high fidelity prototype similar to those found in hospitals.

In the situation where number entry errors are dependent on the people entering the numbers, my research program will help produce a practical, evidence based test that would identify the proficiency of such users. Understanding the subtle

		Design			Usability					Safety			
		Precision	Range	Buttons	Sequential Entry	Movable Decimal	Edit Digits	Adjust Values	Speed	One step error cost	Error Recovery	Syntax Error	Error Detection
Serial	With Decimal Key												
	Without Decimal Key												
Independent digits	Four Key												
	Up Down Array												
Incremental	Chevrons												

(Legend: black = to be determined; gradient from Worst to Best)

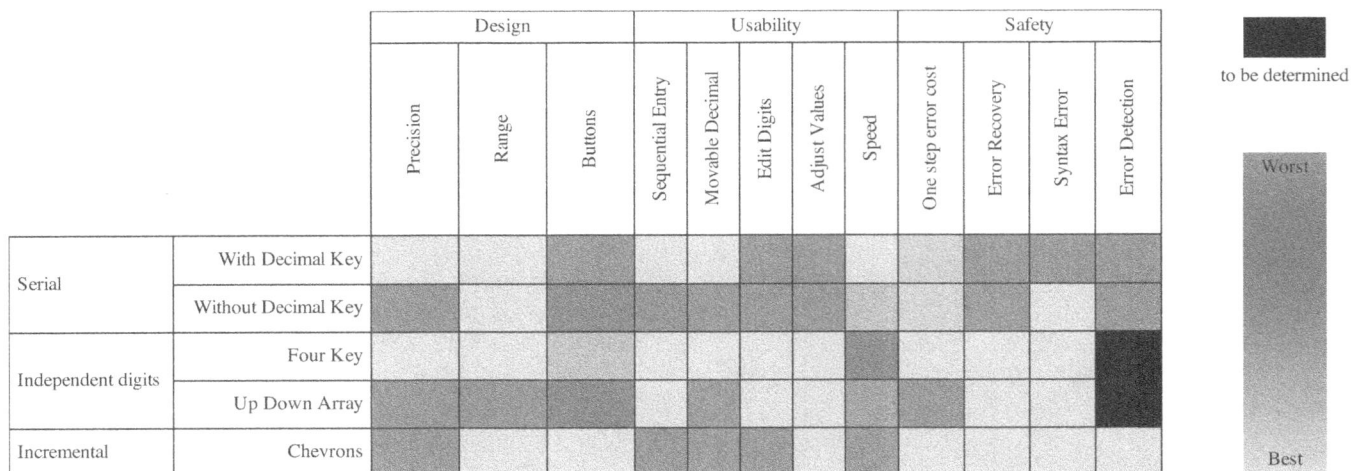

Figure 3. This chart shows the trade-off between design, usability and safety properties using some example number entry user interfaces. The properties are color coded to show relative performance amongst the interfaces that are compared under the given property. Values for cells colored black are yet to be determined in future experiments.

trade-offs between the usability, design and safety properties of number entry interfaces is valuable to the HCI community because this knowledge can contribute to the design of safer medical systems.

Acknowledgments
Funded as part of the CHI+MED (see www.chi-med.ac.uk): EPSRC Grant Number EP/G059063/1. I am grateful to Professor Harold Thimbleby, Dr. Parisa Eslambolchilar and Dr. Anna Cox for their help and feedback.

REFERENCES
1. Barber, N., and Taxis, K. Incidence and severity of intravenous drug errors in a german hospital. *European Journal of Clinical Pharmacology 59*, 11 (Jan. 2004), 815–817.

2. Cauchi, A., Curzon, P., Eslambolchilar, P., Gimblett, A., Huang, H., Lee, P., Li, Y., Masci, P., Oladimeji, P., Ruksenas, R., and Thimbleby, H. Towards dependable number entry for medical devices. In *Proceedings of the 1st International Workshop on engineering interactive computer systems for medicine and healthcare* (Pisa, Italy, June 2011).

3. Conrad, R., and Hull, A. J. The preferred layout for numeral Data-Entry keysets. *Ergonomics 11*, 2 (1968), 165–173.

4. Deininger, R. L. Human factors engineering studies of the design and use of pushbutton telephone sets. *Bell System Technical Journal 39* (1960), 995–1012.

5. Hoefel, H. H., Lautert, L., Schmitt, C., Soares, T., and Jordan, S. Vancomycin administration: mistakes made by nursing staff. *Nursing Standard (Royal College of Nursing (Great Britain): 1987) 22*, 39 (June 2008), 35–42. PMID: 18578131.

6. Marteniuk, R. G., Ivens, C. J., and Brown, B. E. Are there task specific performance effects for differently configured numeric keypads? *Applied Ergonomics 27*, 5 (Oct. 1996), 321–325.

7. Oladimeji, P., Thimbleby, H., and Cox, A. Number entry interfaces and their effects on error detection. In *Human-Computer Interaction INTERACT 2011*, vol. 6949. Springer Berlin Heidelberg, Berlin, Heidelberg, 2011, 178–185.

8. Straub, H. R., and Granaas, M. M. Task-specific preference for numeric keypads. *Applied Ergonomics 24*, 4 (Aug. 1993), 289–290.

9. Taxis, K., and Barber, N. Ethnographic study of incidence and severity of intravenous drug errors. *BMJ 326*, 7391 (Mar. 2003), 684.

10. Thimbleby, H., and Cairns, P. Reducing number entry errors: solving a widespread, serious problem. 1429–1439.

11. Wang, S., Lin, C., Wu, C., and Chaovalitwongse, W. A. Early detection of numerical typing errors using data mining techniques. *IEEE Transactions on Systems, Man and Cybernetics, Part A: Systems and Humans 41*, 6 (Nov. 2011), 1199–1212.

12. Westbrook, J. I., Rob, M. I., Woods, A., and Parry, D. Errors in the administration of intravenous medications in hospital and the role of correct procedures and nurse experience. *BMJ Quality & Safety* (June 2011).

13. Wiseman, S., Cairns, P., and Cox, A. A taxonomy of number entry errors. In *HCI2011: The 25th BCS Conference on Human-Computer Interaction* (Newcastle Upon Tyne, UK, 2011).

Creative and Open Software Engineering Practices and Tools in Maker Community Projects

Konstantinos Chorianopoulos
Ionian University
Plateia Tsirigoti 7, Corfu
49100, Greece
choko@ionio.gr
and NTNU

Letizia Jaccheri
Norwegian University of
Science and Technology
Sem Sælands vei 7-9
Trondheim 7491, Norway
letizia@idi.ntnu.no

Alexander Salveson Nossum
Norwegian University of
Science and Technology
Høgskoleringen 7A
7491 Trondheim, Norway
alexander.nossum@ntnu.no

ABSTRACT

Processing, Arduino and the growth of the associated communities of practice, also called Maker communities, has motivated a broader participation of non-technical users in the engineering of interactive systems. Besides online sharing, Maker communities meet regularly and share knowledge for various purposes (e.g., creative hacking, social networking, lifelong learning). In the context of Maker communities, the understanding of engineering interactive systems (e.g., motivations, objectives, collaboration, process, reports) and the design of the respective tools (e.g., end-user programming for artists, or children) are not well documented. As a remedy, we present a coherent overview of related work, as well as our own experiences in the organization and running of Maker workshops. The tutorial format (lecture and hands-on workshop) benefits both practitioners and researchers with an understanding of creative software tools and practices. Moreover, participants become familiar with the organization of Maker workshops as 1) a research method for understanding users, 2) an engineering process for interactive computer systems, and 3) a practice for teaching and learning.

ACM Classification Keywords: H.5.2 [User Interfaces]: Prototyping; Evaluation/methodology. D.2.2 [Software Engineering]: Design Tools and Techniques; User Interfaces.

Keywords

Open Source, Creative process, Maker, collaboration.

INTRODUCTION

Although the software engineering discipline has mostly evolved in the context of large-scale corporate projects, there have always been small-scale ad-hoc efforts by communities of hobbyists (e.g., shareware, independent games). The skills and motivations of Maker communities are rather broad. Nevertheless, the design of the most popular software tools has mostly regarded corporate users, or only those hobbyists with strong engineering backgrounds (e.g., VisualStudio, Eclipse, XCode). More recently, software developed by makers and for makers [1] has emerged as a new software category at the intersection between software and art. Artists need software technology for creating and evolving their artwork [2]. Technologists have long regarded the contact with artists as a source of inspiration for innovation [3]. Industry is also paying attention, because users have always been recognized as a source of innovation [4]. For example, an increasing number of companies are getting involved in OSS projects [5]. Tools for creativity have emerged as an important subject of study within computer science research [6]. Several popular rapid prototyping tools, such as Processing, Arduino, and Scratch [1] [7] have their roots in this intersection of open source engineering and creativity. In this tutorial, we suggest that the intrinsic motivation of hobbyists and Maker communities have many significant benefits for research, engineering, and learning.

OPEN SOURCE TOOLS

A technology is considered open source if its design (e.g., code, diagram, parts-list) is available to everybody for inspection, use, and modification. Notably, users of open source are not paying customers but potential co-developers. End-user development has considered some issues related with software and tools, but has not considered other emerging aspects of open source, such as community collaboration and open hardware. The most important characteristics and success factor of open source projects are associated with communities of users and of developers. The quality of collaboration in the community is crucial for any software project [8]. Members of each community are connected and assist each other via computer mediated communication tools (e.g., wikis, forums), as well as via real world meetings (e.g., Maker events, Hacker-spaces). In particular, Maker events have built upon the open source approach by offering a localized social gathering, which reinforces community as well as knowledge sharing. Moreover, Maker communities produce tangible interactive systems with the help of affordable fabrication methods (e.g., 3D printers) and tools (e.g., Arduino), thus they have novel needs in terms of tool chain support.

CREATIVE AND COLLABORATIVE PROCESS

The inner joy of creation and unselfish cooperation has often been identified as an important asset of the open source developer culture, bringing it, according to Castells [9] close to the world of art. For Castells, the Internet not only serves as a means for distribution of final blueprints, but also serves as a shared platform for a process that aims to create new blueprints. Innovative and creative businesses are often found within the field of computer science. These are often faced with similar collaboration issues, for instance when one or more stakeholders to a project have different backgrounds than the rest of a team. Or when the task is to "think outside the box" and develop creative solutions. The social issues experienced in these settings may be an obstacle that results in sub-optimal solutions [10].

Collaboration between several, co-located or distant, persons can be a complex task. This is an issue shared with most intellectual activities. In previous creativity work [11] [12], this issue has been identified, when computer engineering practitioners are working together with non-engineers or other branches of engineering. Applying and adapting methods from the field of social psychology have proven to be successful in optimizing the collaboration in heterogeneous groups. These methods approach the issues in a social manner and generally aim at optimizing the social issues and in effect optimizing the end results of the collaboration.

LEARNING OBJECTIVES AND STRUCTURE

Open source tools for creativity: In this tutorial, we are leveraging previous empirical evidence [13] and we chose to focus on open tools and creative processes. The format has also been motivated by significant related work in open source, such as Processing, Arduino, and Scratch.

Community documentation and reporting: The proposed workshop (hands-on) format employs several techniques for documentation and reporting. The ArTe blog links to a set of reusable resources, among which three master level and a PhD course in the interdisciplinary field of software and art. The blog also documents a set of creative workshops that have been offered by our research group during the last years. This documentation includes pictures, videos, and code, which can be reused and reflected upon.

Research issues: The tutorial regards several research questions that are intended to be explored and to be a basis for further elaboration:

- "How can we support Maker communities with updated practices and tools?"

- "How can the creative process of Maker communities contribute to the existing engineering theory of interactive systems?"

Guidelines for organizing and hosting your own Maker workshop: The tutorial includes experience based creativity sessions, which are based on a process that has been documented and validated through interviews with participants and analysis of the collected data and developed artifacts [13]. Thus, participants will become empowered with methods that enhance their research, engineering, and teaching practice.

REFERENCES

1. Noble, J. *Programming Interactivity: A Designer's Guide to Processing, Arduino, and Openframeworks.* O'Reilly Media, 2009.

2. Trifonova, A., Jaccheri, L., and Bergaust, K. Software Engineering Issues in Interactive Installation Art. *International Journal on Arts and Technology (IJART)* 1, 1 (2008), 43-65.

3. Harris, C. Art and innovation: the Xerox PARC Artist-in-Residence program. MIT Press, Cambridge, MA, USA, 1999.

4. E von Hippel. 1986. Lead users: a source of novel product concepts. Management Science 32, 7 (July 1986), 791-805.

5. Herbsleb. J.D. Global Software Engineering: The Future of Socio-technical Coordination. In *Future of Software Engineering (FOSE '07).* IEEE Computer Society, Washington, DC, USA, 188-198.

6. Shneiderman, B. Creativity Support Tools Accelerating Discovery and Innovation. Communication of the ACM 50, 12 (2007), 20-32.

7. Maloney, J., Resnick, M., Rusk, N., Silverman, B., Eastmond, E. The Scratch Programming Language and Environment. Trans. Comput. Educ. 10, 4, Article 16 (November 2010), 15 pages.

8. Dittrich, Y., Randall, D. W., Singer, J. Software Engineering as Cooperative Work. *Comput. Supported Coop. Work* 18, 5-6 (December 2009), 393-399.

9. Castells, M. Rise of The Network Society (Castells, Manuel. Information Age, 1.) (Vol 1). Wiley, 1996.

10. Johnson, D.W. and Johnson, F.P. Joining Together: Group Theory and Group Skills (10th Edition). Pearson, 2008.

11. Jaccheri, L., Sindre, G. Software Engineering Students meet Interdisciplinary Project work and Art. 11th International Conference Information Visualization, IV '07, IEEE Computer Society (2007), 925-934.

12. Chorianopoulos, K., Rieniets, T. City of collision: an interactive video installation to inform and engage. In IET Conference Publications, 2007, 502-509.

13. Høiseth, M. and Jaccheri, L. Art and Technology for Young Creators. Entertainment Computing - ICEC 2011 - 10th International Conference, Springer (2011), 210-221.

Model-based Interactive Ubiquitous Systems

Thomas Schlegel, Stefan Pietschmann, and Romina Kühn
Technische Universität Dresden
01062 Dresden
{thomas.schlegel,stefan.pietschmann,romina.kuehn}@tu-dresden.de

ABSTRACT

Ubiquitous systems today are introducing a new quality of interaction both into our lives and into software engineering. Systems become increasingly dynamic making frequent changes to system structures, distribution, and behavior necessary. Also, adaptation to new user needs and contexts as well as new modalities and communication channels make these systems differ strongly from what has been standard in the last decades.

Models and model-based interaction at runtime and design-time form a promising approach for coping with the dynamics and uncertainties inherent to interactive ubiquitous systems (IUS). Hence, this workshop discusses how model-based approaches can be used to cope with challenges of IUS. It covers the range from design-time to runtime models and from interaction to software engineering, addressing the challenges of interaction with and engineering of interactive ubiquitous systems.

Building on the results of MODIQUITOUS 2011 at EICS 2011, MODIQUITOUS 2012 aims at strengthening the community and allow for deeper discussions, demonstrations as well as inclusion of new developments in ubiquitous systems research.

Author Keywords

Models, MDA, runtime, ubiquitous systems, software engineering, multimodal interaction, adaptive interaction, generation, transformation, interactive systems, context-awareness, self-adaptation, EICS workshop, Modiquitous

ACM Classification Keywords

D.2.2 Design Tools and Techniques: Modules and interfaces; user interfaces. D.2.11 Software Architectures: Patterns. D.2.13 Reusable Software: Domain engineering; reuse models. H.5.2 User Interfaces: Interaction styles; standardization

General Terms

Design, Human Factors

THEME, GOALS, AND RELEVANCE

Model-based interactive ubiquitous systems form a new promising yet challenging domain within the scope of the Engineering of Interactive Computing Systems (EICS) conference. This workshop is intended to discuss these challenges and possible solutions of the EICS community to design and runtime aspects of interactive ubiquitous systems with a focus on model-based approaches.

The related problem space becomes clear when looking at typical future scenarios: users will not only carry their data but also their applications and profiles with them. This may mean switching from planning a project on a desktop system to a collaborative setting in a meeting and further to a mobile or public display setting where a mobile device is used for creating sketches for the first steps in the project. Consequently, applications will evolve from device-oriented to emergent cyber-physical and ubiquitous software in a broad sense, forming interactive and socio-technical systems. This opens manifold possibilities, but also a number of research problems regarding both the development process and the execution environment for those kinds of applications.

The MODIQUITOUS workshop is intended to provide a basis for discussing the adequate solution space. Therefore, it aims to bring together researchers and practitioners focused on different challenges of IUS, including:

- Model-driven architecture (MDA) in the context of IUS, including advantages and potential problems
- Domain and meta models for IUS, specifically for IUS-related aspects like interaction, different modalities, dynamic distribution, etc.
- Model-driven generation of (intelligent) IUS
- Model-to-model and model-to-code transformations for IUS development
- Model-driven development and execution architectures, i.e., runtime systems for IUS
- Tools and frameworks for supporting the model-driven development of IUS
- Concepts for context-awareness and self-adaptation of IUS at the model and runtime level
- Software and Usability Engineering aspects in the context of model-based IUS
- Studies on interaction concepts on IUS
- Innovative ideas and novel application solutions for new interactive ubiquitous settings, e.g., from the fields of mobile computing, pervasive computing and social software
- Requirements, insights and experiences from existing mobile and pervasive settings

All these topics are of high relevance to a big part of the EICS community as their use is not restricted to ubiquitous systems and will show new ways for many kinds of new systems like mobile device settings, pervasive computing and social software.

FORMAT

This full-time workshop aims to provide a forum for discussing new ideas, issues and solutions in the field of model-based interactive ubiquitous systems. The workshop will include introductory statements, the presentations of the participants' contributions, including position statements, research solutions and demonstrations, as well as discussions regarding the single contributions and group specific topics.

The goal of this workshop is to create a result in the form of a poster or paper, which can serve as an initial research agenda for the field of model-based approaches for interactive ubiquitous environments.

ORGANIZATION

Co-Organizers

Thomas Schlegel is Junior Professor for Software Engineering of Ubiquitous Systems at the Institute of Software and Multimedia Technology at the Technical University of Dresden. At Fraunhofer IAO from 2002 on, he has organized different seminars and workshops as well as the conference LIKE in 2005 and 2007 and different scientific events in the frame of the European Network of Excellence I*PROMS (www.iproms.org) as a research cluster leader and member of the executive board. He also serves as reviewer and member of the program committee in diverse national and international conferences.

Stefan Pietschmann is research associate and Ph.D. student at the Institute of Software and Multimedia Technology of the Technical University of Dresden. He has been actively involved in several research projects in the field of collaborative and context-aware web applications. In the project CRUISe he specifically addresses the model-driven development of adaptive interactive applications based on the idea of a universal service composition.

Romina Kühn is research associate and Ph.D. student at the Junior Professorship of Software Engineering of Ubiquitous Systems at the Technical University of Dresden. She is involved in a research project in the field of public transportation and interactive ubiquitous systems.

Program Committee

- Jan van den Bergh
  Hasselt University, Belgium
- Florian Daniel
  University of Trento, Italy
- Alfonso Garcia-Frey

University of Grenoble, France
- Heinrich Hussmann
  Ludwig-Maximilian University Munich, Germany
- Sevan Kavaldjian
  Vienna University of Technology, Austria
- Gerrit Meixner
  DFKI, Germany
- Philippe Palanque
  University of Toulouse, France
- Fabiò Paterno
  CNR-ISTI, Italy
- Michael Raschke
  University of Stuttgart, Germany
- Thomas Springer
  Technical University of Dresden, Germany
- Gerhard Weber
  Technical University of Dresden, Germany
- Anette Weisbecker
  Fraunhofer IAO Stuttgart, Germany
- Jürgen Ziegler
  University Duisburg-Essen, Germany

PARTICIPANTS

The workshop aims to bring together researchers and practitioners working on ubiquitous interactive systems or related areas dealing with sub-problems, such as: model-driven approaches for interactive applications; interaction and distribution modeling; self-adaptive interactive systems, etc.

WORKSHOP CONTENTS

The contributions to the workshop cover a wide range of aspects, which are discussed in the context of existing works and addressed with adequate models and model-based systems.

For one, submissions target the development process of ubiquitous systems, its individual phases and relation to existing models. Few authors introduce new models and methodologies, e.g., to formalize distributed activity-based computing. Further, reusable models and patterns for smart environments are discussed. For the other, some papers focus more on model-driven architectures and model usage including approaches for model-based testing of ubiquitous systems, model-based concepts for interactive, service-enabled appliances, and platform-independent solutions. Finally, highlighting the interaction aspect, new user interface and interaction concepts are presented.

AFTER THE CONFERENCE

The community benefits from a wide distribution and availability of the papers presented at the workshop. The contributions will be published in a publicly accessible way as workshop proceedings including the results of the workshop.

Author Index

www.ingramcontent.com/pod-product-compliance
Lightning Source LLC
Chambersburg PA
CBHW080912220326

41598CB00034B/5549